The Humanities in the Western Tradition

Second Edition

Constance Bouchard | Michael Graham | Michael Levin |
Julius R. Ruff | Merry E. Wiesner | William Bruce Wheeler

169-232

God
|
nous (logos)   Jesus   gnostic-
| saved
World soul   from
| special
individual soul   knowledge

exam 22

CENGAGE
Learning™

Australia • Brazil • Japan • Korea • Mexico • Singapore • Spain • United Kingdom • United States

CENGAGE
Learning™

The Humanities in the Western Tradition: Second Edition

The Humanities in the Western Tradition, A Reader
Michael Graham | Michael Levin | Constance Bouchard |
Stephen Harp | Shelley Baranowski

© 2006 Cengage Learning. All rights reserved.

Discovering the Western Past: A Look at the Evidence, Volume I: To 1789, 6th Edition
Merry E. Wiesner-Hanks | Julius R. Ruff | William Bruce Wheeler

© 2000 Cengage Learning. All rights reserved.

Executive Editors:

Maureen Staudt
Michael Stranz

Senior Project Development Manager:

Linda deStefano

Marketing Specialist:

Courtney Sheldon

Senior Production/
Manufacturing Manager:

Donna M. Brown

PreMedia Manager:

Joel Brennecke

Sr. Rights Acquisition
Account Manager:

Todd Osborne

Cover Image:
Getty Images*

*Unless otherwise noted, all cover images used by Custom Solutions. a part of Cengage Learning, have been supplied courtesy of Getty Images with the exception of the Earthviewcover image, which has been supplied by the National Aeronautics and Space Administration (NASA).

For product information and technology assistance, contact us at
Cengage Learning Customer & Sales Support, 1-800-354-9706

For permission to use material from this text or product,
submit all requests online at **cengage.com/permissions**
Further permissions questions can be emailed to
permissionrequest@cengage.com

This book contains select works from existing Cengage Learning resources and was produced by Cengage Learning Custom Solutions for collegiate use. As such, those adopting and/or contributing to this work are responsible for editorial content accuracy, continuity and completeness.

Compilation © 2011 Cengage Learning.

ISBN-13: 978-1-133-44013-0

ISBN-10: 1-133-44013-4

Cengage Learning
5191 Natorp Boulevard
Mason, Ohio 45040
USA

Cengage Learning is a leading provider of customized learning solutions with office locations around the globe, including Singapore, the United Kingdom, Australia, Mexico, Brazil, and Japan. Locate your local office at:

international.cengage.com/region.
Cengage Learning products are represented in Canada by Nelson Education, Ltd.
For your lifelong learning solutions, visit **www.cengage.com/custom.**
Visit our corporate website at **www.cengage.com.**

Printed in the United States
of America

CONTENTS

Introduction

Michael Graham

General education courses, such as the one for which this reader has been prepared, are often controversial—with students, with faculty, and with the wider public which higher education in part serves. Students may wonder why they are "forced" to take courses which do not on the surface seem directly relevant to their professional preparation. Why do accountants, or engineers, or nurses (just to name three non-humanities professional fields) need to learn about Plato, Thomas Hobbes or the Qu'ran? Faculty are often dissatisfied with what is included in general education curricula compared to what is left out. How can general surveys covering such a broad range of material be expected to give students any depth of understanding of critical issues? Some see them as inherently biased. For example, the limited educational, political and social opportunities given women throughout western (or for that matter, human) history has meant that relatively few words written by women in the first 5,000 years of writing have survived. Do courses like this, which stress what has been written by our human ancestors, merely perpetuate that disenfranchisement? Some members of the general public are suspicious of the ways traditional core beliefs are subject to scrutiny in this type of course. For example, does encouraging students to examine the evolution of Christian beliefs and their relationship to other religious and philosophical systems undermine the foundations of a religion to which so many adhere, providing yet another example of an academy funded in part through tax dollars which is "out of touch" with public opinion?

We are probably guilty as charged on most counts, and that is precisely why courses like this remain, and should remain, part of a strong general education curriculum. A significant proportion of a traditional university education involves preparation for life and responsible citizenship, not just professional training or the upholding of tradition. Preparation for life and responsible citizenship requires the development and honing of skills—in critical reading, in sifting through unfamiliar and sometimes contradictory information, in argumentation and in written and oral communication—as well as the inculcation of a bit of what has been termed "cultural literacy." Such skills take a long time to develop, and their possession is difficult to measure, but those who gain them are empowered for a life of learning, aesthetic appreciation, empathy and adaptability, all of which are very practical attributes in our rapidly—changing and increasingly interconnected world. These attributes are every bit as valuable to the future speech therapist, township trustee or investment banker as they are to the future novelist or theologian. The Humanities in the Western Tradition is aimed at helping students attain them.

The "western" focus of courses like this has also been questioned. Many people around the world have an ambivalent or hostile view of western civilization, seeing it as embodying a legacy of putative cultural superiority coupled with exploitation and a disinclination to value other cultures. Others embrace it, seeing it as representing a tradition which has fostered political representation and concepts of individual rights along with certain kinds of rationality and technological progress. Love it or hate it, what is undeniable is that we live in the midst of it, in a world on which it has left its indelible imprint, from the classically-influenced buildings of Washington, D.C., to Japanese string quartets playing European art music, to the mosques of Istanbul and the Nike sneakers sold in Calcutta or Dakar (and manufactured elsewhere in the developing world). We are better off learning about it, whether we would like to celebrate it, destroy it, or simply make sense of our world and the roots of so many assumptions, beliefs and conflicts.

Plato quoted his mentor and hero Socrates as saying "the unexamined life is not worth living." The sources in this book help us to examine the past lives of the culture that surrounds us. One of the first things that astute readers will notice is that the western tradition is not monolithic. Rather, it is full of contradictions. It is a long-running argument between many voices about the origins of the universe, our place within it, the nature (or existence) of God, the nature of humanity, proper relationships between humans, how we can best govern ourselves and whether our lives ultimately have any meaning. If, in reading through the sources in this book you do not find some things with which you disagree, you are not paying close enough attention. One of our fundamental goals is to give students an understanding, or even appreciation, of views which they may not share. You may be put off by Homer's celebration of masculine violence or his tendency to explain so many things, good or evil, as the results of the interventions of the gods in human affairs. You might think Socrates in the *Phaedo* is far too eager to embrace death. You might not share Ovid's cynicism about love, and you may be offended by the low regard he seems to have had for the female intellect. You might find the account of the creation of the world in the Book of Genesis self-contradictory. In reading Matthew's account of Jesus' teachings, you might find yourself with the Pharisees, searching for consistency in what seemed to be confusing doctrine. You might conclude that Augustine was far too hard on his youthful self. By the time you read the "Conquest of Orange" epic, you will probably be appalled at the author's lack of understanding of Islamic beliefs. You may find it harsh that Dante places Plato in the first circle of Hell, and you might be depressed by the hellish picture Thomas Hobbes presents of humanity in a state of nature (conversely, you may find his portrayal depressingly accurate).

So you will end up reading a seeming cacophony of diverse voices, some pushing ideas you embrace and others ideas you cannot accept. In some cases, you will probably wonder what all the fuss is about. The point is not for you to be improved or seduced by the "great minds" of the past. Rather, it is for you to understand the context from which particular views have emerged, and the ways in which they have been influential. Our world is full of people who do not share our views on any manner of subjects. So is our past. A better understanding of the latter will leave us much better prepared to deal with the former. You will probably find that you have more in common with the people purchasing those Nike shoes in Calcutta today than you do with Homer, Thomas Aquinas or any number of quintessentially "western" figures.

But do not write off our strange cultural ancestors. Sometimes we can learn the most about the past when we focus on what seems at first most odd. If something seems weird to us, but apparently made sense to them, we need to figure out why—what is it that has caused our attitudes to change? Further, you will discover that we take many of our common assumptions, expressions, symbols and even cliches from these people of the distant past. There are things that we think we know as well as behavioral patterns and habits of speech which we take for granted, rarely considering the fact that most aspects of our lives have been shaped by our cultural past, in a process of evolution which is ongoing. Our own distant descendants will probably look on us as strange also, even as they re-enact the patterns of life which we have shaped.

It is appropriate here to define two critical terms found in the title of this reader. "Western" as a cultural label is difficult to pin down. The approach of this reader and the course for which it is intended is to interpret the term broadly, taking it as referring to cultures whose origins can be located in the area of the world where the three major continents of Africa, Asia and Europe meet—today's Middle East, Asia Minor and southeastern Europe. Later, due to the geographic spread of the Roman Empire, the borders of the "west" expanded to include much of Europe. Later still, European exploration and colonial expansion would bring the Americas into the "western" orbit, while today western culture is in many ways global, due to movements in peoples and technologies, as well as the imperial practices of traditionally western societies, in the last few centuries. "Western" in this sense defines more the borders of a long cultural conversation than it does a geographic area, although it certainly has geographic roots. Furthermore, the conversational borders have rarely been impermeable, often taking in voices from outside and in turn influencing those outsiders.

By "humanities" we refer to subjects studied in several academic disciplines, including literature, history, philosophy, religion, art, architecture and music. Certainly, western culture has left behind many artifacts which are studied outside of those disciplines (the Mesopotamian pottery fragments analyzed by archaeologists come to mind), but our approach here is to concentrate on the western past as seen in written works and the fine arts. There are many ways of getting at the past, and ours is but one. The approaches taken by the social sciences and even the physical sciences are also valid and very useful, but this course will focus more on the qualitative analysis of written sources and artistic works; it is in these that the past speaks most eloquently, if imprecisely.

A term which is not part of the book's title, but is also worth pondering here is "civilization." This word comes from Latin roots having to do with cities and citizenship. To the Latin-speaking Romans, a *civitas* was a city or commonwealth, a union of citizens, and an individual citizen was a *civis*. They had a word for the science of politics: *civilitas*, which had the additional meaning of "politeness" or "civility." At first glance, this would seem to suggest that civilization has generally been an urban thing, and the derogative term *pagani*, used by the Romans to refer to the residents of rural villages (from which we get the word "pagan"), reinforces the notion that city life was regarded as more "civilized." But was this always the case? Is "civilization" possible without cities? And does it make us more polite or "civil" to each other? The value of civilization is one of the things you will ponder in this course.

Our general approach with this reader has been to give students substantial excerpts of a few works, rather than short snippets of many. We have resisted the common tendency of primary source collections to abridge texts by removing parts deemed less significant. This is because we believe that authors write things a certain way for their own good reasons, and parts of a work which our modern sensibilities might rate as less important or even unnecessary might have been regarded as critical by an author. If we are to meet the past on its own terms, we must let it speak freely, without us filtering out the parts that do not seem to relate to us. We also feel that this more prolonged exposure to particular writers will allow students a more substantial engagement with the works in question, resulting in more thoughtful and provocative classroom discussions, as well as better retention of the material. We do not want *The Humanities in the Western Tradition* to offer the intellectual equivalent of a fast food meal. Rather, we aim for something more nutritious and long-lasting, even if its preparation takes more time and expense.

With the development of critical reading skills as one of our primary objectives, we hope that students and their instructors engage in some fundamental source criticism as they approach these texts. In assessing everyday information we often caution others to "consider the source," and this is of paramount importance in the text-based study of the past. With every one of the sources in this book, students and instructors should ponder the following questions: who is the author of the work and what was their likely intent in writing it? In what format was the work initially intended to be presented (e.g. oral performance, written down, or—a post-1460s option, publication)? For what audience was it intended? If events are described, are they events that the author is likely to have witnessed? How far removed in time was the writing of the work from the events described? What issues seem to be particularly important for the author? There are many other questions which can also be asked in reference to particular sources. But knowing (or making an educated guess at) the answers to these sorts of questions will put a reader in a much better position to understand why a text is written the way it is and how it can be used to give us a better understanding of the past.

Finally, we are well aware that some of the sources included here are difficult to read and interpret, even in the modern translations which we have used. Styles of writing today are much different than they were a mere century ago, not to mention 2,800 years ago, at the time Homer was composing the *Iliad*. Students may be frustrated that these authors take a long time to "get to the point." In the face of this, we counsel patience. Sifting through material like this can take time. More importantly, what we consider to be "the point" might be something very different from what the author considered it to be. While some of them were writing for posterity, they were not necessarily writing for us. We have just stepped into their long-running conversation. In a situation like that, the best thing to do is to pay close attention to what people are saying to help yourself get up to speed, rather than interrupting the flow of things by rudely demanding an update on what they are talking about! Good things come to those who wait, and listen, and study, and think.

Homer

THE ILIAD

Introduction by Michael Graham

The Iliad is one of the earliest works in western literature. It is an epic poem attributed to an author named Homer, said to have been blind, who lived somewhere in Greece around 800–750 B.C. The Iliad takes its name from Ilium, the Greek word for Troy, a city in Asia Minor (modern-day Turkey). It describes the efforts of the Greeks (referred to in the poem as "Achaeans") to capture the city of Troy. The site of Troy was excavated by archaeologists in the nineteenth century, and there is evidence that a city on the site was destroyed by fire between about 1250 and 1225 B.C., suggesting that Homer's poem may be based on actual events. But the precise details will never be known, and we must treat the Iliad more as a work of literature than history. It may not offer us a documentary history of the Trojan War, but it does offer us substantial insights into the mentality of the Greeks of Homer's time—their values, their beliefs, their ethical codes and how they thought the world operated.

Even in translation (which can almost never do full justice to an original work), the *Iliad* is a feast of language. We must keep in mind that it was intended to be recited aloud. The vast majority of the Greeks of Homer's time were illiterate, so they would have heard this poem, rather than reading it. And while written copies of the poem circulated for centuries, it was not actually published for the first time until 1488, at which point the poem was already more than 2200 years old. Therefore, we should see this poem as part of a Greek oral tradition; indeed, much of the education of a Greek boy in the Classical era would have involved memorizing Homer's poetry for recitation, and it is quite possible, even likely, that details would have been modified as the work was passed on. So when you are reading this section of the *Iliad* (which includes the first two "books" out of a total of twenty-four), take some time to read aloud, and imagine yourself as a listener rather than a reader.

When the poem begins, the Achaeans have been battling the Trojans for ten years. Troy has not fallen, but there has been a falling-out within the ranks of the Achaeans. Achilles, one of the Achaean commanders, is angry at Agamemnon, king of Mycenae and general of all the Achaean forces. As you read it will become clear what the disagreement is about. What caused it, and what does this say about the values of these men? Are either of them presented in a way which makes them seem heroic? What makes someone a hero in this story? The first two books raise other issues as well. In book two you will meet Helen of Troy. What role does she play in this conflict between the Achaeans and the Trojans? What sort of character is she? You might extend this question to all the female characters who appear in the poem. What does this tell you about gender relations in ancient Greek society? You will also notice that the gods seem to take an active interest in the various conflicts presented in the story. For example, Achilles' mother is the sea-goddess Thetis, and she tries to help him out. How does she go about doing this, and what does this tell us about Greek perceptions of the gods? How would you compare the behavior of Zeus, king of the gods, with the behavior of the Judeo-Christian God as presented in the Bible? Do these gods seem trustworthy? What ethical values do these Greeks seem to have held dear? Did they value mercy or compassion? Parts of book two may seem to you like an endless recitation of names. Why do you think the poet thought it was important to include all this information?

We hope that after reading books one and two, you will have become absorbed enough in the story to want to know how it turned out, so we won't spoil things by giving away the outcome here. But even if you find the *Iliad* not to your taste, you will have received a crash course in Greek values the same way that many ancient Greeks learned them: through the poetry of Homer.

The Iliad

BOOK ONE

The Rage of Achilles

Rage—Goddess, sing the rage of Peleus' son Achilles,
murderous, doomed, that cost the Achaeans countless losses,
hurling down to the House of Death so many sturdy souls,
great fighters' souls, but made their bodies carrion,
feasts for the dogs and birds,
and the will of Zeus was moving toward its end.
Begin, Muse, when the two first broke and clashed,
Agamemnon lord of men and brilliant Achilles.

What god drove them to fight with such a fury?
Apollo the son of Zeus and Leto. Incensed at the king   10
he swept a fatal plague through the army—men were dying
and all because Agamemnon spurned Apollo's priest.
Yes, Chryses approached the Achaeans' fast ships
to win his daughter back, bringing a priceless ransom
and bearing high in hand, wound on a golden staff,
the wreaths of the god, the distant deadly Archer.
He begged the whole Achaean army but most of all
the two supreme commanders, Atreus' two sons,
"Agamemnon, Menelaus—all Argives geared for war!
May the gods who hold the halls of Olympus give you   20
Priam's city to plunder, then safe passage home.
Just set my daughter free, my dear one . . . here,
accept these gifts, this ransom. Honor the god
who strikes from worlds away—the son of Zeus, Apollo!"

Homer, *The Iliad* (Robert Fagles, trans.), Penguin, 1990 (ISBN 0-14-044592-7), original pp. 77–127.

And all ranks of Achaeans cried out their assent:
"Respect the priest, accept the shining ransom!"
But it brought no joy to the heart of Agamemnon.
The king dismissed the priest with a brutal order
ringing in his ears: "Never again, old man,   30
let me catch sight of you by the hollow ships!
Not loitering now, not slinking back tomorrow.
The staff and the wreaths of god will never save you then.
The girl—I won't give up the girl. Long before that,
old age will overtake her in *my* house, in Argos,
far from her fatherland, slaving back and forth
at the loom, forced to share my bed!
                                        Now go,
don't tempt my wrath—and you may depart alive."

     The old man was terrified. He obeyed the order,
turning, trailing away in silence down the shore
where the battle lines of breakers crash and drag.   40
And moving off to a safe distance, over and over
the old priest prayed to the son of sleek-haired Leto,
lord Apollo, "Hear me, Apollo! God of the silver bow
who strides the walls of Chryse and Cilla sacrosanct—
lord in power of Tenedos—Smintheus, god of the plague!
If I ever roofed a shrine to please your heart,
ever burned the long rich bones of bulls and goats
on your holy altar, now, now bring my prayer to pass.
Pay the Danaans back—your arrows for my tears!"

     His prayer went up and Phoebus Apollo heard him.   50
Down he strode from Olympus' peaks, storming at heart
with his bow and hooded quiver slung across his shoulders.
The arrows clanged at his back as the god quaked with rage,
the god himself on the march and down he came like night.
Over against the ships he dropped to a knee, let fly a shaft
and a terrifying clash rang out from the great silver bow.
First he went for the mules and circling dogs but then,
launching a piercing shaft at the men themselves,
he cut them down in droves—
and the corpse-fires burned on, night and day, no end in sight.   60

     Nine days the arrows of god swept through the army.
On the tenth Achilles called all ranks to muster—
the impulse seized him, sent by white-armed Hera
grieving to see Achaean fighters drop and die.
Once they'd gathered, crowding the meeting grounds,
the swift runner Achilles rose and spoke among them:
"Son of Atreus, now we are beaten back, I fear,

the long campaign is lost. So home we sail . . .
if we can escape our death—if war and plague
are joining forces now to crush the Argives.   70
But wait: let us question a holy man,
a prophet, even a man skilled with dreams—
dreams as well can come our way from Zeus—
come, someone to tell us why Apollo rages so,
whether he blames us for a vow we failed, or sacrifice.
If only the god would share the smoky savor of lambs
and full-grown goats, Apollo might be willing, still,
somehow, to save us from this plague."

                                        So he proposed
and down he sat again as Calchas rose among them,
Thester's son, the clearest by far of all the seers   80
who scan the flight of birds. He knew all things that are,
all things that are past and all that are to come,
the seer who had led the Argive ships to Troy
with the second sight that god Apollo gave him.
For the armies' good the seer began to speak:
"Achilles, dear to Zeus . . .
you order me to explain Apollo's anger,
the distant deadly Archer? I will tell it all.
But strike a pact with me, swear you will defend me
with all your heart, with words and strength of hand.   90
For there is a man I will enrage—I see it now—
a powerful man who lords it over all the Argives,
one the Achaeans must obey . . . A mighty king,
raging against an inferior, is too strong.
Even if he can swallow down his wrath today,
still he will nurse the burning in his chest
until, sooner or later, he sends it bursting forth.
Consider it closely, Achilles. Will you save me?"

   And the matchless runner reassured him: "Courage!
Out with it now, Calchas. Reveal the will of god,   100
whatever you may know. And I swear by Apollo
dear to Zeus, the power you pray to, Calchas,
when you reveal god's will to the Argives—no one,
not while I am alive and see the light on earth, no one
will lay his heavy hands on you by the hollow ships.
None among all the armies. Not even if you mean
Agamemnon here who now claims to be, by far,
the best of the Achaeans."
                                 The seer took heart
and this time he spoke out, bravely: "Beware—
he casts no blame for a vow we failed, a sacrifice.   110
The god's enraged because Agamemnon spurned his priest,

he refused to free his daughter, he refused the ransom.
That's why the Archer sends us pains and he will send us more
and never drive this shameful destruction from the Argives,
not till we give back the girl with sparkling eyes
to her loving father—no price, no ransom paid—
and carry a sacred hundred bulls to Chryse town.
Then we can calm the god, and only then appease him."

So he declared and sat down. But among them rose   120
the fighting son of Atreus, lord of the far-flung kingdoms,
Agamemnon—furious, his dark heart filled to the brim,
blazing with anger now, his eyes like searing fire.
With a sudden, killing look he wheeled on Calchas first:
"Seer of misery! Never a word that works to my advantage!
Always misery warms your heart, your prophecies—
never a word of profit said or brought to pass.
Now, again, you divine god's will for the armies,
bruit it about, as fact, why the deadly Archer
multiplies our pains: because I, I refused   130
that glittering price for the young girl Chryseis.
Indeed, I prefer *her* by far, the girl herself,
I want her mine in my own house! I rank her higher
than Clytemnestra, my wedded wife—she's nothing less
in build or breeding, in mind or works of hand.
But I am willing to give her back, even so,
if that is best for all. What I really want
is to keep my people safe, not see them dying.
But fetch me another prize, and straight off too,
else I alone of the Argives go without my honor.   140
That would be a disgrace. You are all witness,
look—*my* prize is snatched away!"
                                   But the swift runner
Achilles answered him at once, "Just how, Agamemnon,
great field marshal . . . most grasping man alive,
how can the generous Argives give you prizes now?
I know of no troves of treasure, piled, lying idle,
anywhere. Whatever we dragged from towns we plundered,
all's been portioned out. But collect it, call it back
from the rank and file? *That* would be the disgrace.
So return the girl to the god, at least for now.   150
We Achaeans will pay you back, three, four times over,
if Zeus will grant us the gift, somehow, someday,
to raze Troy's massive ramparts to the ground."

But King Agamemnon countered, "Not so quickly,
brave as you are, godlike Achilles—trying to cheat *me*.
Oh no, you won't get past me, take me in that way!

What do you want? To cling to your own prize
while I sit calmly by—empty-handed here?
No—if our generous Argives *will* give me a prize,
a match for my desires, equal to what I've lost,   160
well and good. But if they give me nothing
I will take a prize myself—your own, or Ajax'
or Odysseus' prize—I'll commandeer her myself
and let that man I go to visit choke with rage!
Enough. We'll deal with all this later, in due time.
Now come, we haul a black ship down to the bright sea,
gather a decent number of oarsmen along her locks
and put abroad a sacrifice, and Chryseis herself,
in all her beauty . . . we embark her too.
Let one of the leading captains take command.   170
Ajax, Idomeneus, trusty Odysseus or you, Achilles,
you—the most violent man alive—so you can perform
the rites for us and calm the god yourself."

                       A dark glance
and the headstrong runner answered him in kind: "Shameless—
armored in shamelessness—always shrewd with greed!
How could an Argive soldier obey your orders,
freely and gladly do your sailing for you
or fight your enemies, full force? Not I, no.
It wasn't Trojan spearmen who brought me here to fight.
The Trojans never did *me* damage, not in the least,   180
they never stole my cattle or my horses, never
in Phthia where the rich soil breeds strong men
did they lay waste my crops. How could they?
Look at the endless miles that lie between us . . .
shadowy mountain ranges, seas that surge and thunder.
No, you colossal, shameless—we all followed you,
to please you, to fight for you, to win your honor
back from the Trojans—Menelaus and you, you dog-face!
What do *you* care? Nothing. You don't look right or left.
And now you threaten to strip me of my prize in person—   190
the one I fought for long and hard, and sons of Achaea
handed her to me.

               My honors never equal yours,
whenever we sack some wealthy Trojan stronghold—
my arms bear the brunt of the raw, savage fighting,
true, but when it comes to dividing up the plunder
the lion's share is yours, and back I go to my ships,
clutching some scrap, some pittance that I love,
when I have fought to exhaustion.

                    No more now—
back I go to Phthia. Better that way by far,
to journey home in the beaked ships of war.   200

I have no mind to linger here disgraced,
brimming your cup and piling up your plunder."

　　But the lord of men Agamemnon shot back,
"*Desert,* by all means—if the spirit drives you home!
I will never beg you to stay, not on *my* account.
Never—others will take my side and do me honor,
Zeus above all, whose wisdom rules the world.
You—I hate you most of all the warlords
loved by the gods. Always dear to your heart,   210
strife, yes, and battles, the bloody grind of war.
What if you are a great soldier? That's just a gift of god.
Go home with your ships and comrades, lord it over your Myrmidons!
You *are* nothing to me—you and your overweening anger!
But let this be my warning on your way:
since Apollo insists on taking my Chryseis,
I'll send her back in my own ships with *my* crew.
But I, I will be there in person at your tents
to take *Briseis* in all her beauty, your own prize—
so you can learn just how much greater I am than you   220
and the next man up may shrink from matching words with me,
from hoping to rival Agamemnon strength for strength!"

　　He broke off and anguish gripped Achilles.
The heart in his rugged chest was pounding, torn . . .
Should he draw the long sharp sword slung at his hip,
thrust through the ranks and kill Agamemnon now?—
or check his rage and beat his fury down?
As his racing spirit veered back and forth,
just as he drew his huge blade from its sheath,
down from the vaulting heavens swept Athena,   230
the white-armed goddess Hera sped her down:
Hera loved both men and cared for both alike.
Rearing behind him Pallas seized his fiery hair—
only Achilles saw her, none of the other fighters—
struck with wonder he spun around, he knew her at once,
Pallas Athena! the terrible blazing of those eyes,
and his winged words went flying: "Why, why now?
Child of Zeus with the shield of thunder, why come now?
To witness the outrage Agamemnon just committed?
I tell you this, and so help me it's the truth—   240
he'll soon pay for his arrogance with his life!"

　　Her gray eyes clear, the goddess Athena answered,
"Down from the skies I come to check your rage
if only you will yield.
The white-armed goddess Hera sped me down:

she loves you both, she cares for you both alike.
Stop this fighting, now. Don't lay hand to sword.
Lash him with threats of the price that he will face.
And I tell you this—and I *know* it is the truth—
one day glittering gifts will lie before you,
three times over to pay for all his outrage.   250
Hold back now. Obey us both."

> So she urged
and the swift runner complied at once: "I must—
when the two of you hand down commands, Goddess,
a man submits though his heart breaks with fury.
Better for him by far. If a man obeys the gods
they're quick to hear his prayers."

> And with that
Achilles stayed his burly hand on the silver hilt
and slid the huge blade back in its sheath.
He would not fight the orders of Athena.
Soaring home to Olympus, she rejoined the gods   260
aloft in the halls of Zeus whose shield is thunder.

  But Achilles rounded on Agamemnon once again,
lashing out at him, not relaxing his anger for a moment:
"Staggering drunk, with your dog's eyes, your fawn's heart!
Never once did you arm with the troops and go to battle
or risk an ambush packed with Achaea's picked men—
you lack the courage, you can see death coming.
Safer by far, you find, to foray all through camp,
commandeering the prize of any man who speaks against you.
King who devours his people! Worthless husks, the men you rule—   270
if not, Atrides, this outrage would have been your last.
I tell you this, and I swear a mighty oath upon it . . .
by this, this scepter, look,
that never again will put forth crown and branches,
now it's left its stump on the mountain ridge forever,
nor will it sprout new green again, now the brazen ax
has stripped its bark and leaves, and now the sons of Achaea
pass it back and forth as they hand their judgments down,
upholding the honored customs whenever Zeus commands—
This scepter will be the mighty force behind my oath: 280
someday, I swear, a yearning for Achilles will strike
Achaea's sons and all your armies! But then, Atrides,
harrowed as you will be, *nothing* you do can save you—
not when your hordes of fighters drop and die,
cut down by the hands of man-killing Hector! Then—
then you will tear your heart out, desperate, raging
that you disgraced the best of the Achaeans!"

> Down on the ground

he dashed the scepter studded bright with golden nails,
then took his seat again. The son of Atreus smoldered,
glaring across at him, but Nestor rose between them,   290
the man of winning words, the clear speaker of Pylos . . .
Sweeter than honey from his tongue the voice flowed on and on.
Two generations of mortal men he had seen go down by now,
those who were born and bred with him in the old days,
in Pylos' holy realm, and now he ruled the third.
He pleaded with both kings, with clear good will,
"No more—or enormous sorrow comes to all Achaea!
How they would exult, Priam and Priam's sons
and all the Trojans. Oh they'd leap for joy   300
to hear the two of you battling on this way,
you who excel us all, first in Achaean councils,
first in the ways of war.
                              Stop. Please.
Listen to Nestor. You are both younger than I,
and in my time I struck up with better men than you,
even you, but never once did they make light of me.
I've never seen such men, I never will again . . .
men like Pirithous, Dryas, that fine captain,
Caeneus and Exadius, and Polyphemus, royal prince,
and Theseus, Aegeus' boy, a match for the immortals.   310
They were the strongest mortals ever bred on earth,
the strongest, and they fought against the strongest too,
shaggy Centaurs, wild brutes of the mountains—
they hacked them down, terrible, deadly work.
And I was in their ranks, fresh out of Pylos,
far away from home—they enlisted me themselves
and I fought on my own, a free lance, single-handed.
And none of the men who walk the earth these days
could battle with those fighters, none, but they,
they took to heart my counsels, marked my words.   320
So now you listen too. Yielding is far better . . .
Don't seize the girl, Agamemnon, powerful as you are—
leave her, just as the sons of Achaea gave her,
his prize from the very first.
And you, Achilles, never hope to fight it out
with your king, pitting force against his force:
no one can match the honors dealt a king, you know,
a sceptered king to whom great Zeus gives glory.
Strong as you are—a goddess was your mother—
he has more power because he rules more men.   330
Atrides, end your anger—look, it's Nestor!
I beg you, cool your fury against Achilles.
Here the man stands over all Achaea's armies,
our rugged bulwark braced for shocks of war."

But King Agamemnon answered him in haste,
"True, old man—all you say is fit and proper—
but this soldier wants to tower over the armies,
he wants to rule over all, to lord it over all,
give out orders to every man in sight. Well,
there's one, I trust, who will never yield to *him*!
What if the everlasting gods have made a spearman of him?   340
Have they entitled him to hurl abuse at *me*?"

"Yes!"—blazing Achilles broke in quickly—
"What a worthless, burnt-out coward I'd be called
if I would submit to you and all your orders,
whatever you blurt out. Fling them at others,
don't give me commands!
Never again, *I* trust, will Achilles yield to *you*.
And I tell you this—take it to heart, I warn you—
my hand will never do battle for that girl,
neither with you, King, nor any man alive.   350
You Achaeans gave her, now you've snatched her back.
But all the rest I possess beside my fast black ship—
not one bit of it can you seize against my will, Atrides.
Come, try it! So the men can see, that instant,
your black blood gush and spurt around my spear!"

Once the two had fought it out with words,
battling face-to-face, both sprang to their feet
and broke up the muster beside the Argive squadrons.
Achilles strode off to his trim ships and shelters,
back to his friend Patroclus and their comrades.   360
Agamemnon had a vessel hauled down to the sea,
he picked out twenty oarsmen to man her locks,
put aboard the cattle for sacrifice to the god
and led Chryseis in all her beauty amidships.
Versatile Odysseus took the helm as captain.

All embarked,
the party launched out on the sea's foaming lanes
while the son of Atreus told his troops to wash,
to purify themselves from the filth of plague.
They scoured it off, threw scourings in the surf
and sacrificed to Apollo full-grown bulls and goats   370
along the beaten shore of the fallow barren sea
and savory smoke went swirling up the skies.

So the men were engaged throughout the camp.
But King Agamemnon would not stop the quarrel,
the first threat he hurled against Achilles.
He called Talthybius and Eurybates briskly,

his two heralds, ready, willing aides:
"Go to Achilles' lodge. Take Briseis at once,
his beauty Briseis by the hand and bring her here.
But if he will not surrender her, I'll go myself,   380
I'll seize her myself, with an army at my back—
and all the worse for him!"
                          He sent them off
with the strict order ringing in their ears.
Against their will the two men made their way
along the breaking surf of the barren salt sea
and reached the Myrmidon shelters and their ships.
They found him beside his lodge and black hull,
seated grimly—and Achilles took no joy
when he saw the two approaching.   390
They were afraid, they held the king in awe
and stood there, silent. Not a word to Achilles,
not a question. But he sensed it all in his heart,
their fear, their charge, and broke the silence for them:
"Welcome, couriers! Good heralds of Zeus and men,
here, come closer. You have done nothing to me.
You are not to blame. No one but Agamemnon—
he is the one who sent you for Briseis.
Go, Patroclus, Prince, bring out the girl
and hand her to them so they can take her back.
But let them both bear witness to my loss . . .
in the face of blissful gods and mortal men,
in the face of that unbending, ruthless king—
if the day should come when the armies need *me*
to save their ranks from ignominious, stark defeat.
The man is raving—with all the murderous fury in his heart.
He lacks the sense to see a day behind, a day ahead,
and safeguard the Achaeans battling by the ships."

    Patroclus obeyed his great friend's command.
He led Briseis in all her beauty from the lodge
and handed her over to the men to take away.   410
And the two walked back along the Argive ships
while she trailed on behind, reluctant, every step.
But Achilles wept, and slipping away from his companions,
far apart, sat down on the beach of the heaving gray sea
and scanned the endless ocean. Reaching out his arms,
again and again he prayed to his dear mother: "Mother!
You gave me life, short as that life will be,
so at least Olympian Zeus, thundering up on high,
should give he honor—but now he gives me nothing.
Atreus' son Agamemnon, for all his far-flung kingdoms—   420

the man disgraces me, seizes and keeps my prize,
he tears her away himself!"
                  So he wept and prayed
and his noble mother heard him, seated near her father,
the Old Man of the Sea in the salt green depths.
Suddenly up she rose from the churning surf
like mist and settling down beside him as he wept,
stroked Achilles gently, whispering his name, "My child—
why in tears? What sorrow has touched your heart?
Tell me, please. Don't harbor it deep inside you.
We must share it all."
                And now from his depths   430
the proud runner groaned: "You know, you know,
why labor through it all? You know it all so well . . .
We raided Thebe once, Eetion's sacred citadel,
we ravaged the place, hauled all the plunder here
and the armies passed it round, share and share alike,
and they chose the beauty Chryseis for Agamemnon.
But soon her father, the holy priest of Apollo
the distant deadly Archer, Chryses approached
the fast trim ships of the Argives armed in bronze
to win his daughter back, bringing a priceless ransom   440
and bearing high in hand, wound on a golden staff,
the wreaths of the god who strikes from worlds away.
He begged the whole Achaean army but most of all
the two supreme commanders, Atreus' two sons,
and all ranks of Achaeans cried out their assent,
'Respect the priest, accept the shining ransom!'
But it brought no joy to the heart of Agamemnon,
our high and mighty king dismissed the priest
with a brutal order ringing in his ears.
And shattered with anger, the old man withdrew   450
but Apollo heard his prayer—he loved him, deeply—
he loosed his shaft at the Argives, withering plague,
and now the troops began to drop and die in droves,
the arrows of god went showering left and right,
whipping through the Achaeans' vast encampment.
But the old seer who knew the cause full well
revealed the will of the archer god Apollo.
And I was the first, mother, I urged them all,
'Appease the god at once!' That's when the fury
gripped the son of Atreus. Agamemnon leapt to his feet   460
and hurled his threat—his threat's been driven home.
One girl, Chryseis, the fiery-eyed Achaeans
ferry out in a fast trim ship to Chryse Island,
laden with presents for the god. The other girl,

just now the heralds came and led her away from camp,
Briseus' daughter, the prize the armies gave me.
But you, mother, if you have any power at all,
protect your son! Go to Olympus, plead with Zeus,
if you ever warmed his heart with a word or any action . . .

    Time and again I heard your claims in father's halls,   470
boasting how you and you alone of all the immortals
rescued Zeus, the lord of the dark storm cloud,
from ignominious, stark defeat . . .
That day the Olympians tried to chain him down,
Hera, Poseidon lord of the sea, and Pallas Athena—
you rushed to Zeus, dear Goddess, broke those chains,
quickly ordered the hundred-hander to steep Olympus,
that monster whom the immortals call Briareus
but every mortal calls the Sea-god's son, Aegaeon,   480
though he's stronger than his father. Down he sat,
flanking Cronus' son, gargantuan in the glory of it all,
and the blessed gods were struck with terror then,
they stopped shackling Zeus.
                        Remind him of that,
now, go and sit beside him, grasp his knees . . .
persuade him, somehow, to help the Trojan cause,
to pin the Achaeans back against their ships,
trap them round the bay and mow them down.
So all can reap the benefits of their king—
so even mighty Atrides can see how mad he was   490
to disgrace Achilles, the best of the Achaeans!"

    And Thetis answered, bursting into tears,
"O my son, my sorrow, why did I ever bear you?
All I bore was doom . . .
Would to god you could linger by your ships
without a grief in the world, without a torment!
Doomed to a short life, you have so little time.
And not only short, now, but filled with heartbreak too,
more than all other men alive—doomed twice over.
Ah to a cruel fate I bore you in our halls!
Still, I shall go to Olympus crowned with snow   500
and repeat your prayer to Zeus who loves the lightning.
Perhaps he will be persuaded.
                      But you, my child,
stay here by the fast ships, rage on at the Achaeans,
just keep clear of every foray in the fighting.
Only yesterday Zeus went off to the Ocean River
to feast with the Aethiopians, loyal, lordly men,
and all the gods went with him. But in twelve days

the Father returns to Olympus. Then, for your sake,
up I go to the bronze floor, the royal house of Zeus—
I'll grasp his knees, I think I'll win him over."

                                    With that vow   510
his mother went away and left him there, alone,
his heart inflamed for the sashed and lovely girl
they'd wrenched away from him against his will.
Meanwhile Odysseus drew in close to Chryse Island,
bearing the splendid sacrifice in the vessel's hold.
And once they had entered the harbor deep in bays
they furled and stowed the sail in the black ship,
they lowered the mast by the forestays, smoothly,
quickly let it down on the forked mast-crutch
and rowed her into a mooring under oars.   520
Out went the bow-stones—cables fast astern—
and the crew themselves swung out in the breaking surf,
leading out the sacrifice for the archer god Apollo,
and out of the deep-sea ship Chryseis stepped too.
Then tactful Odysseus led her up to the altar,
placing her in her loving father's arms, and said,
"Chryses, the lord of men Agamemnon sent me here
to bring your daughter back and perform a sacrifice,
a grand sacrifice to Apollo—for all Achaea's sake—
so we can appease the god   530
who's loosed such grief and torment on the Argives."

    With those words he left her in Chryses' arms
and the priest embraced the child he loved, exultant.
At once the men arranged the sacrifice for Apollo,
making the cattle ring his well-built altar,
then they rinsed their hands and took up barley.
Rising among them Chryses stretched his arms to the sky
and prayed in a high resounding voice, "Hear me, Apollo!
God of the silver bow who strides the walls of Chryse
and Cilla sacrosanct—lord in power of Tenedos!   540
If you honored me last time and heard my prayer
and rained destruction down on all Achaea's ranks,
now bring my prayer to pass once more. Now, at last,
drive this killing plague from the armies of Achaea!"

    His prayer went up and Phoebus Apollo heard him.
And soon as the men had prayed and flung the barley,
first they lifted back the heads of the victims,
slit their throats, skinned them and carved away
the meat from the thighbones and wrapped them in fat,
a double fold sliced clean and topped with strips of flesh.   550
And the old man burned these over dried split wood

and over the quarters poured out glistening wine
while young men at his side held five-pronged forks.
Once they had burned the bones and tasted the organs
they cut the rest into pieces, pierced them with spits,
roasted them to a turn and pulled them off the fire.
The work done, the feast laid out, they ate well
and no man's hunger lacked a share of the banquet.
When they had put aside desire for food and drink,
the young men brimmed the mixing bowls with wine   560
and tipping first drops for the god in every cup
they poured full rounds for all. And all day long
they appeased the god with song, raising a ringing hymn
to the distant archer god who drives away the plague,
those young Achaean warriors singing out his power,
and Apollo listened, his great heart warm with joy.

　　Then when the sun went down and night came on
they made their beds and slept by the stern-cables . . .
When young Dawn with her rose-red fingers shone once more,
they set sail for the main encampment of Achaea.   570
The Archer sent them a bracing following wind,
they stepped the mast, spread white sails wide,
the wind hit full and the canvas bellied out
and a dark blue wave, foaming up at the bow,
sang out loud and strong as the ship made way,
skimming the whitecaps, cutting toward her goal.
And once offshore of Achaea's vast encampment
they eased her in and hauled the black ship high,
far up on the sand, and shored her up with timbers.
Then they scattered, each to his own ship and shelter.   580

　　But *he* raged on, grimly camped by his fast fleet,
the royal son of Peleus, the swift runner Achilles.
Now he no longer haunted the meeting grounds
where men win glory, now he no longer went to war
but day after day he ground his heart out, waiting there,
yearning, always yearning for battle cries and combat.

　　But now as the twelfth dawn after this shone clear
the gods who live forever marched home to Olympus,
all in a long cortege, and Zeus led them on.
And Thetis did not forget her son's appeals.   590
She broke from a cresting wave at first light
and soaring up to the broad sky and Mount Olympus,
found the son of Cronus gazing down on the world,
peaks apart from the other gods and seated high
on the topmost crown of rugged ridged Olympus.

And crouching down at his feet,
quickly grasping his knees with her left hand,
her right hand holding him underneath the chin,
she prayed to the lord god Zeus, the son of Cronus:
"Zeus, Father Zeus! If I ever served you well   600
among the deathless gods with a word or action,
bring this prayer to pass: honor my son Achilles!—
doomed to the shortest life of any man on earth.
And now the lord of men Agamemnon has disgraced him,
seizes and keeps his prize, tears her away himself. But you—
exalt him, Olympian Zeus: your urgings rule the world!
Come, grant the Trojans victory after victory
till the Achaen armies pay my dear son back,
building higher the honor he deserves!"

                    She paused
but Zeus who commands the storm clouds answered nothing.   610
The Father sat there, silent. It seemed an eternity . . .
But Thetis, clasping his knees, held on, clinging,
pressing her question once again: "Grant my prayer,
once and for all, Father, bow your head in assent!
Or deny me outright. What have *you* to fear?
So I may know, too well, just how cruelly
I am the most dishonored goddess of them all."

                        Filled with anger
Zeus who marshals the storm clouds answered her at last:
"Disaster. You will drive me into war with Hera.
She will provoke me, she with her shrill abuse.
Even now in the face of all the immortal gods   620
she harries me perpetually, Hera charges *me*
that I always go to battle for the Trojans.
Away with you now. Hera might catch us here.
I will see to this. I will bring it all to pass.
Look, I will bow my head if that will satisfy you.
That, I remind you, that among the immortal gods
is the strongest, truest sign that I can give.
No word or work of mine—nothing can be revoked,
there is no treachery, nothing left unfinished   630
once I bow my head to say it shall be done."

    So he decreed. And Zeus the son of Cronus bowed
his craggy dark brows and the deathless locks came pouring
down from the thunderhead of the great immortal king
and giant shock waves spread through all Olympus.

    So the two of them made their pact and parted.
Deep in the sea she drove from radiant Mount Olympus.
Zeus went back to his own halls, and all the gods

in full assembly rose from their seats at once
to meet the Father striding toward them now.   640
None dared remain at rest as Zeus advanced,
they all sprang up to greet him face-to-face
as he took his place before them on his throne.
But Hera knew it all. She had seen how Thetis,
the Old Man of the Sea's daughter, Thetis quick
on her glistening feet was hatching plans with Zeus.
And suddenly Hera taunted the Father, son of Cronus:
"So, who of the gods this time, my treacherous one,
was hatching plans with you?
Always your pleasure, whenever my back is turned,   650
to settle things in your grand clandestine way.
You never deign, do you, freely and frankly,
to share your plots with me—never, not a word!"

　　The father of men and gods replied sharply,
"Hera—stop hoping to fathom all my thoughts.
You will find them a trial, though you are my wife.
Whatever is right for you to hear, no one, trust me,
will know of it before you, neither god nor man.
Whatever I choose to plan apart from all the gods—
no more of your everlasting questions, probe and pry no more."   660

　　And Hera the Queen, her dark eyes wide, exclaimed,
"Dread majesty, son of Cronus, what are you saying?
Now surely I've never probed or pried in the past.
Why, you can scheme to your heart's content
without a qualm in the world for me. But now
I have a terrible fear that she has won you over,
Thetis, the Old Man of the Sea's daughter, Thetis
with her glistening feet. I know it. Just at dawn
she knelt down beside you and grasped your knees
and I suspect you bowed your head in assent to her—   670
you granted once and for all to exalt Achilles now
and slaughter hordes of Achaeans pinned against their ships."

　　And Zeus who marshals the thunderheads returned,
"Maddening one . . . you and your eternal suspicions—
I can never escape you. Ah but tell me, Hera,
just what can you *do* about all this? Nothing.
Only estrange yourself from me a little more—
and all the worse for you.
If what you say is true, that must be my pleasure.
Now go sit down. Be quiet now. Obey my orders,   680
for fear the gods, however many Olympus holds,

are powerless to protect you when I come
to throttle you with my irresistible hands."

                              He subsided
but Hera the Queen, her eyes wider, was terrified.
She sat in silence. She wrenched her will to his.
And throughout the halls of Zeus the gods of heaven
quaked with fear. Hephaestus the Master Craftsman
rose up first to harangue them all, trying now
to bring his loving mother a little comfort,
the white-armed goddess Hera: "Oh disaster . . .
that's what it is, and it will be unbearable
if the two of you must come to blows this way,
flinging the gods in chaos just for mortal men.
No more joy for us in the sumptuous feast
when riot rules the day.
I urge you, mother—you know that I am right—
work back into his good graces, so the Father,
our beloved Father will never wheel on us again,
send our banquets crashing! The Olympian lord of lightning—
what if he would like to blast us from our seats?   700
He is far too strong. Go back to him, mother,
stroke the Father with soft, winning words—
at once the Olympian will turn kind to us again."

    Pleading, springing up with a two-handled cup,
he reached it toward his loving mother's hands
with his own winning words: "Patience, mother!
Grieved as you are, bear up, or dear as you are,
I have to see you beaten right before my eyes.
I would be shattered—what could I do to save you?
It's hard to fight the Olympian strength for strength.   710
You remember the last time I rushed to your defense?
He seized my foot, he hurled me off the tremendous threshold
and all day long I dropped, I was dead weight and then,
when the sun went down, down I plunged on Lemnos,
little breath left in me. But the mortals there
soon nursed a fallen immortal back to life."

    At that the white-armed goddess Hera smiled
and smiling, took the cup from her child's hands.
Then dipping sweet nectar up from the mixing bowl
he poured it round to all the immortals, left to right.   720
And uncontrollable laughter broke from the happy gods
as they watched the god of fire breathing hard
and bustling through the halls.
                              That hour then

and all day long till the sun went down they feasted
and no god's hunger lacked a share of the handsome banquet
or the gorgeous lyre Apollo struck or the Muses singing
voice to voice in choirs, their vibrant music rising.

    At last, when the sun's fiery light had set,
each immortal went to rest in his own house,
the splendid high halls Hephaestus built for each   730
with all his craft and cunning, the famous crippled Smith.
And Olympian Zeus the lord of lightning went to his own bed
where he had always lain when welcome sleep came on him.
There he climbed and there he slept and by his side
lay Hera the Queen, the goddess of the golden throne.

BOOK TWO

The Great Gathering of Armies

Now the great array of gods and chariot-driving men
slept all night long, but the peaceful grip of sleep
could not hold Zeus, turning it over in his mind . . .
how to exalt Achilles?—how to slaughter
hordes of Achaeans pinned against their ships?
As his spirit churned, at last one plan seemed best:
he would send a murderous dream to Agamemnon.
Calling out to the vision, Zeus winged it on:
"Go, murderous Dream, to the fast Achaean ships
and once you reach Agamemnon's shelter rouse him,   10
order him, word-for-word, exactly as I command.
Tell Atrides to arm his long-haired Achaeans,
to attack at once, full force—
now he can take the broad streets of Troy.
The immortal gods who hold Olympus clash no more,
Hera's appeals have brought them round and all agree:
griefs are about to crush the men of Troy."
                                  At that command
the dream went winging off, and passing quickly
along the fast trim ships, made for the king
and found him soon, sound asleep in his tent   20
with refreshing godsent slumber drifted round him.
Hovering at his head the vision rose like Nestor,
Neleus' son, the chief Agamemnon honored most.
Inspired with Nestor's voice and sent by Zeus,

the dream cried out, "Still asleep, Agamemnon?
The son of Atreus, that skilled breaker of horses?
How can you sleep all night, a man weighed down with duties?
Your armies turning over their lives to your command—
responsibilities so heavy. Listen to me, quickly!
I bring you a message sent by Zeus, a world away   30
but he has you in his heart, he pities you now . . .
Zeus commands you to arm your long-haired Achaeans,
to attack at once, full force—
now you can take the broad streets of Troy!
The immortal gods who hold Olympus clash no more,
Hera's appeals have brought them round and all agree:
griefs from Zeus are about to crush the men of Troy!
But keep this message firmly in your mind.
Remember—let no loss of memory overcome you
when the sweet grip of slumber sets you free."   40

  With that the dream departed, leaving him there,
his heart racing with hopes that would not come to pass.
He thought he would take the city of Priam then,
that very day, the fool. How could he know
what work the Father had in mind? The Father,
still bent on plaguing the Argives and Trojans both
with wounds and groans in the bloody press of battle.
But rousing himself from sleep, the divine voice
swirling round him, Atrides sat up, bolt awake,
pulled on a soft tunic, linen never worn,
and over it threw his flaring battle-cape,   50
under his smooth feet he fastened supple sandals,
across his shoulder slung his silver-studded sword.
Then he seized the royal scepter of his fathers—
its power can never die—and grasping it tightly
off he strode to the ships of Argives armed in bronze.

  Now the goddess Dawn climbed up to Olympus heights,
declaring the light of day to Zeus and the deathless gods
as the king commanded heralds to cry out loud and clear
and muster the long-haired Achaeans to full assembly.   60
Their cries rang out. Battalions gathered quickly.

  But first he called his ranking chiefs to council
beside the ship of Nestor, the warlord born in Pylos.
Summoning them together there Atrides set forth
his cunning, foolproof plan: "Hear me, friends—
a dream sent by the gods has come to me in sleep.
Down through the bracing godsent night it came
like good Nestor in features, height and build,

the old king himself, and hovering at my head
the dream called me on: 'Still asleep, Agamemnon?   70
The son of Atreus, that skilled breaker of horses?
How can you sleep all night, a man weighed down with duties?
Your armies turning over their lives to your command—
responsibilities so heavy. Listen to me, quickly!
I bring you a message sent by Zeus, a world away
but he has you in his heart, he pities you now . . .
Zeus commands you to arm your long-haired Achaeans,
to attack at once, full force—
now you can take the broad streets of Troy!
The immortal gods who hold Olympus clash no more,   80
Hera's appeals have brought them round and all agree:
griefs from Zeus are about to crush the men of Troy!
But keep this message firmly in your mind.'
                              With that
the dream went winging off and soothing sleep released me.
Come—see if we can arm the Achaeans for assault.
But first, according to time-honored custom,
I will test the men with a challenge, tell them all
to crowd the oarlocks, cut and run in their ships.
But you take up your battle-stations at every point,
command them, hold them back."
                              So much for his plan.   90
Agamemnon took his seat and Nestor rose among them.
Noble Nestor the king of Pylos' sandy harbor
spoke and urged them on with all good will:
"Friends, lords of the Argives, O my captains!
If any other Achaean had told us of this dream
we'd call it false and turn our backs upon it.
But look, the man who saw it has every claim
to be the best, the bravest Achaean we can field.
Come—see if we can arm the Achaeans for assault."

    And out he marched, leading the way from council.   100
The rest sprang to their feet, the sceptered kings
obeyed the great field marshal. Rank and file
streamed behind and rushed like swarms of bees
pouring out of a rocky hollow, burst on endless burst,
bunched in clusters seething over the first spring blooms,
dark hordes swirling into the air, this way, that way—
so the many armed platoons from the ships and tents
came marching on, close-file, along the deep wide beach
to crowd the meeting grounds, and Rumor, Zeus's crier,
like wildfire blazing among them, whipped them on.   110
The troops assembled. The meeting grounds shook.
The earth groaned and rumbled under the huge weight

as soldiers took positions—the whole place in uproar.
Nine heralds shouted out, trying to keep some order,
"Quiet, battalions, silence! Hear your royal kings!"
The men were forced to their seats, marshaled into ranks,
the shouting died away . . . silence.

                       King Agamemnon
rose to his feet, raising high in hand the scepter
Hephaestus made with all his strength and skill.
Hephaestus gave it to Cronus' son, Father Zeus,   120
and Zeus gave it to Hermes, the giant-killing Guide
and Hermes gave it to Pelops, that fine charioteer,
Pelops gave it to Atreus, marshal of fighting men,
who died and passed it on to Thyestes rich in flocks
and he in turn bestowed it on Agamemnon, to bear on high
as he ruled his many islands and lorded mainland Argos.
Now, leaning his weight upon that kingly scepter,
Atrides declared his will to all Achaea's armies:
"Friends—fighting Danaans, aides-in-arms of Ares!
Cronus' son has trapped me in madness, blinding ruin—   130
Zeus is a harsh, cruel god. He vowed to me long ago,
he bowed his head that I should never embark for home
till I had brought the walls of Ilium crashing down.
But now, I see, he only plotted brutal treachery:
now he commands me back to Argos in disgrace,
whole regiments of my men destroyed in battle.
So it must please his overweening heart, who knows?
Father Zeus has lopped the crowns of a thousand cities,
true, and Zeus will lop still more—his power is too great.
What humiliation! Even for generations still to come,   140
to learn that Achaean armies so strong, so vast,
fought a futile war . . . We are still fighting it,
no end in sight, and battling forces we outnumber—
by far. Say that Trojans and Argives both agreed
to swear a truce, to seal their oaths in blood,
and opposing sides were tallied out in full:
count one by one the Trojans who live in Troy
but count our Achaeans out by ten-man squads
and each squad pick a Trojan to pour its wine—
many Achaean tens would lack their steward then!   150
That's how far we outnumber them, I'd say—Achaeans
to Trojans—the men who hail from Troy at least.
But they have allies called from countless cities,
fighters brandishing spears who block my way,
who throw me far off course,
thwarting my will to plunder Ilium's rugged walls.
And now nine years of almighty Zeus have marched by,
our ship timbers rot and the cables snap and fray

and across the sea our wives and helpless children
wait in the halls, wait for our return . . . And we?   160
Our work drags on, unfinished as always, hopeless—
the labor of war that brought us here to Troy.
So come, follow my orders. All obey me now.
Cut and run! Sail home to the fatherland we love!
We'll never take the broad streets of Troy."
                                                        Testing his men
but he only made the spirit race inside their chests,
all the rank and file who'd never heard his plan.
And the whole assembly surged like big waves at sea,
the Icarian Sea when East and South Winds drive it on,   170
blasting down in force from the clouds of Father Zeus,
or when the West Wind shakes the deep standing grain
with hurricane gusts that flatten down the stalks—
so the massed assembly of troops was shaken now.
They cried in alarm and charged toward the ships
and the dust went whirling up from under rushing feet
as the men jostled back and forth, shouting orders—
"Grapple the ships! Drag them down to the bright sea!
Clean out the launching-channels!" Shrill shouts
hitting the heavens, fighters racing for home,   180
knocking the blocks out underneath the hulls.

    And now they might have won their journey home,
the men of Argos fighting the will of fate, yes,
if Hera had not alerted Athena: "Inconceivable!
Child of Zeus whose battle-shield is thunder,
tireless one, Athena—what, is *this* the way?
All the Argives flying home to their fatherland,
sailing over the sea's broad back? Leaving Priam
and all the men of Troy a trophy to glory over,
Helen of Argos, Helen for whom so many Argives   190
lost their lives in Troy, far from native land.
Go, range the ranks of Achaeans armed in bronze.
With your winning words hold back each man you find—
don't let them haul their rolling ships to sea!"

    The bright-eyed goddess Pallas lost no time.
Down she flashed from the peaks of Mount Olympus,
quickly reached the ships and found Odysseus first,
a mastermind like Zeus, still standing fast.
He had not laid a hand on his black benched hull,
such anguish racked his heart and fighting spirit.
Now close beside him the bright-eyed goddess stood   200
and urged him on: "Royal son of Laertes, Odysseus,
great tactician—what, is *this* the way?

All you Argives flying home to your fatherland,
tumbling into your oar-swept ships? Leaving Priam
and all the men of Troy a trophy to glory over,
Helen of Argos, Helen for whom so many Argives
lost their lives in Troy, far from native land!
No, don't give up now. Range the Achaean ranks,
with your winning words hold back each man you find—
don't let them haul their rolling ships to sea!"   210

He knew the goddess' voice—he went on the run,
flinging off his cape as Eurybates picked it up,
the herald of Ithaca always at his side.
Coming face-to-face with Atrides Agamemnon,
he relieved him of his fathers' royal scepter—
its power can never die—and grasping it tightly
off he strode to the ships of Argives armed in bronze.

Whenever Odysseus met some man of rank, a king,
he'd halt and hold him back with winning words:
"My *friend*—it's wrong to threaten you like a coward,   220
but you stand fast, you keep your men in check!
It's too soon to see Agamemnon's purpose clearly.
Now he's only testing us, soon he'll bear down hard.
Didn't we all hear his plan in secret council?
God forbid his anger destroy the army he commands.
The rage of kings is strong, they're nursed by the gods,
their honor comes from Zeus—
they're dear to Zeus, the god who rules the world."

When he caught some common soldier shouting out,
he'd beat him with the scepter, dress him down: 230
"You *fool*—sit still! Obey the commands of others,
your superiors—you, you deserter, rank coward,
you count for nothing, neither in war nor council.
How can all Achaeans be masters here in Troy?
Too many kings can ruin an army—mob rule!
Let there be one commander, one master only,
endowed by the son of crooked-minded Cronus
with kingly scepter and royal rights of custom:
whatever one man needs to lead his people well."

So he ranged the ranks, commanding men to order—   240
and back again they surged from ships and shelters,
back to the meeting grounds with a deep pounding din,
thundering out as battle lines of breakers crash and drag
along some endless beach, and the rough sea roars.

The armies took their seats, marshaled into ranks.
But one man, Thersites, still railed on, nonstop.
His head was full of obscenities, teeming with rant,
all for no good reason, insubordinate, baiting the kings—
anything to provoke some laughter from the troops.
Here was the ugliest man who ever came to Troy.   250
Bandy-legged he was, with one foot clubbed,
both shoulders humped together, curving over
his caved-in chest, and bobbing above them
his skull warped to a point,
sprouting clumps of scraggly, woolly hair.
Achilles despised him most, Odysseus too—
he was always abusing both chiefs, but now
he went for majestic Agamemnon, hollering out,
taunting the king with strings of cutting insults.
The Achaeans were furious with him, deeply offended.   260
But he kept shouting at Agamemnon, spewing his abuse:
"Still moaning and groaning, mighty Atrides—why now?
What are you panting after now? Your shelters packed
with the lion's share of bronze, plenty of women too,
crowding your lodges. Best of the lot, the beauties
we hand you first, whenever we take some stronghold.
Or still more gold you're wanting? More ransom a son
of the stallion-breaking Trojans might just fetch from Troy?—
though I or another hero drags him back in chains . . .
Or a young woman, is it?—to spread and couple,   270
to bed down for yourself apart from all the troops?
How shameful for you, the high and mighty commander,
to lead the sons of Achaea into bloody slaughter!
Sons? No, my soft friends, wretched excuses—
women, not men of Achaea! Home we go in our ships!
Abandon him here in Troy to wallow in all his prizes—
he'll see if the likes of us have propped him up or not.
Look—now it's Achilles, a greater man he disgraces,
seizes and keeps his prize, tears her away himself.
But no gall in Achilles. Achilles lets it go.   280
If not, Atrides, that outrage would have been your last!"

So Thersites taunted the famous field marshal.
But Odysseus stepped in quickly, faced him down
with a dark glance and threats to break his nerve:
"What a flood of abuse, Thersites! Even for you,
fluent and flowing as you are. Keep quiet.
Who are *you* to wrangle with kings, you alone?
No one, I say—no one alive less soldierly than you,
none in the ranks that came to Troy with Agamemnon.

So stop your babbling, mouthing the names of kings,   290
flinging indecencies in their teeth, your eyes
peeled for a chance to cut and run for home.
We can have no idea, no clear idea at all
how the long campaign will end . . .
whether Achaea's sons will make it home unharmed
or slink back in disgrace.
                           But there you sit,
hurling abuse at the son of Atreus, Agamemnon,
marshal of armies, simply because our fighters
give Atrides the lion's share of all our plunder.
You and your ranting slander—*you*'re the outrage.   300
I tell you this, so help me it's the truth:
if I catch you again, blithering on this way,
let Odysseus' head be wrenched off his shoulders,
never again call me the father of Telemachus
if I don't grab you, strip the clothing off you,
cloak, tunic and rags that wrap your private parts,
and whip you howling naked back to the fast ships,
out of the armies' muster—whip you like a cur!"

    And he cracked the scepter across his back and shoulders.
The rascal doubled over, tears streaking his face   310
and a bloody welt bulged up between his blades,
under the stroke of the golden scepter's studs.
He squatted low, cringing, stunned with pain,
blinking like some idiot . . .
rubbing his tears off dumbly with a fist.
Their morale was low but the men laughed now,
good hearty laughter breaking over Thersites' head—
glancing at neighbors they would shout, "A terrific stroke!
A thousand terrific strokes he's carried off—Odysseus,
taking the lead in tactics, mapping battle-plans.   320
But here's the best thing yet he's done for the men—
he's put a stop to this babbling, foulmouthed fool!
Never again, I'd say, will our gallant comrade
risk his skin to attack the kings with insults."

    So the soldiers bantered but not Odysseus.
The raider of cities stood there, scepter in hand,
and close beside him the great gray-eyed Athena
rose like a herald, ordering men to silence. All,
from the first to lowest ranks of Achaea's troops,
should hear his words and mark his counsel well.   330
For the good of all he urged them: "Agamemnon!
Now, my king, the Achaeans are bent on making you

a disgrace in the eyes of every man alive. Yes,
they fail to fulfill their promise sworn that day
they sailed here from the stallion-land of Argos:
that not until you had razed the rugged walls of Troy
would they sail home again. But look at them now,
like green, defenseless boys or widowed women
whimpering to each other, wailing to journey back.
True, they've labored long—they're desperate for home.   340
Any fighter, cut off from his wife for one month,
would chafe at the benches, moaning in his ship,
pinned down by gales and heavy, raging seas.
A month—but look at *us*.
This is the ninth year come round, the ninth
we've hung on here. Who could blame the Achaeans
for chafing, bridling beside the beaked ships?
Ah but still—what a humiliation it would be
to hold out so long, then sail home empty-handed.
Courage, my friends, hold out a little longer.   350
Till we see if Calchas divined the truth or not.
We all recall that moment—who could forget it?
We were all witnesses then. All, at least,
the deadly spirits have not dragged away . . .
                                             Why,
it seems like only yesterday or the day before
when our vast armada gathered, moored at Aulis,
freighted with slaughter bound for Priam's Troy.
We were all busy then, milling round a spring
and offering victims up on the holy altars,
full sacrifice to the gods to guarantee success,   360
under a spreading plane tree where the water splashed,
glittering in the sun—when a great omen appeared.
A snake, and his back streaked red with blood,
a thing of terror! Olympian Zeus himself
had launched him into the clean light of day . . .
He slid from under the altar, glided up the tree
and there the brood of a sparrow, helpless young ones,
teetered high on the topmost branch-tips, cowering
under the leaves there, eight they were all told
and the mother made the ninth, she'd borne them all—   370
chirping to break the heart but the snake gulped them down
and the mother cried out for her babies, fluttering over him . . .
he coiled, struck, fanging her wing—a high thin shriek!
But once he'd swallowed down the sparrow with her brood,
the son of crooked Cronus who sent the serpent forth
turned him into a sign, a monument clear to see—
Zeus struck him to stone! And we stood by,

amazed that such a marvel came to light.
                                        So then,
when those terrible, monstrous omens burst in
on the victims we were offering to the gods,   380
Calchas swiftly revealed the will of Zeus:
'Why struck dumb now, my long-haired Achaeans?
Zeus who rules the world has shown us an awesome sign,
an event long in the future, late to come to birth
but the fame of that great work will never die.
As the snake devoured the sparrow with her brood,
eight and the mother made the ninth, she'd borne them all,
so *we* will fight in Troy that many years and then,
then in the tenth we'll take her broad streets.'
So that day the prophet revealed the future—   390
and now, look, by god, it all comes to pass!
Up with you, all you Argives geared for combat,
stand your ground, right here,
until we take the mighty walls of Priam!"
                                He fired them so
the armies roared and the ships resounded round them,
shattering echoes ringing from their shouts
as Argives cried assent to King Odysseus' words.
And Nestor the noble horseman spurred them more:
"What disgrace! Look at you, carrying on
in the armies' muster just like boys—fools!   400
Not a thought in your heads for works of battle.
What becomes of them now, the pacts and oaths we swore?
Into the flames with councils, all the plans of men,
the vows sealed with the strong, unmixed wine,
the firm clasp of the right hand we trusted!
We battle on in words, as always, mere words,
and what's the cure? We cannot find a thing.
No matter how many years we wrangle here.
                                Agamemnon—
never swerve, hold to your first plan of action,
lead your armies headlong into war!   410
The rest of them? Let them rot, the one or two
who hatch their plans apart from all the troops—
what good can they win from that? Nothing at all.
Why, they'd scuttle home before they can even learn
if the vows of Zeus with his dark cloudy shield
are false or not. Zeus the son of almighty Cronus,
I remind you, bowed his head that day we boarded ship,
all the Argives laden with blood and death for Troy—
his lightning bolts on the right, good omens blazing forth.
So now let no man hurry to sail for home, not yet . . .   420

not till he beds down with a faithful Trojan wife,
payment in full for the groans and shocks of war
we have all borne for Helen.
                              But any soldier
wild with desire to reach his home at once—
just let him lay a hand on his black benched ship
and right in front of the rest he'll reach his death!
But you, my King, be on your guard yourself. Come,
listen well to another man. Here's some advice,
not to be tossed aside, and I will tell it clearly.
Range your men by tribes, even by clans, Agamemnon,   430
so clan fights by the side of clan, tribe by tribe.
Fight this way, if the Argives still obey you,
then you can see which captain is a coward,
which contingent too, and which is loyal, brave,
since they will fight in separate formations of their own.
Then, what's more, if you fail to sack the city,
you will know if the will of god's to blame
or the cowardice of your men—inept in battle."

    And King Agamemnon took his lead, saluting:
"Again, old man, you outfight the Argives in debate!   440
Father Zeus, Athena, Apollo, if only I had ten men
like Nestor to plan with me among Achaea's armies—
then we could topple Priam's citadel in a day,
throttle it in our hands and gut Troy to nothing.
But Cronus' son, Zeus with his shield of storm
insists on embroiling me in painful struggles,
futile wars of words . . .
Imagine—I and Achilles, wrangling over a girl,
battling man-to-man. And I, I was the first
to let my anger flare. Ah if the two of us   450
could ever think as one, Troy could delay
her day of death no longer, not one moment.
Go now, take your meal—the sooner to bring on war.
Quickly—let each fighter sharpen his spear well,
balance his shield well, feed his horses well
with plenty of grain to build their racing speed—
each man look well to his chariot's running order,
nerve himself for combat now, so all day long
we can last out the grueling duels of Ares!
No breathing space, no letup, not a moment, not   460
till the night comes on to part the fighters' fury!
Now sweat will soak the shield-strap round your chest,
your fist gripping the spear will ache with tensing,
now the lather will drench your war-team's flanks,
hauling your sturdy chariot.

But any man I catch,
trying to skulk behind his long beaked ships,
hanging back from battle—he is finished.
No way for *him* to escape the dogs and birds!"

So he commanded
and the armies gave a deep resounding roar like waves
crashing against a cliff when the South Wind whips it,   470
bearing down, some craggy headland jutting out to sea—
the waves will never leave it in peace, thrashed by gales
that hit from every quarter, breakers left and right.
The troops sprang up, scattered back to the ships,
lit fires beside their tents and took their meal.
Each sacrificed to one or another deathless god,
each man praying to flee death and the grind of war.
But the lord of men Agamemnon sacrificed a fat rich ox,
five years old, to the son of mighty Cronus, Zeus,
and called the chiefs of all the Argive forces: 480
Nestor first and foremost, then King Idomeneus,
the Great and Little Ajax, Tydeus' son Diomedes
and Odysseus sixth, a mastermind like Zeus.
The lord of the war cry Menelaus came uncalled,
he knew at heart what weighed his brother down.
They stood in a ring around the ox, took up barley
and then, rising among them, King Agamemnon
raised his voice in prayer: "Zeus, Zeus,
god of greatness, god of glory, lord god
of the dark clouds who lives in the bright sky,   490
don't let the sun go down or the night descend on us!
Not till I hurl the smoke-black halls of Priam headlong—
torch his gates to blazing rubble—rip the tunic of Hector
and slash his heroic chest to ribbons with my bronze—
and a ruck of comrades round him, groveling facedown,
gnaw their own earth!"

And so Agamemnon prayed
but the son of Cronus would not bring his prayer to pass,
not yet . . . the Father accepted the sacrifices, true,
but doubled the weight of thankless, ruthless war.
Once the men had prayed and flung the barley,   500
first they lifted back the heads of the victims,
slit their throats, skinned them and carved away
the meat from the thighbones and wrapped them in fat,
a double fold sliced clean and topped with strips of flesh.
And they burned these on a cleft stick, peeled and dry,
spitted the vitals, held them over Hephaestus' flames
and once they'd charred the thighs and tasted the organs
they cut the rest into pieces, pierced them with spits,
roasted them to a turn and pulled them off the fire.

The work done, the feast laid out, they ate well   510
and no man's hunger lacked a share of the banquet.
When they had put aside desire for food and drink,
Nestor the noble old horseman spoke out first:
"Marshal Atrides, lord of men Agamemnon,
no more trading speeches now. No more delay,
putting off the work the god puts in our hands.
Come, let the heralds cry out to all contingents,
full battle-armor, muster the men along the ships.
Now down we go, united—review them as we pass.   520
Down through the vast encampment of Achaea,
the faster to rouse the slashing god of war!"

    Agamemnon the lord of men did not resist.
He commanded heralds to cry out loud and clear
and summon the long-haired Achaean troops to battle.
Their cries rang out. The battalions gathered quickly.
The warlords dear to the gods and flanking Agamemnon
strode on ahead, marshaling men-at-arms in files,
and down their ranks the fiery-eyed Athena bore
her awesome shield of storm, ageless, deathless—
a hundred golden tassels, all of them braided tight   530
and each worth a hundred oxen, float along the front.
Her shield of lightning dazzling, swirling around her,
headlong on Athena swept through the Argive armies,
driving soldiers harder, lashing the fighting-fury
in each Achaean's heart—no stopping them now,
mad for war and struggle. Now, suddenly,
battle thrilled them more than the journey home,
than sailing hollow ships to their dear native land.

    As ravening fire rips through big stands of timber
high on a mountain ridge and the blaze flares miles away,   540
so from the marching troops the blaze of bronze armor,
splendid and superhuman, flared across the earth,
flashing into the air to hit the skies.
                              Armies gathering now
as the huge flocks on flocks of winging birds; geese or cranes
or swans with their long lancing necks—circling Asian marshes
round the Cayster outflow, wheeling in all directions,
glorying in their wings—keep on landing, advancing,
wave on shrieking wave and the tidal flats resound.
So tribe on tribe, pouring out of the ships and shelters,
marched across the Scamander plain and the earth shook,   550
tremendous thunder from under trampling men and horses
drawing into position down the Scamander meadow flats

breaking into flower—men by the thousands, numberless
as the leaves and spears that flower forth in spring.

The armies massing . . . crowding thick-and-fast
as the swarms of flies seething over the shepherds' stalls
in the first spring days when the buckets flood with milk—
so many long-haired Achaeans swarmed across the plain
to confront the Trojans, fired to smash their lines.

The armies grouping now—as seasoned goatherds   560
split their wide-ranging flocks into packs with ease
when herds have mixed together down the pasture:
so the captains formed their tight platoons,
detaching right and left, moving up for action—
and there in the midst strode powerful Agamemnon,
eyes and head like Zeus who loves the lightning,
great in the girth like Ares, god of battles,
broad through the chest like sea lord Poseidon.
Like a bull rising head and shoulders over the herds,
a royal bull rearing over his flocks of driven cattle—   570
so imposing was Atreus' son, so Zeus made him that day,
towering over fighters, looming over armies.

Sing to me now, you Muses who hold the halls of Olympus!
You are goddesses, you are everywhere, you know all things—
all we hear is the distant ring of glory, we know nothing—
who were the captains of Achaea? Who were the kings?
The mass of troops I could never tally, never name,
not even if I had ten tongues and ten mouths,
a tireless voice and the heart inside me bronze,
never unless you Muses of Olympus, daughter of Zeus   580
whose shield is rolling thunder, sing, sing in memory
all who gathered under Troy. Now I can only tell
the lords of the ships, the ships in all their numbers!

First came the Boeotian units led by Leitus and Peneleos:
Arcesilaus and Prothoënor and Clonius shared command
of the armed men who lived in Hyria, rocky Aulis,
Schoenus, Scolus and Eteonus spurred with hills,
Thespia and Graea, the dancing rings of Mycalessus,
men who lived round Harma, Ilesion and Erythrae
and those who settled Eleon, Hyle and Peteon,   590
Ocalea, Medeon's fortress walled and strong,
Copae, Eutresis and Thisbe thronged with doves,
fighters from Coronea, Haliartus deep in meadows,
and the men who held Plataea and lived in Glisas,

men who held the rough-hewn gates of Lower Thebes,
Onchestus the holy, Poseidon's sun-filled grove,
men from the town of Arne green with vineyards,
Midea and sacred Nisa, Anthedon-on-the-marches.
Fifty ships came freighted with these contingents,
one hundred and twenty young Boeotians manning each.   600

Then men who lived in Aspledon, Orchomenos of the Minyans,
fighters led by Ascalaphus and Ialmenus, sons of Ares
whom Astyoche bore in Actor son of Azeus' halls
when the shy young girl, climbing into the upper rooms,
made love with the god of war in secret, shared his strength.
In her two sons' command sailed thirty long curved ships.

Then Schedius and Epistrophus led the men of Phocis—
two sons of Iphitus, that great heart, Naubolus' son—
the men who held Cyparissus and Pytho's high crags,   610
the hallowed earth of Crisa, Daulis and Panopeus,
men who dwelled round Anemoria, round Hyampolis,
men who lived along the Cephisus' glinting waters,
men who held Lilaea close to the river's wellsprings.
Laden with all their ranks came forty long black ships
and Phocian captains ranged them column by column,
manning stations along the Boeotians' left flank.

Next the Locrians led by racing Ajax, son of Oileus,
Little Ajax—a far cry from the size of Telamonian Ajax—
a smaller man but trim in his skintight linen corslet,
he outthrew all Hellenes, all Achaeans with his spear.   620
He led the men who lived in Opois, Cynus, Calliarus,
Bessa and Scarphe, the delightful town of Augeae,
Tarphe and Thronion down the Boagrius River.
In Oilean Ajax' charge came forty long black ships,
Locrians living across the straits from sacrosanct Euboea.

And the men who held Euboea, Abantes breathing fury,
Chalcis and Eretria, Histiaea covered with vineyards,
Cerinthus along the shore and Dion's hilltop streets,
the men who held Carystus and men who settled Styra.
Elephenor, comrade of Ares, led the whole contingent,   630
Chalcodon's son, a lord of the fierce Abantes.
The sprinting Abantes followed hard at his heels,
their forelocks cropped, hair grown long at the back,
troops nerved to lunge with their tough ashen spears
and slash the enemies' breastplates round their chests.
In Elephenor's command sailed forty long black ships.

Next the men who held the strong-built city of Athens,
realm of high-hearted Erechtheus. Zeus's daughter Athena
tended him once the grain-giving fields had borne him,
long ago, and then she settled the king in Athens,   640
in her own rich shrine, where sons of Athens worship him
with bulls and goats as the years wheel round in season.
Athenians all, and Peteos' son Menestheus led them on,
and no one born on the earth could match that man
in arraying teams of horse and shielded fighters—
Nestor his only rival, thanks to Nestor's age.
And in his command sailed fifty long black ships.

Out of Salamis Great Telamonian Ajax led twelve ships
drawn up where Athenian forces formed their line of battle.

Then men of Argos and Tiryns with her tremendous walls   650
and Hermione and Asine commanding the deep wide gulf,
Troezen, Eionae and Epidaurus green with vines
and Achaea's warrior sons who held Aegina and Mases—
Diomedes lord of the war cry led their crack contingents
flanked by Sthenelus, far-famed Capaneus' favorite son.
Third in the vanguard marched Euryalus strong as a god,
son of King Mecisteus son of Talaus, but over them all,
with cries to marshal men Diomedes led the whole force
and his Argives sailed in eighty long black ships.

Next the men who held Mycenae's huge walled citadel,   660
Corinth in all her wealth and sturdy, strong Cleonae,
men of Orniae, lovely Araethyrea and Sicyon,
Adrastus' domain before he ruled Mycenae,
men of Hyperesia, Gonoëssa perched on hills,
men who held Pellene and those who circled Aegion,
men of the coastal strip and Helice's broad headland.
They came in a hundred ships and Agamemnon led them on,
Atreus' royal son, and marching in his companies
came the most and bravest fighting men by far.
And there in the midst, armed in gleaming bronze,   670
in all his glory, he towered high over all his fighters—
he was the greatest warlord, he led by far the largest army.

Next those who held Lacedaemon's hollows deep with gorges,
Pharis, Sparta and Messe, crowded haunt of the wild doves,
men who lived in Brysiae and Augeae's gracious country,
men who held Amyclae, Helos the seaboard fortress,
men who settled Laas and lived near Oetylus:
Agamemnon's brother, Menelaus lord of the war cry

led their sixty ships, armed them apart, downshore,
and amidst their ranks he marched, ablaze with valor,   680
priming men for attack. And his own heart blazed the most
to avenge the groans and shocks of war they'd borne for Helen.

Next the men who lived in Pylos and handsome Arene,
Thryon, the Alpheus ford and finely-masoned Aepy,
men who lived in Cyparisseis and Amphigenia,
Pteleos, Helos and Dorion where the Muses met
the Thracian Thamyris, stopped the minstrel's song.
From Oechalia he came, from Oechalia's King Eurytus,
boasting to high heaven that he could outsing the very Muses,
the daughters of Zeus whose shield resounds with thunder.   690
They were enraged, they maimed him, they ripped away
his voice, the rousing immortal wonder of his song
and wiped all arts of harping from his mind.
Nestor the noble old horseman led those troops
in ninety sweeping ships lined up along the shore.

And those who held Arcadia under Cyllene's peak,
near Aepytus' ancient tomb where men fight hand-to-hand,
men who lived in Pheneos and Orchomenos rife with sheep,
Stratia, Rhipe and Enispe whipped by the sudden winds,
men who settled Tegea, Mantinea's inviting country,   700
men who held Stymphalus, men who ruled Parrhasia—
the son of Ancaeus led them, powerful Agapenor
with sixty ships in all, and aboard each vessel
crowded full Arcadian companies skilled in war.
Agamemnon himself, the lord of men had given them
those well-benched ships to plow the wine-dark sea,
since works of the sea meant nothing to those landsmen.

Then the men who lived in Buprasion, brilliant Elis,
all the realm as far as Hyrmine and Myrsinus, frontier towns
and Olenian Rock and Alesion bound within their borders.   710
Four warlords led their ranks, ten-ship flotillas each,
and filling the decks came bands of Epean fighters,
two companies under Thalpius and Amphimachus, sons
of the line of Actor, one of Eurytus, one of Cteatus.
Strong Diores the son of Amarynceus led the third
and the princely Polyxinus led the fourth,
the son of King Agasthenes, Augeas' noble stock.

Then ocean men from Dulichion and the Holy Islands,
the Echinades rising over the sea across from Elis—
Meges a match for Ares led their troops to war,   720
a son of the rider Phyleus dear to Zeus who once,

enraged at his father, fled and settled Dulichion.
In his son's command sailed forty long black ships.

Next Odysseus led his Cephallonian companies,
gallant-hearted fighters, the island men of Ithaca,
of Mount Neriton's leafy ridges shimmering in the wind,
and men who lived in Crocylia and rugged Aegilips,
men who held Zacynthus and men who dwelled near Samos
and mainland men who grazed their flocks across the channel.
That mastermind like Zeus, Odyssus led those fighters on.   730
In his command sailed twelve ships, prows flashing crimson.

And Thoas son of Andraemon led Aetolia's units,
soldiers who lived in Pleuron, Pylene and Olenus,
Chalcis along the shore and Calydon's rocky heights
where the sons of wellborn Oeneus were no more
and the king himself was dead
and Meleager with his golden hair was gone.
So the rule of all Aetolian men had passed to Thoas.
In Thoas' command sailed forty long black ships.

And the great spearman Idomeneus led his Cretans,   740
the men who held Cnossos and Gortyn ringed in walls,
Lyctos, Miletus, Lycastus' bright chalk bluffs,
Phaestos and Rhytion, cities a joy to live in—
the men who peopled Crete, a hundred cities strong.
The renowned spearman Idomeneus led them all in force
with Meriones who butchered men like the god of war himself.
And in their command sailed eighty long black ships.

And Heracles' son Tlepolemus tall and staunch
led nine ships of the proud Rhodians out of Rhodes,
the men who lived on Rhodes in three island divisions,   750
Lindos and Ialysus and Camirus' white escarpment,
armies led by the famous spearman Tlepolemus
whom Astyochea bore to Heracles filled with power.
He swept her up from Ephyra, from the Selleis River
after he'd ravaged many towns of brave young warlords
bred by the gods. But soon as his son Tlepolemus
came of age in Heracles' well-built palace walls
the youngster abruptly killed his father's uncle—
the good soldier Licymnius, already up in years—
and quickly fitting ships, gathering partisans,   760
he fled across the sea with threats of the sons
and the sons' sons of Heracles breaking at his back.
But he reached Rhodes at last, a wanderer rocked by storms,
and there they settled in three divisions, all by tribes,

loved by Zeus himself the king of gods and mortals
showering wondrous gold on all their heads.

Nireus led his three trim ships from Syme,
Nireus the son of Aglaea and King Charopus,
Nireus the handsomest man who ever came to Troy,
of all the Achaeans after Peleus' fearless son.   770
But he was a lightweight, trailed by a tiny band.

And men who held Nisyrus, Casus and Crapathus,
Cos, Eurypylus' town, and the islands called Calydnae—
combat troops, and Antiphus and Phidippus led them on,
the two sons of the warlord Thessalus, Heracles' son.
In their command sailed thirty long curved ships.
                                    And now, Muse,
sing all those fighting men who lived in Pelasgian Argos,
the big contingents out of Alus and Alope and Trachis,
men of Phthia and Hellas where the women are a wonder,
all the fighters called Achaeans, Hellenes and Myrmidons   780
ranked in fifty ships, and Achilles was their leader.
But they had no lust for the grind of battle now—
where was the man who marched their lines to war?
The brilliant runner Achilles lay among his ships,
raging over Briseis, the girl with lustrous hair,
the prize he seized from Lyrnessus—
after he had fought to exhaustion at Lyrnessus,
storming the heights, and breached the walls of Thebes
and toppled the vaunting spearmen Epistrophus and Mynes,
sons of King Euenus, Selepius' son. All for Briseis   790
his heart was breaking now . . . Achilles lay there now
but he would soon rise up in all his power.

Then men of Phylace, Pyrasus banked in flowers,
Demeter's closed and holy grove and Iton mother of flocks,
Antron along the shore and Pteleos deep in meadows.
The veteran Protesilaus had led those troops
while he still lived, but now for many years
the arms of the black earth had held him fast
and his wife was left behind, alone in Phylace,
both cheeks torn in grief, their house half-built.   800
Just as he vaulted off his ship a Dardan killed him,
first by far of the Argives slaughtered on the beaches.
But not even then were his men without a captain,
yearn as they did for their lost leader. No,
Podarces a fresh campaigner ranged their units—
a son of Iphiclus son of Phylacus rich in flocks—

Podarces, gallant Protesilaus' blood brother,
younger-born, but the older man proved braver too,
an iron man of war. Yet not for a moment did his army
lack a leader, yearn as they did for the braver dead.   810
Under Podarces sailed their forty long black ships.

And the men who lived in Pherae fronting Lake Boebeis,
in Boebe and Glaphyrae and Iolcos' sturdy ramparts:
their eleven ships were led by Admetus' favored son,
Eumelus, born to Admetus by Alcestis, queen of women,
the most radiant daughter Pelias ever fathered.

Then men who lived in Methone and Thaumacia,
men who held Meliboea and rugged ridged Olizon:
Philoctetes the master archer had led them on
in seven ships with fifty oarsmen aboard each,   820
superbly skilled with the bow in lethal combat.
But their captain lay on an island, racked with pain,
on Lemnos' holy shores where the armies had marooned him,
agonized by his wound, the bite of a deadly water-viper.
There he writhed in pain but soon, encamped by the ships,
the Argives would recall Philoctetes, their great king.
But not even then were his men without a captain,
yearn as they did for their lost leader. No,
Medon formed them up, Oileus' bastard son
whom Rhene bore to Oileus, grim raider of cities.   830

And men who settled Tricca, rocky Ithome terraced high
and men who held Oechalia, Oechalian Eurytus' city:
the two sons of Asclepius led their units now,
both skilled healers, Podalirius and Machaon.
In their command sailed forty curved black ships.

And men who held Ormenion and the Hyperian Spring,
men who held Asterion, Titanos' chalk-white cliffs:
Eurypylus marched them on, Euaemon's shining son.
In his command sailed forty long black ships.

And the men who settled Argissa and Gyrtone,   840
Orthe, Elone, the gleaming citadel Oloosson:
Polypoetes braced for battle led them on,
the son of Pirithous, son of deathless Zeus.
Famous Hippodamia bore the warrior to Pirithous
that day he wreaked revenge on the shaggy Centaurs,
routed them out of Pelion, drove them to the Aethices.
Polypoetes was not alone, Leonteus shared the helm,

companion of Ares, Caeneus' grandson, proud Coronus' son.
And in his command sailed forty long black ships.

And Guneus out of Cyphus led on two and twenty ships   850
and in his platoons came Enienes and battle-tried Peraebians
who pitched homes in the teeth of Dodona's bitter winters,
who held the tilled acres along the lovely Titaressus
that runs her pure crystal currents into Peneus—
never mixed with Peneus' eddies glistening silt
but gliding over the surface smooth as olive oil,
branching, breaking away from the river Styx,
the dark and terrible oath-stream of the gods.

And Prothous son of Tenthredon led the Magnesians,
men who lived around the Peneus, up along Mount Pelion   860
sloped in wind-whipped leaves. Racing Prothous led them on
and in his command sailed forty long black ships.

These, these were the captains of Achaea and the kings.
Now tell me, Muse, who were the bravest of them all,
of the men and chariot-teams that came with Atreus' sons?

The best by far of the teams were Eumelus' mares
and Pheres' grandson drove them—swift as birds,
matched in age and their glossy coats and matched
to a builder's level flat across their backs.
Phoebus Apollo lord of the silver bow   870
had bred them both in Perea, a brace of mares
that raced the War-god's panic through the lines.
But best by far of the men was Telamonian Ajax
while Achilles raged apart. The famed Achilles
towered over them all, he and the battle-team
that bore the peerless son of Peleus into war.
But off in his beaked seagoing ships he lay,
raging away at Atrides Agamemnon, king of armies,
while his men sported along the surf, marking time,
hurling the discus, throwing spears and testing bows.   880
And the horses, each beside its chariot, champing clover
and parsley from the marshes, waited, pawing idly.
Their masters' chariots stood under blankets now,
stored away in the tents while the rank and file,
yearning for their leader, the great man of war,
drifting here and there throughout the encampment,
hung back from the fighting.
                              But on the armies came
as if the whole earth were devoured by wildfire, yes,
and the ground thundered under them, deep as it does

for Zeus who loves the lightning, Zeus in all his rage   890
when he lashes the ground around Typhoeus in Arima,
there where they say the monster makes his bed of pain—
so the earth thundered under their feet, armies trampling,
sweeping through the plain at blazing speed.
                                        Now the Trojans.
Iris the wind-quick messenger hurried down to Ilium,
bearing her painful message, sent by storming Zeus.
The Trojans assembled hard by Priam's gates,
gathered together there, young men and old,
and rushing closer, racing Iris addressed them,
keying her voice to that of Priam's son Polites.   900
He had kept a watch for the Trojans, posted atop
old Aesyetes' tomb and poised to sprint for home
at the first sign of Argives charging from the ships.
Like him to the life, the racing Iris urged, "Old Priam,
words, endless words—that is your passion, always,
as once in the days of peace. But ceaseless war's upon us!
Time and again I've gone to battle, fought with men
but I've never seen an army great as this. Too much—
like piling leaves or sand, and on and on they come,
advancing across the plain to fight before our gates.   910
Hector, I urge you first of all—do as I tell you.
Armies of allies crowd the mighty city of Priam,
true, but they speak a thousand different tongues,
fighters gathered here from all ends of the realm.
Let each chief give commands to the tribe he leads,
move them out, marshal his own contingents—now!"

    Hector missed nothing—that was a goddess' call.
He broke up the assembly at once. They rushed to arms
and all the gates flung wide and the Trojan mass surged out,
horses, chariots, men on foot—a tremendous roar went up.   920

    Now a sharp ridge rises out in front of Troy,
all on its own and far across the plain
with running-room around it, all sides clear.
Men call it Thicket Ridge, the immortals call it
the leaping Amazon Myrine's mounded tomb, and there
the Trojans and allies ranged their troops for battle.

    First, tall Hector with helmet flashing led the Trojans—
Priam's son and in his command by far the greatest, bravest army,
divisions harnessed in armor, veterans bristling spears.

    And the noble son of Anchises led the Dardanians—   930
Aeneas whom the radiant Aphrodite bore Anchises

down the folds of Ida, a goddess bedded with a man.
Not Aeneas alone but flanked by Antenor's two sons,
Acamas and Archelochus, trained for every foray.

And men who lived in Zelea under the foot of Ida,
a wealthy clan that drank the Aesepus' dark waters—
Trojans all, and the shining son of Lycaon led them on,
Pandarus, with the bow that came from Apollo's own hands.

And the men who held the land of Apaesus and Adrestia,   940
men who held Pityea, Terea's steep peaks—the units led
by Adrestus joined by Amphius trim in linen corslet,
the two good sons of Merops out of Percote harbor,
Merops adept beyond all men in the *mantic arts*.
He refused to let his two boys march to war,
this man-killing war, but the young ones fought him
all the way—the forces of black death drove them on.

And the men who lived around Percote and Practios,
men who settled Sestos, Abydos and gleaming Arisbe:
Asius son of Hyrtacus led them on, captain of armies,   950
Hyrtacus' offspring Asius—hulking, fiery stallions
bore him in from Arisbe, from the Selleis River.

Hippothous led the Pelasgian tribes of spearmen,
fighters who worked Larissa's dark rich plowland.
Hippothous and Pylaeus, tested soldier, led them on,
both sons of Pelasgian Lethus, Teutamus' scion.

Acamas and the old hero Pirous led the Thracians,
all the Hellespont bounds within her riptide straits.

Euphemus led the Cicones, fighters armed with spears,
son of Troezenus, Ceas' son, a warlord bred by the gods.

Pyraechmes led the Paeonians, reflex bows in hand,   960
hailing from Amydon far west and the broad river Axius,
Axius, clearest stream that flows across the earth.

That burly heart Pylaemenes led his Paphlagonians
out of Enetian country, land where the wild mules breed:
the men who held Cytorus and lived in range of Sesamus,
building their storied halls along the Parthenius River,
at Cromna, Aegialus and the highland fortress Erythini.

Odius and Epistrophus led the Halizonians out of Alybe
miles east where the mother lode of silver came to birth.

Chromis led the Mysian men with Ennomus seer of birds—   970
but none of his winged signs could beat off black death.
Down he went, crushed by racing Achilles' hands, destroyed
in the river where he slaughtered other Trojans too.

Ascanius strong as a god and Phorcys led the Phrygians
in from Ascania due east, primed for the clash of combat.

Mesthles and Antiphus led Maeonia's proud contingent,
Talaemenes' two sons sprung from the nymph of Gyge Lake
led on Maeonian units born and bred under Mount Tmolus.

Nastes led the Carians wild with barbarous tongues,
men who held Miletus, Phthires' ridges thick with timber,   980
Maeander's currents and Mount Mycale's craggy peaks.
Amphimachus and Nastes led their formations on,
Nastes and Amphimachus, Nomion's flamboyant sons.
Nastes strolled to battle decked in gold like a girl,
the fool! None of his trappings kept off grisly death—
down he went, crushed by racing Achilles' hands, destroyed
at the ford where battle-hard Achilles stripped his gold away.

And last, Sarpedon and valiant Glaucus marched the Lycians on
from Lycia far south, from the Xanthus' swirling rapids.

Plato

THE PHAEDO

Introduction by James Eichler

Plato (circa 427–347 B.C.), a student of Socrates, established the basis for a major strand of Western philosophy called idealism. Like his teacher, he opposed the relativism of the Sophists and sought to define absolute standards of justice, beauty, good, etc. This, coupled with the influences of the Pythagoreans, and of Heraclitus and Parmenides, led him to develop a synthesis that addressed most of the philosophical problems of his day.

Plato is said to have been of aristocratic birth, and a critic of the democratic form of government so highly esteemed in Athens during its "golden age." Because, in 399 B.C., a restored Athenian democracy made Socrates a scapegoat for its ill fortunes in the Peloponnesian War, and because Plato was personally associated with Socrates, and related to members of the short-lived but infamous Thirty Tyrant Regime imposed by the victorious Spartans at the end of that war, he left Athens following Socrates' execution, returning in 387 B.C. to establish a school (The Academy) in which he taught until his death. He also wrote a series of dialogues—among them the *Apology,* the *Crito,* the *Republic,* and the *Laws.* These dialogues preserved his thought for succeeding generations of philosophers.

One theme which permeates these writings is the nature of virtue and the need to live the "good life." In the dialogue entitled the *Phaedo,* which recounts Socrates' death, Plato describes the good life and the key role philosophy plays in its attainment. In reading the *Phaedo,* it will be helpful to keep several questions in mind. How does Plato define reality or truth (ontology)? What are its qualities? How does he think one can know that reality or truth (epistemology)? Given his definition of truth, how then should one apply it to his or her life (ethics)? What will be the reward for doing so and how does this imply order and justice in the universe? What does Plato have to say about God? What about human nature, the soul, or death? What did Socrates mean in the dialogue when he said he had no fear of death, because he had "practiced dying" his entire life? How do Plato's views of reality, humanity, and the afterlife inspire religious and philosophical systems of thought we follow today? Do we define a virtuous life in similar ways? Finally, consider why Plato chose to write in the form of conversations and make Socrates his chief spokesman. What purposes might this have served for him?

In reading this, note that Plato equates the intellect with the soul, and that for him, the improvement of one translates into the improvement of the other. On moral grounds then, Plato makes a strong case for rationalism as a guide to "the good life." His emphasis on the importance of spirit and idea shapes his answers to the questions listed above, and has influenced Western thought so pervasively that philosophers and theologians of the twentieth century still acknowledge their debt to him.

Phaedo

CHARACTERS OF THE DIALOGUE

PHAEDO
The Narrator
ECHECRATES
SOCRATES

APOLLODORUS
CEBES
CRITO
SIMMIAS

THE SERVANT OF THE ELEVEN

SCENE—*The Prison of Socrates*

Echecrates. Were you with Socrates yourself, Phaedo, on that day when he drank the poison in the prison, or did you hear the story from someone else?

Phaedo. I was there myself, Echecrates.

Ech. Then what was it that our master said before his death, and how did he die? I should be very glad if you would tell me. None of our citizens go very much to Athens now; and no stranger has come from there for a long time who could give us any definite account of these things, except that he drank the poison and died. We could learn nothing beyond that.

Phaedo. Then have you not heard about the trial either, how that went?

Ech. Yes, we were told of that, and we were rather surprised to find that he did not die till so long after the trial. Why was that, Phaedo?

Phaedo. It was an accident, Echecrates. The stern of the ship, which the Athenians send to Delos, happened to have been crowned on the day before the trial.

Ech. And what is this ship?

Phaedo. It is the ship, as the Athenians say, in which Theseus took the seven youths and the seven maidens to Crete, and saved them from death, and himself was saved. The Athenians made a vow then to Apollo, the story goes, to send a sacred mission to Delos every year, if they should be saved; and from that time to this they have always sent it to the god, every year. They have a law to keep the city pure as soon as the mission begins, and not to execute any sentence of death until the ship has returned from Delos; and sometimes, when it is detained by contrary winds, that is a long while. The sacred mission begins when the priest of Apollo crowns the

Plato, *Phaedo* (F.J. Church, trans.), Bobbs–Merrill, 1951, original pp. 1–33 (through "deliverance and purification.")

stern of the ship; and as I said, this happened to have been done on the day before the trial. That was why Socrates lay so long in prison between his trial and his death.

Ech.   But tell me about his death, Phaedo. What was said and done, and which of his friends were with our master? Or would not the authorities let them be there? Did he die alone?

Phaedo.   Oh, no; some of them were there, indeed several.

Ech.   It would be very good of you, if you are not busy, to tell us the whole story as exactly as you can.

Phaedo.   No, I have nothing to do, and I will try to relate it. Nothing is more pleasant to me than to recall Socrates to my mind, whether by speaking of him myself or by listening to others.

Ech.   Indeed, Phaedo, you will have an audience like yourself. But try to tell us everything that happened as precisely as you can.

Phaedo.   Well, I myself was strangely moved on that day. I did not feel that I was being present at the death of a dear friend; I did not pity him, for he seemed to me happy, Echecrates, both in his bearing and in his words, so fearlessly and nobly did he die. I could not help thinking that the gods would watch over him still on his journey to the other world, and that when he arrived there it would be well with him, if it was ever well with any man. Therefore I had scarcely any feeling of pity, as you would expect at such a mournful time. Neither did I feel the pleasure which I usually felt at our philosophical discussions; for our talk was of philosophy. A very singular feeling came over me, a strange mixture of pleasure and pain when I remembered that he was presently to die. All of us who were there were in much the same state, laughing and crying by turns; particularly Apollodorus. I think you know the man and his ways.

Ech.   Of course I do.

Phaedo.   Well, he did not restrain himself at all and I myself and the others were greatly agitated too.

Ech.   Who were there, Phaedo?

Phaedo.   Of native Athenians, there was this Apollodorus, and Critobulus, and his father Crito, and Hermogenes, and Epigenes, and Aeschines, and Antisthenes. Then there was Ctesippus the Paeanian, and Menexenus, and some other Athenians. Plato I believe was ill.

Ech.   Were any strangers there?

Phaedo.   Yes, there was Simmias of Thebes, and Cebes, and Phaedondes; and Eucleides and Terpsion from Megara.

Ech.   But Aristippus and Cleombrotus, were they present?

Phaedo.   No, they were not. They were said to be in Aegina.

Ech.   Was anyone else there?

Phaedo.   No, I think that these were all.

Ech.   Then tell us about your conversation.

Phaedo.   I will try to relate the whole story to you from the beginning. On the previous days I and the others had always met in the morning at the court where the trial was held, which was close to the prison; and then we had gone in to Socrates. We used to wait each morning until the prison was opened, conversing, for it was not opened early. When it was opened we used to go in to Socrates, and we generally spent the whole day with him. But on that morning we met earlier than usual; for the evening before we had learned, on leaving the prison, that the ship had arrived from Delos. So

II

59

III

we arranged to be at the usual place as early as possible. When we reached the prison, the porter, who generally let us in, came out to us and bade us wait a little, and not to go in until he summoned us himself: "For the Eleven," he said, "are releasing Socrates from his fetters and giving directions for his death today." In no great while he returned and bade us enter. So we went in and found Socrates just released, and Xanthippe—you know her—sitting by him, holding his child in her arms. When Xanthippe saw us, she wailed aloud, and cried, in her woman's way, "This is the last time, Socrates, that you will talk with your friends, or they with you." And Socrates glanced at Crito, and said, "Crito, let her be taken home." So some of Crito's servants led her away weeping bitterly and beating her breast. But Socrates sat up on the bed, and bent his leg and rubbed it with his hand, and while he was rubbing it said to us, How strange a thing is what men call pleasure! How wonderful is its relation to pain, which seems to be the opposite of it! They will not come to a man together; but if he pursues the one and gains it, he is almost forced to take the other also, as if they were two distinct things united at one end. And I think, said he, that if Aesop had noticed them he would have composed a fable about them, to the effect that God had wished to reconcile them when they were quarreling, and that, when he could not do that, he joined their ends together; and that therefore whenever the one comes to a man, the other is sure to follow. That is just the case with me. There was pain in my leg caused by the chains, and now, it seems, pleasure is come following the pain.

60

Cebes interrupted him and said, By the bye, Socrates, I am glad that you reminded me. Several people have been inquiring about your poems, the hymn to Apollo, and Aesop's fables which you have put into meter, and only a day or two ago Evenus asked me what was your reason for writing poetry on coming here, when you had never written a line before. So if you wish me to be able to answer him when he asks me again, as I know that he will, tell me what to say.

IV

Then tell him the truth, Cebes, he said. Say that it was from no wish to pose as a rival to him, or to his poems. I knew that it would not be easy to do that. I was only testing the meaning of certain dreams and acquitting my conscience about them, in case they should be bidding me make this kind of music. The fact is this. The same dream used often to come to me in my past life, appearing in different forms at different times, but always saying the same words, "Socrates, work at music and compose it." Formerly I used to think that the dream was encouraging me and cheering me on in what was already the work of my life, just as the spectators cheer on different runners in a race. I supposed that the dream was encouraging me to create the music at which I was working already, for I thought that philosophy was the highest music, and my life was spent in philosophy. But then, after the trial, when the feast of the god delayed my death, it occurred to me that the dream might possibly be bidding me create music in the popular sense, and that in that case I ought to do so, and not to disobey. I thought that it would be safer to acquit my conscience by creating poetry in obedience to the dream before I departed. So first I composed a hymn to the god whose feast it was. And then I turned such fables of Aesop as I knew, and had ready to my hand, into verse, taking those which came first; for I reflected that a man who means to be a poet has to use fiction and not facts for his poems; and I could not invent fiction myself.

61

Tell Evenus this, Cebes, and bid him farewell from me; and tell him to follow me as quickly as he can, if he is wise. I, it seems, shall depart today, for that is the will of the Athenians.

V

And Simmias said, What strange advice to give Evenus, Socrates! I have often met him, and from what I have seen of him I think that he is certainly not at all the man to take it, if he can help it.

What, he said, is not Evenus a philosopher?

Yes, I suppose so, replied Simmias.

Then Evenus will wish to die, he said, and so will every man who is worthy of having any part in this study. But he will not lay violent hands on himself; for that, they say, is wrong. And as he spoke he put his legs off the bed on to the ground, and remained sitting thus for the rest of the conversation.

Then Cebes asked him, What do you mean, Socrates, by saying that it is wrong for a man to lay violent hands on himself, but that the philosopher will wish to follow the dying man?

What, Cebes? Have you and Simmias been with Philolaus, and not heard about these things?

Nothing very definite, Socrates.

Well, I myself only speak of them from hearsay, yet there is no reason why I should not tell you what I have heard. Indeed, as I am setting out on a journey to the other world, what could be more fitting for me than to talk about my journey and to consider what we imagine to be its nature? How could we better employ the interval between this and sunset?

Then what is their reason for saying that it is wrong for a man to kill himself, Socrates? It is quite true that I have heard Philolaus say, when he was living at Thebes, that it is not right; and I have heard the same thing from others, too, but I never heard anything definite on the subject from any of them.   VI

You must be of good cheer, said he, possibly you will hear something some day.   62
But perhaps you will be surprised if I say that this law, unlike every other law to which mankind is subject, is absolute and without exception; and that it is not true that death is better than life only for some persons and at some times. And perhaps you will be surprised if I tell you that these men, for whom it would be better to die, may not do themselves a service, but that they must await a benefactor from without.

Oh indeed, said Cebes, laughing quietly, and speaking in his native dialect.

Indeed, said Socrates, so stated it may seem strange, and yet perhaps a reason may be given for it. The reason which the secret teaching[1] gives, that man is in a kind of prison, and that he may not set himself free, nor escape from it, seems to me rather profound and not easy to fathom. But I do think, Cebes, that it is true that the gods are our guardians, and that we men are a part of their property. Do you not think so?

I do, said Cebes.

Well then, said he, if one of your possessions were to kill itself, though you had not signified that you wished it to die, should you not be angry with it? Should you not punish it, if punishment were possible?

Certainly, he replied.

Then in this way perhaps it is not unreasonable to hold that no man has a right to take his own life, but that he must wait until God sends some necessity upon him, as has now been sent upon me.

[1] The Esoteric system of the Pythagoreans.

Yes, said Cebes, that does seem natural. But you were saying just now that the
philosopher will desire to die. Is not that a paradox, Socrates, if what we have just been
saying, that God is our guardian and that we are his property, be true? It is not reasonable to say that the wise man will be content to depart from this service, in which the
gods, who are the best of all rulers, rule him. He will hardly think that when he becomes
free he will take better care of himself than the gods take of him. A fool perhaps might
think so, and say that he would do well to run away from his master; he might not consider that he ought not to run away from a good master, but that he ought to remain with
him as long as possible, and so in his thoughtlessness he might run away. But the wise
man will surely desire to remain always with one who is better than himself. But if this
be true, Socrates, the reverse of what you said just now seems to follow. The wise man
should grieve to die, and the fool should rejoice.

I thought Socrates was pleased with Cebes' insistence. He looked at us, and said,   63
Cebes is always examining arguments. He will not be convinced at once by anything
that one says.

Yes, Socrates, said Simmias, but I do think that now there is something in what
Cebes says. Why should really wise men want to run away from masters who are better
than themselves, and lightly quit their service? And I think Cebes is aiming his argument at you, because you are so ready to leave us, and the gods, who are good rulers, as
you yourself admit.

You are right, he said. I suppose you mean that I must defend myself against your
charge, as if I were in a court of justice.

That is just our meaning, said Simmias.

Well then, he replied, let me try to make a more successful defense to you than I did
to the judges at my trial. I should be wrong, Cebes and Simmias, he went on, not to
grieve at death, if I did not think that I was going to live both with other gods who are
good and wise, and with men who have died and who are better than the men of this
world. But you must know that I hope that I am going to live among good men, though I
am not quite sure of that. But I am so sure as I can be in such matters that I am going to
live with gods who are very good masters. And therefore I am not so much grieved at
death; I am confident that the dead have some kind of existence, and, as has been said of
old, an existence that is far better for the good than for the wicked.

Well, Socrates, said Simmias, do you mean to go away and keep this belief to yourself, or will you let us share it with you? It seems to me that we too have an interest in
this good. And it will also serve as your defense, if you can convince us of what you say.

Only, Socrates, said Crito, that the man who is going to give you the poison has
been telling me to warn you not to talk much. He says that talking heats people, and that
the action of the poison must not be counteracted by heat. Those who excite themselves
sometimes have to drink it two or three times.

Let him be, said Socrates; let him mind his own business, and be prepared to give
me the poison twice, or, if need be, thrice.

I knew that would be your answer, said Crito, but the man has been importunate.

Never mind him, he replied. But I wish not to explain to you, my judges, why it
seems to me that a man who has really spent his life in philosophy has reason to be of
good cheer when he is about to die, and may well hope after death to gain in the other   64
world the greatest good. I will try to show you, Simmias and Cebes, how this may be.

The world, perhaps, does not see that those who rightly engage in philosophy study   IX
only dying and death. And, if this be true, it would be surely strange for a man all
through his life to desire only death, and then, when death comes to him, to be vexed at
it, when it has been his study and his desire for so long.

Simmias laughed, and said: Indeed, Socrates, you make me laugh, though I am
scarcely in a laughing humor now. If the multitude heard that, I fancy they would think
that what you say of philosophers is quite true; and my countrymen would entirely
agree with you that philosophers are indeed eager to die, and they would say that they
know full well that philosophers deserve to be put to death.

And they would be right, Simmias, except in saying that they know it. They do not
know in what sense the true philosopher is eager to die, or what kind of death he
deserves, or in what sense he deserves it. Let us dismiss them from our thoughts, and
converse by ourselves. Do we believe death to be anything?

We do, replied Simmias.

And do we not believe it to be the separation of the soul from the body? Does not
death mean that the body comes to exist by itself, separated from the soul, and that the
soul exists by herself, separated from the body? What is death but that?

It is that, he said.

Now consider, my good friend, if you and I are agreed on another point which I
think will help us to understand the question better. Do you think that a philosopher will
care very much about what are called pleasures, such as the pleasures of eating and
drinking?

Certainly not, Socrates, said Simmias.

Or about the pleasures of sexual passion?

Indeed, no.

And, do you think that he holds the remaining cares of the body in high esteem?
Will he think much of getting fine clothes, and sandals, and other bodily adornments, or
will he despise them, except so far as he is absolutely forced to meddle with them?

The real philosopher, I think, will despise them, he replied.

In short, said he, you think that his studies are not concerned with the body? He
stands aloof from it, as far as he can, and turns toward the soul?

I do.

Well then, in these matters, first, it is clear that the philosopher releases his soul   65
from communion with the body, so far as he can, beyond all other men?

It is.

And does not the world think, Simmias, that if a man has no pleasure in such
things, and does not take his share in them, his life is not worth living? Do not they hold
that he who thinks nothing of bodily pleasures is almost as good as dead?

Indeed you are right.

But what about the actual acquisition of wisdom? If the body is taken as a compan-   X
ion in the search for wisdom, is it a hindrance or not? For example, do sight and hearing
convey any real truth to men? Are not the very poets forever telling us that we neither
hear nor see anything accurately? But if these senses of the body are not accurate or
clear, the others will hardly be so, for they are all less perfect than these, are they not?

Yes, I think so, certainly, he said.

Then when does the soul attain truth? he asked. We see that, as often as she seeks to
investigate anything in company with the body, the body leads her astray.

True.

Is it not by reasoning, if at all, that any real truth becomes manifest to her?

Yes.

And she reasons best, I suppose, when none of the senses, whether hearing, or sight, or pain, or pleasure, harasses her; when she has dismissed the body, and released herself as far as she can from all intercourse or contact with it, and so, coming to be as much alone with herself as is possible, strives after real truth.

That is so.

And here too the soul of the philosopher very greatly despises the body, and flies from it, and seeks to be alone by herself, does she not?

Clearly.

And what do you say to the next point, Simmias? Do we say that there is such a thing as absolute justice, or not?

Indeed we do.

And absolute beauty, and absolute good?

Of course.

Have you ever seen any of them with your eyes?

Indeed I have not, he replied.

Did you ever grasp them with any bodily sense? I am speaking of all absolutes, whether size, or health, or strength; in a word, of the essence or real being of everything. Is the very truth of things contemplated by the body? Is it not rather the case that the man who prepares himself most carefully to apprehend by his intellect the essence of each thing which he examines will come nearest to the knowledge of it?

Certainly.

And will not a man attain to this pure thought most completely if he goes to each thing, as far as he can, with his mind alone, taking neither sight nor any other sense along with his reason in the process of thought, to be an encumbrance? In every case he will pursue pure and absolute being, with his pure intellect alone. He will be set free as far as possible from the eye and the ear and, in short, from the whole body, because intercourse with the body troubles the soul, and hinders her from gaining truth and wisdom. Is it not he who will attain the knowledge of real being, if any man will?   66

Your words are admirably true, Socrates, said Simmias.

And, he said, must not all this cause real philosophers to reflect, and make them say   XI
to each other, It seems that there is a narrow path which will bring us safely to our journey's end, with reason as our guide. As long as we have this body, and an evil of that sort is mingled with our souls, we shall never fully gain what we desire; and that is truth. For the body is forever taking up our time with the care which it needs; and, besides, whenever diseases attack it, they hinder us in our pursuit of real being. It fills us with passions, and desires, and fears, and all manner of phantoms, and much foolishness; and so, as the saying goes, in very truth we can never think at all for it. It alone and its desires cause wars and factions and battles; for the origin of all wars is the pursuit of wealth,[2] and we are forced to pursue wealth because we live in slavery to the cares of the body. And therefore, for all these reasons, we have no leisure for philosophy. And last of all, if we ever are free from the body for a time, and then turn to examine some

---

[2]Cf. *Republic* 373d.

matter, it falls in our way at every step of the inquiry, and causes confusion and trouble and panic, so that we cannot see the truth for it. Verily we have learned that if we are to have any pure knowledge at all, we must be freed from the body; the soul by herself must behold things as they are. Then, it seems, after we are dead, we shall gain the wisdom which we desire, and for which we say we have a passion, but not while we are alive, as the argument shows. For if it be not possible to have pure knowledge while the body is with us, one of two things must be true: either we cannot gain knowledge at all, or we can gain it only after death. For then, and not till then, will the soul exist by herself, separate from the body. And while we live, we shall come nearest to knowledge, if we have no communion or intercourse with the body beyond what is absolutely necessary, and if we are not defiled with its nature. We must live pure from it until God himself releases us. And when we are thus pure and released from its follies, we shall dwell, I suppose, with others who are pure like ourselves, and we shall of ourselves know all that is pure; and that may be the truth. For I think that the impure is not allowed to attain to the pure. Such, Simmias, I fancy must needs be the language and the reflection of the true lovers of knowledge. Do you not agree with me?

67

Most assuredly I do, Socrates.

And, my friend, said Socrates, if this be true, I have good hope that, when I reach the place whither I am going, I shall there, if anywhere, gain fully that which we have sought so earnestly in the past. And so I shall set forth cheerfully on the journey that is appointed me today, and so may every man who thinks that his mind is prepared and purified.

XII

That is quite true, said Simmias.

And does not the purification consist, as we have said, in separating the soul from the body, as far as is possible, and in accustoming her to collect and rally herself as much as she can, both now and hereafter, released from the bondage of the body?

Yes, certainly, he said.

Is not what we call death a release and separation of the soul from the body?

Undoubtedly, he replied.

And the true philosopher, we hold, is alone in his constant desire to set his soul free? His study is simply the release and separation of the soul from the body, is it not?

Clearly.

Would it not be absurd then, as I began by saying for a man to complain at death coming to him, when in his life he has been preparing himself to live as nearly in a state of death as he could? Would not that be absurd?

Yes, indeed.

In truth, then, Simmias, he said, the true philosopher studies to die, and to him of all men is death least terrible. Now look at the matter in this way. In everything he is at enmity with his body, and he longs to possess his soul alone. Would it not then be most unreasonable if he were to fear and complain when he has his desire, instead of rejoicing to go to the place where he hopes to gain the wisdom that he has passionately longed for all his life, and to be released from the company of his enemy? Many a man has willingly gone to the other world, when a human love or wife or son has died, in the hope of seeing there those whom he longed for, and of being with them: and will a man who has a real passion for wisdom, and a firm hope of really finding wisdom in the other world and nowhere else, grieve at death, and not depart rejoicing? Nay, my friend, you ought not to think that, if he be truly a philosopher. He will be firmly convinced that

68

there and nowhere else will he meet with wisdom in its purity. And if this be so, would it not, I repeat, be very unreasonable for such a man to fear death?

Yes, indeed, he replied, it would.

Does not this show clearly, he said, that any man whom you see grieving at the approach of death is after all no lover of wisdom, but a lover of his body? He is also, most likely, a lover either of wealth, or of honor, or, it may be, of both.   XIII

Yes, he said, it is as you say.

Well then, Simmias, he went on, does not what is called courage belong especially to the philosopher?

Certainly I think so, he replied.

And does not temperance, the quality which even the world calls temperance, and which means to despise and control and govern the passions—does not temperance belong only to such men as most despise the body, and pass their lives in philosophy?

Of necessity, he replied.

For if you will consider the courage and the temperance of other men, said he, you will find that they are strange things.

How so, Socrates?

You know, he replied, that all other men regard death as one of the great evils to which mankind is subject?

Indeed they do, he said.

And when the brave men of them submit to death, do not they do so from a fear of still greater evils?

Yes.

Then all men but the philosopher are brave from fear and because they are afraid. Yet it is rather a strange thing for a man to be brave out of fear and cowardice.

Indeed it is.

And are not the orderly men of them in exactly the same case? Are not they temperate from a kind of intemperance? We should say that this cannot be; but in them this state of foolish temperance comes to that. They desire certain pleasures, and fear to lose them; and so they abstain from other pleasures because they are mastered by these.   69
Intemperance is defined to mean being under the dominion of pleasure, yet they only master certain pleasures because they are mastered by others. But that is exactly what I said just now—that, in a way, they are made temperate from intemperance.

It seems to be so.

My dear Simmias, I fear that virtue is not really to be bought in this way, by bartering pleasure for pleasure, and pain for pain, and fear for fear, and the greater for the less, like coins. There is only one sterling coin for which all these things ought to be exchanged, and that is wisdom. All that is bought and sold for this and with this, whether courage, or temperance, or justice, is real; in one word, true virtue cannot be without wisdom, and it matters nothing whether pleasure, and fear, and all other such things are present or absent. But I think that the virtue which is composed of pleasures and fears bartered with one another, and severed from wisdom, is only a shadow of true virtue, and that it has no freedom, nor health, nor truth. True virtue in reality is a kind of purifying from all these things; and temperance, and justice, and courage, and wisdom itself are the purification. And I fancy that the men who established our mysteries had a very real meaning: in truth they have been telling us in parables all the time that whosoever comes to Hades uninitiated and profane will lie in the mire, while he that has been purified and initiated shall dwell with the gods. For "the thyrsus-bearers are many," as they say in the mysteries, "but the inspired few." And by these last, I believe, are meant only the true philosophers. And I in my life have striven as hard as I was able, and have left nothing undone, that I might become one of them. Whether I have striven in the right way, and whether I have succeeded or not, I suppose that I shall learn in a little while, when I reach the other world, if it be the will of God.

That is my defense, Simmias and Cebes, to show that I have reason for not being angry or grieved at leaving you and my masters here. I believe that in the next world, no less than in this, I shall meet with good masters and friends, though the multitude are incredulous of it. And if I have been more successful with you in my defense than I was with my Athenian judges, it is well.

When Socrates had finished, Cebes replied to him, and said, I think that for the most part you are right, Socrates. But men are very incredulous of what you have said of the soul. They fear that she will no longer exist anywhere when she has left the body, but that she will be destroyed and perish on the very day of death. They think that the moment that she is released and leaves the body, she will be dissolved and vanish away like breath or smoke, and thenceforward cease to exist at all. If she were to exist somewhere as a whole, released from the evils which you enumerated just now, we should have good reason to hope, Socrates, that what you say is true. But it will need no little persuasion and assurance to show that the soul exists after death, and continues to possess any power or wisdom.

True, Cebes, said Socrates; but what are we to do? Do you wish to converse about these matters and see if what I say is probable?

I for one, said Cebes, should gladly hear your opinion about them.

I think, said Socrates, that no one who heard me now, even if he were a comic poet, would say that I am an idle talker about things which do not concern me. So, if you wish it, let us examine this question.

Let us consider whether or not the souls of men exist in the next world after death, thus. There is an ancient belief, which we remember, that on leaving this world they exist there, and that they return hither and are born again from the dead. But if it be true that the living are born from the dead, our souls must exist in the other world; otherwise they could not be born again. It will be a sufficient proof that this is so if we can really prove that the living are born only from the dead. But if this is not so, we shall have to find some other argument.

Exactly, said Cebes.

Well, said he, the easiest way of answering the question will be to consider it not in relation to men only, but also in relation to all animals and plants, and in short to all things that are generated. Is it the case that everything which has an opposite is generated only from its opposite? By opposites I mean the honorable and the base, the just and the unjust, and so on in a thousand other instances. Let us consider then whether it is necessary for everything that has an opposite to be generated only from its own opposite. For instance, when anything becomes greater, I suppose it must have been less and then become greater?

Yes.

And if a thing becomes less, it must have been greater, and afterward become less?   71

That is so, said he.

XIV

70

XV

And further, the weaker is generated from the stronger, and the swifter from the slower?

Certainly.

And the worse is generated from the better, and the more just from the more unjust?

Of course.

Then it is sufficiently clear to us that all things are generated in this way, opposites from opposites?

Quite so.

And in every pair of opposites, are there not two generations between the two members of the pair, from the one to the other, and then back again from the other to the first? Between the greater and the less are growth and diminution, and we say that the one grows and the other diminishes, do we not?

Yes, he said.

And there is division and composition, and cold and hot, and so on. In fact, is it not a universal law, even though we do not always express it in so many words, that opposites are generated always from one another, and that there is a process of generation from one to the other?

It is, he replied.

Well, said he, is there an opposite to life, in the same way that sleep is the opposite of being awake?   XVI

Certainly, he answered.

What is it?

Death, he replied.

Then if life and death are opposites, they are generated the one from the other: they are two, and between them there are two generations. Is it not so?

Of course.

Now, said Socrates, I will explain to you one of the two pairs of opposites of which I spoke just now, and its generations, and you shall explain to me the other. Sleep is the opposite of waking. From sleep is produced the state of waking, and from the state of waking is produced sleep. Their generations are, first, to fall asleep; secondly, to awake. Is that clear? he asked.

Yes, quite.

Now then, said he, do you tell me about life and death. Death is the opposite of life, is it not?

It is.

And they are generated the one from the other?

Yes.

Then what is that which is generated from the living?

The dead, he replied.

And what is generated from the dead?

I must admit that it is the living.

Then living things and living men are generated from the dead, Cebes?

Clearly, said he.

Then our souls exist in the other world? he said.

Apparently.

Now of these two generations the one is certain? Death I suppose is certain enough, is it not?

Yes, quite, he replied.

What then shall we do? said he. Shall we not assign an opposite generation to correspond? Or is nature imperfect here? Must we not assign some opposite generation to dying?

I think so, certainly, he said.

And what must it be?

To come to life again.

And if there be such a thing as a return to life, he said, it will be a generation from the dead to the living, will it not?   72

It will, certainly.

Then we are agreed on this point: namely, that the living are generated from the dead no less than the dead from the living. But we agreed that, if this be so, it is sufficient proof that the souls of the dead must exist somewhere, whence they come into being again.

I think, Socrates, that that is the necessary result of our premises.

And I think, Cebes, said he, that our conclusion has not been an unfair one. For if   XVII opposites did not always correspond with opposites as they are generated, moving as it were round in a circle, and there was generation in a straight line forward from one opposite only, with no turning or return to the other, then, you know, all things would come at length to have the same form and be in the same state, and would cease to be generated at all.

What do you mean? he asked.

It is not at all hard to understand my meaning, he replied. If, for example, the one opposite, to go to sleep, existed without the corresponding opposite, to wake up, which is generated from the first, then all nature would at last make the tale of Endymion meaningless, and he would no longer be conspicuous; for everything else would be in the same state of sleep that he was in. And if all things were compounded together and never separated, the Chaos of Anaxagoras would soon be realized. Just in the same way, my dear Cebes, if all things in which there is any life were to die, and when they were dead were to remain in that form and not come to life again, would not the necessary result be that everything at last would be dead, and nothing alive? For if living things were generated from other sources than death, and were to die, the result is inevitable that all things would be consumed by death. Is it not so?

It is indeed, I think, Socrates, said Cebes; I think that what you say is perfectly true.

Yes, Cebes, he said, I think it is certainly so. We are not misled into this conclusion. The dead do come to life again, and the living are generated from them, and the souls of the dead exist; and with the souls of the good it is well, and with the souls of the evil it is evil.   XVIII

And besides, Socrates, rejoined Cebes, if the doctrine which you are fond of stating, that our learning is only a process of recollection, be true, then I suppose we must have learned at some former time what we recollect now. And that would be impossible   73 unless our souls had existed somewhere before they came into this human form. So that is another reason for believing the soul immortal.

But, Cebes, interrupted Simmias, what are the proofs of that? Recall them to me; I am not very clear about them at present.

One argument, answered Cebes, and the strongest of all, is that if you question men about anything in the right way, they will answer you correctly of themselves. But they would not have been able to do that unless they had had within themselves knowledge and right reason. Again, show them such things as geometrical diagrams, and the proof of the doctrine is complete.[3]

And if that does not convince you, Simmias, said Socrates, look at the matter in another way and see if you agree then. You have doubts, I know, how what is called knowledge can be recollection.

Nay, replied Simmias, I do not doubt. But I want to recollect the argument about recollection. What Cebes undertook to explain has nearly brought your theory back to me and convinced me. But I am nonetheless ready to hear you undertake to explain it.

In this way, he returned. We are agreed, I suppose, that if a man remembers anything, he must have known it at some previous time.

Certainly, he said.

And are we agreed that when knowledge comes in the following way, it is recollection? When a man has seen or heard anything, or has perceived it by some other sense, and then knows not that thing only, but has also in his mind an impression of some other thing, of which the knowledge is quite different, are we not right in saying that he remembers the thing of which he has an impression in his mind?

What do you mean?

I mean this. The knowledge of a man is different from the knowledge of a lyre, is it not?

Certainly.

And you know that when lovers see a lyre, or a garment, or anything that their favorites are wont to use, they have this feeling. They know the lyre, and in their mind they receive the image of the youth whose the lyre was. That is recollection. For instance, someone seeing Simmias often is reminded of Cebes; and there are endless examples of the same thing.

Indeed there are, said Simmias.

Is not that a kind of recollection, he said; and more especially when a man has this feeling with reference to things which the lapse of time and inattention have made him forget?

Yes, certainly, he replied.

Well, he went on, is it possible to recollect a man on seeing the picture of a horse, or the picture of a lyre? Or to recall Simmias on seeing a picture of Cebes?

Certainly.

And it is possible to recollect Simmias himself on seeing a picture of Simmias?

No doubt, he said.

74

Then in all these cases there is recollection caused by similar objects, and also by dissimilar objects?

XIX

There is.

But when a man has a recollection caused by similar objects, will he not have a further feeling and consider whether the likeness to that which he recollects is defective in any way or not?

---

[3] For an example of this see *Meno* 82a ff., where, as here, Socrates proves the doctrine of Reminiscence, and therefore the Immortality of the Soul, by putting judicious questions about geometry to a slave who was quite ignorant of geometry, and, with the help of diagrams, obtaining from him correct answers.

He will, he said.

Now see if this is true, he went on. Do we not believe in the existence of equality—not the equality of pieces of wood or of stones, but something beyond that—equality in the abstract? Shall we say that there is such a thing, or not?

Yes indeed, said Simmias, most emphatically we will.

And do we know what this abstract equality is?

Certainly, he replied.

Where did we get the knowledge of it? Was it not from seeing the equal pieces of wood, and stones, and the like, which we were speaking of just now? Did we not form from them the idea of abstract equality, which is different from them? Or do you think that is it not different? Consider the question in this way. Do not equal pieces of wood and stones appear to us sometimes equal and sometimes unequal, though in fact they remain the same all the time?

Certainly they do.

But did absolute equals ever seem to you to be unequal, or abstract equality to be inequality?

No, never, Socrates.

Then equal things, he said, are not the same as abstract equality?

No, certainly not, Socrates.

Yet is was from these equal things, he said, which are different from abstract equality, that you have conceived and got your knowledge of abstract equality?

That is quite true, he replied.

And that whether it is like them or unlike them?

Certainly.

But that makes no difference, he said. As long as the sight of one thing brings another thing to your mind, there must be recollection, whether or not the two things are like.

That is so.

Well then, said he, do the equal pieces of wood, and other similar equal things, of which we have been speaking, affect us at all this way? Do they seem to us to be equal, in the way that abstract equality is equal? Do they come short of being like abstract equality, or not?

Indeed, they come very short of it, he replied.

Are we agreed about this? A man sees something and thinks to himself, "This thing that I see aims at being like some other thing, but it comes short and cannot be like that other thing; it is inferior"; must not the man who thinks that have known at some previous time that other thing, which he says that it resembles, and to which it is inferior?

He must.

Well, have we ourselves had the same sort of feeling with reference to equal things, and to abstract equality?

Yes, certainly.

Then we must have had knowledge of equality before we first saw equal things, and perceived that they all strive to be like equality, and all come short of it.

75

That is so.

And we are agreed also that we have not, nor could we have, obtained the idea of equality except from sight or touch or some other sense; the same is true of all the senses.

Yes, Socrates, for the purposes of the argument that is so.

At any rate it is by the senses that we must perceive that all sensible objects strive to resemble absolute equality, and are inferior to it. Is not that so?

Yes.

Then before we began to see, and to hear, and to use the other senses, we must have received the knowledge of the nature of abstract and real equality; otherwise we could not have compared equal sensible objects with abstract equality, and seen that the former in all cases strive to be like the latter, though they are always inferior to it?

That is the necessary consequence of what we have been saying, Socrates.

Did we not see, and hear, and possess the other senses as soon as we were born?

Yes, certainly.

And we must have received the knowledge of abstract equality before we had these senses?

Yes.

Then, it seems, we must have received that knowledge before we were born?

It does.

Now if we received this knowledge before our birth, and were born with it, we knew, both before and at the moment of our birth, not only the equal, and the greater, and the less, but also everything of the same kind, did we not? Our present reasoning does not refer only to equality. It refers just as much to absolute good, and absolute beauty, and absolute justice, and absolute holiness; in short, I repeat, to everything which we mark with the name of the real, in the questions and answers of our dialectic. So we must have received our knowledge of all realities before we were born.   XX

That is so.

And we must always be born with this knowledge, and must always retain it throughout life, if we have not each time forgotten it, after having received it. For to know means to receive and retain knowledge, and not to have lost it. Do not we mean by forgetting, the loss of knowledge, Simmias?

Yes, certainly, Socrates, he said.

But, I suppose, if it be the case that we lost at birth the knowledge which we received before we were born, and then afterward, by using our senses on the objects of sense, recovered the knowledge which we had previously possessed, then what we call learning is the recovering of knowledge which is already ours. And are we not right in calling that recollection?

Certainly.

For we have found it possible to perceive a thing by sight, or hearing, or any other sense, and thence to form a notion of some other thing, like or unlike, which had been forgotten, but with which this thing was associated. And therefore, I say, one of two things must be true. Either we are all born with this knowledge and retain it all our life; or, after birth, those whom we say are learning are only recollecting, and our knowledge is recollection.   76

Yes indeed, that is undoubtedly true, Socrates.

Then which do you choose, Simmias? Are we born with knowledge or do we recollect the things of which we have received knowledge before our birth?   XXI

I cannot say at present, Socrates.

Well, have you an opinion about this question? Can a man who knows give an account of what he knows, or not? What do you think about that?

Yes, of course he can, Socrates.

And do you think that everyone can give an account of the ideas of which we have been speaking?

I wish I did, indeed, said Simmias, but I am very much afraid that by this time tomorrow there will no longer be any man living able to do so as it should be done.

Then, Simmias, he said, you do not think that all men know these things?

Certainly not.

Then they recollect what they once learned?

Necessarily.

And when did our souls gain this knowledge? It cannot have been after we were born men.

No, certainly not.

Then it was before?

Yes.

Then, Simmias, our souls existed formerly, apart from our bodies, and possessed intelligence before they came into man's shape.[4]

Unless we receive this knowledge at the moment of birth, Socrates. That time still remains.

Well, my friend, and at what other time do we lose it? We agreed just now that we are not born with it; do we lose it at the same moment that we gain it, or can you suggest any other time?

I cannot, Socrates. I did not see that I was talking nonsense.

Then, Simmias, he said, is not this the truth? If, as we are forever repeating, beauty, XXII and good, and the other ideas[5] really exist, and if we refer all the objects of sensible perception to these ideas which were formerly ours, and which we find to be ours still, our souls must have existed before ever we were born. But if they do exist, then our reasoning will have been thrown away. Is it so? If these ideas exist, does it not at once follow that our souls must have existed before we were born, and if they do not exist, then neither did our souls?

Admirably put, Socrates, said Simmias. I think that the necessity is the same for the one as for the other. The reasoning has reached a place of safety in the common proof of   77 the existence of our souls before we were born and of the existence of the ideas of which you spoke. Nothing is so evident to me as that beauty, and good, and the other ideas which you spoke of just now have a very real existence indeed. Your proof is quite sufficient for me.

But what of Cebes? said Socrates. I must convince Cebes too.

I think that he is satisfied, said Simmias, though he is the most skeptical of men in argument. But I think that he is perfectly convinced that our souls existed before we were born.

But I do not think myself, Socrates, he continued, that you have proved that the soul XXIII will continue to exist when we are dead. The common fear which Cebes spoke of, that she may be scattered to the winds at death, and that death may be the end of her exis-

---

[4] Cf. Wordworth's famous *Ode on Intimations of Immortality*. It must be noticed that in one respect Wordsworth exactly reverses Plato's theory. With Wordsworth "Heaven lies about us in our infancy," and as we grow to manhood we gradually forget it. With Plato, we lose the knowledge which we possessed in a prior state of existence, at birth, and recover it, as we grow up.

[5] For a fuller account of the ideas, see 100b ff.

tence, still stands in the way. Assuming that the soul is generated and comes together from some other elements, and exists before she ever enters the human body, why should she not come to an end and be destroyed, after she has entered into the body, when she is released from it?

You are right, Simmias, said Cebes. I think that only half the required proof has been given. It has been shown that our souls existed before we were born; but it must also be shown that our souls will continue to exist after we are dead, no less than that they existed before we were born, if the proof is to be complete.

That has been shown already, Simmias and Cebes, said Socrates, if you will combine this reasoning with our previous conclusion, that all life is generated from death. For if the soul exists in a previous state and if, when she comes into life and is born, she can only be born from death, and from a state of death, must she not exist after death too, since she has to be born again? So the point which you speak of has been already proved.

Still I think that you and Simmias would be glad to discuss this question further. XXIV Like children, you are afraid that the wind will really blow the soul away and disperse her when she leaves the body, especially if a man happens to die in a storm and not in a calm.

Cebes laughed and said, Try and convince us as if we were afraid, Socrates; or rather, do not think that we are afraid ourselves. Perhaps there is a child within us who has these fears. Let us try and persuade him not to be afraid of death, as if it were a bugbear.

You must charm him every day, until you have charmed him away, said Socrates.

And where shall we find a good charmer, Socrates, he asked, now that you are leaving us?   78

Hellas is a large country, Cebes, he replied, and good men may doubtless be found in it; and the nations of the Barbarians are many. You must search them all through for such a charmer, sparing neither money nor labor; for there is nothing on which you could spend money more profitably. And you must search for him among yourselves too, for you will hardly find a better charmer than yourselves.

That shall be done, said Cebes. But let us return to the point where we left off, if you will.

Yes, I will: why not?

Very good, he replied.

Well, said Socrates, must we not ask ourselves this question? What kind of thing is XXV liable to suffer dispersion, and for what kind of thing have we to fear dispersion? And then we must see whether the soul belongs to that kind or not, and be confident or afraid about our own souls accordingly.

That is true, he answered.

Now is it not the compound and composite which is naturally liable to be dissolved in the same way in which it was compounded? And is not what is uncompounded alone not liable to dissolution, if anything is not?

I think that that is so, said Cebes.

And what always remains in the same state and unchanging is most likely to be uncompounded, and what is always changing and never the same is most likely to be compounded, I suppose?

Yes, I think so.

Now let us return to what we were speaking of before in the discussion, he said. Does the being, which in our dialectic we define as meaning absolute existence, remain always in exactly the same state, or does it change? Do absolute equality, absolute beauty, and every other absolute existence, admit of any change at all? Or does absolute existence in each case, being essentially uniform, remain the same and unchanging, and never in any case admit of any sort or kind of change whatsoever?

It must remain the same and unchanging, Socrates, said Cebes.

And what of the many beautiful things, such as men, and horses, and garments, and the like, and of all which bears the names of the ideas, whether equal, or beautiful, or anything else? Do they remain the same or is it exactly the opposite with them? In short, do they never remain the same at all, either in themselves or in their relations?

These things, said Cebes, never remain the same.

You can touch them, and see them, and perceive them with the other senses, while   79 you can grasp the unchanging only by the reasoning of the intellect. These latter are invisible and not seen. Is it not so?

That is perfectly true, he said.

Let us assume then, he said, if you will, that there are two kinds of existence, the   XXVI one visible, the other invisible.

Yes, he said.

And the invisible is unchanging, while the visible is always changing.

Yes, he said again.

Are not we men made up of body and soul?

There is nothing else, he replied.

And which of these kinds of existence should we say that the body is most like, and most akin to?

The visible, he replied; that is quite obvious.

And the soul? Is that visible or invisible?

It is invisible to man, Socrates, he said.

But we mean by visible and invisible, visible and invisible to man; do we not?

Yes; that is what we mean.

Then what do we say of the soul? Is it visible or not visible?

It is not visible.

Then is it invisible?

Yes.

Then the soul is more like the invisible than the body; and the body is like the visible.

That is necessarily so, Socrates.

Have we not also said that, when the soul employs the body in any inquiry, and XXVII makes use of sight, or hearing, or any other sense—for inquiry with the body means inquiry with the senses—she is dragged away by it to the things which never remain the same, and wanders about blindly, and becomes confused and dizzy, like a drunken man, from dealing with things that are ever changing?

Certainly.

But when she investigates any question by herself, she goes away to the pure, and eternal, and immortal, and unchangeable, to which she is akin, and so she comes to be ever with it, as soon as she is by herself, and can be so; and then she rests from her wanderings and dwells with it unchangingly, for she is dealing with what is unchanging. And is not this state of the soul called wisdom?

Indeed, Socrates, you speak well and truly, he replied.

Which kind of existence do you think from our former and our present arguments that the soul is more like and more akin to?

I think, Socrates, he replied, that after this inquiry the very dullest man would agree that the soul is infinitely more like the unchangeable than the changeable.

And the body?

That is like the changeable.

Consider the matter in yet another way. When the soul and the body are united, XXVIII nature ordains the one to be a slave and to be ruled, and the other to be master and to 80 rule. Tell me once again, which do you think is like the divine, and which is like the mortal? Do you not think that the divine naturally rules and has authority, and that the mortal naturally is ruled and is a slave?

I do.

Then which is the soul like?

That is quite plain, Socrates. The soul is like the divine, and the body is like the mortal.

Now tell me, Cebes, is the result of all that we have said that the soul is most like the divine, and the immortal, and the intelligible, and the uniform, and the indissoluble, and the unchangeable; while the body is most like the human, and the mortal, and the unintelligible, and the multiform, and the dissoluble, and the changeable? Have we any other argument to show that this is not so, my dear Cebes?

We have not.

Then if this is so, is it not the nature of the body to be dissolved quickly, and of the XXIX soul to be wholly or very nearly indissoluble?[6]

Certainly.

You observe, he said, that after a man is dead, the visible part of him, his body, which lies in the visible world and which we call the corpse, which is subject to dissolution and decomposition, is not dissolved and decomposed at once? It remains as it was for a considerable time, and even for a long time, if a man dies with his body in good condition and in the vigor of his life. And when the body falls in and is embalmed, like the mummies of Egypt, it remains nearly entire for an immense time. And should it decay, yet some parts of it, such as the bones and muscles, may almost be said to be immortal. Is it not so?

Yes.

And shall we believe that the soul, which is invisible, and which goes hence to a place that is like herself, glorious, and pure, and invisible, to Hades, which is rightly called the unseen world, to dwell with the good and wise God, whither, if it be the will of God, my soul too must shortly go—shall we believe that the soul, whose nature is so glorious, and pure, and invisible, is blown away by the winds and perishes as soon as she leaves the body, as the world says? Nay, dear Cebes and Simmias, it is not so. I will tell you what happens to a soul which is pure at her departure, and which in her life has had no intercourse that she could avoid with the body, and so draws after her, when she dies, no taint of the body, but has shunned it, and gathered herself into herself, for such

---

[6] Compare Bishop Butler's *Analogy*, Pt. I, Ch. I, where a similar argument is used: the soul being indiscerptible is immortal. The argument based on the "divine" nature of the soul is, of course, also a modern one. See *e.g.* Lord Tennyson, *In Memoriam*, LIV-LVI.

has been her constant study—and that only means that she has loved wisdom rightly,   81
and has truly practiced how to die. Is not this the practice of death?

Yes, certainly.

Does not the soul, then, which is in that state, go away to the invisible that is like
herself, and to the divine, and the immortal, and the wise, where she is released from
error, and folly, and fear, and fierce passions, and all the other evils that fall to the lot of
men, and is happy, and for the rest of time lives in very truth with the gods, as they say
that the initiated do? Shall we affirm this, Cebes?

Yes, certainly, said Cebes.

But if she be defiled and impure when she leaves the body, from being ever with it,   XXX
and serving it and loving it, and from being besotted by it and by its desires and pleasures, so that she thinks nothing true but what is bodily and can be touched, and seen,
and eaten, and drunk, and used for men's lusts; if she has learned to hate, and tremble at,
and fly from what is dark and invisible to the eye, and intelligible and apprehended by
philosophy—do you think that a soul which is in that state will be pure and without
alloy at her departure?

No, indeed, he replied.

She is penetrated, I suppose, by the corporeal, which the unceasing intercourse and
company and care of the body has made a part of her nature.

Yes.

And, my dear friend, the corporeal must be burdensome, and heavy, and earthy,
and visible; and it is by this that such a soul is weighed down and dragged back to the
visible world, because she is afraid of the invisible world of Hades, and haunts, it is
said, the graves and tombs, where shadowy forms of souls have been seen, which are
the phantoms of souls which were impure at their release and still cling to the visible;
which is the reason why they are seen.[7]

That is likely enough, Socrates.

That is likely, certainly, Cebes; and these are not the souls of the good, but of the
evil, which are compelled to wander in such places as a punishment for the wicked lives
that they had lived; and their wanderings continue until, from the desire for the corporeal that clings to them, they are again imprisoned in a body.

And, he continued, they are imprisoned, probably, in the bodies of animals with   XXXI
habits similar to the habits which were theirs in their lifetime.

What do you mean by that, Socrates?

I mean that men who have practiced unbridled gluttony, and wantonness, and
drunkenness probably enter the bodies of asses and suchlike animals. Do you not   82
think so?

Certainly that is very likely.

And those who have chosen injustice, and tyranny, and robbery enter the bodies of
wolves, and hawks, and kites. Where else should we say that such souls go?

No doubt, said Cebes, they go into such animals.

In short, it is quite plain, he said, whither each soul goes; each enters an animal
with habits like its own.

Certainly, he replied, that is so.

---

[7] Professor Jowett compares Milton, *Comus*, 463 ff.

And of these, he said, the happiest, who go to the best place, are those who have practiced the popular and social virtues which are called temperance and justice, and which come from habit and practice, without philosophy or reason.

And why are they the happiest?

Because it is probable that they return into a mild and social nature like their own, such as that of bees, or wasps, or ants; or, it may be, into the bodies of men, and that from them are made worthy citizens.

Very likely.

But none but the philosopher or the lover of knowledge, who is wholly pure when he goes hence, is permitted to go to the race of the gods; and therefore, my friends, Simmias and Cebes, the true philosopher is temperate and refrains from all the pleasures of the body, and does not give himself up to them. It is not squandering his substance and poverty that he fears, as the multitude and the lovers of wealth do; nor again does he dread the dishonor and disgrace of wickedness, like the lovers of power and honor. It is not for these reasons that he is temperate. **XXXII**

No, it would be unseemly in him if he were, Socrates, said Cebes.

Indeed it would, he replied, and therefore all those who have any care for their souls, and who do not spend their lives in forming and molding their bodies, bid farewell to such persons, and do not walk in their ways, thinking that they know not whither they are going. They themselves turn and follow whithersoever philosophy leads them, for they believe that they ought not to resist philosophy, or its deliverance and purification.

Ovid

THE ART OF LOVE

Introduction by Michael Graham

Ovid (whose full name was Publius Ovidus Naso) was a Roman poet, born in 43 B.C. His family was prominent, and he was trained as a lawyer. Despite his legal talent, however, he fell in love with poetry and decided to devote all his energies to writing it, and he became one of the leading lights in the literary culture of Augustan Rome—that is, among those writers who were active during the reign of the emperor Augustus (27 B.C.–14 A.D.), a group which also included the poet Virgil and the historian Livy.

Ovid's subject matter was wide-ranging, from tragedy to imaginary love letters to a poem on artificial aids to beauty, but he often returned to what seems to have been his favorite topic— love, or perhaps to be more specific, seduction. We cannot gauge his real expertise in this field, but he was certainly willing to offer advice, and did so in what is generally regarded as his masterpiece, the *Ars Amatoria,* or *Art of Love,* which appeared about 1 B.C. This long poem has been widely-read through the ages, enjoying, for instance, some popularity in the high middle ages as part of the inspiration behind the literary movement which has been labeled "courtly love." The subject is one which continues to fascinate, although today's readers might be disturbed, or even shocked, by some of Ovid's basic assumptions about relations between the sexes.

In order to better understand Ovid as his original audience may have understood him, it is helpful to know a bit about social relations and literary culture in Augustan Rome. First of all, advice literature was a popular form during the period—with works available on fighting, farming and courting, just to name a few popular subjects. The "ars" in the poem's title, which is usually translated as "art," might be better rendered as "technique." Earlier love poets such as Catullus (84–54 B.C.) had offered readers flowery verses overflowing with passion, whereas Ovid adopted a much more businesslike approach; he would dispense cool advice rather than romantic rhapsodies.

Augustan Rome was a city of one million inhabitants, and it often seemed a rowdy, ungovernable place, full of young men with time on their hands. Well-born girls were usually married early in their teenage years, typically to men of similar social standing who were in their mid-twenties. Once married, wealthy women enjoyed a high degree of social freedom, and could control their own property. This left them much freer than the women of classical Athens, for instance. Fearful that Roman society was becoming too decadent, and that the family was breaking down, Augustus issued morality legislation designed to reinforce traditional family and marital ties and to promote childbearing, particularly among upper-class Romans. In 18 B.C., he issued a law against adultery. To prove that he was serious, Augustus in 2 B.C. had to force Julia, his daughter and only child, into exile on a barren island due to her well-known extramarital affairs. It may be significant that Ovid wrote this poem in the year after Julia's banishment. Was it intended to offer ironic commentary on the times? Interestingly, Ovid himself was exiled in 8 A.D., but we do not know why. He died on the Black Sea, having never returned to Rome, in 17 A.D.

The *Art of Love* raises other questions as well. First of all, who do you think Ovid was writing for? Who would be in a position to take his advice? What references did he make to other works which you have read? What picture of Augustan Rome does this poem give you? Who were the women Ovid was writing about, and what basic assumptions about them did he make? Does the poem raise issues of relations between classes as well as genders? Do you think Ovid's advice is still useful today? Why or why not?

The Art of Love

BOOK 1

Should anyone here in Rome lack finesse at love-making, let him
    Try me—read my book, and results are guaranteed!
Technique is the secret. Charioteer, sailor, oarsman,
    All need it. Technique can control
Love himself. As Automedon was charioteer to Achilles,   5
    And Tiphys Jason's steersman, so I,
By Venus' appointment, am made Love's artificer, shall be known as
    The Tiphys, the very Automedon of Love.
He's a wild handful, will often rebel against me,
    But still just a child—   10
Malleable, easily disciplined. Chiron made young Achilles
    A fine musician, hammered that fierce heart
On the anvil of peaceful artistry. So this future terror
    To friend and foe alike went in awe, it's said,
Of his elderly teacher, at whose bidding the hand that in after-   15
    Time bore down Hector was held out for the tawse.
As Chiron taught Achilles, so I am Love's preceptor:
    Wild boys both, both goddess-born—and yet
Even bulls can be broken to plough, or spirited horses
    Subdued with bridle and bit.   20
So Love shall likewise own my mastery, though his bowshots
    Skewer my breast, though his torch
Flicker and sear me. The worse the wounds, the deeper the branding,
    That much keener I to avenge
Such outrage. Nor shall I falsely ascribe my arts to Apollo: 25
    No airy bird comes twittering advice

Ovid, *The Erotic Poems* (Peter Green, trans.), Penguin, 1983 (ISBN 0-140-44360-6), original pp. 166–213. (Books one and two of "The Art of Love")

Into *my* ear, *I* never had a vision of the Muses
    Herding sheep in Ascra's valleys. This work is based
On experience: what I write, believe me, I have practised.
    My poem will deal in truth.   30

Aid my enterprise, Venus! Respectable ladies, the kind who
    Wear hairbands and ankle-length skirts,
Are hereby warned off. Safe love, legitimate liaisons
    Will be my theme. This poem breaks no taboos.
First, then, you fledgling troopers in passion's service,   35
    Comes the task of finding an object for your love.
Next, you must labour to woo and win your lady;
    Thirdly, ensure that the affair will last.
Such are my limitations, such the ground I will cover,
    The race I propose to run.   40

While you are fancy-free still, and can drive at leisure,
    Pick a girl, tell her, 'You're the one I love.
And only you.' But this search means using your eyes: a mistress
    Won't drop out of the sky at your feet.
A hunter's skilled where to spread his nets for the stag, senses   45
    In which glen the wild boar lurks.
A fowler's familiar with copses, an expert angler
    Knows the richest shoaling-grounds for fish.
You too, so keen to establish some long-term relationship,
    Must learn, first, where girl is to be found.   50
Your search need not take you—believe me—on an overseas voyage:
    A short enough trek will bring you to your goal.
True, Perseus fetched home Andromeda from the coloured Indies,
    While Phrygian Paris abducted Helen in Greece,
But Rome can boast of so many and such dazzling beauties   55
    You'd swear the whole world's talent was gathered here.
The girls of your city outnumber Gargara's wheatsheaves,
    Methymna's grape-clusters, all
Birds on the bough, stars in the sky, fish in the ocean:
    Venus indeed still haunts   60
Her son Aeneas' foundation. If you like budding adolescents
    Any number of (guaranteed) maidens are here to delight
Your roving eye. You prefer young women? They'll charm you
    By the thousand, you won't know which to choose.
And if you happen to fancy a more mature, experienced   65
    Age-group, believe me, *they* show up in droves.

Here's what to do. When the sun's on the back of Hercules'
    Lion, stroll down some shady colonnade,

Pompey's, say, or Octavia's (for her dead son Marcellus:
    Extravagant marble facings, R.I.P.), 70
Or Livia's, with its gallery of genuine Old Masters,
    Or the Danaids' Portico (note
The artwork: Danaus' daughters plotting mischief for their cousins,
    Father attitudinizing with drawn sword).
Don't miss the shrine of Adonis, mourned by Venus, 75
    Or the synagogue—Syrian Jews
Worship there each Sabbath—or the linen-clad heifer-goddess's
    Memphian temple: Io makes many a maid what *she*
Was to Jove. The very courts are hunting-grounds for passion;
    Amid lawyers' rebuttals love will often be found. 80
Here, where under Venus' marble temple the Appian
    Fountain pulses its jets high in the air,
Your jurisconsult's entrapped by Love's beguilements—
    Counsel to others, he cannot advise himself.
Here, all too often, words fail the most eloquent pleader, 85
    And a new sort of case comes on—his own. He must
Defend *himself* for a change, while Venus in her nearby
    Temple snickers at this reversal of roles.

But the theatre's curving tiers should form your favourite
    Hunting-ground: here you are sure to find
The richest returns, be your wish for lover or playmate,
    A one-night stand or a permanent affair.
As ants hurry to and fro in column, mandibles
    Clutching grains of wheat
(Their regular diet), as bees haunt fragrant pastures 95
    And meadows, hovering over the thyme,
Flitting from flower to flower, so our fashionable ladies
    Swarm to the games in such crowds, I often can't
Decide which I like. As spectators they come, come to be inspected:
    Chaste modesty doesn't stand a chance. 100
Such incidents at the games go back to Romulus—
    Men without women, Sabine rape.
No marble theatre then, no awnings, no perfumed saffron
    To spray the stage red:
The Palatine woods supplied a leafy backdrop (nature's 105
    Scenery, untouched by art),
While the tiers of seats were plain turf, and spectators shaded
    Their shaggy heads with leaves.
Urgently brooding in silence, the men kept glancing
    About them, each marking his choice 110
Among the girls. To the skirl of Etruscan flutes' rough triple
    Rhythm, the dancers stamped

And turned. Amid cheers (applause then lacked discrimination)
    The king gave the sign for which
They'd so eagerly watched. Project Rape was on. Up they sprang then   115
    With a lusty roar, laid hot hands on the girls.
As timorous doves flee eagles, as a lambkin
    Runs when it sees the hated wolf,
So this wild charge of men left the girls all panic-stricken,
    Not one had the same colour in her cheeks as before—   120
The same nightmare for all, though terror's features varied:
    Some tore their hair, some just froze
Where they sat; some, dismayed, kept silence, others vainly
    Yelled for Mamma; some wailed; some gaped;
Some fled, some just stood there. So they were carried off as   125
    Marriage-bed plunder; even so, many contrived
To make panic look fetching. Any girl who resisted her pursuer
    Too vigorously would find herself picked up
And borne off regardless. 'Why spoil those pretty eyes with weeping?'
    She'd hear, 'I'll be all to you   130
That your Dad ever was to your Mum.' (You alone found the proper
    Bounty for soldiers, Romulus: give me that,
And I'll join up myself!) Ever since that day, by hallowed custom,
    Our theatres have always held dangers for pretty girls.

Don't forget the races, either: the spacious Circus offers   135
    Chances galore. No need,
Here, of private finger-talk, or secret signals,
    Nods conveying messages: you'll sit
Right beside your mistress, without let or hindrance,
    So be sure to press against her wherever you can—   140
An easy task: the seating-divisions restrict her,
    Regulations facilitate contact. Now find
Some excuse to engage in friendly conversation,
    Casual small-talk at first—
Ask, with a show of interest, whose are those horses   145
    Just coming past: find out
Her favourite, back it yourself. When the long procession of ivory
    Deities approaches, be sure you give
A big hand to Lady Venus. If some dust should settle
    In your girl's lap, flick it away   150
With your fingers; and if there's no dust, still flick away—nothing:
    Let any excuse serve to prove your zeal.
If her cloak's trailing, gather it up, make a great business
    Of rescuing it from the dirt—
Instant reward for your gallantry, a licensed peep at   155
    Delectable ankles, and more.

Keep an eye on whoever may be sitting behind you,
    Don't let him rub his knee
Against her smooth back. Light minds are captivated by trifles:
    Plumping out a cushion can often help,   160
Or fanning the lady, or slipping a little footstool
    Under her dainty feet.

Such approaches will the Circus afford to a new courtship,
    Such, too, the crowded forum with its grim
Sanded arena, where Cupid's a regular contestant,   165
    Where the blood-and-guts fancier gets bloodied himself:
While he's chatting, and touching her hand, and checking the programme,
    And anxious (once he's placed his bet) to know
Which contestant will win, the winged steel has transfixed him,
    He groans at the wound, becomes part   170
Of the show he was watching. When Caesar lately staged that
    Naval mock-battle between Persians and Greeks,
Young men and girls converged from east coast and west, the whole wide
    World was packed into Rome—
With such a throng, who could fail to find what caught his fancy?   175
    Many a man was singed by some foreign flame!

Now Caesar is planning to fill in the final gaps of
    Empire: now the furthest East will be ours,
Revenge fall on Parthia, joy lighten the grave of Crassus,
    Redeem the standards profaned   180
By barbarian hands! The avenger's prepared, proclaims his
    Captaincy, though of green years: embraces a war
No boy—no other boy—could direct. Why cravenly reckon
    The age of a god? These Caesars come to courage young,
The surge of heavenly spirit outstrips mere calendars,   185
    Takes mean delays ill. A mere babe
Was Hercules when he strangled those two serpents: even
    In the cradle he proved worthy of Jove.
And you, Bacchus, still a youth, what age were *you* when conquered
    India bowed before your rod?   190
With the years—and luck—of your father, boy, you'll fight this
    Campaign: with his years—and luck—you'll win.
Such a debut befits so great a name: today prince of
    The youths, tomorrow of their seniors! Since
You have brothers, avenge these brothers' insults; since a   195
    Father is yours, uphold a father's rights.
Your father, your country's father, has armed you for battle;
    Your enemy has wrested *his* kingdom from
A reluctant sire. Your righteous javelins shall match his

Treacherous arrows. Justice and right shall march   200
    Before your banners. May these lost-cause Parthians likewise
       Lose every fight, may my prince bring the wealth of the East
    Back home! Mars and Caesar—one god, one god-to-be—endow him
       With your paternal powers as he sets forth!
I prophesy victory for you, vow a song in your honour,   205
       Will extol you with loud praise:
You'll stand and exhort your troops in words I have written—
       May my words, I pray, not fall short
Of your valour! I'll speak of Parthian backs, of Roman courage,
       Of the shafts discharged by the foe   210
As he retreats on horseback. If a Parthian flees to conquer
       What's left him for defeat? That's a bad
Omen for warfare already. The day will come, most splendid
       Of beings, when you'll ride in gold behind
Four snow-white steeds, preceded by captive chieftains, fetters   215
       About their necks to prevent the flight that brought
Them safety before. Cheering youths will look on, and girls beside them,
       A day to make every heart run wild for joy;
And when some girl inquires the names of the monarchs,
       Or the towns, rivers, hills portrayed
On the floats, answer all her questions (and don't draw the line at
       Questions only): pretend
You know even when you don't. *Here comes Euphrates*, tell her,
       With reed-fringed brow; those dark
Blue tresses belong to Tigris, I fancy; there go Armenians,   225
       That's Persia, and that, h'r'm, is some
Upland Achaemenid city. Both those men there are generals—
       Give the names if you know them; if not, invent.

Banquets, too, give you an *entrée,* offer
       More to the palate than wine: 230
There flushed Love has often clasped the horns of reclining
       Bacchus in a seductive embrace,
And when wine has sodden Cupid's bibulous pinions
       He's grounded, too sluggish for the sport he's begun.
Still, it takes *him* no time to shake out his damp plumage—   235
       But if Love merely brushes the breast
You're wounded, it hurts. Wine rouses the heart, inclines to passion:
       Heavy drinking dilutes and banishes care
In a sea of laughter, gives the poor man self-confidence,
       Smooths out wrinkles, puts paid   240
To pain and sorrow. Then our age's rarest endowment,
       Simplicity, opens all hearts, as the god
Dissipates guile. Men's minds have often been enchanted
       By girls at such times: ah, Venus in the wine
Is fire within fire! Night and drink can impair your eye for beauty: 245

Don't trust the lamplight too much,
 It's deceptive. When Paris examined those goddesses, when he said, 'You
  Beat them both, Venus,' he did it in broad
Daylight. But darkness hides faults, each blemish is forgiven:
  Any woman you name will pass   250
As a beauty at night. Judge jewels or fine fabrics,
  A face or a figure, *by day*.

How list every female resort with prospects for the hunter?
  Sand-grains are fewer. Why tell of Baiae with
Its yacht-fringed beaches and hot sulphurous thermal   255
  Baths? I met one tourist who came back
Home from there with a nasty hole in his heart, said the waters
  Weren't half as healthy as report made out.
Then there's Diana's woodland shrine, not far from the city,
  With its murderous slave-priest—   260
Diana's a virgin, detests the shafts of Cupid: that's why
  People who go in the woods
Always get hurt, always will.
       So far my elegiacs
  Have taught you which coverts to draw, where to spread
Your erotic nets. What follows is more subtly artistic—   265
  How to snare the girl of your choice.
All you gallants, mark and attend now; and you, the common
  People, encourage my task with a thumbs-up!

The first thing to get in your head is that every single
  Girl can be caught—and that you'll catch her if   270
You set your toils right. Birds will sooner fall dumb in springtime,
  Cicadas in summer, or a hunting-dog
Turn his back on a hare, than a lover's bland inducements
  Can fail with a woman. Even one you suppose
Reluctant will want it. Like men, girls love stolen passion,   275
  But are better at camouflaging their desires:
If masculine custom precluded courtship of women
  You'd find each besotted girl
Taking the lead herself. A heifer amid lush pastures
  Lows to the bull, a mare   280
Whinnies at stallions; but our male libido's milder,
  Less rabid: man's sex has bounds
Imposed by convention. Incest is out. Think of wretched Byblis—
  Burned up by her brother, expiating her crime
With a suicide's noose. Myrrha loved her father (but hardly   285
  As a daughter should), and now she's straitjacketed
Behind tree-bark, oozing those fragrant tears we use for
  Perfume, named after her: myrrh.
Once in the shady valleys of woodland Ida

There roamed a milk-white bull,   290
   Pride of the herd, spotless save for one single
      Black mark between his horns:
The heifers of Crete all yearned to sustain that burden
      On their backs; but Pasiphaë
Proudly rejoiced in her role as bull's mistress, eyed his   295
      Cows with envious hate.
What I say is well-known: not even Crete of the hundred
      Cities, for all her mendacious ways,
Can deny it. With unpractised hands—they say—the lady
      Plucked leaves and lush grass   300
For this bull, went off with the herds, unrestrained by concern for
      Her husband. A bull won out
Over Minos himself. Why dress richly, Pasiphaë?
      Your lover's blind to your wealth.
Why bother with mirrors when the company you're seeking   305
      Is upland cattle? Why keep fixing your hair,
You silly girl? You're no heifer (on *that* you can trust your mirror)—
      But oh, how you wish you could sprout horns!
If you love Minos, steer clear of *all* adulterers; if you
      Choose to cuckold your man, then at least   310
Cuckold him with a man!
                              See the queen desert her bower
      For woods and glens, like some god—
Frenzied maenad: ah, the times she eyed a cow in fury,
      Crying, 'What can my lord ever see
In *that*? Just watch the silly creature frisking before him   315
      Down there at pasture—I suppose *she* thinks
She's a raving beauty.' With that, she would have the wretched
      Cow dragged from the herd to be yoked to the plough
Or poleaxed at the altar in a bogus sacrifice, just to
      Let her—a rare pleasure—get her hands   320
On her rival's entrails. The times she slaughtered such heifers
      To appease the gods, and cried, as she held out
Their guts, 'Go see how he likes you *now*!' Now she craves to be Io,
      Now Europa: bovine, or bull-borne.
Yet the herd-leader, taken in by a wooden cow, contrived to   325
      Fill her: their offspring betrayed
Its paternity. Had Aerope restrained her love for Thyestes
      (And to forego even one man
Is a serious matter), Phoebus would never have turned backwards   330
      In mid-flight, have driven his steeds
And chariot Dawnwards. From Nisus his daughter stole that purple
      Lock—and now fights down
The mad dogs that swarm from her groin. Agamemnon lived through battles
      On land, and great storms by sea,
To become his wife's victim. Who's not wept for flame-racked   335

Creüsa, for the children whose bloody death
Stained Medea's hands? Amyntor's son Phoenix wept tears
   From sightless orbs; fright-maddened horses tore
Hippolytus limb from limb. Ah Phineus, why blind your
   Innocent sons? On your own head the same   340
Horror will fall. Each one of these crimes was prompted
   By woman's lust—lust that far
Outstrips ours in keenness and frenzy. Why doubt that you can conquer
   Any girl in sight? Few indeed
Will turn you down—and (willing or not) a male proposition   345
   Is something they all enjoy. Draw a blank,
Rejection brings no danger. But why should you be rejected
   When new thrills delight, when what's not ours
Has more allure than what is? The harvest's always richer
   In another man's fields, the herd   350
Of our neighbour has fuller udders.

                   But first you must get acquainted
   With your quarry's maid—she can help
In the early stages. Make sure she enjoys the full confidence
   Of her mistress: make sure you can trust
Her with your secret liaison. Corrupt her with promises,   355
   Corrupt her with prayers. If
She's willing, you'll get what you want. She'll await the propitious
   Time (like a doctor) when her mistress is in
A receptive, seducible mood, when she's bursting out all over
   With cheerfulness, like a wheat-crop in rich soil.   360
When hearts are rejoicing, and have no sorrow to constrict them,
   They're wide open, Venus can steal
In by persuasive guile. Grim Troy long faced her besiegers,
   But a light-hearted change of mood
Fell for that troop-gravid horse.
                 Another time to try her   365
   Is when she's been miffed by a rival. Make it your job
To ensure she gets her revenge. Prime her maid to egg her on while
   Combing her hair each morning, put an oar in
To boost Ma'am's plain sailing, sigh to herself, and murmur:
   'What a pity it is you can't just pay him out   370
With a tit-for-tat,' then talk about *you* in persuasive
   Language, swear you're dying of mad
Passion. But lose no time, don't let the wind subside or
   The sails drop slack. Fury, like brittle ice,
Melts with delay. You may ask, does it pay to seduce the   375
   Maid herself? Such a gambit involves great risk.
Bed makes one girl jealous, takes the edge off another: will she
   Want you for her mistress—or for *her*?
It can go either way. Though the situation calls for

Bold risks, my advice is, *Don't*. I'm not the sort   380
To climb precipitous paths, sharp peaks. With me for leader
    No young man will be caught. But if,
While she carries your letters back and forth, it's not just
    Her zeal but her figure that tickles your fancy, then make
Mistress first, maid second. Never *begin* your wooing   385
    With the lady's companion. And here's one piece of advice
(If you trust in my skill at all, if the greedy winds don't
    Blow my words out to sea):
Lay off—*or make sure of her*. Once she's involved, and guilty,
    There's no longer any fear   390
That she'll turn informer against you. What's the use of liming
    A bird's wings if it escapes? A loose-netted boar
That breaks free is no good. Play your fish on the hook she's taken,
    Press home your assault, don't give up till victory's won.*

But keep such relationships secret: with a secret informer   397
    You'll always know every move your mistress makes.

It's wrong to suppose that only shipmen and toiling farmers
    Must observe due season. Grain   400
Cannot always be trusted to the treacherous furrow, nor curving
    Hulls to the green deep; likewise
It's not always safe to pursue young girls: the occasion
    Will often condition success. Thus, avoid
Her birthday; and April the First (the feast of Venus   405
    In conjunction with Mars); and when
The Circus is decorated, not, as before, with gew-gaws
    But with the wealth of kings: never make
Your attempt at such times—then storms are roughest, the Pleiads
    Sinking horizonwards, or the Kid washed down   410
Under the waves. Best to sit tight: those who venture
    On the high seas now, limp home
With a dismembered vessel. Begin on a day of mourning:
    The anniversary of Rome's bloody defeat
At the Allia—or perhaps on the Jewish sabbath: many   415
    Shops will be shut then. Regard
Your mistress's birthday with superstitious horror,
    Set a black mark against
Any day when you have to buy presents. Yet avoid it as you may, she'll
    Collect all the same. Every woman knows just how   420
To fleece her panting lover. When she's got a spending mood on,

---

* Lines 395–6 do not appear in two of the better MSS, and are omitted as spurious by some editors. I am in two minds about this verdict, so translate them here:

Then guilty complicity will keep her from betraying you,
    And you will learn of all your mistress says or does.

Some loose-garbed pedlar will come and spread out his wares
With you sitting by. She'll ask you to look at the stuff, show off your
    Expert knowledge. Kisses will follow. Then
She'll insist that you buy it, swear it'll satisfy her   425
    For years, say she needs it now, now's a good
Time to buy it. Tell her you haven't the cash in the house, she'll
    Ask for a note-of-hand—just to make
You sorry you learnt how to write. There's the birthday-cake gambit,
    A broad hint for presents: she's born x times a year   430
As the occasion demands. Or she'll come up weeping, pretend she's
    Lost one of her ear-bobs. Such girls
Are always borrowing things that, once they've had loaned them,
    They never return. Your loss in this sort of case
Isn't even offset by gratitude. To list the tricks such gold-digging   435
    Tarts employ, I'd require ten mouths, ten tongues.

Let wax pave the way for you, spread out on smooth tablets,
    Let wax go before as witness to your mind—
Bring her your flattering words, words that ape the lover:
    And remember, whoever you are, to throw in some good   440
Entreaties. Entreaties are what made Achilles give back Hector's
    Body to Priam; even an angry god
Is moved by the voice of prayer. Make promises, what's the harm in
    Promising? Here's where anyone can play rich.
Hope, once entertained, is enduring: a deceptive   445
    Goddess—but useful. Your gift
Once made, you can be abandoned, and with good reason:
    She'll have fleeced you, past tense, at no
Loss to herself. But a present withheld breeds expectations:
    That's how farmers, so often, are fooled by a barren field,   450
That's why the inveterate gambler doubles his losses
    To stave off loss, why the dice-box beckons his hand
Back again and again. *This the task, this the labour,* to win her
    Gift-free: she'll continue to give
Lest she lose what she's given already. A persuasive letter's   455
    The thing to lead off with, explore her mind,
Reconnoitre the landscape. A message scratched on an apple
    Betrayed Cydippe: she was snared by her own words.
My advice, then, young men of Rome, is to learn the noble
    Advocate's arts—not only to let you defend   460
Some trembling client: a woman, no less than the populace,
    Elite senator, or grave judge,
Will surrender to eloquence. Nevertheless, dissemble
    Your powers, avoid long words,
Don't look too highbrow. Who but a mindless ninny   465
    Declaims to his mistress? An over-lettered style
Repels girls as often as not. Use ordinary language,

Familiar yet coaxing words—as though
You were there, in her presence. If she refuses your letter,
   Sends it back unread, persist: 470
Say you hope she'll read it later. Time breaks stubborn oxen
   To the plough, time teaches a horse
To accept the bridle. An iron ring's worn by constant
   Friction, the furrowed soil
Rubs away the curved ploughshare. What is softer than water,   475
   What harder than stone? Yet the soft
Water-drip hollows hard rock. In time, with persistence,
   You'll conquer Penelope. Troy fell late,
But fall it did. Suppose she reads your notes, but won't answer?
   Don't press her, just keep up   480
Your flattering *billets-doux*. The girl who reads letters
   Will reply to them in the end: affairs like these
Go by degrees and stages. First you may get an angry
   Note saying 'Don't pester me, please.'
She's really afraid you'll stop: what she wants (but says she doesn't)   485
   Is for you to go on. Press hard, you'll win through in the end.

What else? If she's out, reclining in her litter,
   Make your approach discreet,
And—just to fox the sharp ears of those around you—
   Cleverly riddle each phrase   490
With ambiguous subtleties. If she's taking a leisurely
   Stroll down the colonnade, then you stroll there too—
Vary your pace to hers, march ahead, drop behind her,
   Dawdling and brisk by turns. Be bold,
Dodge in round the columns between you, brush your person   495
   Lingeringly past hers. You must never fail
To attend the theatre when she does, gaze at her beauty—
   From the shoulders up she's time
Most delectably spent, a feast for adoring glances,
   For the eloquence of eyebrows, the speaking sign.   500
Applaud when some male dancer struts on as the heroine,
   Cheer for each lover's role.
When she leaves, leave too—but sit there as long as she does:
   Waste time at your mistress's whim.

Don't torture your hair, though, with curling-irons: don't pumice   505
   Your legs into smoothness. Leave *that*
To Mother Cybele's votaries, ululating in chorus
   With their Phrygian modes. Real men
Shouldn't primp their good looks. When Theseus abducted Ariadne
   No pins held up *his* locks;   510
Hippolytus was no dandy, yet Phaedra loved him; Adonis,
   That creature of woodland, allured

A goddess. Keep pleasantly clean, take exercise, work up an outdoor
    Tan; make quite sure that your toga fits
And doesn't show spots; don't lace your shoes too tightly   515
    Or ignore any rusty buckles, or slop
Around in too large a fitting. Don't let some incompetent barber
    Ruin your looks: both hair and beard demand
Expert attention. Keep your nails pared, and dirt-free;
    Don't let those long hairs sprout   520
In your nostrils, make sure your breath is never offensive,
    Avoid the rank male stench
That wrinkles noses. Beyond this is for wanton women—
    Or any half-man who wants to attract men.

Lo! Bacchus calls to his poet: Bacchus too helps lovers,   525
    Fosters that flame with which he burns himself—
As Ariadne discovered, ranging the unfamiliar
    Sea-strand of Naxos, crazed
Out of her mind, fresh-roused from sleep, in an ungirt
    Robe, blonde hair streaming loose, barefoot,   530
Calling 'Ah cruel Theseus!' to the deaf waves, tears coursing
    Down her innocent-tender cheeks.
She wept, she besought, yet contrived to remain appealing
    Despite all: not even those tears
Could imperil such beauty. Hands beating her soft bosom,   535
    'He's gone,' she cried, 'he's betrayed me: what, ah what
Will become of me now?' Then, presto, the whole shore echoed
    With frenzied drumming, the clash
Of cymbals. She broke off, speechless, fainted
    In terror, the blood fled   540
From her pale inert limbs, as wild-tressed Bacchanals, wanton
    Satyrs, the god's forerunners, appeared,
With drunken old Silenus, scarce fit to ride his swaybacked
    Ass, hands clutching its mane
As he chased the Maenads—the Maenads would flee and rally—   545
    A dizzy rider, whipping his steed ahead
Till he pitched off the long-eared ass on his head, and the satyrs
    All shouted: 'Up with you, Dad!
Come on up there!' And then came the god, his chariot grape-clustered,
    Paired tigers padding on as he shook   550
The golden reins. Poor girl: lost voice, lost colour—lost Theseus.
    Thrice she tried to run, thrice stood frozen with fear,
Shivering, like the thin breeze-rustled cornstalk,
    Or osiers in a marsh. 'I am here
For you,' the god told her. '*My* love will prove more faithful.   555
    No need for fear. You shall be
Wife to Bacchus, take the sky as your dowry, be seen there
    As a star, the Cretan Crown, a familiar guide

To wandering vessels.' Down he sprang from his chariot, lest the
    Girl take fright at the tigers; set his foot   560
On the shore, then gathered her up in his arms—no resistance—
    And bore her away. No trouble for gods to do
Whatever they please. Loud cheers, a riotous wedding: Bacchus
    And his bride were soon bedded down.
So when the blessings of Bacchus are set out before you   565
    At dinner, with a lady to share your couch,
Then pray the Lord of Darkness and Nocturnal Orgies
    To stop the wine going to your head!
Here double-talk is the vogue: lace your conversation
    With ambiguous phrases designed to make the girl   570
Feel they're specially meant for her. Write flatteries on the table
    In wine, let her read herself your heart's
Mistress: gaze deep in her eyes with open passion—
    One silent glance can speak
Whole volumes. Make sure you're the first to snatch the cup that   575
    Her lips have touched: drink from where she has drunk;
And if there's some piece of food she's fingered, take it,
    Brushing her hand as you reach out.
Let it be your concern, too, to please your lady's escort—
    He'll be more use to you as a friend.   580
When you're dicing to settle the drinking-order, let him take your
    Place, give him the garland off your head,
Never mind if he's placed below you or with you, still let him
    Be served first every time, defer to his words.*
I'll give you specific advice, now, on just what limits
    You should set to your drinking. Keep mind and feet   590
Steady. Above all, avoid drunken quarrels, don't get
    Into a fight too fast.
His stupid swilling killed off Eurytion the Centaur;
    Wine over dinner was rather meant to promote
Fun and games. So if you've a voice, then sing; or if your movements   595
    Are graceful, dance. Please with whatever gifts
You possess to give pleasure. And though real drunkenness can harm you,
    To feign it may prove useful. Let your devious tongue
Stutter and slur: then, however licentious your words or
    Actions, they'll be blamed on the wine. 'A health   600
To the lady,' you'll cry, 'a health to the man she sleeps with!'
    —While silently wishing her present partner in hell.
But when the tables are cleared, and the guests departing,
    And in the confusion you perceive your chance

---

* Lines 585–8 are a spurious (and moralizing) insertion by some post-Ovidian hand:

    It's a safe, well-trodden path to deceive in friendship's name: safe
    And well-trodden perhaps, but still
The path of guilt. That way a collector collects more
    Than is due him, looks to care for more than his charge.

To make contact, then join the crowd, discreetly approach her 605
    On the way out, let your fingers brush against
Her side, touch her foot with yours. Now's the time for chatting
    Her up, no clodhopping bashfulness—the bold
Are favoured by Chance and Venus. Don't think that your eloquence
    Must conform to poetic canons. Just pitch in 610
And you'll find yourself fluent enough. You must play the lover,
    Ape heartache with words, use every subtle device
To compel her belief. It's not hard—what woman doesn't believe she's
    A natural object for love, or, however plain,
Isn't thrilled by her own appearance? Besides, very often 615
    That passion a gallant feigns in his opening round
Will become the real thing. (So, girls, show more kindness to pretenders:
    True love may spring tomorrow from today's
False declaration.) Press on, undermine them with devious
    Flatteries: so a stream will eat away 620
Its overhanging bank. Never weary of praising
    Her face, her hair, her slim fingers, her tiny feet.
Even the chaste like having their good looks published,
    Even virgins are taken up with their own
Cute figures. Why does it still bother Juno and Pallas 625
    That they didn't win first prize in the Phrygian woods?
When it's praised, then Juno's peacock displays its plumage;
    If you stare without comment—no show.
Even racehorses, back in the paddock, respond with pleasure
    To a combed mane, a pat on the neck. 630

Don't be shy about promising: it's promises girls are undone by;
    Invoke any gods you please
To endorse your performance. Jupiter smiles from heaven
    On foresworn lovers, lets all their perjuries blow
Away unrequited. (*He* used to swear falsely, by Styx, to Juno— 635
    So looks now with favour on others who do the same.)
The existence of gods is expedient: let us therefore assume it,
    With gifts of incense and wine on their antique hearths—
No carefree repose, like a drowsy siesta, keeps them
    Remote after all. So, lead an innocent life: 640
Divinity's nigh. Honour bonds, don't embezzle deposits,
    Avoid murder and fraud. If you're wise
Gull only girls, they're no danger. In this one deception
    It's good faith that ought to make you blush.
They're cheats, so cheat *them:* most are dumb and unscrupulous: let them 645
    Fall into the traps they've set themselves.
Egypt had drought for nine years once, no rain to quicken
    Her harvest-fields. Then Thrasius the sage
Told King Busiris the gods could be propitiated
    With a stranger's spilt blood. 650

Busiris replied: '*You* shall be the gods' first victim, you the
  Stranger who brings water to Egypt's soil.'
So Perillus, the inventor of Phalaris' brazen bull, was
  The first, unlucky man, to roast in his own
Cruel contrivance. Both kings did right. No fairer statute   655
  Than that which condemns the artificer of death
To perish by his art. So let perjuries gull the perjured,
  Let Woman smart from the wounds she first dealt out!

Tears, too, will help: with tears you'll shift adamant. Flaunt wet
  Cheeks—if you can—for *her* to see: 660
But if tears won't come (and they sometimes fail in a crisis)
  Just wipe a moist hand across your eyes!
What sensible man will not intersperse his coaxing
  With kisses? Even if she doesn't kiss back,
Still force on regardless! She may struggle, cry 'Naughty!',   665
  Yet she wants to be overcome. Just take care
Not to bruise her tender lips with such hard-snatched kisses,
  Don't give her a chance to protest
You're too rough. Those who grab their kisses, but not what follows,
  Deserve to lose all they've gained. How short were you   670
Of the ultimate goal after all your kissing? That was
  Gaucheness, not modesty, I'm afraid . . .

It's all right to use force—force of *that* sort goes down well with
  The girls: what in fact they love to yield
They'd often rather have stolen. Rough seduction   675
  Delights them, the audacity of near-rape
Is a compliment—so the girl who *could* have been forced, yet somehow
  Got away unscathed, may feign delight, but in fact
Feels sadly let down. Hilaira and Phoebe, both ravished,
  Both fell for their ravishers. Then there's another tale,   680
Well-known, but well worth retelling, which recounts how Achilles
  Made a girl on Scyros his:
It was after the goddess had won that beauty-competition
  Against her peers on Ida, and had given her own
Reward to Paris; after Priam had welcomed his foreign   685
  Daughter-in-law, and a Greek wife came to dwell
Within Troy's walls. All swore allegiance to the injured
  Husband. So one man's hurt became
A national cause. But Achilles—to his shame, were the act not prompted
  By a mother's prayers—concealed his manhood beneath   690
A girl's long robe. What's this? Wool-spinning's not your business.
  Achilles: it's quite another of Pallas' arts
Through which you'll find fame. What have you to do with baskets?
  Your arm should support a shield. Why does the hand
That will one day slay Hector carry a skein? Cast aside your spindle 695

With its laborious threading: the Pelian spear
Is what *you* should wield.
                    The king's daughter, Deidamia,
    Who shared his room soon proved
That manhood through rape. Her seduction must have been forceful,
    But to *be* forced was what she desired.   700
'Don't go,' she cried, when Achilles was hastening from her,
    Distaff forgotten, a warrior under arms.
Where's that violence now? Why coax the perpetrator
    Of your rape to remain, Deidamia? If you take
The initiative, it's true, you may feel some embarrassment: better   705
    To let *him*—and more fun when you submit.
Any lover who waits for his girl to make the running
    Has too much faith in his own
Irresistible charms. The first approaches, the pleading,
    Are the man's concern: *her* place   710
Is to hear his smooth line with kindness. To win her, ask her:
    She's dying to be asked. Just provide a good excuse
For her to fulfil your wishes. Jupiter wooed those antique
    Heroines as a suppliant. No girl seduced
The Almighty. But if you find that your pleading induces   715
    Puffed-up disdain, then ease off,
Take a step back. Many women adore the elusive,
    Hate over-eagerness. So, play hard to get,
Stop boredom developing. And don't let your entreaties
    Sound too confident of possession. Insinuate sex   720
Camouflaged as friendship. I've seen ultra-stubborn creatures
    Fooled by this gambit, the switch from companion to stud.

For sailors a pale complexion is inappropriate,
    They should be tanned and dark,
Fetchingly weatherbeaten; so should husbandmen   725
    Who spend their time out of doors
With plough and harrow; so should the champion athlete—
    If *they're* white, it looks all wrong.
But let every lover be pale: here's the proper complexion
    For lovers; this gambit, please note,   730
Has worked on every occasion. Pale was Orion, roaming
    The woodlands, pining for Side; pale
Daphnis (ah, unkind Naiad!). Look lean and haggard
    As proof of your passion, don't baulk
At hooding your lustrous curls. Sleepless nights, the pangs and worry   735
    Of consuming love—these will reduce young men
To a thin nothing. If you mean to achieve your purpose
    Be an object of pity, so that the passers-by
Will say at once, 'He's in love'.

Now should I complain, or warn you,
    That no one now distinguishes right from wrong?   740
Friendship and honour are empty words, it's not safe to praise your
    Girl to a friend—if he believes what you say
He'll be in there himself. You may ask, 'Did Patroclus cuckold
    Achilles? Wasn't Phaedra perfectly chaste
With Pirithoüs? Didn't Pylades love Hermione as Apollo   745
    Loved Pallas, or Castor his twin?'
If anyone nurses *that* hope, he'll believe that apples grow on
    Tamarisks, that honey's to be found in midstream.
The base alone gives pleasure; men seek only their own enjoyment,
    And find that sweet when it springs from another's pain.   750
How outrageous, when it's not their enemies that lovers
    Most need to fear! Nowadays you'll be safe enough
If you shun those you trust. Cousins, brothers, loyal comrades—
    Here's where your real trouble lies.
One word more before I stop. The characters of women   755
    All differ. To capture a thousand hearts demands
A thousand devices. Some soils are better for olives,
    Some for vines, or for wheat: you can't
Raise them all in one field. Hearts have as many changing
    Moods as the face has expressions. A wise man   760
Will adapt to countless fashions, will resolve himself, like Proteus,
    Into water, now lion, now tree,
Now bristling boar. Some fish are trawled, some netted,
    Some caught with line and hook:
And don't try the same technique on every age-group,   765
    An old doe will spot the trap
From much further off. If a simpleton finds you too highbrow
    Or a prude over-coarse, they'll feel
Self-distrust and dismay. That's how the girl who shies off decent
    Lovers will cheapen herself by giving in   770
To some low cad.
            This concludes the first part of my venture—
    Now throw out the anchor, let my craft ride secure!

BOOK 2

Cry hurrah, and hurrah again, for a splendid triumph—
    The quarry I sought has fallen into my toils.
Each happy lover now rates my verses higher
    Than Homer's or Hesiod's, awards them the palm
Of victory. He's as cheerful as Paris was, sailing away from   5
    Warlike Sparta, the guest who stole a bride,
Or Pelops, the stranger, the winner of Hippodameia
    After that chariot-race.

Why hurry, young man? Your ship's still in mid-passage,
    And the harbour I seek is far away.   10
Through my verses, it's true, you may have *acquired* a mistress,
    But that's not enough. If my art
Caught her, my art must keep her. To guard a conquest's
    As tricky as making it. There was luck in the chase,
But *this* task will call for skill. If ever I needed support from   15
    Venus and Son, and Erato—the Muse
Erotic by name—it's now, for my too-ambitious project
    To relate some techniques that might restrain
That fickle young globetrotter, Love. He's winged and flighty,
    Hard to pin down. Just so   20
Minos might block every line of escape, yet his guest still found a
    Daring way out—by air.
When Daedalus had built his labyrinth to imprison
    The bull-man, man-bull, conceived through a queen's guilt,
He said: 'Most just Minos, put a term, now, to my exile,   25
    Let my native soil receive
My ashes. Since unkind fate would not let me live there,
    Grant me at least to die
In my own country. Release the boy, if you hold his father's
    Services cheap; spare me if you will not spare   30
My son.' So much he said—but might have gone on pleading
    For ever in vain: the king
Would not grant his request. When Daedalus perceived this,
    Now, now is the time, he told himself, *to deploy*
All your skill and craft. Minos rules earth, rules ocean: 35
    No escape by sea or land. All that remains
Is the sky. So, through the sky we'll seek our passage—
    God in high heaven, forgive
Such a project! I do not aspire to touch your starry dwellings:
    This is the only way I have to escape   40
My master. Were there a way by Styx, through Stygian waters
    We'd swim to freedom. I must devise new laws
For human nature. Necessity often mothers invention.
    Who would have believed man could ever fly?
But Daedalus fashioned birds' oarage, trimmed it with feathers   45
    Bonded the flimsy fabric with linen thread,
Melted wax to glue wings in place. Very soon his novel
    Craftsman's task was achieved:
Excitedly the boy studied wings and wax, not guessing   50
    The gear had been made for his own
Shoulders and arms, till his father said: 'These are the craft which
    Must bear us home, with their aid
We must escape from Minos. Though he's blocked all other
    Routes to us, he cannot master the air—as you   55
Can do, through my device. But take care, don't go stargazing

At belted Orion or the Bear:
Take these pinions, fly behind me: I'll go ahead, you
    Follow my lead. That way
You'll be safe. If we fly too close to the sun, through the upper   60
    Air, then the wax will be softened by the heat;
If we stoop too low seaward, then our thrashing pinions
    Will grow waterlogged from the spray.
So, my son, set a middle course—and watch out for turbulent
    Air-currents: spread your wings
To the steady breeze, go with it.' While he talked, he was fitting   65
    The boy's gear, showing him how to move
Like a mother bird with her fledglings. Then he fixed his own harness
    To his shoulders, nervously poised himself for this strange
New journey; paused on the brink of take-off, embraced his
    Son, couldn't fight back his tears.   70
They'd found a hilltop—above the plain, but no mountain—
    And from this they took off
On their hapless flight. Daedalus flexed his wings, glanced back at
    His son's, held a steady course. The new
Element bred delight. Fear forgotten, Icarus flew more   75
    Boldly, with daring skill. The pair
Were glimpsed by an angler, line bobbing, who at the sight of them
    Dropped his rod in surprise. They left
Naxos and Paros behind them, skirted Delos, beloved of
    Apollo, flew on east: to the north   80
Lay Samos, southward Lebynthos, Calýmne with its shady
    Forests, and Astypálaea, set amid fish-rich shoals.
Then the boy, made over-reckless by youthful daring, abandoned
    His father, soared aloft
Too close to the sun: the wax melted, the ligatures   85
    Flew apart, his flailing arms had no hold
On the thin air. From dizzy heaven he gazed down seaward
    In terror. Fright made the scene go black
Before his eyes. No wax, wings gone, a thrash of naked
    Arms, a shuddering plunge   90
Down through the void, a scream—'Father, father, I'm falling—'
    Cut off as he hit the waves.
His unhappy father, a father no longer, cried: 'Icarus!
    Icarus, where are you? In what part of the sky
Do you fly now?'—then saw wings littering the water.   95
    Earth holds his bones; the Icarian Sea, his name.
So Minos failed to clip the wings of a mortal—yet here am
    I now, planning to pin down the winged god.
Delusions abound. Don't mess with Thessalian witchcraft—
    That love-charm torn from the brow   100
Of a foal is no good. Not all Medea's herbs, not every
    Spell and magical cantrip will suffice

To keep love alive—else Circe had held Ulysses,
    And Medea her Jason, by their arts alone.
Giving girls aphrodisiac drugs, too, is useless—and dangerous: 105
    Drugs can affect the brain, induce madness. Avoid
All such nasty tricks. To be loved you must show yourself lovable—
    Something good looks alone
Can never achieve. You may be handsome as Homer's Nireus,
    Or young Hylas, snatched by those bad   110
Naiads; but all the same, to avoid a surprise desertion
    And to keep your girl, it's best you have gifts of mind
In addition to physical charms. Beauty's fragile, the passing
    Years diminish its substance, eat it away.
Violets and bell-mouthed lilies do not bloom for ever,   115
    Hard thorns are all that's left of the blown rose.
So with you, my handsome youth: soon wrinkles will furrow
    Your body; soon, too soon, your hair turn grey.
Then build an enduring mind, add that to your beauty:
    It alone will last till the flames   120
Consume you. Keep your wits sharp, explore the liberal
    Arts, win a mastery over Greek
As well as Latin. Ulysses was eloquent, not handsome—
    Yet he filled sea-goddesses' hearts
With aching passion. How often Calypso lamented   125
    His haste to be off, swore the sea
Was too rough for rowing! Again and again she'd beg him
    To recount Troy's fate, made him find fresh words
For the same old tale. They'd pace the shore; pretty Calypso
    Would say: 'Now tell me how King Rhesus met   130
His bloody end.' Then Ulysses would take the stick he was holding
    And sketch in the wet sand whatever scene
She'd demanded. 'Here's Troy,' he'd say, making walls of shingle.
    'And here's the river. Let's call this bit my camp.
This was the plain—' he levelled it—'where we butchered Dolon,   135
    The spy-by-night, as he dreamed
Of Achilles' horses. There stood the tents of Rhesus;
    I rode back home that night
On the King's captured steeds—'As he spoke, a sudden breaker
    Washed away Rhesus, his camp, and Troy itself.   140
Then the goddess exclaimed: 'You'd trust *these* waves for your voyage?
    Look at the great names they've destroyed!'
So don't rely too much on looks, they can prove deceptive
    Whoever you are: have something more than physique!

Nothing works on a mood like tactful tolerance: harshness   145
    Provokes hatred, makes nasty rows.
We detest the hawk and the wolf, those natural hunters,
    Always preying on timid flocks;

But the gentle swallow goes safe from man's snares, we fashion
    Little turreted houses for doves.   150
Keep clear of all quarrels, sharp-tongued recriminations—
    Love's sensitive, needs to be fed
With gentle words. Leave nagging to wives and husbands,
    Let *them,* if they want, think it a natural law,
A permanent state of feud. Wives thrive on wrangling,   155
    That's their dowry. A mistress should always hear
What she wants to be told. You don't share one bed by legal
    Fiat, with you love substitutes for law.
Use tender blandishments, language that caresses
    The ear, make her glad you came.   160
I'm not here as preceptor of loving to the wealthy; a suitor
    With gifts doesn't need my skills—
Anyone attractive who says 'Here's something for you,'
    Has genius of his own. To such a one
I give place: he's got my tricks beat. I'm the poor man's poet,   165
    Was poor myself as a lover, couldn't afford
Gifts, so spun words. Poor suitors must woo with caution,
    Watch their tongues, bear much that the rich
Would never put up with. I recall how once in anger
    I pulled my girl's hair. The days I lost through that   170
Little outburst! I don't think I tore her dress, I wasn't conscious
    Of doing so—but *she* said I did, and the bill
Was paid for at my expense. Avoid (if you're wise) your teacher's
    Errors, shun what may cost you dear.
Fight Parthians, but keep peace with a civilized mistress,   175
    Have fun together, do all that induces love.

If the girl's curt and unreceptive to your wooing,
    Persist, be obdurate: the time will come
When she's more welcoming. Go with the bough, you'll bend it;
    Use brute force, it'll snap.   180
Go with the current: that's how to swim across rivers—
    Fighting upstream's no good.
Go easy with lions or tigers if you aim to tame them;
    The bull gets inured to the plough by slow degrees.
Was there ever a girl more prickly than Atalanta?   185
    Yet tough as she was, she went down
Before a man's prowess, Milanion, roaming the forest,
    Kept bewailing his lot, and the girl's
Unkindness. She made him hump hunting-nets on his back, he
    Was for ever spearing wild boars;   190
His wounded flesh learnt the strength of Hylaeus the Centaur's
    Taut bow—yet his keener pangs
Came from another bow, Cupid's. I'm not suggesting
    You have to go lugging nets up mountain glens

Or play the hunter, or bare your breast to flying arrows—   195
    A cautious lover will find the rules of my art
Undemanding enough. So, yield if she shows resistance:
    That way you'll win in the end. Just be sure to play
The part she allots you. Censure the things she censures,
    Endorse her endorsements, echo her every word,   200
Pro or con, and laugh whenever she laughs; remember,
    If she weeps, to weep too: take your cue
From her every expression. Suppose she's playing a board-game,
    Then throw the dice carelessly, move
Your pieces all wrong. At knucklebones, when you beat her,   205
    Exact no forfeit, roll low throws yourself
As often as you can manage. If you're playing halma, permit her
    Glass piece to take yours. Open up
Her parasol, hold it over her when she's out walking,
    Clear her a path through the crowd.   210
When she's on her chaise-lounge, make haste to find a footstool
    For those dainty feet of hers, help her on and off
With her slippers. At times she'll feel cold: then (though you're shivering
    Yourself) warm her tiny hand
In your bosom. Don't jib at a slavish task like holding   215
    Her mirror: slavish or not, such attentions please.
When his stepmother Hera tired of sending him monsters
    To vanquish, then the hero who won a place
In the sky he'd formerly shouldered took to the distaff
    And basket, spun wool among Ionian girls.   220
If Hercules, then, obeyed *his* mistress's orders, will you
    Flinch from enduring what he endured?
She says you've a date in town? Be sure you always get there
    Ahead of time: don't give her up
Till it's *really* late. If she asks you to meet her somewhere,   225
    Put everything off, elbow your way through the crowd
At the double. When she comes home, late at night, from a party,
    You still must attend, like her slave,
If she summons you. It's the same when she's in the country:
    Love detests laggards. You've no transport? Walk.   230
Don't be put off by bad weather, or a heatwave,
    Or snowdrifts blocking your road.

Love is a species of warfare. Slack troopers, go elsewhere!
    It takes more than cowards to guard
These standards. Night-duty in winter, long route-marches, every   235
    Hardship, all forms of suffering: these await
The recruit who expects a soft option. You'll often be out in
    Cloudbursts, and bivouack on the bare
Ground. We know how Apollo pastured Admetus' cattle,
    Dossed down in a herdsman's hut. What mere   240

Mortal's too good for conditions a god accepted? Is lasting
    Love your ambition? Then put away all pride.
The simple, straightforward way in may be denied you,
    Doors bolted, shut in your face—
So be ready to slip down from the roof through a lightwell,   245
    Or sneak in by an upper-floor window. She'll be glad
To know you're risking your neck, and for her sake: that will offer
    Any mistress sure proof of your love.
Leander might, often enough, have endured Hero's absence—
    But swam over to show her how he felt.   250
Don't think it beneath you to cultivate madam's houseboys
    And her more important maids:
Greet each one by name (the gesture costs you nothing),
    Clasp their coarse hands in yours—all part of the game.

On Good Luck Day, if you're asked for a present, even   255
    By a slave, then give: the expense
Will be minimal. See that the maids, too, get a handout
    On *their* day (the day those Gauls
Were figged by some dressed-up slaveys). It pays, believe me,
    To keep in with the servants—especially those who watch   260
Her front-door or bedroom entrance.
                              Don't give your mistress costly
    Presents: let them be small, but chosen with skill
And discretion. At harvest-time, when fields are full, boughs heavy,
    Send round a basket of fruit—
Say it came from your country estate (though you really bought it   265
    At some smart city shop). Give her grapes,
Or the chestnuts to which Amaryllis was so devoted—
    No, not chestnuts, she's off them these days:
Much too cheap. Why not try a poulterer's hoop of thrushes
    By way of remembrance? (It's shameful to use such gifts   270
In the hope of a death, to bribe the elderly or barren:
    I've not time for those who give presents a bad name.)
Would you be well advised to send her love-poems?
    Poetry, I fear, is held in small esteem.
Girls praise a poem, but go for expensive presents: 275
    Any illiterate oaf can catch their eye
Provided he's rich. Today is truly the Golden
    Age: gold buys honours, gold
Procures love. If Homer dropped by—with all the Muses,
    But empty-handed—he'd be shown the door.   280
There *are* a few cultured girls (not many, it's true), and others
    Who'd like to be cultured, but aren't;
Flatter any of these with poems: a bravura declamation
    Even of trash—this will suffice to win

Their approval. Clever or stupid, they'll take a poem fashioned   285
   In the small hours, for *them,* as a cute little gift.

Make your mistress ask as a favour for what you intended,
   All along, to do yourself
In the way of self-interest. You've promised manumission
   To one slave? See that he begs it, first, from her.   290
You plan to spare another in his flogging, or the chain-gang?
   Then put her in your debt for a 'change of heart'
That never existed. The benefit's yours, give her the credit,
   Waste not want not, while she
Plays the Lady Bountiful. You're anxious to keep your mistress?   295
   Convince her she's knocked you all of a heap
With her stunning looks. If it's purple she's wearing, praise purple;
   When she's in a silk dress, say silk
Suits her best of all; if her mantle's gold-embroidered
   Say she's dearer than gold to you; if tweeds   300
Take her fancy, back tweeds. She's in her slip? She inflames you
   (Tell her) with passion—but ask, at the same time,
Very shyly, 'Aren't you cold?' Compliment the way she's parted
   Or curled her hair. Admire
Her singing voice, her gestures as she dances,   305
   Cry 'Encore!' when she stops. You can even praise
Her performance in bed, her talent for love-making—
   Spell out what turned you on.
Though she may show fiercer in action than any Medusa,
   Her lover will always describe her as kind   310
And gentle. But take care not to give yourself away while
   Making such tongue-in-cheek compliments, don't allow
Your expression to ruin the message. Art's most effective
   When concealed. Detection discredits you for good.

Often in early autumn, when the year's at its sweetest,   315
   When grapes glow purple and full,
One day we'll be chilled to the bone, the next get heat-exhaustion,
   Our bodies made listless by the changing air.
Let's hope your girl keeps well—but if this unhealthy
   Season turns her sickly, sends her to bed,   320
Then let her see, beyond doubt, how she's loved and cherished,
   Then sow your seed: you'll reap a bumper crop
When the time is ripe. Bear with her fretful sickness,
   Attend in person to all she'll let you do;
Let her see you weeping, comfort her with kisses   325
   Day in, day out; let her parched
Lips drink your tears. Invent cheerful dreams to tell her,
   Make vows galore—and all of them aloud.

Bring round some old crone to purify bed and bedroom,
    Eggs and sulphur clutched in her tremulous hands.   330
All this will be proof of your willing care: such tactics
    Have often led to a legacy. But don't
Let your services risk incurring the invalid's displeasure—
    Sedulous zeal should know its proper bounds.
Never restrict her diet, never make her drink unpleasant   335
    Medicines: leave your rival to deal with such things.

Remember, the wind you spread your sails to when leaving
    Harbour should not be used out on the high
Seas: let your young love, fancy free, gather strength through
    Experience. Nourish it well, in time   340
It will grow steadfast. The bull you now fear began as
    The calf you stroked; the tree
Beneath which you recline was once a sapling. A river's
    Small beginnings swell with progression, embrace
Many confluent waters. Get her accustomed to you: 345
    Habit's the key, spare no pains till that's achieved.
Let her always see you around, always hear you talking,
    Show her your face night and day.
When you're confident you'll be missed, when your absence
    Seems sure to cause her regret,   350
Then give her some respite: a field improves when fallow,
    Parched soil soaks up the rain.
Demophoön's presence gave Phyllis no more than mild excitement;
    It was his sailing caused arson in her heart.
Penelope was racked by crafty Ulysses' absence,   355
    Protesilaus, abroad, made Laodameia burn.
Short partings do best, though: time wears out affections,
    The absent love fades, a new one takes its place.
With Menelaus away, Helen's disinclination for sleeping
    Alone led her into her guest's   360
Warm bed at night. Were you crazy, Menelaus?
    Why go off leaving your wife
With a stranger in the house? Do you trust doves to falcons,
    Full sheepfolds to mountain wolves?
Here Helen's not at fault, the adulterer's blameless—   365
    He did no more than you, or any man else,
Would do yourself. By providing place and occasion
    You precipitated the act. What else did she do
But act on your clear advice? Husband gone; this stylish stranger
    Here on the spot; too scared to sleep alone—   370
Oh, Helen wins my acquittal, the blame's her husband's:
    All *she* did was take advantage of a man's
Human complaisance. And yet, more savage than the tawny
    Boar in his rage, as he tosses the maddened dogs

On lightning tusks, or a lioness suckling her unweaned   375
    Cubs, or the tiny adder crushed
By some careless foot, is a woman's wrath, when some rival
    Is caught in the bed *she* shares. Her feelings show
On her face. Decorum's flung to the wind, a maenadic
    Frenzy grips her, she rushes headlong off   380
After fire and steel. Deserted, barbarian Medea
    Avenged her marital wrongs
On Jason by killing their children—like Procne the swallow,
    Another ruthless mother, breast stained red
With blood. Such acts destroy the most strongly bonded   385
    Passions: all prudent men should avoid
Set-tos of this sort. Such a ruling, though, won't condemn you
    (God forbid!) to one girl alone. No bride can expect
That degree of devotion. Have fun, but play it discreetly—
    Don't broadcast your intrigues   390
As a boost for your ego. Don't make regular assignations,
    Don't give X presents that Y might recognize.
Don't always meet in the same place: the lady may catch you
    If you haunt the milieux that she knows—
And whenever you write, make sure all previous letters   395
    Have been erased from your tablets: many girls read
More than was ever sent them. Venus, when affronted,
    Hits back, inflicts on you
All that she suffered. So long as Agamemnon was faithful,
    Clytemnestra stayed chaste. It was her husband's crimes   400
Turned her to the bad. She'd heard how Chryses, sacerdotal
    Fillet on head and laurel in hand, had failed
To win back his daughter. She'd heard the sad tale of abducted
    Briseis, knew how shameful delay
Had prolonged the war. Yet all this was mere hearsay: Priam's daughter   405
    Cassandra she'd *seen,* the conqueror shamefully caught
By his own captive. It was then she welcomed Thyestes' son to
    Her heart and bed, avenged her husband's ill deed.

Should your carefully camouflaged actions he brought not notwithstanding
    To light, then deny them still, through thick and thin;   410
Don't be over-subservient, don't flatter her more than usual—
    Such traits are clear proof of guilt.
Go to it in bed: that's the one way you'll get round her,
    With cocksmanship so fine it *has* to disprove
Any earlier peccadillo. Some advise taking aphrodisiac   415
    Herbal concoctions—they're poison, believe you me.
Some crush up pepper with nettleseed, an urticant mixture,
    Or blend yellow camomile in vintage wine;
But the goddess worshipped high on Eryx's leafy mountain
    Won't let her joys be forced this way—   420

Try white Megarian onions, and salacious colewort
    Picked from your kitchen-garden; eat eggs;
Enrich your diet with Hymettus honey, with the needled
    Pine-tree's delectable nuts.
Why digress on such hocus-pocus, Muse? I must guide my chariot   425
    Straight down the innermost lane,
Grazing the rail. Just now, at my urging, you were ready
    To keep your affairs a secret. Now change tack
—At my urging—and publish them. Don't chide me for fickle
    Impulses: no ship is always blown   430
By the same prevailing wind. We veer to every quarter
    As the breeze fills our sails. Watch how
A charioteer will handle his horses, first letting them gallop,
    Then skilfully reining them in.
Some women just don't react well to timid complaisance: 435
    If there's no competition in sight
Their love wanes. Success will often breed presumption,
    It's hard to keep your head
Through a run of good luck. You've seen the fire that smoulders
    Down to nothing, grows a crown of pale ash   440
Over its hidden embers (yet a sprinkling of sulphur
    Will suffice to rekindle the flame)?
So with the heart. It grows torpid from lack of worry,
    Needs a sharp stimulus to elicit love.
Get her anxious about you, reheat her tepid passions,   445
    Tell her your guilty secrets, watch her blanch.
Thrice fortunate that man, lucky past calculation,
    Who can make some poor injured girl
Torture herself over him, lose voice, go pale, pass out when
    The unwelcome news reaches her. Ah, may I   450
Be the one whose hair she tears out in her fury, the one whose
    Soft cheeks she rips with her nails,
Whom she sees, eyes glaring, through a rain of tears; without whom,
    Try as she will, she cannot live!
How long (you may ask) should you leave her lamenting her wrong? A little   455
    While only, lest rage gather strength
Through procrastination. By then you should have her sobbing
    All over your chest, your arms tight round her neck.
You want peace? Give her kisses, make love to the girl while she's crying—
    That's the only way to melt her angry mood.   460

When she's been raging at you, when she seems utterly hostile,
    Then is the time to try
An alliance in bed. She'll come through. Bed's where harmony dwells when
    The fighting's done: that's the place
Where loving-kindness was born. The doves that lately fought now   465
    Call softly, bill and coo.

The world at first was mere mass, confused and patternless, one great
    Mingled vista: stars, earth, sea. But soon
Heaven was set above earth, land ringed with water,
    And the void withdrew to its own place.   470
Birds made their home in the air, beasts in the forest:
    Deep underwater, fish lurked.
Mankind was nomadic then, went wandering through an empty
    Landscape, mere muscular brutes
Whose home was the woodland, who ate grass, used leaves for bedding,   475
    Went solitary, long avoided their own kind.
What softened those fierce hearts? Voluptuous pleasure
    When a man and a woman stopped
In the same place. They found what to do by themselves. No teacher
    Was needed. Venus saw the sweet game through   480
Without subtle trimmings. The bird has his mate, the fish will
    Find a partner out in the deep,
Hind follows stag, serpent tangles with serpent,
    Dog mounts random dog, the ewe
Thrills to be covered, bulls rouse their heifers, the snub-nosed   485
    She-goat's back sustains
Her rank male partner. Mares are driven to frenzy,
    Cross rivers in hot pursuit
Of their stallions. So get moving with this potent medicine
    When your lady's angry: nothing else will relieve   490
Her fierce distress, this dose surpasses even Machaon's
    Drugs: if you've been unfaithful, this will make your peace.

As I was reciting these lines, Apollo abruptly
    Materialized beside me, thrumming a chord
On his gilded lyre, bay in hand, bay wreathed about his sacred   495
    Hair (to poets he will sometimes appear
In visible form). 'Preceptor,' he told me, 'of wanton
    Love, come, lead your disciples to my shrine,
Show them the world-famous sign, that brief commandment:
    Know yourself. Only with true   500
Self-knowledge will a man love wisely, pursue the matter
    By exploiting the gifts he's got.
If nature's made him handsome, let him flash his best profile;
    If smooth-skinned, he should recline
Bare-shouldered. The brilliant talker can fill in those awkward   505
    Silences; the good singer should sing,
The good drinker—drink. But brilliant declamations
    And highflown poetic recitals are out of place
In common-or-garden discourse.' Such was Apollo's counsel,
    Counsel to be obeyed: this god speaks truth.   510
Back to my theme, then. Any intelligent lover
    Will win in the end: my techniques

Are sure to bring him fulfilment. Not every sown furrow
  Repays its investment with interest, not every wind
Blows your wandering ship on course. Lovers get less pleasure   515
  Than pain: let them steel their hearts
To endless hardship. As thick as Sicily's swarming
  Bees, or hares on Athos, or the grey
Olive-tree's clustering yield, or shells on the shore, so many
  Are the pains of love: there's gall for us in those pricks.   520

She's out, they'll announce, although you well may glimpse her
  Somewhere inside. So, she's out,
You were seeing visions. Suppose she locks the door against you
  Come the promised night? Then doss down
On the bare ground. It's dirty? Too bad. Even when some lying   525
  And snotty maid asks, 'What's this
Fellow hanging around for?' still coax door and cruel mistress,
  Take off your wreath of roses, hang it up
On the knocker. When she's willing, move in; when she avoids you,
  Take yourself off: no gentleman should become   530
An importunate bore. Why force your mistress to say, 'You
  Just can't get rid of old so-and-so'? She won't
Always be set against you. And don't think it demeaning
  To endure a girl's blows or curses, to kiss her feet.

Why waste time over trifles? My mind's on greater matters,   535
  Great themes will I tackle—your full
Attention, please, reader! The task will be arduous—but no credit
  Otherwise: hard and exacting the toil
My art demands. Bear patiently with a rival, and victory
  Will be yours, you'll triumph in the end.   540
Take this not as mere human opinion, believe it rather
  Prophetic utterance: nothing in my art
Is of greater importance. Put up with her flirtations,
  Leave her billets-doux alone, let her come or go
As she pleases. Husbands allow this latitude to lawful   545
  Wives—they nod off, let sleep assist the fun.
At this game, I must confess, I fall short of perfection,
  But what to do? I just can't follow my own
Instructions. What, sit by while someone's making passes
  At my girl? Let that go, not blow my top?   550
Her own incumbent, as I remember, had kissed her: I resented
  The kisses: my love abounds with wild
Uncivilized instincts (a fault that has caused me trouble
  On more than one occasion). Wiser the man
Who oils doors for his rivals. But it's best to know nothing,   555
  Let guilty secrets be hidden; don't make her confess,
Spare her blushes. Observe, you young blades, don't catch out your girls: no,

Let them cheat you—and while they're cheating, believe
They've eluded discovery. Passion's fanned by detection,
    A guilty pair revealed will always persist   560
In the love that undid them. Take one famous example—
    Vulcan's crafty snaring of Mars
And Venus. Driven wild by a frantic passion
    For the goddess, Mars was transformed
From grim captain to lover. Nor did Venus play the rustic   565
    And hold out against his entreaties: there's no
Goddess more willing. Ah, the times she mocked her husband's
    Limp, the wanton, or his hands, made hard
By toil at the forge and bellows! To ape him in Mars' presence
    Lent her chic, gave added charm   570
To her beauty. At first they concealed their adulterous
    Meetings: guilt blushed, shame kept
The affair quite dark. But who could deceive the Sun? He
    Saw all—and told Vulcan what acts
His wife was performing. Sun, that's a bad example   575
    You set there. Just ask, she'll oblige
You too in return for your silence. So Vulcan set hidden
    Snares round and over the bed (no eye
Could detect them), then put about he was off to Lemnos. The lovers
    Met as arranged, were trapped   580
In the toils, lay naked: tableau. Then Vulcan invited
    All the gods round. Venus came close to tears—
She and Mars couldn't cover their faces, couldn't even
    Move a hand to their private parts.
Someone laughed and said: 'If you find your chains a burden,   585
    Brave Mars, transfer them to me!'
At Neptune's urging, reluctantly, Vulcan released them:
    Venus ran off to Paphos, Mars to Thrace.
So much for Vulcan's plotting: once their shameful
    Secret was out, the lovers did as they pleased   590
Without thought for concealment. Later Vulcan admitted
    His folly, they say, and would curse the fatal skill
He'd deployed to catch them. So, be warned by the fate of Venus,
    Don't set up the kind of snare
She had to endure. Don't organize traps for your rivals,   595
    Don't intercept secret letters—that's a job
More proper to husbands (if they reckon such correspondence
    Worth interception). Once more, let me repeat,
There's no sport here that isn't legitimate, no long-skirted
    Respectable ladies figure in *my* fun.   600

Who'd dare to profane the rites of Ceres, who would publish
    The high mysteries held on Samothrace? To keep
Silence is no great virtue, but blurting out religious

Secrets—that's a most heinous crime.
Garrulous Tantalus, vainly reaching up for apples,   605
    In water, yet parched with thirst,
Deserved his fate: Venus expressly commands that her holy
    Rites be kept private. I'm warning you, let no
Kiss-and-tell gossip come near them. These mysteries may not
    Lurk in a box, may not echo to the wild   610
Clash of bronze cymbals; yet, though so popular among us,
    Among us they still insist
On concealment. Venus herself, when she poses naked,
    Bends down, places one hand
Over her mons. Brute beasts may couple in public,   615
    Promiscuously, a sight to make girls blush
And avert their eyes; but our more furtive passions call for
    Locked doors and bedrooms, we hide
Our private parts under the bedclothes, and prefer, if not darkness,
    At least something less than bright   620
Noonday, a touch of shadow. In the old days, when sun and weather
    Weren't yet kept off by roof-tiles, when oaks
Provided both food and shelter, love-making was restricted
    To caves or woods. Even these simple folk
Would have blushed to be seen in the act. But now we flaunt our prowess   625
    At such nocturnal pursuits, pay a high price
Just for the kick of bragging. Will you give every girl in town the
    Treatment, just to be able to tell your friends
'I had her, too?' Will you find some circumstantial scandal
    To repeat about each as she's mentioned, never lack   630
For a victim to point at? That's mild, though: some fabricate stories
    They'd deny if true, claim there's no
Woman they haven't slept with. If they cannot touch girls'
    Bodies, they'll smear their names: though the flesh escape
Defilement, repute is tarnished. So, bar the lady's chamber,   635
    You crabby old doorkeeper, fix on a hundred bolts—
What's left secure when her name's fair game for 'adulterers'
    Who work to convince the world of what never took place?
Myself, I remain discreet about my erotic encounters
    Even when they're true: keep such secrets under seal.   640

Take care not to criticize girls for their shortcomings: many
    Have found it advantageous to pretend
Such things didn't exist. Andromeda's dusky complexion
    Left wing-footed Perseus silent. Although
Everyone else thought Andromache too large a woman,   645
    To Hector alone she looked
Just the right size. Habit breeds tolerance: a long-established
    Love will condone much, whereas
At first it's all-sensitive. While a new graft's growing

In the green cortex, a light   650
Breeze can detach it; but soon, time-strengthened, the tree will
    Outface all winds, hold firm,
Bear adopted fruit. Time heals each physical blemish,
    The erstwhile flaw will fade:
Young nostrils cannot abide the stink of tanning leather,   655
    But age inures them to it, after a while
They don't even notice the smell. Labels minimize feelings—
    She's blacker than pitch? Try 'brunette'.
If she squints, compare her to Venus. She croaks? She's Minerva!
    A living skeleton? 'Svelte' is the word. Call her 'trim'   660
When she's minuscule, or 'plumpish' when she's a Fat Lady—
    Use proximate virtues to camouflage each fault.

Don't ask her age, don't inquire under just which consul
    She was born—leave that kind of chore
To the Censor's office, especially if she's past her girlish   665
    Prime, and already plucking those first
White hairs. Such ladies, in this (or even a higher) age-group
    Are good value, a field worth sowing, ready to bear.*
Besides, they possess a wider range of knowledge   675
    And experience, the sole source
Of true skill: they make up for their years with sophistication,
    Camouflaging their age through art; they know
A thousand postures—name yours—for making love in,
    More ways than any pillow-book could reveal.   680
They need no stimuli to warm up their passions—
    Men and women should share the same
Pleasures. I hate it unless both lovers reach a climax:
    That's why I don't much go for boys.
I can't stand a woman who puts out because she has to,   685
    Who lies there dry as a bone
With her mind on her knitting. Pleasure by way of duty
    Holds no charm for me, I don't want
Any dutiful martyrs. I love the sighs that betray their rapture,
    That beg me to go slow, to keep it up   690
Just a little longer. It's great when my mistress comes, eyes swooning,
    Then collapses, can't take any more
For a long while. Such joys attend you in your thirties:
    Nature does not bestow them on green youth.
For the hasty, new-bottled wine; for me, a vintage   695
    Laid down long years before.
Only an ageing plane-tree can block the sunlight,

---

*Editors have often remarked that lines 669–74 are out of place here, but no truly satisfactory place was found for them until it was shown that they properly belong at the *end* of Book 2, between lines 732 and 733. I have therefore transposed them in the present version.

Bare feet are crippled by a new-grown field.
Would you rate Helen's daughter Hermione over Helen? Was Medusa
    An improvement on *her* mother? Any man   700
Willing to get involved with mature passions,
    And to stay the course, will win a worthwhile prize.

So the bed, as though consciously, has received its two lovers.
    And the door is shut. Muse, you must wait outside:
They don't need you, now, to prompt their whispered endearments,   705
    Their hands won't be idle, fingers will learn
What to do in those hidden parts where Love's unnoticed
    Darts transfix the flesh.
Andromache got this treatment from most valiant Hector—
    His talents extended beyond war: 710
Captive Briseis was handled thus by the great Achilles,
    Who came, battle-weary, to her soft bed.
Those hands, Briseis, you let those bloody hands caress you
    Though daily they claimed their stint
Of Phrygian dead. Or was that just what you found so exciting—   715
    The hands of a conqueror on your limbs?
Believe me, love's acme of pleasure must not be hurried,
    But drawn insensibly on—and when you've found
Those places a woman adores to have touched up, don't let any
    Feeling of shame prevent you, go right in.   720
You'll see that tremulous glint in her eyes, like the dazzle
    Of sunlight on a lake;
She'll moan and gasp, murmur words of sweet endearment
    Well matched to the sport you're playing, heave soft sighs.
But take care not to cram on sail and outrace your mistress,   725
    Or let *her* overtake *you;* both should pass
The winning-post neck and neck—that's the height of pleasure,
    When man and woman lie knocked out at once.
This is the pace you should keep when time's no object,
    And your stolen pleasures take no prick from fear;   730
When delay isn't safe, though, it helps to press on regardless,
    Step up the strike-rate, spur that galloping horse.
While strength and age permit it, keep at such labours: 669
    Bent age will come soon enough   670
On stealthy feet. Cleave the sea with oars, the soil with a ploughshare,   671
    Turn your fierce hands to war—   672
Or expend your strength and toil and vigour on women: 673
    This too is military service, this too needs sweat.   674

My task is ended: give me the palm, you grateful   733
    Young lovers, wreathe myrtle in my scented hair!
As great as Podalirius was among the Achaeans   735
    For his healing arts, or Achilles for his strength,

Or Nestor in counsel, or Calchas as prophet, or Ajax
    In arms, or Automedon as charioteer,
So great am I at the love-game. Sing my praises, declare me
    Your prophet and poet, young men: let my name   740
Be broadcast world-wide. As Vulcan made arms for Achilles,
    So have I done for you: then use
My gift, as he did, to conquer! And when you've brought down your
    Amazon, write on the trophy *Ovid was my guide*.

Now the girls (hullo there!) are begging me for lessons: 745
    The next part of this poem will be yours.

The Bible

THE OLD TESTAMENT

Introduction by Michael Levin

The Bible is arguably the single most important work of Western literature; it has had a profound effect on the culture, philosophy, and even the languages of Western civilization. It is also perhaps the most controversial work you will find in this sourcebook, precisely because it is so important to so many people. For all these reasons, no course on the Humanities in the Western Tradition would be complete without a close look at the Bible. Our ideas about human nature, human society, the role of religion — in short, most of the themes of this course — have all been shaped by this one work.

More specifically, the first half of the Bible, or the Hebrew Scriptures (referred to as the Old Testament after the development of Christianity) is at the heart of the Jewish religion and people. The various individual books of the Hebrew Scriptures, written by different people over the course of many centuries, collectively tell the story of the Israelites. We can follow the development of this particular group of people, from their origins (or Genesis), through their first encounters with God, who tells the Israelites that they are his Chosen People. Eventually the Israelites become a people of Law, guided by divine wisdom as revealed to them by God. But the Israelites are very human — they often doubt, and they sometimes fail to live up to God's expectations, leading to divine punishment. When reading these stories, it is important to remember that the Hebrew Scriptures are a combination of religious instruction and historical narrative. Modern day Jews regard these scriptures as both a moral guide and a record of where they came from.

Our selections from the Hebrew Scriptures begin with the beginning of everything, from the Book of Genesis (which means origin or creation). Many of the stories included in this section may be familiar to you — the Garden of Eden, Cain and Abel, Noah and Flood. But do not skip this section! Read these stories carefully — you might be surprised. Ask yourself what is really going on here. What is God's purpose in placing the Tree of the Knowledge of Good and Evil in the Garden of Eden? Why does God decide to cause the Flood? These stories are not as simple as you might think. Also, in chapter nine pay close attention to the idea of a "covenant," or a contract between God and Noah. This is a key concept in the Hebrew Scriptures, the idea that people (and in particular the Chosen People) can make agreements with God.

In the Book of Exodus, we see evidence that God honors his side of the convenant he made with the Israelites; he rescues the Israelites from slavery in Egypt. But he acts through a human agent, a reluctant hero named Moses. And initially, the Israelites are not all that grateful to be rescued. They wander through the desert for forty years, and go through several crises of faith. What message is being given here about human nature? Eventually, they arrive at Mount Sinai, where God gives Moses the Ten Commandments as well as many other laws. This section is one of the foundation stones of Western society. What do the laws emphasize? How are we supposed to live our lives?

The Book of Isaiah takes place much later in the history of the Israelites, after they have settled in the land of Canaan. By this time, the Israelites have become prosperous, but they have begun to neglect their religious duties. Isaiah is one of a series of prophets who warn the Israelites that if they do not correct the error of their ways, God will punish them. And this is exactly what happens — the Babylonians conquer Canaan and enslave the Israelites. Isaiah also predicts that one day a child will be born who will be a Messiah, or a savior. Centuries later, followers of Jesus would claim that Jesus was in fact the Messiah who Isaiah had foreseen.

Finally, in the Book of Job we have a fascinating (and perhaps troubling) story about how God sometimes tests our faith. Job is a virtuous man, who, for no apparent reason, loses everything. Eventually, even Job's famous patience begins to wear thin, and he dares to question God. How does God respond? Compare the vision of God presented here with the Greek gods you read about earlier in the semester. What makes the God of the Hebrew Scriptures different from all other gods?

THE FIRST BOOK OF MOSES COMMONLY CALLED

Genesis

IN THE BEGINNING God CREATED*a* the heavens and the earth. ² The earth was without form and void, and darkness was upon the face of the deep; and the Spirit*b* of God was moving over the face of the waters.

3 And God said, "Let there be light"; and there was light. ⁴ And God saw that the light was good; and God separated the light from the darkness. ⁵ God called the light Day, and the darkness he called Night. And there was evening and there was morning, one day.

6 And God said, "Let there be a firmament in the midst of the waters, and let it separate the waters from the waters." ⁷ And God made the firmament and separated the waters which were under the firmament from the waters which were above the firmament. And it was so. ⁸ And God called the firmament Heaven. And there was evening and there was morning, a second day.

a Or *When God began to create*   *b* Or *wind*

1.1–2.4a: The Priestly story of creation. Out of original chaos God created an orderly world in which he assigned a preeminent place to man. **1:** Probably a preface to the whole story, though possibly introductory to v. 3: *When God began to create* (note *a*) . . . *God said* (compare 2.4b–7). The ancients believed the world originated from and was founded upon a watery chaos (*the deep;* compare Ps.24.1,2), portrayed as a dragon in various myths (Is.51.9). **3–5:** Creation by the word of God (Ps.33.6–9) expresses God's absolute lordship and prepares for the doctrine of creation out of nothing (2 Macc.7.28). Light was created first (2 Cor.4.6), even before the sun, and was *separated* from *night,* a remnant of uncreated darkness (v. 2). Since the Jewish day began with sundown, the order is *evening* and *morning.* **6–8:** A *firmament,* or solid dome (Job 37.18), separated the upper from the lower waters (Ex.20.4; Ps.148.4).

Bible, THE NEW OXFORD ANNOTATED BIBLE WITH THE APOCRYPHA Revised Standard Edition, Genesis 1–9.

9 And God said, "Let the waters under the heavens be gathered together into one place, and let the dry land appear." And it was so. [10] God called the dry land Earth, and the waters that were gathered together he called Seas. And God saw that it was good. [11] And God said, "Let the earth put forth vegetation, plants yielding seed, and fruit trees bearing fruit in which is their seed, each according to its kind, upon the earth." And it was so. [12] The earth brought forth vegetation, plants yielding seed according to their own kinds, and trees bearing fruit in which is their seed, each according to its kind. And God saw that it was good. [13] And there was evening and there was morning, a third day.

14 And God said, "Let there be lights in the firmament of the heavens to separate the day from the night; and let them be for signs and for seasons and for days and years, [15] and let them be lights in the firmament of the heavens to give light upon the earth." And it was so. [16] And God made the two great lights, the greater light to rule the day, and the lesser light to rule the night; he made the stars also. [17] And God set them in the firmament of the heavens to give light upon the earth, [18] to rule over the day and over the night, and to separate the light from the darkness. And God saw that it was good. [19] And there was evening and there was morning, a fourth day.

20 And God said, "Let the waters bring forth swarms of living creatures, and let birds fly above the earth across the firmament of the heavens." [21] So God created the great sea monsters and every living creature that moves, with which the waters swarm, according to their kinds, and every winged bird according to its kind. And God saw that it was good. [22] And God blessed them, saying, "Be fruitful and multiply and fill the waters in the seas, and let birds multiply on the earth." [23] And there was evening and there was morning, a fifth day.

24 And God said, "Let the earth bring forth living creatures according to their kinds: cattle and creeping things and beasts of the earth according to their kinds." And it was so. [25] And God made the beasts of the earth according to their kinds and the cattle according to their kinds, and everything that creeps upon the ground according to its kind. And God saw that it was good.

26 Then God said, "Let us make man in our image, after our likeness; and let them have dominion over the fish of the sea, and over the birds of the air, and over the cattle, and over all the earth, and over every creeping thing that creeps upon the earth." [27] So God created man in his own image, in the image of God he created him; male and female he created them. [28] And God blessed them, and God said to them, "Be fruitful and multiply, and fill the earth and subdue it; and have dominion over the fish of the sea and over the birds of the air and over every living thing that moves upon the earth." [29] And God said, "Behold, I have given you every plant yielding seed which is upon the face of all the earth, and every tree with seed in its fruit; you shall have them for food. [30] And to every beast of the earth, and to every bird of the air, and to

---

See 7.11 n. **9–10:** The *seas,* a portion of the watery chaos, were assigned boundaries at the edge of the earth (Ps.139.9; Pr.8.29), where they continue to menace God's creation (Jer.5.22; Ps.104.7–9). **11–13:** *Vegetation* was created only indirectly by God; his creative command was directed to *the earth.* **14–19:** The sun, moon, and stars are not divine powers that control man's destiny, as was believed in antiquity, but are only *lights.* Implicitly worship of the heavenly host is forbidden (Dt.4.19; Zeph.1.5). **20–23:** The creation of birds and fishes. *Sea monsters,* see Pss.74.13; 104.25–26. **24–25:** God's command for the earth to *bring forth* (compare v. 11) suggests that the animals are immediately bound to *the ground* and only indirectly related to God, in contrast with man. **26–27:** The solemn divine decision emphasizes man's supreme place at the climax of God's creative work. **26:** The plural *us, our* (3.22; 11.7; Is.6.8) probably refers to the divine beings who compose God's heavenly court (1 Kg.22.19; Job 1.6). Made in *the image of God,* man is the creature through whom God manifests his rule on earth. The language reflects "royal theology" in which, as in Egypt, the king was the "image of God." **27:** *Him, them:* man was not created to be alone but is *male and female* (2.18–24). *Man,* the Hebrew word is "adam," a collective, referring to mankind. **28:** As God's representative, man is given *dominion* (Ps.8.6–8). **29–30:** His dominion is limited, as shown by the vegetarian requirement, modified in

everything that creeps on the earth, everything that has the breath of life, I have given every green plant for food." And it was so. [31] And God saw everything that he had made, and behold, it was very good. And there was evening and there was morning, a sixth day.

2 Thus the heavens and the earth were finished, and all the host of them. [2] And on the seventh day God finished his work which he had done, and he rested on the seventh day from all his work which he had done. [3] So God blessed the seventh day and hallowed it, because on it God rested from all his work which he had done in creation.

4 These are the generations of the heavens and the earth when they were created.

In the day that the LORD God made the earth and the heavens, [5] when no plant of the field was yet in the earth and no herb of the field had yet sprung up — for the LORD God had not caused it to rain upon the earth, and there was no man to till the ground; [6] but a mist[c] went up from the earth and watered the whole face of the ground — [7] then the LORD God formed man of dust from the ground, and breathed into his nostrils the breath of life; and man became a living being. [8] And the LORD God planted a garden in Eden, in the east; and there he put the man whom he had formed. [9] And out of the ground the LORD God made to grow every tree that is pleasant to the sight and good for food, the tree of life

also in the midst of the garden, and the tree of the knowledge of good and evil.

10 A river flowed out of Eden to water the garden, and there it divided and became four rivers. [11] The name of the first is Pishon; it is the one which flows around the whole land of Hav'ilah, where there is gold; [12] and the gold of that land is good; bdellium and onyx stone are there. [13] The name of the second river is Gihon; it is the one which flows around the whole land of Cush. [14] And the name of the third river is Tigris, which flows east of Assyria. And the fourth river is the Euphra'tes.

15 The LORD God took the man and put him in the garden of Eden to till it and keep it. [16] And the LORD God commanded the man, saying, "You may freely eat of every tree of the garden; [17] but of the tree of the knowledge of good and evil you shall not eat, for in the day that you eat of it you shall die."

18 Then the LORD God said, "It is not good that the man should be alone; I will make him a helper fit for him." [19] So out of the ground the LORD God formed every beast of the field and every bird of the air, and brought them to the man to see what he would call them; and whatever the man called every living creature, that was its name. [20] The man gave names to all cattle, and to the birds of the air, and to every beast of the field; but for the man there was not found a helper fit for him.

c Or *flood*

Noah's time (9.2–3); it is to be benevolent and peaceful (compare Is.11.6–8). **31:** *Very good* (vv. 4,10,12. etc.), corresponding perfectly to God's purpose. **2.1–3:** The verb *rested* (Hebrew *"shabat"*) is the basis of the noun sabbath (Ex.31.12–17).

2.4b–3.24: The creation and the fall of man. This is a different tradition from that in 1.1–2.4a, as evidenced by the flowing style and the different order of events, e.g. man is created before vegetation, animals, and woman. **6:** *A mist* (or *flood*) probably refers to the water which surged up from the subterranean ocean, the source of fertility (49.25). **7:** The word-play on *man* ('adham) and *ground* ('adhamah) introduces a motif characteristic of this early tradition: man's relation to the ground from which he was *formed*, like a potter molds clay (Jer.18.6). Man is not body and soul (a Greek distinction) but is dust animated by the LORD God's *breath* or "spirit" which constitutes him *a living being* or psycho-physical self (Ps.104.29–30; Job 34.14–15). **8–9:** *Eden,* meaning "delight," is a "garden of God" (Is.51.3; Ezek.31.8–9; Jl.2.3) or divine park. **9:** The *tree of life* was believed to confer eternal life (3.22; see Pr.3.18 n.; Rev.22.2,14,19), as the *tree of the knowledge of good and evil* confers wisdom (see 2 Sam.14.17; Is.7.15). **10–14:** The rivers, springing from the subterranean ocean (v. 6), flowed out to the four corners of the known historical world. **15–17:** Man is given a task: to *till* and *keep* the garden. The prohibition against eating the forbidden fruit (3.3) stresses God's lordship and man's obedience. **18:** *To be alone* is not good, for man is social by nature (see 1.27 n.). *A helper fit for him* means a partner who is suitable for him, who completes his being. **19:** Naming the animals signifies man's

21 So the LORD God caused a deep sleep to fall upon the man, and while he slept took one of his ribs and closed up its place with flesh; 22 and the rib which the LORD God had taken from the man he made into a woman and brought her to the man. 23 Then the man said,

> "This at last is bone of my bones
>   and flesh of my flesh;
> she shall be called Woman,*d*
>   because she was taken out of Man."*e*

24 Therefore a man leaves his father and his mother and cleaves to his wife, and they become one flesh. 25 And the man and his wife were both naked, and were not ashamed.

3 Now the serpent was more subtle than any other wild creature that the LORD God had made. He said to the woman, "Did God say, 'You shall not eat of any tree of the garden'?" 2 And the woman said to the serpent, "We may eat of the fruit of the trees of the garden; 3 but God said, 'You shall not eat of the fruit of the tree which is in the midst of the garden, neither shall you touch it, lest you die.'" 4 But the serpent said to the woman, "You will not die. 5 For God knows that when you eat of it your eyes will be opened, and you will be like God, knowing good and evil." 6 So when the woman saw that the tree was good for food, and that it was a delight to the eyes, and that the tree was to be desired to make one wise, she took of its fruit and ate; and she also gave some to her husband, and he ate. 7 Then the eyes of both were opened, and they knew that they were naked; and they sewed fig leaves together and made themselves aprons.

8 And they heard the sound of the LORD God walking in the garden in the cool of the day, and the man and his wife hid themselves from the presence of the LORD God among the trees of the garden. 9 But the LORD God called to the man, and said to him, "Where are you?" 10 And he said, "I heard the sound of thee in the garden, and I was afraid, because I was naked; and I hid myself." 11 He said, "Who told you that you were naked? Have you eaten of the tree of which I commanded you not to eat?" 12 The man said, "The woman whom thou gavest to be with me, she gave me fruit of the tree, and I ate." 13 Then the LORD God said to the woman, "What is this that you have done?" The woman said, "The serpent beguiled me, and I ate." 14 The LORD God said to the serpent,

> "Because you have done this,
>   cursed are you above all cattle,
>   and above all wild animals;
> upon your belly you shall go,
>   and dust you shall eat
>   all the days of your life.

15 I will put enmity between you and the woman,
>   and between your seed and her seed;
> he shall bruise your head,
>   and you shall bruise his heel."

16 To the woman he said,

> "I will greatly multiply your pain in childbearing;
>   in pain you shall bring forth children,
> yet your desire shall be for your husband,
>   and he shall rule over you."

d Heb *ishshah*   *e* Heb *ish*

---

dominion over them (compare 1.28). **21–23:** The deep affinity between man and woman is portrayed in the statement that God made the woman from the man's *rib.* **24–25:** Sex is not regarded as evil but as a God-given impulse which draws man and woman together so that *they become one flesh.* **25:** The two were unashamedly *naked,* a symbol of their guiltless relation to God and to one another. **3.1–7:** The temptation begins with the insinuation of doubt (vv. 1–3), increases as suspicion is cast upon God's motive (vv. 4–5), and becomes irresistible when the couple sense the possibilities of freedom (v. 6). **1:** *The serpent,* one of the wild creatures, distinguished by uncanny wisdom (Mt.10.16); there is a hint of a seductive power in man's environment, hostile to God. **5:** *Like God:* perhaps "like gods" (Septuagint), the divine beings of the heavenly court (v. 22; 1.26 n.). *Knowing good and evil,* see 2.9 n. **7:** Bodily shame (2.25) symbolizes anxiety about broken relationship with God. **8–13:** Anxiety leads to a guilty attempt to hide from God (Ps.139.7–12), described anthropomorphically as strolling in his garden. **14–15:** The curse contains an old explanation of why the serpent crawls rather than walks and why men are instinctively hostile to it. **16:** This divine judgment contains an old explanation of woman's pain in childbirth, her sexual *desire* for her husband (i.e. her motherly

¹⁷ And to Adam he said,
"Because you have listened to the voice of
your wife,
and have eaten of the tree
of which I commanded you,
'You shall not eat of it,'
cursed is the ground because of you;
in toil you shall eat of it all the days of
your life;
¹⁸ thorns and thistles it shall bring forth to
you;
and you shall eat the plants of the field.
¹⁹ In the sweat of your face
you shall eat bread
till you return to the ground,
for out of it you were taken;
you are dust,
and to dust you shall return."

20 The man called his wife's name Eve,^f because she was the mother of all living. ²¹ And the LORD God made for Adam and for his wife garments of skins, and clothed them.

22 Then the LORD God said, "Behold, the man has become like one of us, knowing good and evil; and now, lest he put forth his hand and take also of the tree of life, and eat, and live for ever"— ²³ therefore the LORD God sent him forth from the garden of Eden, to till the ground from which he was taken. ²⁴ He drove out the man; and at the east of the garden of Eden he placed the cherubim, and a flaming sword which turned every way, to guard the way to the tree of life.

4 Now Adam knew Eve his wife, and she conceived and bore Cain, saying, "I have gotten^g a man with the help of the LORD." ² And again, she bore his brother Abel. Now Abel was a keeper of sheep, and Cain a tiller of the ground. ³ In the course of time Cain brought to the LORD an offering of the fruit of the ground, ⁴ and Abel brought of the firstlings of his flock and of their fat portions. And the LORD had regard for Abel and his offering, ⁵ but for Cain and his offering he had no regard. So Cain was very angry, and his countenance fell. ⁶ The LORD said to Cain, "Why are you angry, and why has your countenance fallen? ⁷ If you do well, will you not be accepted? And if you do not do well, sin is couching at the door; its desire is for you, but you must master it."

8 Cain said to Abel his brother, "Let us go out to the field."^h And when they were in the field, Cain rose up against his brother Abel, and killed him. ⁹ Then the LORD said to Cain, "Where is Abel your brother?" He said, "I do not know; am I my brother's keeper?" ¹⁰ And the LORD said, "What have you done? The voice of your brother's blood is crying to me from the ground. ¹¹ And now you are cursed from the ground, which has opened its mouth to receive your brother's blood from your hand. ¹² When you till the ground, it shall no longer yield to you its strength; you shall be a

f The name in Hebrew resembles the word for *living*
g Heb *qanah,* get

---

impulse, compare 30.1), and her subordinate position to man in ancient society. **17–19:** An explanation of man's struggle to eke an existence from the soil. Work is not essentially evil (2.15) but it becomes *toil* as a result of man's broken relationship with his Creator. **17:** The Hebrew word *Adam* is usually translated "man" in this story (see 1.27 n.). Note that the curse is upon the ground, not man. **19:** *Till you return to the ground:* The mortal nature of man was implicit in the circumstances of his origin (2.7); because of man's disobedience, God now makes death an inevitable fate that haunts man throughout life. **21:** *Garments of skins,* a sign of God's protective care even in the time of judgment (4.15). **22:** *Like one of us,* see 3.5 n. *The tree of life* (2.9) does not figure in the temptation story, which explicitly speaks of only one tree in the center of the garden (3.3–6, 11–12, 17). **24:** *The cherubim,* guardians of sacred areas (1 Kg.8.6–7), were represented as winged creatures like the Sphinx of Egypt, half human and half lion (Ezek.41.18–19). *A flaming sword* (compare Jer.47.6) was placed near the cherubim to remind banished man of the impossibility of overstepping his creaturely bounds (compare Ezek.28.13–16).

4.1–26: Cain, Abel, and Seth. 2–5: The story reflects the tension between farmers and semi-nomads, two different ways of life that are symbolized in the two types of offerings. No reason is given for the acceptance of Abel's offering (compare Ex.33.19). **7:** Perhaps the meaning is that Cain himself will be *accepted,* even though his offering is not, if his deed springs from the right motive. Sin is pictured as a predatory animal, *couching at the door.* **10–11:** Blood is sacred to God, for it is the seat of life (Dt.12.23) and cries *from the ground* for vindication. **13–14:** Cain concludes that

fugitive and a wanderer on the earth." [13] Cain said to the LORD, "My punishment is greater than I can bear. [14] Behold, thou hast driven me this day away from the ground; and from thy face I shall be hidden; and I shall be a fugitive and a wanderer on the earth, and whoever finds me will slay me." [15] Then the LORD said to him, "Not so![i] If any one slays Cain, vengeance shall be taken on him sevenfold." And the LORD put a mark on Cain, lest any who came upon him should kill him. [16] Then Cain went away from the presence of the LORD, and dwelt in the land of Nod,[j] east of Eden.

17 Cain knew his wife, and she conceived and bore Enoch; and he built a city, and called the name of the city after the name of his son, Enoch. [18] To Enoch was born Irad; and Irad was the father of Me-hu'ja-el, and Me-hu'ja-el the father of Me-thu'sha-el, and Me-thu'sha-el the father of Lamech. [19] And Lamech took two wives; the name of the one was Adah, and the name of the other Zillah. [20] Adah bore Jabal; he was the father of those who dwell in tents and have cattle. [21] His brother's name was Jubal; he was the father of all those who play the lyre and pipe. [22] Zillah bore Tubal-cain; he was the forger of all instruments of bronze and iron. The sister of Tubal-cain was Na'amah.

23 Lamech said to his wives:

"Adah and Zillah, hear my voice;
    you wives of Lamech, hearken to what I
        say:
I have slain a man for wounding me,
    a young man for striking me.

24 If Cain is avenged sevenfold,
    truly Lamech seventy-sevenfold."

25 And Adam knew his wife again, and she bore a son and called his name Seth, for she said, "God has appointed for me another child instead of Abel, for Cain slew him." [26] To Seth also a son was born, and he called his name Enosh. At that time men began to call upon the name of the LORD.

5 This is the book of the generations of Adam. When God created man, he made him in the likeness of God. [2] Male and female he created them, and he blessed them and named them Man when they were created. [3] When Adam had lived a hundred and thirty years, he became the father of a son in his own likeness, after his image, and named him Seth. [4] The days of Adam after he became the father of Seth were eight hundred years; and he had other sons and daughters. [5] Thus all the days that Adam lived were nine hundred and thirty years; and he died.

6 When Seth had lived a hundred and five years, he became the father of Enosh. [7] Seth lived after the birth of Enosh eight hundred and seven years, and had other sons and daughters. [8] Thus all the days of Seth were nine hundred and twelve years; and he died.

9 When Enosh had lived ninety years, he became the father of Kenan. [10] Enosh lived after the birth of Kenan eight hundred and fifteen years, and had other sons and daughters.

h Sam Gk Syr Compare Vg: Heb lacks *Let us go out to the field*   *i* Gk Syr Vg: Heb *Therefore*   *j* That is *Wandering*

exile from the farmland is also exile from the LORD's *face,* i.e. protective presence, exposing him to blood revenge. **15:** The "mark of Cain" was a protective mark, perhaps a tattoo, signifying divine mercy. **17:** Here Cain is not the ancestor of nomadic tribesmen (vv. 11–16) but the founder of sedentary culture. **19–22:** Cultural advance is evidenced by the three occupations of Lamech's sons: shepherds, musicians, and smiths. **23–24:** An ancient song, probably once sung in praise of Lamech, is here quoted to illustrate the development of wickedness from murder to measureless blood revenge. **25–26:** From Cain's genealogy the narrator returns to the sequel of Cain's banishment (vv. 11–16) and introduces the new line of Seth. **26b:** This tradition traces the worship of the LORD (Yahweh) back to the time of Adam's grandson, in contrast to other traditions which claim that the sacred name was introduced in Moses' time (Ex.3.13–15; 6.2–3).

5.1–32: The generations from Adam to Noah. This priestly tradition bridges the times from the creation to the flood. **1:** *The book of the generations* was evidently a separate source from which the writer drew genealogical data (6.9; 10.1; 11.10,27; etc.). **1b–2:** See 1.26–28. **3:** The divine *likeness* (v. 1; see 1.26 n.) was continued in Adam's son Seth, born *in his own likeness,* and thus was transmitted to succeeding generations without effacement (9.6). Priestly tradition makes no reference to the account of the fall of man. **4–32:** Babylonian tradition also reckons ten heroes

¹¹ Thus all the days of Enosh were nine hundred and five years; and he died.

12 When Kenan had lived seventy years, he became the father of Ma-hal'-alel. ¹³ Kenan lived after the birth of Ma-hal'alel eight hundred and forty years, and had other sons and daughters. ¹⁴ Thus all the days of Kenan were nine hundred and ten years; and he died.

15 When Ma-hal'alel had lived sixty-five years, he became the father of Jared. ¹⁶ Ma-hal'alel lived after the birth of Jared eight hundred and thirty years, and had other sons and daughters. ¹⁷ Thus all the days of Ma-hal'-alel were eight hundred and ninety-five years; and he died.

18 When Jared had lived a hundred and sixty-two years he became the father of Enoch. ¹⁹ Jared lived after the birth of Enoch eight hundred years, and had other sons and daughters. ²⁰ Thus all the days of Jared were nine hundred and sixty-two years; and he died.

21 When Enoch had lived sixty-five years, he became the father of Methu'selah. ²² Enoch walked with God after the birth of Methu'selah three hundred years, and had other sons and daughters. ²³ Thus all the days of Enoch were three hundred and sixty-five years. ²⁴ Enoch walked with God; and he was not, for God took him.

25 When Methu'selah had lived a hundred and eighty-seven years, he became the father of Lamech. ²⁶ Methu'selah lived after the birth of Lamech seven hundred and eighty-two years, and had other sons and daughters. ²⁷ Thus all the days of Methu'selah were nine hundred and sixty-nine years; and he died.

28 When Lamech had lived a hundred and eighty-two years, he became the father of a son, ²⁹ and called his name Noah, saying, "Out of the ground which the LORD has cursed this one shall bring us relief from our work and from the toil of our hands." ³⁰ Lamech lived after the birth of Noah five hundred and ninety-five years, and had other sons and daughters. ³¹ Thus all the days of Lamech were seven hundred and seventy-seven years; and he died.

32 After Noah was five hundred years old, Noah became the father of Shem, Ham, and Japheth.

6 When men began to multiply on the face of the ground, and daughters were born to them, ² the sons of God saw that the daughters of men were fair; and they took to wife such of them as they chose. ³ Then the LORD said, "My spirit shall not abide in man for ever, for he is flesh, but his days shall be a hundred and twenty years." ⁴ The Nephilim were on the earth in those days, and also afterward, when the sons of God came in to the daughters of men, and they bore children to them. These were the mighty men that were of old, the men of renown.

5 The LORD saw that the wickedness of man was great in the earth, and that every imagination of the thoughts of his heart was only evil continually. ⁶ And the LORD was sorry that he had made man on the earth, and it grieved him to his heart. ⁷ So the LORD said, "I will blot out man whom I have created from the face of the ground, man and beast and creeping things and birds of the air, for I am

---

before the flood but ascribes fantastically higher ages. In Hebrew tradition the ages decrease from 900–1000 (Adam to Noah), to 200–600 (Noah to Abraham), to 100–200 (the patriarchs), to the normal three-score years and ten (Ps.90.10). This list is somehow related to the genealogy of Cain (4.17–21) as shown by the resemblance of some of the names. **24:** Babylonian tradition also reports that the seventh hero before the flood was taken by God, i.e. translated (2 Kg.2.11). **29:** This verse, the only connection with the early traditions of Eden (3.17–19) and Cain and Abel, anticipates the new age inaugurated with Noah (9.20).

6.1–4: The birth of the Nephilim is related to demonstrate the increase of wickedness on the earth. **1:** This old fragment of mythology connects immediately with chs. 2–4. **2:** *The sons of God* were divine beings who belonged to the heavenly court (1.26 n.). **3:** Despite the lustful intrusion of divine beings into the human sphere, man did not become semi-divine (compare 3.22–24) but remained a mortal creature in whom the LORD's *spirit* dwells temporarily (see 2.7 n.). **4:** Originally the story accounted for *the Nephilim* (Num.13.33; Dt.2.10–11), men of gigantic stature whose superhuman power was thought to result from divine-human marriage.

sorry that I have made them." [8] But Noah found favor in the eyes of the LORD.

9 These are the generations of Noah. Noah was a righteous man, blameless in his generation; Noah walked with God. [10] And Noah had three sons, Shem, Ham, and Japheth.

11 Now the earth was corrupt in God's sight, and the earth was filled with violence. [12] And God saw the earth, and behold, it was corrupt; for all flesh had corrupted their way upon the earth. [13] And God said to Noah, "I have determined to make an end of all flesh; for the earth is filled with violence through them; behold, I will destroy them with the earth. [14] Make yourself an ark of gopher wood; make rooms in the ark, and cover it inside and out with pitch. [15] This is how you are to make it: the length of the ark three hundred cubits, its breadth fifty cubits, and its height thirty cubits. [16] Make a roof[k] for the ark, and finish it to a cubit above; and set the door of the ark in its side; make it with lower, second, and third decks. [17] For behold, I will bring a flood of waters upon the earth, to destroy all flesh in which is the breath of life from under heaven; everything that is on the earth shall die. [18] But I will establish my covenant with you; and you shall come into the ark, you, your sons, your wife, and your sons' wives with you. [19] And of every living thing of all flesh, you shall bring two of every sort into the ark, to keep them alive with you; they shall be male and female. [20] Of the birds according to their kinds, and of the animals according to their kinds, and of the animals according to their kinds, of every creeping thing of the ground according to its kind, two of every sort shall come in to you, to keep them alive. [21] Also take with you every sort of food that is eaten, and store it up; and it shall serve as food for you and for them." [22] Noah did this; he did all that God commanded him.

7 Then the LORD said to Noah, "Go into the ark, you and all your household, for I have seen that you are righteous before me in this generation. [2] Take with you seven pairs of all clean animals, the male and his mate; and a pair of the animals that are not clean, the male and his mate; [3] and seven pairs of the birds of the air also, male and female, to keep their kind alive upon the face of all the earth. [4] For in seven days I will send rain upon the earth forty days and forty nights; and every living thing that I have made I will blot out from the face of the ground." [5] And Noah did all that the LORD had commanded him.

6 Noah was six hundred years old when the flood of waters came upon the earth. [7] And Noah and his sons and his wife and his sons' wives with him went into the ark, to escape the waters of the flood. [8] Of clean animals, and of animals that are not clean, and of birds, and of everything that creeps on the ground, [9] two and two, male and female, went into the ark with Noah, as God had commanded Noah. [10] And after seven days the waters of the flood came upon the earth.

k Or *window*

6.5–8.22: The great flood. God's judgment took the form of a destructive flood, and his mercy was shown in saving a remnant with whom he made a new historical beginning. **5–8:** An introduction, belonging to the old literary tradition found in 2.4b–3.24; 4.1–26; 6.1–4. **5:** The *heart* includes the will and reason, as shown by its capacity for *imagination* of thought. **7:** The Biblical account is superficially similar to the Babylonian Gilgamesh Epic. The Biblical perspective, however, is basically different, for the flood was not the expression of polytheistic caprice but of God's judgment upon the *wickedness of man*. **9:** Noah was *a righteous man,* i.e. he stood in right relationship to God (15.6). **11–22:** A parallel version. It is generally recognized that an earlier and a later (priestly) tradition have been combined. **11:** The earth, once seen to be "good" (1.31), is called *corrupt* owing to man's *violence* or wilful, lawless deeds. **14–16:** In the Babylonian epic too, the hero is commanded to build a houseboat, sealing it with pitch. **15:** The dimensions: about $450 \times 75 \times 45$ feet.

7.1–10: This section is essentially a continuation of the early tradition (6.5–8). **2–3:** On clean and unclean animals, see Lev. ch. 11. (The priestly version mentions two animals of every sort [v.9; 6.19], presuming that the clean-unclean distinction was introduced at Sinai.) **4:** The flood was caused by heavy rainfall, lasting *forty days and forty nights*

11 In the six hundredth year of Noah's life, in the second month, on the seventeenth day of the month, on that day all the fountains of the great deep burst forth, and the windows of the heavens were opened. [12] And rain fell upon the earth forty days and forty nights. [13] On the very same day Noah and his sons, Shem and Ham and Japheth, and Noah's wife and the three wives of his sons with them entered the ark, [14] they and every beast according to its kind, and all the cattle according to their kinds, and every creeping thing that creeps on the earth according to its kind, and every bird according to its kind, every bird of every sort. [15] They went into the ark with Noah, two and two of all flesh in which there was the breath of life. [16] And they that entered, male and female of all flesh, went in as God had commanded him; and the LORD shut him in.

17 The flood continued forty days upon the earth; and the waters increased, and bore up the ark, and it rose high above the earth. [18] The waters prevailed and increased greatly upon the earth; and the ark floated on the face of the waters. [19] And the waters prevailed so mightily upon the earth that all the high mountains under the whole heaven were covered; [20] the waters prevailed above the mountains, covering them fifteen cubits deep. [21] And all flesh died that moved upon the earth, birds, cattle, beasts, all swarming creatures that swarm upon the earth, and every man; [22] everything on the dry land in whose nostrils was the breath of life died. [23] He blotted out every living thing that was upon the face of the ground, man and animals and creeping things and birds of the air; they were blotted out from the earth. Only Noah was left, and those that were with him in the ark. [24] And the waters prevailed upon the earth a hundred and fifty days.

8 But God remembered Noah and all the beasts and all the cattle that were with him in the ark. And God made a wind blow over the earth, and the waters subsided; [2] the fountains of the deep and the windows of the heavens were closed, the rain from the heavens was restrained, [3] and the waters receded from the earth continually. At the end of a hundred and fifty days the waters had abated; [4] and in the seventh month, on the seventeenth day of the month, the ark came to rest upon the mountains of Ar′arat. [5] And the waters continued to abate until the tenth month; in the tenth month, on the first day of the month, the tops of the mountains were seen.

6 At the end of forty days Noah opened the window of the ark which he had made, [7] and sent forth a raven; and it went to and fro until the waters were dried up from the earth. [8] Then he sent forth a dove from him, to see if the waters had subsided from the face of the ground; [9] but the dove found no place to set her foot, and she returned to him to the ark, for the waters were still on the face of the whole earth. So he put forth his hand and took her and brought her into the ark with him. [10] He waited another seven days, and again he sent forth the dove out of the ark; [11] and the dove came back to him in the evening, and lo, in her mouth a freshly plucked olive leaf; so Noah knew that the waters had subsided from the earth. [12] Then he waited another seven days, and sent forth the dove; and she did not return to him any more.

(v. 12; compare the difference in the priestly version, v. 24). **11–24:** Largely from the priestly tradition. **11:** Here the flood was not caused by a rain storm but was a cosmic catastrophe resulting from opening the *windows of the heavens* (or the firmament) and the upsurging of the *fountains of the great deep* (or the subterranean watery chaos; see 1.6–8 n.). Thus the earth was threatened with a return to pre-creation chaos (1.2). **15:** The animals went in *two by two* (6.19; see 7.2 n.). **16b:** *The LORD shut him in,* a note from the early tradition, which delights in anthropomorphic touches. **18–20:** The waters covered *all the high mountains,* thus threatening a confluence of the upper and lower waters (1.6). Archaeological evidence suggests that traditions of a prehistoric flood covering the whole earth are heightened versions of local inundations, e.g. in the Tigris-Euphrates basin. **8.1–5:** In the main a continuation of the priestly tradition. Because God *remembered Noah,* he stayed the cosmic destruction by water from above and below (v. 2a). **4:** In the Babylonian epic the boat also rested on a mountain. *Ararat* (2 Kg.19.37; Jer.51.27) is the name of a region in Armenia. **6–12:** Essentially from the early tradition. In the Babylonian epic the hero sent out two birds, a dove and a swallow,

13 In the six hundred and first year, in the first month, the first day of the month, the waters were dried from off the earth; and Noah removed the covering of the ark, and looked, and behold, the face of the ground was dry. 14 In the second month, on the twenty-seventh day of the month, the earth was dry. 15 Then God said to Noah, 16 "Go forth from the ark, you and your wife, and your sons and your sons' wives with you. 17 Bring forth with you every living thing that is with you of all flesh — birds and animals and every creeping thing that creeps on the earth — that they may breed abundantly on the earth, and be fruitful and multiply upon the earth." 18 So Noah went forth, and his sons and his wife and his sons' wives with him. 19 And every beast, every creeping thing, and every bird, everything that moves upon the earth, went forth by families out of the ark.

20 Then Noah built an altar to the LORD, and took of every clean animal and of every clean bird, and offered burnt offerings on the altar. 21 And when the LORD smelled the pleasing odor, the LORD said in his heart, "I will never again curse the ground because of man, for the imagination of man's heart is evil from his youth; neither will I ever again destroy every living creature as I have done. 22 While the earth remains, seedtime and harvest, cold and heat, summer and winter, day and night, shall not cease."

9 And God blessed Noah and his sons, and said to them, "Be fruitful and multiply, and fill the earth. 2 The fear of you and the dread of you shall be upon every beast of the earth, and upon every bird of the air, upon everything that creeps on the ground and all the fish of the sea; into your hand they are delivered. 3 Every moving thing that lives shall be food for you; and as I gave you the green plants, I give you everything. 4 Only you shall not eat flesh with its life, that is, its blood. 5 For your lifeblood I will surely require a reckoning; of every beast I will require it and of man; of every man's brother I will require the life of man. 6 Whoever sheds the blood of man, by man shall his blood be shed; for God made man in his own image. 7 And you, be fruitful and multiply, bring forth abundantly on the earth and multiply in it."

8 Then God said to Noah and to his sons with him. 9 "Behold, I establish my covenant with you and your descendants after you, 10 and with every living creature that is with you, the birds, the cattle, and every beast of the earth with you, as many as came out of the ark.*/ 11 I establish my covenant with you, that never again shall all flesh be cut off by the waters of a flood, and never again shall there be a flood to destroy the earth." 12 And God said, "This is the sign of the covenant which I make between me and you and every living creature that is with you, for all future generations: 13 I set my bow in the cloud, and it shall be a sign of the covenant between me and the earth. 14 When I bring clouds over the earth

l Gk: Heb repeats *every beast of the earth*

---

each of which came back; the third, a raven, did not return. **13–19:** A continuation of the priestly account. **20–22:** The early tradition relates that Noah sacrificed *burnt offerings* (Lev. ch. 1) of clean animals (see 7.2–3 n.). In the Babylonian epic the hero offered sacrifices and "the gods smelt [compare v. 21] the goodly savor." For the curse, compare 3.17. Despite the evil *imagination of man's heart* (6.5), the LORD's steadfast mercy will be expressed in the regularities of nature, *seedtime and harvest,* etc.

9.1–19: God's covenant with Noah included all mankind under divine promise and law. **1:** The new age opened with a renewal of the blessing which had been given at creation (v. 7; compare 1.28). **3–6:** The command to exercise dominion (1.28–30) is qualified by the permission to eat animal flesh but not with *its life,* i.e. *its blood* (see 4.10–11 n.). The violence which had corrupted the earth (6.11) is restrained by a very old law against murder, the validity of which is grounded in the creation: man is made in God's *image* (1.26–27). These verses set forth the laws given to Noah, binding not only on Israel but on all men (Acts 15.20; 21.25). **8–11:** The preservation of the natural order from the waters of chaos is guaranteed by a *covenant* (see 17.2 n.). Unlike later covenants (ch. 17; Ex. ch. 24), this is a universal covenant with Noah, his *descendants,* and *every living creature,* for Noah's three sons (6.10; 9.18–19) are regarded as the ancestors of all the nations (see ch. 10). **13:** Ancients imagined the rainbow as God's weapon (bow) from which the lightnings of his arrows were shot (Ps.7.12–13; Hab.3.9–11). God places his weapon in the heavens as a *sign,* or visible token, that his wrath has abated.

and the bow is seen in the clouds, [15] I will remember my covenant which is between me and you and every living creature of all flesh; and the waters shall never again become a flood to destroy all flesh. [16] When the bow is in the clouds, I will look upon it and remember the everlasting covenant between God and every living creature of all flesh that is upon the earth." [17] God said to Noah, "This is the sign of the covenant which I have established between me and all flesh that is upon the earth."

18 The sons of Noah who went forth from the ark were Shem, Ham, and Japheth. Ham was the father of Canaan. [19] These three were the sons of Noah; and from these the whole earth was peopled.

20 Noah was the first tiller of the soil. He planted a vineyard; [21] and he drank of the wine, and became drunk, and lay uncovered in his tent. [22] And Ham, the father of Canaan, saw the nakedness of his father, and told his two brothers outside. [23] Then Shem and Japheth took a garment, laid it upon both their shoulders, and walked backward and covered the nakedness of their father; their faces were turned away, and they did not see their father's nakedness. [24] When Noah awoke from his wine and knew what his youngest son had done to him, [25] he said,

"Cursed be Canaan;
 a slave of slaves shall he be to his
  brothers."

[26] He also said,

"Blessed by the LORD my God be Shem;[m]
 and let Canaan be his slave.

[27] God enlarge Japheth,
 and let him dwell in the tents of Shem;
 and let Canaan be his slave."

28 After the flood Noah lived three hundred and fifty years. [29] All the days of Noah were nine hundred and fifty years; and he died.

m Or *Blessed be the* LORD, *the God of Shem*

9.18–27: Noah's curse upon Canaan. 20: In the new age, Noah was the *first tiller of the soil.* His success in agriculture fulfilled the prophecy made at his birth (5.29). **22:** Since the curse was later put on Canaan rather than Ham (v. 25), it is likely that Canaan was the actor originally. **24:** Here Noah's *youngest son* is clearly Canaan, not Ham as in v. 22. **25:** The curse implies that Canaan's subjugation to Israel was the result of Canaanite sexual perversions (Lev.18.24–30). **26:** *Shem,* 10.21. **27:** *Japheth,* 10.2–5. The verse may refer to the Philistines, one of the sea-peoples who dwelt *in the tents of Shem,* i.e. conquered the coast of Canaan.

Exodus

12 The LORD said to Moses and Aaron in the land of Egypt, ² "This month shall be for you the beginning of months; it shall be the first month of the year for you. ³ Tell all the congregation of Israel that on the tenth day of this month they shall take every man a lamb according to their fathers' houses, a lamb for a household; ⁴ and if the household is too small for a lamb, then a man and his neighbor next to his house shall take according to the number of persons; according to what each can eat you shall make your count for the lamb. ⁵ Your lamb shall be without blemish, a male a year old; you shall take it from the sheep or from the goats; ⁶ and you shall keep it until the fourteenth day of this month, when the whole assembly of the congregation of Israel shall kill their lambs in the evening.*ᵒ* ⁷ Then they shall take some of the blood, and put it on the two doorposts and the lintel of the houses in which they eat them. ⁸ They shall eat the flesh that night, roasted; with unleavened bread and bitter herbs they shall eat it. ⁹ Do not eat any of it raw or boiled with water, but roasted, its head with its legs and its inner parts. ¹⁰ And you shall let none of it remain until the morning, anything that remains until the morning you shall burn. ¹¹ In this manner you shall eat it: your loins girded, your sandals on your feet, and your staff in your hand; and you shall eat it in haste. It is the LORD's passover. ¹² For I will pass through the land of Egypt that night, and I will smite all the first-born in the land of Egypt, both man and beast; and on all the gods of Egypt I will execute judgments: I am the LORD. ¹³ The blood shall be a sign for you, upon the houses where you are; and when I see the blood, I will pass over

o Heb *between the two evenings*

12.1–28: The feasts of passover and unleavened bread. 1–13 (and vv. 43–49): This is priestly tradition concerning the passover, an ancient nomadic spring festival which Israel reinterpreted as a memorial of the LORD's deliverance of his people from Egypt (Dt.16.1–8; Num.9.1–14; Ezek.45.21–25). **2:** *This month* refers to Nisan (March–April) which in the post-exilic ecclesiastical calendar was *the beginning of months* (see Lev.23.5,23–25 n.). According to the older agricultural calendar, the new year began in the autumn (Ex.23.16; 34.22). **3–4:** Priestly tradition assumes that Israel in Egypt was already an organized *congregation* under the leadership of tribal princes (16.22). *Fathers' houses,* see Num.1.2–4 n. The passover was a nocturnal festival, celebrated during full moon (v. 8; see Is. 30.29). **7:** Blood, regarded as the deity's portion of the sacrifice (Lev.1.5), was smeared on the doorposts and the lintel, the holy places of the house (21.6; Dt.6.9), as a protection against the destroyer (vv. 22–23; see 4.24 n.). **11:** The feast must be eaten in readiness for the march, in commemoration of Israel's hasty exodus. **12–13:** Here *passover* is

---

Bible, THE NEW OXFORD ANNOTATED BIBLE WITH THE APOCRYPHA Revised Standard Edition, Exodus 12–24.

you, and no plague shall fall upon you to destroy you, when I smite the land of Egypt.

14 "This day shall be for you a memorial day, and you shall keep it as a feast to the LORD; throughout your generations you shall observe it as an ordinance for ever. [15] Seven days you shall eat unleavened bread; on the first day you shall put away leaven out of your houses, for if any one eats what is leavened, from the first day until the seventh day, that person shall be cut off from Israel. [16] On the first day you shall hold a holy assembly, and on the seventh day a holy assembly; no work shall be done on those days; but what every one must eat, that only may be prepared by you. [17] And you shall observe the feast of unleavened bread, for on this very day I brought your hosts out of the land of Egypt: therefore you shall observe this day, throughout your generations, as an ordinance for ever. [18] In the first month, on the fourteenth day of the month at evening, you shall eat unleavened bread, and so until the twenty-first day of the month at evening. [19] For seven days no leaven shall be found in your houses; for if any one eats what is leavened, that person shall be cut off from the congregation of Israel, whether he is a sojourner or a native of the land. [20] You shall eat nothing leavened; in all your dwellings you shall eat unleavened bread."

21 Then Moses called all the elders of Israel, and said to them, "Select lambs for yourselves according to your families, and kill the passover lamb. [22] Take a bunch of hyssop and dip it in the blood which is in the basin, and touch the lintel and the two doorposts with the blood which is in the basin; and none of you shall go out of the door of his house until the morning. [23] For the LORD will pass through to slay the Egyptians; and when he sees the blood on the lintel and on the two doorposts, the LORD will pass over the door, and will not allow the destroyer to enter your houses to slay you. [24] You shall observe this rite as an ordinance for you and for your sons for ever. [25] And when you come to the land which the LORD will give you, as he has promised, you shall keep this service. [26] And when your children say to you, 'What do you mean by this service?' [27] you shall say, 'It is the sacrifice of the LORD's passover, for he passed over the houses of the people of Israel in Egypt, when he slew the Egyptians but spared our houses.'" And the people bowed their heads and worshiped.

28 Then the people of Israel went and did so; as the LORD had commanded Moses and Aaron, so they did.

29 At midnight the LORD smote all the first-born in the land of Egypt, from the first-born of Pharaoh who sat on his throne to the first-born of the captive who was in the dungeon, and all the first-born of the cattle. [30] And Pharaoh rose up in the night, he, and all his servants, and all the Egyptians; and there was a great cry in Egypt, for there was not a house where one was not dead. [31] And he summoned Moses and Aaron by night, and said, "Rise up, go forth from among my people, both you and the people of Israel; and

---

interpreted from a verb meaning "to pass over," referring to the LORD's passing over Israelite houses during the plague of the first-born (vv. 24–27). **14–20:** The feast of unleavened cakes, originally an agricultural festival held at the time of barley harvest, was also converted into an historical commemoration and came to be closely connected with the passover (Dt.16.1–8; Ezek.45.21–25). **14:** The passover was celebrated on the 14th of Nisan (v. 6); *this day* refers to the 15th (Lev.23.6; Num.28.17). The seven day festival is regarded as a continuation of the passover. **15:** The absence of leaven (yeast) is interpreted as due to hasty preparations for flight (vv. 34,39; Dt.16.3). Originally leaven, owing to its fermenting or corrupting power (23.18; Mt.16.6; 1 Cor.5.7), was regarded as a ritually unclean substance (compare Lev.2.11) which could contaminate the whole harvest. **18:** So closely is the festival combined with the passover that it is said to begin on the evening of the 14th, i.e. the night of the passover (see v. 14). **21–28:** An older tradition concerning the passover. **22:** See v. 7 n. *Hyssop,* the foliage of an aromatic plant. Because of its presumed magical powers, it was used for ritual purposes (Lev.14.4; Num.19.6,18; Ps.51.7). **23:** *The destroyer,* or the angel of death (2 Sam.24.16; Is.37.36), was regarded as a manifestation of the LORD's power.

12.29–50: Israel's departure from Egypt. 29–32: The conclusion of the tenth plague (11.1–10). **33–34:** See v. 15 n. **35–36:** See 3.21–22 and 11.2–3. **37:** Rameses (1.11) and Succoth (13.20) were the starting places on Israel's itinerary

go, serve the LORD, as you have said. ³² Take your flocks and your herds, as you have said, and be gone; and bless me also!"

33 And the Egyptians were urgent with the people, to send them out of the land in haste; for they said, "We are all dead men." ³⁴ So the people took their dough before it was leavened, their kneading bowls being bound up in their mantles on their shoulders. ³⁵ The people of Israel had also done as Moses told them, for they had asked of the Egyptians jewelry of silver and of gold, and clothing; ³⁶ and the LORD had given the people favor in the sight of the Egyptians, so that they let them have what they asked. Thus they despoiled the Egyptians.

37 And the people of Israel journeyed from Ram′eses to Succoth, about six hundred thousand men on foot, besides women and children. ³⁸ A mixed multitude also went up with them, and very many cattle, both flocks and herds. ³⁹ And they baked unleavened cakes of the dough which they had brought out of Egypt, for it was not leavened, because they were thrust out of Egypt and could not tarry, neither had they prepared for themselves any provisions.

40 The time that the people of Israel dwelt in Egypt was four hundred and thirty years. ⁴¹ And at the end of four hundred and thirty years, on that very day, all the hosts of the LORD went out from the land of Egypt. ⁴² It was a night of watching by the LORD, to bring them out of the land of Egypt; so this same night is a night by watching kept to the LORD by all the people of Israel throughout their generations.

43 And the LORD said to Moses and Aaron, "This is the ordinance of the passover: no foreigner shall eat of it; ⁴⁴ but every slave that is bought for money may eat of it after you have circumcised him. ⁴⁵ No sojourner or hired servant may eat of it. ⁴⁶ In one house shall it be eaten; you shall not carry forth any of the flesh outside the house; and you shall not break a bone of it. ⁴⁷ All the congregation of Israel shall keep it. ⁴⁸ And when a stranger shall sojourn with you and would keep the passover to the LORD, let all his males be circumcised, then he may come near and keep it; he shall be as a native of the land. But no uncircumcised person shall eat of it. ⁴⁹ There shall be one law for the native and for the stranger who sojourns among you."

50 Thus did all the people of Israel; as the LORD commanded Moses and Aaron, so they did. ⁵¹ And on that very day the LORD brought the people of Israel out of the land of Egypt by their hosts.

13 The LORD said to Moses, ² "Consecrate to me all the first-born; whatever is the first to open the womb among the people of Israel, both of man and of beast, is mine."

3 And Moses said to the people, "Remember this day, in which you came out from Egypt, out of the house of bondage, for by strength of hand the LORD brought you out from this place; no leavened bread shall be eaten. ⁴ This day you are to go forth, in the month of Abib. ⁵ And when the LORD brings you into the land of the Canaanites, the Hittites,

(Num.33.5). *Six hundred thousand men on foot* (Num.11.21), in addition to women and children, is an exaggeration, for neither the land of Goshen nor the southern Palestinian wilderness could have supported so large a population (at least two and a half million). The number apparently reflects the census list in Num.1.17–46. **38:** The *mixed multitude* (Num.11.4) included other "Hebrews" (see 1.15 n.) or rootless people. **40:** If the four hundred and thirty years (see Gen.15.13; Acts 7.6 n.; Gal.3.17 n.) covers the total time of the Egyptian sojourn, then the descent into Egypt coincided with the Hyksos invasion (about 1720 B.C.; see Gen.45.10 n.) and the Exodus occurred during the reign of Rameses II, about 1290 B.C. (see 1.8 n.). **42:** The *night of watching* refers to the passover. **43–49:** A supplement to the priestly tradition about the passover (12.1–13). A *foreigner* (v. 43), a visiting *sojourner,* and a *hired servant* (v. 45) are excluded on the ground that they are related to other gods; however, the purchased slave who becomes a part of the family (v. 44) and the sojourner who resides permanently within Israel may eat the passover, if the *one law* of circumcision is kept (Gen.17.9–14).

13.1–16: The consecration of the first-born. 2: According to ancient belief, the devotion of the first-born of man and beast to God, the giver of fertility, was necessary for continuing increase and well-being (22.29b–30; Lev.27.26–27; Num.3.13; 8.17–18; 18.15). **3–10:** Old tradition about the feast of unleavened bread (compare the

the Amorites, the Hivites, and the Jeb'usites, which he swore to your fathers to give you, a land flowing with milk and honey, you shall keep this service in this month. [6] Seven days you shall eat unleavened bread, and on the seventh day there shall be a feast to the LORD. [7] Unleavened bread shall be eaten for seven days; no leavened bread shall be seen with you, and no leaven shall be seen with you in all your territory. [8] And you shall tell your son on that day, 'It is because of what the LORD did for me when I came out of Egypt.' [9] And it shall be to you as a sign on your hand and as a memorial between your eyes, that the law of the LORD may be in your mouth; for with a strong hand the LORD has brought you out of Egypt. [10] You shall therefore keep this ordinance at its appointed time from year to year.

11 "And when the LORD brings you into the land of the Canaanites, as he swore to you and your fathers, and shall give it to you, [12] you shall set apart to the LORD all that first opens the womb. All the firstlings of your cattle that are males shall be the LORD's. [13] Every firstling of an ass you shall redeem with a lamb, or if you will not redeem it you shall break its neck. Every first-born of man among your sons you shall redeem. [14] And when in time to come your son asks you, 'What does this mean?' you shall say to him, 'By strength of hand the LORD brought us out of Egypt, from the house of bondage. [15] For when Pharaoh stubbornly refused to let us go, the LORD slew all the first-born in the land of Egypt, both the first-born of man and the first-

born of cattle. Therefore I sacrifice to the LORD all the males that first open the womb; but all the first-born of my sons I redeem.' [16] It shall be as a mark on your hand or frontlets between your eyes; for by a strong hand the LORD brought us out of Egypt."

17 When Pharaoh let the people go, God did not lead them by way of the land of the Philistines, although that was near; for God said, "Lest the people repent when they see war, and return to Egypt." [18] But God led the people round by the way of the wilderness toward the Red Sea. And the people of Israel went up out of the land of Egypt equipped for battle. [19] And Moses took the bones of Joseph with him; for Joseph had solemnly sworn the people of Israel, saying, "God will visit you; then you must carry my bones with you from here." [20] And they moved on from Succoth, and encamped at Etham, on the edge of the wilderness. [21] And the LORD went before them by day in a pillar of cloud to lead them along the way, and by night in a pillar of fire to give them light, that they might travel by day and by night; [22] the pillar of cloud by day and the pillar of fire by night did not depart from before the people.

14 Then the LORD said to Moses, [2] "Tell the people of Israel to turn back and encamp in front of Pi-ha-hi'roth, between Migdol and the sea, in front of Ba'al-ze'phon; you shall encamp over against it, by the sea. [3] For Pharaoh will say of the people of Israel, 'They are entangled in the land; the wilderness has shut them in.' [4] And I will harden

---

parallel priestly version, 12.14–20). **4:** *Abib,* the older name for the month of the Exodus (23.15; see 12.2 n.). **5:** See 3.8. **8:** In later times a man could tell *what the LORD did for me when I came out of Egypt,* for in worship the redemptive event was made present (12.26–27; see Dt.5.2–3 n.). **9:** See Dt.6.8. **11–16:** An old tradition about the consecration of the first-born. **13:** Unclean animals, of which the ass is typical (Lev. ch. 11; Dt. ch. 14), may be redeemed by substituting a lamb. In early times the custom arose of substituting an animal for the human first-born (34.19–20; compare Gen.22.13), although pagan human sacrifice persisted (1 Kg.16.34; 2 Kg.16.3; Ezek.20.26; Mic.6.7). **14–15:** The practice, rooted in ancient fertility beliefs, is here reinterpreted in the light of the Exodus.

13.17–14.22. Israel's deliverance. 17–18: *Philistines,* see Gen.21.34 n. The route mentioned was the main military road into Canaan. To avoid attack, the people were providentially led *round by the way of the wilderness.* On the *Red Sea,* see 14.2 n. **19:** See Gen.50.25–26 n. **21–22:** The *pillar of cloud* and the *pillar of fire* may reflect the ancient custom of carrying a burning brazier at the head of a marching army or caravan to indicate the line of march by day and night. Whatever the nature of the phenomenon originally, cloud and fire have become traditional ways of expressing God's presence and guidance (see 3.2 n.; 19.9; 33.9; 40.34–38; 1 Kg.8.10–11). **14.2:** The places mentioned, like Etham (13.20), were probably Egyptian frontier fortresses. Apparently the Israelites were unable to break through and

Pharaoh's heart, and he will pursue them and I will get glory over Pharaoh and all his host; and the Egyptians shall know that I am the LORD." And they did so.

5 When the king of Egypt was told that the people had fled, the mind of Pharaoh and his servants was changed toward the people, and they said, "What is this we have done, that we have let Israel go from serving us?" [6] So he made ready his chariot and took his army with him, [7] and took six hundred picked chariots and all the other chariots of Egypt with officers over all of them. [8] And the LORD hardened the heart of Pharaoh king of Egypt and he pursued the people of Israel as they went forth defiantly. [9] The Egyptians pursued them, all Pharaoh's horses and chariots and his horsemen and his army, and overtook them encamped at the sea, by Pi-ha-hi′roth, in front of Ba′al-ze′phon.

10 When Pharaoh drew near, the people of Israel lifted up their eyes, and behold, the Egyptians were marching after them; and they were in great fear. And the people of Israel cried out to the LORD; [11] and they said to Moses, "Is it because there are no graves in Egypt that you have taken us away to die in the wilderness? What have you done to us, in bringing us out of Egypt? [12] Is not this what we said to you in Egypt, 'Let us alone and let us serve the Egyptians'? For it would have been better for us to serve the Egyptians than to die in the wilderness." [13] And Moses said to the people, "Fear not, stand firm, and see the salvation of the LORD, which he will work for you today; for the Egyptians whom you see today, you shall never see again. [14] The LORD will fight for you, and you have only to be still." [15] The LORD said to Moses, "Why do you cry to me? Tell the people of Israel to go forward. [16] Lift up your rod, and stretch out your hand over the sea and divide it, that the people of Israel may go on dry ground through the sea. [17] And I will harden the hearts of the Egyptians so that they shall go in after them, and I will get glory over Pharaoh and all his host, his chariots, and his horsemen. [18] And the Egyptians shall know that I am the LORD, when I have gotten glory over Pharaoh, his chariots, and his horsemen."

19 Then the angel of God who went before the host of Israel moved and went behind them; and the pillar of cloud moved from before them and stood behind them, [20] coming between the host of Egypt and the host of Israel. And there was the cloud and the darkness; and the night passed[p] without one coming near the other all night.

21 Then Moses stretched out his hand over the sea; and the LORD drove the sea back by a strong east wind all night, and made the sea dry land, and the waters were divided. [22] And the people of Israel went into the midst of the sea on dry ground, the waters being a wall to them on their right hand and on their left. [23] The Egyptians pursued, and went in after them into the midst of the sea, all Pharaoh's horses, his chariots, and his horsemen. [24] And in the morning watch the LORD in the pillar of fire and of cloud looked down upon the host of the Egyptians, and discomfited the host of the Egyptians, [25] clogging[q] their chariot wheels so that they drove heavily; and the Egyptians said, "Let us flee from before Israel; for the LORD fights for them against the Egyptians."

p Gk: Heb *and it lit up the night*
q Or *binding.* Sam Gk Syr: Heb *removing*

had to *turn back,* with the result that they were trapped (v. 3) between the water barrier and the Egyptian forces. *The sea,* known in Hebrew as the "sea of reeds," was not the Red Sea itself but a shallow body of water farther north, perhaps in the area of Lake Timsah. **11–12:** See 15.24 n. **13–14:** Viewed in faith, the victory was a mighty act of the LORD who was fighting for his people in a contest with the powerful Pharaoh (v. 25). *Salvation,* see Gen.49.18. **19–20:** One tradition expresses the divine presence as *the angel of God* (see Gen.16.7 n.), another as the shining pillar of cloud (v. 24; see 13.21–22 n.). **21–29:** The divine victory was rooted in a natural phenomenon: during a storm the shallow waters were driven back by *a strong east wind* (v. 21), making it possible for the Israelites to cross on foot. Egyptian chariots, however, were mired in the mud and engulfed by the returning waters. Tradition heightened the miracle by

26 Then the Lord said to Moses, "Stretch out your hand over the sea, that the water may come back upon the Egyptians, upon their chariots, and upon their horsemen." 27 So Moses stretched forth his hand over the sea, and the sea returned to its wonted flow when the morning appeared; and the Egyptians fled into it, and the Lord routed[r] the Egyptians in the midst of the sea. 28 The waters returned and covered the chariots and the horsemen and all the host[s] of Pharaoh that had followed them into the sea; not so much as one of them remained. 29 But the people of Israel walked on dry ground through the sea, the waters being a wall to them on their right hand and on their left.

30 Thus the Lord saved Israel that day from the hand of the Egyptians; and Israel saw the Egyptians dead upon the seashore. 31 And Israel saw the great work which the Lord did against the Egyptians, and the people feared the Lord; and they believed in the Lord and in his servant Moses.

15 Then Moses and the people of Israel sang this song to the Lord, saying,
"I will sing to the Lord, for he has
    triumphed gloriously;
the horse and his rider[t] he has thrown
    into the sea.
2 The Lord is my strength and my song,
    and he has become my salvation;
this is my God, and I will praise him,
    my father's God, and I will exalt him.
3 The Lord is a man of war;
    the Lord is his name.

4 "Pharaoh's chariots and his host he cast
    into the sea;
and his picked officers are sunk in the
    Red Sea.

5 The floods cover them;
    they went down into the depths like
    a stone.
6 Thy right hand, O Lord, glorious in
    power,
    thy right hand, O Lord, shatters the
    enemy.
7 In the greatness of thy majesty thou
    overthrowest thy adversaries;
    thou sendest forth thy fury, it consumes
    them like stubble.
8 At the blast of thy nostrils the waters
    piled up,
    the floods stood up in a heap;
    the deeps congealed in the heart of the
    sea.
9 The enemy said, 'I will pursue, I will
    overtake,
    I will divide the spoil, my desire shall
    have its fill of them.
    I will draw my sword, my hand shall
    destroy them.'
10 Thou didst blow with thy wind, the sea
    covered them;
    they sank as lead in the mighty waters.

11 "Who is like thee, O Lord, among the
    gods?
    Who is like thee, majestic in holiness,
    terrible in glorious deeds, doing
    wonders?
12 Thou didst stretch out thy right hand,
    the earth swallowed them.

13 "Thou hast led in thy steadfast love the
    people whom thou hast redeemed,
    thou hast guided them by thy strength
    to thy holy abode.

r Heb shook off   s Gk Syr: Heb to all the host
t Or its chariot

attributing it to Moses' wonder-working rod (vv. 16,21a,26–27) and by saying that the waters stood up like walls (vv. 22b,29b).

15.1–21: Two songs of praise which celebrate the Lord's deliverance of his people. **1:** The song of Moses (vv. 1–18) is introduced by quoting the ancient song of Miriam (v. 21). **2:** See 14.13–14 n. *My father's God* refers to "the God of the fathers" (3.6). **3:** *A man of war*, i.e. Divine Warrior (Ps.24.8). In the following vv. Canaanite mythical motifs are used to confess the Lord's saving action in behalf of Israel (14.14,25). **4–10:** Recital of the Divine Warrior's victory at the Sea (Ps.78.12–13). **8–10:** The language seems influenced by the myth of a divine battle against the *sea*, the chaotic power hostile to God's rule (see Ps.77.16–19; 114.3–6; Hab. 3.8–15). **11:** The Lord's *glorious deeds* demonstrate that he is incomparable *among the gods* who compose his heavenly council (Pss.86.8; 89.7–8; Gen.1.26 n.). **13–17:** The guidance into Canaan. **13:** *Thy holy abode*, i.e. Canaan (Ps.78.54). **14:** *Philistia* was settled by the

14 The peoples have heard, they tremble;
   pangs have seized on the inhabitants
      of Philistia.
15 Now are the chiefs of Edom dismayed;
   the leaders of Moab, trembling seizes
      them;
   all the inhabitants of Canaan have
      melted away.
16 Terror and dread fall upon them;
   because of the greatness of thy arm,
      they are as still as a stone,
   till thy people, O LORD, pass by,
      till the people pass by whom thou hast
         purchased.
17 Thou wilt bring them in, and plant them on
      thy own mountain,
   the place, O LORD, which thou hast
      made for thy abode,
   the sanctuary, O LORD, which thy hands
      have established.
18 The LORD will reign for ever and ever."

19 For when the horses of Pharaoh with his chariots and his horsemen went into the sea, the LORD brought back the waters of the sea upon them; but the people of Israel walked on dry ground in the midst of the sea. 20 Then Miriam, the prophetess, the sister of Aaron, took a timbrel in her hand; and all the women went out after her with timbrels and dancing. 21 And Miriam sang to them:

"Sing to the LORD, for he has triumphed
   gloriously;
the horse and his rider he has thrown into
   the sea."

22 Then Moses led Israel onward from the Red Sea, and they went into the wilderness of Shur; they went three days in the wilderness and found no water. 23 When they came to Marah, they could not drink the water of Marah because it was bitter; therefore it was named Marah.*u* 24 And the people murmured against Moses, saying, "What shall we drink?" 25 And he cried to the LORD; and the LORD showed him a tree, and he threw it into the water, and the water became sweet.

There the LORD*v* made for them a statute and an ordinance and there he proved them, 26 saying, "If you will diligently hearken to the voice of the LORD your God, and do that which is right in his eyes, and give heed to his commandments and keep all his statutes, I will put none of the diseases upon you which I put upon the Egyptians; for I am the LORD, your healer."

27 Then they came to Elim, where there were twelve springs of water and seventy palm trees; and they encamped there by the water.

16 They set out from Elim, and all the congregation of the people of Israel came to the wilderness of Sin, which is between Elim and Sinai, on the fifteenth day of the second month after they had departed from the land of Egypt. 2 And the whole congregation of the people of Israel murmured against Moses and Aaron in the wilderness, 3 and said to them, "Would that we had died

u That is *Bitterness* *v* Heb *he*

Philistines (Gen.21.32 n.) about 1175 B.C.; hence the poem was written afterwards. **15:** See Num.20.18–21; 21.13. **16:** *Purchased,* possibly "created." **17:** Canaan is described as the mythical cosmic mountain, Zaphon, where God has his *abode* and *sanctuary* (see Ps.48.1–3 n.). **19–21:** Miriam's victory dance. Miriam (Num.26.59) is called a prophetess (compare Jg.4.4) because of her ecstatic rousing of devotion to the LORD through song and dance. Compare 1 Sam.18.6–7). **21:** The Song of Miriam, one of the oldest poetic couplets in the Old Testament, was probably composed by an eyewitness of the event.

15.22–16.36: Crises in the wilderness. In times of need, when faith was put to the test, Israel perceived signs of the LORD's care and protection. **22:** *The Wilderness of Shur,* identified with the wilderness of Etham in Num.33.8, was on the border of Egypt. **24:** Israel's continual murmuring in the wilderness is a dominant theme of the tradition (16.2–3; 17.3; 32.1–4,25; Num.11.4–6; 12.1–2; 14.2–3; 16.13–14; 20.2–13; 21.4–5). **25:** It was believed that the leaves or bark of certain trees had magical properties for sweetening or "healing" water (2 Kg.2.21). **26:** *Diseases,* i.e. the Egyptian plagues. *Your healer,* Num.21.4–9; Dt.7.15; Ps.103.3. **16.1–36:** The provision of food in the wilderness. **1:** *The wilderness of Sin* (17.1; Num.33.11–12), probably on the Sinaitic Peninsula. **3:** The murmuring wanderers

by the hand of the LORD in the land of Egypt, when we sat by the fleshpots and ate bread to the full; for you have brought us out into this wilderness to kill this whole assembly with hunger."

4 Then the LORD said to Moses, "Behold, I will rain bread from heaven for you; and the people shall go out and gather a day's portion every day, that I may prove them, whether they will walk in my law or not. 5 On the sixth day, when they prepare what they bring in, it will be twice as much as they gather daily." 6 So Moses and Aaron said to all the people of Israel, "At evening you shall know that it was the LORD who brought you out of the land of Egypt, 7 and in the morning you shall see the glory of the LORD, because he has heard your murmurings against the LORD. For what are we, that you murmur against us?" 8 And Moses said, "When the LORD gives you in the evening flesh to eat and in the morning bread to the full, because the LORD has heard your murmurings which you murmur against him — what are we? Your murmurings are not against us but against the LORD."

9 And Moses said to Aaron, "Say to the whole congregation of the people of Israel, 'Come near before the LORD, for he has heard your murmurings.'" 10 And as Aaron spoke to the whole congregation of the people of Israel, they looked toward the wilderness, and behold, the glory of the LORD appeared in the cloud. 11 And the LORD said to Moses, 12 "I have heard the murmurings of the people of Israel; say to them, 'At twilight you shall eat flesh, and in the morning you shall be filled with bread; then you shall know that I am the LORD your God.'"

13 In the evening quails came up and covered the camp; and in the morning dew lay round about the camp. 14 And when the dew had gone up, there was on the face of the wilderness a fine, flake-like thing, fine as hoarfrost on the ground. 15 When the people of Israel saw it, they said to one another, "What is it?"[w] For they did not know what it was. And Moses said to them, "It is the bread which the LORD has given you to eat. 16 This is what the LORD has commanded: 'Gather of it, every man of you, as much as he can eat; you shall take an omer apiece, according to the number of the persons whom each of you has in his tent.'" 17 And the people of Israel did so; they gathered, some more, some less. 18 But when they measured it with an omer, he that gathered much had nothing over, and he that gathered little had no lack; each gathered according to what he could eat. 19 And Moses said to them, "Let no man leave any of it till the morning." 20 But they did not listen to Moses; some left part of it till the morning, and it bred worms and became foul; and Moses was angry with them. 21 Morning by morning they gathered it, each as much as he could eat; but when the sun grew hot, it melted.

22 On the sixth day they gathered twice as much bread, two omers apiece; and when all the leaders of the congregation came and told Moses, 23 he said to them, "This is what the LORD has commanded: 'Tomorrow is a day of solemn rest, a holy sabbath to the LORD; bake what you will bake and boil what you will boil, and all that is left over lay by to be kept till the morning.'" 24 So they laid it by till the

w Or *"It is manna."* Heb *man hu*

---

preferred the seasoned food of *the fleshpots of Egypt* to the precarious freedom of the wilderness. **4:** *Prove,* i.e. test their faith by providing only a *portion* sufficient for one day (see Dt.8.3,16; Mt.6.11). **5:** See vv. 22–30. **6–7:** *At evening* when the quails come; *in the morning* when the manna is found (vv. 8,12). In the priestly view, *the glory of the LORD* was an envelope of light (associated with the pillar of cloud and fire; see 13.21–22 n.) which veiled his being. Though men could not see God they could behold the glory which signified his presence (40.34; Num.14.10b,22; 16.19; Ezek.11.23). **9–10:** *Before the LORD,* see vv. 33–34 n. **13–21:** An early tradition concerning the provision of bread (v. 15). **13:** On the quails, see Num.11.1–35. **14:** The description here (see also v. 31 and Num.11.7–9) corresponds fairly closely to the "honey-dew" excretion of two scale-insects which feed on the twigs of the tamarisk tree. **15:** The name of the food, *manna* (v. 31), is explained by an expression meaning "What is it?" For men of faith the answer was that the natural phenomenon was *bread which the LORD has given.* **22–36:** The provision of manna

morning, as Moses bade them; and it did not become foul, and there were no worms in it. [25] Moses said, "Eat it today, for today is a sabbath to the Lord; today you will not find it in the field. [26] Six days you shall gather it; but on the seventh day, which is a sabbath, there will be none." [27] On the seventh day some of the people went out to gather, and they found none. [28] And the Lord said to Moses, "How long do you refuse to keep my commandments and my laws? [29] See! The Lord has given you the sabbath, therefore on the sixth day he gives you bread for two days; remain every man of you in his place, let no man go out of his place on the seventh day." [30] So the people rested on the seventh day.

31 Now the house of Israel called its name manna; it was like coriander seed, white, and the taste of it was like wafers made with honey. [32] And Moses said, "This is what the Lord has commanded: 'Let an omer of it be kept throughout your generations, that they may see the bread with which I fed you in the wilderness, when I brought you out of the land of Egypt.'" [33] And Moses said to Aaron, "Take a jar, and put an omer of manna in it, and place it before the Lord, to be kept throughout your generations." [34] As the Lord commanded Moses, so Aaron placed it before the testimony, to be kept. [35] And the people of Israel ate the manna forty years, till they came to a habitable land; they ate the manna, till they came to the border of the land of Canaan. [36] (An omer is the tenth part of an ephah.)

17 All the congregation of the people of Israel moved on from the wilderness of Sin by stages, according to the commandment of the Lord, and camped at Reph'idim; but there was no water for the people to drink. [2] Therefore the people found fault with Moses, and said, "Give us water to drink." And Moses said to them, "Why do you find fault with me? Why do you put the Lord to the proof?" [3] But the people thirsted there for water, and the people murmured against Moses, and said, "Why did you bring us up out of Egypt, to kill us and our children and our cattle with thirst?" [4] So Moses cried to the Lord, "What shall I do with this people? They are almost ready to stone me." [5] And the Lord said to Moses, "Pass on before the people, taking with you some of the elders of Israel; and take in your hand the rod with which you struck the Nile, and go. [6] Behold, I will stand before you there on the rock at Horeb; and you shall strike the rock, and water shall come out of it, that the people may drink." And Moses did so, in the sight of the elders of Israel. [7] And he called the name of the place Massah[x] and Mer'ibah,[y] because of the fault-finding of the children of Israel, and because they put the Lord to the proof by saying, "Is the Lord among us or not?"

8 Then came Am'alek and fought with Israel at Reph'idim. [9] And Moses said to Joshua, "Choose for us men, and go out, fight with Am'alek; tomorrow I will stand on the top of the hill with the rod of God in my hand." [10] So Joshua did as Moses told him, and fought with Am'alek; and Moses, Aaron, and Hur went up to the top of the hill. [11] Whenever Moses held up his hand, Israel prevailed; and whenever he lowered his hand, Am'alek prevailed. [12] But Moses' hands grew weary; so they took a stone and put it under

x That is *Proof*   *y* That is *Contention*

is the occasion for the insertion of priestly teaching concerning the sabbath, *a day of solemn rest* (31.15; 35.2). **33–34:** *Before the Lord,* i.e. before the ark. In priestly tradition the ark is sometimes designated by its chief contents, *the Testimony* or tablets of law (27.21; Lev.16.13; Num.17.4).

17.1–16: Other trying experiences in the wilderness. 1–7: Israel's thirst was quenched with water from the rock (compare Num.20.2–13). **1:** *By stages,* see Num.33.1–49. **2–3:** See 15.24 n. *Put the Lord to proof,* i.e. challenged him to show that he was in their midst (v. 7b). **6:** Water lies below the limestone surface in the region of Sinai. **7:** The place is named both *Massah* from the Hebrew verb "test" and *Meribah* from the verb "find fault"— names which became memorials of Israel's faithlessness (Dt.6.16; 9.22; 33.8; Ps.95.8). Meribah was one of the springs at Kadesh (Num.20.13; 27.14; Dt.32.51). Marah (15.23) and Massah were evidently springs at the same oasis. Some traditions in 15.23–18.27 come from this oasis south of Beer-sheba (see Num.13.26 n.). **8–15:** The battle with the Amalekites.

him, and he sat upon it, and Aaron and Hur held up his hands, one on one side, and the other on the other side; so his hands were steady until the going down of the sun. [13] And Joshua mowed down Am'alek and his people with the edge of the sword.

14 And the LORD said to Moses, "Write this as a memorial in a book and recite it in the ears of Joshua, that I will utterly blot out the remembrance of Am'alek from under heaven." [15] And Moses built an altar and called the name of it, The LORD is my banner, [16] saying, "A hand upon the banner of the LORD![z] The LORD will have war with Am'alek from generation to generation."

18 Jethro, the priest of Mid'ian, Moses' father-in-law, heard of all that God had done for Moses and for Israel his people, how the LORD had brought Israel out of Egypt. [2] Now Jethro, Moses' father-in-law, had taken Zippo'rah, Moses' wife, after he had sent her away, [3] and her two sons, of whom the name of the one was Gershom (for he said, "I have been a sojourner[a] in a foreign land"), [4] and the name of the other, Elie'zer[b] (for he said, "The God of my father was my help, and delivered me from the sword of Pharaoh"). [5] And Jethro, Moses' father-in-law, came with his sons and his wife to Moses in the wilderness where he was encamped at the mountain of God. [6] And when one told Moses, "Lo,[c] your father-in-law Jethro is coming to you with your wife and her two sons with her," [7] Moses went out to meet his father-in-law, and did obeisance and kissed him; and they asked each other of their welfare, and went into the tent. [8] Then Moses told his father-in-law all that the LORD had done to Pharaoh and to the Egyptians for Israel's sake, all the hardship that had come upon them in the way, and how the LORD had delivered them. [9] And Jethro rejoiced for all the good which the LORD had done to Israel, in that he had delivered them out of the hand of the Egyptians.

10 And Jethro said, "Blessed be the LORD, who has delivered you out of the hand of the Egyptians and out of the hand of Pharaoh. [11] Now I know that the LORD is greater than all gods, because he delivered the people from under the hand of the Egyptians,[d] when they dealt arrogantly with them." [12] And Jethro, Moses' father-in-law, offered[e] a burnt offering and sacrifices to God; and Aaron came with all the elders of Israel to eat bread with Moses' father-in-law before God.

13 On the morrow Moses sat to judge the people, and the people stood about Moses from morning till evening. [14] When Moses' father-in-law saw all that he was doing for the people, he said, "What is this that you are doing for the people? Why do you sit alone, and all the people stand about you from morning till evening?" [15] And Moses said to his father-in-law, "Because the people come to me to inquire of God; [16] when they have a dis-

z Cn: Heb obscure   a Heb ger   b Heb Eli, my God, ezer, help   c Sam Gk Syr: Heb I   d Transposing the last clause of v. 10 to v. 11   e Syr Tg Vg: Heb took

---

8: The Amalekites, a fierce desert tribe, claimed control of the wilderness in the region of Kadesh (Gen.14.7; Num.13.29; 14.25). **9–13:** *Choose for us men* implies holy war (v. 16) with a select group (compare Jg. ch. 7). The young warrior, Joshua, here mentioned for the first time, was at the head of the Israelite army. Moses, however, led the battle from a hilltop and ensured victory by the power of his rod and outstretched arms and perhaps by the power of the curse (Num.22.4–6). **10:** *Hur,* elsewhere mentioned only in 24.14. **14:** *Utterly blot out,* i.e. the foe will be subjected to the sacrificial ban, a practice of holy war. **16:** The bitter feud with Amalek persisted (Num.24.20; Dt.25.17–19; 1 Sam.15.7–8; 27.8; ch. 30) until the foe was exterminated during the reign of Hezekiah (1 Chr.4.41–43).

18.1–27: Jethro's visit. The priest of Midian celebrated a sacred meal and counseled Moses about the administration of law. **1:** *Jethro,* see 2.18 n. **2–4:** Zipporah and her sons (2.21–22) apparently had been sent back from Egypt to Midian. **5:** The narrative is out of order, for Israel reached *the mountain of God* later (19.2). **9–12:** This passage may imply that the priest of Midian was already a worshiper of the LORD (see 3.1 n.). As the priest of the cult, Jethro came to rejoice in the LORD's great deeds and to officiate at a cultic celebration. **12:** *Eat bread,* an allusion to a sacred meal held *before God* (24.9–11). Moses was not invited, perhaps because he had already been initiated into the cult (3.1–6). **13–27:** Jethro's plan for the reorganization of legal administration (compare Dt.1.9–18). **13:** Like a bedouin chief,

pute, they come to me and I decide between a man and his neighbor, and I make them know the statutes of God and his decisions." [17] Moses' father-in-law said to him, "What you are doing is not good. [18] You and the people with you will wear yourselves out, for the thing is too heavy for you; you are not able to perform it alone. [19] Listen now to my voice; I will give you counsel, and God be with you! You shall represent the people before God, and bring their cases to God; [20] and you shall teach them the statutes and the decisions, and make them know the way in which they must walk and what they must do. [21] Moreover choose able men from all the people, such as fear God, men who are trustworthy and who hate a bribe; and place such men over the people as rulers of thousands, of hundreds, of fifties, and of tens. [22] And let them judge the people at all times; every great matter they shall bring to you, but any small matter they shall decide themselves; so it will be easier for you, and they will bear the burden with you. [23] If you do this, and God so commands you, then you will be able to endure, and all this people also will go to their place in peace."

24 So Moses gave heed to the voice of his father-in-law and did all that he had said. [25] Moses chose able men out of all Israel, and made them heads over the people, rulers of thousands, of hundreds, of fifties, and of tens. [26] And they judged the people at all times; hard cases they brought to Moses, but any small matter they decided themselves. [27] Then Moses let his father-in-law depart, and he went his way to his own country.

19 On the third new moon after the people of Israel had gone forth out of the land of Egypt, on that day they came into the wilderness of Sinai. [2] And when they set out from Reph'-idim and came into the wilderness of Sinai, they encamped in the wilderness; and there Israel encamped before the mountain. [3] And Moses went up to God, and the LORD called to him out of the mountain, saying, "Thus you shall say to the house of Jacob, and tell the people of Israel: [4] You have seen what I did to the Egyptians, and how I bore you on eagles' wings and brought you to myself. [5] Now therefore, if you will obey my voice and keep my covenant, you shall be my own possession among all peoples; for all the earth is mine, [6] and you shall be to me a kingdom of priests and a holy nation. These are the words which you shall speak to the children of Israel."

7 So Moses came and called the elders of the people, and set before them all these words which the LORD had commanded him. [8] And all the people answered together and said, "All that the LORD has spoken we will do." And Moses reported the words of the people to the LORD. [9] And the LORD said to Moses, "Lo, I am coming to you in a thick cloud, that the people may hear when I speak with you, and may also believe you for ever."

Then Moses told the words of the people to the LORD. [10] And the LORD said to Moses,

---

Moses acted as judge in the people's disputes (2 Sam.15.1–6). **15–16:** *Inquire of God,* i.e. seek a verdict by oracle (Jg.4.4–5). **21–22:** Moses was to deal with cases without legal precedent which required a special oracle (compare Dt.17.8–13); ordinary cases were to be handled by lay leaders (Num.11.16–17, 24–25) or appointed judges (compare Dt.16.18–20). *Rulers of thousands,* see Num.1.17–46 n.

19.1–25 (20.18–21): The theophany at Sinai. At the sacred mountain the LORD offered to make a covenant with Israel. **2:** *Sinai,* see 3.1 n. **3:** The account assumes that the LORD dwells in heaven, whence he "comes down" (v. 20; 3.8) to the mountain top for meeting with men (24.9–11). Compare the similar view reflected in the Babylonian temple-tower (Gen.11.1–9). **4:** *You have seen what I did,* the background and presupposition of the *covenant* (see Gen.17.2 n.) is the LORD's mighty acts of deliverance. *On eagles' wings,* Dt.32.11–12. **5:** On Israel's side, the covenant rests upon a condition, *if you will obey my voice* — an allusion to the covenant laws to be given. *My own possession,* or "treasure," is a metaphor for Israel's special relationship to God. In freedom and grace he chose this people for his own (Dt.7.6; 14.2; 26.18), though all the earth belongs to him (Ex.9.29b). **6:** That which is holy is set apart as belonging to God; thus Israel is to be *a kingdom of priests and a holy nation,* consecrated for his service (see Is.61.6; 1 Pet.2.5,9). **7–8:** Compare 24.7. **9:** This tradition stresses Moses' role as the covenant mediator whom the people are to believe *for ever* (20.19; 24.1–2,9–11). **10–15:** In this tradition all the people are to prepare for participation in the

"Go to the people and consecrate them today and tomorrow, and let them wash their garments, [11] and be ready by the third day; for on the third day the LORD will come down upon Mount Sinai in the sight of all the people. [12] And you shall set bounds for the people round about, saying, 'Take heed that you do not go up into the mountain or touch the border of it; whoever touches the mountain shall be put to death; [13] no hand shall touch him, but he shall be stoned or shot; whether beast or man, he shall not live.' When the trumpet sounds a long blast, they shall come up to the mountain." [14] So Moses went down from the mountain to the people, and consecrated the people; and they washed their garments. [15] And he said to the people, "Be ready by the third day; do not go near a woman."

16 On the morning of the third day there were thunders and lightnings, and a thick cloud upon the mountain, and a very loud trumpet blast, so that all the people who were in the camp trembled. [17] Then Moses brought the people out of the camp to meet God; and they took their stand at the foot of the mountain. [18] And Mount Sinai was wrapped in smoke, because the LORD descended upon it in fire; and the smoke of it went up like the smoke of a kiln, and the whole mountain quaked greatly. [19] And as the sound of the trumpet grew louder and louder, Moses spoke, and God answered him in thunder. [20] And the LORD came down upon Mount Sinai, to the top of the mountain; and the LORD called Moses to the top of the mountain, and Moses went up. [21] And the LORD said to Moses, "Go down and warn the people, lest they break through to the LORD to gaze and many of them perish. [22] And also let the priests who come near to the LORD consecrate themselves, lest the LORD break out upon them." [23] And Moses said to the LORD, "The people cannot come up to Mount Sinai; for thou thyself didst charge us, saying, 'Set bounds about the mountain, and consecrate it.'" [24] And the LORD said to him, "Go down, and come up bringing Aaron with you; but do not let the priests and the people break through to come up to the LORD, lest he break out against them." [25] So Moses went down to the people and told them.

20 And God spoke all these words, saying,

2 "I am the LORD your God, who brought you out of the land of Egypt, out of the house of bondage.

3 "You shall have no other gods before[f] me.

4 "You shall not make for yourself a graven image, or any likeness of anything that is in heaven above, or that is in the earth beneath, or that is in the water under the earth; [5] you shall not bow down to them or serve them; for I the LORD your God am a jealous God, visiting the iniquity of the fathers upon the children to the third and the fourth generation of those who hate me, [6] but showing steadfast love to thousands of those who love me and keep my commandments.

f Or *besides*

covenant ceremony (24.3–8). **12:** The setting of bounds so that the people do not come near the mountain (v. 21) reflects the ancient view of holiness as a mysterious, threatening power with which the mountain is charged (see 3.6 n.; 2 Sam.6.6–9). No hand may touch the offender who has become affected with the contagion of holiness (Lev.6.27–28). **14–15:** Washing or changing of garments (Gen.35.2) and sexual abstinence (1 Sam.21.4–6) were forms of ceremonial purification. **16–19:** The theophany is portrayed primarily in the imagery of a violent thunderstorm (Jg.5.4–5; Pss.18.7–15; 29.3–9; etc.). This traditional language — "earthquake, wind, and fire" (1 Kg.19.11–13) — depicts the wonder and majesty of God's revelation. **16:** The trumpet (v. 13) was sounded on cultic occasions (2 Sam.6.15).

20.1–17: The Ten Commandments, the epitome of man's duties toward God and his neighbor. **1:** *These words,* i.e. "the ten words" or the Decalogue (34.28; Dt.4.13; 10.4). Originally each commandment was a short utterance (see vv. 13,14,15), lacking the explanatory comments found, e.g. in vv. 5,6,9–11. **2:** Jewish tradition considers this to be the first commandment. Actually it is a preface which summarizes the meaning of the Exodus, thus setting law within the context of God's redemptive action. **3:** The first commandment asserts that for Israel there shall be no other gods, because the LORD is *a jealous God* (v. 5; 34.14) who will tolerate no rivals for his people's devotion. **4–6:** Imageless worship of the LORD made Israel's faith unique in the ancient world where natural powers were personified and statues

7 "You shall not take the name of the Lord your God in vain; for the Lord will not hold him guiltless who takes his name in vain.

8 "Remember the sabbath day, to keep it holy. ⁹ Six days you shall labor, and do all your work; ¹⁰ but the seventh day is a sabbath to the Lord your God; in it you shall not do any work, you, or your son, or your daughter, your manservant, or your maidservant, or your cattle, or the sojourner who is within your gates; ¹¹ for in six days the Lord made heaven and earth, the sea, and all that is in them, and rested the seventh day; therefore the Lord blessed the sabbath day and hallowed it.

12 "Honor your father and your mother, that your days may be long in the land which the Lord your God gives you.

13 "You shall not kill.

14 "You shall not commit adultery.

15 "You shall not steal.

16 "You shall not bear false witness against your neighbor.

17 "You shall not covet your neighbor's house; you shall not covet your neighbor's wife, or his manservant, or his maidservant, or his ox, or his ass, or anything that is your neighbor's."

18 Now when all the people perceived the thunderings and the lightnings and the sound of the trumpet and the mountain smoking, the people were afraid and trembled; and they stood afar off, ¹⁹ and said to Moses, "You speak to us, and we will hear; but let not God speak to us, lest we die." ²⁰ And Moses said to the people, "Do not fear; for God has come to prove you, and that the fear of him may be before your eyes, that you may not sin."

21 And the people stood afar off, while Moses drew near to the thick darkness where God was. ²² And the Lord said to Moses, "Thus you shall say to the people of Israel: 'You have seen for yourselves that I have talked with you from heaven. ²³ You shall not make gods of silver to be with me, nor shall you make for yourselves gods of gold. ²⁴ An altar of earth you shall make for me and sacrifice on it your burnt offerings and your peace offerings, your sheep and your oxen; in every place where I cause my name to be remembered I will come to you and bless you. ²⁵ And if you make me an altar of stone, you shall not build it of hewn stones; for if you wield your tool upon it you profane it. ²⁶ And you shall not go up by steps to my altar, that your nakedness be not exposed on it.'

21 "Now these are the ordinances which you shall set before them. ² When you buy a Hebrew slave, he shall serve six years, and in the seventh he shall go out free, for nothing. ³ If he comes in single, he shall go

of them (animal or human) were worshiped. Some interpreters consider vv. 3–6 as one commandment and divide v. 17 into two commandments. **7:** The third commandment prohibits the misuse of the Lord's name in magic, divination, or false swearing (Lev.19.12). It reflects the ancient view that knowledge of the name could be used to exert magical control (see Gen.32.27,29 n.). **8–11:** Keeping the sabbath *holy* means to observe it as a day separated from others, a segment of time belonging especially to God. **10:** 16.22–30. **11:** Compare Dt.5.15. **12:** 21.15,17; Dt.27.16. **13:** This commandment forbids murder (see Gen.9.5,6 n.), not the forms of killing authorized for Israel, e.g. war or capital punishment. **16:** This law demands telling the truth in a law suit involving the neighbor (23.1; Dt.19.15–21; 1 Kg.21.8–14). **17:** Some regard the first sentence as a separate commandment; however, *neighbor's house* probably includes what is enumerated in the second part of the verse: wife, manservant, etc. **18–21:** The conclusion to the theophany scene (ch. 19). The people request that Moses be the covenant mediator (see 19.9 n.) so that they need not hear God's law directly (compare Dt.5.4–5).
20.22–23.33: The Covenant Code. These laws are largely neutral in regard to Israelite faith and presuppose a settled agricultural society. They reflect a situation after Israel's invasion of Canaan, when prevailing laws were borrowed and adapted to the covenant tradition. **22–26:** Cultic regulations. **23:** See 20.4–6 n. **24–26:** The Israelite altar, in contrast to pagan models, is to be the simplest kind and is to be built wherever the Lord *causes his name to be remembered*, i.e. chooses to reveal himself. Contrast the reform demanded in Dt.12.5–14. **21.1–11:** The rights of a slave (compare Dt.15.12–18). **1:** *Ordinances* refers to laws formulated (usually in the third person) to deal with various cases, in contrast to the apodictic or unconditional law of the Israelite theocracy (e.g. the Decalogue). These case laws reflect the agricultural way of life in Canaan (e.g. 22.5–6) and are similar in style and content to other legal codes of the ancient Near East. **2:** *Hebrew,* see Ex.1.15 n. An Israelite could go into servitude because of debts (Ex.22.1;

out single; if he comes in married, then his wife shall go out with him. [4] If his master gives him a wife and she bears him sons or daughters, the wife and her children shall be her master's and he shall go out alone. [5] But if the slave plainly says, 'I love my master, my wife, and my children; I will not go out free,' [6] then his master shall bring him to God, and he shall bring him to the door or the doorpost; and his master shall bore his ear through with an awl; and he shall serve him for life.

[7] "When a man sells his daughter as a slave, she shall not go out as the male slaves do. [8] If she does not please her master, who has designated her[g] for himself, then he shall let her be redeemed; he shall have no right to sell her to a foreign people, since he has dealt faithlessly with her. [9] If he designates her for his son, he shall deal with her as with a daughter. [10] If he takes another wife to himself, he shall not diminish her food, her clothing, or her marital rights. [11] And if he does not do these three things for her, she shall go out for nothing, without payment of money.

[12] "Whoever strikes a man so that he dies shall be put to death. [13] But if he did not lie in wait for him, but God let him fall into his hand, then I will appoint for you a place to which he may flee. [14] But if a man willfully attacks another to kill him treacherously, you shall take him from my altar, that he may die.

[15] "Whoever strikes his father or his mother shall be put to death.

[16] "Whoever steals a man, whether he sells him or is found in possession of him, shall be put to death.

[17] "Whoever curses his father or his mother shall be put to death.

[18] "When men quarrel and one strikes the other with a stone or with his fist and the man does not die but keeps his bed, [19] then if the man rises again and walks abroad with his staff, he that struck him shall be clear; only he shall pay for the loss of his time, and shall have him thoroughly healed.

[20] "When a man strikes his slave, male or female, with a rod and the slave dies under his hand, he shall be punished. [21] But if the slave survives a day or two, he is not to be punished; for the slave is his money.

[22] "When men strive together, and hurt a woman with child, so that there is a miscarriage, and yet no harm follows, the one who hurt her shall[h] be fined, according as the woman's husband shall lay upon him; and he shall pay as the judges determine. [23] If any harm follows, then you shall give life for life, [24] eye for eye, tooth for tooth, hand for hand, foot for foot, [25] burn for burn, wound for wound, stripe for stripe.

[26] "When a man strikes the eye of his slave, male or female, and destroys it, he shall let the slave go free for the eye's sake. [27] If he knocks out the tooth of his slave, male or female, he shall let the slave go free for the tooth's sake.

[28] "When an ox gores a man or a woman to death, the ox shall be stoned, and its flesh shall not be eaten; but the owner of the ox shall be clear. [29] But if the ox has been accustomed to gore in the past, and its owner has been warned but has not kept it in, and it kills a man or a woman, the ox shall be stoned, and its owner also shall be put to death. [30] If a

g Another reading is *so that he has not designated her*
h Heb *he shall*

Lev.25.39; 2 Kg.4.1). **6:** *To God,* i.e. the legal act had to be performed at the sacred doorpost of the house (see 12.7 n.), perhaps in the presence of the household gods (Gen.31.19). **7–11:** The rights of a female slave or concubine (compare Dt.15.12,17). **8:** *Redeemed,* i.e. by a relative or another buyer who pays the purchase price.

21.12–32: Laws protecting human beings. 12–14: A distinction is drawn between intentional and unintentional murder. As protection from the swift justice of the blood-avenger, the man-slayer is guaranteed asylum (Num.35.12; Dt.4.41–43; 19.1–13; Jos. ch. 20), so that the case may be adjudicated soberly by legal authorities. The asylum in ancient times was at the altar (1 Kg.2.28–34). **17:** The curse, according to ancient belief, released an inexorable power (Num.22.6), thus making it as serious to curse parents as to strike them. **22–25:** This lex talionis (see Lev.24.20) was not an expression of vengeance but a limitation upon measureless vengeance.

ransom is laid on him, then he shall give for the redemption of his life whatever is laid upon him. [31] If it gores a man's son or daughter, he shall be dealt with according to this same rule. [32] If the ox gores a slave, male or female, the owner shall give to their master thirty shekels of silver, and the ox shall be stoned.

33 "When a man leaves a pit open, or when a man digs a pit and does not cover it, and an ox or an ass falls into it, [34] the owner of the pit shall make it good; he shall give money to its owner, and the dead beast shall be his.

35 "When one man's ox hurts another's, so that it dies, then they shall sell the live ox and divide the price of it; and the dead beast also they shall divide. [36] Or if it is known that the ox has been accustomed to gore in the past, and its owner has not kept it in, he shall pay ox for ox, and the dead beast shall be his.

22 [i] "If a man steals an ox or a sheep, and kills it or sells it, he shall pay five oxen for an ox, and four sheep for a sheep.[j] He shall make restitution; if he has nothing, then he shall be sold for his theft. [4] If the stolen beast is found alive in his possession, whether it is an ox or an ass or a sheep, he shall pay double.

2[k] "If a thief is found breaking in, and is struck so that he dies, there shall be no bloodguilt for him; [3] but if the sun has risen upon him, there shall be bloodguilt for him.

5 "When a man causes a field or vineyard to be grazed over, or lets his beast loose and it feeds in another man's field, he shall make restitution from the best in his own field and in his own vineyard.

6 "When fire breaks out and catches in thorns so that the stacked grain or the standing grain or the field is consumed, he that kindled the fire shall make full restitution.

7 "If a man delivers to his neighbor money or goods to keep, and it is stolen out of the man's house, then, if the thief is found, he shall pay double. [8] If the thief is not found, the owner of the house shall come near to God, to show whether or not he has put his hand to his neighbor's goods.

9 "For every breach of trust, whether it is for ox, for ass, for sheep, for clothing, or for any kind of lost thing, of which one says, 'This is it,' the case of both parties shall come before God; he whom God shall condemn shall pay double to his neighbor.

10 "If a man delivers to his neighbor an ass or an ox or a sheep or any beast to keep, and it dies or is hurt or is driven away, without any one seeing it, [11] an oath by the LORD shall be between them both to see whether he has not put his hand to his neighbor's property; and the owner shall accept the oath, and he shall not make restitution. [12] But if it is stolen from him, he shall make restitution to its owner. [13] If it is torn by beasts, let him bring it as evidence; he shall not make restitution for what has been torn.

14 "If a man borrows anything of his neighbor, and it is hurt or dies, the owner not being with it, he shall make full restitution. [15] If the owner was with it, he shall not make restitution; if it was hired, it came for its hire.[l]

16 "If a man seduces a virgin who is not betrothed, and lies with her, he shall give the marriage present for her, and make her his wife. [17] If her father utterly refuses to give her to him, he shall pay money equivalent to the marriage present for virgins.

i Ch 21.37 in Heb
j Restoring the second half of verse 3 with 4 to their place immediately following verse 1
k Ch 22.1 in Heb
l Or *it is reckoned in* (Heb *comes into*) *its hire*

21.33–22.17: Laws dealing with property. 33–36: These laws establish responsibility in cases of carelessness. **22:1–4:** Case laws regulating stealing. **2–3:** These verses may mean that if the invader is caught in the act (at night) he may be slain with impunity, but if he is slain in broad daylight there is blood guilt. **5–6:** Cases of neglect. **7–15:** Cases involving trusteeship. **9:** *Before God* (v. 8), i.e. to the sanctuary (possibly to the doorpost; 21.6) for an oracular decision or the sacred oath (v. 11; 1 Kg.8.31–32). **16–17:** This law is included here because it deals with a financial matter, the *marriage present* (Dt.22.29). Laws concerning sexual relations are found in Dt.22.13–30.

18 "You shall not permit a sorceress to live.

19 "Whoever lies with a beast shall be put to death.

20 "Whoever sacrifices to any god, save to the LORD only, shall be utterly destroyed.

21 "You shall not wrong a stranger or oppress him, for you were strangers in the land of Egypt. [22] You shall not afflict any widow or orphan. [23] If you do afflict them, and they cry out to me, I will surely hear their cry; [24] and my wrath will burn, and I will kill you with the sword, and your wives shall become widows and your children fatherless.

25 "If you lend money to any of my people with you who is poor, you shall not be to him as a creditor, and you shall not exact interest from him. [26] If ever you take your neighbor's garment in pledge, you shall restore it to him before the sun goes down; [27] for that is his only covering, it is his mantle for his body; in what else shall he sleep? And if he cries to me, I will hear, for I am compassionate.

28 "You shall not revile God, nor curse a ruler of your people.

29 "You shall not delay to offer from the fulness of your harvest and from the outflow of your presses.

"The first-born of your sons you shall give to me. [30] You shall do likewise with your oxen and with your sheep: seven days it shall be with its dam; on the eighth day you shall give it to me.

31 "You shall be men consecrated to me; therefore you shall not eat any flesh that is torn by beasts in the field; you shall cast it to the dogs.

23 "You shall not utter a false report. You shall not join hands with a wicked man, to be a malicious witness. [2] You shall not follow a multitude to do evil; nor shall you bear witness in a suit, turning aside after a multitude, so as to pervert justice; [3] nor shall you be partial to a poor man in his suit.

4 "If you meet your enemy's ox or his ass going astray, you shall bring it back to him. [5] If you see the ass of one who hates you lying under its burden, you shall refrain from leaving him with it, you shall help him to lift it up.[m]

6 "You shall not pervert the justice due to your poor in his suit. [7] Keep far from a false charge, and do not slay the innocent and righteous, for I will not acquit the wicked. [8] And you shall take no bribe, for a bribe blinds the officials, and subverts the cause of those who are in the right.

9 "You shall not oppress a stranger; you know the heart of a stranger, for you were strangers in the land of Egypt.

10 "For six years you shall sow your land and gather in its yield; [11] but the seventh year you shall let it rest and lie fallow, that the poor of your people may eat; and what they leave the wild beasts may eat. You shall do likewise with your vineyard, and with your olive orchard.

12 "Six days you shall do your work, but on the seventh day you shall rest; that your ox and your ass may have rest, and the son of your bondmaid, and the alien, may be refreshed. [13] Take heed to all that I have said to you; and make no mention of the names of other gods, nor let such be heard out of your mouth.

l Or *it is reckoned in* (Heb *comes into*) *its hire*
m Gk: Heb obscure

22.18–23.9: Miscellaneous social and cultic laws. The laws of vv. 18–20 (compare 21.12,15–17) are in the unconditional style of the Decalogue. **20:** Compare 20.3; Dt.13.12–18. **21–27:** Israel's God is the protector of the legally defenseless: the stranger (sojourner), orphan, widow, and poor. **25:** Being a farming people, Israel frowned upon the mercantile way of life (Hos.12.7–8) and specifically upon the exaction of interest from a fellow-Israelite (Lev.25.35–38). **26:** A loan with a garment as security could only be for the day, lest a poor man suffer (Dt.24.12–13; Am.2.8). **28:** Lev.24.15–16; 2 Sam.16.9; 1 Kg.2.8–9; 21.10. **29–30:** See 13.2 n. **31:** Flesh torn by beasts was regarded as unclean because it was not properly drained of blood (Lev.7.24; 17.15). **23.1–9:** Laws expounding Israel's sense of justice. **4–5:** Justice extends even to helping *your enemy* (Dt.22.1–4).

23.10–19: A cultic calendar (34.18–26; Lev.23.1–44; Dt.16.1–17). **10–11:** See Lev.25.2–7. **12:** Here the observance of the sabbath is based upon humanitarian concern (compare 20.11). **14–17:** This law reflects the practice of

14 "Three times in the year you shall keep a feast to me. [15] You shall keep the feast of unleavened bread; as I commanded you, you shall eat unleavened bread for seven days at the appointed time in the month of Abib, for in it you came out of Egypt. None shall appear before me empty-handed. [16] You shall keep the feast of harvest, of the first fruits of your labor, of what you sow in the field. You shall keep the feast of ingathering at the end of the year, when you gather in from the field the fruit of your labor. [17] Three times in the year shall all your males appear before the Lord God.

18 "You shall not offer the blood of my sacrifice with leavened bread, or let the fat of my feast remain until the morning.

19 "The first of the first fruits of your ground you shall bring into the house of the Lord your God.

"You shall not boil a kid in its mother's milk.

20 "Behold, I send an angel before you, to guard you on the way and to bring you to the place which I have prepared. [21] Give heed to him and hearken to his voice, do not rebel against him, for he will not pardon your transgression; for my name is in him.

22 "But if you hearken attentively to his voice and do all that I say, then I will be an enemy to your enemies and an adversary to your adversaries.

23 "When my angel goes before you, and brings you in to the Amorites, and the Hittites, and the Per'izzites, and the Canaanites, the Hivites, and the Jeb'usites, and I blot them out, [24] you shall not bow down to their gods, nor serve them, nor do according to their works, but you shall utterly overthrow them and break their pillars in pieces. [25] You shall serve the Lord your God, and I[n] will bless your bread and your water; and I will take sickness away from the midst of you. [26] None shall cast her young or be barren in your land; I will fulfil the number of your days. [27] I will send my terror before you, and will throw into confusion all the people against whom you shall come, and I will make all your enemies turn their backs to you. [28] And I will send hornets before you, which shall drive out Hivite, Canaanite, and Hittite from before you. [29] I will not drive them out from before you in one year, lest the land become desolate and the wild beasts multiply against you. [30] Little by little I will drive them out from before you, until you are increased and possess the land. [31] And I will set your bounds from the Red Sea to the sea of the Philistines, and from the wilderness to the Euphra'tes; for I will deliver the inhabitants of the land into your hand, and you shall drive them out before you. [32] You shall make no covenant with them or with their gods. [33] They shall not dwell in your land, lest they make you sin against me; for if you serve their gods, it will surely be a snare to you."

24 And he said to Moses, "Come up to the Lord, you and Aaron, Nadab, and Abi'hu, and seventy of the elders of Israel, and worship afar off. [2] Moses alone shall come

n Gk Vg: Heb *he*

making a pilgrimage to the central sanctuary of the tribal confederacy (1 Sam.1.3,21). **15:** *Empty-handed,* i.e. without a gift of the first fruits of the barley harvest. **16:** The *feast of harvest,* i.e. the feast of weeks (or pentecost, see Lev.23.15–21 n.) which was celebrated at the time of the wheat harvest (June). The third feast, *the feast of ingathering,* or feast of booths, was celebrated *at the end of the year* (autumn), according to the old agricultural calendar (see 12.2 n.), when fruit, grapes, and olives were harvested. **17:** According to ancient practice, men were the chief participants in the cult (34.23; see 10.7–11 n.). **18–19:** 34.25–26. The prohibition against seething a kid in its mother's milk (Dt.14.21) is a protest against a Canaanite method of preparing a sacrifice.

23.20–33: The conclusion to the Covenant Code (beginning 20.22). **20–21:** The *angel* is the Lord himself (14.19; see Gen.16.7 n.). On *the name,* see Gen.32.27 n. **27.28:** Here the language of "holy war" is used. *Terror,* Gen.35.5 n. The term *hornets* apparently is used figuratively to portray the panic aroused in holy war (Dt.7.20; Jos.24.12 n.).

24.1–18: The ceremony of covenant ratification. 1–2: This tradition is continued in vv. 9–11. *Moses alone,* an indication of Moses' special role as covenant mediator (19.9; 20.19). **3–8:** The first version of the covenant ceremony

near to the LORD; but the others shall not come near, and the people shall not come up with him."

3 Moses came and told the people all the words of the LORD and all the ordinances; and all the people answered with one voice, and said, "All the words which the LORD has spoken we will do." [4] And Moses wrote all the words of the LORD. And he rose early in the morning, and built an altar at the foot of the mountain, and twelve pillars, according to the twelve tribes of Israel. [5] And he sent young men of the people of Israel, who offered burnt offerings and sacrificed peace offerings of oxen to the LORD. [6] And Moses took half of the blood and put it in basins, and half of the blood he threw against the altar. [7] Then he took the book of the covenant, and read it in the hearing of the people; and they said, "All that the LORD has spoken we will do, and we will be obedient." [8] And Moses took the blood and threw it upon the people, and said, "Behold the blood of the covenant which the LORD has made with you in accordance with all these words."

9 Then Moses and Aaron, Nadab, and Abi'hu, and seventy of the elders of Israel went up, [10] and they saw the God of Israel; and there was under his feet as it were a pavement of sapphire stone, like the very heaven for clearness. [11] And he did not lay his hand on the chief men of the people of Israel; they beheld God, and ate and drank.

12 The LORD said to Moses, "Come up to me on the mountain, and wait there; and I will give you the tables of stone, with the law and the commandment, which I have written for their instruction." [13] So Moses rose with his servant Joshua, and Moses went up into the mountain of God. [14] And he said to the elders, "Tarry here for us, until we come to you again; and, behold, Aaron and Hur are with you; whoever has a cause, let him go to them."

15 Then Moses went up on the mountain, and the cloud covered the mountain. [16] The glory of the LORD settled on Mount Sinai, and the cloud covered it six days; and on the seventh day he called to Moses out of the midst of the cloud. [17] Now the appearance of the glory of the LORD was like a devouring fire on the top of the mountain in the sight of the people of Israel. [18] And Moses entered the cloud, and went up on the mountain. And Moses was on the mountain forty days and forty nights.

---

stresses the people's participation (19.10–15). **3:** *The words,* i.e. the Decalogue; *the ordinances,* i.e. the laws of the Covenant Code (see 21.1 n.). **4:** The participation of all the people is symbolized by *twelve pillars,* one for each tribe. **5:** On the types of sacrifice, see Lev. chs. 1 and 3. **6–8:** The ritual dramatizes the uniting of the two parties: the LORD, whose presence is represented by the altar, and the people. Compare the ancient covenant ceremony found in Gen. ch. 15. **7:** *The book of the covenant* (Jos.24.25–26) apparently contained the covenant laws, here tacitly identified with *the words* and *the ordinances* (v. 3). **8:** *The blood of the covenant* (compare Mt.26.28; 1 Cor.11.25) reflects the ancient view that blood was efficacious in establishing community between God and man (see Lev.1.5 n.). **9–11:** The second version of the covenant ceremony (continuing vv. 1–2). **9:** The people did not take part but were represented by the seventy *elders* or *chief men.* Moses, the covenant mediator, was accompanied by the priestly family, Aaron, Nadab, and Abihu (6.14–25; Lev, 10.1–3). **10:** The leaders did not see God directly; they saw only the lower part of his heavenly throne-room — the sapphire pavement (the firmament) above which the LORD was enthroned (compare Is.6.1; Ezek.1.1,26–28). **11:** Unharmed by divine holiness (see 3.6 n.), the leaders partook of the covenant meal (18.12). **12–14:** A separate tradition about the gift of *the tables of stone* on which the Decalogue was written (32.15; 34.28; Dt.9.9,11,15). **14:** 18.16. This verse sets the stage for the episode of ch. 32. *Hur,* see 17.10 n. **15–18:** This theophany introduces the priestly material of chs. 25–31, which apparently has replaced the early tradition about Moses making the ark and putting the tables of law in it (Dt.10.1–5). *The glory,* see 16.6–7 n.

The Book of Job

THERE WAS A MAN IN THE LAND OF UZ, whose name was Job; and that man was blameless and upright, one who feared God, and turned away from evil. ² There were born to him seven sons and three daughters. ³ He had seven thousand sheep, three thousand camels, five hundred yoke of oxen, and five hundred she-asses, and very many servants; so that this man was the greatest of all the people of the east. ⁴ His sons used to go and hold a feast in the house of each on his day; and they would send and invite their three sisters to eat and drink with them. ⁵ And when the days of the feast had run their course, Job would send and sanctify them, and he would rise early in the morning and offer burnt offerings according to the number of them all; for Job said, "It may be that my sons have sinned, and cursed God in their hearts." Thus Job did continually.

6 Now there was a day when the sons of God came to present themselves before the LORD, and Satan*a* also came among them. ⁷ The LORD said to Satan, "Whence have you come?" Satan answered the LORD, "From going to and fro on the earth, and from walking up and down on it." ⁸ And the LORD said to Satan, "Have you considered my servant Job, that there is none like him on the earth, a blameless and upright man, who fears God and turns away from evil?" ⁹ Then Satan answered the LORD, "Does Job fear God for nought? ¹⁰ Hast thou not put a hedge about him and his house and all that he has, on every side? Thou hast blessed the work of his hands, and his possessions have increased in the land. ¹¹ But put forth thy hand now, and touch all that he has, and he will curse thee to thy face." ¹² And the LORD said to Satan, "Behold, all that he has is in your power; only upon him-self do not put forth your hand." So Satan went forth from the presence of the LORD.

13 Now there was a day when his sons and daughters were eating and drinking wine in their eldest brother's house; ¹⁴ and there came a messenger to Job, and said, "The oxen were plowing and the asses feeding beside them; ¹⁵ and the Sabe′ans fell upon them and took them, and slew the servants with the edge of the sword; and I alone have escaped to tell you." ¹⁶ While he was yet speaking, there came another, and said, "The fire of God fell from heaven and burned up the sheep and the servants, and consumed them; and I alone have escaped to tell you." ¹⁷ While he was yet speaking, there came another, and said, "The Chalde′-ans formed three companies, and made a raid upon the camels and took them, and slew the servants with the edge of the sword; and I alone have escaped to tell you." ¹⁸ While he was yet speaking, there came another, and said, "Your sons and daughters were eating and drinking wine in their eldest brother's house; ¹⁹ and behold, a great wind came across the wilderness, and struck the four corners of the house, and it fell upon the young people, and they are dead; and I alone have escaped to tell you."

20 Then Job arose, and rent his robe, and shaved his head, and fell upon the ground, and worshiped. ²¹ And he said, "Naked I came from my mother's womb, and naked shall I return; the LORD gave, and the LORD has taken away; blessed be the name of the LORD."

22 In all this Job did not sin or charge God with wrong.

2 Again there was a day when the sons of God came to present themselves before

a Heb *the adversary*

1.1–2.13: The prologue. A blameless man is deprived of wealth, posterity, and health, but keeps his faith in God. **1:** *The land of Uz* is probably Edom, although some locate it in north Transjordan. The name *Job* may mean "hostile" or "penitent." *Blameless,* i.e. healthy, whole, and socially responsible. **6–8:** *Satan* (see note *a;* Zech.3.1 n.) is *among the sons of God.* He is not yet the demonic personification of later Judaism (compare 1 Chr.21.1) and Christianity. **15:** *Sabeans,* nomads from Arabia. **17:** *Chaldeans,* originally from southern Mesopotamia. The folk-teller respects archaic and local color. **21:** *Naked shall I return,* Hebrew adds "there," suggesting correspondence between *mother's womb* and "mother earth." Although a foreigner, Job uses the covenant-name, Yahweh (the LORD); this is an indication of early date. In the poem, the sacred name Yahweh is never used by the speakers (except in 12.9, a proverbial quotation). **22:** The Deity is not accused of capricious malevolence. **2.4:** *Skin for skin,* a hide for a hide, a proverb probably

Bible, THE NEW OXFORD ANNOTATED BIBLE WITH THE APOCRYPHA Revised Standard Edition, Job 1–7, 40–42.

the LORD, and Satan also came among them to present himself before the LORD. [2] And the LORD said to Satan, "Whence have you come?" Satan answered the LORD, "From going to and fro on the earth, and from walking up and down on it." [3] And the LORD said to Satan, "Have you considered my servant Job, that there is none like him on the earth, a blameless and upright man, who fears God and turns away from evil? He still holds fast his integrity, although you moved me against him, to destroy him without cause." [4] Then Satan answered the LORD, "Skin for skin! All that a man has he will give for his life. [5] But put forth thy hand now, and touch his bone and his flesh, and he will curse thee to thy face." [6] And the LORD said to Satan, "Behold, he is in your power; only spare his life."

7 So Satan went forth from the presence of the LORD, and afflicted Job with loathsome sores from the sole of his foot to the crown of his head. [8] And he took a potsherd with which to scrape himself, and sat among the ashes.

9 Then his wife said to him, "Do you still hold fast your integrity? Curse God, and die." [10] But he said to her, "You speak as one of the foolish women would speak. Shall we receive good at the hand of God, and shall we not receive evil?" In all this Job did not sin with his lips.

11 Now when Job's three friends heard of all this evil that had come upon him, they came each from his own place, Eli'phaz the Te'manite, Bildad the Shuhite, and Zophar the Na'amathite. They made an appointment together to come to condole with him and comfort him. [12] And when they saw him from afar, they did not recognize him; and they raised their voices and wept; and they rent their robes and sprinkled dust upon their heads toward heaven. [13] And they sat with him on the ground seven days and seven nights, and no one spoke a word to him, for they saw that his suffering was very great.

3 After this Job opened his mouth and cursed the day of his birth. [2] And Job said:
3   "Let the day perish wherein I was born,
    and the night which said,
    'A man-child is conceived.'
4   Let that day be darkness!
    May God above not seek it,
    nor light shine upon it.
5   Let gloom and deep darkness claim it.
    Let clouds dwell upon it;
    let the blackness of the day terrify it.
6   That night — let thick darkness seize it!
    let it not rejoice among the days
      of the year,
    let it not come into the number
      of the months.
7   Yea, let that night be barren;
    let no joyful cry be heard[b] in it.
8   Let those curse it who curse the day,
    who are skilled to rouse up Leviathan.
9   Let the stars of its dawn be dark;
    let it hope for light, but have none,
    nor see the eyelids of the morning;
10 because it did not shut the doors of my
      mother's womb,
    nor hide trouble from my eyes.

11   "Why did I not die at birth,
    come forth from the womb and expire?
12 Why did the knees receive me?
    Or why the breasts, that I should suck?
13 For then I should have lain down and been
      quiet;
    I should have slept; then I should have
      been at rest,

b Heb *come*

---

used by tradesmen. **7:** *Loathsome sores,* not necessarily leprosy (Hansen's disease) but a skin ailment, one of many in the Near East. **9:** *Curse God, and die,* Job's wife still believed in his *integrity* (see 4.6 n.) but wished to shorten his torture. **10:** *Foolish women,* i.e. those who do not believe in divine intervention into human affairs (see Ps.14.1 n.). **11:** The friends of Job came from northwest Arabia.

    3.1–26: Job's soliloquy. 8: Those *who are skilled to rouse Leviathan* are magicians, astrologers, and calendar-makers who were believed to produce as well as announce eclipses. *Leviathan,* the sea monster (7.12), like Rahab (9.13; 26.12; Is.51.9), threatens to engulf the created order and the succession of days and nights, especially during

14 with kings and counselors of the earth
   who rebuilt ruins for themselves,
15 or with princes who had gold,
   who filled their houses with silver.
16 Or why was I not as a hidden untimely birth,
   as infants that never see the light?
17 There the wicked cease from troubling,
   and there the weary are at rest.
18 There the prisoners are at ease together;
   they hear not the voice of the taskmaster.
19 The small and the great are there,
   and the slave is free from his master.

20 "Why is light given to him that is in misery,
   and life to the bitter in soul,
21 who long for death, but it comes not,
   and dig for it more than for hid treasures;
22 who rejoice exceedingly,
   and are glad, when they find the grave?
23 Why is light given to a man whose way is hid,
   whom God has hedged in?
24 For my sighing comes as^c my bread,
   and my groanings are poured out like water.
25 For the thing that I fear comes upon me,
   and what I dread befalls me.
26 I am not at ease, nor am I quiet;
   I have no rest; but trouble comes."

4 Then Eli′phaz the Te′manite answered:
2 "If one ventures a word with you, will you be offended?
   Yet who can keep from speaking?
3 Behold, you have instructed many,
   and you have strengthened the weak hands.
4 Your words have upheld him who was stumbling,
   and you have made firm the feeble knees.
5 But now it has come to you, and you are impatient;
   it touches you, and you are dismayed.
6 Is not your fear of God your confidence,
   and the integrity of your ways your hope?

7 "Think now, who that was innocent ever perished?
   Or where were the upright cut off?
8 As I have seen, those who plow iniquity
   and sow trouble reap the same.
9 By the breath of God they perish,
   and by the blast of his anger they are consumed.
10 The roar of the lion, the voice of the fierce lion,
   the teeth of the young lions, are broken.
11 The strong lion perishes for lack of prey,
   and the whelps of the lioness are scattered.

12 "Now a word was brought to me stealthily,
   my ear received the whisper of it.
13 Amid thoughts from visions of the night,
   when deep sleep falls on men,
14 dread came upon me, and trembling,
   which made all my bones shake.
15 A spirit glided past my face;
   the hair of my flesh stood up.
16 It stood still,
   but I could not discern its appearance.
   A form was before my eyes;
   there was silence, then I heard a voice:

c Heb *before*

eclipses of the sun or moon. **14:** *Ruins,* probably pyramids. The thought of a happy afterlife is not Hebraic but Egyptian. **23:** *God,* Hebrew Eloah, a name which stresses the terrible aspect of the Deity, whose omnipotence is never doubted by Job. Job's dilemma is directly related to his theological view that God is the cause of both good and evil (disaster, calamities, etc.); see 2.10; Is.45.7; Am.3.6.

4.1–5.27: First discourse of Eliphaz. 1–4: The opening words are courteous. The poet insists on the sincerity of Job's comforters. **6:** Job's *integrity* (Hebrew word related to "blameless" in 1.1; see 2.9 n.) is not yet questioned. **7:** The dogma of individual, this-worldly retribution is upheld. **12–16:** Eliphaz appeals to a supranatural, almost prophetic, source of authority. He does not speak in the name of tradition or experience, as wise men generally do. **17:** Surely no *mortal man is righteous before God,* and Job should adopt an attitude of humility instead of rebelling

17 'Can mortal man be righteous before[d] God?
Can a man be pure before[d] his Maker?

18 Even in his servants he puts no trust,
and his angels he charges with error;

19 how much more those who dwell in houses
of clay,
whose foundation is in the dust,
who are crushed before the moth.

20 Between morning and evening they are
destroyed;
they perish for ever without any
regarding it.

21 If their tent-cord is plucked up within
them,
do they not die, and that without
wisdom?'

5 "Call now; is there any one who will
answer you?
To which of the holy ones will you turn?

2 Surely vexation kills the fool,
and jealousy slays the simple.

3 I have seen the fool taking root,
but suddenly I cursed his dwelling.

4 His sons are far from safety,
they are crushed in the gate,
and there is no one to deliver them.

5 His harvest the hungry eat,
and he takes it even out of thorns;[e]
and the thirsty[f] pant after his[g] wealth.

6 For affliction does not come from the dust,
nor does trouble sprout from the
ground;

7 but man is born to trouble
as the sparks fly upward.

8 "As for me, I would seek God,
and to God would I commit my cause;

9 who does great things and unsearchable,
marvelous things without number:

10 he gives rain upon the earth
and sends waters upon the fields;

11 he sets on high those who are lowly,
and those who mourn are lifted to safety.

12 He frustrates the devices of the crafty,
so that their hands achieve no success.

13 He takes the wise in their own craftiness;
and the schemes of the wily are brought
to a quick end.

14 They meet with darkness in the daytime,
and grope at noonday as in the night.

15 But he saves the fatherless from their mouth,[h]
the needy from the hand of the mighty.

16 So the poor have hope,
and injustice shuts her mouth.

17 "Behold, happy is the man whom God
reproves;
therefore despise not the chastening of
the Almighty.

18 For he wounds, but he binds up;
he smites, but his hands heal.

19 He will deliver you from six troubles;
in seven there shall no evil touch you.

20 In famine he will redeem you from death,
and in war from the power of the sword.

21 You shall be hid from the scourge of the
tongue,
and shall not fear destruction when it
comes.

22 At destruction and famine you shall laugh,
and shall not fear the beasts of the earth.

23 For you shall be in league with the stones
of the field,
and the beasts of the field shall be at
peace with you.

24 You shall know that your tent is safe,
and you shall inspect your fold and miss
nothing.

25 You shall know also that your descendants
shall be many,

d Or more than   e Heb obscure   f Aquila Symmachus
Syr Vg: Heb snare   g Heb their   h Cn: Heb uncertain

against the divine will. **21:** The word translated *tent-cord* has two separate meanings; here it should be translated "pre-eminence" or "excellency"; men's pre-eminence or excellency is of no avail. They have only an illusion of *wisdom.* **5.1:** *The holy ones,* divine beings (see 15.15; Ex.15.11 n.; Ps.82.1 n.); members of the heavenly court cannot be intercessors. Eliphaz suspects, perhaps, that Job has attempted to justify himself by invoking other gods. **8:** *I would,* that is, were I in Job's place; if Job would only turn from his arrogance, his present misery would be ended. **17–27:** Suffering must be accepted as *the chastening of the Almighty.* The poet refers to the doctrine of *musar* (chastening or correction), which is characteristic of Jewish orthodoxy.

and your offspring as the grass of the earth.

26 You shall come to your grave in ripe old age,
as a shock of grain comes up to the threshing floor in its season.

27 Lo, this we have searched out; it is true.
Hear, and know it for your good."[i]

6 Then Job answered:
2 "O that my vexation were weighed,
and all my calamity laid in the balances!

3 For then it would be heavier than the sand of the sea;
therefore my words have been rash.

4 For the arrows of the Almighty are in me;
my spirit drinks their poison;
the terrors of God are arrayed against me.

5 Does the wild ass bray when he has grass,
or the ox low over his fodder?

6 Can that which is tasteless be eaten without salt,
or is there any taste in the slime of the purslane?[j]

7 My appetite refuses to touch them;
they are as food that is loathsome to me.[k]

8 "O that I might have my request,
and that God would grant my desire;

9 that it would please God to crush me,
that he would let loose his hand and cut me off!

10 This would be my consolation;
I would even exult[l] in pain unsparing;
for I have not denied the words of the Holy One.

11 What is my strength, that I should wait?
And what is my end, that I should be patient?

12 Is my strength the strength of stones,
or is my flesh bronze?

13 In truth I have no help in me,
and any resource is driven from me.

14 "He who withholds[m] kindness from a friend
forsakes the fear of the Almighty.

15 My brethren are treacherous as a torrent-bed,
as freshets that pass away,

16 which are dark with ice,
and where the snow hides itself.

17 In time of heat they disappear;
when it is hot, they vanish from their place.

18 The caravans turn aside from their course;
they go up into the waste, and perish.

19 The caravans of Tema look,
the travelers of Sheba hope.

20 They are disappointed because they were confident;
they come thither and are confounded.

21 Such you have now become to me;[n]
you see my calamity, and are afraid.

22 Have I said, 'Make me a gift'?
Or, 'From your wealth offer a bribe for me'?

23 Or, 'Deliver me from the adversary's hand'?
Or, 'Ransom me from the hand of oppressors'?

24 "Teach me, and I will be silent;
make me understand how I have erred.

25 How forceful are honest words!
But what does reproof from you reprove?

i Heb *for yourself*   *j* The meaning of the Hebrew word is uncertain   *k* Heb obscure   *l* The meaning of the Hebrew word is uncertain   *m* Syr Vg Compare Tg: Heb obscure   *n* Cn Compare Gk Syr: Heb obscure

6.1–7.21: Reply of Job. The orthodox explanation cannot be valid in Job's case, for his *calamity* exceeds all ordinary misfortunes. **6:** *Slime of the purslane,* an insipid and repulsive food. Purslane is a potherb. **8–11:** The Egyptian theme of desire for an early death reappears (see ch. 3). Moreover Job fears that, if his days (and hence, his tortures) are prolonged, he may deny *the words of the Holy One* (v. 10). The poet suggests thereby the complexity of the hero's personality; Job is an unwilling blasphemer. **14:** The test of true religion lies in human compassion for others. Another rendering is: "A man should show kindness to a man in despair, even to one who forsakes the fear of the Almighty." Some commentators suggest that the verse is a marginal note made by a scribe. **15–20:** Friendship fails precisely when it is needed. **24:** Job is willing to admit that he has *erred,* if only convincing evidence is brought forward. **30:** His con-

26 Do you think that you can reprove words,
    when the speech of a despairing man is
      wind?
27 You would even cast lots over the fatherless,
    and bargain over your friend.

28 "But now, be pleased to look at me;
    for I will not lie to your face.
29 Turn, I pray, let no wrong be done.
    Turn now, my vindication is at stake.
30 Is there any wrong on my tongue?
    Cannot my taste discern calamity?

7 "Has not man a hard service upon earth,
    and are not his days like the days of a
      hireling?
2 Like a slave who longs for the shadow,
    and like a hireling who looks for his
      wages,
3 so I am allotted months of emptiness,
    and nights of misery are apportioned
      to me.
4 When I lie down I say, 'When shall I arise?'
    But the night is long,
    and I am full of tossing till the dawn.
5 My flesh is clothed with worms and dirt;
    my skin hardens, then breaks out afresh.
6 My days are swifter than a weaver's shuttle,
    and come to their end without hope.

7 "Remember that my life is a breath;
    my eye will never again see good.
8 The eye of him who sees me will behold
    me no more;
    while thy eyes are upon me, I shall be
      gone.
9 As the cloud fades and vanishes,

so he who goes down to Sheol does not
    come up;
10 he returns no more to his house,
    nor does his place know him any more.

11 "Therefore I will not restrain my mouth;
    I will speak in the anguish of my spirit;
    I will complain in the bitterness of my
      soul.
12 Am I the sea, or a sea monster,
    that thou settest a guard over me?
13 When I say, 'My bed will comfort me,
    my couch will ease my complaint,'
14 then thou dost scare me with dreams
    and terrify me with visions,
15 so that I would choose strangling
    and death rather than my bones.
16 I loathe my life; I would not live for ever.
    Let me alone, for my days are a breath.
17 What is man, that thou dost make so much
    of him,
    and that thou dost set thy mind upon him,
18 dost visit him every morning,
    and test him every moment?
19 How long wilt thou not look away from
    me,
    nor let me alone till I swallow my
      spittle?
20 If I sin, what do I do to thee, thou watcher
    of men?
    Why hast thou made me thy mark?
    Why have I become a burden to thee?
21 Why dost thou not pardon my transgression
    and take away my iniquity?
    For now I shall lie in the earth;
    thou wilt seek me, but I shall not be."

---

science, however, is able to *discern* the right of his case. **7.1–6:** The life of mortal man in general is comparable to that of *a slave who longs for the shadow;* moreover, its transient nature is the source of new anguish. **7–21:** A prayer. It is at the moment of despair that man begins to pray. **7–9:** *Remember that my life is a breath.* Job appeals to divine compassion with the implied mockery that God will act when it will be too late. Job has heard of foreign speculations on the descent of men and gods to the underworld, only to deny any return from there. **12:** *Am I the sea, or a sea monster?* Again the hero alludes to the personification of evil (see 3.8 n.) in a context of sarcastic humor. Job compares himself in jest to the primeval forces which in Semitic polytheism threaten the security of the inhabited earth. His pain and his destitution are likened to the watch or *guard* which Marduk posted around the conquered dragon in the Babylonian poem on creation. **17–18:** A parody of Ps. 8. While the psalmist praised the creator who assigns to insignificant and mortal man a place of pre-eminence in nature, Job ironically prefers to receive minimal attention (see also Ps.144.3–4). **20:** Human sin cannot justify God's hostility to man. **21:** *Thou wilt seek me,* i.e. thou wilt grope in the darkness after me, *but I shall not be.* Job threatens the Almighty with his own non-being! He at once reaffirms his former trust in a loving God and sarcastically implies the frustration of that love.

40

And the LORD said to Job:

2 "Shall a faultfinder contend with the
Almighty?
He who argues with God, let him
answer it."
3 Then Job answered the LORD:
4 "Behold, I am of small account; what shall
I answer thee?
I lay my hand on my mouth.
5 I have spoken once, and I will not answer;
twice, but I will proceed no further."
6 Then the LORD answered Job out of the
whirlwind:
7 "Gird up your loins like a man;
I will question you, and you declare to
me.
8 Will you even put me in the wrong?
Will you condemn me that you may be
justified?
9 Have you an arm like God,
and can you thunder with a voice like
his?
10 "Deck yourself with majesty and dignity;
clothe yourself with glory and splendor.
11 Pour forth the overflowings of your anger,
and look on every one that is proud, and
abase him.
12 Look on every one that is proud, and bring
him low;
and tread down the wicked where they
stand.
13 Hide them all in the dust together;
bind their faces in the world below.*n*
14 Then will I also acknowledge to you,
that your own right hand can give you
victory.
15 "Behold, Be'hemoth,*o*
which I made as I made you;
he eats grass like an ox.
16 Behold, his strength in his loins,
and his power in the muscles of his
belly.

17 He makes his tail stiff like a cedar;
the sinews of his thighs are knit
together.
18 His bones are tubes of bronze,
his limbs like bars of iron.
19 "He is the first of the works*p* of God;
let him who made him bring near his
sword!
20 For the mountains yield food for him
where all the wild beasts play.
21 Under the lotus plants he lies,
in the covert of the reeds and in the
marsh.
22 For his shade the lotus trees cover him;
the willows of the brook surround him.
23 Behold, if the river is turbulent he is not
frightened;
he is confident though Jordan rushes
against his mouth.
24 Can one take him with hooks,*q*
or pierce his nose with a snare?

41

r "Can you draw out Levi'athan*s* with
a fishhook,
or press down his tongue with a cord?
2 Can you put a rope in his nose,
or pierce his jaw with a hook?
3 Will he make many supplications to you?
Will he speak to you soft words?
4 Will he make a covenant with you
to take him for your servant for ever?
5 Will you play with him as with a bird,
or will you put him on leash for your
maidens?
6 Will traders bargain over him?
Will they divide him up among the
merchants?
7 Can you fill his skin with harpoons,
or his head with fishing spears?
8 Lay hands on him;

n Heb *hidden place*   *o* Or *the hippopotamus*
p Heb *ways*   *q* Cn: Heb *in his eyes*
r Ch 40.25 in Heb   *s* Or *the crocodile*

40.1–5: Job refuses the challenge to fight. **1:** *Shall a faultfinder contend with the Almighty?* Read, with some ancient versions, "Will he who disputes with the Almighty yield?" The Deity never condemns Job for moral faults but clearly implies that he has been guilty of theological insolence.

40.6–41.34: Second discourse of the LORD. 40.6–9: The divine challenge of man is renewed, apparently because Job is only silenced but not convinced. **8:** *Will you condemn me that you may be justified?* The poet indicates here the

think of the battle; you will not do it
   again!

⁹ᵗ Behold, the hope of a man is disappointed;
   he is laid low even at the sight of him.

¹⁰ No one is so fierce that he dares to stir
   him up.
   Who then is he that can stand before
   me?

¹¹ Who has given to me,ᵘ that I should
   repay him?
   Whatever is under the whole heaven
   is mine.

¹² "I will not keep silence concerning his
   limbs,
   or his mighty strength, or his goodly
   frame.

¹³ Who can strip off his outer garment?
   Who can penetrate his double coat
   of mail?ᵛ

¹⁴ Who can open the doors of his face?
   Round about his teeth is terror.

¹⁵ His backʷ is made of rows of shields,
   shut up closely as with a seal.

¹⁶ One is so near to another
   that no air can come between them.

¹⁷ They are joined one to another;
   they clasp each other and cannot be
   separated.

¹⁸ His sneezings flash forth light,
   and his eyes are like the eyelids of the
   dawn.

¹⁹ Out of his mouth go flaming torches;
   sparks of fire leap forth.

²⁰ Out of his nostrils comes forth smoke,
   as from a boiling pot and burning
   rushes.

²¹ His breath kindles coals,
   and a flame comes forth from his
   mouth.

²² In his neck abides strength,
   and terror dances before him.

²³ The folds of his flesh cleave together,
   firmly cast upon him and immovable.

²⁴ His heart is hard as a stone,
   hard as the nether millstone.

²⁵ When he raises himself up the mightyˣ are
   afraid;
   at the crashing they are beside
   themselves.

²⁶ Though the sword reaches him, it does not
   avail;
   nor the spear, the dart, or the javelin.

²⁷ He counts iron as straw,
   and bronze as rotten wood.

²⁸ The arrow cannot make him flee;
   for him slingstones are turned to
   stubble.

²⁹ Clubs are counted as stubble;
   he laughs at the rattle of javelins.

³⁰ His underparts are like sharp potsherds;
   he spreads himself like a threshing
   sledge on the mire.

³¹ He makes the deep boil like a pot;
   he makes the sea like a pot of ointment.

³² Behind him he leaves a shining wake;
   one would think the deep to be hoary.

³³ Upon earth there is not his like,
   a creature without fear.

³⁴ He beholds everything that is high;
   he is king over all the sons of pride."

42 Then Job answered the LORD:
² "I know that thou canst do all
   things,
   and that no purpose of thine can be
   thwarted.

---

t Ch 41.1 in Heb   *u* The meaning of the Hebrew is
uncertain   *v* Gk: Heb *bridle*   *w* Cn Compare Gk Vg:
Heb *pride*   *x* Or *gods*

---

central theme of the work. Self-righteousness leads man to condemn God. **15–24:** This portrait of *Behemoth* (like that of Leviathan, 41.1–34) may have received literary amplification, but it plays an integral part of the poet's purpose: the creating God is in control of all forces of evil, despite appearances to the contrary. **15:** The primeval monster (compare v. 19) is not a mere hippopotamus, but a mythical symbol. *Which I made as I made you*, the mystery of evil is not dissolved, but the divine sway embraces all. **41.1–34:** *Leviathan*, not an ordinary crocodile, but the sea-monster (3.8; 26.13; Ps.74.14), which was associated with chaos. Like the psalmist (Ps.104.26), the poet shows that it is only a plaything in the eyes of God.

42.1–6: The answer of Job. Having contemplated divine activity, the sufferer now knows the purposefulness of God (v. 2). **3a:** A quotation from 38.2; Job acknowledges his finitude. **4:** An echo of the divine questioning (40.7),

3 'Who is this that hides counsel without
knowledge?'
Therefore I have uttered what I did not
understand,
things too wonderful for me, which I
did not know.
4 'Hear, and I will speak;
I will question you, and you declare
to me.'
5 I had heard of thee by the hearing of the
ear,
but now my eye sees thee;
6 therefore I despise myself,
and repent in dust and ashes."

7 After the LORD had spoken these words
to Job, the LORD said to Eli'phaz the Te'manite: "My wrath is kindled against you and
against your two friends; for you have not
spoken of me what is right, as my servant Job
has. 8 Now therefore take seven bulls and
seven rams, and go to my servant Job, and
offer up for yourselves a burnt offering; and
my servant Job shall pray for you, for I will
accept his prayer not to deal with you according to your folly; for you have not spoken of
me what is right, as my servant Job has." 9 So
Eli'phaz the Te'manite and Bildad the Shuhite
and Zophar the Na'amathite went and did
what the LORD had told them; and the LORD
accepted Job's prayer.

10 And the LORD restored the fortunes of
Job, when he had prayed for his friends; and
the LORD gave Job twice as much as he had
before. 11 Then came to him all his brothers
and sisters and all who had known him before,
and ate bread with him in his house; and they
showed him sympathy and comforted him for
all the evil that the LORD had brought upon
him; and each of them gave him a piece of
money*y* and a ring of gold. 12 And the LORD
blessed the latter days of Job more than his
beginning; and he had fourteen thousand
sheep, six thousand camels, a thousand yoke
of oxen, and a thousand she-asses. 13 He had
also seven sons and three daughters. 14 And he
called the name of the first Jemi'mah; and the
name of the second Kezi'ah; and the name of
the third Ker'en-hap'puch. 15 And in all the
land there were no women so fair as Job's
daughters; and their father gave them inheritance among their brothers. 16 And after this
Job lived a hundred and forty years, and saw
his sons, and his sons' sons, four generations.
17 And Job died, an old man, and full of days.

y Heb *qesitah*

preparing for the confession of the following lines. **5:** The contrast between belief through tradition and faith through
prophetic vision. God has not justified Job, but he has come to him personally; the upholder of the universe cares for a
lonely man so deeply that he offers him the fulness of his communion. Job is not vindicated but he has obtained far
more than a recognition of his innocence: he has been accepted by the ever-present master-worker, and intimacy with
the Creator makes vindication superfluous. The philosophical problem is not solved, but it is transfigured by the theological reality of the divine-human rapport. **6:** *I despise myself;* the Hebrew verb is obscure, but is probably related to
a root meaning "to melt into nothing." *I repent,* the Hebrew verb used here is not the usual one for repentance of sins,
but a word expressing the utmost grief and self-depreciation. Such an experience follows rather than precedes the
vision of God.

42.7–17: The epilogue. The style, language, and situation of the folktale (1.1–2.13) reappear abruptly (see Introduction). **8:** *Burnt offering,* sacrificial ritual, absent from the poem, is a characteristic of the archaic story (1.5).
10: Job's restoration follows not his repentance but his intercession on behalf of his friends (v. 8). Intercessory power
is a feature which is in accord with the figure of the ancient legend (Ezek.14.14,20). **10–17:** Job receives a double
restitution, although no healing of his disease is explicitly mentioned. **11:** *A piece of money,* a qesitah (see note *y* and
Gen.33.19; Jos.24.32). **14:** The names of Job's new daughters have a flavor of folklore: *Jemimah,* Dove; *Keziah,*
Cinnamon; *Keren-happuch,* Horn of eye-shadow. **15b:** An exceptional procedure (contrast Num.27.1–11). **16–17:** A
patriarchal theme (Gen.25.8; 35.29; 50.23; see also Ps.128.6; Pr.17.6; 1 Chr.29.28).

The Book of Isaiah

THE VISION OF ISAIAH THE SON OF AMOZ,
which he saw concerning Judah and
Jerusalem in the days of Uzzi′ah, Jotham,
Ahaz, and Hezeki′ah, kings of Judah.
2 Hear, O heavens, and give ear, O earth;
for the LORD has spoken:
"Sons have I reared and brought up,
but they have rebelled against me.
3 The ox knows its owner,
and the ass its master's crib;
but Israel does not know,
my people does not understand."

4 Ah, sinful nation,
a people laden with iniquity,
offspring of evildoers,
sons who deal corruptly!
They have forsaken the LORD,
they have despised the Holy One of
Israel,
they are utterly estranged.

5 Why will you still be smitten,
that you continue to rebel?
The whole head is sick,
and the whole heart faint.
4 From the sole of the foot even to the
head,
there is no soundness in it,
but bruises and sores
and bleeding wounds;
they are not pressed out, or bound up,
or softened with oil.

7 Your country lies desolate,
your cities are burned with fire;
in your very presence
aliens devour your land;
it is desolate, as overthrown by aliens.
8 And the daughter of Zion is left
like a booth in a vineyard,
like a lodge in a cucumber field,
like a besieged city.

9 If the LORD of hosts
had not left us a few survivors,
we should have been like Sodom,
and become like Gomor′rah.

1.1–5.24: Oracles against rebellious Judah. 1.1: Superscription. *Vision of Isaiah* (6.1–13; Jer. ch. 1; Ezek. chs. 1–3) identifies Is. chs. 1–39 as God's message to Judah through the prophet. The name *Isaiah* means "The LORD [Yahweh] gives salvation." The latter part of the verse beginning with "in the days of" may be an editorial expansion.
    1.2–31: First series of oracles, serving as a kind of prologue. **2–3:** Poetic exhortation reminiscent of God's address to the heavenly host in 40.1–2. *Sons* compare Jer.3.19–22. The Biblical word *know* implies a profound, identifying comprehension of the right relationship with God; it is a recurring prophetic theme (Jer.1.5; Hos.2.20; 4.1,6; 5.4). **4–9:** An appeal to a people heedless of the significance of Judah's devastation by Tiglath-Pileser III (734–733 B.C.; 7.1–2) or Sennacherib (701 B.C.; 36.1) and Jerusalem's isolation (*daughter of Zion,* see Jer.4.29–31 n.). **4:** Note the poetic parallelism: *nation, people; offspring, sons.* The expression, *Holy One of Israel* (5.19,24; 10.20; 12.6; 17.7; 29.19; 30.11,12,15; 37.23), emphasizes God's unapproachable separateness, which he has bridged by his gracious

---

10 Hear the word of the Lord,
　　you rulers of Sodom!
　Give ear to the teaching of our God,
　　you people of Gomor'rah!
11 "What to me is the multitude of your
　　　sacrifices?
　　says the Lord;
　I have had enough of burnt offerings of
　　　rams
　　and the fat of fed beasts;
　I do not delight in the blood of bulls,
　　or of lambs, or of he-goats.

12 "When you come to appear before me,
　　who requires of you
　　this trampling of my courts?
13 Bring no more vain offerings;
　　incense is an abomination to me.
　New moon and sabbath and the calling of
　　　assemblies —
　　I cannot endure iniquity and solemn
　　　assembly.
14 Your new moons and your appointed
　　　feasts
　　my soul hates;
　they have become a burden to me,
　　I am weary of bearing them.
15 When you spread forth your hands,
　　I will hide my eyes from you;
　even though you make many prayers,
　　I will not listen;
　your hands are full of blood.
16 Wash yourselves; make yourselves clean;
　　remove the evil of your doings
　　from before my eyes;
　cease to do evil,
17 　learn to do good;
　seek justice,
　　correct oppression;

　defend the fatherless,
　　plead for the widow.

18 "Come now, let us reason together,
　　says the Lord:
　though your sins are like scarlet,
　　they shall be as white as snow;
　though they are red like crimson,
　　they shall become like wool.
19 If you are willing and obedient,
　　you shall eat the good of the land;
20 But if you refuse and rebel,
　　you shall be devoured by the sword;
　for the mouth of the Lord has spoken."

21 How the faithful city
　　has become a harlot,
　　she that was full of justice!
　Righteousness lodged in her,
　　but now murderers.
22 Your silver has become dross,
　　your wine mixed with water,
23 Your princes are rebels
　　and companions of thieves.
　Every one loves a bribe
　　and runs after gifts.
　They do not defend the fatherless,
　　and the widow's cause does not come to
　　　them.

24 Therefore the Lord says,
　　the Lord of hosts,
　　the Mighty One of Israel:
　"Ah, I will vent my wrath on my enemies,
　　and avenge myself on my foes.
25 I will turn my hand against you
　　and will smelt away your dross as with
　　　lye
　　and remove all your alloy.

---

election of Israel as his people (Hos.8.1, Jer.3.20). **10–20:** God's pronouncement concerning Judah's religious superficiality (Am.5.21–24; Jer.6.20). Judah may repent and return (Jer.7.5–7); the alternative is destruction (Jer.7.22–34). **10:** *Teaching,* the Hebrew word is "torah," which is frequently translated "law." On *Sodom* and *Gomorrah* see Gen.18.16–19.28; Jer.23.14; Ezek.16.46–58. **14:** *My soul,* a Hebrew idiom which in this context means "I" (compare Lev.26.11,30). *Burden,* see Jer.23.33–40. **16–17:** Compare Ex.22.21,22; Am.5.6–7. **18:** *Reason,* as one argues a case before a judge (Job 23.7). *White* for holiness (Rev.19.8); *scarlet* for wickedness (garments of Babylon, Rev.17.4). **21–23:** Lamentation over Jerusalem. **21:** *Harlot,* Jer.3.6–10; Ezek. chs. 16 and 23. *Justice* and *righteousness* express Isaiah's ideal for the people of God. **24:** *Mighty one of Israel* recalls Israel's patriarchal traditions (49.26; Gen.49.24; Ps.132.2,5). **25:** *As with lye,* or "thoroughly." **26:** Isaiah frequently uses symbolic names (7.14; 8.1; 9.6; see also

26 And I will restore your judges as at the
first,
and your counselors as at the beginning.
Afterward you shall be called the city of
righteousness,
the faithful city."

27 Zion shall be redeemed by justice,
and those in her who repent, by
righteousness.
28 But rebels and sinners shall be destroyed
together,
and those who forsake the LORD shall
be consumed.
29 For you shall be ashamed of the oaks
in which you delighted;
and you shall blush for the gardens
which you have chosen.
30 For you shall be like an oak
whose leaf withers,
and like a garden without water.
31 And the strong shall become tow,
and his work a spark,
and both of them shall burn together,
with none to quench them.

2 The word which Isaiah the son of Amoz
saw concerning Judah and Jerusalem.
2 It shall come to pass in the latter days
that the mountain of the house of the LORD
shall be established as the highest of the
mountains,
and shall be raised above the hills;
and all the nations shall flow to it,
3 and many peoples shall come, and say:
"Come, let us go up to the mountain of the
LORD,
to the house of the God of Jacob;

that he may teach us his ways
and that we may walk in his paths."
For out of Zion shall go forth the law,
and the word of the LORD from
Jerusalem.
4 He shall judge between the nations,
and shall decide for many peoples;
and they shall beat their swords into
plowshares,
and their spears into pruning hooks;
nation shall not lift up sword against
nation,
neither shall they learn war any more.

5 O house of Jacob,
come, let us walk
in the light of the LORD.

6 For thou hast rejected thy people,
the house of Jacob,
because they are full of diviners[a] from the
east
and of soothsayers like the Philistines,
and they strike hands with foreigners.
7 Their land is filled with silver and gold,
and there is no end to their treasures;
their land is filled with horses,
and there is no end to their chariots.
8 Their land is filled with idols;
they bow down to the work of their
hands,
to what their own fingers have made.
9 So man is humbled,
and men are brought low —
forgive them not!
10 Enter into the rock,
and hide in the dust

a Cn: Heb lacks *of diviners*

Jer.33.16; Ezek.48.35 n.). There will be a new creation; compare Am.9.11; Rev.3.12; 21.1–4. **29–31:** An allegory on Judah's faithlessness based on one of Isaiah's rare references to pagan religious practices; compare 57.5; Jer.2.27 Ezek.6.1–14.

    2.1: Second superscription, perhaps for chs. 2–4. *Word* connotes "message" (Jer.7.1; 11.1). **2–5: The new age,** involving the elevation of Zion, the acknowledgment of the nations, and the age of peace. This oracle (vv. 2–4) is also found in Mic.4.1–4. **3:** *Law,* i.e. "teaching" (1.10), which is more suitable to the thought of the passage. **4:** The age of peace will follow the judgment of the LORD (compare 5.25; 30.27–28). **5:** Compare v. 3, paraphrased in Mic.4.5.

    2.4–22: The day of the LORD. This is probably to be taken as three stanzas, vv. 6–11,12–17,18–22. The first two have a similar conclusion (compare vv. 11,17), and it is suggested that the third ended similarly, for the present v. 22 is missing in the Septuagint and is grammatically corrupt. **6–11:** Judgment on idolatry. **6:** *Diviners* were forbidden in

from before the terror of the LORD,
and from the glory of his majesty.
[11] The haughty looks of man shall be brought
low,
and the pride of men shall be humbled;
and the LORD alone will be exalted
in that day.

[12] For the LORD of hosts has a day
against all that is proud and lofty,
against all that is lifted up and high;[b]
[13] against all the cedars of Lebanon,
lofty and lifted up;
and against all the oaks of Bashan;
[14] against all the high mountains,
and against all the lofty hills;
[15] against every high tower,
and against every fortified wall;
[16] against all the ships of Tarshish,
and against all the beautiful craft.
[17] And the haughtiness of man shall be
humbled,
and the pride of men shall be brought low;
and the LORD alone will be exalted in
that day.
[18] And the idols shall utterly pass away.
[19] And men shall enter the caves of the rocks
and the holes of the ground,
from before the terror of the LORD,
and from the glory of his majesty,
when he rises to terrify the earth.

[20] In that day men will cast forth
their idols of silver and their idols of
gold,
which they made for themselves to
worship,
to the moles and the bats,

[21] to enter the caverns of the rocks
and the clefts of the cliffs,
from before the terror of the LORD,
and from the glory of his majesty,
when he rises to terrify the earth.
[22] Turn away from man
in whose nostrils is breath,
for of what account is he?

3 For, behold, the Lord, the LORD of hosts,
is taking away from Jerusalem and from
Judah
stay and staff,
the whole stay of bread,
and the whole stay of water;
[2] the mighty man and the soldier,
the judge and the prophet,
the diviner and the elder,
[3] the captain of fifty
and the man of rank,
the counselor and the skilful magician
and the expert in charms.
[4] And I will make boys their princes,
and babes shall rule over them.
[5] And the people will oppress one another,
every man his fellow
and every man his neighbor;
the youth will be insolent to the elder,
and the base fellow to the honorable.

[6] When a man takes hold of his brother
in the house of his father, saying:
"You have a mantle;
you shall be our leader,
and this heap of ruins
shall be under your rule";
[7] in that day he will speak out, saying:

b Cn Compare Gk: Heb low

Israel (Ex.22.18; Lev.20.27; Dt.18.10–11; compare 8.19; 1 Sam.28.8–25; Ezek.13.9). The situation fits Uzziah's reign 2.Kg.15.1–7; 2 Chr. ch. 26). **7:** Judah's prosperity (Dt.17.16–17; 1 Kg.10.14–29). **11:** *In that day,* the day of the LORD, in which God judges his enemies and manifests his glory is a recurring prophetic theme (13.6; Am.5.18–20; Jer.17.16–18; Ezek.30.3; J.1.15). **12–17:** pride and punishment. **13:** *Lebanon, Bashan,* Ezek.27.5–6; Jer.22.20. **16:** *Ships of Tarshish,* the phrase may mean "refinery fleet" (see 1 Kg.10.22 n.; Jer.10.9 n.). **18–22:** Judgment on idolatry. **19:** The innumerable *caves* in Palestine's limestone hills are age-old places of refuge.

3.1–15: Anarchy in Jerusalem. 1–7: Without key men, society breaks down. **1:** *Stay and staff,* everything which supports life, including food and drink (economic resources), and perhaps also the functionaries in vv. 2–3. **2–3:** Offices deemed necessary for the continuity and stability of the state. **4:** The inexperienced and naïve will rule. **5–6:** Civil unrest will become open violence. **8–12:** A commentary on vv. 1–7. Judah's brazen sinfulness and rejection of

"I will not be a healer;
in my house there is neither bread nor
mantle;
you shall not make me
leader of the people."
8 For Jerusalem has stumbled,
and Judah has fallen;
because their speech and their deeds are
against the LORD,
defying his glorious presence.

9 Their partiality witnesses against them;
they proclaim their sin like Sodom,
they do not hide it.
Woe to them!
For they have brought evil upon
themselves.
10 Tell the righteous that it shall be well with
them,
for they shall eat the fruit of their deeds.
11 Woe to the wicked! It shall be ill with him,
for what his hands have done shall be
done to him.
12 My people — children are their oppressors,
and women rule over them.
O my people, your leaders mislead you,
and confuse the course of your paths.

13 The LORD has taken his place to contend,
he stands to judge his people.*d*
14 The LORD enters into judgment
with the elders and princes of his people:
"It is you who have devoured the vineyard,
the spoil of the poor is in your houses.
15 What do you mean by crushing my people,
by grinding the face of the poor?" says
the Lord GOD of hosts.

16 The LORD said:
Because the daughters of Zion are haughty
and walk with outstretched necks,

glancing wantonly with their eyes,
mincing along as they go,
tinkling with their feet;
17 the Lord will smite with a scab
the heads of the daughters of Zion,
and the LORD will lay bare their secret
parts.

18 In that day the Lord will take away the
finery of the anklets, the headbands, and the
crescents; 19 the pendants, the bracelets, and
the scarfs; 20 the headdresses, the armlets, the
sashes, the perfume boxes, and the amulets;
21 the signet rings and nose rings; 22 the festal
robes, the mantles, the cloaks, and the hand-
bags; 23 the garments of gauze, the linen garments, the turbans, and the veils.
24 Instead of perfume there will be
rottenness;
and instead of a girdle, a rope;
and instead of well-set hair, baldness;
and instead of a rich robe, a girding of
sackcloth;
instead of beauty, shame.*e*
25 Your men shall fall by the sword
and your mighty men in battle.
26 And her gates shall lament and mourn;
ravaged, she shall sit upon the ground.

4 And seven women shall take hold of one
man in that day, saying, "We will eat our
own bread and wear our own clothes, only let
us be called by your name; take away our
reproach."
2 In that day the branch of the LORD shall
be beautiful and glorious, and the fruit of the
land shall be the pride and glory of the survivors of Israel. 3 And he who is left in Zion
and remains in Jerusalem will be called holy,
every one who has been recorded for life in

d Gk Syr: Heb *judge peoples*
e One ancient Ms: Heb lacks *shame*

God's leadership has ruined the people. **13–15:** God will judge the corrupt judges. *Elders,* primary administrators of justice (Ex.19.7; Jos.20.4; Dt.21.19–21). *Princes,* royal appointees (1 Kg.4.2; 2 Kg.10.1; Jer.34.19). *Vineyard,* see 5.1–7.
    3.16–4.1: The humiliation of Jerusalem's women (Am.4.1–3). **18–24:** Detailed expansion of v. 17. **3.25–**
4.1: War's decimation of the male population forces the women to resort to desperate measures to preserve themselves
and their self-respect. *Our reproach* summarizes 3.16–4.1.
    4.2–6: Jerusalem's restoration. 2: *Branch,* the righteous remnant (3.10; compare the Messiah to a Branch in
11.1; Jer.23.5); *fruit of the land,* a "return to paradise." **3:** *Recorded for life,* compare Ex.32.32; Mal.3.16; Dan.12.1;

Jerusalem, [4] when the Lord shall have washed away the filth of the daughters of Zion and cleansed the bloodstains of Jerusalem from its midst by a spirit of judgment and by a spirit of burning. [5] Then the LORD will create over the whole site of Mount Zion and over her assemblies a cloud by day, and smoke and the shining of a flaming fire by night; for over all the glory there will be a canopy and a pavilion. [6] It will be for a shade by day from the heat, and for a refuge and a shelter from the storm and rain.

5 Let me sing for my beloved
a love song concerning his vineyard:
My beloved had a vineyard
on a very fertile hill.
[2] He digged it and cleared it of stones,
and planted it with choice vines;
he built a watchtower in the midst of it,
and hewed out a wine vat in it;
and he looked for it to yield grapes,
but it yielded wild grapes.

[3] And now, O inhabitants of Jerusalem
and men of Judah,
judge, I pray you, between me
and my vineyard.
[4] What more was there to do for my vineyard,
that I have not done in it?
When I looked for it to yield grapes,
why did it yield wild grapes?

[5] And now I will tell you
what I will do to my vineyard.

I will remove its hedge,
and it shall be devoured;
I will break down its wall,
and it shall be trampled down.
[6] I will make it a waste;
it shall not be pruned or hoed,
and briers and thorns shall grow up;
I will also command the clouds
that they rain no rain upon it.

[7] For the vineyard of the LORD of hosts
is the house of Israel,
and the men of Judah
are his pleasant planting;
and he looked for justice,
but behold, bloodshed;
for righteousness,
but behold, a cry!

[8] Woe to those who join house to house,
who add field to field,
until there is no more room,
and you are made to dwell alone
in the midst of the land.
[9] The LORD of hosts has sworn in my hearing:
"Surely many houses shall be desolate,
large and beautiful houses, without
inhabitant.
[10] For ten acres of vineyard shall yield but
one bath,
and a homer of seed shall yield but an
ephah."

[11] Woe to those who rise early in the
morning,

Rev.20.12,15. **5:** *Smoke and flaming fire,* the signs of God's presence among his people at the Exodus (Ex.13.21–22; 40.34–38).

5.1–7: Song of the vineyard (Hos.10.1; Jer.2.21; Ezek.19.10–14), an allegory. This unique didactic poem may have been composed for a celebration of the feast of tabernacles during Jotham's reign, the prophet imitating a vintage festival song. **1a:** Introduction to the poem. **2:** *Choice vines,* the Hebrew word ("soreq") means either red grapes, or grapes native to the valley of Sorek, west of Jerusalem. **3–4:** Judah's only possible answer would be judgment against the vineyard. Judah is asked to pass judgment on herself, much as Nathan through a parable had David pass judgment on himself (2 Sam.12.1–12). **7:** *Justice,* the faithful application of God's will to daily living. *Righteousness,* the living, dynamic relationship between man and God wherein man is spiritually and morally acceptable to God (1.27; 9.7; 16.5; 28.17). Righteousness and justice are naturally coupled (1.21) and grow out of the covenant relationship, the existence of which is assumed (Ex. chs. 19–20). *A cry,* from the oppressed.

5.8–23: Six reproaches (vv. 8,11,18,20,21,22; perhaps 10.1–4 is a seventh). Compare Am.5.7,18; 6.1; Jer.22.13. **8–10:** Against covetousness (Mic.2.1–5,8–9; Ex.20.17). *Bath, ephah,* 6.07 gallons; *homer,* 6.5 bushels (see Ezek. 45.11 n.). **11–12:** Against carousing (Am.6.4–6). **13–17:** *Knowledge,* 1.3. The severity of Judah's punishment will

that they may run after strong drink,
who tarry late into the evening
till wine inflames them!

¹² They have lyre and harp,
timbrel and flute and wine at their
feasts;
but they do not regard the deeds of the
Lord,
or see the work of his hands.

¹³ Therefore my people go into exile
for want of knowledge;
their honored men are dying of hunger,
and their multitude is parched with
thirst.

¹⁴ Therefore Sheol has enlarged its appetite
and opened its mouth beyond measure,
and the nobility of Jerusalem*ᶠ* and her multitude go down,
her throng and he who exults in her.

¹⁵ Man is bowed down, and men are brought
low,
and the eyes of the haughty are
humbled.

¹⁶ But the Lord of hosts is exalted in justice,
and the Holy God shows himself holy in
righteousness.

¹⁷ Then shall the lambs graze as in their pas-
ture,
fatlings and kids*ᵍ* shall feed among the
ruins.

¹⁸ Woe to those who draw iniquity with cords
of falsehood,
who draw sin as with cart ropes,

¹⁹ who say: "Let him make haste,
let him speed his work
that we may see it;
let the purpose of the Holy One of Israel
draw near,
and let it come, that we may know it!"

²⁰ Woe to those who call evil good and good
evil,

who put darkness for light and light for
darkness,
who put bitter for sweet and sweet for
bitter!

²¹ Woe to those who are wise in their own eyes,
and shrewd in their own sight!

²² Woe to those who are heroes at drinking
wine,
and valiant men in mixing strong drink,

²³ who acquit the guilty for a bribe,
and deprive the innocent of his right!

²⁴ Therefore, as the tongue of fire devours the
stubble,
and as dry grass sinks down in the
flame,
so their root will be as rottenness,
and their blossom go up like dust;
for they have rejected the law of the Lord
of hosts,
and have despised the word of the Holy
One of Israel.

²⁵ Therefore the anger of the Lord was
kindled against his people,
and he stretched out his hand against
them and smote them,
and the mountains quaked;
and their corpses were as refuse
in the midst of the streets.
For all this his anger is not turned away
and his hand is stretched out still.

²⁶ He will raise a signal for a nation afar off,
and whistle for it from the ends of the
earth;
and lo, swiftly, speedily it comes!

²⁷ None is weary, none stumbles,
none slumbers or sleeps,
not a waistcloth is loose,
not a sandal-thong broken;

²⁸ their arrows are sharp,
all their bows bent,

f Heb *her nobility*   *g* Cn Compare Gk: Heb *aliens*

---

require the enlargement of *Sheol* (the underworld, 14.9–18). **16:** In all he does, God is just and right. **18–19:** Against mocking God. **20:** Against moral depravity (32.5; Pr.17.15). **21:** Against conceit. **22–23:** Against bravado and bribery. **24b–30:** These verses should probably follow 10.4 (see 9.8–10.4 n.). *Law,* here also in the sense of "teaching" (see 1.10 n.). The Assyrians (*a nation afar off;* Jer.5.15, referring to Babylon) will be the executors of God's judgment.

their horses' hoofs seem like flint,
  and their wheels like the whirlwind.
29 Their roaring is like a lion,
  like young lions they roar;
they growl and seize their prey,
  they carry it off, and none can rescue.
30 They will growl over it on that day,
  like the roaring of the sea.
And if one look to the land,
  behold, darkness and distress;
and the light is darkened by its clouds.

6 In the year that King Uzzi'ah died I saw the Lord sitting upon a throne, high and lifted up; and his train filled the temple. ² Above him stood the seraphim; each had six wings: with two he covered his face, and with two he covered his feet, and with two he flew. ³ And one called to another and said:

"Holy, holy, holy is the LORD of hosts;
  the whole earth is full of his glory."

4 And the foundations of the thresholds shook at the voice of him who called, and the house was filled with smoke. ⁵ And I said: "Woe is me! For I am lost; for I am a man of unclean lips, and I dwell in the midst of a people of unclean lips; for my eyes have seen the King, the LORD of hosts!"

6 Then flew one of the seraphim to me, having in his hand a burning coal which he had taken with tongs from the altar. ⁷ And he touched my mouth, and said: "Behold, this has touched your lips; your guilt is taken away, and your sin forgiven." ⁸ And I heard the voice of the Lord saying, "Whom shall I send, and who will go for us?" then I said, "Here am I! Send me." ⁹ And he said, "Go, and say to this people:

'Hear and hear, but do not understand;
  see and see, but do not perceive.'
10 Make the heart of this people fat,
  and their ears heavy,
  and shut their eyes;
lest they see with their eyes,
  and hear with their ears,
and understand with their hearts,
  and turn and be healed."
¹¹ Then I said, "How long, O Lord?"
And he said:
"Until cities lie waste
  without inhabitant,
and houses without men,
  and the land is utterly desolate,
12 and the LORD removes men far away,
  and the forsaken places are many in the
    midst of the land.
13 And though a tenth remain in it,
  it will be burned again,
like a terebinth or an oak,
  whose stump remains standing
  when it is felled."
The holy seed is its stump.

7 In the days of Ahaz the son of Jotham, son of Uzzi'ah, king of Judah, Rezin the king of Syria and Pekah the son of Remali'ah the king of Israel came up to Jerusalem to wage war against it, but they could not conquer it. ² When the house of David was told, "Syria is in league with E'phraim," his heart and the heart of his people shook as the trees of the forest shake before the wind.

3 And the LORD said to Isaiah, "Go forth to meet Ahaz, you and She'ar-jash'ub[h] your son, at the end of the conduit of the upper pool

h That is A remnant shall return

6.1–13: The call of Isaiah. God's appearance is described in the setting of the Jerusalem temple (compare the description of the enthroned deity in 1 Kg.22.19–23; Ezek.1.4–2.1). 1: Year, 742 B.C. Throne, ark of the covenant. 2: Seraphim, possibly griffin-like creatures; compare the cherubim, also associated with the glory of the Lord (Ezek. ch. 1). 3: Thrice-holy for emphasis (Jer.7.4). 5: Before the holy God, sinful man cannot stand (Ex.33.18–20). 6–8: Cleansed by God's forgiving act, Isaiah may now speak for God. 9–12: Compare Jer.1.10,13–19. Verses 9b–10 are quoted in Mt.13.10–15; compare Mk.4.12; Lk.8.10; Jn.12.39–41; Acts 28.26–27. 13: The last part of the verse is obscure and textually corrupt and perhaps should be restored to read, ". . . . like the terebinth [of the goddess] and the oak of Asherah, cast out with the pillar of the high places," that is, like the destroyed furnishings of a pagan high place.
7.1–8.15: Isaiah and the Syro-Ephraimite War (734–733 B.C.). For the historical background see 2 Kg.16.1–20. 1–9: Sign of Shear-jashub. 2: The continuation of the Davidic monarchy was threatened (see v. 6). 3: Shear-jashub, "A remnant shall return"; assuming the worst eventuality, God's promise to David (2 Sam.7.8–16) will be preserved in

on the highway to the Fuller's Field, [4] and say to him, 'Take heed, be quiet, do not fear, and do not let your heart be faint because of these two smoldering stumps of firebrands, at the fierce anger of Rezin and Syria and the son of Remali'ah. [5] Because Syria, with E'phraim and the son of Remali'ah, has devised evil against you, saying, [6] "Let us go up against Judah and terrify it; and let us conquer it for ourselves, and set up the son of Ta'be-el as king in the midst of it," [7] thus says the Lord GOD:

It shall not stand,
  and it shall not come to pass.
[8] For the head of Syria is Damascus,
  and the head of Damascus is Rezin.
(Within sixty-five years E'phraim will be broken to pieces so that it will no longer be a people.)
[9] And the head of E'phraim is Sama'ria,
  and the head of Sama'ria is the son of
    Remali'ah.
If you will not believe,
  surely you shall not be established.'

10 Again the LORD spoke to Ahaz, [11] "Ask a sign of the LORD your God; let it be deep as Sheol or high as heaven." [12] But Ahaz said, "I will not ask, and I will not put the LORD to the test." [13] And he said, "Hear then, O house of David! Is it too little for you to weary men, that you weary my God also? [14] Therefore the Lord himself will give you a sign. Behold, a young woman[i] shall conceive and bear[j] a son, and shall call his name Imman'u-el.[k] [15] He shall eat curds and honey when he knows how to refuse the evil and choose the good. [16] For before the child knows how to refuse the evil and choose the good, the land before whose two kings you are in dread will be deserted. [17] The LORD will bring upon you and upon your people and upon your father's house such days as have not come since the day that E'phraim departed from Judah — the king of Assyria."

18 In that day the LORD will whistle for the fly which is at the sources of the streams of Egypt, and for the bee which is in the land of Assyria. [19] And they will all come and settle in the steep ravines, and in the clefts of the rocks, and on all the thornbushes, and on all the pastures.

20 In that day the Lord will shave with a razor which is hired beyond the River — with the king of Assyria — the head and the hair of the feet, and it will sweep away the beard also.

21 In that day a man will keep alive a young cow and two sheep; [22] and because of the abundance of milk which they give, he will eat curds; for every one that is left in the land will eat curds and honey.

23 In that day every place where there used to be a thousand vines, worth a thousand shekels of silver, will become briers and thorns. [24] With bow and arrows men will come there, for all the land will be briers and thorns; [25] and as for all the hills which used to be hoed with a hoe, you will not come there for fear of briers and thorns; but they will become a place where cattle are let loose and where sheep tread.

8 Then the LORD said to me, "Take a large tablet and write upon it in common characters, 'Belonging to Ma'her-shal'al-hash-baz.'"[l] [2] And I got reliable witnesses, Uri'ah the priest and Zechari'ah the son of Jeberechi'ah, to attest for me. [3] And I went to the prophet-

---

i Or *virgin*   *j* Or *is with child and shall bear*   *k* That is *God is with us*

---

the remnant (10.20–23). *Upper pool,* reservoir south of the Pool of Siloam. **5:** *Son of Tabeel,* perhaps a prince of Judah whose mother came from Tabeel, a region of northern Transjordan. **8–9a:** The text and meaning are unclear.

7.10–17: Sign of Immanuel. 13: This expresses Isaiah's impatience. **14:** The sign is *Immanuel,* "God with us"; a second (compare vv. 3–9) assurance to the frightened, wavering Ahaz. *Young woman,* Hebrew '*almah,* feminine of '*elem,* young man (1 Sam.17.56; 20.22); the word appears in Gen.24.43; Ex.2.8; Ps.68.25, and elsewhere, where it is translated "young woman," "girl," "maiden." **15:** *Curds, honey,* simple foods suggesting difficult times; *good and evil,* age of moral discrimination. **18–25:** Four threats amplifying v. 17. **20:** Feet, see Ex.4.25 n.

8.1–4: The sign of Maher-shalal-hash-baz, "The spoil speeds, the prey hastes"; Isaiah's third assurance to Ahaz. **1:** *Tablet,* of wood. **2:** *Uriah,* 2 Kg.16.10–16. *Zechariah,* perhaps Ahaz's father-in-law (2 Kg.18.2). **3:** *Prophetess,* Isa-

ess, and she conceived and bore a son. Then the LORD said to me, "Call his name Ma'her-shal'al-hash-baz; [4] for before the child knows how to cry 'My father' or 'My mother,' the wealth of Damascus and the spoil of Sama'ria will be carried away before the king of Assyria."

5 The LORD spoke to me again: [6] "Because this people have refused the waters of Shilo'ah that flow gently, and melt in fear before[m] Rezin and the son of Remali'ah; [7] therefore, behold, the Lord is bringing up against them the waters of the River, mighty and many, the king of Assyria and all his glory; and it will rise over all his channels and go over all its banks; [8] and it will sweep on into Judah, it will overflow and pass on, reaching even to the neck; and its outspread wings will fill the breadth of your land, O Imman'u-el."

[9]   Be broken, you peoples, and be dismayed;
        give ear, all you far countries;
    gird yourselves and be dismayed;
        gird yourselves and be dismayed.
[10] Take counsel together, but it will come to
        nought;
        speak a word, but it will not stand,
        for God is with us.[x]

11 For the LORD spoke thus to me with his strong hand upon me, and warned me not to walk in the way of this people, saying: [12] "Do not call conspiracy all that this people call conspiracy, and do not fear what they fear, nor be in dread. [13] But the LORD of hosts, him you shall regard as holy; let him be your fear, and let him be your dread. [14] And he will become a sanctuary, and a stone of offense, and a rock of stumbling to both houses of Israel, a trap and a snare to the inhabitants of Jerusalem. [15] And many shall stumble thereon; they shall fall and be broken; they shall be snared and taken."

16 Bind up the testimony, seal the teaching among my disciples. [17] I will wait for the LORD, who is hiding his face from the house of Jacob, and I will hope in him. [18] Behold, I and the children whom the LORD has given me are signs and portents in Israel from the LORD of hosts, who dwells on Mount Zion. [19] And when they say to you, "Consult the mediums and the wizards who chirp and mutter," should not a people consult their God? Should they consult the dead on behalf of the living? [20] To the teaching and to the testimony! Surely for this word which they speak there is no dawn. [21] They will pass through the land,[n] greatly distressed and hungry; and when they are hungry, they will be enraged and will curse[o] their king and their God, and turn their faces upward; [22] and they will look to the earth, but behold, distress and darkness, the gloom of anguish; and they will be thrust into thick darkness.

9[p] But there will be no gloom for her that was in anguish. In the former time he brought into contempt the land of Zeb'ulun and the land of Naph'tali, but in the latter time he will make glorious the way of the sea, the land beyond the Jordan, Galilee of the nations.
[2q] The people who walked in darkness
        have seen a great light;

l That is *The spoil speeds, the prey hastes*
m Cn; Heb *rejoices in*   x Heb *immanu el*
n Heb *it*   o Or *curse by*   p Ch 8.23 in Heb

iah's wife. **5–8:** Oracle of Shiloah and the Euphrates; Judah also is included in Assyria's sweep. *Shiloah,* a conduit flanking Ophel from the spring Gihon (see 1 Kg.1.33 n.) to the reservoir (7.3), is contrasted with the *River,* the great Euphrates. Ahaz's mighty ally, Assyria, will inundate tiny Judah, God's people. **9–10:** God is with his people (see 7.14 n.) to deliver them (Ps. 46, esp. vv. 7,11).
    8.11–22: The testimony and the teaching. 11–15: "Man proposes — God disposes" (Pr.16.9). **16:** *Bind, seal,* as one binds and seals a scroll (Jer.32.10). **18:** *Signs,* 7.3; 7.14; 8.1. **19–20:** Condemnation of superstition (2.6). for necromancy (consultation of the dead), see 1 Sam.28.7 n. **9.1:** Transitional verse from doom to promise. *Zebulun, Naphtali,* and Issachar constituted later *Galilee. Way of the sea,* the highway from Damascus to the sea, probable route of the Assyrian invasion in 733–732 B.C. (2 Kg.15.29).
    9.2–7: The messianic king (compare 11.1–9). Filled with borrowed phrases referring to the Davidic monarchy, this passage may have originally celebrated the accession of a Judean king, perhaps Hezekiah; in its present context it

those who dwelt in a land of deep
darkness,
on them has light shined.

3 Thou hast multiplied the nation,
thou hast increased its joy;
they rejoice before thee
as with joy at the harvest,
as men rejoice when they divide the
spoil.

4 For the yoke of his burden,
and the staff for his shoulder,
the rod of his oppressor,
thou hast broken as on the day of
Mid′ian.

5 For every boot of the tramping warrior in
battle tumult
and every garment rolled in blood
will be burned as fuel for the fire.

6 For to us a child is born,
to us a son is given;
and the government will be upon his
shoulder,
and his name will be called
"Wonderful Counselor, Mighty God,
Everlasting Father, Prince of Peace."

7 Of the increase of his government and of
peace
there will be no end,
upon the throne of David, and over his
kingdom,
to establish it, and to uphold it
with justice and with righteousness
from this time forth and for evermore.
The zeal of the LORD of hosts will do this.

8 The Lord has sent a word against Jacob,
and it will light upon Israel;

9 and all the people will know,
E′phraim and the inhabitants of
Sama′ria,

who say in pride and in arrogance of
heart:

10 "The bricks have fallen,
but we will build with dressed stones;
the sycamores have been cut down,
but we will put cedars in their place."

11 So the LORD raises adversaries[r] against
them,
and stirs up their enemies.

12 The Syrians on the east and the Philistines
on the west
devour Israel with open mouth.
For all this his anger is not turned away
and his hand is stretched out still.

13 The people did not turn to him who smote
them,
nor seek the LORD of hosts.

14 So the LORD cut off from Israel head and
tail,
palm branch and reed in one day —

15 the elder and honored man is the head,
and the prophet who teaches lies is the
tail;

16 for those who lead this people lead them
astray,
and those who are led by them are
swallowed up.

17 Therefore the Lord does not rejoice over
their young men,
and has no compassion on their
fatherless and widows;
for every one is godless and an evildoer,
and every mouth speaks folly.
For all this his anger is not turned away
and his hand is stretched out still.

18 For wickedness burns like a fire,
it consumes briers and thorns;
it kindles the thickets of the forest,

q Ch 9.1 in Heb   *r* Cn: Heb *the adversaries of Rezin*

describes the coming Messiah as the ideal king. **4:** *Midian,* Jg.7.15–25. **6:** *Government,* symbol of authority. *Mighty God,* divine in might. *Everlasting Father,* continuing fatherly love and care. *Prince of Peace,* the king who brings peace and prosperity. The king represents the best qualities of Israel's heroes (Ezek.37.25).

9.8–10.4: Ephraim's judgment an object lesson for Judah (five stanzas, including 5.24b–30; with the same refrain, 9.12,17,21; 10.4; 5.25; compare Jer.3.6–10; Ezek.16.44–58). **8–12:** Punishment for pride and unrepented wickedness. **8:** *Word,* more than a statement; it includes the potential and fact of accomplishment (55.10–11; Jer.23.18–20). **10:** *Bricks, sycamore,* for ordinary houses; *dressed stone, cedar* for palaces (Jer.22.7,23). **13–17:** Corrupt leaders misled their people (Jer.6.14). **18–21:** Moral decay consumes like a forest fire (Hos.7.6); civil war breaks

and they roll upward in a column of
   smoke.
[19] Through the wrath of the LORD of hosts
   the land is burned,
  and the people are like fuel for the fire;
   no man spares his brother.
[20] They snatch on the right, but are still
   hungry,
  and they devour on the left, but are not
   satisfied;
  each devours his neighbor's[s] flesh,
[21] Manas'seh E'phraim, and E'phraim
   Manas'seh,
  and together they are against Judah.
For all this his anger is not turned away
  and his hand is stretched out still.

10 Woe to those who decree iniquitous
   decrees,
  and the writers who keep writing
   oppression,
[2] to turn aside the needy from justice
  and to rob the poor of my people of
   their right,
  that widows may be their spoil,
  and that they may make the fatherless
   their prey!
[3] What will you do on the day of punishment,
  in the storm which will come from afar?
To whom will you flee for help,
  and where will you leave your wealth?
[4] Nothing remains but to crouch among the
   prisoners
  or fall among the slain.
For all this his anger is not turned away
  and his hand is stretched out still.

[5] Ah, Assyria, the rod of my anger,
  the staff of my fury![t]
[6] Against a godless nation I send him,

and against the people of my wrath I
   command him,
to take spoil and seize plunder,
  and to tread them down like the mire of
   the streets.
[7] But he does not so intend,
  and his mind does not so think;
but it is in his mind to destroy,
  and to cut off nations not a few;
[8] for he says:
  "Are not my commanders all kings?
[9] Is not Calno like Car'chemish?
  Is not Hamath like Arpad?
  Is not Sama'ria like Damascus?
[10] As my hand has reached to the kingdoms
   of the idols
  whose graven images were greater than
   those of Jerusalem and Sama'ria,
[11] shall I not do to Jerusalem and her idols
  as I have done to Sama'ria and her
   images?"

12 When the Lord has finished all his
work on Mount Zion and on Jerusalem he[u]
will punish the arrogant boasting of the king
of Assyria and his haughty pride. [12] For he
says:
  "By the strength of my hand I have done it,
  and by my wisdom, for I have
   understanding;
I have removed the boundaries of peoples,
  and have plundered their treasures;
  like a bull I have brought down those
   who sat on thrones.
[14] My hand has found like a nest
  the wealth of the peoples;
and as men gather eggs that have been
   forsaken
  so I have gathered all the earth;

s Tg Compare Gk: Heb *the flesh of his arm*
t Heb *a staff it is in their hand my fury*   u Heb *I*

---

out (2 Kg.15.23–31; 16.5). **20:** *His neighbor's flesh;* the Hebrew consonantal text may be read "the flesh of his off-spring" (on cannibalism, see Jer.19.9). Some treat this passage as a proverb. **10.1–4:** Justice is miscarried (3.13–15; Jer.8.8).

    10.5–19: Woe, O Assyria! Unaware that he was serving as God's instrument, powerful Assyria was doomed by his pride to destruction (Jer.25.8–14; 50.23). **9:** In northern Syria, Tiglath-Pileser III captured *Calno* (742 B.C.), *Carchemish, Hamath* (738), *Arpad* (741), southern Syria, *Damascus* (732). Menahem of Israel paid him tribute (2 Kg.15.19–20). **10–11:** To Assyria, the LORD was another idol. **12:** Prose summation of vv. 5–11,13–19. **13–14:** Assyria's boast.

and there was none that moved a wing,
    or opened the mouth, or chirped."

15 Shall the axe vaunt itself over him who
    hews with it,
    or the saw magnify itself against him
    who wields it?
As if a rod should wield him who lifts it,
    or as if a staff should lift him is not
    wood!
16 Therefore the Lord, the LORD of hosts,
    will send wasting sickness among his
    stout warriors,
and under his glory a burning will be
    kindled,
    like the burning of fire.
17 The light of Israel will become a fire,
    and his Holy One a flame;
and it will burn and devour
    his thorns and briers in one day.
18 The glory of his forest and of his fruitful
    land
    the LORD will destroy, both soul and
    body,
and it will be as when a sick man wastes
    away.
19 The remnant of the trees of his forest will
    be so few
    that a child can write them down.

20 In that day the remnant of Israel and the survivors of the house of Jacob will no more lean upon him that smote them, but will lean upon the LORD, the Holy One of Israel, in truth. 21 A remnant will return, the remnant of Jacob, to the mighty God. 22 For though your people Israel be as the sand of the sea, only a remnant of them will return. Destruction is decreed, overflowing with righteousness. 23 For the Lord, the LORD of hosts, will make a full end, as decreed, in the midst of all the earth.

24 Therefore thus says the Lord, the LORD of hosts: "O my people, who dwell in Zion, be not afraid of the Assyrians when they smite with the rod and lift up their staff against you as the Egyptians did. 25 For in a very little while my indignation will come to an end, and my anger will be directed to their destruction. 26 And the LORD of hosts will wield against them a scourge, as when he smote Mid'ian at the rock of Oreb; and his rod will be over the sea, and he will lift it as he did in Egypt. 27 And in that day his burden will depart from your shoulder, and his yoke will be destroyed from your neck."

He has gone up from Rommon,[v]
28   has come to Ai'ath;
he has passed through Migron,
    at Michmash he stores his baggage;
29 they have crossed over the pass,
    at Geba they lodge for the night;
Ramah trembles,
    Gib'e-ah of Saul has fled.
30 Cry aloud, O daughter of Gallim!
    Hearken, O La'ishah!
    Answer her, O An'athoth!

v Cn: Heb *and his yoke from your neck, and a yoke will be destroyed because of fatness*

Removed boundaries, to discourage rebellion, Assyria transplanted subject peoples. **15:** Rhetorical question recalling v. 5 (45.9). **16–19:** Light of Israel, God's majestic glory (2.10; 29.6; Ezek.1.26–28). God will ravage Assyria like a forest fire.

10.20–23: Only a remnant will return. 21: *A remnant will return,* in Hebrew this is the same as the name of Isaiah's son Shear-jashub; in 7.3–4 it stands in an oracle of encouragement, but here in an oracle of doom. **22:** *Sand of the sea* recalls God's oath to the patriarchs (Gen.22.17; compare Rom.9.27). In Isaiah (4.2–3; 6.13; 7.3; 28.5–6; 37.4; 37.31–32; compare Mic.4.7; 5.2–9; Zeph.2.7) *remnant* refers to those remaining after Judah's punishment, from whom a great people will arise. During the Exile the remnant was the deported people (Ezek.6.8–10; Jer.23.3; 31.7), whom God would bring back and make great. After the Exile Jewish faithlessness evoked again the pre-exilic concept (Zech.8.11; Hag.1.12; Zech.14.2).

10.24–27c: Oracle of promise. *Oreb,* Jg.7.25; *rod,* Ex.14.16.

10.27d–32: The approach of the Assyrians. The invader (Tiglath-Pileser III or Sennacherib, 1.4–9 n.) approached from the north toward the outskirts of Jerusalem (Jer.6.1–3). This may be a "traditional" description of the northern invasion route; for a southern route, see Mic.1.10–15. **33–34:** The LORD, the forester, will cut down Assyria.

31 Madme'nah is in flight,
    the inhabitants of Gebim flee for safety.
32 This very day he will halt at Nob,
    he will shake his fist
      at the mount of the daughter of Zion,
    the hill of Jerusalem.

33 Behold, the Lord, the LORD of hosts
    will lop the boughs with terrifying
      power;
    the great in height will be hewn down,
    and the lofty will be brought low.
34 He will cut down the thickets of the forest
    with an axe,
    and Lebanon with its majestic trees[w]
    will fall.

11 There shall come forth a shoot from
the stump of Jesse,
    and a branch shall grow out of his roots.
2 And the Spirit of the LORD shall rest upon
    him,
    the spirit of wisdom and understanding,
    the spirit of counsel and might,
    the spirit of knowledge and the fear of
      the LORD.
3 And his delight shall be in the fear of the
    LORD.

He shall not judge by what his eyes see,
    or decide by what his ears hear;
4 but with righteousness he shall judge the
    poor,
    and decide with equity for the meek of
      the earth;
and he shall smite the earth with the rod of
    his mouth,
    and with the breath of his lips he shall
    slay the wicked.

5 Righteousness shall be the girdle of his
    waist,
    and faithfulness the girdle of his loins.

6 The wolf shall dwell with the lamb,
    and the leopard shall lie down with the
      kid,
    and the calf and the lion and the fatling
      together,
    and a little child shall lead them.
7 The cow and the bear shall feed;
    their young shall lie down together;
    and the lion shall eat straw like the ox.
8 The sucking child shall play over the hole
    of the asp,
    and the weaned child shall put his hand
    on the adder's den.
9 They shall not hurt or destroy
    in all my holy mountain;
for the earth shall be full of the knowledge
    of the LORD
    as the waters cover the sea.

10 In that day the root of Jesse shall stand as
an ensign to the peoples; him shall the nations
seek, and his dwellings shall be glorious.

11 In that day the Lord will extend his
hand yet a second time to recover the remnant
which is left of his people, from Assyria, from
Egypt, from Pathros, from Ethiopia, from
Elam, from Shinar, from Hamath, and from
the coastlands of the sea.
12 He will raise an ensign for the nations,
    and will assemble the outcasts of Israel,
    and gather the dispersed of Judah
    from the four corners of the earth.
13 The jealousy of E'phraim shall depart,
    and those who harass Judah shall be cut
    off;

w Cn Compare Gk Vg: Heb *with a majestic one*

11.1–9: The messianic king (compare 9.2–7). For the occasion of the original oracle, see 9.2–7 n. **1–3a:** The Messiah will manifest the characteristics of Israel's great men. **1:** *Jesse,* David's father (1 Sam.16.1–20). **2:** To these six "Gifts of the Spirit" the Septuagint adds "piety." **3b–5:** Wisdom and justice (5.7) were traditionally associated in the ideal king (1 Kg. ch. 3; Ps. 72). **6–8:** His reign will be "paradise regained"; the disorder of nature will be restored to its pristine harmony (Ezek.47.1–12). **9:** *My holy mountain,* 65.25; Ezek.20.40.

    11.10–16: The messianic age. 10: *Root* is a person, not the dynasty (v. 1). **11–16:** Restored and reunited Israel takes vengeance against her oppressors. The terminology and mood of vv. 11–16 indicate a post-exilic date. **11:** *Pathros,* Upper Egypt; *Shinar,* Babylonia; *coastlands,* Aegean seacoast and islands. **12:** *Ensign,* here a standard, not a person (v. 10). **15:** *The tongue of the sea,* the Red Sea (Ex. ch. 14), *River,* Euphrates.

E′phraim shall not be jealous of Judah,
and Judah shall not harass E′phraim.
14 But they shall swoop down upon the
shoulder of the Philistines in the west,
and together they shall plunder the
people of the east.
They shall put forth their hand against
Edom and Moab,
and the Ammonites shall obey them.
15 And the LORD will utterly destroy
the tongue of the sea of Egypt;
and will wave his hand over the River
with his scorching wind,
and smite it into seven channels
that men may cross dryshod.
16 And there will be a highway from Assyria
for the remnant which is left of his people,
as there was for Israel
when they came up from the land of
Egypt.

12 You will say in that day: "I will give
thanks to thee, O LORD,
for though thou wast angry with me,

thy anger turned away,
and thou didst comfort me.

2 "Behold, God is my salvation;
I will trust, and will not be afraid;
for the LORD GOD is my strength and my
song,
and he has become my salvation."

3 With joy you will draw water from the
wells of salvation. 4 And you will say in that
day:

"Give thanks to the LORD,
call upon his name;
make known his deeds among the nations,
proclaim that his name is exalted.

5 "Sing praises to the LORD, for he has done
gloriously;
let this be known^x in all the earth.
6 Shout, and sing for joy, O inhabitant of
Zion,
for great in your midst is the Holy One
of Israel."

x Or *this is made known*

12.1–6: **Two songs** conclude Section I of the book of Isaiah. (a) **1–3**: Song of deliverance (compare Ps. 116). **1a**
and **4a** are liturgical rubrics. **2b**: Ex.15.2; Ps.118.14. (b) **4–6**: Song of thanksgiving. *Shout and sing for joy,* compare
Zeph.3.14. *In your midst,* God in his temple. *Holy One,* see 1.4.

THE NEW TESTAMENT

Introduction by Constance Bouchard

Because Christianity began as a sect of Judaism, the original Christian Bible was exactly the same as the Jewish Bible. However, both oral and written accounts of the life and death of Jesus soon began taking on a significance for believers equal to the teachings of the Bible they already had. Although it took close to two centuries to decide which accounts belonged in the "new" Bible, and although some people argued, unsuccessfully, that Christians needed to reject the Jewish Bible, eventually a general agreement was reached on what belonged in the "New" Testament, to put alongside the "Old" Testament they already had. The New Testament was written in Greek, the language of all educated people in the eastern parts of the Roman Empire, which in the first few centuries A.D. included the entire Mediterranean region.

The New Testament, as it was put together by the second century A.D., begins with four different accounts of Jesus and his teachings. They are generally credited with having been written by Matthew, Mark, Luke, and John, all names of apostles of Jesus; in fact, it is not known who actually wrote them, but the names are convenient labels. The four accounts, or "gospels," take quite different positions on the significance of the life of Jesus, a Jewish teacher who was put to death by the Romans, on grounds of sedition, around 30 A.D. All four gospels were written within a generation or so after 70 A.D., when the Romans cracked down on Jewish rebellion against Roman domination and destroyed the Temple in Jerusalem. The Gospel of Mark is the earliest, and that of John the last, to be written. All four gospels were written by men who thought that they, and they alone, understood the true significance of Jesus. But in the second century A.D., rather than argue about which version was the best, the Christian community decided to accept all four, putting them back to back. From then on, Christians put parts of all four gospels together for a coherent story of Jesus, ignoring or reconciling the gospels' differences.

The gospels are not, however, the oldest part of the New Testament. The oldest part is the letters of Paul. Paul was a highly-educated Jew who was also a Roman citizen (as not many Jews were in the first century A.D.). Although he never met Jesus personally, he became an early leader of the new Christian sect. He helped spread Christianity through the Roman Empire, wandering from one Christian community to another. His letters were sent to friends in these communities when he was elsewhere. His significance, however, lies in his theology. Paul was the first to apply Hellenistic philosophy, in which he was highly learned, to Christian doctrine.

Hence, from the beginning, Christianity was influenced by a combination of Jewish thought, Greek philosophy, and Roman culture, as well as the specific teachings of Jesus.

The following selections begin with the Gospel of Matthew, which was an account of the life of Jesus composed specifically for a Jewish audience. One of the earliest questions within the Christian community was whether it would continue, as it had begun, as a form of Judaism, or whether non-Jews could be admitted. This gospel was written to argue that Christianity was the culmination of Jewish prophecy. Thus it begins by invoking Abraham, the original Jewish patriarch, and by demonstrating that Jesus was descended from Abraham via King David. In this gospel the Roman governors, like Pilate, or the kings like Herod who ruled as puppets of the Romans, are the chief enemies of the Jews, but the Jewish priests are also portrayed as bitterly opposed to Jesus. Here the author is suggesting that Jews ought to realize that Christianity was the culmination of Judaism, but that many Jewish leaders wrongly refused to recognize this.

The Gospel of John begins quite differently, not with Jewish antecedents, but with a statement on the nature of the Word that incorporates Hellenistic philosophy with Christianity. Although the author indicated that Jesus had fulfilled Jewish prophecy (especially that of Isaiah), he was at pains to distinguish Judaism and Christianity. This gospel author wrote about two generations after Paul wrote his Letter to the Romans, which set out very clearly the philosophical underpinnings which he saw in Christianity, and also distinguished Jewish and Christian beliefs. Paul's discussion of sin and salvation in this letter became the basis of all later Christian theology.

The Gospel According to Matthew

THE BOOK OF THE GENEALOGY OF Jesus Christ, the son of David, the son of Abraham.

2 Abraham was the father of Isaac, and Isaac the father of Jacob, and Jacob the father of Judah and his brothers, ³ and Judah the father of Perez and Zerah by Tamar, and Perez the father of Hezron, and Hezron the father of Ram,ᵃ ⁴ and Ramᵃ the father of Ammin′adab, and Ammin′adab the father of Nahshon, and Nahshon the father of Salmon, ⁵ and Salmon the father of Bo′az by Rahab, and Bo′az the father of Obed by Ruth, and Obed the father of Jesse, ⁶ and Jesse the father of David the king.

And David was the father of Solomon by the wife of Uri′ah, ⁷ and Solomon the father of Rehobo′am, and Rehobo′am the father of Abi′jah, and Abi′jah the father of Asa,ᵇ ⁸ and Asaᵇ the father of Jehosh′aphat, and Jehosh′aphat the father of Joram, and Joram the father of Uzzi′ah, ⁹ and Uzzi′ah the father of Jotham, and Jotham the father of Ahaz, and Ahaz the father of Hezeki′ah, ¹⁰ and Hezeki′ah the father of Manas′seh, and Manas′seh the father of Amos,ᶜ and Amosᶜ the father of Josi′ah,¹¹ and Josi′ah the father of Jechoni′ah and his brothers, at the time of the deportation to Babylon.

12 And after the deportation to Babylon: Jechoni′ah was the father of She-al′ti-el,ᵈ and She-al′ti-elᵈ the father of Zerub′babel, ¹³ and Zerub′babel the father of Abi′ud, and Abi′ud the father of Eli′akim, and Eli′akim the father of Azor, ¹⁴ and Azor the father of Zadok, and Zadok the father of Achim, and Achim the father of Eli′ud, ¹⁵ and Eli′ud the father of Elea′zar, and Elea′zar the father of Matthan, and Matthan the father of Jacob, ¹⁰ and Jacob the father of Joseph the husband of Mary, of whom Jesus was born, who is called Christ.

17 So all the generations from Abraham to David were fourteen generations, and from David to the deportation to Babylon fourteen generations, and from the deportation to Babylon to the Christ fourteen generations.

18 Now the birth of Jesus Christᶠ took place in this way. When his mother Mary had been betrothed to Joseph, before they came together she was found to be with child of the Holy Spirit; ¹⁹ and her husband Joseph, being a just man and unwilling to put her to shame, resolved to divorce her quietly. ²⁰ But as he considered this, behold, an angel of the Lord appeared to him in a dream, saying, "Joseph, son of David, do not fear to take Mary your wife, for that which is conceived in her is of the Holy Spirit; ²¹ she will bear a son, and you shall call his name Jesus, for he will save his people from their sins." ²² All this took place to fulfil what the Lord had spoken by the prophet:

²³ "Behold, a virgin shall conceive and bear a son,

and his name shall be called Emman′u-el"
(which means, God with us). ²⁴ When Joseph woke from sleep, he did as the angel of the Lord commanded him; he took his wife, ²⁵ but knew her not until she had borne a son; and he called his name Jesus.

a Greek *Aram* b Greek *Asaph* c Other authorities read *Amon* d Greek *Salathiel* f Other ancient authorities read *of the Christ*

1.1–17: Jesus' royal descent (Lk.3.23–38) is traced through *David the king* (22.41–45; Rom. 1.3) back to Abraham the patriarch (Gal.3.16). **3–6:** Ru.4.18–22; 1 Chr.2.1–15. **11:** *The deportation,* 2 Kg.24.8–16; Jer.27.20. **12:** *Jeconiah,* or Jehoiachin (2 Kg.24.6; 1 Chr.3.16). *Shealtiel* apparently transmitted the line of legal descent from *Jeconiah* to *Zerubbabel* (Ezra 3.2; Hag.2.2; Lk.3.27), although the Chronicler traces it through Pedaiah (1 Chr.3.16–19). **13–16:** The persons from *Abiud* to *Jacob* are otherwise unknown. **16:** *Christ,* the Greek translation of the Hebrew word "Messiah," which means "anointed one" (compare Lev.4.3,5,16; 2 Sam.1.14,16).

1.18–2.23: Jesus' birth and infancy (Lk.1.26–2.40). **20:** *Angel,* see Heb.1.14 n. **21:** The Hebrew and Aramaic forms of *Jesus* and *he will save* are similar. The point could be suggested by translating, "You shall call his name 'Savior' because he will save." **22–23:** See Is.7.14 n. **25:** *Until:* According to Catholic teaching, the Semitic idiom in the use of *until* here does not imply that they had conjugal relations after the birth of Jesus.

Bible, THE NEW OXFORD ANNOTATED BIBLE WITH THE APOCRYPHA Revised Standard Edition, All of Matthew's Gospel.

2 Now when Jesus was born in Bethlehem of Judea in the days of Herod the king, behold, wise men from the East came to Jerusalem, saying [2] "Where is he who has been born king of the Jews? For we have seen his star in the East, and have come to worship him." [3] When Herod the king heard this, he was troubled, and all Jerusalem with him; [4] and assembling all the chief priests and scribes of the people, he inquired of them where the Christ was to be born. [5] They told him, "In Bethlehem of Judea; for so it is written by the prophet:
[6] 'And you, O Bethlehem, in the land of Judah,
are by no means least among the rulers of Judah;
for from you shall come a ruler
who will govern my people Israel.'"
[7] Then Herod summoned the wise men secretly and ascertained from them what time the star appeared; [8] and he sent them to Bethlehem, saying, "Go and search diligently for the child, and when you have found him bring me word, that I too may come and worship him." [9] When they had heard the king they went their way; and lo, the star which they had seen in the East went before them, till it came to rest over the place where the child was. [10] When they saw the star, they rejoiced exceedingly with great joy; [11] and going into the house they saw the child with Mary his mother, and they fell down and worshiped him. Then, opening their treasures, they offered him gifts, gold and frankincense and myrrh. [12] And being warned in a dream not to return to Herod, they departed to their own country by another way.

[13] Now when they had departed, behold, an angel of the Lord appeared to Joseph in a dream and said, "Rise, take the child and his mother, and flee to Egypt, and remain there till I tell you; for Herod is about to search for the child, to destroy him." [14] And he rose and took the child and his mother by night, and departed to Egypt, [15] and remained there until the death of Herod. This was to fulfil what the Lord had spoken by the prophet, "Out of Egypt have I called my son."

[16] Then Herod, when he saw that he had been tricked by the wise men, was in a furious rage, and he sent and killed all the male children in Bethlehem and in all that region who were two years old or under, according to the time which he had ascertained from the wise men. [17] Then was fulfilled what was spoken by the prophet Jeremiah:
[18] "A voice was heard in Ramah,
wailing and loud lamentation,
Rachel weeping for her children;
she refused to be consoled,
because they were no more."
[19] But when Herod died, behold, an angel of the Lord appeared in a dream to Joseph in Egypt, saying, [20] "Rise, take the child and his mother, and go to the land of Israel, for those who sought the child's life are dead." [21] And he rose and took the child and his mother, and went to the land of Israel. [22] But when he heard that Archela'us reigned over Judea in place of his father Herod, he was afraid to go there, and being warned in a dream he withdrew to the district of Galilee. [23] And he went and dwelt in a city called Nazareth, that what was spoken by the prophets might be fulfilled, "He shall be called a Nazarene."

2.1–12: The wise men (Magi). **1:** *Herod* the Great died early in 4 B.C. The *wise men,* a learned class in ancient Persia. **2:** Jer.23.5; Num.24.17. **5:** Jn.7.42. **6:** Mic.5.2. **11:** See Lk.2.7 n.
 2.13–23: Escape to Egypt and return. 15: *Out of Egypt. . .* , a quotation from Hos.11.1, where the reference is to Israel (compare Ex.4.22). **18:** Quoted from Jer.31.15. *Rachel,* wife of Jacob, died in childbirth and according to Gen.35.16–20 was buried near Bethlehem. *Ramah,* north of Jerusalem, was the scene of national grief (Jer.40.1) inflicted by an enemy. **22:** *Archelaus* reigned from 4 B.C. to A.D. 6 and was replaced by a Roman procurator. **23:** There is a similarity in sound and possibly in meaning between the Aramaic word for *Nazareth* and the Hebrew word translated *branch* (Is.11.1).

3 In those days came John the Baptist, preaching in the wilderness of Judea, ² "Repent, for the kingdom of heaven is at hand." ³ For this is he who was spoken of by the prophet Isaiah when he said,

"The voice of one crying in the wilderness:
Prepare the way of the Lord,
make his paths straight."

⁴ Now John wore a garment of camel's hair, and a leather girdle around his waist; and his food was locusts and wild honey. ⁵ Then went out to him Jerusalem and all Judea and all the region about the Jordan, ⁶ and they were baptized by him in the river Jordan, confessing their sins.

7 But when he saw many of the Pharisees and Sad'ducees coming for baptism, he said to them, "You brood of vipers! Who warned you to flee from the wrath to come? ⁸ Bear fruit that befits repentance, ⁹ and do not presume to say to yourselves, 'We have Abraham as our father'; for I tell you, God is able from these stones to raise up children to Abraham. ¹⁰ Even now the axe is laid to the root of the trees; every tree therefore that does not bear good fruit is cut down and thrown into the fire.

11 "I baptize you with water for repentance, but he who is coming after me is mightier than I, whose sandals I am not worthy to carry; he will baptize you with the Holy Spirit and with fire. ¹² His winnowing fork is in his hand, and he will clear his threshing floor and gather his wheat into the granary, but the chaff he will burn with unquenchable fire."

13 Then Jesus came from Galilee to the Jordan to John, to be baptized by him. ¹⁴ John would have prevented him, saying, "I need to be baptized by you, and do you come to me?" ¹⁵ But Jesus answered him, "Let it be so now; for thus it is fitting for us to fulfil all righteousness." Then he consented. ¹⁶ And when Jesus was baptized, he went up immediately from the water, and behold, the heavens were opened[g] and he saw the Spirit of God descending like a dove, and alighting on him; ¹⁷ and lo, a voice from heaven, saying, "This is my beloved Son,[h] with whom I am well pleased."

4 Then Jesus was led up by the Spirit into the wilderness to be tempted by the devil. ² And he fasted forty days and forty nights, and afterward he was hungry. ³ And the tempter came and said to him, "If you are the Son of God, command these stones to become loaves of bread." ⁴ But he answered, "It is written,

'Man shall not live by bread alone,
but by every word that proceeds from the mouth of God.' "

g Other ancient authorities add *to him*   *h* Or *my Son, my* (or *the*) *Beloved*

3.1–12: Activity of John the Baptist (Mk.1.1–8; Lk.3.1–18; Jn.1.6–8,19–28). **1:** *John* resembled the Old Testament prophets (compare v. 4 with 2 Kg.1.8; Zech.13.4). Christian faith understood him to fulfil Is.40.3; Mal.3.1; 4.5 (see 3.3; 17.10–12). His influence outside Christianity is attested by Acts 18.25; 19.1–7. *Those days*, namely, when Jesus began his public life. *The wilderness of Judea* lay east and southeast of Jerusalem. **2:** *Repent*, literally "return," meant to come back to the way of life charted by the covenant between God and Israel (Ex.19.3–6; 24.3–8; Jer.31.31–34). *The kingdom*, see 4.17 n. **3:** Is.40.3 **6:** See Mk.1.4 n. **7:** *Pharisees* and *Sadducees* formed two major divisions among the Jews (for differences between them, see 22.23 n. and Acts 23.6–10). A third Jewish sect in Palestine was the Essenes (see Josephus, *B. J.*, II, viii, 2–13); their beliefs and practices are reflected in the Dead Sea Scrolls found at Qumran (see "Survey of . . . Bible Lands," §15, end). *The wrath to come*, God's judgment (1 Th. 1.10). **8–10:** See Lk.3.7–9 n.; Jn.8.33. **11–12:** See Lk.12.49 n.; Acts 2.17–21; 19.1–7; 18.24–26.

3.13–17: Jesus' baptism (Mk.1.9–11; Lk.3.21–22; Jn.1.31–34). **13–15:** Jesus recognized John's authority and identified himself with those who responded in faith to John's call. **16–17:** A description of the surge of certainty and self-understanding that came to Jesus at his baptism. The language, akin to Old Testament speech, portrays a spiritual experience which words cannot adequately describe. *Beloved Son*, see Mk.1.11 n.

4.1–11: Jesus' temptation (Mk.1.12–13; Lk.4.1–13; Heb.2.18; 4.15). The accounts illustrate Jesus' habitual refusal to allow his sense of mission to be influenced by concern for his safety or for merely practical interests. **1:** *The devil, tempter* (v. 3), and *Satan* (v. 10) are names for evil conceived as a personal will actively hostile to God (see Lk.13.11,16 n.). **2:** *Forty*, compare Ex.34.28; 1 Kg.19.8. **3:** *If you are the Son of God;* but see the declaration in 3.17. **4:** Dt.8.3. **5:** *The holy city,* Jerusalem. **6:** Ps.91.11–12. **7:** Dt.6.16. **10:** Dt.6.13.

5 Then the devil took him to the holy city, and set him on the pinnacle of the temple, 6 and said to him, "If you are the Son of God, throw yourself down; for it is written,

'He will give his angels charge of you,'

and

'On their hands they will bear you up,

lest you strike your foot against a stone.'" 7 Jesus said to him, "Again it is written, 'You shall not tempt the Lord your God.'" 8 Again, the devil took him to a very high mountain, and showed him all the kingdoms of the world and the glory of them; 9 and he said to him, "All these I will give you, if you will fall down and worship me." 10 Then Jesus said to him, "Begone, Satan! for it is written,

'You shall worship the Lord your God

and him only shall you serve.'"

11 Then the devil left him, and behold, angels came and ministered to him.

12 Now when he heard that John had been arrested, he withdrew into Galilee; 13 and leaving Nazareth he went and dwelt in Caper'na-um by the sea, in the territory of Zeb'ulun and Naph'tali, 14 that what was spoken by the prophet Isaiah might be fulfilled:

15 "The land of Zeb'ulun and the land of
        Naph'tali,
    toward the sea, across the Jordan,
    Galilee of the Gentiles —
16 the people who sat in darkness
        have seen a great light,
    and for those who sat in the region and
        shadow of death
    light has dawned."

17 From that time Jesus began to preach, saying, "Repent, for the kingdom of heaven is at hand."

18 As he walked by the Sea of Galilee, he saw two brothers, Simon who is called Peter and Andrew his brother, casting a net into the sea; for they were fishermen. 19 And he said to them, "Follow me, and I will make you fishers of men." 20 Immediately they left their nets and followed him. 21 And going on from there he saw two other brothers, James the son of Zeb'edee and John his brother, in the boat with Zeb'edee their father, mending their nets, and he called them. 22 Immediately they left the boat and their father, and followed him.

23 And he went about all Galilee, teaching in their synagogues and preaching the gospel of the kingdom and healing every disease and every infirmity among the people. 24 So his fame spread throughout all Syria, and they brought him all the sick, those afflicted with various diseases and pains, demoniacs, epileptics, and paralytics, and he healed them. 25 And great crowds followed him from Galilee and the Decap'olis and Jerusalem and Judea and from beyond the Jordan.

5 Seeing the crowds, he went up on the mountain, and when he sat down his disciples came to him. 2 And he opened his mouth and taught them, saying:

3 "Blessed are the poor in spirit, for theirs is the kingdom of heaven.

4 "Blessed are those who mourn, for they shall be comforted.

4.12–25: Beginnings of Jesus' activity in Galilee. 12–17: Mk.1.14–15; Lk.4.14–15. **15–16:** Is.9.1–2. **17:** *From that time,* the arrest of John (v. 12). *The kingdom of heaven* is Matthew's usual way of expressing the equivalent phrase, "the kingdom of God," found in parallel accounts in the other gospels. In asserting that God's *kingdom is at hand* Jesus meant that all God's past dealings with his creation were coming to climax and fruition. Jesus taught both the present reality of God's rule (Lk.10.18; 11.20; 17.21) and its future realization (Mt.6.10). See Mk.1.15 n. **18–22:** Mk.1.16–20; Lk.5.1–11; Jn.1.35–42. **24:** *Demoniacs,* persons controlled in body or will, or in both, by evil forces (Mt.8.16,28; 9.32; 15.22; Mk.5.15; see Lk.13.11,16 n.). *Demons,* see Lk.4.33 n. **25:** *Decapolis,* see Mk.5.20 n.

5.1–7.27: The Sermon on the Mount sounds the keynote of the new age which Jesus came to introduce. Internal analysis and comparison with Luke's Gospel suggest that the Evangelist (in accord with his habit of synthesis) has inserted into this account of the Sermon portions of Jesus' teaching given on other occasions. **1:** *He sat down,* the usual position of Jewish rabbis while teaching (compare Lk.4.20–21).

5.3–12: The Beatitudes (Lk.6.17,20–23) proclaim God's favor toward those who aspire to live under his rule. **3:** *Poor in spirit,* those who feel a deep sense of spiritual poverty (Is.66.2). **4:** *Comforted,* the word implies strengthening

5 "Blessed are the meek, for they shall inherit the earth.

6 "Blessed are those who hunger and thirst for righteousness, for they shall be satisfied.

7 "Blessed are the merciful, for they shall obtain mercy.

8 "Blessed are the pure in heart, for they shall see God.

9 "Blessed are the peacemakers, for they shall be called sons of God.

10 "Blessed are those who are persecuted for righteousness' sake, for theirs is the kingdom of heaven.

11 "Blessed are you when men revile you and persecute you and utter all kinds of evil against you falsely on my account. [12] Rejoice and be glad, for your reward is great in heaven, for so men persecuted the prophets who were before you.

13 "You are the salt of the earth; but if salt has lost its taste, how shall its saltness be restored? It is no longer good for anything except to be thrown out and trodden under foot by men.

14 "You are the light of the world. A city set on a hill cannot be hid. [15] Nor do men light a lamp and put it under a bushel, but on a stand, and it gives light to all in the house. [16] Let your light so shine before men, that they may see your good works and give glory to your Father who is in heaven.

17 "Think not that I have come to abolish the law and the prophets; I have come not to abolish them but to fulfil them. [18] For truly, I say to you, till heaven and earth pass away, not an iota, not a dot, will pass from the law until all is accomplished. [19] Whoever then relaxes one of the least of these commandments and teaches men so, shall be called least in the kingdom of heaven; but he who does them and teaches them shall be called great in the kingdom of heaven. [20] For I tell you, unless your righteousness exceeds that of the scribes and Pharisees, you will never enter the kingdom of heaven.

21 "You have heard that it was said to the men of old, 'You shall not kill; and whoever kills shall be liable to judgment.' [22] But I say to you that every one who is angry with his brother[i] shall be liable to judgment; whoever insults[j] his brother shall be liable to the council, and whoever says, 'You fool!' shall be liable to the hell[k] of fire. [23] So if you are offering your gift at the altar, and there remember that your brother has something against you, [24] leave your gift there before the altar and go; first be reconciled to your brother, and then come and offer your gift. [25] Make friends quickly with your accuser, while you are going with him to court, lest your accuser hand you over to the judge, and the judge to the guard, and you be put in prison; [26] truly, I say to you, you will never get out till you have paid the last penny.

27 "You have heard that it was said, 'You shall not commit adultery.' [28] But I say to you that every one who looks at a woman lustfully

i Other ancient authorities insert *without cause*
j Greek *says Raca to* (an obscure term of abuse)
k Greek *Gehenna*

---

as well as consolation. **5:** Ps.37.11. **6:** Is.55.1–2; Jn.4.14; 6.48–51. **8:** Purity of *heart* is single-mindedness or sincerity, freedom from mixed motives; it is not synonymous with chastity, but includes it (Ps.24.4; Heb.12.14). *See God,* 1 Cor.13.12; 1 Jn.3.2; Rev. 22.4. **9:** *Peacemakers* are not merely "peaceable," but those who work earnestly to "make" peace. **10:** 1 Pet.3.14; 4.14. **12:** 2 Chr.36.15–16; Mt.23–3; Acts 7.52.

   5.13–16: The witness of the disciples. 13: Mk.9.49–50; Lk.14.34–35. **14:** Phil.2.15; Jn.8.12. **15:** See Mk.4.21 n. **16:** 1 Pet.2.12.

   5.17–20: The relation of Jesus' message to the Jewish law was a great concern to followers with a Jewish background. **17:** *The prophets* in the Hebrew Scriptures comprise the books of Joshua, Judges, Samuel, Kings, Isaiah, Jeremiah, Ezekiel, and the twelve minor prophets (see Lk.24.27 n., 44 n.). **18:** Mk.13.31; Lk.16.17. **19:** *Relaxes,* or "sets aside." *Teaches,* Jas.3.1. **20:** *Righteousness,* one's acceptance of God's requirements and one's being accepted by God (Lk.18.10–14).

   5.21–48: Illustrations of the true understanding of the Law. 21: Ex.20.13; Dt.5.17; 16.18. **25–26:** Lk.12.57–59. **26:** *Penny,* see Lk.12.59 n. **27:** Ex.20.14; Dt.5.18. **29–30:** Mk.9.43–48; Mt.18.8–9. **31:** *It was also said,*

has already committed adultery with her in his heart. ²⁹ If your right eye causes you to sin, pluck it out and throw it away; it is better that you lose one of your members than that your whole body be thrown into hell.ᵏ ³⁰ And if your right hand causes you to sin, cut if off and throw it away; it is better that you lose one of your members than that your whole body go into hell.ᵏ

31 "It was also said, 'Whoever divorces his wife, let him give her a certificate of divorce.' ³² But I say to you that every one who divorces his wife, except on the ground of unchastity, makes her an adulteress; and whoever marries a divorced woman commits adultery.

33 "Again you have heard that it was said to the men of old, 'You shall not swear falsely, but shall perform to the Lord what you have sworn.' ³⁴ But I say to you, Do not swear at all, either by heaven, for it is the throne of God, ³⁵ or by the earth, for it is his footstool, or by Jerusalem, for it is the city of the great King. ³⁶ And do not swear by your head, for you cannot make one hair white or black. ³⁷ Let what you say be simply 'Yes' or 'No'; anything more than this comes from evil.ˡ

38 "You have heard that it was said, 'An eye for an eye and a tooth for a tooth.' ³⁹ But I say to you, Do not resist one who is evil. But if any one strikes you on the right cheek, turn to him the other also; ⁴⁰ and if any one would sue you and take your coat, let him have your cloak as well; ⁴¹ and if any one forces you to go one mile, go with him two miles. ⁴² Give to him who begs from you, and do not refuse him who would borrow from you.

43 "You have heard that it was said, 'You shall love your neighbor and hate your enemy.' ⁴⁴ But I say to you, Love your enemies and pray for those who persecute you, ⁴⁵ so that you may be sons of your Father who is in heaven; for he makes his sun rise on the evil and on the good, and sends rain on the just and on the unjust. ⁴⁶ For if you love those who love you, what reward have you? Do not even the tax collectors do the same? ⁴⁷ And if you salute only your brethren, what more are you doing than others? Do not even the Gentiles do the same? ⁴⁸ You, therefore, must be perfect, as your heavenly Father is perfect.

6 "Beware of practicing your piety before men in order to be seen by them; for then you will have no reward from your Father who is in heaven.

2 "Thus, when you give alms, sound no trumpet before you, as the hypocrites do in the synagogues and in the streets, that they may be praised by men. Truly, I say to you, they have received their reward. ³ But when you give alms, do not let your left hand know what your right hand is doing, ⁴ so that your alms may be in secret; and your Father who sees in secret will reward you.

5 "And when you pray, you must not be like the hypocrites; for they love to stand and pray in the synagogues and at the street corners, that they may be seen by men. Truly, I say to you, they have received their reward. ⁶ But when you pray, go into your room and shut the door and pray to your Father who is in secret; and your Father who sees in secret will reward you.

k Greek *Gehenna*   l Or *the evil one*

Dt.24.1–4. **32:** The expression *except . . . unchastity* occurs also in 19.9; it is absent from the accounts in Mk.10.11–12 and Lk.16.18 (compare also Rom.7.2–3; 1 Cor.7.10–11). **33–37:** Lev.19.12; Num.30.2; Dt.23.21; Mt.23.16–22; Jas.5.12. **35:** Is.66.1. **38:** Ex.21.23–24; Lev.24.19–20; Dt.19.21. Though this principle *controlled* retaliation in primitive society, it did not justify it. **39–42:** Lk.6.29–30; Rom.12.17; 1 Cor.6.7; 1 Pet.2.19; 3.9. **43–48:** Lk.6.27–28,32–36. **45:** To be *sons of* God is to pattern attitudes after God's. The words *son of* commonly mean that one shows the quality named or trait of character implied (see 23.31 n.; Lk.6.35; 10.6; Jn.8.39–47).

6.1–34: Teachings in practical piety; Jesus emphasizes a sincere response to God that identifies oneself with his purposes. **1:** 23.5. **5:** Lk.18.10–14. **9–13:** The Lord's Prayer (compare Lk.11.2–4) falls into two parts relating to God and to man; after the opening invocation, there are three petitions concerning God's glory, followed by those concerning our needs. The phrase, *on earth as it is in heaven* (v. 10), belongs to each of the first three petitions. On the basis of

7 "And in praying do not heap up empty phrases as the Gentiles do; for they think that they will be heard for their many words. 8 Do not be like them, for your Father knows what you need before you ask him. 9 Pray then like this:

Our Father who art in heaven,
Hallowed be thy name.
10 Thy kingdom come.
Thy will be done,
    On earth as it is in heaven.
11 Give us this day our daily bread;*m*
12 And forgive us our debts,
    As we also have forgiven our debtors;
13 And lead us not into temptation,
    But deliver us from evil.*n*

14 For if you forgive men their trespasses, your heavenly Father also will forgive you; 15 but if you do not forgive men their trespasses, neither will your Father forgive your trespasses.

16 "And when you fast, do not look dismal, like the hypocrites, for they disfigure their faces that their fasting may be seen by men. Truly, I say to you, they have received their reward. 17 But when you fast, anoint your head and wash your face, 18 that your fasting may not be seen by men but by your Father who is in secret; and your Father who sees in secret will reward you.

19 "Do not lay up for yourselves treasures on earth, where moth and rust*o* consume and where thieves break in and steal, 20 but lay up for yourselves treasures in heaven, where neither moth nor rust*o* consumes and where thieves do not break in and steal. 21 For where your treasure is, there will your heart be also.

22 "The eye is the lamp of the body. So, if your eye is sound, your whole body will be full of light; 23 but if your eye is not sound, your whole body will be full of darkness. If then the light in you is darkness, how great is the darkness!

24 "No one can serve two masters; for either he will hate the one and love the other, or he will be devoted to the one and despise the other. You cannot serve God and mammon.*x*

25 "Therefore I tell you, do not be anxious about your life, what you shall eat or what you shall drink, nor about your body, what you shall put on. Is not life more than food, and the body more than clothing? 26 Look at the birds of the air: they neither sow nor reap nor gather into barns, and yet your heavenly Father feeds them. Are you not of more value than they? 27 And which of you by being anxious can add one cubit to his span of life?*p* 28 And why are you anxious about clothing? Consider the lilies of the field, how they grow; they neither toil nor spin; 29 yet I tell you, even Solomon in all his glory was not arrayed like one of these. 30 But if God so clothes the grass of the field, which today is alive and tomorrow is thrown into the oven, will he not much more clothe you, O men of little faith? 31 Therefore do not be anxious, saying, 'What shall we eat?' or 'What shall we drink?' or 'What shall we wear?' 32 For the Gentiles seek all these things; and your heavenly Father knows that you need them all. 33 But seek first his kingdom and his righteousness, and all these things shall be yours as well.

m Or *our bread for the morrow*   *n* Or *the evil one.*
Other authorities, some ancient, add, in some form, *For thine is the kingdom and the power and the glory, for ever. Amen.*   *o* Or *worm*   *x* *Mammon* is a Semitic word for money or riches   *p* Or *to his stature*

David's prayer (1 Chr.29.11–13) the early church added an appropriate concluding doxology (see note *n*). **9:** Is.63.16; 64.8. **13:** 2 Th.3.3; Jas.1.13. **14–15:** 18.35; Mk.11.25–26; Eph.4.32; Col.3 13. **16–18:** Acceptable fasting (Is.58.5). **19–21:** The uselessness of trusting in worldly goods (Jas.5.2–3). **22–23:** Lk.11.34–36. **24:** Lk.16.13. **25–33:** Lk.12.22–31. **25:** Lk.10.41; 12.11; Phil.4.6. **27:** A *cubit,* about 18 inches. "Cubit" may be used figuratively of length of life (see Ps.39.5 for a similar usage); or in the literal sense Jesus could note that growing in stature (see note *p*) is natural to life and beyond control by anxiety. **29:** 1 Kg.10.4–7. **30:** *Men of little faith* are unwilling to rest in the assurance that God cares about their lives (8.26; 14.31; 16.8). **33:** Mk.10.29–30; Lk.18.29–30.

34 "Therefore do not be anxious about tomorrow, for tomorrow will be anxious for itself. Let the day's own trouble be sufficient for the day.

7 "Judge not, that you be not judged. [2] For with the judgment you pronounce you will be judged, and the measure you give will be the measure you get. [3] Why do you see the speck that is in your brother's eye, but do not notice the log that is in your own eye? [4] Or how can you say to your brother, 'Let me take the speck out of your eye,' when there is the log in your own eye? [5] You hypocrite, first take the log out of your own eye, and then you will see clearly to take the speck out of your brother's eye.

6 "Do not give dogs what is holy; and do not throw your pearls before swine, lest they trample them under foot and turn to attack you.

7 "Ask, and it will be given you; seek, and you will find; knock, and it will be opened to you. [8] For every one who asks receives, and he who seeks finds, and to him who knocks it will be opened. [9] Or what man of you, if his son asks him for bread, will give him a stone? [10] Or if he asks for a fish, will give him a serpent? [11] If you then, who are evil, know how to give good gifts to your children, how much more will your Father who is in heaven give good things to those who ask him! [12] So whatever you wish that men would do to you, do so to them; for this is the law and the prophets.

13 "Enter by the narrow gate; for the gate is wide and the way is easy,[q] that leads to destruction, and those who enter by it are many. [14] For the gate is narrow and the way is hard, that leads to life, and those who find it are few.

15 "Beware of false prophets, who come to you in sheep's clothing but inwardly are ravenous wolves. [16] You will know them by their fruits. Are grapes gathered from thorns, or figs from thistles? [17] So, every sound tree bears good fruit, but the bad tree bears evil fruit. [18] A sound tree cannot bear evil fruit, nor can a bad tree bear good fruit. [19] Every tree that does not bear good fruit is cut down and thrown into the fire. [20] Thus you will know them by their fruits.

21 "Not every one who says to me, 'Lord, Lord,' shall enter the kingdom of heaven, but he who does the will of my Father who is in heaven. [22] On that day many will say to me, 'Lord, Lord, did we not prophesy in your name, and cast out demons in your name, and do many mighty works in your name?' [23] And then will I declare to them, 'I never knew you; depart from me, you evildoers.'

24 "Every one then who hears these words of mine and does them will be like a wise man who built his house upon the rock; [25] and the rain fell, and the floods came, and the winds blew and beat upon that house, but it did not fall, because it had been founded on the rock. [26] And every one who hears these words of mine and does not do them will be like a foolish man who built his house upon the sand; [27] and the rain fell, and the floods came, and the winds blew and beat against that house, and it fell; and great was the fall of it."

28 And when Jesus finished these sayings, the crowds were astonished at his teaching, [29] for he taught them as one who had authority, and not as their scribes.

q Other ancient authorities read *for the way is wide and easy*

7.1–27: Illustrations of the practical meaning of Jesus message. 1–5: Judgment of others (Lk.6.37–38,41–42; Mk.4.24; Rom.2.1; 14.10). **7–11:** Encouragement to prayer (6.8; Mk.11.23–24; Jn.15.7; 1 Jn.3.22; 5.14). **12:** Lk.6.31; Mt.22.39–40; Rom.13.8–10. **13–14:** Lk.13.23–24; Jer.21.8; Ps.1; Dt.30.19; Jn.10.7; 14.6. **15–20:** Lk.6.43–45. **15:** 24.11,24; Ezek.22.27; 1 Jn.4.1; Jn.10.12. *Sheep* often symbolize a group of followers in a religious sense (Ezek.34.1–24; Lk.12.32). **16:** 3.8; 12.33–35; Lk.6.43–45. **19:** 3.10; Lk.13.6–9; Jas.3.10–12. **22:** *That day,* the day of judgment, Jesus speaks as the divine judge. **24–27:** Lk.6.47–49; Jas.1.22–25. **28:** *When Jesus finished these sayings,* this (or a similar) formula marks the conclusion of each of the five main discourses in the gospel (see Introduction and 11.1; 13.53; 19.1; 26.1). **29:** *Unlike their scribes,* Jesus speaks on his own responsibility without appeal to traditional authority (Mk.1.22; 11.18; Lk.4.32).

8 When he came down from the mountain, great crowds followed him; [2] and behold, a leper came to him and knelt before him, saying, "Lord, if you will, you can make me clean." [3] And he stretched out his hand and touched him, saying, "I will; be clean." And immediately his leprosy was cleansed. [4] And Jesus said to him, "See that you say nothing to any one; but go, show yourself to the priest, and offer the gift that Moses commanded, for a proof to the people."[r]

5 As he entered Caper'na-um, a centurion came forward to him, beseeching him [6] and saying, "Lord, my servant is lying paralyzed at home, in terrible distress." [7] And he said to him, "I will come and heal him." [8] But the centurion answered, "Lord, I am not worthy to have you come under my roof; but only say the word, and my servant will be healed. [9] For I am a man under authority, with soldiers under me; and I say to one, 'Go,' and he goes, and to another, 'Come,' and he comes, and to my slave, 'Do this,' and he does it." [10] When Jesus heard him, he marveled, and said to those who followed him, "Truly, I say to you, not even[s] in Israel have I found such faith. [11] I tell you, many will come from east and west and sit at table with Abraham, Isaac, and Jacob in the kingdom of heaven, [12] while the sons of the kingdom will be thrown into the outer darkness; there men will weep and gnash their teeth." [13] And to the centurion Jesus said, "Go; be it done for you as you have believed." And the servant was healed at that very moment.

14 And when Jesus entered Peter's house, he saw his mother-in-law lying sick with a fever; [15] he touched her hand, and the fever left her, and she rose and served him. [16] That evening they brought to him many who were possessed with demons; and he cast out the spirits with a word, and healed all who were sick. [17] This was to fulfil what was spoken by the prophet Isaiah, "He took our infirmities and bore our diseases."

18 Now when Jesus saw great crowds around him, he gave orders to go over to the other side. [19] And a scribe came up and said to him, "Teacher, I will follow you wherever you go." [20] And Jesus said to him, "Foxes have holes, and birds of the air have nests; but the Son of man has nowhere to lay his head." [21] Another of the disciples said to him, "Lord, let me first go and bury my father." [22] But Jesus said to him, "Follow me, and leave the dead to bury their own dead."

23 And when he got into the boat, his disciples followed him. [24] And behold, there arose a great storm on the sea, so that the boat was being swamped by the waves; but he was asleep. [25] And they went and woke him, saying, "Save, Lord; we are perishing." [26] And he said to them, "Why are you afraid, O men of little faith?" Then he rose and rebuked the winds and the sea; and there was a great calm. [27] And the men marveled, saying, "What sort of man is this, that even winds and sea obey him?"

28 And when he came to the other side, to the country of the Gadarenes,[t] two demoniacs met him, coming out of the tombs, so fierce

r Greek *to them*   *s* Other ancient authorities read *with no one*   *t* Other ancient authorities read *Gergesenes;* some, *Gerasenes*   *u* Other ancient authorities read *seeing*

8.1–9.38: Events in Galilee. 8.2–4: Mk.1.40–44; Lk.5.12–14. *Leprosy,* a skin disorder of an uncertain nature. Several diseases were possibly referred to by this name (see Lev.13.1–59 n.; Num.5.1–4). Its presence excluded the sufferer from associating with others. *Make me clean,* the leper seeks not merely healing but the freedom to rejoin the Jewish community. **4:** Lev.14.2–32. **5–13:** Lk.7.1–10; Jn.4.46–53. The *centurion,* a non-Jewish military officer, is convinced that diseases are as obedient to Jesus as soldiers are to him. **10:** *Faith* refers to the centurion's trust and recognition of Jesus' power (v. 13; Mk.11.23 n., 24 n.). **11–12:** See Lk.14.15 n.; Is.49.12; 59.19; Mt.13.42,50; 22.13; 24.51; 25.30. **14–17:** Mk.1.29–34; Lk.4.38–41. **16:** *Demons,* see 4.24 n.; 12.22 n.; Lk.4.33 n.; 7.33 n.; 13.16 n. **17:** Is.53.4. **18–22:** Mk.4.35; Lk.8.22; 9.57–60. **18:** *The other side,* the eastern shore of the Sea of Galilee. **20:** *Son of man,* see Mk.2.10 n. **22:** *Follow me,* Jesus implies that obedience to his call must take precedence over every other duty or love (compare 10.37). *Leave the dead,* i.e. the spiritually dead, who are not alive to the greater demands of the kingdom of God. **23–27:** Mk.4.36–41; Lk.8.22–24. **25:** See Lk.8.24 n. **28–34:** Mk.5.1–20; Lk.8.26–39. **31:** See v. 16 n.

that no one could pass that way. [29] And behold, they cried out, "What have you to do with us, O Son of God? Have you come here to torment us before the time?" [30] Now a herd of many swine was feeding at some distance from them. [31] And the demons begged him, "If you cast us out, send us away into the herd of swine." [32] And he said to them, "Go." So they came out and went into the swine; and behold, the whole herd rushed down the steep bank into the sea, and perished in the waters. [33] The herdsmen fled, and going into the city they told everything, and what had happened to the demoniacs. [34] And behold, all the city came out to meet Jesus; and when they saw him, they begged him to leave their neighborhood.

9 And getting into a boat he crossed over and came to his own city. [2] And behold, they brought to him a paralytic, lying on his bed; and when Jesus saw their faith he said to the paralytic, "Take heart, my son; your sins are forgiven." [3] And behold; some of the scribes said to themselves, "This man is blaspheming." [4] But Jesus, knowing[u] their thoughts, said, "Why do you think evil in your hearts? [5] For which is easier, to say, 'Your sins are forgiven,' or to say, 'Rise and walk'? [6] But that you may know that the Son of man has authority on earth to forgive sins"— he then said to the paralytic —"Rise, take up your bed and go home." [7] And he rose and went home. [8] When the crowds saw it, they were afraid, and they glorified God, who had given such authority to men.

9 As Jesus passed on from there, he saw a man called Matthew sitting at the tax office; and he said to him, "Follow me." And he rose and followed him.

10 And as he sat at table[v] in the house, behold, many tax collectors and sinners came and sat down with Jesus and his disciples. [11] And when the Pharisees saw this, they said to his disciples, "Why does your teacher eat with tax collectors and sinners?" [12] But when he heard it, he said, "Those who are well have no need of a physician, but those who are sick. [13] Go and learn what this means, 'I desire mercy, and not sacrifice.' For I came not to call the righteous, but sinners."

14 Then the disciples of John came to him, saying, "Why do we and the Pharisees fast,[w] but your disciples do not fast?" [15] And Jesus said to them, "Can the wedding guests mourn as long as the bridegroom is with them? The days will come, when the bridegroom is taken away from them, and then they will fast. [16] And no one puts a piece of unshrunk cloth on an old garment, for the patch tears away from the garment, and a worse tear is made. [17] Neither is new wine put into old wineskins; if it is, the skins burst, and the wine is spilled, and the skins are destroyed; but new wine is put into fresh wineskins, and so both are preserved."

18 While he was thus speaking to them, behold, a ruler came in and knelt before him, saying, "My daughter has just died; but come and lay your hand on her, and she will live." [19] And Jesus rose and followed him, with his disciples. [20] And behold, a woman who had suffered from a hemorrhage for twelve years came up behind him and touched the fringe of his garment; [21] for she said to herself, "If I only touch his garment, I shall be made well." [22] Jesus turned, and seeing her he said, "Take heart, daughter; your faith has made you

v Greek *reclined*   w Other ancient authorities add *much or often*

9.1–8: Healing a paralytic (Mk.2.1–12; Lk.5.17–26). **1:** *His own city*, Capernaum. **8:** 7.28–29. **9–13:** Mk.2.13–17; Lk.5.27–32. **10:** Lk.7.34; 15.1–2. **13:** Hos.6.6; Mt.12.7; 15.2–6. Jesus uses a Biblical quotation to challenge a conventional religious idea (see Lk.5.32 n.). **14–17:** Mk.2.18–22; Lk.5.33–39. **15:** Jesus recognizes the principle of fasting, but denies that it fits the circumstances of his life. **16–17:** The two pictorial sayings defend the practices of John's disciples and the practices of his own disciples; Jesus insists that the two ways should not be joined. **18–26:** Mk.5.21–43; Lk.8.40–56. **18:** *A ruler*, a leader in a synagogue. **21:** The Greek word here translated *be made well* (also v. 22; Mk.5.23,28,34; 10.52; Lk.8.36,48,50; 17.19; 18.42) carries with it the idea of rescue from impending destruc-

well." And instantly the woman was made well. [23] And when Jesus came to the ruler's house, and saw the flute players, and the crowd making a tumult, [24] he said, "Depart; for the girl is not dead but sleeping." And they laughed at him. [25] But when the crowd had been put outside, he went in and took her by the hand, and the girl arose. [26] And the report of this went through all that district.

[27] And as Jesus passed on from there, two blind men followed him, crying aloud, "Have mercy on us, Son of David." [28] When he entered the house, the blind men came to him; and Jesus said to them, "Do you believe that I am able to do this?" They said to him, "yes, Lord." [29] Then he touched their eyes, saying, "According to your faith be it done to you." [30] And their eyes were opened. And Jesus sternly charged them, "See that no one knows it." [31] But they went away and spread his fame through all that district.

[32] As they were going away, behold, a dumb demoniac was brought to him. [33] And when the demon had been cast out, the dumb man spoke; and the crowds marveled, saying, "Never was anything like this seen in Israel." [34] But the Pharisees said, "He casts out demons by the prince of demons."[a]

[35] And Jesus went about all the cities and villages, teaching in their synagogues and preaching the gospel of the kingdom, and healing every disease and every infirmity. [36] When he saw the crowds, he had compassion for them, because they were harassed and helpless, like sheep without a shepherd. [37] Then he said to his disciples, "The harvest is plentiful, but the laborers are few; [38] pray therefore the Lord of the harvest to send out laborers into his harvest."

10 And he called to him his twelve disciples and gave them authority over unclean spirits, to cast them out, and to heal every disease and every infirmity. [2] The names of the twelve apostles are these: first, Simon, who is called Peter, and Andrew his brother; James the son of Zeb'edee, and John his brother; [3] Philip and Bartholomew; Thomas and Matthew the tax collector; James the son of Alphaeus, and Thaddaeus;[x] [4] Simon the Cananaean, and Judas Iscariot, who betrayed him.

[5] These twelve Jesus sent out, charging them, "Go nowhere among the Gentiles, and enter no town of the Samaritans, [6] but go rather to the lost sheep of the house of Israel. [7] And preach as you go, saying, 'The kingdom of heaven is at hand.' [8] Heal the sick, raise the dead, cleanse lepers, cast out demons. You received without paying, give without pay. [9] Take no gold, nor silver, nor copper in your belts, [10] no bag for your journey, nor two tunics, nor sandals, nor a staff; for the laborer deserves his food. [11] And whatever town or village you enter, find out who is worthy in it, and stay with him until you depart. [12] As you enter the house, salute it. [13] And if the house is worthy, let your peace come upon it; but if it is not worthy, let your peace return to you. [14] And if any one will not receive you or listen to your words, shake off the dust from your feet as you leave that house or town. [15] Truly, I say to you, it shall be more

a Other ancient authorities omit this verse   *x* Other ancient authorities read *Lebbaeus* or *Lebbaeus called Thaddaeus*

---

tion or from a superior power. **22:** Mk.11.23 n., 24 n. **23:** Jer.9.17–18. **24:** Jesus speaks in the perspective of the kingdom of God in which physical death is not finally destructive of a person's existence but is a temporary cessation of personal activity (and analogous to sleeping). Verse 18 and the crowd's attitude clearly assert the fact of physical death. **27–31:** 20.29–34. **29:** 9.22 n. **30:** 8.4. **32–34:** 12.22–24; Lk.11.14–15. **34:** See 12.24 n.; Mk.3.22 n.; Jn.7.20. **35–38:** 4.23–25. **36:** Mk.6.34; Mt.14.14; 15.32; Num.27.17; Ezek.34.1–6; Zech.10.2.
   10.1–11.1: Commissioning and instruction of the Twelve. 10.1–4: Mk.6.7; 3.13–19; Lk.9.1; 6.12–16. **1:** *Unclean spirits,* see Mk.1.23 n. **5–15:** Mk.6.8–11; Lk.9.2–5; 10.3–12. **5:** 15.21–28; Lk.9.52; Jn.4.9. **6:** 15.24. **7:** The primary message. Through acceptance, or at least openness to this message and its bearer, healing would follow (see 4.17 n.; 4.23; 9.21,35). **9:** Lk.22.35–36. **10:** *Tunic,* a short-sleeved garment of knee-length, held in at the waist by a girdle (Mk.1.6). *Deserves,* 1 Cor.9.14. **15:** Life and death depend on man's response to God's kingdom.

tolerable on the day of judgment for the land of Sodom and Gomor'rah than for that town.

16 "Behold, I send you out as sheep in the midst of wolves; so be wise as serpents and innocent as doves. [17] Beware of men; for they will deliver you up to councils, and flog you in their synagogues, [18] and you will be dragged before governors and kings for my sake, to bear testimony before them and the Gentiles. [19] When they deliver you up, do not be anxious how you are to speak or what you are to say; for what you are to say will be given to you in that hour; [20] for it is not you who speak, but the Spirit of your Father speaking through you. [21] Brother will deliver up brother to death, and the father his child, and children will rise against parents and have them put to death; [22] and you will be hated by all for my name's sake. But he who endures to the end will be saved. [23] When they persecute you in one town, flee to the next; for truly, I say to you, you will not have gone through all the towns of Israel, before the Son of man comes.

24 "A disciple is not above his teacher, nor a servant[y] above his master; [25] it is enough for the disciple to be like his teacher, and the servant[y] like his master. If they have called the master of the house Be-el'zebul, how much more will they malign those of his household.

26 "So have no fear of them; for nothing is covered that will not be revealed, or hidden that will not be known. [27] What I tell you in the dark, utter in the light; and what you hear whispered, proclaim upon the housetops. [28] And do not fear those who kill the body but cannot kill the soul; rather fear him who can destroy both soul and body in hell.[z] [29] Are not two sparrows sold for a penny? And not one of them will fall to the ground without your Father's will. [30] But even the hairs of your head are all numbered. [31] Fear not, therefore; you are of more value than many sparrows. [32] So every one who acknowledges me before men, also will acknowledge before my Father who is in heaven; [33] but whoever denies me before men, I also will deny before my Father who is in heaven.

34 "Do not think that I have come to bring peace on earth; I have not come to bring peace, but a sword. [35] For I have come to set a man against his father, and a daughter against her mother, and a daughter-in-law against her mother-in-law; [36] and a man's foes will be those of his own household. [37] He who loves father or mother more than me is not worthy of me; and he who loves son or daughter more than me is not worthy of me; [38] and he who does not take his cross and follow me is not worthy of me. [39] He who finds his life will lose it, and he who loses his life for my sake will find it.

40 "He who receives you receives me, and he who receives me receives him who sent me. [41] He who receives a prophet because he is a prophet shall receive a prophet's reward, and he who receives a righteous man because he is a righteous man shall receive a righteous man's reward. [42] And whoever gives to one of these little ones even a cup of cold water because he is a disciple, truly, I say to you, he shall not lose his reward."

y Or *slave*   *z* Greek *Gehenna*

Sodom and Gomorrah illustrate God's judgment on wickedness (Gen.18.16–33; ch. 19). **16–25:** 24.9,13; Mk.13.9–13; Lk.21.12–17,19. **20:** Jn.16.7–11. **21:** 10.35–36; Lk.12.52–53. **22:** *My name's sake,* "because of me and my cause." **23:** The words stress the urgency of the disciples' task. **25:** Lk.6.40; Jn.13.16; 15.20; Mt.9.34; 12.24; Mk.3.22. **26–33:** Lk.12.2–9. **28:** Heb.10.31. **29–33:** 6.26–33. **29:** See Lk.12.6 n. **31:** 12.12. **32–33:** Jesus claims to mediate God's will; a favorable response to him is a response to God (compare vv. 40–42). **34–36:** Lk.12.51–53. **35:** Mic.7.6. **37–39:** 16.24–25; Mk.8.34–35; Lk.9.23–24; 14.26–27; 17.33. **37:** Compare the stronger form of expression in Lk.14.26. **38:** A *cross,* a Roman means of execution, was carried by the condemned man to the scene of death. Jesus sees that the acceptance of his message with its promise also brings seeming destruction (v. 34). Only those who in faith accept the threat of destruction will find life (v. 39; 5.11–12; 16.24; Mk.8.34–35; 10.29–31; Lk.9.24–25; 14.27; 17.33; Jn.12.25). **42:** *Little ones,* see 18.6 n.

11 And when Jesus had finished instructing his twelve disciples, he went on from there to teach and preach in their cities.

2 Now when John heard in prison about the deeds of the Christ, he sent word by his disciples [3] and said to him, "Are you he who is to come, or shall we look for another?" [4] And Jesus answered them, "Go and tell John what you hear and see: [5] the blind receive their sight and the lame walk, lepers are cleansed and the deaf hear, and the dead are raised up, and the poor have good news preached to them. [6] And blessed is he who takes no offense at me."

7 As they went away, Jesus began to speak to the crowds concerning John: "What did you go out into the wilderness to behold? A reed shaken by the wind? [8] Why then did you go out? To see a man[a] clothed in soft raiment? Behold, those who wear soft raiment are in kings' houses. [9] Why then did you go out? To see a prophet?[b] Yes, I tell you, and more than a prophet. [10] This is he of whom it is written,

'Behold, I send my messenger before thy face,
who shall prepare thy way before thee.'

[11] Truly, I say to you, among those born of women there has risen no one greater than John the Baptist; yet he who is least in the kingdom of heaven is greater than he. [12] From the days of John the Baptist until now the kingdom of heaven has suffered violence,[c] and men of violence take it by force. [13] For all the prophets and the law prophesied until John; [14] and if you are willing to accept it, he is Eli'jah who is to come. [15] He who has ears to hear,[d] let him hear.

16 "But to what shall I compare this generation? It is like children sitting in the market places and calling to their playmates,

[17] 'We piped to you, and you did not dance;
we wailed, and you did not mourn.'

[18] For John came neither eating nor drinking, and they say, 'He has a demon'; [19] the Son of man came eating and drinking, and they say, 'Behold, a glutton and a drunkard, a friend of tax collectors and sinners!' Yet wisdom is justified by her deeds.'[e]

20 Then he began to upbraid the cities where most of his mighty works had been done, because they did not repent. [21] "Woe to you, Chora'zin! woe to you, Beth-sa'ida! for if the mighty works done in you had been done in Tyre and Sidon, they would have repented long ago in sackcloth and ashes. [22] But I tell you, it shall be more tolerable on the day of judgment for Tyre and Sidon than for you. [23] And you, Caper'na-um, will you be exalted to heaven? You shall be brought down to Hades. For if the mighty works done in you had been done in Sodom, it would have remained until this day. [24] But I tell you that it shall be more tolerable on the day of judgment for the land of Sodom than for you."

25 At that time Jesus declared, "I thank thee, Father, Lord of heaven and earth, that thou hast hidden these things from the wise and understanding and revealed them to babes; [26] yea, Father, for such was thy gracious will.[f] [27] All things have been delivered

a Or *What then did you go out to see? A man . . .*
b Other ancient authorities read *What then did you go out to see? A prophet?*   c Or *has been coming violently*
d Other ancient authorities omit *to hear*   e Other ancient authorities read *children* (Lk 7.35)   f Or *so it was well-pleasing before thee*

11.1: *Finished,* see 7.28 n. **11.2–12.50: Narratives illustrating the authority claimed by Jesus. 11.2–19:** Jesus and John (Lk.7.18–35; 16.16). **2–3:** *The Christ,* i.e. the Messiah who *is to come.* **4–5:** Jesus performs the works of the predicted Messiah (Is.29.18–19; 35.5–6; 61.1; compare Lk.4.18–19). **6:** Jesus invites John to answer his own question, basing his decision on what he hears of Jesus' activities interpreted in comparison with Isaiah's words (compare Lk.4.17–21. **7–15:** John was important because he introduced the new manifestation (or "coming") of God's kingdom. **10:** From Mal.3.1; compare Mk.1.2. **14:** Mal.4.5; Lk.1.17; Mk.9.11–13. Biblical prophecy depends on human acceptance of God's terms for fulfilment. If John's message were accepted, his activity would become that foretold in Elijah's name. Jesus seems not to have expected the literal return of *Elijah* (17.10–13; Mk.9.9–13). **18:** See Lk.7.33 n. **23:** Is.14.13,15. **25–30:** Lk.10.21–22. **25:** 9.13; 10.42; see 16.17 n.; Lk.10.21–22; 24.16. **27:** Jesus claimed a special

to me by my Father; and no one knows the Son except the Father, and no one knows the Father except the Son and any one to whom the Son chooses to reveal him. [28] Come to me, all who labor and are heavy laden, and I will give you rest. [29] Take my yoke upon you, and learn from me; for I am gentle and lowly in heart, and you will find rest for your souls. [30] For my yoke is easy, and my burden is light."

12 At that time Jesus went through the grainfields on the sabbath; his disciples were hungry, and they began to pluck heads of grain and to eat. [2] But when the Pharisees saw it, they said to him, "Look, your disciples are doing what is not lawful to do on the sabbath." [3] He said to them, "Have you not read what David did, when he was hungry, and those who were with him: [4] how he entered the house of God and ate the bread of the Presence, which it was not lawful for him to eat nor for those who were with him, but only for the priests? [5] Or have you not read in the law how on the sabbath the priests in the temple profane the sabbath, and are guiltless? [6] I tell you, something greater than the temple is here. [7] And if you had known what this means, 'I desire mercy, and not sacrifice,' you would not have condemned the guiltless. [8] For the Son of man is lord of the sabbath."

9 And he went on from there, and entered their synagogue, [10] And behold, there was a man with a withered hand. And they asked him, "Is it lawful to heal on the sabbath?" so that they might accuse him. [11] He said to them, "What man of you, if he has one sheep and it falls into a pit on the sabbath, will not lay hold of it and lift it out? [12] Of how much more value is a man than a sheep! So it is lawful to do good on the sabbath." [13] Then he said to the man, "Stretch out your hand." And the man stretched it out, and it was restored, whole like the other. [14] But the Pharisees went out and took counsel against him, how to destroy him.

15 Jesus, aware of this, withdrew from there. And many followed him, and he healed them all, [16] and ordered them not to make him known. [17] This was to fulfil what was spoken by the prophet Isaiah:

[18] "Behold, my servant whom I have chosen,
    my beloved with whom my soul is well
        pleased.
I will put my Spirit upon him,
    and he shall proclaim justice to the
        Gentiles.
[19] He will not wrangle or cry aloud,
    nor will any one hear his voice in the
        streets;
[20] he will not break a bruised reed
    or quench a smoldering wick,
        till he brings justice to victory;
[21]   and in his name will the Gentiles hope."

22 Then a blind and dumb demoniac was brought to him, and he healed him, so that the dumb man spoke and saw. [23] And all the people were amazed, and said, "Can this be the Son of David?" [24] But when the Pharisees

relation to God which he could share with others (Jn.3.35; 13.3). **29:** The rabbis spoke of the *yoke* of the Law. Jesus regarded his claim as more demanding and more rewarding (5.17–20).

12.1–14: Jesus and sabbath laws (Mk.2.23–3.6; Lk.6.1–11). **1:** Dt.23.25. **2:** The objection rested on the traditional interpretation that plucking grain by hand was an activity forbidden by Ex.20.8–11. **3–4:** 1 Sam.21.1–6; Lev.24.5–9. **5:** Num.28.9–10. **6:** Since no penalty was exacted from those who set aside provisions of the Law for the sake of some human need or some more significant service to God, Jesus' disciples eat because of their need and serve him who is greater than the institutions of the Law (see vv. 41–42). **7:** Hos.6.6; Mt.9.13. **8:** Jesus claims, by virtue of his mission as the Messiah, authority over man's obedience to God (11.27; Is.5.1–18). **11–12:** The rabbis agreed with the principle of attending to accidental injury and danger on the sabbath, but they thought that chronic conditions should wait (Lk.13.14). For Jesus it was important to restore a person to useful life. **12:** 10.31.

12.15–21: Work of healing (Mk.3.7–12; Lk.6.17–19; 4.40). **17–21:** Is.42.1–4.

12.22–37: Sources of Jesus' power (Mk.3.20–30; Lk.11.14–23; 12.10). **22–24:** The dumbness here said to be caused by demonic possession is said in Lk.11.14 to describe the demon itself. The Biblical writers speak either of *healing* the victim or casting out the demon (v. 24; 9.32–33; Lk.11.14–15). **23:** *Son of David*, a title of the Messiah (21.9). **24:** The issue is how to account for Jesus' manifest power. The Pharisees attribute it to evil forces hostile to

heard it they said, "It is only by Be-el'zebul, the prince of demons, that this man casts out demons." 25 Knowing their thoughts, he said to them, "Every kingdom divided against itself is laid waste, and no city or house divided against itself will stand; 26 and if Satan casts out Satan, he is divided against himself; how then will his kingdom stand? 27 And if I cast out demons by Be-el'zebul, by whom do your sons cast them out? Therefore they shall be your judges. 28 But if it is by the Spirit of God that I cast out demons, then the kingdom of God has come upon you. 29 Or how can one enter a strong man's house and plunder his goods, unless he first binds the strong man? Then indeed he may plunder his house. 30 He who is not with me is against me, and he who does not gather with me scatters. 31 Therefore I tell you, every sin and blasphemy will be forgiven men, but the blasphemy against the Spirit will not be forgiven. 32 And whoever says a word against the Son of man will be forgiven; but whoever speaks against the Holy Spirit will not be forgiven, either in this age or in the age to come.

33 "Either make the tree good, and its fruit good; or make the tree bad, and its fruit bad; for the tree is known by its fruit. 34 You brood of vipers! how can you speak good, when you are evil? For out of the abundance of the heart the mouth speaks. 35 The good man out of his good treasure brings forth good, and the evil man out of his evil treasure brings forth evil. 36 I tell you, on the day of judgment men will render account for every careless word they utter; 37 for by your words you will be justified, and by your words you will be condemned."

38 Then some of the scribes and Pharisees said to him, "Teacher, we wish to see a sign from you." 39 But he answered them, "An evil and adulterous generation seeks for a sign; but no sign shall be given to it except the sign of the prophet Jonah. 40 For as Jonah was three days and three nights in the belly of the whale, so will the Son of man be three days and three nights in the heart of the earth. 41 The men of Nin'eveh will rise at the judgment with this generation and condemn it; for they repented at the preaching of Jonah, and behold, something greater than Jonah is here. 42 The queen of the South will arise at the judgment with this generation and condemn it; for she came from the ends of the earth to hear the wisdom of Solomon, and behold, something greater than Solomon is here.

43 "When the unclean spirit has gone out of a man, he passes through waterless places seeking rest, but he finds none. 44 Then he says, 'I will return to my house from which I came.' And when he comes he finds it empty, swept, and put in order. 45 Then he goes and brings with him seven other spirits more evil than himself, and they enter and dwell there; and the last state of that man becomes worse than the first. So shall it be also with this evil generation."

46 While he was still speaking to the people, behold, his mother and his brothers stood outside, asking to speak to him.*g* 48 But he replied to the man who told him, "Who is my mother, and who are my brothers?" 49 And

g Other ancient authorities insert verse 47, *Some one told him, "Your mother and your brothers are standing outside, asking to speak to you"*

---

mankind (see Lk.7.33 n.). *Beelzebul,* see 2 Kg.1.2 n.; Mk.3.22 n. **27:** *Your sons,* your disciples (compare 1 Pet.5.13). Exorcising demons was not limited to Jesus and his followers (7.22–23; Mk.9.38; Acts 19.13–19). **28:** Lk.4.18–20. **31–32:** The unforgivable sin is the utter rebellion against God that denies him as the doer of his own acts (Lk.12.10). **32:** Mk.3.28–30. **33–36:** 7.16–20; Mk.7.14–23; Lk.6.43–45. **33:** *Make,* recognize that fruit and tree will be alike (Jas.3.11–12). **36:** *Careless,* useless; "barren" in Jas.2.20. **37:** Compare Rom.2.6.

  12.38–42: Request for a sign (Lk.11.16,29–32). **39:** *Adulterous* was used by Old Testament prophets to describe Israel's turning away from God (Jer.3.8; Ezek.23.37; Hos.2.2–10). *Sign,* compare v. 40. **40:** *Whale,* "sea monster" (compare Jon.1.17). **41:** Jon.3.5; Mt.11.20–24; 12.6. **42:** 1 Kg.10.1–10; 2 Chr.9.1–9.

  12.43–45: The return of the unclean spirit (Lk.11.24–26; see Mk.1.23 n.). **43:** Waterless places, or deserts, supposed to be the favorite abode of demons (compare Is.13.21–22; 34.14). **44:** *My house,* the man himself. *Empty,* though evil has been temporarily expelled, nothing good has been put in its place.

  12.46–50: Jesus' true family (Mk.3.31–35; Lk.8.19–21). See 13.55 n.

stretching out his hand toward his disciples, he said, "Here are my mother and my brothers! [50] For whoever does the will of my Father in heaven is my brother, and sister, and mother."

13 That same day Jesus went out of the house and sat beside the sea. [2] And great crowds gathered about him, so that he got into a boat and sat there; and the whole crowd stood on the beach. [3] And he told them many things in parables, saying: "A sower went out to sow. [4] And as he sowed, some seeds fell along the path, and the birds came and devoured them. [5] Other seeds fell on rocky ground, where they had not much soil, and immediately they sprang up, since they had no depth of soil, [6] but when the sun rose they were scorched; and since they had no root they withered away. [7] Other seeds fell upon thorns, and the thorns grew up and choked them. [8] Other seeds fell on good soil and brought forth grain, some a hundredfold, some sixty, some thirty. [9] He who has ears,[h] let him hear."

10 Then the disciples came and said to him, "Why do you speak to them in parables?" [11] And he answered them, "To you it has been given to know the secrets of the kingdom of heaven, but to them it has not been given. [12] For to him who has will more be given, and he will have abundance; but from him who has not, even what he has will be taken away. [13] This is why I speak to them in parables, because seeing they do not see, and hearing they do not hear, nor do they understand. [14] With them indeed is fulfilled the prophecy of Isaiah which says:

'You shall indeed hear but never understand,
　and you shall indeed see but never perceive.
[15] For this people's heart has grown dull,
　and their ears are heavy of hearing,
　and their eyes they have closed,
lest they should perceive with their eyes,
　and hear with their ears,
and understand with their heart,
　and turn for me to heal them.'

[16] But blessed are your eyes, for they see, and your ears, for they hear. [17] Truly, I say to you, many prophets and righteous men longed to see what you see, and did not see it, and to hear what you hear, and did not hear it.

18 "Hear then the parable of the sower. [19] When any one hears the word of the kingdom and does not understand it, the evil one comes and snatches away what is sown in his heart; this is what was sown along the path. [20] As for what was sown on rocky ground, this is he who hears the word and immediately receives it with joy; [21] yet he has no root in himself, but endures for a while, and when tribulation or persecution arises on account of the word, immediately he falls away.[i] [22] As for what was sown among thorns, this is he who hears the word, but the cares of the world and the delight in riches choke the word, and it proves unfruitful. [23] As for what was sown on good soil, this is he who hears the word and understands it; he indeed bears fruit, and yields, in one case a hundredfold, in another sixty, and in another thirty."

h Other ancient authorities add here and in verse 43 *to hear*   i Or *stumbles*

13.1–52: Teaching in parables (Mk.4.1–34; Lk.8.4–18; 13.18–21). **1:** *The sea,* of Galilee. **3:** *Parables* are stories describing situations in everyday life which, as Jesus used them, convey a spiritual meaning. In general the teaching of each parable relates to a single point, and apart from this the details may, or may not, have a particular meaning. Jesus used this method of teaching because: (a) it gave vivid, memorable expression to his teachings; (b) it led those who heard to reflect on his words and bear responsibility for their decision to accept or oppose his claim; (c) it probably reduced specific grounds for contention by hostile listeners. **3b–8:** The sower, explained in vv. 18–23 (see Mk.4.1–9). **11:** The disciples heard and accepted the message about God's kingdom and by their faith had access to deeper understanding (see Mk.4.11 n). **12:** 25.29; Mk.4.24–25; Lk.8.18; 19.26. **13:** The parables do not obscure truth but present it; men receive the message through their physical senses but do not comprehend (see 11.25 n.). **14–15:** Is.6.9–10; Mk.8.18; see Acts 28.26 n. **16–17:** See Lk.10.23–24 n. **17:** *See . . . hear,* Jesus' message about God's kingdom. **18–23:** Response

24 Another parable he put before them, saying, "The kingdom of heaven may be compared to a man who sowed good seed in his field; [25] but while men were sleeping, his enemy came and sowed weeds among the wheat, and went away. [26] So when the planets came up and bore grain, then the weeds appeared also. [27] And the servants[j] of the householder came and said to him, 'Sir, did you not sow good seed in your field? How then has it weeds?' [28] He said to them, 'An enemy has done this.' The servants[j] said to him, 'Then do you want us to go and gather them?' [29] But he said, 'No; lest in gathering the weeds you root up the wheat along with them. [30] Let both grow together until the harvest; and at harvest time I will tell the reapers, Gather the weeds first and bind them in bundles to be burned, but gather the wheat into my barn.'"

31 Another parable he put before them, saying, "The kingdom of heaven is like a grain of mustard seed which a man took and sowed in his field; [32] it is the smallest of all seeds, but when it has grown it is the greatest of shrubs and becomes a tree, so that the birds of the air come and make nests in its branches."

33 He told them another parable. "The kingdom of heaven is like leaven which a woman took and hid in three measures of flour, till it was all leavened."

34 All this Jesus said to the crowds in parables; indeed he said nothing to them without a parable. [35] This was to fulfil what was spoken by the prophet:[k]

"I will open my mouth in parables,
I will utter what has been hidden since the foundation of the world."

36 Then he left the crowds and went into the house. And his disciples came to him, saying, "Explain to us the parable of the weeds of the field." [37] He answered, "He who sows the good seed is the Son of man; [38] the field is the world, and the good seed means the sons of the kingdom; the weeds are the sons of the evil one, [39] and the enemy who sowed them is the devil; the harvest is the close of the age, and the reapers are angels. [40] Just as the weeds are gathered and burned with fire, so will it be at the close of the age. [41] The Son of man will send his angels, and they will gather out of his kingdom all causes of sin and all evildoers, [42] and throw them into the furnace of fire; there men will weep and gnash their teeth. [43] Then the righteous will shine like the sun in the kingdom of their Father. He who has ears, let him hear.

44 "The kingdom of heaven is like treasure hidden in a field, which a man found and covered up; then in his joy he goes and sells all that he has and buys that field.

45 "Again, the kingdom of heaven is like a merchant in search of fine pearls, [46] who, on finding one pearl of great value, went and sold all that he had and bought it.

47 "Again, the kingdom of heaven is like a net which was thrown into the sea and gathered fish of every kind; [48] when it was full, men drew it ashore and sat down and sorted the good into vessels but threw away the bad. [49] So it will be at the close of the age. The angels will come out and separate the evil from the righteous, [50] and throw them into the furnace of fire; there men will weep and gnash their teeth.

j Or *slaves*   *k* Other ancient authorities read *the prophet Isaiah*

to Jesus' message affected by the circumstances of human life. **22:** 19.23. **24–30: Weeds in the wheat.** God allows good and evil to exist together until the close of human history (vv. 36–43). **31–32: The mustard seed.** (Lk.13.18–19). The beginnings of God's kingdom are small, but it has an inherent nature that will grow to its intended end, startlingly different in size from its beginning. **32:** Dan.4.12. **33: Leaven** (Lk.13.20–21). God's rule, like *leaven* working in a hidden way, will pervade man's life, giving it a new quality. **35:** *The prophet*, i.e. Asaph the seer (2 Chr.29.30), the author of Ps. 78, from which (v. 2) the quotation is taken. **42:** See Lk.12.49 n. **43:** Dan.12.3. **44–46: Hidden treasure and the pearl of great value. 44:** Some men respond in whole-hearted dedication to Jesus' message without any other thought than to have what it yields. **45–46:** Some men dedicate themselves to God's kingdom because, being able to judge the value of other claims being made on them, they value it more. **47–50: The drag-**

51 "Have you understood all this?" They said to him, "Yes." 52 And he said to them, "Therefore every scribe who has been trained for the kingdom of heaven is like a householder who brings out of his treasure what is new and what is old."

53 And when Jesus had finished these parables, he went away from there, 54 and coming to his own country he taught them in their synagogue, so that they were astonished, and said, "Where did this man get this wisdom and these mighty works? 55 Is not this the carpenter's son? Is not his mother called Mary? And are not his brothers James and Joseph and Simon and Judas? 56 And are not all his sisters with us? Where then did this man get all this?" 57 And they took offense at him. But Jesus said to them, "A prophet is not without honor except in his own country and in his own house." 58 And he did not do many mighty works there, because of their unbelief.

14 At that time Herod the tetrarch heard about the fame of Jesus; 2 and he said to his servants, "This is John the Baptist, he has been raised from the dead; that is why these powers are at work in him." 8 For Herod had seized John and bound him and put him in prison, for the sake of Hero'di-as, his brother Philip's wife;*l* 4 because John said to him, "It is not lawful for you to have her." 5 And though he wanted to put him to death, he feared the people, because they held him to be a prophet. 6 But when Herod's birthday came, the daughter of Hero'di-as danced before the company, and pleased Herod, 7 so that he promised with an oath to give her whatever

she might ask. 8 Prompted by her mother, she said, "Give me the head of John the Baptist here on a platter." 9 And the king was sorry; but because of his oaths and his guests he commanded it to be given; 10 he sent and had John beheaded in the prison, 11 and his head was brought on a platter and given to the girl, and she brought it to her mother. 12 And his disciples came and took the body and buried it; and they went and told Jesus.

13 Now when Jesus heard this, he withdrew from there in a boat to a lonely place apart. But when the crowds heard it, they followed him on foot from the towns. 14 As he went ashore he saw a great throng; and he had compassion on them, and healed their sick. 15 When it was evening, the disciples came to him and said, "This is a lonely place, and the day is now over; send the crowds away to go into the villages and buy food for themselves." 16 Jesus said, "They need not go away; you give them something to eat." 17 They said to him, "We have only five loaves here and two fish." 18 And he said, "Bring them here to me." 19 Then he ordered the crowds to sit down on the grass; and taking the five loaves and the two fish he looked up to heaven, and blessed, and broke and gave the loaves to the disciples, and the disciples gave them to the crowds. 20 And they all ate and were satisfied. And they took up twelve baskets full of the broken pieces left over. 21 And those who ate were about five thousand men, besides women and children.

j Or *slaves*   *k* Other ancient authorities read *the prophet Isaiah*   *l* Other ancient authorities read *his brother's wife*

net. 52: *Scribe,* an expert in the Mosaic law, having become a disciple of Jesus is able to preserve past insights and enlarge them.

13.53–17.27: Events of decisive acceptance or rejection of Jesus. 13.53–58: Rejection at home. 53: *Finished,* see 7.28 n. 54: *His own country,* Nazareth (Lk.4.16,23). 55: *Brothers,* regarded by Protestants as children of Mary, younger than Jesus. In Semitic usage, besides its ordinary meaning, the word *brothers* may also refer to persons of varying degrees of blood relationship; here (and in Mt.12.46; Mk.3.31–32; 6.3; Lk.8.19–20; Jn.2.12; 7.3,5; Acts 1.14; 1 Cor.9.5; Gal.1.19) Catholic tradition regards them as relatives of Jesus, not blood brothers (see also Mt.1.25 n.; Lk.2.7 n.). 58: See Mk.6.5–6 n.

14.1–12: Death of John (Mk.6.14–29; Lk.9.7–9). 1: *Herod* Antipas, son of Herod the Great *Tetrarch,* ruler of a minor political unit. 3: *Philip,* not the tetrarch of Lk.3.1, but a half-brother of *Herod* Antipas. 4: Lev.18.16; 20.21. 6: *The daughter of Herodias* was Salome.

14.13–21: Five thousand fed (Mk.6.30–44; Lk.9.10–17; Jn.6.1–13). 13: After John's death Jesus faced a new stage in his life (compare his reaction to John's imprisonment, Mk.1.14–15). 14: 20.25–28.

22 Then he made the disciples get into the boat and go before him to the other side, while he dismissed the crowds. 23 And after he had dismissed the crowds, he went up on the mountain by himself to pray. When evening came, he was there alone, 24 but the boat by this time was many furlongs distant from the land,*m* beaten by the waves; for the wind was against them. 25 And in the fourth watch of the night he came to them, walking on the sea. 26 But when the disciples saw him walking on the sea, they were terrified, saying, "It is a ghost!" And they cried out for fear. 27 But immediately he spoke to them, saying, "Take heart, it is I; have no fear."

28 And Peter answered him, "Lord, if it is you, bid me come to you on the water." 29 He said, "Come." So Peter got out of the boat and walked on the water and came to Jesus; 30 but when he saw the wind,*n* he was afraid, and beginning to sink he cried out, "Lord, save me."31 Jesus immediately reached out his hand and caught him, saying to him, "O man of little faith, why did you doubt?" 32 And when they got into the boat, the wind ceased. 33 And those in the boat worshiped him, saying, "Truly you are the Son of God."

34 And when they had crossed over, they came to land at Gennes'aret. 35 And when the men of that place recognized him, they sent round to all that region and brought to him all that were sick, 36 and besought him that they might only touch the fringe of his garment; and as many as touched it were made well.

15 Then Pharisees and scribes came to Jesus from Jerusalem and said, 2 "Why do your disciples transgress the tradition of the elders? For they do not wash their hands when they eat." 3 He answered them, "And why do you transgress the commandment of God for the sake of your tradition? 4 For God commanded, 'Honor your father and your mother,' and, 'He who speaks evil of father or mother, let him surely die.' 5 But you say, 'If any one tells his father or his mother, What you would have gained from me is given to God,*o* he need not honor his father.' 6 So, for the sake of your tradition, you have made void the word*p* of God. 7 You hypocrites! Well did Isaiah prophesy of you, when he said:

8 'This people honors me with their lips,
   but their heart is far from me;
9 in vain do they worship me,
   teaching as doctrines the precepts of
   men.'"

10 And he called the people to him and said to them, "Hear and understand: 11 not what goes into the mouth defiles a man, but what comes out of the mouth, this defiles a man." 12 Then the disciples came and said to him, "Do you know that the Pharisees were offended when they heard this saying?" 13 He answered, "Every plant which my heavenly Father has not planted will be rooted up. 14 Let them alone; they are blind guides. And if a blind man leads a blind man, both will fall into a pit." 15 But Peter said to him, "Explain the parable to us." 16 And he said, "Are you also still without understanding? 17 Do you not see that whatever goes into the mouth passes into the stomach, and so passes on?*q* 18 But what comes out of the mouth proceeds from the heart, and this defiles a man. 19 For out of the heart come evil thoughts, murder, adultery, fornication, theft, false witness, slander. 20 These are what defile a man; but to eat with unwashed hands does not defile a man."

m Other ancient authorities read *was out on the sea*
n Other ancient authorities read *strong wind*
o Or *an offering*   *p* Other ancient authorities read *law*
q Or *is evacuated*

14.22–36: Jesus walks on water (Mk.6.45–52; Jn.6.15–21). **24:** A *furlong,* about one-eighth of a mile. **25:** *The fourth watch,* see Mk.6.48 n. **26:** Lk.24.37. **33:** Mk.6.51–52.

15.1–20: Tradition of the elders (Mk.7.1–23). **2:** *The tradition of the elders,* the rabbinical exposition of the Law of Moses. **4:** Ex.20.12; Dt.5.16; Ex.21.17; Lev.20.9. **7–9:** Is.29.13 (see Mk.7.6–7 n.). **10–20:** The teaching here depends on the principle in the Law that certain physical conditions can and do render an individual unfit to share in the worship of the community. **11:** *Defiles,* renders unfit to share in public ritual (Acts 10.14–15; 1 Tim.4.3). **13:** Is.60.21. **14:** Lk.6.39; Mt.23.16,24. **19–20:** Violations of the rights and interests of another hinder worship (5.23–24).

21 And Jesus went away from there and withdrew to the district of Tyre and Sidon. [22] And behold, a Canaanite woman from that region came out and cried, "Have mercy on me, O Lord, Son of David; my daughter is severely possessed by a demon." [23] But he did not answer her a word. And his disciples came and begged him, saying, "Send her away, for she is crying after us." [24] He answered, "I was sent only to the lost sheep of the house of Israel." [25] But she came and knelt before him, saying, "Lord, help me." [26] And he answered, "It is not fair to take the children's bread and throw it to the dogs." [27] She said, "Yes, Lord, yet even the dogs eat the crumbs that fall from their masters' table." [28] Then Jesus answered her, "O woman, great is your faith! Be it done for you as you desire." And her daughter was healed instantly.

29 And Jesus went on from there and passed along the Sea of Galilee. And he went up on the mountain, and sat down there. [30] And great crowds came to him, bringing with them the lame, the maimed, the blind, the dumb, and many others, and they put them at his feet, and he healed them, [31] so that the throng wondered, when they saw the dumb speaking, the maimed whole, the lame walking, and the blind seeing; and they glorified the God of Israel.

32 Then Jesus called his disciples to him and said, "I have compassion on the crowd, because they have been with me now three days, and have nothing to eat; and I am unwilling to send them away hungry, lest they faint on the way." [33] And the disciples said to him, "Where are we to get bread enough in the desert to feed so great a crowd?" [34] And Jesus said to them, "How many loaves have you?" They said, "Seven, and a few small fish." [35] And commanding the crowd to sit down on the ground, [36] he took the seven loaves and the fish, and having given thanks he broke them and gave them to the disciples, and the disciples gave them to the crowds. [37] And they all ate and were satisfied; and they took up seven baskets full of the broken pieces left over. [38] Those who ate were four thousand men, besides women and children. [39] And sending away the crowds, he got into the boat and went to the region of Mag'adan.

16 And the Pharisees and Sad'ducees came, and to test him they asked him to show them a sign from heaven. [2] He answered them,[r] "When it is evening, you say, 'It will be fair weather; for the sky is red.' [3] And in the morning, 'It will be stormy today, for the sky is red and threatening.' You know how to interpret the appearance of the sky, but you cannot interpret the signs of the times. [4] An evil and adulterous generation seeks for a sign, but no sign shall be given to it except the sign of Jonah." So he left them and departed.

5 When the disciples reached the other side, they had forgotten to bring any bread. [6] Jesus said to them, "Take heed and beware of the leaven of the Pharisees and Sad'ducees." [7] And they discussed it among themselves, saying, "We brought no bread." [8] But Jesus, aware of this, said, "O men of little faith, why do you discuss among yourselves the fact that you have no bread? [9] Do you not yet

r Other ancient authorities omit the following words to the end of verse 3

15.21–28: The Canaanite woman (Mk.7.24–30). **22:** The woman, though a Gentile, speaks to Jesus as the Jewish Messiah. **24:** 10.6,23. Jesus consistently said that his primary mission was to call Jews back to God. The Gentile woman's claim must be based on her own personal acceptance of his message. The distinction is between his mission and his willingness to respond to faith wherever found. **27:** The woman accepts Jesus' mission and as a Gentile asks his help.

15.29–31: Healings (Mk.7.31–37).

15.32–39: Four thousand fed (see Mk.8.1–10 n.). **39:** *Magadan* was apparently on the west side of the Sea of Galilee.

16.1–4: Demand for signs (Mk.8.11–13; Lk.11.16,29; 12.54–56). **3:** *The signs of the times* may refer to 15.29–31; compare 11.2–6. **4:** See 12.39 n., 40 n.; Jon.3.4–5.

16.5–12: Leaven of the Pharisees (Mk.8.14–21; Lk.12.1). **5:** *The other side,* the eastern shore of the Sea of Galilee. **6:** *Leaven,* see Mk.8.15 n. **9:** 14.17–21. **10:** 15.34–38.

perceive? Do you not remember the five loaves of the five thousand, and how many baskets you gathered? [10] Or the seven loaves of the four thousand, and how many baskets you gathered? [11] How is it that you fail to perceive that I did not speak about bread? Beware of the leaven of the Pharisees and Sad'ducees." [12] Then they understood that he did not tell them to beware of the leaven of bread, but of the teaching of the Pharisees and Sad'ducees.

13 Now when Jesus came into the district of Caesare'a Philip'pi, he asked his disciples, "Who do men say that the Son of man is?" [14] And they said, "Some say John the Baptist, others say Eli'jah, and others Jeremiah or one of the prophets." [15] He said to them, "But who do you say that I am?" [16] Simon Peter replied, "You are the Christ, the Son of the living God." [17] And Jesus answered him, "Blessed are you, Simon Bar-Jona! For flesh and blood has not revealed this to you, but my Father who is in heaven. [18] And I tell you, you are Peter,*s* and on this rock*t* I will build my church, and the powers of death*u* shall not prevail against it. [19] I will give you the keys of the kingdom of heaven, and whatever you bind on earth shall be bound in heaven, and whatever you loose on earth shall be loosed in heaven." [29] Then he strictly charged the disciples to tell no one that he was the Christ.

21 From that time Jesus began to show his disciples that he must go to Jerusalem and suffer many things from the elders and chief priests and scribes, and be killed, and on the third day be raised. [22] And Peter took him and began to rebuke him, saying, "God forbid, Lord! This shall never happen to you." [23] But he turned and said to Peter, "Get behind me, Satan! You are a hindrance*v* to me; for you are not on the side of God, but of men."

24 Then Jesus told his disciples, "If any man would come after me, let him deny himself and take up his cross and follow me. [25] For whoever would save his life will lose it, and whoever loses his life for my sake will find it. [26] For what will it profit a man, if he gains the whole world and forfeits his life? Or what shall a man give in return for his life? [27] For the Son of man is to come with his angels in the glory of his Father, and then he will repay every man for what he has done. [28] Truly, I say to you, there are some standing here who will not taste death before they see the Son of man coming in his kingdom."

17 And after six days Jesus took with him Peter and James and John his brother, and led them up a high mountain apart. [2] And he was transfigured before them, and his face shone like the sun, and his garments became white as light. [3] And behold, there appeared to them Moses and Eli'jah, talking with him. [4] And Peter said to Jesus, "Lord, it is well that we are here; if you wish, I will make three

s Greek *Petros*   *t* Greek *petra*   *u* Greek *the gates of Hades*   *v* Greek *stumbling block*

16.13–23: Peter's confession (Mk.8.27–33; Lk.9.18–22). **13:** See Mk.8.27 n. *Son of man* here is equivalent to "I." **16:** Peter asserts that Jesus is the Messiah, not merely one of the prophets (v. 14). He identifies Jesus with the figure of Mal.3.1–4 (compare Mk.1.2; Mt.1.16; Jn.1.49; 11.27). **17:** *Simon* was Peter's personal name. *Bar-Jona* identifies Simon as "son of John." *Flesh and blood,* human beings (1 Cor.15.50; Gal.1.16; Eph.6.12). *Revealed,* understanding spiritual realities involves God's disclosure (see 11.25 n.; Lk.24.16; 1 Cor.1.18–25; 2.6–16). **18:** The Greek text involves a play on two words, *Petros* ("Peter") and *petra* ("rock"). Palestinian Aramaic, which Jesus usually spoke, used the same word for both proper name and common noun: "You are *Kepha* [Cephas; compare 1 Cor.15.5; Gal.2.9], and on this *kepha* [rock] I will build . . ." For the view that all the apostles also form the foundation of the church, see Eph.2.20; Rev.21.14. *Church,* see Gal.1.13 n. **19:** *The keys of the kingdom* are a symbol of Peter's power as the leader of the church. *Bind* and *loose* are technical rabbinic terms meaning "forbid" and "permit" some action about which a question has arisen. Later the authority of binding and loosing was also conferred upon all the apostles (18.18). **20:** See Mk.8.30 n. **21:** See Lk.9.22 n. **22–23:** See Mk.8.32 n., 33 n.

16.24–28: On discipleship (Mk.8.34–9.1; Lk.9.23–27). **24:** See 10.38 n. **25:** See Mk.8.35 n. **26:** Here *life* is not merely physical existence, but the higher or spiritual life of man, his real self (compare Lk.9.25; 12.15). **27:** Ps.62.12; Mt.10.33; Lk.12.8–9; Rom.2.6; 1 Jn.2.28; Rev.22.12. **28:** See Mk.9.1 n.; 1 Cor.16.22; 1 Th.4.15–18; Jas.5.7; Rev.1.7.

17.1–8: The transfiguration. See notes on the parallel passages, Mk.9.2–8; Lk.9.28–36.

booths here, one for you and one for Moses and one for Eli′jah." [5] He was still speaking, when lo, a bright cloud overshadowed them, and a voice from the cloud said, "This is my beloved Son,[w] with whom I am well pleased; listen to him." [6] When the disciples heard this, they fell on their faces, and were filled with awe. [7] But Jesus came and touched them, saying, "Rise, and have no fear." [8] And when they lifted up their eyes, they saw no one but Jesus only.

[9] And as they were coming down the mountain, Jesus commanded them, "Tell no one the vision, until the Son of man is raised from the dead." [10] And the disciples asked him, "Then why do the scribes say that first Eli′jah must come?" [11] He replied, "Eli′jah does come, and he is to restore all things; [12] but I tell you that Eli′jah has already come, and they did not know him, but did to him whatever they pleased. So also the Son of man will suffer at their hands." [13] Then the disciples understood that he was speaking to them of John the Baptist.

[14] And when they came to the crowd, a man came up to him and kneeling before him said, [15] "Lord, have mercy on my son, for he is an epileptic and he suffers terribly; for often he falls into the fire, and often into the water. [16] And I brought him to your disciples, and they could not heal him." [17] And Jesus answered, "O faithless and perverse generation, how long am I to be with you? How long am I to bear with you? Bring him here to me." [18] And Jesus rebuked him, and the demon came out of him, and the boy was cured instantly. [19] Then the disciples came to Jesus privately and said, "Why could we not cast it out?" [20] He said to them, "Because of your little faith. For truly, I say to you, if you have faith as a grain of mustard seed, you will say to this mountain, 'Move from here to there,' and it will move; and nothing will be impossible to you."[x]

22 As they were gathering[y] in Galilee, Jesus said to them, "The Son of man is to be delivered into the hands of men, [23] and they will kill him, and he will be raised on the third day." And they were greatly distressed.

24 When they came to Caper′na-um, the collectors of the half-shekel tax went up to Peter and said, "Does not your teacher pay the tax?" [25] He said, "Yes." And when he came home, Jesus spoke to him first, saying, "What do you think, Simon? From whom do kings of the earth take toll or tribute? From their sons or from others?" [26] And when he said, "From others," Jesus said to him, "Then the sons are free. [27] However, not to give offense to them, go to the sea and cast a hook, and take the first fish that comes up, and when you open its mouth you will find a shekel; take that and give it to them for me and for yourself."

18 At that time the disciples came to Jesus, saying, "Who is the greatest in the kingdom of heaven?" [2] And calling to him a child, he put him in the midst of them, [3] and said, "Truly, I say to you, unless you turn and become like children, you will never enter the kingdom of heaven. [4] Whoever humbles him-

w Or *my Son, my* (or *the*) *Beloved*   x Other ancient authorities insert verse 21, *"But this kind never comes out except by prayer and fasting"*   y Other ancient authorities read *abode*

17.9–13: Prophecies about Elijah (Mk.9.9–13). **9:** See Mk.8.30 n. **10:** See 11.14 n. **12:** *Elijah has already come,* in the person of John the Baptist.

17.14–21: An epileptic child healed (Mk.9.14–29; Lk.9.37–42). **15:** To be *epileptic* was attributed to the baleful influences of the moon, a demonic force (compare Ps.121.6). **20:** *Little faith* as distinguished from unbelief (13.58). Jesus' saying is in figurative language; faith is concerned with God's will, not with moving mountains (compare 21.21–22; Mk.11.22–23; Lk.17.6; 1 Cor.13.2; Jas.1.6).

17.22–23: The Passion foretold a second time (Mk.9.30–32; Lk.9.43–45). Compare 16.21; 20.17–19.

17.24–27: Money for the temple tax. 24: The half-shekel tax was paid by Jewish males annually to support the temple. On the value see 26.15 n. (Ex.30.13; 38.26).

18.1–35: Sayings on humility and forgiveness. 1–5: True greatness (Mk.9.33–37; Lk.9.46–48). **3:** *Turn and become like children,* turn away from self-chosen goals and relate oneself to God as to a father. Childlike relations to a

self like this child, he is the greatest in the kingdom of heaven.

5 "Whoever receives one such child in my name receives me; [6] but whoever causes one of these little ones who believe in me to sin,[z] it would be better for him to have a great millstone fastened round his neck and to be drowned in the depth of the sea.

7 "Woe to the world for temptations to sin![a] For it is necessary that temptations come, but woe to the man by whom the temptation comes! [8] And if your hand or your foot causes you to sin,[z] cut it off and throw it away; it is better for you to enter life maimed or lame than with two hands or two feet to be thrown into the eternal fire. [9] And if your eye causes you to sin,[z] pluck it out and throw it away; it is better for you to enter life with one eye than with two eyes to be thrown into the hell[b] of fire.

10 "See that you do not despise one of these little ones; for I tell you that in heaven their angels always behold the face of my Father who is in heaven.[c] [12] What do you think? If a man has a hundred sheep, and one of them has gone astray, does he not leave the ninety-nine on the mountains and go in search of the one that went astray? [13] And if he finds it, truly, I say to you, he rejoices over it more than over the ninety-nine that never went astray. [14] So it is not the will of my[d] Father who is in heaven that one of these little ones should perish.

15 "If your brother sins against you, go and tell him his fault, between you and him alone. If he listens to you, you have gained your brother. [16] But if he does not listen, take one or two others along with you, that every word may be confirmed by the evidence of two or three witnesses. [17] If he refuses to listen to them, tell it to the church; and if he refuses to listen even to the church, let him be to you as a Gentile and a tax collector. [18] Truly, I say to you, whatever you bind on earth shall be bound in heaven, and whatever you loose on earth shall be loosed in heaven. [19] Again I say to you, if two of you agree on earth about anything they ask, it will be done for them by my Father in heaven. [20] For where two or three are gathered in my name, there am I in the midst of them."

21 Then Peter came up and said to him, "Lord, how often shall my brother sin against me, and I forgive him? As many as seven times?" [22] Jesus said to him, "I do not say to you seven times, but seventy times seven.[e]

23 "Therefore the kingdom of heaven may be compared to a king who wished to settle accounts with his servants. [24] When he began the reckoning, one was brought to him who owed him ten thousand talents;[f] [25] and as he could not pay, his lord ordered him to be sold, with his wife and children and all that he had, and payment to be made. [26] So the servant fell on his knees, imploring him, 'Lord, have patience with me, and I will pay you everything.' [27] And out of pity for him the lord of that servant released him and forgave him the debt. [28] But that same servant, as he went out, came upon one of his fellow servants who owed him a hundred denarii;[g] and seizing him

z Greek *causes . . . to stumble*   a Greek *stumbling blocks*   b Greek *Gehenna*   c Other ancient authorities add verse 11, *For the Son of man came to save the lost*   d Other ancient authorities read *your*   e Or *seventy-seven times*   f This talent was more than fifteen years' wages of a laborer   g The denarius was a day's wage for a laborer

parent, not childish behavior, are in view (Mk.10.15; Lk.18.17; 1 Pet.2.2). **6:** *Little ones,* disciples of Jesus, whom he calls "children" (Mk.10.24; compare Mt.11.25).

     18.7–9: Warnings of hell (Mk.9.42–48; Lk.17.1–2). **8–9:** In vivid language Jesus speaks of the terrible danger in yielding to temptation (5.29–30).

     18.10–14: The lost sheep (Lk.15.3–7). **10:** *Little ones,* see v. 6 n. *Angels,* see Acts 12,15 n.

     18.15–20: Discipline among followers (Lk.17.3). 1 Cor.6.1–6; Gal.6.1; Jas.5.19–20; Lev.19.17. **16:** Dt.19.15. **17:** The guilty person excludes himself from the group of followers. **18:** See 16.19 n.; Jn.20.21–23 n.

     18.21–35: Forgiveness. 21–22: Lk.17.4. Forgiveness is beyond calculating. **23:** 25.19. **25:** Lk.7.42. **26:** 8.2; 17.14. **32–33:** Lk.7.41–43.

by the throat he said, 'Pay what you owe,' [29] So his fellow servant fell down and besought him, 'Have patience with me, and I will pay you.' [30] He refused and went and put him in prison till he should pay the debt. [31] When his fellow servants saw what had taken place, they were greatly distressed, and they went and reported to their lord all that had taken place. [32] Then his lord summoned him and said to him, 'You wicked servant! I forgave you all that debt because you besought me; [33] and should not you have had mercy on your fellow servant, as I had mercy on you?' [34] And in anger his lord delivered him to the jailers,[h] till he should pay all his debt. [35] So also my heavenly Father will do to every one of you, if you do not forgive your brother from your heart."

19 Now when Jesus had finished these sayings, he went away from Galilee and entered the region of Judea beyond the Jordan; [2] and large crowds followed him, and he healed them there.

[3] And Pharisees came up to him and tested him by asking, "Is it lawful to divorce one's wife for any cause?" [4] He answered, "Have you not read that he who made them from the beginning made them male and female, [5] and said, 'For this reason a man shall leave his father and mother and be joined to his wife, and the two shall become one flesh'? [6] So they are no longer two but one flesh. What therefore God has joined together, let not man put asunder." [7] They said to him, "Why then did Moses command one to give a certificate of divorce, and to put her away?" [8] He said to them, "For your hardness of heart Moses allowed you to divorce your wives, but from

the beginning it was not so. [9] And I say to you: whoever divorces his wife, except for unchastity,[j] and marries another, commits adultery."[k]

[10] The disciples said to him, "If such is the case of a man with his wife, it is not expedient to marry." [11] But he said to them, "Not all men can receive this saying, but only those to whom it is given. [12] For there are eunuchs who have been so from birth, and there are eunuchs who have been made eunuchs by men, and there are eunuchs who have made themselves eunuchs for the sake of the kingdom of heaven. He who is able to receive this, let him receive it."

[13] Then children were brought to him that he might lay his hands on them and pray. The disciples rebuked the people; [14] but Jesus said, "Let the children come to me, and do not hinder them; for to such belongs the kingdom of heaven." [15] And he laid his hands on them and went away.

[16] And behold, one came up to him, saying, "Teacher, what good deed must I do, to have eternal life?" [17] And he said to him, "Why do you ask me about what is good? One there is who is good. If you would enter life, keep the commandments." [18] He said to him, "Which?" And Jesus said, "You shall not kill, You shall not commit adultery, You shall not steal, You shall not bear false witness, [19] Honor your father and mother, and, You shall love your neighbor as yourself." [20] The young man said to him, "All these I have

h Greek *torturers*   j Other ancient authorities, after *unchastity,* read *makes her commit adultery*   k Other ancient authorities insert *and he who marries a divorced woman commits adultery*

19.1–20.34: From Galilee to Jerusalem (Mk.10.1–52; Lk.18.15–19.27).
19.1–12: Marriage and divorce (Mk.10.1–12). **1:** *Finished,* see 7.28 n. **3:** The Mosaic law gives no answer to this question and the rabbis differed in their opinions. **4–6:** Gen.1.27; 2.24. Jesus appeals to God's purpose of unity in marriage as shown in the account of creation. **7:** Dt.24.1–4. **8:** See Mk.10.5 n. **9:** See 5.32 n.; Lk.16.18; 1 Cor.7.10–13. **11–12:** Jesus recognizes a place for voluntary celibacy in the service of God's kingdom (compare 1 Cor.7.1–9).
19.13–15: Blessing the children (Mk.10.13–16; Lk.18.15–17). **14:** See Mk.10.15 n.; compare Mt.18.2–4; 1 Cor.14.20.
19.16–30: The rich young man (Mk.10.17–31; Lk.18.18–30). **16:** Lk.10.25; Lev.18.5. The question concerns the way of life which Jesus will guarantee as satisfying God (see Lk.18.26 n.). **17:** Jesus replies that the good way of life is obedience to God's will (15.2–3,6). **18:** Ex.20.12–16; Dt.5.16–20; Rom.13.9; Jas.2.11. **19:** Lev.19.18; Mt.22.39;

observed; what do I still lack?" [21] Jesus said to him, "If you would be perfect, go, sell what you possess and give to the poor, and you will have treasure in heaven; and come, follow me." [22] When the young man heard this he went away sorrowful; for he had great possessions.

23 And Jesus said to his disciples, "Truly, I say to you, it will be hard for a rich man to enter the kingdom of heaven. [24] Again I tell you, it is easier for a camel to go through the eye of a needle than for a rich man to enter the kingdom of God." [25] When the disciples heard this they were greatly astonished, saying, "Who then can be saved?" [26] But Jesus looked at them and said to them, "With men this is impossible, but with God all things are possible." [27] Then Peter said in reply, "Lo, we have left everything and followed you. What then shall we have?" [28] Jesus said to them, "Truly, I say to you, in the new world, when the Son of man shall sit on his glorious throne, you who have followed me will also sit on twelve thrones, judging the twelve tribes of Israel. [29] And every one who has left houses or brothers or sisters or father or mother or children or lands, for my name's sake, will receive a hundredfold,[l] and inherit eternal life. [30] But many that are first will be last, and the last first.

20 "For the kingdom of heaven is like a householder who went out early in the morning to hire laborers for his vineyard. [2] After agreeing with the laborers for a denarius[m] a day, he sent them into his vineyard. [3] And going out about the third hour he saw others standing idle in the market place; [4] and to them he said, 'You go into the vineyard too, and whatever is right I will give you.' So they went. [5] Going out again about the sixth hour and the ninth hour, he did the same. [6] And about the eleventh hour he went out and found others standing; and he said to them, 'Why do you stand here idle all day?' [7] They said to him, 'Because no one has hired us.' He said to them, 'You go into the vineyard too.' [8] And when evening came, the owner of the vineyard said to his steward, 'Call the laborers and pay them their wages, beginning with the last, up to the first.' [9] And when those hired about the eleventh hour came, each of them received a denarius. [10] Now when the first came, they thought they would receive more; but each of them also received a denarius. [11] And on receiving it they grumbled at the householder, [12] saying, 'These last worked only one hour, and you have made them equal to us who have borne the burden of the day and the scorching heat.' [13] But he replied to one of them, 'Friend, I am doing you no wrong; did you not agree with me for a denarius? [14] Take what belongs to you, and go; I choose to give to this last as I give to you. [15] Am I not allowed to do what I choose with what belongs to me? Or do you begrudge my generosity?'[n] [16] So the last will be first, and the first last."

17 And as Jesus was going up to Jerusalem, he took the twelve disciples aside, and

l Other ancient authorities read *manifold*   *m* The denarius was a day's wage for a laborer   *n* Or *is your eye evil because I am good?*

Rom.13.8; Jas.2.8–9. **21:** Jesus consistently turned men's attention from concern over their own religious standing, calling them to involve themselves in the basic, vital interests of others. Neither wealth, poverty, nor formal piety was so important as sharing in the working out of God's life-giving design for all men (5.23–24,43–48; 6.33). Eternal life will be found through utter dependence on God, not through a ritual that wealth makes possible (see Lk.12.33 n.; Acts 2.44–45; 4.34,35). **24:** See Mk.10.25 n. **28:** *The new world* refers to the consummation of God's purpose (compare Rom.8.18–25). **29:** *Inherit eternal life* means *enter the kingdom of God* (vv. 23,24), and *inherit the kingdom* (25.34). **30:** 20.16; Mk.10.31; Lk.13.30. **20.1–16: Laborers in the vineyard. 1:** *Early,* approximately 6 a.m. **3:** About nine a.m. **5:** About noon and three p.m. **6:** About five p.m. **8:** Lev.19.13; Dt.24.14–15. **9:** *Denarius,* smaller coins existed (see Lk.12.59 n.); therefore payment could have been made on an hourly basis. **14:** The point of the parable is the willingness of the owner to exceed conventional practices, and his freedom to do so within the limits of agreement. **15:** The first sentence is not a statement of economic theory except as it claims the right to enter into differing contracts. The second sentence expresses the sense of the Greek text, which is literally translated in note *n.* **16:** Compare 19.30. **20.17–19: The Passion foretold a third time** (Mk.10.32–34; Lk.18.31–34); compare 16.21; 17.22.

on the way he said to them, [18] "Behold, we are going up to Jerusalem; and the Son of man will be delivered to the chief priests and scribes, and they will condemn him to death, [19] and deliver him to the Gentiles to be mocked and scourged and crucified, and he will be raised on the third day."

20 Then the mother of the sons of Zeb'edee came up to him, with her sons, and kneeling before him she asked him for something. [21] And he said to her, "What do you want?" She said to him, "Command that these two sons of mine may sit, one at your right hand and one at your left, in your kingdom." [22] But Jesus answered, "You do not know what you are asking. Are you able to drink the cup that I am to drink?" They said to him, "We are able." [23] He said to them, "You will drink my cup, but to sit at my right hand and at my left is not mine to grant, but it is for those whom it has been prepared by my Father." [24] And when the ten heard it, they were indignant at the two brothers. [25] But Jesus called them to him and said, "You know that the rulers of the Gentiles lord it over them, and their great men exercise authority over them. [26] It shall not be so among you; but whoever would be great among you must be your servant, [27] and whoever would be first among you must be your slave; [28] even as the Son of man came not to be served but to serve, and to give his life as a ransom for many."

29 And as they went out of Jericho, a great crowd followed him. [30] And behold, two blind men sitting by the roadside, when they heard that Jesus was passing by, cried out,[o] "Have mercy on us, Son of David!" [31] The crowd rebuked them, telling them to be silent; but they cried out the more, "Lord, have mercy on us, Son of David!" [32] And Jesus stopped and called them, saying, "What do you want me to do for you?" [33] They said to him, "Lord, let our eyes be opened." [34] And Jesus in pity touched their eyes, and immediately they received their sight and followed him.

21 And when they drew near to Jerusalem and came to Beth'phage, to the Mount of Olives, then Jesus sent two disciples, [2] saying to them, "Go into the village opposite you, and immediately you will find an ass tied, and a colt with her; untie them and bring them to me. [3] If any one says anything to you, you shall say, 'The Lord has need of them,' and he will send them immediately." [4] This took place to fulfil what was spoken by the prophet, saying,

[5] "Tell the daughter of Zion,
   Behold, your king is coming to you,
   humble, and mounted on an ass,
   and on a colt, the foal of an ass."

[6] The disciples went and did as Jesus had directed them; [7] they brought the ass and the colt, and put their garments on them, and he sat thereon. [8] Most of the crowd spread their garments on the road, and others cut branches from the trees and spread them on the road. [9] And the crowds that went before him and that followed him shouted, "Hosanna to the Son of David! Blessed is he who comes in the name of the Lord! Hosanna in the highest!" [10] And when he entered Jerusalem, all the city was stirred, saying, "Who is this?" [11] And the

o Other ancient authorities insert Lord

20.20–28: James and John seek honor (Mk.10.35–45; Lk.22.24–27). **22:** *Cup,* see Lk.22.42 n. **23:** Acts 12.2; Rev.1.9; Mt.13.11. **26:** See Mk.9.35. **28:** 26.39; 1 Tim.2.5–6; Jn.13.15–16; Tit.2.14; 1 Pet.1.18. The thought seems to be based on Is. ch. 53.

20.29–34: Two blind men of Jericho (Mk.10.46–52; Lk.18.35–43). Jesus responds not to the Messianic title *Son of David* (v. 30) but to the cry of need (v. 34; compare 15.22–28).

21.1–27.66: The last week (Mk.11.1–15.47; Lk.19.28–23.56).

21.1–9: Palm Sunday (Mk.11.1–10; Lk.19.28–38; Jn.12.12–18). **1:** See Mk.11.1 n. **5:** Is. 62.11; Zech.9.9. The Hebrew text refers not to two animals but to one. The reference to the two in v. 7 may have arisen through misunderstanding the form of Hebrew poetic expression in Zech.9.9. **8:** Tokens of honor (2 Kg.9.13). **9:** Ps.118.26. *Hosanna,* originally a Hebrew invocation addressed to God, meaning, "O save!"; later it was used as a cry of joyous acclamation. **11:** The identification reflects an unchanged attitude toward Jesus. His parable (see Mk.11.1 n.) is seen and not understood (Jn.6.14; 7.40; Acts 3.22; Mk.6.15; Lk.13.33).

crowds said, "This is the prophet Jesus from Nazareth of Galilee."

12 And Jesus entered the temple of God[p] and drove out all who sold and bought in the temple, and he overturned the tables of the money-changers and the seats of those who sold pigeons. [13] He said to them, "It is written, 'My house shall be called a house of prayer'; but you make it a den of robbers."

14 And the blind and the lame came to him in the temple, and he healed them. [15] But when the chief priests and the scribes saw the wonderful things that he did, and the children crying out in the temple, "Hosanna to the Son of David!" they were indignant; [16] and they said to him, "Do you hear what these are saying?" And Jesus said to them, "Yes; have you never read,

'Out of the mouth of babes and sucklings thou hast brought perfect praise'?"

[17] And leaving them, he went out of the city to Bethany and lodged there.

18 In the morning, as he was returning to the city, he was hungry. [19] And seeing a fig tree by the wayside he went to it, and found nothing on it but leaves only. And he said to it, "May no fruit ever come from you again!" And the fig tree withered at once. [20] When the disciples saw it they marveled, saying, "How did the fig tree wither at once?" [21] And Jesus answered them, "Truly, I say to you, if you have faith and never doubt, you will not only do what has been done to the fig tree, but even if you say to this mountain, 'Be taken up and cast into the sea,' it will be done. [22] And whatever you ask in prayer, you will receive, if you have faith."

23 And when he entered the temple, the chief priests and the elders of the people came up to him as he was teaching, and said, "By what authority are you doing these things, and who gave you this authority?" [24] Jesus answered them, "I also will ask you a question; and if you tell me the answer, then I also will tell you by what authority I do these things. [25] The baptism of John, whence was it? From heaven or from men?" And they argued with one another, "If we say, 'From heaven,' he will say to us, 'Why then did you not believe him?' [26] But if we say, 'From men,' we are afraid of the multitude; for all hold that John was a prophet." [27] So they answered Jesus, "We do not know." And he said to them, "Neither will I tell you by what authority I do these things.

28 "What do you think? A man had two sons; and he went to the first and said, 'Son, go and work in the vineyard today.' [29] And he answered, 'I will not'; but afterward he repented and went. [30] And he went to the second and said the same; and he answered, 'I go, sir,' but did not go. [31] Which of the two did the will of his father?" They said, "The first." Jesus said to them, "Truly, I say to you, the tax collectors and the harlots go into the kingdom of God before you. [32] For John came to you in the way of righteousness, and you did not believe him, but the tax collectors and the harlots believed him; and even when you saw it, you did not afterward repent and believe him.

33 "Hear another parable. There was a householder who planted a vineyard, and set a hedge around it, and dug a wine press in it,

p Other ancient authorities omit *of God*

21.12–17: **Cleansing the temple** (Mk.11.11,15–19; Lk.19.45–48; Jn.2.13–17). **12:** The animals for sale were acceptable for sacrifice; the money changers converted Gentile coins into Jewish money that could properly be presented in the temple (Ex.30.13; Lev.1.14). **13:** Is.56.7; Jer.7.11. **15:** Lk.19.39; Mt.21.9. *Hosanna*, see v. 9 n. **16:** Ps.8.2.
21.18–22: **Fig tree cursed** (Mk.11.12–14,20–25). See Mk.11.13 n. **19:** The leaves of the fig tree normally appear after the fruit. **21:** See 17.20 n.
21.23–32: **Jesus' authority** (Mk.11.27–33; Lk.20.1–8). Jn.2.18–22. **26:** 11.9; 14.5; Lk.1.76. **27:** Jesus declined to answer because his listeners declined to heed. **28–32:** 20.1; 21.33; Lk.15.11–32. **32:** Lk.7.29–30. *The way of righteousness* led to reconciliation with God by Faith.
21.33–46: **Parable of the vineyard** (Mk.12.1–12; Lk.20.9–19). **33:** Compare Is.5.1–7, which forms the background of Jesus' parable. **34:** 22.3. **41:** 8.11; Acts 13.46; 18.6; 28.28. **42:** Jesus agrees with his listeners' answer (v. 41) and quotes Ps.118.22–23 to support his teaching (Acts 4.11; 1 Pet.2.7).

and built a tower, and let it out to tenants, and went into another country. [34] When the season of fruit drew near, he sent his servants to the tenants, to get his fruit; [35] and the tenants took his servants and beat one, killed another, and stoned another. [36] Again he sent other servants, more than the first; and they did the same to them. [37] Afterward he sent his son to them, saying, 'They will respect my son.' [38] But when the tenants saw the son, they said to themselves, 'This is the heir; come, let us kill him and have his inheritance.' [39] And they took him and cast him out of the vineyard, and killed him. [40] When therefore the owner of the vineyard comes, what will he do to those tenants?" [41] They said to him, "He will put those wretches to a miserable death, and let out the vineyard to other tenants who will give him the fruits in their seasons."

42 Jesus said to them, "Have you never read in the scriptures:

'The very stone which the builders rejected
has become the head of the corner;
this was the Lord's doing,
and it is marvelous in our eyes'?

[43] Therefore I tell you, the kingdom of God will be taken away from you and given to a nation producing the fruits of it."[q]

45 When the chief priests and the Pharisees heard his parables, they perceived that he was speaking about them. [46] But when they tried to arrest him, they feared the multitudes, because they held him to be a prophet.

22 And again Jesus spoke to them in parables, saying, [2] "The kingdom of heaven may be compared to a king who gave a marriage feast for his son, [3] and sent his servants to call those who were invited to the marriage feast; but they would not come. [4] Again he sent other servants, saying, 'Tell those who are invited, Behold, I have made ready my dinner, my oxen and my fat calves

are killed, and everything is ready; come to the marriage feast.' [5] But they made light of it and went off, one to his farm, another to his business, [6] while the rest seized his servants, treated them shamefully, and killed them. [7] The king was angry, and he sent his troops and destroyed those murderers and burned their city. [8] Then he said to his servants, 'The wedding is ready, but those invited were not worthy. [9] Go therefore to the thoroughfares, and invite to the marriage feast as many as you find.' [10] And those servants went out into the streets and gathered all whom they found, both bad and good; so the wedding hall was filled with guests.

11 "But when the king came in to look at the guests, he saw there a man who had no wedding garment; [12] and he said to him, 'Friend, how did you get in here without a wedding garment?' And he was speechless. [13] Then the king said to the attendants, 'Bind him hand and foot, and cast him into the outer darkness; there men will weep and gnash their teeth.' [14] For many are called, but few are chosen."

15 Then the Pharisees went and took counsel how to entangle him in his talk. [16] And they sent their disciples to him, along with the Hero'dians, saying, "Teacher, we know that you are true, and teach the way of God truthfully, and care for no man; for you do not regard the position of men. [17] Tell us, then, what you think. Is it lawful to pay taxes to Caesar, or not?" [18] But Jesus, aware of their malice, said, "Why put me to the test, you hypocrites? [19] Show me the money for the tax." And they brought him a coin.[r] [20] And Jesus said to them, "Whose likeness and inscription is this?" [21] They said, "Caesar's."

q Other ancient authorities add verse 44, *"And he who falls on this stone will be broken to pieces; but when it falls on any one, it will crush him"*   r Greek *a denarius*

22.1–14: The marriage feast (Lk.14.16–24). **3:** 21.34. **10:** 13.47. **13:** 8.12.
     22.15–22: Paying taxes to Caesar (Mk.12.13–17; Lk.20.20–26). **15:** Mk.3.6; 8.15. **16:** *Herodians,* Mk.3.6 n. In asking Jesus for a pronouncement affecting all Jews, his enemies thought to bring him into conflict with sectarian views. **17:** If Jesus approved paying taxes he would offend the nationalistic parties; if he disapproved payment he could be reported as disloyal to the empire. **21:** Rom.13.7; 1 Pet.2.17.

Then he said to them, "Render therefore to Caesar the things that are Caesar's, and to God the things that are God's." [22] When they heard it, they marveled; and they left him and went away.

23 The same day Sad'ducees came to him, who say that there is no resurrection; and they asked him a question, [24] saying, "Teacher, Moses said, 'If a man dies, having no children, his brother must marry the widow, and raise up children for his brother.' [25] Now there were seven brothers among us; the first married, and died, and having no children left his wife to his brother. [26] So too the second and third, down to the seventh. [27] After them all, the woman died. [28] In the resurrection, therefore, to which of the seven will she be wife? For they all had her."

29 But Jesus answered them, "You are wrong, because you know neither the scriptures nor the power of God. [30] For in the resurrection they neither marry nor are given in marriage, but are like angels[s] in heaven. [31] And as for the resurrection of the dead, have you not read what was said to you by God, [32] 'I am the God of Abraham, and the God of Isaac, and the God of Jacob'? He is not God of the dead, but of the living." [33] And when the crowd heard it, they were astonished at his teaching.

34 But when the Pharisees heard that he had silenced the Sad'ducees, they came together. [35] And one of them, a lawyer, asked him a question, to test him. [36] "Teacher, which is the great commandment in the law?" [37] And he said to him, "You shall love the Lord your God with all your heart, and with all your soul, and with all your mind. [38] This is the great and first commandment. [39] And a second is like it, You shall love your neighbor as yourself. [40] On these two commandments depend all the law and the prophets."

41 Now while the Pharisees were gathered together, Jesus asked them a question, [42] saying, "What do you think of the Christ? Whose son is he?" They said to him, "The son of David." [43] He said to them, "How is it then that David, inspired by the Spirit,[t] calls him Lord, saying,

[44] 'The Lord said to my Lord,

Sit at my right hand,

till I put thy enemies under they feet'?

[45] If David thus calls him Lord, how is he his son?" [46] And no one was able to answer him a word, nor from that day did any one dare to ask him any more questions.

23 Then said Jesus to the crowds and to his disciples, [2] "The scribes and the Pharisees sit on Moses' seat; [3] so practice and observe whatever they tell you, but not what they do; for they preach, but do not practice. [4] They bind heavy burdens, hard to bear,[u] and lay them on men's shoulders; but they themselves will not move them with their finger. [5] They do all their deeds to be seen by men; for they make their phylacteries broad and their fringes long, [6] and they love the place of honor at feasts and the best seats in the synagogues, [7] and salutations in the market places, and being called rabbi by men. [8] But you are not to be called rabbi, for you have one

s Other ancient authorities add *of God* t Or *David in the Spirit* u Other ancient authorities omit *hard to bear*

22.23–33: Question about the resurrection (Mk.12.18–27; Lk.20.27–40). **23:** Belief in the *resurrection* was held by the Pharisees in Jesus' day, but rejected by the Sadducees (Acts 4.1–2; 23.6–10). **24; Dt.25.5. 29:** The Sadducees fail to see God's purpose and do not trust his *power.* **31–32:** Ex.3.6. The idea here is that men who are related to God in faith have life even though physically dead. Resurrection is the divine act by which men will achieve the fulness of life intended in creation and lost through sin and death (see Lk.20.34–36 n.).
22.34–40: The great commandment (Mk.12.28–34; Lk.10.25–28). **37:** Dt.6.5. **39:** Lev.19.18; Compare Mt.19.19; Rom.13.9; Gal.5.14; Jas.2.8. **40:** The Law contains many ways of applying to life the principle of love.
22.41–46: David's son (Mk.12.35–37; Lk.20.41–44). **44:** The first *Lord* refers to God, the second *Lord* is taken here to refer to the Messiah (see Ps.110.1; Acts 2.34–35; Heb.1.13; 10.12–13).
23.1–36: Woe to scribes and Pharisees. 4: Lk.11.46; Mt.11.28–30; Acts 15.10. **5:** 6.1; 5.16; Ex.13.9; Dt.6.8. **6–7:** Mk.12.38–39; Lk.11.43; 14.7–11; 20.46. **8:** Jas.3.1. **12:** Lk.14.11; 18.14; Mt.18.4; 1 Pet.5.6. **13:** Lk.11.52. **15:**

teacher, and you are all brethren. [9] And call no man your father on earth, for you have one Father, who is in heaven. [10] Neither be called masters, for you have one master, the Christ. [11] He who is greatest among you shall be your servant; [12] whoever exalts himself will be humbled, and whoever humbles himself will be exalted.

[13] "But woe to you, scribes and Pharisees, hypocrites! because you shut the kingdom of heaven against men; for you neither enter yourselves, nor allow those who would enter to go in.[v] [15] Woe to you, scribes and Pharisees, hypocrites! for you traverse sea and land to make a single proselyte, and when he becomes a proselyte, you make him twice as much a child of hell[w] as yourselves.

[16] "Woe to you, blind guides, who say, 'If any one swears by the temple, it is nothing; but if any one swears by the gold of the temple, he is bound by his oath.' [17] You blind fools! For which is greater, the gold or the temple that has made the gold sacred? [18] And you say, 'If any one swears by the altar, it is nothing; but if any one swears by the gift that is on the altar, he is bound by his oath.' [18] You blind men! For which is greater, the gift or the altar that makes the gift sacred? [20] So he who swears by the altar, swears by it and by everything on it; [21] and he who swears by the temple, swears by it and by him who dwells in it; [22] and he who swears by heaven, swears by the throne of God and by him who sits upon it.

[23] "Woe to you, scribes and Pharisees, hypocrites! for you tithe mint and dill and cummin, and have neglected the weightier matters of the law, justice and mercy and faith; these you ought to have done, without neglecting the others. [24] You blind guides, straining out a gnat and swallowing a camel!

[25] "Woe to you, scribes and Pharisees, hypocrites! for you cleanse the outside of the cup and of the plate, but inside they are full of extortion and rapacity. [26] You blind Pharisee! first cleanse the inside of the cup and of the plate, that the outside also may be clean.

[27] "Woe to you, scribes and Pharisees, hypocrites! for you are like white-washed tombs, which outwardly appear beautiful, but within they are full of dead men's bones and all uncleanness. [28] So you also outwardly appear righteous to men, but within you are full of hypocrisy and iniquity.

[29] "Woe to you, scribes and Pharisees, hypocrites! for you build the tombs of the prophets and adorn the monuments of the righteous, [30] saying, 'If we had lived in the days of our fathers, we would not have taken part with them in shedding the blood of the prophets.' [31] Thus you witness against yourselves, that you are sons of those who murdered the prophets. [32] Fill up, then, the measure of your fathers. [33] You serpents, you brood of vipers, how are you to escape being sentenced to hell?[w] [34] Therefore I send you prophets and wise men and scribes, some of whom you will kill and crucify, and some you will scourge in your synagogues and persecute from town to town, [35] that upon you may come all the righteous blood shed on earth, from the blood of innocent Abel to the blood of Zechari'ah

---

v Other authorities add here (or after verse 12) verse 14, *Woe to you, scribes and Pharisees, hypocrites! for you devour widows' houses and for a pretense you make long prayers; therefore you will receive the greater condemnation*   w Greek *Gehenna*

Acts 2.10; 6.5; 13.43. **16:** 5.33–37; 15.14. **17:** Ex.30.29. **21:** 1 Kg.8.13; Ps.26.8. **23–24:** Lk.11.42; Lev.27.30; Mic.6.8. **25–26:** Lk.11.39–41; Mk.7.4. **27–28:** Lk.11.44; Acts 23.3; Ps.5.9. **28:** See Lk.20.20 n. **29–32:** Lk.11.47–48; Acts 7.51–53. **31:** *Sons of* has two meanings: descendants, or, those of similar character. The scribes and Pharisees would admit to being descendants *of those who murdered the prophets.* Jesus insists that their attitudes are also similar (v. 28). **33:** 3.7; Lk.3.7. **34–36:** Lk.11.49–51. **34:** See Lk.11.49 n.; Mt.10.17,23; 2 Chr.36.15–16. *Prophets and wise men and scribes* are terms of Jewish origin applied here to Christian missionaries. **35:** Gen.4.8; Heb.11.4; 2 Chr.24.20–22; Zech.1.1. The identifying words *son of Barachiah* (not in Lk.11.51) probably were mistakenly added to the text of Matthew at an early date because of confusion over which *Zechariah* was meant. The meaning of the sentence is to indicate the sweep of time from the first to the last victim of murder mentioned in the Old Testament (2 Chronicles stands last in the order of books in the Hebrew Bible).

the son of Barachi'ah, whom you murdered between the sanctuary and the altar. [38] Truly, I say to you, all this will come upon this generation.

37 "O Jerusalem, Jerusalem, killing the prophets and stoning those who are sent to you! How often would I have gathered your children together as a hen gathers her brood under her wings, and you would not! [38] Behold, your house is forsaken and desolate.[x] [39] For I tell you, you will not see me again, until you say, 'Blessed is he who comes in the name of the Lord.'"

24 Jesus left the temple and was going away, when his disciples came to point out to him the buildings of the temple. [2] But he answered them, "You see all these, do you not? Truly, I say to you, there will not be left here one stone upon another, that will not be thrown down."

3 As he sat on the Mount of Olives, the disciples came to him privately, saying, "Tell us, when will this be, and what will be the sign of your coming and the close of the age?" [4] And Jesus answered them, "Take heed that no one leads you astray. [5] For many will come in my name, saying, 'I am the Christ,' and they will lead many astray. [6] And you will hear of wars and rumors of wars; see that you are not alarmed; for this must take place, but the end is not yet. [7] For nation will rise against nation, and kingdom against kingdom, and there will be famines and earthquakes in various places: [8] all this is but the beginning of the birth-pangs.

9 "Then they will deliver you up to tribulation, and put you to death; and you will be hated by all nations for my name's sake. [10] And then many will fall away,[y] and betray one another, and hate one another. [11] And many false prophets will arise and lead many astray. [12] And because wickedness is multiplied, most men's love will grow cold. [18] But he who endures to the end will be saved. [14] And this gospel of the kingdom will be preached throughout the whole world, as a testimony to all nations; and then the end will come.

15 "So when you see the desolating sacrilege spoken of by the prophet Daniel, standing in the holy place (let the reader understand), [16] then let those who are in Judea flee to the mountains; [17] let him who is on the housetop not go down to take what is in his house; [18] and let him who is in the field not turn back to take his mantle. [19] And alas for those who are with child and for those who give suck in those days! [20] Pray that your flight may not be in winter or on a sabbath. [21] For then there will be great tribulation, such as has not been from the beginning of the world until now, no, and never will be. [22] And if those days had not been shortened, no human being would be saved; but for the sake of the elect those days will be shortened. [23] Then if any one says to you, 'Lo, here is the Christ!' or 'There he is!' do not believe it. [24] For false Christs and false prophets will arise and show great signs and wonders, so as to lead astray, if possible, even the elect. [25] Lo, I have told you beforehand. [26] So, if they say to you, 'Lo, he is in the wilderness,'

x Other ancient authorities omit *and desolate*
y Or *stumble*

23.37–39: Lament over Jerusalem (Lk.13.34–35). **37:** The words *how often* suggest repeated efforts, made perhaps during an earlier Judean ministry (see Lk.4.44 n.). **38:** 1 Kg.9.7; Jer.12.7; 22.5. **39:** 21.9; Ps.118.26.

24.1–3: Destruction of the temple foretold (Mk.13.1–2; Lk.21.5–7). **1:** These verses, together with the discourse that follows, seem to merge teachings about an immediate destruction of Jerusalem with details associated in Scripture with the end of human history. These teachings were set down by the Evangelist in the light of events between A.D. 30 and 70. It is difficult to be certain what the original form of Jesus' words was. **3:** Lk.17.20–21; Mt.13.39,40,49; 16.27.

24.4–36: On the end of the age (Mk.13.3–37; Lk.21.8–36). **5:** 1 Jn.2.18. **6–7:** Rev.6.3–8; **12–17. 8:** *The birth-pangs* signal the imminence of the new age, which was announced at the beginning of Jesus' public ministry as "at hand" (4.17), but is to be realized only after a period of witness to Jesus' message (v. 14). Verses 5–14 seem to include a larger community of followers than the original disciples. **9:** 10.17–18,22; Jn.15.18; 16.2. **13:** 10.22; Rev.2.7. **14:** 28.19; Rom. 10.18. **15:** Dan.9.27; 11.31; 12.11; see Mk.13.14 n. **17–18:** Lk.17.31. **21:** Dan.12.1; Jl.2.2.

do not go out; if they say, 'Lo, he is in the inner rooms,' do not believe it. [27] For as the lightning comes from the east and shines as far as the west, so will be the coming of the Son of man. [28] Wherever the body is, there the eagles[z] will be gathered together.

29 "Immediately after the tribulation of those days the sun will be darkened, and the moon will not give its light, and the stars will fall from heaven, and the powers of the heavens will be shaken; [30] then will appear the sign of the Son of man in heaven, and then all the tribes of the earth will mourn, and they will see the Son of man coming on the clouds of heaven with power and great glory; [31] and he will send out his angels with a loud trumpet call, and they will gather his elect from the four winds, from one end of heaven to the other.

32 "From the fig tree learn its lesson: as soon as its branch becomes tender and puts forth its leaves, you know that summer is near. [33] So also, when you see all these things, you know that he is near, at the very gates. [34] Truly, I say to you, this generation will not pass away till all these things take place. [35] Heaven and earth will pass away, but my words will not pass away.

36 "But of that day and hour no one knows, not even the angels of heaven, nor the Son,[a] but the Father only. [37] As were the days of Noah, so will be the coming of the Son of man. [38] For as in those days before the flood they were eating and drinking, marrying and giving in marriage, until the day when Noah entered the ark, [39] and they did not know until the flood came and swept them all away, so will be the coming of the Son of man. [40] Then two men will be in the field; one is taken and one is left. [41] Two women will be grinding at the mill; one is taken and one is left. [42] Watch therefore, for you do not know on what day your Lord is coming. [43] But know this, that if the householder had known in what part of the night the thief was coming, he would have watched and would not have let his house be broken into. [44] Therefore you also must be ready; for the Son of man is coming at an hour you do not expect.

45 "Who then is the faithful and wise servant, whom his master has set over his household, to give them their food at the proper time? [46] Blessed is that servant whom his master when he comes will find so doing. [47] Truly, I say to you, he will set him over all his possessions. [48] But if that wicked servant says to himself, 'My master is delayed,' [49] and begins to beat his fellow servants, and eats and drinks with the drunken, [50] the master of that servant will come on a day when he does not expect him and at an hour he does not know, [51] and will punish[b] him, and put him with the hypocrites; there men will weep and gnash their teeth.

25 "Then the kingdom of heaven shall be compared to ten maidens who took their lamps and went to meet the bridegroom.[c] [2] Five of them were foolish, and five were wise. [3] For when the foolish took their lamps, they took no oil with them; [4] but the wise took flasks of oil with their lamps. [5] As the bridegroom was delayed, they all slumbered and slept. [6] But at midnight there was a cry, 'Behold, the bridegroom! Come out to meet him.' [7] Then all those maidens rose and trimmed their lamps. [8] And the foolish said to

z Or *vultures*   a Other ancient authorities omit *nor the Son*   b Or *cut him in pieces*   c Other ancient authorities add *and the bride*

28: See Lk.17.37 n.; Job 39.30. **29–31:** The language here is drawn from the Old Testament; God's victory over sin is to be established by the Son of man whom he sends (Rev.8.12; Is.13.10; 34.4; Ezek.32.7; Jl.2.10–11; Zeph.1.15). **30:** 16.27; Dan.7.13; Rev.1.7. **31:** 1 Cor.15.52; 1 Th.4.16; Is.27.13; Zech.2.10; 9.14. **34:** 10.23; 16.28. The normal meaning of *this generation* would be "men of our time," and the words would refer to a period of 20–30 years. What Jesus meant, however, is uncertain. **35:** 5.18; Lk.16.17. **36:** Acts 1.6–7. **37–39:** Lk.17.26–27; Gen.6.5–8; 7.6–24. **40–41:** Lk.17.34–35. **42:** Mk.13.35; Lk.12.40; 21.34–46; Mt.25.13. **43–51:** Lk.12.39–46. **43:** 1 Th.5.2; Rev.3.3.
25.1–46: Teachings on the coming of the kingdom. 1–13: The parable of the wise and foolish maidens is based on the Palestinian custom that *the bridegroom* fetched his bride from her parents' home to his own. **1:** Lk.12.35–38; Mk.13.34. **2:** 7.24–27. **10:** Rev.19.9. **11–12:** Lk.13.25; Mt.7.21–23. **13:** 24.42; Mk.13.35; Lk.12.40.

the wise, 'Give us some of your oil, for our lamps are going out.' [9] But the wise replied, 'Perhaps there will not be enough for us and for you; go rather to the dealers and buy for yourselves.' [10] And while they went to buy, the bridegroom came, and those who were ready went in with him to the marriage feast; and the door was shut. [11] Afterward the other maidens came also, saying, 'Lord, lord, open to us.' [12] But he replied, 'Truly, I say to you, I do not know you.' [13] Watch therefore, for you know neither the day nor the hour.

[14] "For it will be as when a man going on a journey called his servants and entrusted to them his property; [15] to one he gave five talents,[d] to another two, to another one, to each according to his ability. Then he went away. [16] He who had received the five talents went at once and traded with them; and he made five talents more. [17] So also, he who had the two talents made two talents more. [18] But he who had received the one talent went and dug in the ground and hid his master's money. [19] Now after a long time the master of those servants came and settled accounts with them. [20] And he who had received the five talents came forward, bringing five talents more, saying, 'Master, you delivered to me five talents; here I have made five talents more.' [21] His master said to him, 'Well done, good and faithful servant; you have been faithful over a little. I will set you over much; enter into the joy of your master.' [22] And he also who had the two talents came forward, saying, 'Master, you delivered to me two talents; here I have made two talents more.' [23] His master said to him, 'Well done, good and faithful servant; you have been faithful over a little, I will set you over much; enter into the joy of your master.' [24] He also who had received the one talent came forward, saying, 'Master, I knew you to be a hard man, reaping where you did not sow, and gathering where you did not winnow; [25] so I was afraid, and I went and hid your talent in the ground. Here you have what is yours.' [26] But his master answered him, 'You wicked and slothful servant! You knew that I reap where I have not sowed, and gather where I have not winnowed? [27] Then you ought to have invested my money with the bankers, and at my coming I should have received what was my own with interest. [28] So take the talent from him, and give it to him who has the ten talents. [29] For to every one who has will more be given, and he will have abundance; but from him who has not, even what he has will be taken away. [30] And cast the worthless servant into the outer darkness; there men will weep and gnash their teeth.'

[31] "When the Son of man comes in his glory, and all the angels with him, then he will sit on his glorious throne. [32] Before him will be gathered all the nations, and he will separate them one from another as a shepherd separates the sheep from the goats, [33] and he will place the sheep at his right hand, but the goats at the left. [34] Then the King will say to those at his right hand, 'Come, O blessed of my Father, inherit the kingdom prepared for you from the foundation of the world; [35] for I was hungry and you gave me food, I was thirsty and you gave me drink, I was a stranger and you welcomed me, [36] I was naked and you clothed me, I was sick and you visited me, I was in prison and you came to me.' [37] Then the righteous will answer him, 'Lord, when did we see thee hungry and feed thee, or thirsty and give thee drink? [38] And when did we see thee a stranger and welcome thee, or naked and clothe thee? [39] And when did we

d This talent was more than fifteen years' wages of a laborer

---

25.14–30: Parable of the talents. Lk.19.12–27. **15:** On the value of this *talent* see note *d*. **21:** Lk.16.10. **29:** The statement, *From him who has not . . . taken away,* illustrates Jesus' way of speaking in two settings at once: as the master's servant had his original talent, yet had earned nothing by it, so men can have their earthly existence and all that derives from it, yet lack merit in the final judgment (v. 30). **30:** *Worthless,* without value to his master.

25.31–46: The Great Judgment. 31: 16.27; 19.28. **32:** Ezek.34.17. *The nations,* probably those who do not know the God of Israel (compare Rom.2.13–16). **34:** Lk.12.32; Mt.5.3; Rev.13.8; 17.8. **35–36:** Is.58.7; Jas.1.27; 2.15–16;

see thee sick or in prison and visit thee?' [40] And the King will answer them, 'Truly, I say to you, as you did it to one of the least of these my brethren, you did it to me.' [41] Then he will say to those at his left hand, 'Depart from me, you cursed, into the eternal fire prepared for the devil and his angels; [42] for I was hungry and you gave me no food, I was thirsty and you gave me no drink, [43] I was a stranger and you did not welcome me, naked and you did not clothe me, sick and in prison and you did not visit me.' [44] Then they also will answer, 'Lord, when did we see thee hungry or thirsty or a stranger or naked or sick or in prison, and did not minister to thee?' [45] Then he will answer them, 'Truly, I say to you, as you did it not to one of the least of these, you did it not to me.' [46] And they will go away into eternal punishment, but the righteous into eternal life."

26 When Jesus had finished all these sayings, he said to his disciples, [2] "You know that after two days the Passover is coming, and the Son of man will be delivered up to be crucified."

[3] Then the chief priests and the elders of the people gathered in the palace of the high priest, who was called Ca'iaphas, [4] and took counsel together in order to arrest Jesus by stealth and kill him. [5] But they said, "Not during the feast, lest there be a tumult among the people."

[6] Now when Jesus was at Bethany in the house of Simon the leper, [7] a woman came up to him with an alabaster flask of very expensive ointment, and she poured it on his head, as he sat at table. [8] But when the disciples saw

it, they were indignant, saying, "Why this waste? [9] For this ointment might have been sold for a large sum, and given to the poor." [10] But Jesus, aware of this, said to them, "Why do you trouble the woman? For she has done a beautiful thing to me. [11] For you always have the poor with you, but you will not always have me. [12] In pouring this ointment on my body she has done it to prepare me for burial. [13] Truly, I say to you, wherever this gospel is preached in the whole world, what she has done will be told in memory of her."

[14] Then one of the twelve, who was called Judas Iscariot, went to the chief priests [15] and said, "What will you give me if I deliver him to you?" And they paid him thirty pieces of silver. [16] And from that moment he sought an opportunity to betray him.

[17] Now on the first day of Unleavened Bread the disciples came to Jesus, saying, "Where will you have us prepare for you to eat the passover?" [18] He said, "Go into the city to a certain one, and say to him, 'The Teacher says, My time is at hand; I will keep the passover at your house with my disciples.'" [19] And the disciples did as Jesus had directed them, and they prepared the passover.

[20] When it was evening, he sat at table with the twelve disciples;[e] [21] and as they were eating, he said, "Truly, I say to you, one of you will betray me." [22] And they were very sorrowful, and began to say to him one after another, "Is it I, Lord?" [23] He answered, "He who has dipped his hand in the dish with me, will betray me. [24] The Son of man goes as it

e Other authorities omit *disciples*

Heb.13.2; 2 Tim.1.16. **40:** 10.42; Mk.9.41; Heb.6.10; Pr.19.17. **41:** Mk.9.48; Rev.20.10. **46:** Dan.12.2; Jn.5.29. *Go away into eternal life* expresses the same idea as *inherit the kingdom* (v. 34).

26.1–27.66: Jesus' death (Mk.14.1–15.47; Lk.22.1–23.56; Jn.13.1–19.42). **26.1:** *Finished,* see 7.28 n. **2–5:** Mk.14.1–2; Lk.22.1–2; Jn.11.47–53. **2:** *The Passover* commemorated the escape from Egypt under Moses (Ex.12.1–20). **6–13:** Mk.14.3–9; Jn.12.1–8. A similar event is reported in Lk.7.36–50. **6:** The identity of this Simon is unknown. **7:** Jn.12.3; see Lk.7.37 n., 46. **10:** The *beautiful thing* is what is good and fitting under the circumstances of impending death. The same Greek words are translated "good works" in 5.16. **12:** Jn.19.40. **14–16:** Mk.14.10–11; Lk.22.3–6. **14:** See Mk.14.10 n. **15:** Ex.21.32; Zech.11.12. The value of the *thirty pieces of silver* is uncertain. Matthew's quotation refers to silver shekels; at four denarii to the shekel this was one hundred and twenty days' wages (20.2).

26.17–29: The Last Supper. 17–19: Mk.14.12–16; Lk.22.7–13. **17:** See Lk.22.7 n. **18:** Lk.22.10 n., 11 n. Jn.7.6; 12.23; 13.1; 17.1. **19:** 21.6; Dt.16.5–8. **20–25:** Mk.14.17–21; Lk.22.14,21–23; Jn.13.21–30. **24:** Ps.41.9; Lk.24.25; 1

is written of him, but woe to that man by whom the Son of man is betrayed! It would have been better for that man if he had not been born." [25] Judas, who betrayed him, said, "Is it I, Master?"[f] He said to him, "You have said so."

26 Now as they were eating, Jesus took bread, and blessed, and broke it, and gave it to the disciples and said, "Take, eat, this is my body." [27] And he took a cup, and when he had given thanks he gave it to them, saying, "Drink of it, all of you; [28] for this is my blood of the[g] covenant, which is poured out for many for the forgiveness of sins. [29] I tell you I shall not drink again of this fruit of the vine until that day when I drink it new with you in my Father's kingdom."

30 And when they had sung a hymn, they went out to the Mount of Olives. [31] Then Jesus said to them, "You will all fall away because of me this night; for it is written, 'I will strike the shepherd, and the sheep of the flock will be scattered.' [32] But after I am raised up, I will go before you to Galilee." [33] Peter declared to him, "Though they all fall away because of you, I will never fall away." [34] Jesus said to him, "Truly, I say to you, this very night, before the cock crows, you will deny me three times." [35] Peter said to him, "Even if I must die with you, I will not deny you." And so said all the disciples.

36 Then Jesus went with them to a place called Gethsem'ane, and he said to his disciples, "Sit here, while I go yonder and pray." [37] And taking with him Peter and the two sons of Zeb'edee, he began to be sorrowful and troubled. [38] Then he said to them, "My soul is very sorrowful, even to death; remain here, and watch[h] with me." [39] And going a little farther he fell on his face and prayed, "My Father, if it be possible, let this cup pass from me; nevertheless, not as I will, but as thou wilt." [40] And he came to the disciples and found them sleeping; and he said to Peter, "So, could you not watch[h] with me one hour? [41] Watch[h] and pray that you may not enter into temptation; the spirit indeed is willing, but the flesh is weak." [42] Again, for the second time, he went away and prayed, "My Father, if this cannot pass unless I drink it, thy will be done." [43] And again he came and found them sleeping, for their eyes were heavy. [44] So, leaving them again, he went away and prayed for the third time, saying the same words. [45] Then he came to the disciples and said to them, "Are you still sleeping and taking your rest? Behold, the hour is at hand, and the Son of man is betrayed into the hands of sinners. [46] Rise, let us be going; see, my betrayer is at hand."

47 While he was still speaking, Judas came, one of the twelve, and with him a great crowd with swords and clubs, from the chief priests and the elders of the people. [48] Now the betrayer had given them a sign, saying, "The one I shall kiss is the man; seize him." [49] And he came up to Jesus at once and said, "Hail, Master!"[i] And he kissed him. [50] Jesus said to him, "Friend, why are you here?"[j] Then they came up and laid hands on Jesus and seized him. [51] And behold, one of those

f Or *Rabbi* *g* Other ancient authorities insert *new*
h Or *keep awake* *i* Or *Rabbi* *j* Or *do that for which you have come*

Cor.15.3; Acts 17.2–3; Mt.18.7. **25:** Judas' question is phrased to imply that the answer will be in the negative. **26–29:** Mk.14.22–25; Lk.22.15–20; 1 Cor.10.16; 11.23–26; Mt.14.19; 15.36; see Lk.22.17 n. **28:** Heb.9.20; Mt.20.28; Mk.1.4; Ex.24.6–8; see Mk.14.24 n. In the background of Jesus' words are several important ideas of Jewish religion: man's sins lead to death; God has rescued his people, as from Egypt, and may be trusted to deliver from death itself; God forgives men in mercy if they obey him; God will make a new covenant (Jer.31.31–34). **29:** See Lk.14.15; 22.18,30; Rev.19.9.

26.30–56: Gethsemane. 30–35: Mk.14.26–31; Lk.22.31–34,39; Jn.14.31; 18.1; 13.36–38. **30:** Probably the *hymn* was Psalms 115–118. **31:** Zech.13.7; Jn.16.32. **32:** 28.7,10,16. **36–46:** Mk.14.32–42; Lk.22.40–46. **38:** Jn.12.27; Heb.5.7–8; Ps.42.6. *My soul,* i.e. "I." **39:** Ezek. 23.31–34; Jn.18.11; Mt.20.22. Jesus does not desire death but accepts God's will even including death. *Cup,* see Lk.22.42 n. **41:** 6.13; Lk.11.4. *Temptation,* "testing," in which man's best intentions may give way. **42:** Jn.4.34; 5.30; 6.38. **45:** 26.18 n.; Jn.12.23; 13.1; 17.1. **47–56:** Mk.14.43–52; Lk.22.47–53; Jn.18.2–11. **50:** *Friend,* "comrade." The synoptic gospels do not report Judas' movements on this night

who were with Jesus stretched out his hand and drew his sword, and struck the slave of the high priest, and cut off his ear. [52] Then Jesus said to him, "Put your sword back into its place; for all who take the sword will perish by the sword. [53] Do you think that I cannot appeal to my Father, and he will at once send me more than twelve legions of angels? [54] But how then should the scriptures be fulfilled, that it must be so?" [55] At that hour Jesus said to the crowds, "Have you come out as against a robber, with swords and clubs to capture me? Day after day I sat in the temple teaching, and you did not seize me. [56] But all this has taken place, that the scriptures of the prophets might be fulfilled." Then all the disciples forsook him and fled.

57 Then those who had seized Jesus led him to Ca'iaphas the high priest, where the scribes and the elders had gathered. [58] But Peter followed him at a distance, as far as the courtyard of the high priest, and going inside he sat with the guards to see the end. [59] Now the chief priests and the whole council sought false testimony against Jesus that they might put him to death, [60] but they found none, though many false witnesses came forward. At last two came forward [61] and said, "This fellow said, 'I am able to destroy the temple of God, and to build it in three days.'" [62] And the high priest stood up and said, "Have you no answer to make? What is it that these men testify against you?" [63] But Jesus was silent. And the high priest said to him, "I adjure you by the living God, tell us if you are the Christ, the Son of God." [64] Jesus said to him, "You have said so. But I tell you, hereafter you will see the Son of man seated at the right hand of Power, and coming on the clouds of heaven."

[65] Then the high priest tore his robes, and said, "He has uttered blasphemy. Why do we still need witnesses? You have now heard his blasphemy. [66] What is your judgment?" They answered, "He deserves death." [67] Then they spat in his face, and struck him; and some slapped him, [68] saying, "Prophesy to us, you Christ! Who is it that struck you?

69 Now Peter was sitting outside in the courtyard. And a maid came up to him, and said, "You also were with Jesus the Galilean." [70] But he denied it before them all, saying, "I do not know what you mean." [71] And when he went out to the porch, another maid saw him, and she said to the bystanders, "This man was with Jesus of Nazareth." [72] And again he denied it with an oath, "I do not know the man." [73] After a little while the bystanders came up and said to Peter, "Certainly you are also one of them, for your accent betrays you." [74] Then he began to invoke a curse on himself and to swear, "I do not know the man." And immediately the cock crowed.[75] And Peter remembered the saying of Jesus, "Before the cock crows, you will deny me three times." And he went out and wept bitterly.

27 When morning came, all the chief priests and the elders of the people took counsel against Jesus to put him to death; [2] and they bound him and led him away and delivered him to Pilate the governor.

3 When Judas, his betrayer, saw that he was condemned, he repented and brought back the thirty pieces of silver to the chief priest and the elders, [4] saying, "I have sinned in betraying innocent blood." They said, "What is that to us? See it to yourself." [5] And throwing down the pieces of silver in the temple, he departed; and he went and hanged

---

(compare Jn.13.30; 18.3). **51:** Jn.18.10. **52:** Gen.9.6; Rev.13.10. **53:** *Twelve legions,* 72,000. **54:** Faith in God can not claim his promise (4.6) so as to counteract his purpose. **55:** Lk.19.47; Jn.18.19–21.

26.57–75: Jesus before Caiaphas. 57: The reference is to the Jewish supreme court (the Sanhedrin; see Jn.11.47 n.). **59:** See Mk.14.55 n. **61:** 24.2; 27.40; Acts 6.14; Jn.2.19. **63:** 27.11; Jn.18.33. **64:** 16.28; Dan.7.13; Ps.110.1. **65:** Num.14.6; Acts 14.14; Lev.24.16. **66:** Lev.24.16. **73:** Peter spoke with a Galilean accent differing from the Judean. **75:** Compare v. 34.

27.1–26: Jesus before Pilate. 1–2: Mk.15.1; Lk.23.1; Jn.18.28–32. Jewish law required that the Sanhedrin take formal action by daylight. Apparently 26.57–68 describes a pre-dawn hearing. **3–10:** Acts 1.16–20. The details of

himself. ⁶ But the chief priests, taking the pieces of silver, said, "It is not lawful to put them into the treasury, since they are blood money." ⁷ So they took counsel, and bought with them the potter's field, to bury strangers in. ⁸ Therefore that field has been called the Field of Blood to this day. ⁹ Then was fulfilled what had been spoken by the prophet Jeremiah, saying, "And they took the thirty pieces of silver, the price of him on whom a price had been set by some of the sons of Israel, ¹⁰ and they gave them for the potter's field, as the Lord directed me."

11 Now Jesus stood before the governor; and the governor asked him, "Are you the King of the Jews?" Jesus said, "You have said so." ¹² But when he was accused by the chief priests and elders, he made no answer. ¹³ Then Pilate said to him, "Do you not hear how many things they testify against you?" ¹⁴ But he gave him no answer, not even to a single charge; so that the governor wondered greatly.

15 Now at the feast the governor was accustomed to release for the crowd any one prisoner whom they wanted. ¹⁶ And they had then a notorious prisoner, called Barab'bas.ᵏ ¹⁷ So when they had gathered, Pilate said to them, "Whom do you want me to release for you, Barab'basᵏ or Jesus who is called Christ?" ¹⁸ For he knew that it was out of envy that they had delivered him up. ¹⁹ Besides, while he was sitting on the judgment seat, his wife sent word to him, "Have nothing to do with that righteous man, for I have suffered much over him today in a dream." ²⁰ Now the chief priests and the elders persuaded the people to ask for Barab'bas and destroy Jesus. ²¹ The governor again said to them, "Which of the two do you want me to release for you?"

And they said, "Barab'bas." ²² Pilate said to them, "Then what shall I do with Jesus who is called Christ?" They all said, "Let him be crucified." ²³ And he said, "Why, what evil has he done?" But they shouted all the more, "Let him be crucified."

24 So when Pilate saw that he was gaining nothing, but rather that a riot was beginning, he took water and washed his hands before the crowd, saying, "I am innocent of this man's blood;ˡ see to it yourselves." ²⁵ And all the people answered, "His blood be on us and on our children!" ²⁶ Then he released for them Barab'bas, and having scourged Jesus, delivered him to be crucified.

27 Then the soldiers of the governor took Jesus into the praetorium, and they gathered the whole battalion before him. ²⁸ And they stripped him and put a scarlet robe upon him, ²⁹ and plaiting a crown of thorns they put it on his head, and put a reed in his right hand. And kneeling before him they mocked him, saying, "Hail, King of the Jews!" ³⁰ And they spat upon him, and took the reed and struck him on the head. ³¹ And when they had mocked him, they stripped him of the robe, and put his own clothes on him, and led him away to crucify him.

32 As they went out, they came upon a man of Cyre'ne, Simon by name; this man they compelled to carry his cross. ³³ And when they came to a place called Gol'gotha (which means the place of a skull), ³⁴ they offered him wine to drink, mingled with gall; but when he tasted it, he would not drink it. ³⁵ And when they had crucified him, they divided his garments among them by casting

k Other ancient authorities read *Jesus Barabbas*
l Other authorities read *this righteous blood* or *this righteous man's blood*

Judas' end are obscure. Each account connects him in death with a cemetery for foreigners in Jerusalem. **9–10:** Zech.11.12–13; Jer.18.1–3; 32.6–15. **11–14:** Mk.15.2–5; Lk.23.2–5; Jn.18.29–19.16. **14:** Lk.23.9; Mt.26.62; Mk.14.60; 1 Tim.6.13. **15–26:** Mk.15.6–15; Lk.23.18–25; Jn.18.38–40; 19.4–16. **19:** Lk.23.4. **21:** Acts 3.13–14. **24:** Dt.21.6–9; Ps.26.6. **25:** Acts 5.28; Jos.2.19. **26:** Scourging with a multi-thonged whip ordinarily preceded execution.
    27.27–44: The crucifixion. 27–31: Mk.15.16–20; Jn.19.1–3. **27:** The *praetorium* was the governor's residence. *The battalion* at full strength numbered about five hundred men. **32–44:** Mk.15.21–32; Lk.23.26,33–43; Jn.19.17–24. **32:** The procession included Jesus, two other prisoners, a centurion, and a few soldiers. *Simon,* see Mk.15.21 n. **34:** *Gall,* any bitter liquid, possibly the myrrh of Mk.15.23. **35:** Ps.22.18. **37:** Indication of the offense was customary.

lots; [36] then they sat down and kept watch over him there. [37] And over his head they put the charge against him, which read, "This is Jesus the King of the Jews." [38] Then two robbers were crucified with him, one on the right and one on the left. [39] And those who passed by derided him, wagging their heads [40] and saying, "You who would destroy the temple and build it in three days, save yourself! If you are the Son of God, come down from the cross." [41] So also the chief priests, with the scribes and elders, mocked him, saying, [42] "He saved others; he cannot save himself. He is the King of Israel; let him come down now from the cross, and we will believe in him. [43] He trusts in God; let God deliver him now, if he desires him; for he said, 'I am the Son of God.'" [44] And the robbers who were crucified with him also reviled him in the same way.

45 Now from the sixth hour there was darkness over all the land[m] until the ninth hour. [46] And about the ninth hour Jesus cried with a loud voice, "Eli, Eli, la'ma sabach-tha'ni?" that is, "My God, my God, why hast thou forsaken me?" [47] And some of the bystanders hearing it said, "This man is calling Eli'jah." [48] And one of them at once ran and took a sponge, filled it with vinegar, and put it on a reed, and gave it to him to drink. [49] But the others said, "Wait, let us see whether Eli'jah will come to save him."[n] [50] And Jesus cried again with a loud voice and yielded up his spirit.

51 And behold, the curtain of the temple was torn in two, from top to bottom; and the earth shook, and the rocks were split; [52] the tombs also were opened, and many bodies of the saints who had fallen asleep were raised, [53] and coming out of the tombs after his resurrection they went into the holy city and appeared to many. [54] When the centurion and those who were with him, keeping watch over Jesus, saw the earthquake and what took place, they were filled with awe, and said, "Truly this was the Son[x] of God!"

55 There were also many women there, looking on from afar, who had followed Jesus from Galilee, ministering to him; [56] among whom were Mary Mag'dalene, and Mary the mother of James and Joseph, and the mother of the sons of Zeb'edee.

57 When it was evening, there came a rich man from Arimathe'a, named Joseph, who also was a disciple of Jesus. [58] He went to Pilate and asked for the body of Jesus. Then Pilate ordered it to be given to him. [59] And Joseph took the body, and wrapped it in a clean linen shroud, [60] and laid it in his own new tomb, which he had hewn in the rock; and he rolled a great stone to the door of the tomb, and departed. [61] Mary Mag'dalene and the other Mary were there, sitting opposite the sepulchre.

62 Next day, that is, after the day of Preparation, the chief priests and the Pharisees gathered before Pilate [63] and said, "Sir, we remember how that impostor said, while he was still alive, 'After three days I will rise again.' [64] Therefore order the sepulchre to be made secure until the third day, lest his disciples go and steal him away, and tell the

m Or *earth*   n Other ancient authorities insert *And another took a spear and pierced his side, and out came water and blood*   x Or *a son*

Since the Romans recognized the ruling Herods, it seems implied that Jesus was alleged to be a pretender and revolutionary. **39:** Ps.22.7–8; 109.25. **40:** 26.61; Acts 6.14; Jn.2.19. **42–43:** The taunts stress religious aspects of Jesus' works and words. *Israel* (rather than *the Jews*, v. 37) refers to the religious community rather than the political state. **43:** Ps.22.8.

27.45–66: The death of Jesus. 45–56: Mk.15.33–41; Lk.23.44–49; Jn.19.28–37. **45:** From about noon to about three p.m. **46:** *Eli . . . sabachthani,* quoted from Ps.22.1. **47:** *Elijah* (similar in sound to *Eli*) was expected to usher in the final period (Mal.4.5–6; Mt.27.49). **48:** Ps.69.21. The *vinegar* was a cheap, sour wine of the poor. The motive in offering it may have been to revive him and hence prolong the ordeal. **51:** Heb.9.8; 10.19; Ex.26.31–35; Mt.28.2; see Mk.15.38 n. **56:** *James,* possibly the James of 10.3; Lk.24.10; Acts 1.13. **57–61:** Mk.15.42–47; Lk.23.50–56; Jn.19.38–42; Acts 13.29. **58:** Bodies of the executed were normally denied burial. **60:** See Mk.16.3–5 n.; Acts 13.29. **61:** 27.56. **62:** *Next day,* the sabbath (Mk.15.42).

people, 'He has risen from the dead,' and the last fraud will be worse than the first." [65] Pilate said to them, "You have a guard[o] of soldiers; go, make it as secure as you can."[p] [66] So they went and made the sepulchre secure by sealing the stone and setting a guard.

28 Now after the sabbath, toward the dawn of the first day of the week, Mary Mag'dalene and the other Mary went to see the sepulchre. [2] And behold, there was a great earthquake; for an angel of the Lord descended from heaven and came and rolled back the stone, and sat upon it. [3] His appearance was like lightning, and his raiment white as snow. [4] And for fear of him the guards trembled and became like dead men. [5] But the angel said to the women, "Do not be afraid; for I know that you seek Jesus who was crucified. [6] He is not here; for he has risen, as he said. Come, see the place where he[q] lay. [7] Then go quickly and tell his disciples that he has risen from the dead, and behold, he is going before you to Galilee; there you will see him. Lo, I have told you." [8] So they departed quickly from the tomb with fear and great joy, and ran to tell his disciples. [9] And behold, Jesus met them and said, "Hail!" And they came up and took hold of his feet and worshiped him. [10] Then Jesus said to them, "Do not be afraid; go and tell my brethren to go to Galilee, and there they will see me."

[11] While they were going, behold, some of the guard went into the city and told the chief priests all that had taken place. [12] And when they had assembled with the elders and taken counsel, they gave a sum of money to the soldiers [13] and said, "Tell people, 'His disciples came by night and stole him away while we were asleep.' [14] And if this comes to the governor's ears, we will satisfy him and keep you out of trouble." [15] So they took the money and did as they were directed; and this story has been spread among the Jews to this day.

[16] Now the eleven disciples went to Galilee, to the mountain to which Jesus had directed them. [17] And when they saw him they worshiped him; but some doubted. [18] And Jesus came and said to them, "All authority in heaven and on earth has been given to me. [19] Go therefore and make disciples of all nations, baptizing them in the name of the Father and of the Son and of the Holy Spirit, [20] teaching them to observe all that I have commanded you; and lo, I am with you always, to the close of the age."

o Or *Take a guard* *p* Greek *know*
q Other ancient authorities read *the Lord*

28.1–15: The first Easter (Mk.16.1–8; Lk.24.1–11; Jn.20.1–10). **4:** *The guards,* 27.62–66. **7:** 26.32; 28.16; Jn.21.1–23; 1 Cor.15.3–4,12,20. **8:** Compare Lk.24.9,22–23; the sequence of events cannot be worked out. Each account is a separate summary of early Christian testimony to the fact of Jesus' resurrection. **9:** Jn.20.14–18.

28.11–15: Bribing the guard. 11: 27.62–66. **15:** *This day,* i.e. the time when the Gospel according to Matthew was written.

28:16–20: Jesus' commission to his disciples. 17: 1 Cor.15.5–6; Jn.21.1–23; Lk.24.11. **18:** 11.27; Lk.10.22; Phil.2.9; Eph.1.20–22. *All authority,* compare Dan.7.14. **19:** *All nations,* contrast 10.5, and compare Mk.16.15; Lk.24.47; Acts 1.8. According to Hebrew usage *in the name of* means in the possession and protection of (Ps.124.8). **20:** *I am with you,* 18.20; Acts 18.10.

The Gospel According to John

IN THE BEGINNING WAS THE WORD, and the Word was with God, and the Word was God. [2] He was in the beginning with God; [3] all things were made through him, and without him was not anything made that was made. [4] In him was life,[a] and the life was the light of men. [5] The light shines in the darkness, and the darkness has not overcome it.

6 There was a man sent from God, whose name was John. [7] He came for testimony, to bear witness to the light, that all might believe through him. [8] He was not the light, but came to bear witness to the light.

9 The true light that enlightens every man was coming into the world. [10] He was in the world, and the world was made through him, yet the world knew him not. [11] He came to his own home, and his own people received him not. [12] But to all who received him, who believed in his name, he gave power to become children of God; [13] who were born, not of blood nor of the will of the flesh nor of the will of man, but of God.

14 And the Word became flesh and dwelt among us, full of grace and truth; we have beheld his glory, glory as of the only Son from the Father. [15] (John bore witness to him, and cried, "This was he of whom I said, 'He who comes after me ranks before me, for he was before me.'") [16] And from his fulness have we all received, grace upon grace. [17] For the law was given through Moses; grace and truth came through Jesus Christ. [18] No one has ever seen God; the only Son,[b] who is in the bosom of the Father, he has made him known.

19 And this is the testimony of John, when the Jews sent priests and Levites from Jerusalem to ask him, "Who are you?" [20] He confessed, he did not deny, but confessed, "I am not the Christ." [21] And they asked him, "What then? Are you Eli'jah?" He said, "I am not." "Are you the prophet?" And he answered, "No." [22] They said to him then, "Who are you? Let us have an answer for those who sent us. What do you say about yourself?" [23] He said, "I am the voice of one crying in the wilderness, 'Make straight the way of the Lord,' as the prophet Isaiah said."

24 Now they had been sent from the Pharisees. [25] They asked him, "Then why are you baptizing, if you are neither the Christ, nor Eli'jah, nor the prophet?" [26] John answered them, "I baptize with water; but among you stands one whom you do not know, [27] even he who comes after me, the thong of whose sandal I am not worthy to untie." [28] This took place in Bethany beyond the Jordan, where John was baptizing.

29 The next day he saw Jesus coming toward him, and said, "Behold, the Lamb of God, who takes away the sin of the world! [30] This is he of whom I said, 'After me comes a man who ranks before me, for he was before

a Or *was not anything made. That which has been made was life in him*   *b* Other ancient authorities read *God*

1.1–18: The Prologue. 1–2: The *Word* (Greek "logos") of God is more than speech; it is God in action, creating (Gen.1.3; Ps.33.6), revealing (Amos 3.7–8), redeeming (Ps.107.19–20). Jesus is this *Word* (v. 14). He was eternal (*in the beginning:* compare Gen.1.1); personal *(with God);* divine *(was God). Was,* not "became" (contrast v. 14). **3:** He was sole agent of creation (Gen. 1.1; Pr.8.27–30; Col.1.16–17; Heb.1.2). **4:** Apart from him both physical (Col.1.17) and spiritual life would recede into nothingness (5.39–40; 8.12). **5:** *Darkness* is total evil in conflict with God; it cannot *overcome.* **6–8:** John, climaxing the Old Testament prophets, was *sent* (commissioned by God, Mal.3.1) to point to Jesus (vv. 19–34). **9:** *True light* is real, underived light, contrasted not with false light, but with such as John, who was but a lamp (5.35). **11:** *His own people,* the Jews. **14–17:** God's *glory* dwelt ("tabernacled") in the *flesh* (human nature) of Jesus, as did his *grace* (redeeming love) and *truth* (faithfulness to his promises). These are available to *all,* exhaustless *(grace upon grace),* a fulfilment of the *law of Moses.* **18:** *The bosom of the Father,* complete communion (vv. 1–2). Men *see* God in Jesus (14.9).

1.19–34: The testimony of John. 19: *Jews,* the religious authorities. **20:** *The Christ,* the Messiah. **21:** *Elijah* (2 Kg.2.11) was expected to return to prepare the Messiah's way (Mal.4.5). John is unconscious of this role, but Jesus later ascribed it to him (see Mt.11.14 n.; Mk.9.13 n.). *The prophet* was likewise an expected Messianic forerunner (6.14; 7.40; see Dt.18.15). **23:** As a *voice* John fulfils a prophetic role announcing the Messiah's coming (Is.40.3). **25:** *Why are you baptizing,* performing an official rite, without official status? **27:** *To untie a sandal thong* was a slave's task. **29:** *Lamb,* Ex. ch. 12; Is.53.7. *Of God,* provided by God. **30:** He outranks me, *for he was* (existed) *before me.*

Bible, THE NEW OXFORD ANNOTATED BIBLE WITH THE APOCRYPHA Revised Standard Edition, Gospel of John, chaps 1–6.

me.' [31] I myself did not know him; but for this I came baptizing with water, that he might be revealed to Israel." [32] And John bore witness, "I saw the Spirit descend as a dove from heaven, and it remained on him. [33] I myself did not know him; but he who sent me to baptize with water said to me, 'He on whom you see the Spirit descend and remain, this is he who baptizes with the Holy Spirit.' [34] And I have seen and have borne witness that this is the Son of God."

35 The next day again John was standing with two of his disciples; [36] and he looked at Jesus as he walked, and said, "Behold, the Lamb of God!" [37] The two disciples heard him say this, and they followed Jesus. [38] Jesus turned, and saw them following, and said to them, "What do you seek?" And they said to him, "Rabbi" (which means Teacher), "where are you staying?" [39] He said to them, "Come and see." They came and saw where he was staying; and they stayed with him that day, for it was about the tenth hour. [40] One of the two who heard John speak, and followed him, was Andrew, Simon Peter's brother. [41] He first found his brother Simon, and said to him, "We have found the Messiah" (which means Christ). [42] He brought him to Jesus. Jesus looked at him, and said, "So you are Simon the son of John? You shall be called Cephas" (which means Peter[c]).

43 The next day Jesus decided to go to Galilee. And he found Philip and said to him, "Follow me." [44] Now Philip was from Beth-sa′ida, the city of Andrew and Peter. [45] Philip found Nathan′a-el, and said to him, "We have found him of whom Moses in the law and also the prophets wrote, Jesus of Nazareth, the son of Joseph." [46] Nathan′a-el said to him, "Can anything good come out of Nazareth?" Philip said to him, "Come and see." [47] Jesus saw Nathan′a-el coming to him, and said of him, "Behold, an Israelite indeed, in whom is no guile!" [48] Nathan′a-el said to him, "How do you know me?" Jesus answered him, "Before Philip called you, when you were under the fig tree, I saw you." [49] Nathan′a-el answered him, "Rabbi, you are the Son of God! You are the King of Israel!" [50] Jesus answered him, "Because I said to you, I saw you under the fig tree, do you believe? You shall see greater things than these." [51] And he said to him, "Truly, truly, I say to you, you will see heaven opened, and the angels of God ascending and descending upon the Son of man."

2 On the third day there was a marriage at Cana in Galilee, and the mother of Jesus was there; [2] Jesus also was invited to the marriage, with his disciples. [3] When the wine gave out, the mother of Jesus said to him, "They have no wine." [4] And Jesus said to her, "O woman, what have you to do with me? My hour has not yet come." [5] His mother said to the servants, "Do whatever he tells you." [6] Now six stone jars were standing there, for the Jewish rites of purification, each holding twenty or thirty gallons. [7] Jesus said to them, "Fill the jars with water." And they filled them up to the brim. [8] He said to them, "Now draw some out, and take it to the steward of the feast." So they took it. [9] When the steward of the feast tasted the water now become wine,

c From the word for *rock* in Aramaic and Greek respectively

31–33: John's knowledge of Jesus' significance was given him by God at the baptism. **34:** *Son of God,* the Messiah (v. 49; 11.27).

1.35–51: The testimony of Jesus' first disciples. 39: *Come and see,* a call to personal following (8.12). *The tenth hour,* about 4 p.m. **42:** In Aramaic *Cephas* (Greek *Peter*) means Rock. **45:** *Moses . . . prophets,* the Old Testament points to Christ. **46:** *Nathanael,* probably the same person as Bartholomew (Mt.10.3; Mk.3.18; Lk.6.14), lived in Cana, near Nazareth (21.2). **47:** *No guile,* no qualities of Jacob before he became Israel (Gen.27.35; 32.28). **51:** What Jacob saw in vision (Gen.28.12) is now a reality in Jesus. *Son of man,* a messenger from heaven to make God known (3.13), and to be the final judge (5.27; see Mk.2.10 n.).

2.1–12: The wedding at Cana. 4: *Woman,* a term of solemn and respectful address (compare 19.26). The *hour* of Jesus' self-disclosure was determined by God, not by Mary's desires. His final manifestation was at the cross (7.30; 8.20; 12.23,27; 13.1; 17.1). **6:** *Rites of purification* were ceremonial, not hygienic. **8:** *Steward,* head-waiter or toast-

and did not know where it came from (though the servants who had drawn the water knew), the steward of the feast called the bridegroom [10] and said to him, "Every man serves the good wine first; and when men have drunk freely, then the poor wine; but you have kept the good wine until now." [11] This, the first of his signs, Jesus did at Cana in Galilee, and manifested his glory; and his disciples believed in him.

[12] After this he went down to Caper'na-um, with his mother and his brothers and his disciples; and there they stayed for a few days.

[13] The Passover of the Jews was at hand, and Jesus went up to Jerusalem. [14] In the temple he found those who were selling oxen and sheep and pigeons, and the money-changers at their business. [15] And making a whip of cords, he drove them all, with the sheep and oxen, out of the temple; and he poured out the coins of the money-changers and overturned their tables. [16] And he told those who sold the pigeons, "Take these things away; you shall not make my Father's house a house of trade." [17] His disciples remembered that it was written, "Zeal for thy house will consume me." [18] The Jews then said to him, "What sign have you to show us for doing this?" [19] Jesus answered them, "Destroy this temple, and in three days I will raise it up." [20] The Jews then said, "It has taken forty-six years to build this temple, and will you raise it up in three days?" [21] But he spoke of the temple of his body. [22] When therefore he was raised from the dead, his disciples remembered that he had said this; and they believed the scripture and the word which Jesus had spoken.

[23] Now when he was in Jerusalem at the Passover feast, many believed in his name when they saw the signs which he did; [24] but Jesus did not trust himself to them, [25] because he knew all men and needed no one to bear witness of man; for he himself knew what was in man.

3 Now there was a man of the Pharisees, named Nicode'mus, a ruler of the Jews. [2] This man came to Jesus[d] by night and said to him, "Rabbi, we know that you are a teacher come from God; for no one can do these signs that you do, unless God is with him." [3] Jesus answered him, "Truly, truly, I say to you, unless one is born anew,[e] he cannot see the kingdom of God." [4] Nicode'mus said to him, "How can a man be born when he is old? Can he enter a second time into his mother's womb and be born?" [5] Jesus answered, "Truly, truly, I say to you, unless one is born of water and the Spirit, he cannot enter the kingdom of God. [6] That which is born of the flesh is flesh, and that which is born of the Spirit is spirit.[f] [7] Do not marvel that I said to you, 'You must be born anew.'[e] [8] The wind[f] blows where it wills, and you hear the sound of it, but you do not know whence it comes or whither it goes; so it is with every one who is born of the Spirit." [9] Nicode'mus said to him, "How can this be?" [10] Jesus answered him, "Are you a teacher of Israel, and yet you do not understand this? [11] Truly, truly, I say to you, we speak of what we know, and bear witness to what we have seen; but you do not receive our testimony. [12] If I have told you earthly things

d Greek *him* *e* Or *from above* *f* The same Greek word means both *wind* and *spirit*

---

master. **11:** Jesus' miracles were not wonders to astound, but *signs* pointing to *his glory* (God's presence in him). *First,* for the second see 4.46–54. **12:** *Brothers,* see Mt.13.55 n.

2.13–25: The cleansing of the temple (compare Mt.21.12–17; Mk.11.15–19; Lk.19.45–48). **14:** Animals were sold for sacrifice; Roman money was changed into Jewish money to pay the temple tax. **15–16:** Not an outburst of temper, but the energy of righteousness against religious leaders to whom religion had become a business. *My Father's house* is a claim to lordship. **17:** Ps.69.9. **23–25:** Faith which rests merely on *signs* and not on him to whom they point is shallow and unstable.

3.1–21: Jesus and official Judaism. 1: *The Pharisees* were the most devout of Jews. *A ruler,* a member of the Sanhedrin (see 11.47 n.). **3:** *The kingdom of God* is entered, not by moral achievement, but by a transformation wrought by God. **5:** Birth into the new order is through *water* (referring to baptism; 1.33; Eph.5.26) and *the Spirit* (Ezek.36.25–27; Tit.3.5). **6:** Like begets like. **8–9:** See note *f* and Ezek.37.5–10. **12:** *Earthly things,* such as the para-

and you do not believe, how can you believe if I tell you heavenly things? [13] No one has ascended into heaven but he who descended from heaven, the Son of man.*g* [14] And as Moses lifted up the serpent in the wilderness, so must the Son of man be lifted up, [15] that whoever believes in him may have eternal life."*h*

16 For God so loved the world that he gave his only Son, that whoever believes in him should not perish but have eternal life. [17] For God sent the Son into the world, not to condemn the world, but that the world might be saved through him. [18] He who believes in him is not condemned; he who does not believe is condemned already, because he has not believed in the name of the only Son of God. [19] And this is the judgment, that the light has come into the world, and men loved darkness rather than light, because their deeds were evil. [20] For every one who does evil hates the light, and does not come to the light, lest his deeds should be exposed. [21] But he who does what is true comes to the light, that it may be clearly seen that his deeds have been wrought in God.

22 After this Jesus and his disciples went into the land of Judea; there he remained with them and baptized. [23] John also was baptizing at Ae'non near Salim, because there was much water there; and people came and were baptized. [24] For John had not yet been put in prison.

25 Now a discussion arose between John's disciples and a Jew over purifying. [26] And they came to John, and said to him, "Rabbi, he who was with you beyond the Jordan, to whom you bore witness, here he is, baptizing,

and all are going to him," [27] John answered, "No one can receive anything except what is given him from heaven. [28] You yourselves bear me witness, that I said, I am not the Christ, but I have been sent before him. [29] He who has the bride is the bridegroom; the friend of the bridegroom, who stands and hears him, rejoices greatly at the bridegroom's voice; therefore this joy of mine is now full. [30] He must increase, but I must decrease."*i*

31 He who comes from above is above all; he who is of the earth belongs to the earth, and of the earth he speaks; he who comes from heaven is above all. [32] He bears witness to what he has seen and heard, yet no one receives his testimony; [33] he who receives his testimony sets his seal to this, that God is true. [34] For he whom God has sent utters the words of God, for it is not by measure that he gives the Spirit; [35] the Father loves the Son, and has given all things into his hand. [36] He who believes in the Son has eternal life; he who does not obey the Son shall not see life, but the wrath of God rests upon him.

4 Now when the Lord knew that the Pharisees had heard that Jesus was making and baptizing more disciples than John [2] (although Jesus himself did not baptize, but only his disciples), [3] he left Judea and departed again to Galilee. [4] He had to pass through Sama'ria. [5] So he came to a city of Sama'ria, called Sy'char, near the field that Jacob gave to his son Joseph. [6] Jacob's well was there, and so Jesus, wearied as he was with his journey,

g Other ancient authorities add *who is in heaven*
h Some interpreters hold that the quotation continues through verse 21   *i* Some interpreters hold that the quotation continues through verse 36

ble of the wind; *heavenly things,* supreme spiritual realities. **13–15:** Jesus *descended from heaven* to bring *eternal life* (participation in God's life), through being *lifted up* on the cross (Num.21.9). **16:** Luther called this verse "the Gospel in miniature." **17–20:** God's purpose is to save; men judge themselves by hiding their *evil deeds* from the *light* of Christ's holiness.

3.22–36: Further testimony of John (compare 1.19–34). **25:** *Purifying,* Jewish religious ceremonies. **27–29:** John was only the *friend of the bridegroom,* leading Israel, the bride, to Jesus, the bridegroom. He *rejoices* in their union (see Mk.2.19–20 n.). **32–35:** *No one,* a generalization about the Jews. The author and others do believe, and attest that Jesus authentically speaks *the words of God.* **36:** Unbelief is disobedience. *Wrath* is the consuming fire of God's holiness.

4.1–42: Jesus and the Samaritans. 1–3: *The Pharisees,* hostile to John, now turn on Jesus. **4:** *Samaria,* between Judea and Galilee, with a mixed people (see Acts 8.5 n.). **5:** Gen.33.19; 48.22; Jos.24.32. **6:** *Wearied,* shows Jesus'

sat down beside the well. It was about the sixth hour.

7 There came a woman of Sama'ria to draw water. Jesus said to her, "Give me a drink." [8] For his disciples had gone away into the city to buy food. [9] The Samaritan woman said to him, "How is it that you, a Jew, ask a drink of me, a woman of Sama'ria?" For Jews have no dealings with Samaritans. [10] Jesus answered her, "If you knew the gift of God, and who it is that is saying to you, 'Give me a drink,' you would have asked him, and he would have given you living water." [11] The woman said to him, "Sir, you have nothing to draw with, and the well is deep; where do you get that living water? [12] Are you greater than our father Jacob, who gave us the well, and drank from it himself, and his sons, and his cattle?" [13] Jesus said to her, "Every one who drinks of this water will thirst again, [14] but whoever drinks of the water that I shall give him will never thirst; the water that I shall give him will become in him a spring of water welling up to eternal life." [15] The woman said to him, "Sir, give me this water, that I may not thirst, nor come here to draw."

16 Jesus said to her, "Go, call your husband, and come here." [17] The woman answered him, "I have no husband." Jesus said to her, "You are right in saying, 'I have no husband'; [18] for you have had five husbands, and he whom you now have is not your husband; this you said truly." [19] The woman said to him, "Sir, I perceive that you are a prophet. [20] Our fathers worshiped on this mountain; and you say that in Jerusalem is the place where men ought to worship." [21] Jesus said to her, "Woman, believe me, the hour is coming when neither on this mountain nor in Jerusalem will you worship the Father. [22] You wor-

ship what you do not know; we worship what we know, for salvation is from the Jews. [23] But the hour is coming, and now is, when the true worshipers will worship the Father in spirit and truth, for such the Father seeks to worship him. [24] God is spirit, and those who worship him must worship in spirit and truth." [25] The woman said to him, "I know that Messiah is coming (he who is called Christ); when he comes, he will shows us all things." [26] Jesus said to her, "I who speak to you am he."

27 Just then his disciples came. They marveled that he was talking with a woman, but none said, "What do you wish?" or, "Why are you talking with her?" [28] So the woman left her water jar, and went away into the city, and said to the people, [29] "Come, see a man who told me all that I ever did. Can this be the Christ?" [30] They went out of the city and were coming to him.

31 Meanwhile the disciples besought him, saying, "Rabbi, eat." [32] But he said to them, "I have food to eat of which you do not know." [33] So the disciples said to one another, "Has any one brought him food?" [34] Jesus said to them, "My food is to do the will of him who sent me, and to accomplish his work. [35] Do you not say, 'There are yet four months, then comes the harvest'? I tell you, lift up your eyes, and see how the fields are already white for harvest. [36] He who reaps receives wages, and gathers fruit for eternal life, so that sower and reaper may rejoice together. [37] For here the saying holds true, 'One sows and another reaps.' [38] I sent you to reap that for which you did not labor; others have labored, and you have entered into their labor."

39 Many Samaritans from that city believed in him because of the woman's testi-

humanity. *The sixth hour,* about noon. **5:** Gen.33.19; 48.22; Jos.24.32. **9:** Rabbis avoided speaking to a *woman* in public (v. 27). *Jews* held *Samaritans* in contempt, as religious apostates (2 Kg.17.24–34). **10:** *Living water,* Jer.2.13; 17.13. **14:** Jesus' gift is God's life in man. **19–20:** *A prophet* should be able to settle rival religious claims. **21:** *This mountain,* i.e. Mount Gerizim, where the Samaritans had had a temple. Jesus means that the place of worship is not of primary importance. **24:** Worship *in spirit* is man's response to God's gift of himself (*the Father seeks,* v. 23). *In truth,* in accord with God's nature seen in Christ. **27:** See v. 9 n. **35:** *Already,* see v. 30. **36:** *Wages,* the reward of gathering believers. **37–38:** Jesus *sows* (vv. 7–26), the disciples *reap;* the harvest comes from the *labor* of Jesus' life, death, and resurrection (12.23–24). **39–42:** Faith based on the testimony of another (*the woman*) is vindicated in personal experience.

mony, "He told me all that I ever did." ⁴⁰ So when the Samaritans came to him, they asked him to stay with them; and he stayed there two days. ⁴¹ And many more believed because of his word. ⁴² They said to the woman, "It is no longer because of your words that we believe, for we have heard for ourselves, and we know that this is indeed the Savior of the world."

43 After the two days he departed to Galilee. ⁴⁴ For Jesus himself testified that a prophet has no honor in his own country. ⁴⁵ So when he came to Galilee, the Galileans welcomed him, having seen all that he had done in Jerusalem at the feast, for they too had gone to the feast.

46 So he came again to Cana in Galilee, where he had made the water wine. And at Caper'na-um there was an official whose son was ill. ⁴⁷ When he heard that Jesus had come from Judea to Galilee, he went and begged him to come down and heal his son, for he was at the point of death. ⁴⁸ Jesus therefore said to him, "Unless you see signs and wonders you will not believe." ⁴⁹ The official said to him, "Sir, come down before my child dies." ⁵⁰ Jesus said to him, "Go; your son will live." The man believed the word that Jesus spoke to him and went his way. ⁵¹ As he was going down, his servants met him and told him that his son was living. ⁵² So he asked them the hour when he began to mend, and they said to him, "Yesterday at the seventh hour the fever left him." ⁵³ The father knew that was the hour when Jesus had said to him, "Your son will live"; and he himself believed, and all his household. ⁵⁴ This was now the second sign that Jesus did when he had come from Judea to Galilee.

5 After this there was a feast of the Jews, and Jesus went up to Jerusalem.

2 Now there is in Jerusalem by the Sheep Gate a pool, in Hebrew called Beth-za'tha,^j which has five porticoes. ³ In these lay a multitude of invalids, blind, lame, paralyzed.^k ⁵ One man was there, who had been ill for thirty-eight years. ⁶ When Jesus saw him and knew that he had been lying there a long time, he said to him, "Do you want to be healed?" ⁷ The sick man answered him, "Sir, I have no man to put me into the pool when the water is troubled, and while I am going another steps down before me." ⁸ Jesus said to him, "Rise, take up your pallet, and walk." ⁹ And at once the man was healed, and he took up his pallet and walked.

Now that day was the sabbath. ¹⁰ So the Jews said to the man who was cured, "It is the sabbath, it is not lawful for you to carry your pallet." ¹¹ But he answered them, "The man who healed me said to me; 'Take up your pallet, and walk.'" ¹² They asked him, "Who is the man who said to you, 'Take up your pallet, and walk'?" ¹³ Now the man who had been healed did not know who it was, for Jesus had withdrawn, as there was a crowd in the place. ¹⁴ Afterward, Jesus found him in the temple, and said to him, "See, you are well! Sin no more, that nothing worse befall you." ¹⁵ The man went away and told the Jews that it was Jesus who had healed him. ¹⁶ And this was why the Jews persecuted Jesus, because he did

j Other ancient authorities read *Bethesda,* others *Beth-saida* *k* Other ancient authorities insert, wholly or in part, *waiting for the moving of the water;* ⁴ *for an angel of the Lord went down at certain seasons into the pool, and troubled the water; whoever stepped in first after the troubling of the water was healed of whatever disease he had*

4.43–54: Jesus and the Gentiles. Illustrates v. 42, Jesus as *Savior of the world* (Jew, Samaritan, Gentile — everyone; compare Is.43.3,11; 45.22). **46:** *An official,* a Gentile military officer. **48:** *You* is plural here, addressed to all who base faith on mere signs (compare v. 45). **49:** He desires life for his child, not a display. **50:** The official *believed* that Jesus' *word* had effected the cure, and he did not return to his home (which was only about eighteen miles away) until the next day (v. 52). **52:** *Seventh hour,* about 1 p.m. **53:** *Believed,* in the deepest sense. **54:** *Second,* for the first see 2.1–11.

5.1–18: Healing the lame man on the sabbath. 3: After the word *paralyzed* later manuscripts add an explanatory statement; see note *k.* **7:** *When the water is troubled* is explained by the addition to v. 3. Movement caused by an intermittent spring was attributed to divine action. **13:** *Jesus had withdrawn* to avoid publicity. **14:** There are *worse* things

this on the sabbath. [17] But Jesus answered them, "My Father is working still, and I am working." [18] This was why the Jews sought all the more to kill him, because he not only broke the sabbath but also called God his own Father, making himself equal with God.

[19] Jesus said to them, "Truly, truly, I say to you, the Son can do nothing of his own accord, but only what he sees the Father doing; for whatever he does, that the Son does likewise. [20] For the Father loves the Son, and shows him all that he himself is doing; and greater works than these will he show him, that you may marvel. [21] For as the Father raises the dead and gives them life, so also the Son gives life to whom he will. [22] The Father judges no one, but has given all judgment to the Son, [23] that all may honor the Son, even as they honor the Father. He who does not honor the Son does not honor the Father who sent him. [24] Truly, truly, I say to you, he who hears my word and believes him who sent me, has eternal life; he does not come into judgment, but has passed from death to life.

[25] "Truly, truly, I say to you, the hour is coming, and now is, when the dead will hear the voice of the Son of God, and those who hear will live. [26] For as the Father has life in himself, so he has granted the Son also to have life in himself, [27] and has given him authority to execute judgment, because he is the Son of man. [28] Do not marvel at this; for the hour is coming when all who are in the tombs will hear his voice [29] and come forth, those who have done good, to the resurrection of life, and those who have done evil, to the resurrection of judgment.

[30] "I can do nothing on my own authority; as I hear, I judge; and my judgment is just, because I seek not my own will but the will of him who sent me. [31] If I bear witness to myself, my testimony is not true; [32] there is another who bears witness to me, and I know that the testimony which he bears to me is true. [33] You sent to John, and he has borne witness to the truth. [34] Not that the testimony which I receive is from man; but I say this that you may be saved. [35] He was a burning and shining lamp, and you were willing to rejoice for a while in his light. [36] But the testimony which I have is greater than that of John; for the works which the Father has granted me to accomplish, these very works which I am doing, bear me witness that the Father has sent me. [37] And the Father who sent me has himself borne witness to me. His voice you have never heard, his form you have never seen; [38] and you do not have his word abiding in you, for you do not believe him whom he has sent. [39] You search the scriptures, because you think that in them you have eternal life; and it is they that bear witness to me; [40] yet you refuse to come to me that you may have life. [41] I do not receive glory from men. [42] But I know that you have not the love of God within you. [43] I have come in my Father's name, and you do not receive me; if another comes in his own name, him you will receive. [44] How can you believe, who receive glory from one another and do not seek the glory that comes from the only God? [45] Do not think that I shall accuse you to the Father; it is Moses who accuses you, on whom you set your hope. [46] If you believed Moses, you would believe me, for he wrote of me. [47] But

than illness. **16:** *The Jews,* the religious authorities, opposed Jesus for his break with their legalism. **17:** God continually gives life and judges evil, as does Jesus. **18:** *Equal,* see 10.30–33.

5.19–29: Jesus' relation to God. 19–20: Jesus' sonship involves the identity of his will and actions with the Father's. The *greater works* are giving life (v. 21) and judgment (v. 22). **24:** He who *believes* on the basis of Jesus' word *has passed* into the realm where death does not reign. **25:** The *coming* age is already present in Jesus. To *hear* with the comprehension of faith makes the spiritually *dead* live. **26–29:** They will share in the final *resurrection of life.*

5.30–40: Evidence of Jesus' relation to God. 30: Jesus' judgment is that of God, and therefore *just,* without favoritism or error. **32:** *Another,* the Father. **33–40:** God witnesses to Jesus through the ministry of *John* the Baptist (vv. 33–35), through Jesus' *works* (v. 36), and through *the scriptures* (vv. 37–40).

5.41–47: Jesus condemns the Jews. 41: No human standards apply to him. **42:** No *love of God,* no love of Jesus. **43–44:** Judgment based on human pride. **45:** 9.28; Rom.2.17. **47:** Lk.16.29,31.

if you do not believe his writings, how will you believe my words?"

6 After this Jesus went to the other side of the Sea of Galilee, which is the Sea of Tibe′ri-as. ² And a multitude followed him, because they saw the signs which he did on those who were diseased. ³ Jesus went up on the mountain, and there sat down with his disciples. ⁴ Now the Passover, the feast of the Jews, was at hand. ⁵ Lifting up his eyes, then, and seeing that a multitude was coming to him, Jesus said to Philip, "How are we to buy bread, so that these people may eat?" ⁶ This he said to test him, for he himself knew what he would do. ⁷ Philip answered him, "Two hundred denarii*l* would not buy enough bread for each of them to get a little." ⁸ One of his disciples, Andrew, Simon Peter's brother, said to him, ⁹ "There is a lad here who has five barley loaves and two fish; but what are they among so many?" ¹⁰ Jesus said, "Make the people sit down." Now there was much grass in the place; so the men sat down, in number about five thousand. ¹¹ Jesus then took the loaves, and when he had given thanks, he distributed them to those who were seated; so also the fish, as much as they wanted. ¹² And when they had eaten their fill, he told his disciples, "Gather up the fragments left over, that nothing may be lost." ¹³ So they gathered them up and filled twelve baskets with fragments from the five barley loaves, left by those who had eaten. ¹⁴ When the people saw the sign which he had done, they said, "This is indeed the prophet who is to come into the world!"

15 Perceiving then that they were about to come and take him by force to make him king, Jesus withdrew again to the mountain by himself.

16 When evening came, his disciples went down to the sea, ¹⁷ got into a boat, and started across the sea to Caper′na-um. It was now dark, and Jesus had not yet come to them. ¹⁸ The sea rose because a strong wind was blowing. ¹⁹ When they had rowed about three or four miles,*m* they saw Jesus walking on the sea and drawing near to the boat. They were frightened, ²⁰ but he said to them, "It is I; do not be afraid." ²¹ Then they were glad to take him into the boat, and immediately the boat was at the land to which they were going.

22 On the next day the people who remained on the other side of the sea saw that there had been only one boat there, and that Jesus had not entered the boat with his disciples, but that his disciples had gone away alone. ²³ However, boats from Tibe′ri-as came near the place where they ate the bread after the Lord had given thanks. ²⁴ So when the people saw that Jesus was not there, nor his disciples, they themselves got into the boats and went to Caper′na-um, seeking Jesus.

25 When they found him on the other side of the sea, they said to him, "Rabbi, when did you come here?" ²⁶ Jesus answered them, "Truly, truly, I say to you, you seek me, not because you saw signs, but because you ate your fill of the loaves. ²⁷ Do not labor for the food which perishes, but for the food which endures to eternal life, which the Son of man will give to you; for on him has God the Father set his seal." ²⁸ Then they said to him, "What must we do, to be doing the works of

l The denarius was a day's wage for a laborer
m Greek *twenty-five or thirty stadia*

6.1–15: Feeding the five thousand; the only miracle recorded by all four gospels (Mt.14.13–21; Mk.6.32–44; Lk.9.10–17). **1:** *Tiberias,* named for the Emperor Tiberius. **6:** *To test* Philip's faith. **7:** *Two hundred denarii,* for the value of the denarius, see note *l.* **9:** *Barley loaves,* food of the poor. **12:** *Gather,* an act of reverential economy toward the gift of God. **13:** *Twelve baskets,* one for each disciple. **15:** *To make him king,* as a political Messiah opposing Rome; but Jesus would not accept this (18.36).

6.16–21: Jesus walks on the sea (Mt.14.22–27; Mk.6.45–51). Jesus is greater than a political ruler (v. 15); he is Lord of the elements (Ps.107.29–30). **17:** *Not yet come,* probably they expected to meet Jesus along the shore. **20–21:** Jesus' presence dispels fear.

6.22–71: Jesus, the bread of life. 22–25: Note the clamor for more bread. **26:** *Signs,* pointing to Jesus as food for the soul. **27:** *Son of man,* see 1.51 n. *Seal,* God's authentication, perhaps at the baptism (1.32). **28:** *Works,* 3.21;

God?" [29] Jesus answered them, "This is the work of God, that you believe in him whom he has sent." [30] So they said to him, "Then what sign do you do, that we may see, and believe you? What work do you perform? [31] Our fathers ate the manna in the wilderness; as it is written, 'He gave them bread from heaven to eat.'" [32] Jesus then said to them, "Truly, truly, I say to you, it was not Moses who gave you the bread from heaven; my Father gives you the true bread from heaven. [33] For the bread of God is that which comes down from heaven, and gives life to the world." [34] They said to him, "Lord, give us this bread always."

[35] Jesus said to them, "I am the bread of life; he who comes to me shall not hunger, and he who believes in me shall never thirst. [36] But I said to you that you have seen me and yet do not believe. [37] All that the Father gives me will come to me; and him who comes to me I will not cast out. [38] For I have come down from heaven, not to do my own will, but the will of him who sent me; [39] and this is the will of him who sent me, that I should lose nothing of all that he has given me, but raise it up at the last day. [40] For this is the will of my Father, that every one who sees the Son and believes in him should have eternal life; and I will raise him up at the last day."

[41] The Jews then murmured at him, because he said, "I am the bread which came down from heaven." [42] They said, "Is not this Jesus, the son of Joseph, whose father and mother we know? How does he now say, 'I have come down from heaven'?" [43] Jesus answered them, "Do not murmur among yourselves. [44] No one can come to me unless the Father who sent me draws him; and I will raise him up at the last day. [45] It is written in the prophets, 'And they shall all be taught by God.' Every one who has heard and learned from the Father comes to me. [46] Not that any one has seen the Father except him who is from God; he has seen the Father. [47] Truly, truly, I say to you, he who believes has eternal life. [48] I am the bread of life. [49] Your fathers ate the manna in the wilderness, and they died. [50] This is the bread which comes down from heaven, that a man may eat of it and not die. [51] I am the living bread which came down from heaven; if any one eats of this bread, he will live for ever; and the bread which I shall give for the life of the world is my flesh."

[52] The Jews then disputed among themselves, saying, "How can this man give us his flesh to eat?" [53] So Jesus said to them, "Truly, truly, I say to you, unless you eat the flesh of the Son of man and drink his blood, you have no life in you; [54] he who eats my flesh and drinks my blood has eternal life, and I will raise him up at the last day. [55] For my flesh is food indeed, and my blood is drink indeed. [56] He who eats my flesh and drinks my blood abides in me, and I in him. [57] As the living Father sent me, and I live because of the Father, so he who eats me will live because of me. [58] This is the bread which came down from heaven, not such as the fathers ate and died; he who eats this bread will live for ever." [59] This he said in the synagogue, as he taught at Caper'na-um.

[60] Many of his disciples, when they heard it, said, "This is a hard saying; who can listen to it?" [61] But Jesus, knowing in himself that

---

Rev.2.26. **29:** *Work,* singular number; not many works (v. 28), but obedient trust *(believe)* is the one thing pleasing to God (1 Jn.3.23). *Him . . . sent,* Jesus who reveals God. **30:** *See,* as a proof; but faith cannot be proved. **31:** The Messiah was expected to reproduce the miracle of the giving of manna (Ex.16.4,15; Num.11.8; Ps.78.24; 105.40). **36–40:** Jesus himself is God's gift of sustenance for time and eternity. Belief, or unbelief involves a mystery known only to God, but no one who *comes* is rejected (v. 37). Faith is God's gift, not a human achievement; it gives *eternal life* now and issues in resurrection *at the last day.* **44–45:** The *drawing* is not coercive or mechanical. *Prophets,* Is.54.13; compare Jl.2.28–29. Had they *heard* and *learned* God's voice in their scriptures, they would have recognized its accents in him who alone has direct communion with God. **51:** *The living bread . . . is my flesh,* the One who became flesh (assumed complete human nature, 1.14) offered himself to God in death, thus releasing his life *for the life of the world.* **53:** The separation of the *blood* from the *flesh* emphasizes the reality of Jesus' death. **54:** To *eat* and *drink* is to believe (v. 47), to appropriate, assimilate, and *abide* in Christ (v. 56). **58:** Since Christ is *bread . . . from heaven* (compare vv. 32–35), to eat him is to *live for ever.* **60:** *Hard saying* means offensive or difficult, but not obscure. **62–63:** The ascen-

his disciples murmured at it, said to them, "Do you take offense at this? [62] Then what if you were to see the Son of man ascending where he was before? [63] It is the spirit that gives life, the flesh is of no avail; the words that I have spoken to you are spirit and life. [64] But there are some of you that do not believe." For Jesus knew from the first who those were that did not believe, and who it was that would betray him. [65] And he said, "This is why I told you that no one can come to me unless it is granted him by the Father."

[66] After this many of his disciples drew back and no longer went about with him. [67] Jesus said to the twelve, "Do you also wish to go away?" [68] Simon Peter answered him, "Lord, to whom shall we go? You have the words of eternal life; [69] and we have believed, and have come to know, that you are the Holy One of God." [70] Jesus answered them, "Did I not choose you, the twelve, and one of you is a devil?" [71] He spoke of Judas the son of Simon Iscariot, for he, one of the twelve, was to betray him.

sion, by which Jesus will be taken away as regards the flesh, will indicate that he has been speaking of spiritual realities and not the actual eating of his flesh. **64–65:** These truths can be discerned only by faith, which is God's gift, not man's achievement (Eph.2.8). **66–71:** To receive God's gift of faith is to *know* God in Christ; to refuse it is to become an ally of the *devil*. Faith and unbelief mark the great divisions among men.

Romans

3 Then what advantage has the Jew? Or what is the value of circumcision? [2] Much in every way. To begin with, the Jews are entrusted with the oracles of God. [3] What if some were unfaithful? Does their faithlessness nullify the faithfulness of God? [4] By no means! Let God be true though every man be false, as it is written,

"That thou mayest be justified in thy words,
and prevail when thou art judged."

[5] But if our wickedness serves to show the justice of God, what shall we say? That God is unjust to inflict wrath on us? (I speak in a human way.) [6] By no means! For then how could God judge the world? [7] But if through my falsehood God's truthfulness abounds to his glory, why am I still being condemned as a sinner? [8] And why not do evil that good may come? — as some people slanderously charge us with saying. Their condemnation is just.

[9] What then? Are we Jews any better off?[c] No, not at all; for I[d] have already charged that all men, both Jews and Greeks, are under the power of sin, [10] as it is written:

"None is righteous, no, not one;
[11] no one understands, no one seeks for God.
[12] All have turned aside, together they have gone wrong;
no one does good, not even one."
[13] "Their throat is an open grave,
they use their tongues to deceive."
"The venom of asps is under their lips."
[14] "Their mouth is full of curses and bitterness."
[15] "Their feet are swift to shed blood,
[16] in their paths are ruin and misery,
[17] and the way of peace they do not know."
[18] "There is no fear of God before their eyes."

[19] Now we know that whatever the law says it speaks to those who are under the law, so that every mouth may be stopped, and the whole world may be held accountable to God. [20] For no human being will be justified in his sight by works of the law, since through the law comes knowledge of sin.

c Or *at any disadvantage?*   d Greek *we*

3.1–8: **The advantage of the Jews** as the covenant people cannot be denied. To them were given the *oracles,* i.e. the Scriptures, and particularly the promises they contain. God's *faithfulness* in making the promises is not invalidated by the failure of the Jews to keep their part of the covenant; nor can that failure be excused on the plea that, because of it, God's truth will shine more brightly when he fulfils his part (Paul will discuss this problem more fully in chs. 9–11). **4:** Ps.51.4.
3.9–20: **All are guilty.** Jew and Greek, despite the former's advantages, stand on the same ground, *under the power of sin.* **10–18:** Ps.14.1–2; 53.1–2; 5.9; 140.3; 10.7; Is.59.7–8; Ps.36.1. The law succeeds only in making men aware of their condition. That indeed was God's purpose in giving it (7.7; see Gal.3.19–29 n.).

21 But now the righteousness of God has been manifested apart from law, although the law and the prophets bear witness to it, 22 the righteousness of God through faith in Jesus Christ for all who believe. For there is no distinction; 23 since all have sinned and fall short of the glory of God, 24 they are justified by his grace as a gift, through the redemption which is in Christ Jesus, 25 whom God put forward as an expiation by his blood, to be received by faith. This was to show God's righteousness, because in his divine forbearance he had passed over former sins; 26 it was to prove at the present time that he himself is righteous and that he justifies him who has faith in Jesus.

27 Then what becomes of our boasting? It is excluded. On what principle? On the principle of works? No, but on the principle of faith. 28 For we hold that a man is justified by faith apart from works of law. 29 Or is God the God of Jews only? Is he not the God of Gentiles also? Yes, of Gentiles also, 30 since God is one; and he will justify the circumcised on the ground of their faith and the uncircumcised through their faith. 31 Do we then overthrow the law by this faith? By no means! On the contrary, we uphold the law.

4 What then shall we say about*e* Abraham, our forefather according to the flesh? 2 For if Abraham was justified by works, he has something to boast about, but not before God. 3 For what does the scripture say? "Abraham believed God, and it was reckoned to him as righteousness." 4 Now to one who works, his wages are not reckoned as a gift but as his due. 5 And to one who does not work but trusts him who justifies the ungodly, his faith is reckoned as righteousness. 6 So also David pronounces a blessing upon the man to whom God reckons righteousness apart from works:

7 "Blessed are those whose iniquities are
        forgiven, and whose sins are covered;
8 blessed is the man against whom the Lord
        will not reckon his sin."

9 Is this blessing pronounced only upon the circumcised, or also upon the uncircumcised? We say that faith was reckoned to Abraham as righteousness. 10 How then was it reckoned to him? Was it before or after he had been circumcised? It was not after, but before he was circumcised. 11 He received circumcision as a sign or seal of the righteousness which he had by faith while he was still uncircumcised. The purpose was to make him the father of all who believe without being circumcised and who thus have righteousness reckoned to them, 12 and likewise the father of the circumcised who are not merely circumcised but also follow the example of the faith which our father Abraham had before he was circumcised.

13 The promise to Abraham and his descendants, that they should inherit the world, did not come through the law but through the righteousness of faith. 14 If it is the adherents of the law who are to be the heirs, faith is null

e Other ancient authorities read *was gained by*

3.21–26: The true righteousness, now revealed in Christ, rests not upon obedience to law, but on faith in God's act of *redemption . . . in Christ Jesus*. **21:** *The law and the prophets,* the Hebrew scriptures. **24:** *Redemption* means a ransoming or "buying back" (as of a slave or captive), and therefore emancipation or deliverance. Slaves of sin are set free through God's act in Christ (Eph.1.7; Col.1.14; Heb.9.15). **25:** *Expiation by his blood,* a reference to the death of Christ as a sacrifice for sin (1 Jn.2.2), demonstrating the seriousness with which God regards sin (despite his *forbearance*); it also reveals the measure of his love (Jn.3.16).

3.27–31: Boasting is excluded. *On the principle of works* there might be ground for boasting, but if salvation is by faith, pride *is excluded*. **30:** Since *God is one,* he will deal with Jews and Gentiles on the same basis.

4.1–8: Abraham justified by faith, not by works. **2:** *But not before God;* the full statement would be: "But actually if he had anything to boast about, it was not before God." **3:** According to Paul's understanding of Gen.15.6, Abraham's faith in God was credited to him as righteousness. **6–8:** God's blessing belongs not to those who perfectly obey the law (as though that were possible), but to those who in faith accept God's free gift of forgiveness (Ps.32.1–2). **9–12:** This justification of Abraham occurred *before he was circumcised,* and therefore cannot have been dependent upon circumcision; it depended only upon faith. **11:** Gen.17.10. **12:** *Follow the example,* i.e. rely only on faith, as Abraham did.

and the promise is void. [15] For the law brings wrath, but where there is no law there is no transgression.

16 That is why it depends on faith, in order that the promise may rest on grace and be guaranteed to all his descendants — not only to the adherents of the law but also to those who share the faith of Abraham, for he is the father of us all, [17] as it is written, "I have made you the father of many nations"— in the presence of the God in whom he believed, who gives life to the dead and calls into existence the things that do not exist. [18] In hope he believed against hope, that he should become the father of many nations; as he had been told, "So shall your descendants be." [19] He did not weaken in faith when he considered his own body, which was as good as dead because he was about a hundred years old, or when he considered the barrenness of Sarah's womb. [20] No distrust made him waver concerning the promise of God, but he grew strong in his faith as he gave glory to God, [21] fully convinced that God was able to do what he had promised. [22] That is why his faith was "reckoned to him as righteousness." [23] But the words, "it was reckoned to him," were written not for his sake alone, [24] but for ours also. It will be reckoned to us who believe in him that raised from the dead Jesus our Lord, [25] who was put to death for our trespasses and raised for our justification.

5 Therefore, since we are justified by faith, we[f] have peace with God through our Lord Jesus Christ. [2] Through him we have obtained access[g] to this grace in which we stand, and we[h] rejoice in our hope of sharing the glory of God. [3] More than that, we[h] rejoice in our sufferings, knowing that suffering produces endurance, [4] and endurance produces character, and character produces hope, [5] and hope does not disappoint us, because God's love has been poured into our hearts through the Holy Spirit which has been given to us.

6 While we were still weak, at the right time Christ died for the ungodly. [7] Why, one will hardly die for a righteous man — though perhaps for a good man one will dare even to die. [8] But God shows his love for us in that while we were yet sinners Christ died for us. [9] Since, therefore, we are now justified by his blood, much more shall we be saved by him from the wrath of God. [10] For if while we were enemies we were reconciled to God by the death of his Son, much more, now that we are reconciled, shall we be saved by his life. [11] Not only so, but we also rejoice in God through our Lord Jesus Christ, through whom we have now received our reconciliation.

12 Therefore as sin came into the world through one man and death through sin, and so death spread to all men because all men sinned — [13] sin indeed was in the world before the law was given, but sin is not counted where there is no law. [14] Yet death reigned from Adam to Moses, even over those whose sins were not like the transgression of Adam, who was a type of the one who was to come.

15 But the free gift is not like the trespass. For if many died through one man's trespass, much more have the grace of God and the free

---

f Other ancient authorities read *let us* *g* Other ancient authorities add *by faith* *h* Or *let us*

4.13–25: The true descendants of Abraham are those who have faith in Christ, whether Jews or Gentiles. To them the benefits promised to Abraham belong (Gen.17.4–6; 22.17–18; Gal.3.29). **17:** Gen.17.5. **18:** Gen.15.5. **19:** Gen.17.17; 18.11; Heb.11.12. **22–23:** See v. 3.

5.1–11: Consequences of justification. 1–5: When we rely utterly upon God's grace and not at all upon ourselves, *we have peace,* i.e. reconciliation, or a state of harmony *with God. Hope of . . . the glory of God,* though we had fallen short of the glorious destiny God intended for us (3.23), we now find ourselves confidently expecting it. **6–11:** Christ in his death has borne the consequences of our sin and thus has reconciled us to God. Note that Paul never speaks of a reconciliation of God to us; it is we who were estranged. **9–10:** Being *now justified* (and reconciled) *by Christ's death,* we *shall . . . be saved* in the final Judgment *by his life,* i.e. through our participation in his present *life* as the risen Lord. **11:** *Now,* under the gospel.

5.12–21: Adam and Christ; analogy and contrast. Sin and death for all men followed upon Adam's disobedi-

gift in the grace of that one man Jesus Christ abounded for many. [16] And the free gift is not like the effect of that one man's sin. For the judgment following one trespass brought condemnation, but the free gift following many trespasses brings justification. [17] If, because of one man's trespass, death reigned through that one man, much more will those who receive the abundance of grace and the free gift of righteousness reign in life through the one man Jesus Christ.

[18] Then as one man's trespass led to condemnation for all men, so one man's act of righteousness leads to acquittal and life for all men. [19] For as by one man's disobedience many were made sinners, so by one man's obedience many will be made righteous. [20] Law came in, to increase the trespass; but where sin increased, grace abounded all the more, [21] so that, as sin reigned in death, grace also might reign through righteousness to eternal life through Jesus Christ our Lord.

6 What shall we say then? Are we to continue in sin that grace may abound? [2] By no means! How can we who died to sin still live in it? [3] Do you not know that all of us who have been baptized into Christ Jesus were baptized into his death? [4] We were buried therefore with him by baptism into death, so that as Christ was raised from the dead by the glory of the Father, we too might walk in newness of life.

[5] For if we have been united with him in a death like his, we shall certainly be united with him in a resurrection like his. [6] We know that our old self was crucified with him so that the sinful body might be destroyed, and we might no longer be enslaved to sin. [7] For he who has died is freed from sin. [8] But if we have died with Christ, we believe that we shall also live with him. [9] For we know that Christ being raised from the dead will never die again; death no longer has dominion over him. [10] The death he died he died to sin, once for all, but the life he lives he lives to God. [11] So you also must consider yourselves dead to sin and alive to God in Christ Jesus.

[12] Let not sin therefore reign in your mortal bodies, to make you obey their passions. [13] Do not yield your members to sin as instruments of wickedness, but yield yourselves to God as men who have been brought from death to life, and your members to God as instruments of righteousness. [14] For sin will have no dominion over you, since you are not under law but under grace.

[15] What then? Are we to sin because we are not under law but under grace? By no means! [16] Do you not know that if you yield yourselves to any one as obedient slaves, you are slaves of the one whom you obey, either of sin, which leads to death, or of obedience, which leads to righteousness? [17] But thanks be to God, that you who were once slaves of sin have become obedient from the heart to the standard of teaching to which you were committed, [18] and, having been set free from sin, have become slaves of righteousness. [19] I am speaking in human terms, because of your natural limitations. For just as you once yielded your members to impurity and to greater and greater iniquity, so now yield your members to righteousness for sanctification.

[20] When you were slaves of sin, you were free in regard to righteousness. [21] But then

---

ence (Gen.2.17; 3.17–19). **13–16:** 1 Cor.15.21–23,45–49. **18:** *Acquittal and life for all* followed upon Christ's perfect obedience. **20:** *Law . . . to increase the trespass,* this is explained in 7.7–13.

6.1–14: Dying and rising with Christ. Paul's insistence that salvation is entirely a gracious and undeserved gift of God may seem to have laid him open to the charge of encouraging sin. This charge Paul vigorously rejects. When the Christian is *baptized,* he is united with Christ. We share in his death and in the *newness of life* (v. 4), which his resurrection has made possible for us. But this death is a *death . . . to sin,* and the new life is *life . . . to God* (v. 10). *How then can we who died to sin still live in it?* (v. 2). **6:** *The sinful body,* not the physical body as such, but the sinful self. **13:** *Your members,* all the organs and functions of the person.

6.15–23: The two slaveries. In rejecting again the same charge (see v. 1 n.), Paul draws an analogy from slavery. The sinner is sin's slave; but if he becomes God's slave, how can he longer obey his old master? **19:** *Sanctification,* the process and result of being entirely devoted, consecrated, to God (v. 22).

what return did you get from the things of which you are now ashamed? The end of those things is death. ²² But now that you have been set free from sin and have become slaves of God, the return you get is sanctification and its end, eternal life. ²³ For the wages of sin is death, but the free gift of God is eternal life in Christ Jesus our Lord.

7 Do you not know, brethren — for I am speaking to those who know the law — that the law is binding on a person only during his life? ² Thus a married woman is bound by law to her husband as long as he lives; but if her husband dies she is discharged from the law concerning the husband. ³ Accordingly, she will be called an adulteress if she lives with another man while her husband is alive. But if her husband dies she is free from that law, and if she marries another man she is not an adulteress.

4 Likewise, my brethren, you have died to the law through the body of Christ, so that you may belong to another, to him who has been raised from the dead in order that we may bear fruit for God. ⁵ While we were living in the flesh, our sinful passions, aroused by the law, were at work in our members to bear fruit for death. ⁶ But now we are discharged from the law, dead to that which held us captive, so that we serve not under the old written code but in the new life of the Spirit.

7 What then shall we say? That the law is sin? By no means! Yet, if it had not been for the law, I should not have known sin. I should not have known what it is to covet if the law had not said, "You shall not covet." ⁸ But sin, finding opportunity in the commandment, wrought in me all kinds of covetousness. Apart from the law sin lies dead. ⁹ I was once alive apart from the law, but when the commandment came, sin revived and I died; ¹⁰ the very commandment which promised life proved to be death to me. ¹¹ For sin, finding opportunity in the commandment, deceived me and by it killed me. ¹² So the law is holy, and the commandment is holy and just and good.

13 Did that which is good, then, bring death to me? By no means! It was sin, working death in me through what is good, in order that sin might be shown to be sin, and through the commandment might become sinful beyond measure. ¹⁴ We know that the law is spiritual; but I am carnal, sold under sin. ¹⁵ I do not understand my own actions. For I do not do what I want, but I do the very thing I hate. ¹⁶ Now if I do what I do not want, I agree that the law is good. ¹⁷ So then it is no longer I that do it, but sin which dwells within me. ¹⁸ For I know that nothing good dwells within me, that is, in my flesh. I can will what is right, but I cannot do it. ¹⁹ For I do not do the good I want, but the evil I do not want is what I do. ²⁰ Now if I do what I do not want, it is no longer I that do it, but sin which dwells within me.

21 So I find it to be a law that when I want to do right, evil lies close at hand. ²² For I delight in the law of God, in my inmost self, ²³ but I see in my members another law at war

---

7.1–6: An analogy from marriage. One who has died to sin is no more bound to it than is a woman to her deceased husband. **1–2:** *The law* here probably means Roman law. **4–6:** *The law* here refers to God's commandments, as in chs. 2–4.

7.7–13: The law and sin. 7: Though the law is *holy . . . and good* (v. 12), it not only makes man conscious of sin (see Gal.3.19 n.), but also incites to sin (e.g. coveteousness; compare Ex.20.17; Dt.5.21). **9:** Probably a reminiscence of a thoughtless, carefree boyhood brought to an end *(death)* by the dawning sense of moral obligation and guilt. **10:** Lev.18.5. **13:** The real enemy is sin, which uses even *what is good* (the law) to make a man more sinful than he would otherwise be.

7.14–23: The inner conflict. Sin is personified as an evil power that enters a man's life and brings his true self into slavery to its rule or *law* (still another use of this term). **14:** *The law is spiritual,* divine in origin and nature, and holy (v. 12). *I am carnal,* Greek "fleshly," referring not merely to man's physical nature, but to his whole nature in so far as he is ruled by selfish interests (compare v. 18 and v. 25). **17:** In emphasizing the reality of sin's power over a man's *inmost self* (v. 22), Paul seems almost to deny one's responsibility for sin (compare v. 20). Other passages in his letters, however, prevent our inferring that he means this (e.g. Rom.1.31–2.5).

with the law of my mind and making me captive to the law of sin which dwells in my members. [24] Wretched man that I am! Who will deliver me from this body of death? [25] Thanks be to God through Jesus Christ our Lord! So then, I of myself serve the law of God with my mind, but with my flesh I serve the law of sin.

8 There is therefore now no condemnation for those who are in Christ Jesus. [2] For the law of the Spirit of life in Christ Jesus has set me free from the law of sin and death. [3] For God has done what the law, weakened by the flesh, could not do: sending his own Son in the likeness of sinful flesh and for sin,[i] he condemned sin in the flesh, [4] in order that the just requirement of the law might be fulfilled in us, who walk not according to the flesh but according to the Spirit. [5] For those who live according to the flesh set their minds on the things of the flesh, but those who live according to the Spirit set their minds on the things of the Spirit. [6] To set the mind on the flesh is death, but to set the mind on the Spirit is life and peace. [7] For the mind that is set on the flesh is hostile to God; it does not submit to God's law, indeed it cannot; [8] and those who are in the flesh cannot please God.

9 But you are not in the flesh, you are in the Spirit, if in fact the Spirit of God dwells in you. Any one who does not have the Spirit of Christ does not belong to him. [10] But if Christ is in you, although your bodies are dead because of sin, your spirits are alive because of righteousness. [11] If the Spirit of him who raised Jesus from the dead dwells in you, he who raised Christ Jesus from the dead will give life to your mortal bodies also through his Spirit which dwells in you.

12 So then, brethren, we are debtors, not to the flesh, to live according to the flesh — [13] for if you live according to the flesh you will die, but if by the Spirit you put to death the deeds of the body you will live. [14] For all who are led by the Spirit of God are sons of God. [15] For you did not receive the spirit of slavery to fall back into fear, but you have received the spirit of sonship. When we cry. "Abba! Father!" [16] it is the Spirit himself bearing witness with our spirit that we are children of God, [17] and if children, then heirs, heirs of God and fellow heirs with Christ, provided we suffer with him in order that we may also be glorified with him.

18 I consider that the sufferings of this present time are not worth comparing with the glory that is to be revealed to us. [19] For the creation waits with eager longing for the revealing of the sons of God; [20] for the creation was subjected to futility, not of its own will but by the will of him who subjected it in hope; [21] because the creation itself will be set free from its bondage to decay and obtain the

i Or and as a sin offering

7.24–25: Despair and release. Threatened by utter defeat in the struggle with our enemy entrenched in our own souls, we cast ourselves upon God's mercy in Christ; only then do we find freedom from both the guilt and the power of sin. **24:** _This body of death,_ i.e. the body, which is the instrument of sin, is under the dominion of death. **25:** _Flesh,_ compare "carnal," v. 14 n.

8.1–4: God's saving act. 1: _Condemnation_ means more than judgment; it means doom. There is to be no doom or death _for us,_ because God has sentenced sin to death (_condemned sin,_ v. 3). **2:** _The Spirit_ is the divine principle _(law)_ of life in the new order which God has created through Christ. To be _in Christ_ is to belong to this new order and thus to know the Spirit, who is the actual presence of God in our midst and in our hearts. **4:** Only through the power of _the Spirit_ can we hope for the righteousness which _the law_ requires but cannot enable us in our weakness to attain.

8.5–11: Life in the flesh and in the Spirit. 5: To live _according to the flesh_ (see 7.14 n.) is to be dominated by selfish passions; to _live according to_ (or _in,_ v. 9) _the Spirit_ is to belong to the new community of faith where God dwells as the Spirit. **9–10:** Note the similar, almost interchangeable, use of "the Spirit of God," "the Spirit of Christ," and "Christ." **10:** Gal.2.20; Eph.3.17. **11:** Jn.5.21.

8.12–17: The Spirit and sonship. The Spirit does not make slaves of us, but sons. **15:** _Abba,_ the Aramaic word meaning "Father," which Jesus used in his own prayers (Mk.14.36) and which passed into the liturgy of the early church. **16:** The fact that _the Spirit_ prompts this ecstatic prayer proves our sonship (Gal.4.6).

8.18–25: The hope of fulfillment. 18: The Christian life involves _sufferings_ (this was more obviously true then than now), but Paul rejoices in the sure hope of _glory_ (5.2). **20:** _Of him,_ God (Gen.3.17). **21:** When man (in Christ) is

glorious liberty of the children of God. [22] We know that the whole creation has been groaning in travail together until now; [23] and not only the creation, but we ourselves, who have the first fruits of the Spirit, groan inwardly as we wait for adoption as sons, the redemption of our bodies. [24] For in this hope we were saved. Now hope that is seen is not hope. For who hopes for what he sees? [25] But if we hope for what we do not see, we wait for it with patience.

26 Likewise the Spirit helps us in our weakness; for we do not know how to pray as we ought, but the Spirit himself intercedes for us with sighs too deep for words. [27] And he who searches the hearts of men knows what is the mind of the Spirit, because[j] the Spirit intercedes for the saints according to the will of God.

28 We know that in everything God works for good[k] with those who love him,[l] who are called according to his purpose. [29] For those whom he foreknew he also predestined to be conformed to the image of his Son, in order that he might be the first-born among many brethren. [30] And those whom he predestined he also called; and those whom he called he also justified; and those whom he justified he also glorified.

31 What then shall we say to this? If God is for us, who is against us? [32] He who did not spare his own Son but gave him up for us all, will he not also give us all things with him? [33] Who shall bring any charge against God's elect? It is God who justifies; [34] who is to condemn? Is it Christ Jesus, who died, yes, who was raised from the dead, who is at the right hand of God, who indeed intercedes for us?[m] [35] Who shall separate us from the love of Christ? Shall tribulation, or distress, or persecution, or famine, or nakedness, or peril, or sword? [36] As it is written,

"For thy sake we are being killed all the
    day long;
we are regarded as sheep to be slaugh-
    tered."

[37] No, in all these things we are more than conquerors through him who loved us. [38] For I am sure that neither death, nor life, nor angels, nor principalities, nor things present, nor things to come, nor powers, [39] nor height, nor depth, nor anything else in all creation, will be able to separate us from the love of God in Christ Jesus our Lord.

9 I am speaking the truth in Christ, I am not lying; my conscience bears me witness in the Holy Spirit [2] that I have great sorrow and unceasing anguish in my heart. [3] For I could wish that I myself were accursed and cut off from Christ for the sake of my brethren, my kinsmen by race. [4] They are Israelites, and to them belong the sonship, the glory, the covenants, the giving of the law, the worship, and the promises; [5] to them belong the patriarchs, and of their race, according to the flesh, is the

---

j Or *that*   *k* Other ancient authorities read *in everything he works for good,* or *everything works for good*
l Greek *God*   *m* Or *It is Christ Jesus . . . for us*

---

finally restored to his true nature and destiny, nature will also share in the freedom from *bondage to decay* and in the *glorious liberty.* **22–23:** Nature is thought of as sharing in the stress, anxiety, and pain which we ourselves feel as we wait for the promised *redemption. The first fruits of the Spirit,* the Spirit, already received, is an advanced installment of the full sonship we are yet to receive. *Our bodies,* as usually in Paul, our "selves," our "personalities." **24–25:** 1 Cor.2.9; 2 Cor.5.7; Heb.11.1.

8.26–30: Human weakness is sustained by the Spirit's intercession and by the knowledge of God's loving purpose. **28:** *His purpose,* or plan, is set forth in vv. 29–30. **29:** *To be conformed to . . . his Son* is to share the resurrection life of Christ, to be a "fellow heir" (compare v. 17), to be *glorified.*

8.31–39: Our confidence in God. 31: Ps.118.6. **32:** 4.25; 5.8; Jn.3.16. **35:** To be a Christian in the first century was both difficult and dangerous. **36:** Ps.44.22. **38:** *Neither death, nor life,* i.e. whether we live or die we shall not be separated. *Angels . . . principalities . . . powers* are supernatural beings, whether evil or good, and of various ranks (see Eph.6.12.n.). **39:** *Height* and *depth,* the highest point to which the stars rise and the abyss out of which they were thought to ascend; i.e. no supposed astrological power can separate us from Christ or defeat God's purpose for us.

9.1–5: The problem of Israel's unbelief. 3: Ex.32.32. **4:** *Sonship,* Ex.4.22; Jer.31.9. *Glory,* God's presence (Ex.16.10; 24.16). *Covenants,* plural because the covenant with Israel was often renewed (Gen.6.18; 9.9; 15.8; 17.2,7,9; Ex.2.24). *Giving the law,* Ex.20.1–17; Dt.5.1–21. *Worship,* in tabernacle and temple.

Christ. God who is over all be blessed for ever.[n] Amen.

6 But it is not as though the word of God had failed. For not all who are descended from Israel belong to Israel, [7] and not all are children of Abraham because they are his descendants; but "Through Isaac shall your descendants be named." [8] This means that it is not the children of the flesh who are the children of God, but the children of the promise are reckoned as descendants. [9] For this is what the promise said, "About this time I will return and Sarah shall have a son." [10] And not only so, but also when Rebecca had conceived children by one man, our forefather Isaac, [11] though they were not yet born and had done nothing either good or bad, in order that God's purpose of election might continue, not because of works but because of his call, [12] she was told, "The elder will serve the younger." [13] As it is written, "Jacob I loved, but Esau I hated."

14 What shall we say then? Is there injustice on God's part? By no means! [15] For he says to Moses, "I will have mercy on whom I have mercy, and I will have compassion on whom I have compassion." [16] So it depends not upon man's will or exertion, but upon God's mercy. [17] For the scripture says to Pharaoh, "I have raised you up for the very purpose of showing my power in you, so that my name may be proclaimed in all the earth." [18] So then he has mercy upon whomever he wills, and he hardens the heart of whomever he wills.

19 You will say to me then, "Why does he still find fault? For who can resist his will?" [20] But who are you, a man, to answer back to God? Will what is molded say to its molder, "Why have you made me thus?" [21] Has the potter no right over the clay, to make out of the same lump one vessel for beauty and another for menial use? [22] What if God, desiring to show his wrath and to make known his power, has endured with much patience the vessels of wrath made for destruction, [23] in order to make known the riches of his glory for the vessels of mercy, which he has prepared beforehand for glory, [24] even us whom he has called, not from the Jews only but also from the Gentiles? [25] As indeed he says in Hose'a,

"Those who were not my people
I will call 'my people,'
and her who was not beloved
I will call 'my beloved.'"
[26] "And in the very place where it was said to
them, 'You are not my people,'
they will be called 'sons of the living
God.'"

27 And Isaiah cries out concerning Israel: "Though the number of the sons of Israel be as the sand of the sea, only a remnant of them will be saved; [28] for the Lord will execute his sentence upon the earth with rigor and dispatch." [29] And as Isaiah predicted,

"If the Lord of hosts had not left us children,
we would have fared like Sodom and been
made like Gomor'rah."

30 What shall we say, then? That Gentiles who did not pursue righteousness have attained it, that is, righteousness through faith; [31] but that Israel who pursued the righteousness which is based on law did not succeed in fulfilling that law. [32] Why? Because they did not pursue it through faith, but as if it were based on works. They have stumbled over the stumbling stone, [33] as it is written,

n Or *Christ, who is God over all, blessed for ever*

9.6–13: God's promise to Israel has not failed, because the promise was not made to Abraham's physical descendants merely as such, but to those whom God chose. **7:** Gen.21.12. **9:** Gen.18.10. **10–12:** Gen.25.21,23. **13:** Mal.1.2–3.

9.14–29: God's right to choose. 15: Ex.33.19. **17:** Ex.9.16. **19–21:** Is.29,16; 45.9; 64.8; Jer.18.6. **24:** God's choice or election is not limited to *the Jews* (compare 3.29). **25–26:** The passage *in Hosea* (Hos.2.23; 1.10) refers to God's reclaiming of Israel after she had forsaken God and lost her covenant status; Paul (as also 1 Pet.2.10) applies the promise to the Gentiles. **27–29:** God's promise never included all Israelites (Is.10.22; 1.9). *Sodom* and *Gomorrah,* Gen.19.24–25.

9.30–10.13: True righteousness is by faith. 9.30: 3.22; 10.6,20; Gal.2.16; 3.24; Phil.3.9; Heb.11.7. **33:** Is.28.16

"Behold, I am laying in Zion a stone that
will make men stumble,
a rock that will make them fall;
and he who believes in him will not be put
to shame."

10 Brethren, my heart's desire and prayer
to God for them is that they may be
saved. [2] I bear them witness that they have a
zeal for God, but it is not enlightened. [3] For,
being ignorant of the righteousness that
comes from God, and seeking to establish
their own, they did not submit to God's righteousness. [4] For Christ is the end of the law,
that every one who has faith may be justified.

[5] Moses writes that the man who practices
the righteousness which is based on the law
shall live by it. [6] But the righteousness based
on faith says, Do not say in your heart, "Who
will ascend into heaven?" (that is, to bring
Christ down) [7] or "Who will descend into the
abyss?" (that is, to bring Christ up from the
dead). [8] But what does it say? The word is
near you, on your lips and in your heart (that
is, the word of faith which we preach);
[9] because, if you confess with your lips that
Jesus is Lord and believe in your heart that
God raised him from the dead, you will be
saved. [10] For man believes with his heart and
so is justified, and he confesses with his lips
and so is saved. [11] The scripture says, "No one
who believes in him will be put to shame."
[12] For there is no distinction between Jew and
Greek; the same Lord is Lord of all and
bestows his riches upon all who call upon
him. [13] For, "every one who calls upon the
name of the Lord will be saved."

[14] But how are men to call upon him in
whom they have not believed? And how are
they to believe in him of whom they have
never heard? And how are they to hear without a preacher? [15] And how can men preach
unless they are sent? As it is written, "How
beautiful are the feet of those who preach
good news!" [16] But they have not all obeyed
the gospel; for Isaiah says, "Lord, who has
believed what he has heard from us?" [17] So
faith comes from what is heard, and what is
heard comes by the preaching of Christ.

[18] But I ask, have they not heard? Indeed
they have; for
"Their voice has gone out to all the earth,
and their words to the ends of the world."
[19] Again I ask, did Israel not understand?
First Moses says,
"I will make you jealous of those who are
not a nation;
with a foolish nation I will make you
angry."
[20] Then Isaiah is so bold as to say,
"I have been found by those who did not
seek me;
I have shown myself to those who did not
ask for me."
[21] But of Israel he says, "All day long I have
held out my hands to a disobedient and contrary people."

11 I ask, then, has God rejected his people?
By no means! I myself am an Israelite,
a descendant of Abraham, a member of the
tribe of Benjamin. [2] God has not rejected his
people whom he foreknew. Do you not know
what the scripture says of Eli′jah, how he
pleads with God against Israel? [3] "Lord, they
have killed thy prophets, they have demol-
ished thy altars, and I alone am left, and they
seek my life." [4] But what is God's reply to

---

and 8.14–15. The "stone" is a symbol of God's help, but if neglected it becomes an instrument of judgment. Christ is this *stone*. **10.4:** Gal.3.23–26. **5:** Lev.18.5; Gal.3.12. One must actually *practice* the law if one is to find life through it; this Paul has already shown to be impossible (3.9–20). But one has only to *accept* the free gift of the salvation in Christ (vv. 6–9; compare Dt.30.11–14). **10:** Both faith and confession are essential for justification and salvation. **11:** Is.28.16. **13:** Jl.2.32. The early Christians often applied to Jesus Old Testament references to the *Lord,* which in their original context refer to God.

10.14–21: Israel responsible for its failure. 14–18: The nation cannot claim that it has not had the opportunity of hearing the gospel. **15:** Is.52.7. **16:** Is.53.1. **18:** Ps.19.4. **19–21:** Nor can Israel claim that it has not understood the gospel; even Gentiles have been able to understand it. **19:** Dt.32.21. **20–21:** Is.65.1–2.

11.1–16: Israel's rejection not final. 1–6: As in Elijah's time (1 Kg.19.10,18), there is a *remnant* of the faithful.

him? "I have kept for myself seven thousand men who have not bowed the knee to Ba'al." [5] So too at the present time there is a remnant, chose by grace. [6] But if it is by grace, it is no longer on the basis of works; otherwise grace would no longer be grace.

[7] What then? Israel failed to obtain what it sought. The elect obtained it, but the rest were hardened, [8] as it is written,

"God gave them a spirit of stupor,
eyes that should not see and ears that
    should not hear,
down to this very day."

[9] And David says,

"Let their table become a snare and a trap,
a pitfall and a retribution for them;
[10] let their eyes be darkened so that they can-
    not see,
and bend their backs for ever."

[11] So I ask, have they stumbled so as to fall? By no means! But through their trespass salvation has come to the Gentiles, so as to make Israel jealous. [12] Now if their trespass means riches for the world, and if their failure means riches for the Gentiles, how much more will their full inclusion mean!

[13] Now I am speaking to you Gentiles. Inasmuch then as I am an apostle to the Gentiles, I magnify my ministry [14] in order to make my fellow Jews jealous, and thus save some of them. [15] For if their rejection means the reconciliation of the world, what will their acceptance mean but life from the dead? [16] If the dough offered as first fruits is holy, so is the whole lump; and if the root is holy, so are the branches.

[17] But if some of the branches were broken off, and you, a wild olive shoot, were grafted in their place to share the richness[o] of the olive tree, [18] do not boast over the branches. If you do boast, remember it is not you that support the root, but the root that supports you. [19] You will say, "Branches were broken off so that I might be grafted in." [20] That is true. They were broken off because of their unbelief, but you stand fast only through faith. So do not become proud, but stand in awe. [21] For if God did not spare the natural branches, neither will he spare you. [22] Note then the kindness and the severity of God: severity toward those who have fallen, but God's kindness to you, provided you continue in his kindness; otherwise you too will be cut off. [23] And even the others, if they do not persist in their unbelief, will be grafted in, for God has the power to graft them in again. [24] For if you have been cut from what is by nature a wild olive tree, and grafted, contrary to nature, into a cultivated olive tree, how much more will these natural branches be grafted back into their own olive tree.

[25] Lest you be wise in your own conceits, I want you to understand this mystery, brethren: a hardening has come upon part of Israel, until the full number of the Gentiles come in; [26] and so all Israel will be saved; as it is written,

"The Deliverer will come from Zion,
he will banish ungodliness from Jacob";
[27] "and this will be my covenant with them
when I take away their sins."

o Other ancient authorities read *rich root*

Paul as a Jew is no more alone than Elijah was. **7–12:** The resistance to the gospel on the part of the masses of Jews is providential; God has *hardened* their *hearts* for a loving purpose, namely, that the Gentiles might have an opportunity to hear and receive the gospel. **8:** Is.29.10. **9:** Ps.69.22–23. **13–16:** The *reconciliation* of Gentiles will have the effect of making Israelites *jealous* and thus of drawing *some of them* to Christ. **16:** *The dough* and *the root* (Num.15.19–20 Septuagint; Jer.11.16–17) stand for the patriarchs, through whom all Israel has been consecrated.

11.17–24: The metaphor of the olive tree. The tree, including root and branches, is Israel. The branches broken off are the unbelieving Jews; the branches grafted in are Gentiles who believe in Christ. **20–22:** Having been made a part of the tree only because of faith (not merit or works), Gentile believers have no reason for pride, else God who has grafted them into the tree may later cut them off. **24:** The restoration of Israel will be easier than the call of the Gentiles.

11.25–36: All Israel will be saved. 25–26: A *mystery*, a truth once hidden, but now revealed by God. The *full number of the Gentiles* may mean the elect from among the Gentiles; and *all Israel* may mean Israel as a whole, not every

28 As regards the gospel they are enemies of
God, for your sake; but as regards election
they are beloved for the sake of their forefathers. 29 For the gifts and the call of God are
irrevocable. 30 Just as you were once disobedient to God but now have received mercy
because of their disobedience, 31 so they have
now been disobedient in order that by the
mercy shown to you they also may[p] receive
mercy. 32 For God has consigned all men to
disobedience, that he may have mercy upon all.

33 O the depth of the riches and wisdom
and knowledge of God! How unsearchable are
his judgments and how inscrutable his ways!

34 "For who has known the mind of the Lord,
or who has been his counselor?"

35 "Or who has given a gift to him
that he might be repaid?"

36 For from him and through him and to him
are all things. To him be glory for ever. Amen.

12 I appeal to you therefore, brethren, by
the mercies of God, to present your
bodies as a living sacrifice, holy and acceptable to God, which is your spiritual worship.
2 Do not be conformed to this world[q] but be
transformed by the renewal of your mind, that
you may prove what is the will of God, what is
good and acceptable and perfect.[r]

3 For by the grace given to me I bid every
one among you not to think of himself more
highly than he ought to think, but to think with
sober judgment, each according to the measure of faith which God has assigned him.
4 For as in one body we have many members,
and all the members do not have the same
function, 5 so we, though many, are one body
in Christ, and individually members one of
another. 6 Having gifts that differ according to
the grace given to us, let us use them: if
prophecy, in proportion to our faith; 7 if service, in our serving; he who teaches, in his
teaching; 8 he who exhorts, in his exhortation;
he who contributes, in liberality; he who gives
aid, with zeal; he who does acts of mercy, with
cheerfulness.

9 Let love be genuine; hate what is evil,
hold fast to what is good; 10 love one another
with brotherly affection; outdo one another in
showing honor. 11 Never flag in zeal, be aglow
with the Spirit, serve the Lord. 12 Rejoice in
your hope, be patient in tribulation, be constant in prayer. 13 Contribute to the needs of
the saints, practice hospitality.

14 Bless those who persecute you; bless
and do not curse them. 15 Rejoice with those
who rejoice, weep with those who weep.
16 Live in harmony with one another; do not
be haughty, but associate with the lowly;[s]
never be conceited. 17 Repay no one evil for
evil, but take thought for what is noble in the
sight of all. 18 If possible, so far as it depends
upon you, live peaceably with all. 19 Beloved,
never avenge yourselves, but leave it[t] to the
wrath of God; for it is written, "Vengeance is
mine, I will repay, says the Lord." 20 No, "if
your enemy is hungry, feed him; if he is
thirsty, give him drink; for by so doing you
will heap burning coals upon his head." 21 Do
not be overcome by evil, but overcome evil
with good.

p Other ancient authorities add *now* *q* Greek *age*
r Or *what is the good and acceptable and perfect will of God* *s* Or *give yourselves to humble tasks*
t Greek *give place*

particular Israelite. **26–27:** Is.59.20–21; 27.9. **28–32:** Although temporarily *enemies* of the *gospel,* the *election* of the Jews is *irrevocable.* **33:** The wonder of God's providence. **34:** Is.40.13. **35:** Job 35.7; 41.11. **36:** 1 Cor.8.6; 11.12; Col.1.16; Heb.2.10.

12.1–8: The consecrated life. 1: *Bodies,* as usually in Paul, means "selves." *Living sacrifice,* as contrasted to the sacrifice of a slain beast. **2:** Christians are to live as belonging to the coming age, not this present age (Eph.4.23; 1 Jn.2.15). *Prove* means "have sure knowledge of." **3:** *Measure of faith,* measure of the Spirit which one has received by faith (1 Cor.4.7). **4–8:** 1 Cor.12.4–31. **8:** *He who gives aid,* or "he who rules."

12.9–21: The Christian's duty. 9–18: The law of love (compare 1 Cor.13). **13:** *Hospitality,* see 16.1–2 n.; Heb.13.2 n.; 3 Jn.5–8 n. **14:** Mt.5.44. **19:** The vindication of justice is God's prerogative, not ours (Dt.32.35). We are neither wise enough nor good enough to punish our enemies justly. **20:** To *heap burning coals. . . ,* is to make the enemy feel ashamed by meeting his *evil* with *good* (Pr.25.21–22).

13 Let every person be subject to the governing authorities. For there is no authority except from God, and those that exist have been instituted by God. [2] Therefore he who resists the authorities resists what God has appointed, and those who resist will incur judgment. [3] For rulers are not a terror to good conduct, but to bad. Would you have no fear of him who is in authority? Then do what is good, and you will receive his approval, [4] for he is God's servant for your good. But if you do wrong, be afraid, for he does not bear the sword in vain; he is the servant of God to execute his wrath on the wrongdoer. [5] Therefore one must be subject, not only to avoid God's wrath but also for the sake of conscience. [6] For the same reason you also pay taxes, for the authorities are ministers of God, attending to this very thing. [7] Pay all of them their dues, taxes to whom taxes are due, revenue to whom revenue is due, respect to whom respect is due, honor to whom honor is due.

[8] Owe no one anything, except to love one another; for he who loves his neighbor has fulfilled the law. [9] The commandments, "You shall not commit adultery, You shall not kill, You shall not steal, You shall not covet," and any other commandment, are summed up in this sentence, "You shall love your neighbor as yourself." [10] Love does no wrong to a neighbor; therefore love is the fulfilling of the law.

[11] Besides this you know what hour it is, how it is full time now for you to wake from sleep. For salvation is nearer to us now than when we first believed; [12] the night is far gone, the day is at hand. Let us then cast off the works of darkness and put on the armor of light; [13] let us conduct ourselves becomingly as in the day, not in reveling and drunkenness, not in debauchery and licentiousness, not in quarreling and jealousy. [14] But put on the Lord Jesus Christ, and make no provision for the flesh, to gratify its desires.

13.1–7: The Christian and the state. Though the Christian has no right to punish (12.19–21), the state does have that right and the Christian must respect it. Paul's confidence that the Roman state is, on the whole, just and beneficent is matched in 1 Pet.2.13–17; 3.13.

13.8–10: Love fulfils the law. 8a: Pay every debt; do not stand under any obligation except the obligation to love. **8b–10:** Mk.12.31; Jas.2.8.

13.11–14: The imminence of Christ's second coming makes it the more urgent that Christians *conduct* themselves *becomingly*. **14:** To *put on the Lord Jesus Christ* is to enter fully into the new order of existence which God has created through Christ (see 6.1–14 n.).

Augustine

CONFESSIONS

Introduction by Michael Graham

Augustine, second only to St. Paul in his influence on Christian theology, was born in 354 in a town which is today in Algeria. In his late teens, he went off to study at Carthage, a major city in north Africa. After a short stint teaching in his native town, he returned to Carthage for several years, before departing for Italy in 383. The following year he became a professor of rhetoric in Milan, the northern Italian city which had become home to the Roman emperor, and came under the influence of Ambrose, bishop of Milan. In 386, at the age of 32, he converted to Christianity, the religion of his mother Monica as well as his friend Ambrose. In 388 he returned to north Africa, and in 391, at the age of 37, became a priest there, in the port city of Hippo. In 396 he became bishop of Hippo, a post he held for the rest of his life. Augustine died in 430 while Hippo was under siege by the Vandals, invaders from Germany.

Augustine was charismatic, intelligent and curious. These qualities made him popular with friends, and helped him rise to prominence once he embarked on a career in the Church. His best-known theological work was *City of God,* a book he was moved to write after the Visigoths, another Germanic tribe, sacked Rome in 410. Many Romans blamed this historic defeat on the suppression of Roman pagan cults by Christian rulers, and suggested that if Christianity had been the right choice for Rome, the city would not have fallen. In *City of God,* Augustine, who was a great admirer of many aspects of Roman civilization, responded that empires would rise and fall but only God's kingdom was eternal. No earthly empire could remain impregnable, Augustine argued, because life on earth was a passing thing. God's kingdom, ultimately far more important, would last. Augustine was also an active controversialist, defending (and in the process helping to define) Church doctrines against various heresies, including the Pelagians, who rejected the idea of Original Sin and claimed that people could earn eternal salvation through their own good behavior.

But most interestingly for our purposes, Augustine was a seeker. In his youth he experimented with many lifestyles and philosophies, before deciding that Christianity offered the answers for which he had been searching. He became well-acquainted with Roman culture and Greek philosophy, as well as the ideas of the Manicheans, who saw the world as sharply divided between the forces of good and evil. Also, as a teenager he became involved with a girl by whom he had a child, and with whom he lived for many years, although they never married.

Years later, he recorded his spiritual and philosophical journey in his *Confessions,* a landmark in autobiographical literature, which covers Augustine's life up to age 35. It is important to remember that the *Confessions,* only a part of which you are about to read, is an autobiography, not a diary. Rather than copying down a daily or weekly record of events, Augustine was, as a mature adult, recalling his early years. He was thus telling a story for which he already knew the outcome—that he would convert to Christianity. How might this have affected the way he told the story? Not surprisingly, Augustine's father and mother loomed large in his recollection of his early life. What roles did they, particularly his mother, play in his upbringing? What particular sins and temptations did Augustine seem most troubled by? Many of us go through long periods of personal development, often labeled "growing up," before choosing a course to follow in life. Some never find that course. Do you see something of yourself in Augustine? Also of interest in this work is the extent to which Greek and Roman culture dominated the Mediterranean world, including Augustine's corner of north Africa. What were some of his major intellectual influences? Do you think this work is timeless, or does it no longer carry a message for us?

Confessions

BOOK I

14

If this was so, why did I dislike Greek literature, which tells these tales, as much as the Greek language itself? Homer, as well as Virgil, was a skilful spinner of yarns and he is most delightfully imaginative. Nevertheless, as a boy, I found him little to my taste. I suppose that Greek boys think the same about Virgil when they are forced to study him as I was forced to study Homer. There was of course the difficulty which is found in learning any foreign language, and this soured the sweetness of the Greek romances. For I understood not a single word and I was constantly subjected to violent threats and cruel punishments to make me learn. As a baby, of course, I knew no Latin either, but I learned it without fear and fret, simply by keeping my ears open while my nurses fondled me and everyone laughed and played happily with me. I learned it without being forced by threats of punishment, because it was my own wish to be able to give expression to my thoughts. I could never have done this if I had not learnt a few words, not from schoolmasters, but from people who spoke to me and listened when I delivered to their ears whatever thoughts I had conceived. This clearly shows that we learn better in a free spirit of curiosity than under fear and compulsion. But your law, O God, permits the free flow of curiosity to be stemmed by force. From the schoolmaster's cane to the ordeals of martyrdom, your law prescribes bitter medicine to retrieve us from the noxious pleasures which cause us to desert you.

15

Grant my prayer, O Lord, and do not allow my soul to wilt under the discipline which you prescribe. Let me not tire of thanking you for your mercy in rescuing me from all my wicked ways, so that you may be sweeter to me than all the joys which used to tempt me; so that I may love you most intensely and clasp your hand with all the power of my devotion; so that you may save me from all temptation until the end of my days.

You, O Lord, are my King and my God, and in your service I want to use whatever good I learned as a boy. I can speak and write, read and count, and I want these things to be used to serve you, because when I studied other subjects you checked me and forgave me the sins I committed by taking pleasure in such worthless things. It is true that these studies taught me many useful words, but the same words can be learnt by studying something that matters, and this is the safe course for a boy to follow.

Augustine, *Confessions* (R.S. Pine-Coffin, trans.), Penguin, 1961, original pp. 35–70 (Book I, chap. 14–end of Book III).

16

But we are carried away by custom to our own undoing and it is hard to struggle against the stream. Will this torrent never dry up? How much longer will it sweep the sons of Adam down to that vast and terrible sea which cannot easily be passed, even by those who climb upon the ark of the Cross?

This traditional education taught me that Jupiter punishes the wicked with his thunderbolts and yet commits adultery himself. The two roles are quite incompatible. All the same he is represented in this way, and the result is that those who follow his example in adultery can put a bold face on it by making false pretences of thunder. But can any schoolmaster in his gown listen unperturbed to a man who challenges him on his own ground and says 'Homer invented these stories and attributed human sins to the gods. He would have done better to provide men with examples of divine goodness'?[1] It would be nearer the truth to say that Homer certainly invented the tales but peopled them with wicked human characters in the guise of gods. In this way their wickedness would not be reckoned a crime, and all who did as they did could be shown to follow the example of the heavenly gods, not that of sinful mortals.

And yet human children are pitched into this hellish torrent, together with the fees which are paid to have them taught lessons like these. Much business is at stake, too, when these matters are publicly debated, because the law decrees that teachers would be paid a salary in addition to the fees paid by their pupils. And the roar of the torrent beating upon its boulders seems to say 'This is the school where men are made masters of words. This is where they learn the art of persuasion, so necessary in business and debate'—as much as to say that, but for a certain passage in Terence, we should never have heard of words like 'shower', 'golden', 'lap', 'deception', 'sky', and the other words which occur in the same scene. Terence brings on to the stage a dissolute youth who excuses his own fornication by pointing to the example of Jupiter. He looks at a picture painted on the wall, which 'shows how Jupiter is said to have deceived the girl Danae by raining a golden shower into her lap.'[2] These are the words with which he incites himself to lechery, as though he had heavenly authority for it: 'What a god he is! His mighty thunder rocks the sky from end to end. You may say that I am only a man, and thundering is beyond my power. But I played the rest of the part well enough, and willingly too'![2]

The words are certainly not learnt any the more easily by reason of the filthy mortal, but filth is committed with greater confidence as a result of learning the words. I have nothing against the words themselves. They are like choice and costly glasses, but they contain the wine of error which had already gone to the heads of the teachers who poured it out for us to drink. If we refused to drink, we were beaten for it, without the right to appeal to a sober judge. With your eyes upon me, my God, my memory can safely recall those days. But it is true that I learned all these things gladly and took a sinful pleasure in them. And for this very reason I was called a promising boy.

17

Let me tell you, my God, how I squandered the brains you gave me on foolish delusions. I was set a task which troubled me greatly, for if I were successful, I might win some praise: if not, I was afraid of disgrace or a beating. I had to recite the speech of Juno,[3] who was pained and angry because she could not prevent Aeneas from sailing to Italy. I had been told that Juno had never really spoken the words, but we were compelled to make believe and follow the flight of the poet's fancy by repeating in prose what he had said in verse. The contest was to be won by the boy who found the best words to suit the meaning and best expressed feelings of sorrow and anger appropriate to the majesty of the character he impersonated.

What did all this matter to me, my God, my true Life? Why did my recitation win more praise than those of the many other boys in my class? Surely it was all so much smoke without fire? Was there no other subject on which I might have sharpened my wits and my tongue? I might have used them, O Lord, to praise you in the words of your Scriptures, which could have been a prop to support my heart, as if it were a young vine, so that it would not have produced this crop of worthless fruit, fit only for the birds to peck at. For offerings can be made to those birds of prey, the fallen angels, in more ways than one.

18

But was it surprising that I was lured into these fruitless pastimes and wandered away from you, my God? I was expected to model myself upon men who were disconcerted by the rebukes they received if they used outlandish words or strange idioms to tell of some quite harmless thing they might have done, but revelled in the applause they earned for the fine flow of well-ordered and nicely balanced phrases with which they described their own acts of indecency. You see all these things, Lord, and yet you keep silence, because you are patient and full of compassion and can tell no lie.[4] Will you be silent for ever? This very day you are ready to rescue from this fearsome abyss any soul that searches for you, any man who says from the depths of his heart, *I have eyes only for you; I long, Lord, for your presence;*[5] for the soul that is blinded by wicked passions is far from you and cannot see your face. The path that leads us away from you and brings us back again is not measured by footsteps or milestones. The prodigal son of the Scriptures went to live in a distant land to waste in dissipation all the wealth which his father had given him when he set out. But, to reach that land, he did not hire horses, carriages, or ships; he did not take to the air on real wings to set one foot before the other. For you were the Father who gave him riches. You loved him when he set out and you loved him still more when he came home without a penny. But he set his heart on pleasure and his soul was blinded, and this blindness was the measure of the distance he travelled away from you, so that he could not see your face.

O Lord my God, be patient, as you always are, with the men of this world as you watch them and see how strictly they obey the rules of grammar which have been handed down to them, and yet ignore the eternal rules of everlasting salvation which they have received from you. A man who has learnt the traditional rules of pronunciation, or teaches them to others, gives greater scandal if he breaks them by dropping the aitch from 'human being' than if he breaks your rules and hates another human, his fellow man. This is just as perverse as to imagine that our enemies can do us more harm than we do to ourselves by hating them, or that by persecuting another man we can damage him more fatally than we damage our own hearts in the process. O God, alone in majesty, high in the silence of heaven, unseen by man! we can see how your unremitting justice punishes unlawful ambition with blindness, for a man who longs for fame as a fine speaker will stand up before a human judge, surrounded by a human audience, and lash his opponent with malicious invective, taking the greatest care not to say ''uman' instead of 'human' by a slip of the tongue, and yet the thought that the frenzy in his own mind may condemn a human being to death disturbs him not at all.

19

It was at the threshold of a world such as this that I stood in peril as a boy. I was already being prepared for its tournaments by a training which taught me to have a horror of faculty grammar instead of teaching me, when I committed these faults, not to envy others who avoided them. All this, my God, I admit and confess to you. By these means I won praise from the people whose favour I sought, for I thought that the right way to live was to do as they wished. I was blind to the whirlpool of debasement in which I had been plunged away from the sight of your eyes. For in your eyes nothing could be more debased than I was then, since I was even troublesome to the people whom I set out to please. Many and many a time I lied to my tutor, my masters, and my parents, and deceived them because I wanted to play games or watch some futile show or was impatient to imitate what I saw on the stage. I even stole from my parents' larder and from their table, either from greed or to get something to give to other boys in exchange for their favourite toys, which they were willing to barter with me. And in the games I played with them I often cheated in order to come off the better, simply because a vain desire to win had got the better of me. And yet there was nothing I could less easily endure, nothing that made me quarrel more bitterly, than to find others cheating me as I cheated them. All the same, if they found me out and blamed me for it, I would lose my temper rather than give in.

Can this be the innocence of childhood? Far from it, O Lord! But I beg you to forgive it. For commanders and kings may take the place of tutors and schoolmasters, nuts and balls and pet birds may give way to money and estates and servants, but these same passions remain with us while one stage of life follows upon another, just as more severe punishments follow upon the schoolmaster's cane. It was, then, simply because they are small that you used children to symbolize humility when, as our King, you commended it by saying that *the kingdom of heaven belongs to such as these.*[6]

20

And yet, Lord, even if you had willed that I should not survive my childhood, I should have owed you gratitude, because you are our God, the supreme God, the Creator and Ruler of the universe. For even as a child I existed, I was alive, I had the power of feeling; I had an instinct to keep myself safe and sound, to preserve my own being, which was a trace of the single unseen Being from whom it was derived; I had an inner sense which watched over my bodily senses and kept them in full vigour; and even in the small things which occupied my thoughts I found pleasure in the truth. I disliked finding myself in the wrong; my memory was good; I was acquiring the command of words; I enjoyed the company of friends; and I shrank from pain, ignorance, and sorrow. Should I not be grateful that so small a creature possessed such wonderful qualities? But they were all gifts from God, for I did not give them to myself. His gifts are good and the sum of them all is my own self. Therefore, the God who made me must be good and all the good in me is his. I thank him and praise him for all the good in my life, even my life as a boy. But my sin was this, that I looked for pleasure, beauty, and truth not in him but in myself and his other creatures, and the search led me instead to pain, confusion, and error. My God, in whom is my delight, my glory, and my trust, I thank you for your gifts and beg you to preserve and keep them for me. Keep me, too, and so your gifts will grow and reach perfection and I shall be with you myself, for I should not even exist if it were not by your gift.

BOOK II

1

I must now carry my thoughts back to the abominable things I did in those days, the sins of the flesh which defiled my soul. I do this, my God, not because I love those sins, but so that I may love you. For love of your love I shall retrace my wicked ways. The memory is bitter, but it will help me to savour your sweetness, the sweetness that does not deceive but brings real joy and never fails. For love of your love I shall retrieve myself from the havoc of disruption which tore me to pieces when I turned away from you, whom alone I should have sought, and lost myself instead on many a different quest. For as I grew to manhood I was inflamed with desire for a surfeit of hell's pleasures. Foolhardy as I was, I ran wild with lust that was manifold and rank. In your eyes my beauty vanished and I was foul to the core, yet I was pleased with my own condition and anxious to be pleasing in the eyes of men.

2

I cared for nothing but to love and be loved. But my love went beyond the affection of one mind for another, beyond the arc of the bright beam of friendship. Bodily desire, like a morass, and adolescent sex welling up within me exuded mists which clouded over and obscured my heart, so that I could not distinguish the clear light of true love from the murk of lust. Love and lust together seethed within me. In my tender youth they swept me away over the precipice of my body's appetites and plunged me in the whirlpool of sin. More and more I angered you, unawares. For I had been deafened by the clank of my chains, the fetters of the death which was my due to punish the pride in my soul. I strayed still farther from you and you did not restrain me. I was tossed and spilled, floundering in the broiling sea of my fornication, and you said no word. How long it was before I learned that you were my true joy! You were silent then, and I went on my way, farther and farther from you, proud in my distress and restless in fatigue, sowing more and more seeds whose only crop was grief.

Was there no one to lull my distress, to turn the fleeting beauty of these new-found attractions to good purpose and set up a goal for their charms, so that the high tide of my youth might have rolled in upon the shore of marriage? The surge might have been calmed and contented by the procreation of children, which is the purpose of marriage, as your law prescribes, O Lord. By this means you form the offspring of our fallen nature, and with a gentle hand you prune back the thorns that have no place in your paradise. For your almighty power is not far from us, even when we are far from you. Or, again, I might have listened more attentively to your voice from the clouds, saying of those who marry that they will *meet with outward distress, but I leave you your freedom;*[7] that *a man does well to abstain from all commerce with women,*[8] and that *he who is unmarried is concerned with God's claim, asking how he is to please God; whereas the married man is concerned with the world's claim, asking how he is to please his wife.*[9] These were the words to which I should have listened with more care, and if I had made myself a *eunuch for love of the kingdom of heaven,*[10] I should have awaited your embrace with all the greater joy.

But instead, I was in a ferment of wickedness. I deserted you and allowed myself to be carried away by the sweep of the tide. I broke all your lawful bounds and did not escape your lash. For what man can escape it? You were always present, angry and merciful at once, strewing the pangs of bitterness over all my lawless pleasures to lead me on to look for others unallied with pain. You meant me to find them nowhere but in yourself, O Lord, for you teach us by inflicting pain,[11] you smite so that you may heal,[12] and you kill us so that we may not die away from you. Where was I then and how far was I banished from the bliss of your house in that sixteenth year of my life? This was the age at which the frenzy gripped me and I surrendered myself entirely to lust, which your law forbids but human hearts are not ashamed to sanction. My family made no effort to save me from my fall by marriage. Their only concern was that I should learn how to make a good speech and how to persuade others by my words.

3

In the same year my studies were interrupted. I had already begun to go to the near-by town of Madaura to study literature and the art of public speaking, but I was brought back home while my father, a modest citizen of Thagaste whose determination was greater than his means, saved up the money to send me farther afield to Carthage. I need not tell all this to you, my God, but in your presence I tell it to my own kind, to those other men, however few, who may perhaps pick up this book. And I tell it so that I and all who read my words may realize the depths from which we are to cry to you. Your ears will surely listen to the cry of a penitent heart which lives the life of faith.

No one had anything but praise for my father who, despite his slender resources, was ready to provide his son with all that was needed to enable him to travel so far for the purpose of study. Many of our townsmen, far richer than my father, went to no such trouble for their children's sake. Yet this same father of mine took no trouble at all to see how I was growing in your sight or whether I was chaste or not. He cared only that I should have a fertile tongue, leaving my heart to bear none of your fruits, my God, though you are the only Master, true and good, of its husbandry.

In the meanwhile, during my sixteenth year, the narrow means of my family obliged me to leave school and live idly at home with my parents. The brambles of lust grew high above my head and there was no one to root them out, certainly not my father. One day at the public baths he saw the signs of active virility coming to life in me and this was enough to make him relish the thought of having grandchildren. He was happy to tell my mother about it, for his happiness was due to the intoxication which causes the world to forget you, its Creator, and to love the things you have created instead of loving you, because the world is drunk with the invisible wine of its own perverted, earthbound will. But in my mother's heart you had already begun to build your temple and laid the foundations of your holy dwelling, while my father was still a catechumen and a new one at that. So in her piety, she became alarmed and apprehensive, and although I had not yet been baptized, she began to dread that I might follow in the crooked path of those who do not keep their eyes on you but turn their backs instead.

How presumptuous it was of me to say that you were silent, my God, when I drifted farther and farther away from you! Can it be true that you said nothing to me at that time? Surely the words which rang in my ears, spoken by your faithful servant, my mother, could have come from none but you? Yet none of them sank into my heart to make me do as you said. I well remember what her wishes were and how she most earnestly warned me not to commit fornication and above all not to seduce any man's wife. It all seemed womanish advice to me and I should have blushed to accept it. Yet the words were yours, though I did not know it. I thought that you were silent and that she was speaking, but all the while you were speaking to me through her, and when I disregarded her, your handmaid, I was disregarding you, though I was both her son and your servant. But I did this unawares and continued headlong on my way. I was so blind to the truth that among my companions I was ashamed to be less dissolute than they were. For I heard them bragging of their depravity, and the greater the sin the more they gloried in it, so that I took pleasure in the same vices not only for the enjoyment of what I did, but also for the applause I won.

Nothing deserves to be despised more than vice; yet I gave in more and more to vice simply in order not to be despised. If I had not sinned enough to rival other sinners, I used to pretend that I had done things I had not done at all, because I was afraid that innocence would be taken for cowardice and chastity for weakness. These were the companions with whom I walked the streets of Babylon. I wallowed in its mire as if it were made of spices and precious ointments, and to fix me all the faster in the very depths of sin the unseen enemy trod me underfoot and enticed me to himself, because I was an easy prey for his seductions. For even my mother, who by now had escaped from the centre of Babylon, though she still loitered in its outskirts, did not act upon what she had heard about me from her husband with the same earnestness as she had advised me about chastity. She saw that I was already infected with a disease that would become dangerous later on, but if the growth of my passions could not be cut back to the quick, she did not think it right to restrict them to the bounds of married love. This was because she was afraid that the bonds of marriage might be a hindrance to my hopes for the future—not of course the hope of the life to come, which she reposed in you, but my hopes of success at my studies. Both my parents were unduly eager for me to learn, my father because he gave next to no thought to you and only shallow thought to me, and my mother because she thought the usual course of study would certainly not hinder me, but would even help me, in my approach to you. To the best of my memory this is how I construe the characters of my parents. Furthermore, I was given a free rein to amuse myself beyond the strict limits of discipline, so that I lost myself in many kinds of evil ways, in all of which a pall of darkness hung between me and the bright light of your truth, my God. What malice proceeded from my pampered heart![13]

4

It is certain, O Lord, that theft is punished by your law, the law that is written in men's hearts and cannot be erased however sinful they are. For no thief can bear that another thief should steal from him, even if he is rich and the other is driven to it by want. Yet I was willing to steal, and steal I did, although I was not compelled by any lack, unless it were the lack of a sense of justice or a distaste for what was right and a greedy love of doing wrong. For what I stole I already had plenty, and much better at that, and I had no wish to enjoy the things I coveted by stealing, but only to enjoy the theft itself and the sin. There was a pear-tree near our vineyard, loaded with fruit that was attractive neither to look at nor to taste. Late one night a band of ruffians, myself included, went off to shake down the fruit and carry it away, for we had continued our games out of doors until well after dark, as was our pernicious habit. We took away an enormous quantity of pears, not to eat them ourselves, but simply to throw them to the pigs. Perhaps we ate some of them, but our real pleasure consisted in doing something that was forbidden.

Look into my heart, O God, the same heart on which you took pity when it was in the depths of the abyss. Let my heart now tell you what prompted me to do wrong for no purpose, and why it was only my own love of mischief that made me do it. The evil in me was foul, but I loved it. I loved my own perdition and my own faults, not the things for which I committed wrong, but the wrong itself. My soul was vicious and broke away from your safe keeping to seek its own destruction, looking for no profit in disgrace but only for disgrace itself.

5

The eye is attracted by beautiful objects, by gold and silver and all such things. There is great pleasure, too, in feeling something agreeable to the touch, and material things have various qualities to please each of the other senses. Again, it is gratifying to be held in esteem by other men and to have the power of giving them orders and gaining the mastery over them. This is also the reason why revenge is sweet. But our ambition to obtain all these things must not lead us astray from you, O Lord, nor must we depart from what your law allows. The life we live on earth has its own attractions as well, because it has a certain beauty of its own in harmony with all the rest of this world's beauty. Friendship among men, too, is a delightful bond, uniting many souls in one. All these things and their like can be occasions of sin because, good though they are, they are of the lowest order of good, and if we are too much tempted by them we abandon those higher and better things, your truth, your law, and you yourself, O Lord our God. For these earthly things, too, can give joy, though not such joy as my God, who made them all, can give, because *honest men will rejoice in the Lord; upright hearts will not boast in vain.*[14]

When there is an inquiry to discover why a crime has been committed, normally no one is satisfied until it has been shown that the motive might have been either the desire of gaining, or the fear of losing, one of those good things which I said were of the lowest order. For such things are attractive and have beauty, although they are paltry trifles in comparison with the worth of God's blessed treasures. A man commits murder and we ask the reason. He did it because he wanted his victim's wife or estates for himself, or so that he might live on the proceeds of robbery, or because he was afraid that the other might defraud him of something, or because he had been wronged and was burning for revenge. Surely no one would believe that he would commit murder for no reason but the sheer delight of killing? Sallust tells us that Catiline was a man of insane ferocity, 'who chose to be cruel and vicious without apparent reason';[15] but we are also told that his purpose was 'not to allow his men to lose heart or waste their skill through lack of practice'.[16] If we ask the reason for this, it is obvious that he meant that once he had made himself master of the government by means of this continual violence, he would obtain honour, power, and wealth and would no longer go in fear of the law because of his crimes or have to face difficulties through lack of funds. So even Catiline did not love crime for crime's sake. He loved something quite different, for the sake of which he committed his crimes.

6

If the crime of theft which I committed that night as a boy of sixteen were a living thing, I could speak to it and ask what it was that, to my shame, I loved in it. I had no beauty because it was a robbery. It is true that the pears which we stole had beauty, because they were created by you, the good God, who are the most beautiful of all beings and the Creator of all things, the supreme Good and my own true Good. But it was not the pears that my unhappy soul desired. I had plenty of my own, better than those, and I only picked them so that I might steal. For no sooner had I picked them than I threw them away, and tasted nothing in them but my own sin, which I relished and enjoyed. If any part of one of those pears passed my lips, it was the sin that gave it flavour.

And now, O Lord my God, now that I ask what pleasure I had in that theft, I find that it had no beauty to attract me. I do not mean beauty of the sort that justice and prudence possess, nor the beauty that is in man's mind and in his memory and in the life that animates him, nor the beauty of the stars in their allotted places or of the earth and sea, teeming with new life born to replace the old as it passes away. It did not even have the shadowy, deceptive beauty which makes vice attractive—pride, for instance, which is a pretence of superiority, imitating yours, for you alone are God, supreme over all; or ambition, which is only a craving for honour and glory, when you alone are to be honoured before all and you alone are glorious for ever. Cruelty is the weapon of the powerful, used to make others fear them: yet no one is to be feared but God alone, from whose power nothing can be snatched away or stolen by any man at any time or place or by any means. The lustful use caresses to win the love they crave for, yet no one caress is sweeter than your charity and no love is more rewarding than the love of your truth, which shines in beauty above all else. Inquisitiveness has all the appearance of a thirst for knowledge, yet you have supreme knowledge of all things. Ignorance, too, and stupidity choose to go under the mask of simplicity and innocence, because you are simplicity itself and no innocence is greater than yours. You are innocent even of the harm which overtakes the wicked, for it is the result of their own actions. Sloth poses as the love of peace: yet what certain peace is there besides the Lord? Extravagance masquerades as fullness and abundance: but you are the full, unfailing store of never-dying sweetness. The spendthrift makes a pretence of liberality: but you are the most generous dispenser of all good. The covetous want many possessions for themselves: you possess all. The envious struggle for preferment: but what is to be preferred before you? Anger demands revenge: but what vengeance is as just as yours? Fear shrinks from any sudden, unwonted danger which threatens the things that it loves, for its only care is safety: but to you nothing is strange, nothing unforeseen. No one can part you from the things that you love, and safety is assured nowhere but in you. Grief eats away its heart for the loss of things which it took pleasure in desiring, because it wants to be like you, from whom nothing can be taken away.

So the soul defiles itself with unchaste love when it turns away from you and looks elsewhere for things which it cannot find pure and unsullied except by returning to you. All who desert you and set themselves up against you merely copy you in a perverse way; but by this very act of imitation they only show that you are the Creator of all nature and, consequently, that there is no place whatever where man may hide away from you.

What was it, then, that pleased me in the act of theft? Which of my Lord's powers did I imitate in a perverse and wicked way? Since I had no real power to break his law, was it that I enjoyed at least the pretence of doing so, like a prisoner who creates for himself the illusion of liberty by doing something wrong, when he has no fear of punishment, under a feeble hallucination of power? Here was the slave who ran away from his master and chased a shadow instead! What an abomination! What a parody of life! What abysmal death! Could I enjoy doing wrong for no other reason than that it was wrong?

7

What return shall I make to the Lord[17] for my ability to recall these things with no fear in my soul? I will love you, Lord, and thank you, and praise your name, because you have forgiven me such great sins and such wicked deeds. I acknowledge that it was by your grace and mercy that you melted away my sins like ice. I acknowledge, too, that by your grace I was preserved from whatever sins I did not commit, for there was no knowing what I might have done, since I loved evil even if it served no purpose. I avow that you have forgiven me all, both the sins which I committed of my own accord and those which by your guidance I was spared from committing.

What man who reflects upon his own weakness can dare to claim that his own efforts have made him chaste and free from sin, as though this entitled him to love you the less, on the ground that he had less need of the mercy by which you forgive the sins of the penitent? There are some who have been called by you and because they have listened to your voice they have avoided the sins which I here record and confess for them to read. But let them not deride me for having been cured by the same Doctor who preserved them from sickness, or at least from such grave sickness as mine. Let them love you just as much, or even more, than I do, for they can see that the same healing hand which rid me of the great fever of my sins protects them from falling sick of the same disease.

8

It brought me no happiness, for *what harvest did I reap from acts which now make me blush,*[18] particularly from the act of theft? I loved nothing in it except the thieving, though I cannot truly speak of that as a 'thing' that I could love, and I was only the more miserable because of it. And yet, as I recall my feelings at the time, I am quite sure that I would not have done it on my own. Was it then that I also enjoyed the company of those with whom I committed the crime? If this is so, there was something else I loved besides the act of theft; but I cannot call it 'something else', because companionship, like theft, is not a thing at all.

No one can tell me the truth of it except my God, who enlightens my mind and dispels its shadows. What conclusion am I trying to reach from these questions and this discussion? It is true that if the pears which I stole had been to my taste, and if I had wanted to get them for myself, I might have committed the crime on my own if I had needed to do no more than that to win myself the pleasure. I should have had no need to kindle my glowing desire by rubbing shoulders with a gang of accomplices. But as it was not the fruit that gave me pleasure, I must have got it from the crime itself, from the thrill of having partners in sin.

9

How can I explain my mood? It was certainly a very vile frame of mind and one for which I suffered; but how can I account for it? *Who knows his own frailties?*[19]

We were tickled to laughter by the prank we had played, because no one suspected us of it although the owners were furious. Why was it, then, that I thought it fun not to have been the only culprit? Perhaps it was because we do not easily laugh when we are alone. True enough: but even when a man is all by himself and quite alone, sometimes he cannot help laughing if he thinks or hears or sees something especially funny. All the same, I am quite sure that I would never have done this thing on my own.

My God, I lay all this before you, for it is still alive in my memory. By myself I would not have committed that robbery. It was not the takings that attracted me but the raid itself, and yet to do it by myself would have been no fun and I should not have done it. This was friendship of a most unfriendly sort, bewitching my mind in an inexplicable way. For the sake of a laugh, a little sport, I was glad to do harm and anxious to damage another; and that without thought of profit for myself or retaliation for injuries received! And all because we are ashamed to hold back when others say 'Come on! Let's do it!'

10

Can anyone unravel this twisted tangle of knots? I shudder to look at it or think of such abomination. I long instead for innocence and justice, graceful and splendid in eyes whose sight is undefiled. My longing fills me and yet it cannot cloy. With them is certain peace and life that cannot be disturbed. The man who enters their domain goes to *share the joy of his Lord.*[20] He shall know no fear and shall lack no good. In him that is goodness itself he shall find his own best way of life. But I deserted you, my God. In my youth I wandered away, too far from your sustaining hand, and created of myself a barren waste.

BOOK III

1

I went to Carthage, where I found myself in the midst of a hissing cauldron of lust. I had not yet fallen in love, but I was in love with the idea of it, and this feeling that something was missing made me despise myself for not being more anxious to satisfy the need. I began to look around for some object for my love, since I badly wanted to love something. I had no liking for the safe path without pitfalls, for although my real need was for you, my God, who are the food of the soul, I was not aware of this hunger. I felt no need for the food that does not perish, not because I had had my fill of it, but because the more I was starved of it the less palatable it seemed. Because of this my soul fell sick. It broke out in ulcers and looked about desperately for some material, worldly means of relieving the itch which they caused. But material things, which have no soul, could not be true objects for my love. To love and to have my love returned was my heart's desire, and it would be all the sweeter if I could also enjoy the body of the one who loved me.

So I muddied the stream of friendship with the filth of lewdness and clouded its clear waters with hell's black river of lust. And yet, in spite of this rank depravity, I was vain enough to have ambitions of cutting a fine figure in the world. I also fell in love, which was a snare of my own choosing. My God, my God of mercy, how good you were to me, for you mixed much bitterness in that cup of pleasure! My love was returned and finally shackled me in the bonds of its consummation. In the midst of my joy I was caught up in the coils of trouble, for I was lashed with the cruel, fiery rods of jealousy and suspicion, fear, anger, and quarrels.

2

I was much attracted by the theatre, because the plays reflected my own unhappy plight and were tinder to my fire. Why is it that men enjoy feeling sad at the sight of tragedy and suffering on the stage, although they would be most unhappy if they had to endure the same fate themselves? Yet they watch the plays because they hope to be made to feel sad, and the feeling of sorrow is what they enjoy. What miserable delirium this is! The more a man is subject to such suffering himself, the more easily he is moved by it in the theatre. Yet when he suffers himself, we call it misery: when he suffers out of sympathy with others, we call it pity. But what sort of pity can we really feel for an imaginary scene on the stage? The audience is not called upon to offer help but only to feel sorrow, and the more they are pained the more they applaud the author. Whether this human agony is based on fact or is simply imaginary, if it is acted so badly that the audience is not moved to sorrow, they leave the theatre in a disgruntled and critical mood; whereas, if they are made to feel pain, they stay to the end watching happily.

This shows that sorrow and tears can be enjoyable. Of course, everyone wants to be happy; but even if no one likes being sad, is there just the one exception that, because we enjoy pitying others, we welcome their misfortunes, without which we could not pity them? If so, it is because friendly feelings well up in us like the waters of a spring. But what course do these waters follow? Where do they flow? Why do they trickle away to join that stream of boiling pitch, the hideous flood of lust? For by their own choice they lose themselves and become absorbed in it. They are diverted from their true course and deprived of their original heavenly calm.

Of course this does not mean that we must arm ourselves against compassion. There are times when we must welcome sorrow on behalf of others. But for the sake of our souls we must beware of uncleanness. My God must be the Keeper of my soul, the God of our fathers, who is to be exalted and extolled for ever more. My soul must guard against uncleanness.

I am not nowadays insensible to pity. But in those days I used to share the joy of stage lovers and their sinful pleasure in each other even though it was all done in make-believe for the sake of entertainment; and when they were parted, pity of a sort led me to share their grief. I enjoyed both these emotions equally. But now I feel more pity for a man who is happy in his sins than for one who has to endure the ordeal of forgoing some harmful pleasure or being deprived of some enjoyment which was really an affliction. Of the two, this sort of pity is certainly the more genuine, but the sorrow which it causes is not a source of pleasure. For although a man who is sorry for the sufferings of others deserves praise for his charity, nevertheless, if his pity is genuine, he would prefer that there should be no cause for his sorrow. If the impossible could happen and kindness were unkind, a man whose sense of pity was true and sincere might want others to suffer so that he could pity them. Sorrow may therefore be commendable but never desirable. For it is powerless to stab you, Lord God, and this is why the love you bear for our souls and the compassion you show for them are pure and unalloyed, far purer than the love and pity which we feel ourselves. But *who can prove himself worthy of such a calling?*[21]

However, in those unhappy days I enjoyed the pangs of sorrow. I always looked for things to wring my heart and the more tears an actor caused me to shed by his performance on the stage, even though he was portraying the imaginary distress of others, the more delightful and attractive I found it. Was it any wonder that I, the unhappy sheep who strayed from your flock, impatient of your shepherding, became infected with a loathsome mange? Hence my love of things which made me sad. I did not seek the kind of sorrow which would wound me deeply, for I had no wish to endure the sufferings which I saw on the stage; but I enjoyed fables and fictions, which could only graze the skin. But where the fingers scratch, the skin becomes inflamed. It swells and festers with hideous pus. And the same happened to me. Could the life I led be called true life, my God?

3

Yet all the while, far above, your mercy hovered faithfully about me. I exhausted myself in depravity, in the pursuit of an unholy curiosity. I deserted you and sank to the bottom-most depths of scepticism and the mockery of devil-worship. My sins were a sacrifice to the devil, and for all of them you chastised me. I defied you even so far as to relish the thought of lust, and gratify it too, within the walls of your church during the celebration of your mysteries. For such a deed I deserved to pluck the fruit of death, and you punished me for it with a heavy lash. But, compared with my guilt, the penalty was nothing. How infinite is your mercy, my God! You are my Refuge from the terrible dangers amongst which I wandered, head on high, intent upon withdrawing still further from you. I loved my own way, not yours, but it was a truant's freedom that I loved.

Besides these pursuits I was also studying for the law. Such ambition was held to be honourable and I determined to succeed in it. The more unscrupulous I was, the greater my reputation was likely to be, for men are so blind that they even take pride in their blindness. By now I was at the top of the school of rhetoric. I was pleased with my superior status and swollen with conceit. All the same, as you well know, Lord, I behaved far more quietly than the 'Wreckers', a title of ferocious devilry which the fashionable set chose for themselves. I had nothing whatever to do with their outbursts of violence, but I lived amongst them, feeling a perverse sense of shame because I was not like them. I kept company with them and there were times when I found their friendship a pleasure, but I always had a horror of what they did when they lived up to their name. Without provocation they would set upon some timid newcomer, gratuitously affronting his sense of decency for their own amusement and using it as fodder for their spiteful jests. This was the devil's own behaviour or not far different. 'Wreckers' was a fit name for them, for they were already adrift and total wrecks themselves. The mockery and trickery which they loved to practise on others was a secret snare of the devil, by which they were mocked and tricked themselves.

4

These were the companions with whom I studied the art of eloquence at that impressionable age. It was my ambition to be a good speaker, for the unhallowed and inane purpose of gratifying human vanity. The prescribed course of study brought me to a work by an author named Cicero, whose writing nearly everyone admires, if not the spirit of it. The title of the book is *Hortensius* and it recommends the reader to study philosophy. It altered my outlook on life. It changed my prayers to you, O Lord, and provided me with new hopes and aspirations. All my empty dreams suddenly lost their charm and my heart began to throb with a bewildering passion for the wisdom of eternal truth. I began to climb out of the depths to which I had sunk, in order to return to you. For I did not use the book as a whetstone to sharpen my tongue. It was not the style of it but the contents which won me over, and yet the allowance which my mother paid me was supposed to be spent on putting an edge on my tongue. I was now in my nineteenth year and she supported me, because my father had died two years before.

My God, how I burned with longing to have wings to carry me back to you, away from all earthly things, although I had no idea what you would do with me! For *yours is the wisdom.*[22] In Greek the word 'philosophy' means 'love of wisdom', and it was with this love that the *Hortensius* inflamed me. There are people for whom philosophy is a means of misleading others, for they misuse its great name, its attractions, and its integrity to give colour and gloss to their own errors. Most of these so-called philosophers who lived in Cicero's time and before are noted in the book. He shows them up in their true colours and makes quite clear how wholesome is the admonition which the Holy Spirit gives in the words of your good and true servant, Paul: *Take care not to let anyone cheat you with his philosophizings, with empty fantasies drawn from human tradition, from worldly principles; they were never Christ's teaching. In Christ the whole plenitude of Deity is embodied and dwells in him.*[23]

But, O Light of my heart, you know that at that time, although Paul's words were not known to me, the only thing that pleased me in Cicero's book was his advice not simply to admire one or another of the schools of philosophy, but to love wisdom itself, whatever it might be, and to search for it, pursue it, hold it, and embrace it firmly. These were the words which excited me and set me burning with fire, and the only check to this blaze of enthusiasm was that they made no mention of the name of Christ. For by your mercy, Lord, from the time when my mother fed me at the breast my infant heart had been suckled dutifully on his name, the name of your Son, my Saviour. Deep inside my heart his name remained, and nothing could entirely captivate me, however learned, however neatly expressed, however true it might be, unless his name were in it.

5

So I made up my mind to examine the holy Scriptures and see what kind of books they were. I discovered something that was at once beyond the understanding of the proud and hidden from the eyes of children. Its gait was humble, but the heights it reached were sublime. It was enfolded in mysteries, and I was not the kind of man to enter into it or bow my head to follow where it led. But these were not the feelings I had when I first read the Scriptures. To me they seemed quite unworthy of comparison with the stately prose of Cicero, because I had too much conceit to accept their simplicity and not enough insight to penetrate their depths. It is surely true that as the child grows these books grow with him. But I was too proud to call myself a child. I was inflated with self-esteem, which made me think myself a great man.

6

I fell in with a set of sensualists, men with glib tongues who ranted and raved and had the snares of the devil in their mouths. They baited the traps by confusing the syllables of the names of God the Father, God the Son Our Lord Jesus Christ, and God the Holy Ghost, the Paraclete, who comforts us. These names were always on the tips of their tongues, but only as sounds which they mouthed aloud, for in their hearts they had no inkling of the truth. Yet 'Truth and truth alone' was the motto which they repeated to me again and again, although the truth was nowhere to be found in them. All that they said was false, both what they said about you, who truly are the Truth, and what they said about this world and its first principles, which were your creation. But I ought not to have been content with what the philosophers said about such things, even when they spoke the truth. I should have passed beyond them for love of you, my supreme Father, my good Father, in whom all beauty has its source.

Truth! Truth! How the very marrow of my soul within me yearned for it as they dinned it in my ears over and over again! To them it was no more than a name to be voiced or a word to be read in their libraries of huge books. But while my hunger was for you, for Truth itself, these were the dishes on which they served me up the sun and the moon, beautiful works of yours but still only your works, not you yourself nor even the greatest of your created things.[24] For your spiritual works are greater than these material things, however brightly they may shine in the sky.

But my hunger and thirst were not even for the greatest of your works, but for you, my God, because you are Truth itself *with whom there can be no change, no swerving from your course.*[25] Yet the dishes they set before me were still loaded with dazzling fantasies, illusions with which the eye deceives the mind. It would have been better to love the sun itself, which at least is real as far as we can see. But I gulped down this food, because I thought that it was you. I had no relish for it, because the taste it left in my mouth was not the taste of truth—it could not be, for it was not you but an empty sham. And it did not nourish me, but starved me all the more. The food we dream of is very like the food we eat when we are awake, but it does not nourish because it is only a dream. Yet the things they gave me to eat were not in the least like you, as now I know since you have spoken to me. They were dream-substances, mock realities, far less true than the real things which we see with the sight of our eyes in the sky or on the earth. These things are seen by bird and beast as well as by ourselves, and they are far more certain than any image we conceive of them. And in turn we can picture them to ourselves with greater certainty than the vaster, infinite things which we surmise from them. Such things have no existence at all, but they were the visionary foods on which I was then fed but not sustained.

But you, O God whom I love and on whom I lean in weakness so that I may be strong, you are not the sun and the moon and the stars, even though we see these bodies in the heavens; nor are you those other bodies which we do not see in the sky, for you created them and, in your reckoning, they are not even among the greatest of your works. How far, then, must you really be from those fantasies of mine, those imaginary material things which do not exist at all! The images we form in our mind's eyes, when we picture things that really do exist, are far better founded than these inventions; and the things themselves are still more certain than the images we form of them. But you are not these things. Neither are you the soul, which is the life of bodies and, since it gives them life, must be better and more certain than they are themselves. But you are the life of souls, the life of lives. You live, O Life of my soul, because you are life itself, immutable.

Where were you in those days? How far away from me? I was wandering far from you and I was not even allowed to eat the husks on which I fed the swine. For surely the fables of the poets and the penmen are better than the traps which those impostors set! There is certainly more to be gained from verses and poems and tales like the flight of Medea than from their stories of the five elements disguised in various ways because of the five dens of darkness. These things simply do not exist and they are death to those who believe in them. Verses and poems can provide real food for thought, but although I used to recite verses about Medea's flight through the air, I never maintained that they were true; and I never believed the poems which I heard others recite. But I did believe the tales which these men told.

These were the stages of my pitiful fall into the depths of hell, as I struggled and strained for lack of the truth. My God, you had mercy on me even before I had confessed to you; but I now confess that all this was because I tried to find you, not through the understanding of the mind, by which you meant us to be superior to the beasts, but through the senses of the flesh. Yet you were deeper than my inmost understanding and higher than the topmost height that I could reach. I had blundered upon that woman in Solomon's parable who, ignorant and unabashed, sat at her door and said *Stolen waters are sweetest, and bread is better eating when there is none to see.*[26] She inveigled me because she found me living in the outer world that lay before my eyes, the eyes of the flesh, and dwelling upon the food which they provided for my mind.

7

There is another reality besides this, though I knew nothing of it. My own specious reasoning induced me to give in to the sly arguments of fools who asked me what was the origin of evil, whether God was confined to the limits of a bodily shape, whether he had hair and nails, and whether men could be called just if they had more than one wife at the same time, or killed other men, or sacrificed living animals. My ignorance was so great that these questions troubled me, and while I thought I was approaching the truth, I was only departing the further from it. I did not know that evil is nothing but the removal of good until finally no good remains. How could I see this when with the sight of my eyes I saw no more than material things and with the sight of my mind no more than their images? I did not know that God is a spirit, a being without bulk and without limbs defined in length and breadth. For bulk is less in the part than in the whole, and if it is infinite, it is less in any part of it which can be defined within fixed limits than it is in its infinity. It cannot, therefore, be everywhere entirely whole, as a spirit is and as God is. Nor had I the least notion what it is in us that gives us our being, or what the Scriptures mean when they say that we are made in God's image.

I knew nothing of the true underlying justice which judges, not according to convention, but according to the truly equitable law of Almighty God. This is the law by which each age and place forms rules of conduct best suited to itself, although the law itself is always and everywhere the same and does not differ from place to place or from age to age. I did not see that by the sanction of this law Abraham and Isaac, Jacob, Moses, David, and the others whom God praised were just men, although they have been reckoned sinners by men who are not qualified to judge, for they try them by human standards and assess all the rights and wrongs of the human race by the measure of their own customs. Anyone who does this behaves like a man who knows nothing about armour and cannot tell which piece is meant for which part of the body, so that he tries to cover his head with a shin-piece and fix a helmet on his foot, and then complains because they will not fit; or like a shopkeeper who is allowed to sell his wares in the morning, but grumbles because the afternoon is a public holiday and he is not allowed to trade; or like a man who sees one of the servants in a house handling things which the cellar-man is not allowed to touch, or finds something being done in the stableyard which is not allowed in the dining-room, and is then indignant because the members of the household, living together in one house, are not all given the same privileges in all parts of the house.

The people of whom I am speaking have the same sort of grievance when they hear that things which good men could do without sin in days gone by are not permitted in ours, and that God gave them one commandment and has given us another. He has done this because the times have demanded it, although men were subject to the same justice in those days as we are in these. Yet those who complain about this understand that when we are dealing with a single man, a single day, or a single house, each part of the whole has a different function suited to it. What may be done at one time of day is not allowed at the next, and what may be done, or must be done, in one room is forbidden and punished in another. This does not mean that justice is erratic or variable, but that the times over which it presides are not always the same, for it is the nature of time to change. Man's life on earth is short and he cannot, by his own perception, see the connexion between the conditions of earlier times and of other nations, which he has not experienced himself, and those of his own times, which are familiar to him. But when only one individual, one day, or one house is concerned, he can easily see what is suitable for each part of the whole and for each member of the household, and what must be done at which times and places. These things he accepts: but with the habits of other ages he finds fault.

I knew nothing of this at that time. I was quite unconscious of it, quite blind to it, although it stared me in the face. When I composed verses, I could not fit any foot in any position that I pleased. Each metre was differently scanned and I could not put the same foot in every position in the same line. And yet the art of poetry, by which I composed, does not vary from one line to another: it is the same for all alike. But I did not discern that justice, which those good and holy men obeyed, in a far more perfect and sublime way than poetry contains in itself at one and the same time all the principles which it prescribes, without discrepancy; although, as times change, it prescribes and apportions them, not all at once, but according to the needs of the times. Blind to this, I found fault with the holy patriarchs not only because, in their own day, they acted as God commanded and inspired them, but also because they predicted the future as he revealed it to them.

8

Surely it is never wrong at any time or in any place for a man to *love God with his whole heart and his whole soul and his whole mind* and to *love his neighbour as himself*?[27] Sins against nature, therefore, like the sin of Sodom, are abominable and deserve punishment wherever and whenever they are committed. If all nations committed them, all alike would be held guilty of the same charge in God's law, for our Maker did not prescribe that we should use each other in this way. In fact the relationship which we ought to have with God is itself violated when our nature, of which he is the Author, is desecrated by perverted lust.

On the other hand, offences against human codes of conduct vary according to differences of custom, so that no one, whether he is a native or a foreigner, may, to suit his own pleasure, violate the conventions established by the customary usage or the law of the community or the state. For any part that is out of keeping with the whole is at fault. But if God commands a nation to do something contrary to its customs or constitutions, it must be done even if it has never been done in that country before. If it is a practice which has been discontinued, it must be resumed, and if it was not a law before, it must be enacted. In his own kingdom a king has the right to make orders which neither he nor any other has ever made before. Obedience to his orders is not against the common interest of the community; in fact, if they were disobeyed, the common interest would suffer, because it is the general agreement in human communities that the ruler is obeyed. How much more right, then, has God to give commands, since he is the Ruler of all creation and all his creatures must obey his commandments without demur! For all must yield to God just as, in the government of human society, the lesser authority must yield to the greater.

With sins of violence the case is the same as with sins against nature. Here the impulse is to injure others, either by word or by deed, but by whichever means it is done, there are various reasons for doing it. A man may injure his enemy for the sake of revenge; a robber may assault a traveller to secure for himself something that is not his own; or a man may attack someone whom he fears in order to avoid danger to himself. Or the injury may be done from envy, which will cause an unhappy man to harm another more fortunate than himself or a rich man to harm someone whose rivalry he fears for the future or already resents. Again, it may be done for the sheer joy of seeing others suffer, as is the case with those who watch gladiators or make fun of other people and jeer at them.

These are the main categories of sin. They are hatched from the lust for power, from gratification of the eye, and from gratification of corrupt nature—from one or two of these or from all three together. Because of them, O God most high, most sweet, our lives offend against your *ten-stringed harp,*[28] your commandments, the three which proclaim our duty to you and the seven which proclaim our duty to men.

But how can sins of vice be against you, since you cannot be marred by perversion? How can sins of violence be against you, since nothing can injure you? Your punishments are for the sins which men commit against themselves, because although they sin against you, they do wrong to their own souls and their malice is self-betrayed.[29] They corrupt and pervert their own nature, which you made and for which you shaped the rules, either by making wrong use of the things which you allow, or by becoming inflamed with passion to make unnatural use of things which you do not allow. Or else their guilt consists in raving against you in their hearts and with their tongues and *kicking against the goad,*[30] or in playing havoc with the restrictions of human society and brazenly exulting in private feuds and factions, each according to his fancies or his fads.

This is what happens, O Fountain of life, when we abandon you, who are the one true Creator of all that ever was or is, and each of us proudly sets his heart on some one part of your creation instead of on the whole. So it is by the path of meekness and devotion that we must return to you. You rid us of our evil habits and forgive our sins when we confess to you. You *listen to the groans of the prisoners*[31] and free us from the chains which we have forged for ourselves. This you do for us unless we toss our heads against you in the illusion of liberty and in our greed for gain, at the risk of losing all, love our own good better than you yourself, who are the common good of all.

9

Among these vices and crimes and all the endless ways in which men do wrong there are also the sins of those who follow the right path but go astray. By the rule of perfection these lapses are condemned, if we judge them aright, but the sinners may yet be praised, for they give promise of better fruit to come, like the young shoots which later bear the ears of corn. Sometimes we also do things which have every appearance of being sins against nature or against our fellow men, but are not sins because they offend neither you, the Lord our God, nor the community in which we live. For example, a man may amass a store of goods to meet the needs of life or some contingency, but it does not necessarily follow that he is a miser. Or he may be punished by those whose duty it is to correct misdemeanours, but it is by no means certain that they do it out of wanton cruelty. Many of the things we do may therefore seem wrong to men but are approved in the light of your knowledge, and many which men applaud are condemned in your eyes. This is because the appearance of what we do is often different from the intention with which we do it, and the circumstances at the time may not be clear.

But when you suddenly command us to do something strange and unforeseen, even if you had previously forbidden it, none can doubt that the command must be obeyed, even though, for the time being, you may conceal the reason for it and it may conflict with the established rule of custom in some forms of society; for no society is right and good unless it obeys you. But happy are they who know that the commandment was yours. For all that your servants do is done as an example of what is needed for the present or as a sign of what is yet to come.

10

I was ignorant of this and derided those holy servants and prophets of yours. But all that I achieved by deriding them was to earn your derision for myself, for I was gradually led to believe such nonsense as that a fig wept when it was plucked, and that the tree which bore it shed tears of mother's milk. But if some sanctified member of the sect were to eat the fig— someone else, of course, would have committed the sin of plucking it—he would digest it and breathe it out again in the form of angels or even as particles of God, retching them up as he groaned in prayer. These particles of the true and supreme God were supposed to be imprisoned in the fruit and could only be released by means of the stomach and teeth of one of the elect. I was foolish enough to believe that we should show more kindness to the fruits of the earth than to mankind, for whose use they were intended. If a starving man, not a Manichee, were to beg for a mouthful, they thought it a crime worthy of mortal punishment to give him one.

11

But *you sent down your help from above*[32] and rescued my soul from the depths of this darkness because my mother, your faithful servant, wept to you for me, shedding more tears for my spiritual death than other mothers shed for the bodily death of a son. For in her faith and in the spirit which she had from you she looked on me as dead. You heard her and did not despise the tears which streamed down and watered the earth in every place where she bowed her head in prayer. You heard her, for how else can I explain the dream with which you consoled her, so that she agreed to live with me and eat at the same table in our home? Lately she had refused to do this, because she loathed and shunned the blasphemy of my false beliefs.

She dreamed that she was standing on a wooden rule, and coming towards her in a halo of splendour she saw a young man who smiled at her in joy, although she herself was sad and quite consumed with grief. He asked her the reason for her sorrow and her daily tears, not because he did not know, but because he had something to tell her, for this is what happens in visions. When she replied that her tears were for the soul I had lost, he told her to take heart for, if she looked carefully, she would see that where she was, there also was I. And when she looked, she saw me standing beside her on the same rule.

Where could this dream have come from, unless it was that you listened to the prayer of her heart? For your goodness is almighty; you take good care of each of us as if you had no others in your care, and you look after all as you look after each. And surely it was for the same reason that, when she told me of the dream and I tried to interpret it as a message that she need not despair of being one day such as I was then, she said at once and without hesitation 'No! He did not say "Where he is, you are", but "Where you are, he is".'

I have often said before and, to the best of my memory, I now declare to you, Lord, that I was much moved by this answer, which you gave me through my mother. She was not disturbed by my interpretation of her dream, plausible though it was, but quickly saw the true meaning, which I had not seen until she spoke. I was more deeply moved by this than by the dream itself, in which the joy for which this devout woman had still so long to wait was foretold so long before to comfort her in the time of her distress. For nearly nine years were yet to come during which I wallowed deep in the mire and the darkness of delusion. Often I tried to lift myself, only to plunge the deeper. Yet all the time this chaste, devout, and prudent woman, a widow such as is close to your heart, never ceased to pray at all hours and to offer you the tears she shed for me. The dream had given new spirit to her hope, but she gave no rest to her sighs and her tears. *Her prayers reached your presence*[33] and yet you still left me to twist and turn in the dark.

12

I remember that in the meantime you gave her another answer to her prayers, though there is much besides this that escapes my memory and much too that I must omit, because I am in haste to pass on to other things, which I am more anxious to confess to you.

This other answer you gave her through the mouth of one of your priests, a bishop who had lived his life in the Church and was well versed in the Scriptures. My mother asked him, as a favour, to have a talk with me, so that he might refute my errors, drive the evil out of my mind, and replace it with good. He often did this when he found suitable pupils, but he refused to do it for me—a wise decision, as I afterwards realized. He told her that I was still unripe for instruction because, as she had told him, I was brimming over with the novelty of the heresy and had already upset a great many simple people with my casuistry. 'Leave him alone', he said. 'Just pray to God for him. From his own reading he will discover his mistakes and the depth of his profanity.'

At the same time he told her that when he was a child his misguided mother had handed him over to the Manichees. He had not only read almost all their books, but had also made copies of them, and even though no one argued the case with him or put him right, he had seen for himself that he ought to have nothing to do with the sect; and accordingly he had left it. Even after she had heard this my mother still would not be pacified, but persisted all the more with her tears and her entreaties that he should see me and discuss the matter. At last he grew impatient and said 'Leave me and go in peace. It cannot be that the son of these tears should be lost.'

In later years, as we walked together, she used to say that she accepted these words as a message from heaven.

Notes

1. Cicero, *Tusculanae disputationes* I, 26.
2. Terence, *Eunuchus* III, 5.
3. Virgil, *Aeneid* I, 37–49.
4. See Ps. 85: 15 (86: 15).
5. Ps. 26: 8 (27: 8).
6. Matt. 19: 14.
7. I Cor. 7: 28.
8. I Cor. 7: 1.
9. I Cor. 7:32, 33.
10. Matt. 19: 12.
11. See Ps. 93: 20 (94: 20).
12. See Deut. 32: 39.

13. See Ps. 72: 7 (73: 7).
14. Ps. 63: 11 (64: 10).
15. Sallust, *Catilina* XVI.
16. Sallust, *Catilina* XVI.
17. Ps. 115: 12 (116: 12).
18. Rom. 6: 21.
19. Ps. 18: 13 (19: 12).
20. Matt. 25: 21.
21. II Cor. 2: 16.
22. Job 12: 13.
23. Col. 2: 8, 9.
24. Saint Augustine is here speaking of the Manichees, for whom astronomy was a part of theology.
25. James I: 17.
26. Prov. 9: 17.
27. Matt. 22: 37, 39.
28. Ps. 143: 9 (144: 9)
29. See Ps. 26: 12 (27: 12).
30. Acts, 9:5.
31. Ps. 101: 21 (102: 20).
32. Ps. 143: 7 (144: 7).
33. Ps. 87: 3 (88: 2).

THE KORAN

Introduction by Michael Levin

In the year 610 A.D., a man named Muhammed was praying alone in a cave just outside the city of Mecca, in what is now Saudi Arabia. Suddenly he heard a great voice command him to "read!" Mystified Muhammed asked "what should I read?" The voice answered, "read that which man knew not." Then Muhammed turned and saw who was speaking to him—the angel Gabriel (or, in Arabic, Jibrail), who told Muhammed that God had chosen him to receive the last and greatest of divine revelations. When Muhammed emerged from the cave, he had the words of the Koran (which means "reading" or "recitation") inscribed in his heart. Muhammed began to preach the message of God (Allah) in Mecca, and quickly won many converts. Thus was born the religion of Islam.

The Koran is the sacred text for Moslems, as the Bible is for Jews and Christians. Like the Bible, the Koran is a source of moral instruction and practical laws for society, as well as a guide for getting into Heaven. And also like the Bible, the Koran contains beautiful poetry. In fact, the poetic nature of the Koran may be its most confusing aspect for those reading it for the first time. The Koran has little narrative structure; stories and poetic images appear side-by-side with discussions of legal problems. This may seem strange, but new readers may also be surprised by how many similarities there are between the Koran and the Bible. The values and ideals of Islam derive from the Judeo-Christian tradition, a fact which should become clear upon reading the Koran.

The Koran is divided into chapters, called "suras," each with its own title. We have chosen the first two suras, "The Opening" and "The Cow." The first is only a few lines long, but it is important because it encapsulates many of the basics of Islam. We are told here about Allah—who He is, and what His relationship with humanity is like. Compare this vision of God with the God of the Old Testament, or with Jesus as he is described in the Gospel of Matthew. Does it seem familiar?

The second sura is much longer, and contains a great deal of information. One of the key themes of this section is the relationship between Islam and the two older religions, Judaism and Christianity. Jews and Christians are often addressed directly—what are they told? Also, note how many references to the Hebrew Scriptures there are in this sura. What purpose do they serve in the text? Incidentally, the title of this sura is a reference to the Golden Calf which the Israelites worshipped at the foot of Mount Sinai, when they lost faith in God (Exodus 32). In this sura there is a different account of this event. What point is being made about the Israelites?

Another important theme in the second sura is the question of social laws and how to be a righteous person. When reading this section, keep in mind the laws described in the Book of Exodus, as well as Jesus' explication of the Mosaic laws in the Sermon on the Mount in the Gospel of Matthew. What is similar, and what is different? Again, those encountering Islam for the first time may be surprised at how familiar much of it seems. In the modern Western world, Islam has received a great deal of bad press. Hopefully, the more we read about Islam, the less alien it will seem. Today Islam is one of the fastest growing religions in the world. As you read in the Koran, ask yourself what makes this religion so appealing to so many people?

The Koran Interpreted

I

The Opening

In the Name of God, the Merciful, the Compassionate

Praise belongs to God, the Lord of all Being,
the All-merciful, the All-compassionate,
the master of the Day of Doom.

Thee only we serve; to Thee alone we pray for succour.   5
Guide us in the straight path,
the path of those whom Thou hast blessed,
not of those against whom Thou art wrathful,
nor of those who are astray.

II

The Cow

In the Name of God, the Merciful, the Compassionate

Alif Lam Mim

That is the Book, wherein is no doubt,
a guidance to the godfearing
who believe in the Unseen, and perform the prayer,
and expend of that We have provided them;
who believe in what has been sent down to thee
and what has been sent down before thee,
and have faith in the Hereafter;
those are upon guidance from their Lord,
those are the ones who prosper.

The Koran, Oxford University Press, 1964 (ISBN 0192505963), original pp. 1–44 (Suras 1 and 2).

As for the unbelievers, alike it is to them   5
whether thou hast warned them or hast not warned them,
they do not believe.
God has set a seal on their hearts and on their hearing,
and on their eyes is a covering,
and there awaits them a mighty chastisement.

And some men there are who say,
'We believe in God and the Last Day';
but they are not believers.
They would trick God and the believers,
and only themselves they deceive,
and they are not aware.
In their hearts is a sickness,
and God has increased their sickness,
and there awaits them a painful chastisement
for that they have cried lies.
When it is said to them, 'Do not corruption in the land',   10
they say, 'We are only ones that put things right.'
Truly, they are the workers of corruption
but they are not aware.
When it is said to them, 'Believe as the people believe',
they say, 'Shall we believe, as fools believe?'
Truly, they are the foolish ones,
but they do not know.
When they meet those who believe, they say, 'We believe';
but when they go privily to their Satans, they say,
'We are with you; we were only mocking.'
God shall mock them, and shall lead them on
blindly wandering in their insolence.
Those are they that have bought error   15
at the price of guidance,
and their commerce has not profited them,
and they are not right-guided.
The likeness of them is as the likeness of a man
who kindled a fire, and when it lit all about him
God took away their light, and left them in darkness
unseeing,
deaf, dumb, blind—
so they shall not return;
or as a cloudburst out of heaven
in which is darkness, and thunder, and lightning—
they put their fingers in their ears
against the thunderclaps, fearful of death;
and God encompasses the unbelievers;
the lightning wellnigh snatches away their sight;

whensoever it gives them light, they walk in it,
and when the darkness is over them, they halt;
had God willed, He would have taken away
their hearing and their sight.
Truly, God is powerful over everything.

O you men, serve your Lord Who created you,
and those that were before you; haply so
you will be godfearing;
who assigned to you the earth for a couch,   20
and heaven for an edifice, and sent down
out of heaven water, wherewith He brought forth
fruits for your provision; so set not up
compeers to God wittingly.
And if you are in doubt concerning that We have
sent down on Our servant, then bring a sura
like it, and call your witnesses, apart from
God, if you are truthful.
And if you do not—and you will not—then
fear the Fire, whose fuel is men and stones,
prepared for unbelievers.

Give thou good tidings to those who believe
and do deeds of righteousness, that for them
await gardens underneath which rivers flow;
whensoever they are provided with fruits therefrom
they shall say, 'This is what wherewithal
we were provided before'; that they shall be
given in perfect semblance; and there
for them shall be spouses purified; therein
they shall dwell forever.

God is not ashamed to strike a similitude
even of a gnat, or aught above it.
As for the believers, they know it is the truth
from their Lord; but as for unbelievers,
they say, 'What did God desire by this
for a similitude?' Thereby He leads
many astray, and thereby He guides
many; and thereby He leads none astray
save the ungodly
such as break the covenant of God   25
after its solemn binding, and such as cut
what God has commanded should be joined,
and such as do corruption in the land—
they shall be the losers.

How do you disbelieve in God, seeing you were dead
and He gave you life, then He shall make you dead,
then He shall give you life, then unto Him
you shall be returned?
It is He who created for you all that is
in the earth, then He lifted Himself to heaven
and levelled them seven heavens; and He has
knowledge of everything.

And when thy Lord said to the angels,
'I am setting the earth a viceroy.'
They said, 'What, wilt Thou set therein one
who will do corruption there, and shed blood,
while We proclaim Thy praise and call Thee Holy?'
He said, 'Assuredly I know
that you know not.'
And He taught Adam the names, all of them;
then He presented them unto the angels
and said, 'Now tell Me the names of these,
if you speak truly.'
They said, "Glory be to Thee! We know not   30
save what Thou hast taught us. Surely Thou art
the All-knowing, the All-wise.'
He said, 'Adam, tell them their names.'
And when he had told them their names
He said, 'Did I not tell you I know
the unseen things of the heavens and earth?
And I know what things you reveal, and
what you were hiding.'
And when We said to the angels, 'Bow
yourselves to Adam'; so they bowed
themselves, save Iblis; he refused,
and waxed proud, and so he became
one of the unbelievers.
And We said, 'Adam, dwell thou, and thy wife,
in the Garden, and eat thereof easefully
where you desire; but draw not nigh this tree,
lest you be evildoers.'
Then Satan caused them to slip therefrom
and brought them out of that they were in;
and We said, 'Get you all down, each
of you an enemy of each; and in
the earth a sojourn shall be yours, and
enjoyment for a time.'
Thereafter Adam received certain words   35
from his Lord, and He turned towards him;
truly He turns, and is All-compassionate.

We said, 'Get you down out of it, all together;
yet there shall come to you guidance from Me,
and whosoever follows My guidance,
no fear shall be on them, neither shall they sorrow.
As for the unbelievers who cry lies to Our signs,
those shall be the inhabitants of the Fire,
therein dwelling forever.'

Children of Israel, remember My blessing
wherewith I blessed you, and fulfil My covenant
and I shall fulfil your covenant; and have awe of Me.
And believe in that I have sent down, confirming
that which is with you, and be not the first
to disbelieve in it. And sell not My signs
for a little price; and fear you Me.
And do not confound the truth with vanity,
and do not conceal the truth wittingly.
And perform the prayer, and pay the alms,   40
and how with those that bow. Will you bid
others to piety, and forget yourselves
while you recite the Book? Do you not understand?
Seek you help in patience and prayer,
for grievous it is, save to the humble
who reckon that they shall meet their Lord
and that unto Him they are returning.

Children of Israel, remember My blessing
wherewith I blessed you, and that I
have preferred you above all beings;
and beware of a day when no soul for another
shall give satisfaction, and no intercession   45
shall be accepted from it, nor any counterpoise
be taken, neither shall they be helped.

And when We delivered you from the folk of Pharaoh
who were visiting you with evil chastisement,
slaughtering your sons, and sparing your women;
and in that was a grievous trial from your Lord.
And when We divided for you the sea
and delivered you, and drowned Pharaoh's folk
while you were beholding.
And when We appointed with Moses forty nights
then you took to yourselves the Calf after him
and you were evildoers;
then We pardoned you after that, that haply
you should be thankful.

And when We gave to Moses the Book   50
and the Salvation, that haply
you should be guided.
And when Moses said to his people,
'My people, you have done wrong against yourselves
by your taking the Calf; now turn to your Creator
and slay one another. That will be better for you
in your Creator's sight, and He will turn to you;
truly He turns, and is All-compassionate.'
And when you said, 'Moses, we will not believe thee
till we see God openly'; and the thunderbolt took you
while you were beholding.
Then We raised you up after you were dead, that haply
you should be thankful.
And We outspread the cloud to overshadow you,
and We sent down manna and quails upon you:
'Eat of the good things wherewith We have provided you.
And they worked no wrong upon Us, but
themselves they wronged.
And when We said, 'Enter this township,   55
and eat easefully of it wherever you will,
and enter in at the gate, prostrating,
and say, Unburdening; We will forgive you
your transgressions, and increase the good-doers.'
Then the evildoers substituted a saying
other than that which had been said to them;
so We sent down upon the evildoers
wrath out of heaven for their ungodliness.
And when Moses sought water for his people,
so We said, 'Strike with thy staff the rock';
and there gushed forth from it twelve fountains;
all the people knew now their drinking-place.
'Eat and drink of God's providing, and
mischief not in the earth, doing corruption.'
And when you said, 'Moses, we will not endure
one sort of food; pray to thy Lord for us, that He
may bring forth for us of that the earth produces—
green herbs, cucumbers, corn, lentils, onions.'
He said, 'Would you have in exchange what is meaner
for what is better? Get you down to Egypt;
you shall have there that you demanded.'
And abasement and poverty were pitched upon them,
and they were laden with the burden of God's anger;
that, because they had disbelieved the signs of God
and slain the Prophets unrightfully; that,
because they disobeyed, and were transgressors.
Surely they that believe, and those of Jewry,

and the Christians, and those Sabaeans,
whoso believes in God and the Last Day, and works
righteousness—their wage awaits them with their Lord,
and no fear shall be on them, neither shall they sorrow.

And when We took compact with you, and raised above you   60
the Mount: 'Take forcefully what We have given you, and
remember what is in it; haply you shall be godfearing.'
Then you turned away thereafter, and but for the bounty
and mercy of God towards you, you had been of the losers.
And well you know there were those among you
that transgressed the Sabbath, and We said to them,
'Be you apes, miserably slinking!'
And We made it a punishment exemplary
for all the former times and for the latter,
and an admonition to such as are godfearing.
And when Moses said to his people,
'God commands you to sacrifice a cow.' They said,
'Dost thou take us in mockery?' He said,
'I take refuge with God, lest I should be
one of the ignorant.' They said, 'Pray to thy Lord
for us, that He may make clear to us what she may be.'
He said, 'He says she is a cow neither old, nor virgin,
middling between the two; so do that you are bidden.'
They said, 'Pray to thy Lord for us, that He make clear   65
to us what her colour may be.' He said, 'He says
she shall be a golden cow, bright her colour,
gladdening the beholders.' They said, 'Pray
to thy Lord for us, that He make clear to us
what she may be; cows are much alike to us;
and, if God will, we shall then be guided.'
He said, 'He says she shall be a cow not broken
to plough the earth or to water the tillage,
one kept secure, with no blemish on her.' They said,
'Now thou hast brought the truth'; and therefore they
sacrificed her, a thing they had scarcely done.
And when you killed a living soul, and disputed
thereon—and God disclosed what you were hiding—
so We said, 'Smite him with part of it'; even so
God brings to life the dead, and He shows you
His signs, that haply you may have understanding.
Then your hearts became hardened thereafter
and are like stones, or even yet harder;
for there are stones from which rivers come gushing,
and others split, so that water issues from them,
and others crash down in the fear of God.
And God is not heedless of the things you do.

Are you then so eager that they should believe you,   70
seeing there is a party of them that heard
God's word, and then tampered with it, and that
after they had comprehended it, wittingly?
And when they meet those who believe, they say
'We believe'; and when they go privily
one to another, they say, 'Do you speak to them
of what God has revealed to you, that they may
thereby dispute with you before your Lord?
Have you no understanding?'
Know they not that God knows what they keep secret
and what they publish?
And some there are of them that are common folk
not knowing the Book, but only fancies
and mere conjectures. So woe to those
who write the Book with their hands, then say,
'This is from God,' that they may sell it
for a little price; so woe to them
for what their hands have written, and woe
to them for their earnings.
And they say, 'The Fire shall not touch us
save a number of days.' Say: 'Have you taken
with God a covenant? God will not fail in His
covenant; or say you things against God
of which you know nothing?
Not so; whoso earns evil, and is encompassed by   75
his transgression—those are the inhabitants of the Fire;
there they shall dwell forever.
And those that believe, and do deeds of
righteousness—those are the inhabitants of Paradise;
there they shall dwell forever.'

And when We took compact with the Children of Israel:
'You shall not serve any save God;
and to be good to parents, and the near kinsman,
and to orphans, and to the needy;
and speak good to men, and perform the prayer,
and pay the alms.' Then you turned away,
all but a few of you, swerving aside.
And when We took compact with you: 'You shall not
shed your own blood, neither expel your own
from your habitations'; then you confirmed it
and yourselves bore witness. Then there you are
killing one another, and expelling a party of you
from their habitations, conspiring against them
in sin and enmity; and if they come to you
as captives, you ransom them; yet their expulsion

was forbidden you. What, do you believe
in part of the Book, and disbelieve in part?
What shall be the recompense of those of you who
do that, but degradation in the present life,
and on the Day of Resurrection to be returned
unto the most terrible of chastisement?
And God is not heedless of the things you do.
Those who have purchased the present life at the price   80
of the world to come—for them the chastisement
shall not be lightened, neither shall they be helped.

And We gave to Moses the Book, and after him
sent succeeding Messengers; and We gave Jesus
son of Mary the clear signs, and confirmed him
with the Holy Spirit; and whensoever
there came to you a Messenger with that your souls
had not desire for, did you become arrogant,
and some cry lies to, and some slay?

And they say, 'Our hearts are uncircumcised.'
Nay, but God has cursed them for their unbelief;
little will they believe. When there came to them
a Book from God, confirming what was with them—
and they aforetimes prayed for victory
over the unbelievers—when there came to them
that they recognized, they disbelieved in it;
and the curse of God is on the unbelievers.
Evil is the thing they have sold themselves for,
disbelieving in that which God sent down,
grudging that God should send down of His bounty
on whomsoever He will of His servants,
and they were laden with anger upon anger;
and for unbelievers awaits a humbling chastisement.
And when they were told, 'Believe in that   85
God has sent down,' they said, 'We believe
in what was sent down on us'; and they disbelieve
in what is beyond that, yet it is the truth
confirming what is with them. Say: 'Why then
were you slaying the Prophets of God
in former time, if you were believers?'

And Moses came to you with the clear signs,
then you took to yourselves the Calf after him
and you were evildoers.
And when We took compact with you, and raised over you
the Mount: 'Take forcefully what We have given you
and give ear.' They said, 'We hear, and rebel';

and they were made to drink the Calf in their hearts
for their unbelief. Say: 'Evil is the thing
your faith bids you to, if you are believers.
Say: 'If the Last Abode with God is yours
exclusively, and not for other people,
then long for death—if you speak truly.'
But they will never long for it, because of that
their hands have forwarded; God knows the evildoers;
and thou shalt find them the eagerest of men   90
for life. And of the idolaters; there is one of them
wishes if he might be spared a thousand years,
yet his being spared alive shall not remove him
from the chastisement. God sees the things they do.
Say: 'Whosoever is an enemy to Gabriel—
he it was that brought it down upon thy heart
by the leave of God, confirming what was before it,
and for a guidance and good tidings to the believers.
Whosoever is an enemy to God and His angels
and His Messengers, and Gabriel, and Michael—
surely God is an enemy to the unbelievers.'
And We have sent down unto thee signs, clear signs,
and none disbelieves in them except the ungodly.

Why, whensoever they have made a covenant,
does a party of them reject it?
Nay, but the most of them are unbelievers.
When there has come to them a Messenger from God   95
confirming what was with them, a party of them
that were given the Book reject the Book of God
behind their backs, as though they knew not,
and they follow what the Satans recited
over Solomon's kingdom. Solomon disbelieved not,
but the Satans disbelieved, teaching
the people sorcery, and that which was sent down
upon Babylon's two angels, Harut and Marut;
they taught not any man, without they said,
'We are but a temptation; do not disbelieve.'
From them they learned how they might divide
a man and his wife, yet they did not hurt
any man thereby, save by the leave of God,
and they learned what hurt them, and did not
profit them, knowing well that whoso buys it
shall have no share in the world to come;
evil then was that they sold themselves for,
if they had but known.
Yet had they believed, and been godfearing,

a recompense from God had been better,
if they had but known.

O believers; do not say, 'Observe us,'
but say, 'Regard us'; and give ear;
for unbelievers awaits a painful chastisement.

Those unbelievers of the People of the Book
and the idolaters wish not that any good
should be sent down upon you from your Lord;
but God singles out for His mercy whom He will;
God is of bounty abounding.

And for whatever verse We abrogate   100
or cast into oblivion, We bring a better
or the like of it; knowst thou not that God
is powerful over everything?
Knowest thou not that to God belongs
the kingdom of the heavens and the earth,
and that you have none, apart from God,
neither protector nor helper?
Or do you desire to question your Messenger
as Moses was questioned in former time?
Whoso exchanges belief for unbelief has surely
strayed from the right way.

Many of the People of the Book wish they might
restore you as unbelievers, after you have believed,
in the jealousy of their souls, after the truth
has become clear to them; yet do you pardon
and be forgiving, till God brings His command;
truly God is powerful over everything.
And perform the prayer, and pay the alms; whatever
good you shall forward to your souls' account,
you shall find it with God; assuredly God
sees the things you do.
And they say, 'None shall enter Paradise   105
except that they be Jews or Christians.'
Such are their fancies. Say: 'Produce your proof,
if you speak truly.'
Nay, but whosoever submits his will to God,
being a good-doer, his wage is with his Lord,
and no fear shall be on them, neither shall they sorrow.

The Jews say, 'The Christians stand not on anything';
the Christians say, 'The Jews stand not on anything';

yet they recite the Book. So too the ignorant
say the like of them. God shall decide between them
on the Day of Resurrection touching their differences.
And who does greater evil than he who bars
God's places of worship, so that His Name
be not rehearsed in them, and strives to destroy them?
Such men might never enter them, save in fear;
for them is degradation in the present world,
and in the world to come a mighty chastisement.

To God belong the East and West;
whithersoever you turn, there is the Face of God;
God is All-embracing, All-knowing.

And they say, 'God has taken to Him a son.'   110
Glory be to Him! Nay, to Him belongs
all that is in the heavens and the earth;
all obey His will—
the Creator of the heavens and the earth;
and when He decrees a thing, He but says to it
'Be,' and it is.
And they that know not say, 'Why does God not
speak to us? Why does a sign not come to us?'
So spoke those before them as these men say;
their hearts are much alike. Yet We have made
clear the signs unto a people who are sure.
We have sent thee with the truth, good tidings
to bear, and warning. Thou shalt not be questioned
touching the inhabitants of Hell.
Never will the Jews be satisfied with thee,
neither the Christians, not till thou followest
their religion. Say: 'God's guidance
is the true guidance.' If thou followest
their caprices, after the knowledge that
has come to thee, thou shalt have against God
neither protector nor helper.
Those to whom We have given the Book   115
and who recite it with true recitation,
they believe in it; and whoso disbelieves in it,
they shall be the losers

Children of Israel, remember My blessing
wherewith I blessed you, and that I
have preferred you above all beings;
and beware a day when no soul for another
shall give satisfaction, and no counterpoise
shall be accepted from it, nor any

intercession shall be profitable to it,
neither shall they be helped.

And when his Lord tested Abraham
with certain words, and he fulfilled them.
He said, 'Behold, I make you a leader
for the people.' Said he, 'And of my seed?'
He said 'My covenant shall not reach
the evildoers.'
And when We appointed the House to be
a place of visitation for the people,
and a sanctuary,
and: 'Take to yourselves Abraham's station
for a place of prayer.' And We made covenant
with Abraham and Ishmael: 'Purify
My House for those that shall go about it
and those that cleave to it, to those who bow
and prostrate themselves.'
And when Abraham said, 'My Lord, make this   120
a land secure, and provide its people
with fruits, such of them as believe in
God and the Last Day.'
He said, 'And whoso disbelieves, to him
I shall give enjoyment a little, then I
shall compel him to the chastisement of the Fire—
how evil a homecoming!'
And when Abraham, and Ishmael with him,
raised up the foundations of the House:
'Our Lord, receive this from us; Thou art
the All-hearing, the All-knowing;
and, our Lord, make us submissive to Thee,
and of our seed a nation submissive
to Thee; and show us our holy rites, and
turn towards us; surely Thou turnest, and art
All-compassionate;
and, our Lord, do Thou send among them
a Messenger, one of them, who shall recite
to them Thy signs, and teach them the Book
and the Wisdom, and purify them; Thou art
the All-mighty, the All-wise.'
Who therefore shrinks from the religion
of Abraham, except he be foolish-minded?
Indeed, We chose him in the present world,
and in the world to come he shall be
among the righteous.
When his Lord said to him, 'Surrender,'   125
he said, 'I have surrendered me to

the Lord of all Being.'
And Abraham charged his sons with this
and Jacob likewise: 'My sons, God has chosen
for you the religion; see that you die not
save in surrender.'
Why, were you witnesses, when death came
to Jacob? When he said to his sons,
'What will you serve after me?' They said,
'We will serve thy God and the God of thy fathers
Abraham, Ishmael and Isaac, One God;
to Him we surrender.'
That is a nation that has passed away;
there awaits them that they have earned,
and there awaits you that you have earned;
you shall not be questioned concerning
the things they did.

And they say, 'Be Jews or Christians and
you shall be guided.' Say thou: 'Nay, rather
the creed of Abraham, a man of pure faith;
he was no idolater.'
Say you: 'We believe in God, and   130
in that which has been sent down on us
and sent down on Abraham, Ishmael,
Isaac and Jacob, and the Tribes,
and that which was given to Moses and Jesus
and the Prophets, of their Lord; we
make no division between any of them, and
to Him we surrender.
And if they believe in the like of that you
believe in, then they are truly guided; but if
they turn away, then they are clearly in schism;
God will suffice you for them; He is
the All-hearing, the All-knowing;
the baptism of God; and who is there
that baptizes fairer than God?
Him we are serving.
Say: 'Would you then dispute with us
concerning God, who is our Lord
and your Lord? Our deeds belong to us,
and to you belong your deeds; Him
we serve sincerely.
Or do you say, "Abraham, Ishamel,
Isaac and Jacob, and the Tribes—
they were Jews, or they were Christians"?'
Say: 'Have you then greater knowledge,

or God? And who does greater evil than
he who conceals a testimony received
from God? And God is not heedless of
the things you do.'
That is a nation that has passed away;   135
there awaits them that they have earned,
and there awaits you that you have earned;
you shall not be questioned concerning
the things they did.

The fools among the people will say,
'What has turned them from the direction
they were facing in their prayers aforetime?'
Say:
'To God belong the East and the West;
He guides whomsoever He will
to a straight path.'

Thus We appointed you a midmost nation
that you might be witnesses to the people,
and that the Messenger might be a witness
to you; and We did not appoint the direction
thou wast facing, except that We might know
who followed the Messenger from him who turned
on his heels—though it were a grave thing
save for those whom God has guided; but
God would never leave your faith to waste—
truly, God is All-gentle with the people,
All-compassionate.
We have seen thee turning thy face about
in the heaven; now We will surely turn thee
to a direction that shall satisfy thee.
Turn thy face towards the Holy Mosque; and
wherever you are, turn your faces towards it.
Those who have been given the Book know it is
the truth from their Lord; God is not heedless of
the things they do.
Yet if thou shouldst bring to those that have been   140
given the Book every sign, they will not follow
thy direction; thou art not a follower
of their direction, neither are they followers
of one another's direction. If thou followest
their caprices, after the knowledge
that has come to three, then thou wilt surely be
among the evildoers
whom We have given the Book, and they recognize

as they recognize their sons, even though
there is a party of them conceal the truth
and that wittingly.
The truth comes from thy Lord; then be not
among the doubters.
Every man has his direction to which he turns;
so be you forward in good works. Wherever
you may be, God will bring you all together;
surely God is powerful over everything.
From whatsoever place thou issuest, turn
thy face towards the Holy Mosque; it is
the truth from thy Lord. God is not heedless of
the things you do.
From whatsoever place thou issuest, turn   145
thy face towards the Holy Mosque; and
wherever you may be, turn your faces
towards it, that the people may not have
any argument against you, excepting
the evildoers of them; and fear you them not,
but fear you Me; and that I may perfect
My blessing upon you, and that haply so
you may be guided;
as also We have sent among you, of yourselves,
a Messenger, to recite Our signs to you
and to purify you, and to teach you
the Book and the Wisdom, and to teach you
that you knew not.
So remember Me, and I will remember
you; and be thankful to Me; and be you not
ungrateful towards Me.
O all you who believe, seek you help
in patience and prayer; surely God is
with the patient.
And say not of those slain in God's way,
'They are dead'; rather they are living,
but you are not aware.
Surely We will try you with something of fear   150
and hunger, and diminution of goods
and lives and fruits; yet give thou good tidings
unto the patient
who, when they are visited by an affliction,
say, 'Surely we belong to God, and
to Him we return';
upon those rest blessings and mercy
from their Lord, and those—they are
the truly guided.

Safa and Marwa are among the waymarks
of God; so whosoever makes the Pilgrimage
to the House, or the Visitation,
it is no fault in him to circumambulate
them; and whoso volunteers good, God is
All-grateful, All-knowing.

Those who conceal the clear signs and the guidance
that We have sent down, after We have shown them
clearly in the Book—they shall be cursed by
God and the cursers,
save such as repent and make amends, and show   155
clearly—towards them I shall turn; I turn,
All-compassionate.
But those who disbelieve, and die disbelieving—
upon them shall rest the curse of God
and the angels, and of men altogether,
therein dwelling forever; the chastisement
shall not be lightened for them; no respite
shall be given them.

Your God is One God;
there is no god but He,
the All-merciful, the All-compassionate.

Surely in the creation of the heavens and the earth
and the alternation of night and day
and the ship that runs in the sea with profit
to men, and the water God sends down from heaven
therewith reviving the earth after it is dead
and His scattering abroad in it all manner of
crawling thing, and the turning about of the winds
and the clouds compelled between heaven and earth—
surely there are signs for a people having understanding.

Yet there be men who take to themselves compeers   160
apart from God, loving them as God is loved;
but those that believe love God more ardently.
O if the evildoers might see, when they see
the chastisement, that the power altogether
belongs to God, and that God is terrible
in chastisement,
when those that were followed disown their followers,
and they see the chastisement, and their cords
are cut asunder,
and those that followed say, 'O if only we might

return again and disown them, as they have disowned
us!' Even so God shall show them their works.
O bitter regrets for them! Never shall they
issue from the Fire.

O men, eat of what is in the earth
lawful and good; and follow not the steps
of Satan; he is a manifest foe to you.
he only commands you to evil and indecency,
and that you should speak against God such things
as you know not.

And when it is said to them, 'Follow what God   165
has sent down,' they say, 'No; but we will follow
such things as we found our fathers doing.'
What? And if their fathers had no understanding
of anything, and if they were not guided?
The likeness of those who disbelieve is as
the likeness of one who shouts to that
which hears nothing, save a call and a cry;
deaf, dumb, blind—they do not understand.

O believers, eat of the good things
wherewith We have provided you, and give thanks
to God, if it be Him that you serve.
These things only has He forbidden you:
carrion, blood, the flesh of swine,
what has been hallowed to other than God.
Yet whoso is constrained, not desiring
nor transgressing, no sin shall be on him;
God is All-forgiving, All-compassionate.

Those who conceal what of the Book God has sent down
on them, and sell it for a little price—they shall eat
naught but the Fire in their bellies; God shall not
speak to them on the Day of Resurrection
neither purify them; there awaits them
a painful chastisement.
Those are they that have bought error at   170
the price of guidance, and chastisement at
the price of pardon; how patiently they
shall endure the Fire!
That, because God has sent down the Book
with the truth; and those that are
at variance regarding the Book
are in wide schism.

It is not piety, that you turn your faces
to the East and to the West.
True piety is this:
to believe in God, and the Last Day,
the angels, the Book, and the Prophets,
to give of one's substance, however cherished,
to kinsmen, and orphans,
the needy, the traveller, beggars,
and to ransom the slave,
to perform the prayer, to pay the alms.
And they who fulfil their covenant
when they have engaged in a covenant,
and endure with fortitude
misfortune, hardship and peril,
these are they who are true in their faith,
these are the truly godfearing.

O believers, prescribed for you is
retaliation, touching the slain;
freeman for freeman, slave for slave,
female for female. But if aught is pardoned
a man by his bother, let the pursuing
be honourable, and let the payment be
with kindliness. That is a lightening
granted you by your Lord, and a mercy;
and for him who commits aggression
after that—for him there awaits
a painful chastisement.
In retaliation there is life for you,   175
men possessed of minds; haply you
will be godfearing.

Prescribed for you, when any of you
is visited by death, and he leaves behind
some goods, is to make testament
in favour of his parents and kinsmen
honourably—an obligation
on the godfearing.
Then if any man changes it after
hearing it, the sin shall rest upon
those who change it; surely God is
All-hearing, All-knowing.
But if any man fears injustice or
sin from one making testament, and so
makes things right between them, then
sin shall not rest upon him; surely God is
All-forgiving, All-compassionate.

O believers, prescribed for you is
the Fast, even as it was prescribed for
those that were before you—haply you
will be godfearing—
for days numbered; and if any of you
be sick, or if he be on a journey,   180
then a number of other days; and for those
who are able to fast, a redemption
by feeding a poor man. Yet better
it is for him who volunteers good,
and that you should fast is better for you,
if you but know;
the month of Ramadan, wherein the Koran
was sent down to be a guidance
to the people, and as clear signs
of the Guidance and the Salvation
So let those of you, who are present
at the month, fast it; and if any of you be sick, or if he be on a journey,
then a number of other days; God desires
ease for you, and desires not hardship
for you; and that you fulfil the number, and
magnify God that He has guided you, and haply
you will be thankful.

And when My servants question thee
concerning Me—I am near to answer
the call of the caller, when he calls
to Me; so let them respond to Me,
and let them believe in Me; haply so
they will go aright.

Permitted to you, upon the night of
the Fast, is to go to your wives;
they are a vestment for you, and you are
a vestment for them. God knows that you have been
betraying yourselves, and has turned to you
and pardoned you. So now lie with them,
and seek what God has prescribed for you.
And eat and drink, until the white thread
shows clearly to you from the black thread
at the dawn; then complete the Fast
unto the night, and do not lie with them
while you cleave to the mosques. Those are
God's bounds; keep well within them. So God
makes clear His signs to men; haply they
will be godfearing.

Consume not your goods between you
in vanity; neither proffer it
to the judges, that you may sinfully
consume a portion of other men's goods,
and that wittingly.

They will question thee concerning   185
the new moons. Say: 'They are appointed
times for the people, and the Pilgrimage.'

It is not piety to come to the houses
from the backs of them; but piety is
to be godfearing; so come to the houses
by the doors, and fear God; haply so
you will prosper.

And fight in the way of God with those
who fight with you, but aggress not: God loves
not the aggressors.
And slay them wherever you come upon them,
and expel them from where they expelled you;
persecution is more grievous than slaying.
But fight them not by the Holy Mosque
until they should fight you there;
then, if they fight you, slay them—
such is the recompense of unbelievers—
but if they give over, surely God is
All-forgiving, All-compassionate.
Fight them, till there is no persecution
and the religion is God's; then if they
give over, there shall be no enmity
save for evildoers.
The holy month for the holy month;   190
holy things demand retaliation.
Whoso commits aggression against you,
do you commit aggression against him
like as he has committed against you;
and fear you God, and know that God is
with the godfearing.

And expend in the way of God;
and cast not yourselves by your own hands
into destruction, but be good-doers; God
loves the good-doers.

Fulfil the Pilgrimage and the Visitation
unto God; but if you are prevented,

then such offering as may be feasible.
And shave not your heads, till the offering
reaches its place of sacrifice. If any
of you is sick, or injured in his head,
then redemption by fast, or freewill offering,
or ritual sacrifice. When you are secure,
then whosoever enjoys the Visitation
until the Pilgrimage, let his offering
be such as may be feasible; or if he
finds none, then a fast of three days
in the Pilgrimage, and of seven when
you return, that is ten completely;
that is for him whose family are not
present at the Holy Mosque. And fear
God, and know that God is terrible
in retribution.

The Pilgrimage is in months well-known;
whoso undertakes the duty of Pilgrimage
in them shall not go in to his womenfolk
nor indulge in ungodliness and disputing
in the Pilgrimage.Whatever good you do,
God knows it. And take provision;
but the best provision is godfearing,
so fear you Me, men possessed of minds!
It is no fault in you, that you should seek
bounty from your Lord; but when you press on
from Arafat, then remember God
at the Holy Waymark, and remember Him
as He has guided you, though formerly you
were gone astray.
Then press on from where the people
press on, and pray for God's forgiveness;
God is All-forgiving, All-compassionate.
And when you have performed your holy rites
remember God, as you remember your fathers
or yet more devoutly. Now some men
there are who say, 'Our Lord, give to us
in this world'; such men shall have no part
in the world to come.
And others there are who say, 'Our Lord,
give to us in this world good, and good
in the world to come, and guard us against the
chastisement of the Fire';
those—they shall have a portion from
what they have earned; and God is swift

195

at the reckoning.
And remember God during certain days
numbered. If any man hastens on
in two days, that is no sin in him;
and if any delays, it is not a sin
in him, if he be godfearing. And
fear you God, and know that unto Him
you shall be mustered.

And some men there are whose saying   200
upon the present world pleases thee,
and such a one calls on God to witness
what is in his heart, yet he is most stubborn
in altercation,
and when he turns his back, he hastens about
the earth, to do corruption there and to
destroy the tillage and the stock; and God
loves not corruption;
and when it is said to him, 'Fear God',
vainglory seizes him in his sin.
So Gehenna shall be enough for him—how
evil a cradling!
But other men there are that sell themselves
desiring God's good pleasure; and God is gentle
with His servants.
O believers, enter the peace, all of you,
and follow not the steps of Satan;
he is a manifest foe to you. But   205
if you slip, after the clear signs
have come to you, know then that God is
All-mighty, All-wise.

What do they look for, but that God
shall come to them in the cloud-shadows,
and the angels? The matter is determined,
and unto God all matters are returned.
Ask the Children of Israel how many a clear sign
We gave them. Whoso changes God's blessing
after it has come to him, God is terrible
in retribution.
Decked out fair to the unbelievers
is the present life, and they deride
the believers; but those who were godfearing
shall be above them on the Resurrection Day;
and God provides whomsoever He will
without reckoning.

The people were one nation; then God sent forth
the Prophets, good tidings to bear
and warning, and He sent down with them
the Book with the truth, that He might
decide between the people touching their differences;
and only those who had been given it
were at variance upon it, after the
clear signs had come to them, being insolent
one to another; then God guided those
who believed to the truth, touching which
they were at variance, by His leave;
and God guides whomsoever He will
to a straight path.
Or did you suppose you should enter Paradise   210
without there had come upon you the like
of those who passed away before you?
They were afflicted by misery and hardship
and where so convulsed, that the Messenger
and those who believed with him said,
'When comes God's help?' Ah, but surely
God's help is nigh.

They will question thee concerning
what they should expend. Say: 'Whatsoever good
you expend is for parents and kinsmen,
orphans, the needy, and the traveller;
and whatever good you may do, God has
knowledge of it.'

Prescribed for you is fighting, though it be
hateful to you.
Yet it may happen that you will hate a thing
which is better for you;
and it may happen that you
will love a thing which is worse for you; God knows,
and you know not.

They will question thee concerning
the holy month, and fighting in it.
Say: 'Fighting in it is a henious thing,
but to bar from God's way, and disbelief in Him,
and the Holy Mosque, and to expel its people
from it—that is more heinous in God's sight;
and persecution is more heinous than slaying.'
They will not cease to fight with you,
till they turn you from your religion,
if they are able; and whosoever of you

turns from his religion, and dies disbelieving—
their works have failed in this world and the next;
those are the inhabitants of the Fire; therein
they shall dwell forever.
But the believers, and those who emigrate   215
and struggle in God's way—those have hope of
God's compassion; and God is All-forgiving,
All-compassionate.

They will question thee concerning
wine, and arrow-shuffling. Say: 'In both
is heinous sin, and uses for men,
but the sin in them is more heinous
than the usefulness.'

They will question thee concerning
what they should expend. Say: 'The abundance.'
So god makes clear His signs to you; haply
you will reflect;
in this world, and the world to come.

They will question thee concerning
the orphans. Say: 'To set their affairs
aright is good.
And if you intermix with them, they are
your brothers. God knows well
him who works corruption from him
who sets aright; and had He willed
He would have harassed you. Surely God is
All-mighty, All-wise.'

Do not marry idolatresses, until   220
they believe; a believing slavegirl
is better than an idolatress, though
you may admire her. And do not marry
idolaters, until they believe. A believing
slave is better than an idolater, though
you may admire him.
Those call unto the Fire; and God calls unto
Paradise, and pardon, by His leave, and He
makes clear His signs to the people; haply
they will remember.

They will question thee concerning
the monthly course. Say: 'It is hurt;
so go apart from women during
the monthly course, and do not approach them

till they are clean. When they have cleansed
themselves, then come unto them as God
has commanded you.' Truly, God loves
those who repent, and He loves those
who cleanse themselves.
Your women are a tillage for you; so come
unto your tillage as you wish, and forward
for your souls; and fear God, and know that
you shall meet Him. Give thou good tidings
to the believers.

Do not make God a hindrance, through your oath
to being pious and godfearing, and putting
things right between men. Surely God is
All-hearing, All-knowing.
God will not take you to task for a slip   225
in your oaths; but He will take you to task
for what your hearts have earned; and God is
All-forgiving, All-clement.

For those who foreswear their women
a wait of four months; if they revert,
God is All-forgiving, All-compassionate;
but if they resolve on divorce, surely God is
All-hearing, All-knowing.
Divorced women shall wait by themselves
for three periods; and it is not lawful
for them to hide what God has created
in their wombs; if they believe in God
and the Last Day. In such time their mates
have better right to restore them, if they
desire to set things right. Women have
such honourable rights as obligations, but
their men have a degree above them; God is
All-mighty, All-wise.
Divorce is twice; then honourable retention
or setting free kindly. It is not lawful
for you to take of what you have given them
unless the couple fear they may not maintain
Gods' bounds; if you fear they may not maintain
God's bounds, it is no fault in them for her
to redeem herself. Those are God's bounds;
do not transgress them. Whosoever
transgresses the bounds of God—those
are the evildoers.
If he divorces her finally, she shall not   230

be lawful to him after that, until she
marries another husband. If he divorces her,
then it is no fault in them to return
to each other, if they suppose that they will
maintain God's bounds. Those are God's bounds;
He makes them clear unto a people
that have knowledge.
When you divorce women, and they have reached
their term, then retain them honourably
or set them free honourably; do not retain them
by force, to transgress; whoever does that
has wronged himself. Take not God's signs
in mockery, and remember God's blessing
upon you, and the Book and the Wisdom He
has sent down on you, to admonish you.
And fear God, and know that God has knowledge
of everything.
When you divorce women, and they have reached
their term, do not debar them from marrying
their husbands, when they have agreed together
honourably. That is an admonition for
whoso of you believes in God and the Last Day;
that is cleaner and purer for you; God knows,
and you know not.

Mothers shall suckle their children two years
completely, for such as desire to fulfil
the suckling. It is for the father to provide them
and clothe them honourably. No soul is charged
save to its capacity; a mother shall not be pressed
for her child, neither a father for his child.
The heir has a like duty. But if the couple
desire by mutual consent and consultation
to wean, then it is no fault in them.
And if you desire to seek nursing
for your children, it is no fault in you
provide you hand over what you have given
honourably; and fear God, and know that God sees
the things you do.

And those of you who die, leaving wives,
they shall wait by themselves for four months
and ten nights; when they have reached their term
then it is no fault in you what they may do
with themselves honourably. God is aware of
the things you do.

There is no fault in you touching the proposal   235
to women you offer, or hide in your hearts;
God knows that you will be mindful of them;
but do not make troth with them secretly
without you speak honourable words.
And do not resolve on the knot of marriage
until the book has reached its term; and know
that God knows what is in your hearts,
so be fearful of Him; and know that God is
All-forgiving, All-clement.

There is no fault in you, if you divorce
women while as yet you have not touched them
nor appointed any marriage-portion for them;
yet make provision for them, the affluent man
according to his means, and according to his means
the needy man, honourably—an obligation
on the good-doers.
And if you divorce them before you have
touched them, and you have already appointed
for them a marriage-portion, then one-half
of what you have appointed, unless it be
they make remission, or he makes remission
in whose hand is the knot of marriage;
yet that you should remit is nearer
to godfearing. Forget not to be bountiful
one towards another. Surely God sees
the things you do.

Be you watchful over the prayers,
and the middle prayer; and do you stand
obedient to God.
And if you are in fear, then afoot   240
or mounted; but when you are secure, then
remember God, as He taught you the things
that you knew not.

And those of you who die, leaving wives,
let them make testament for their wives,
provision for a year without expulsion; but if
they go forth, there is no fault in you what
they may do with themselves honourably; God is
All-mighty, All-wise.
There shall be for divorced women
provision honourable—an obligation
on the godfearing.

So God makes clear His signs for you; haply
you will understand.

Hast thou not regarded those who went forth
from their habitations in their thousands
fearful of death? God said to them, 'Die!'
Then He gave them life. Truly God is bounteous
to the people, but most of the people
are not thankful.
So fight in God's way, and know that God is   245
All-hearing, All-knowing.
Who is he that will lend God a good loan,
and He will multiply it for him manifold?
God grasps, and outspreads; and unto Him
you shall be returned.

Hast thou not regarded the Council
of the Children of Israel, after Moses,
when they said to a Prophet of theirs,
'Raise up for us a king, and we will fight
in God's way.' He said, 'Might it be
that, if fighting is prescribed for you,
you will not fight?' They said, 'Why should we
not fight in God's way, who have been
expelled from our habitations
and our children?' Yet when fighting was
prescribed for them, they turned their backs
except a few of them; and God has knowledge
of the evildoers.
Then their Prophet said to them, 'Verily
God has raised up Saul for you as king.'
They said, 'How should he be king over us
who have better right than he to kingship,
seeing he has not been given amplitude
of wealth?' He said, 'God has chosen him
over you, and has increased him
broadly in knowledge and body. God gives
the kingship to whom He will; and God is
All-embracing, All-knowing.'
And their Prophet said to them, 'The sign
of his kingship is that the Ark will come to you,
in it a Shechina from your Lord, and a remnant
of what the folk of Moses and Aaron's folk
left behind, the angels bearing it.
Surely in that shall be a sign for you if
you are believers.'

And when Saul went forth with the hosts   250
he said, 'God will try you with a river;
whosoever drinks of it is not of me,
and whoso tastes it not, he is of me,
saving him who scoops up with his hand.'
But they drank of it, except a few
of them; and when he crossed it, and those
who believed with him, they said, 'We have no
power today against Goliath and his hosts.'
Said those who reckoned they should meet God,
'How often a little company has overcome
a numerous company, by God's leave! And God
is with the patient.'
So, when they went forth against Goliath
and his hosts, they said, 'Our Lord, pour out
upon us patience, and make firm our feet,
and give us aid against the people of
the unbelievers!'
And they routed them, by the leave of God,
and David slew Goliath; and God gave him
the kingship, Wisdom, and He taught him
such as He willed. Had God not driven back
the people, some by the means of others,
the earth had surely corrupted; but God is bounteous
unto all beings.

These are the signs of God We recite to thee
in truth,
and assuredly thou art of the number
of the Envoys.
And those Messengers, some We have preferred
above others;
some there are to whom god spoke, and some He
raised in rank.

And We gave Jesus son of Mary the clear signs
and confirmed him with the Holy Spirit.
And had God willed, those who came after him
would not have fought one against the other
after the clear signs had come to them;
but they fell into variance, and some of them
believed, and some disbelieved; and had God willed
they would not have fought one against the other;
but God does whatsoever He desires.

O believers, expend of that wherewith
We have provided you, before there comes a day

wherein shall be neither traffick, nor friendship,
nor intercession; and the unbelievers—they
are the evildoers.

God
there is no god but He, the
Living, the Everlasting.
Slumber seizes Him not, neither sleep;
to Him belongs
all that is in the heavens and the earth.
Who is there that shall intercede with Him
save by His leave?
He knows what lies before them
and what is after them,
and they comprehend not anything of His knowledge
save such as He wills.
His Throne comprises the heavens and earth;
the preserving of them oppresses Him not;
He is the All-high, the All-glorious.

No compulsion is there in religion.
Rectitude has become clear from error.
So whosoever disbelieves in idols
and believes in God, has laid hold of
the most firm handle, unbreaking; God is
All-hearing, All-knowing.

God is the Protector of the believers;
He brings them forth from the shadows
into the light.
And the unbelievers—their protectors are
idols, that bring them forth from the light
into the shadows;
those are the inhabitants of the Fire,
therein dwelling forever.

Hast thou not regarded him who disputed   260
with Abraham, concerning his Lord,
that God had given him the kingship? When
Abraham said, 'My Lord is He who gives
life, and makes to die,' he said, 'I give
life, and make to die.' Said Abraham, 'God
brings the sun from the east; so bring thou
it from the west.' Then the unbeliever
was confounded. God guides not the people
of the evildoers.
Or such as he who passed by a city

that was fallen down upon its turrets;
he said, 'How shall God give life to this
now it is dead?' So God made him die
a hundred years, then He raised him up,
saying, 'How long hast thou tarried?' He said,
'I have tarried a day, or part of a day.'
Said He, 'Nay; thou hast tarried a hundred years.
Look at thy food and drink—it has not spoiled;
and look at thy ass. So We would make thee
a sign for the people. And look at the bones,
how We shall set them up, and then clothe them
with flesh.' So, when it was made clear
to him, he said, 'I know that God is powerful
over everything.'
And when Abraham said, 'My Lord, show me
how Thou wilt give life to the dead,' He said,
'Why, dost thou not believe?' 'Yes,' he said,
'but that my heart may be at rest.' Said He,
'Take four birds, and twist them to thee,
then set a part of them on every hill,
then summon them, and they will come to thee
running. And do thou know that God is
All-mighty, All-wise.'

The likeness of those who expend their wealth
in the way of God is as the likeness
of a grain of corn that sprouts seven ears,
in every ear a hundred grains. So God
multiplies unto whom He will; God is
All-embracing, All-knowing.
Those who expend their wealth in the way of God
then follow not up what they have expended with
reproach and injury, their wage is with their Lord,
and no fear shall be on them, neither shall they sorrow.
Honourable words, and forgiveness, are better than
a freewill offering followed by injury; and God is
All-sufficient, All-clement.
O believers, void not your freewill offerings
with reproach and injury, as one who expends
of his substance to show off to men
and believes not in God and the Last Day.
The likeness of him is as the likeness
of a smooth rock on which is soil,
and a torrent smites it, and leaves it barren.
They have no power over anything that they
have earned. God guides not the people
of the unbelievers.

But the likeness of those who expend their
wealth, seeking God's good pleasure, and to
confirm themselves, is as the likeness
of a garden upon a hill; a torrent smites it
and it yields its produce twofold; if no
torrent smites it, yet dew; and God sees
the things you do.
Would any of you wish to have a garden
of palms and vines, with rivers flowing
beneath it, and all manner of fruit there
for him, then old age smites him, and he has
seed, but weaklings, then a whirlwind with
fire smites it, and it is consumed?
So God makes clear the signs to you; haply
you will reflect.
O believers, expend of the good things
you have earned, and of that We
have produced for you from the earth,
and intend not the corrupt of it for
your expending;
for you would never take it yourselves, except   270
you closed an eye on it; and know that God is
All-sufficient, All-laudable.
Satan promises you poverty, and bids you
unto indecency; but God promises you
His pardon and His bounty; and God is
All-embracing, All-knowing.
He gives the Wisdom to whomsoever He will,
and whoso is given the Wisdom, has been
given much good; yet none remembers but men
possessed of minds.
And whatever expenditure you expend,
and whatever vow you vow, surely God
knows it. No helpers have the evildoers.
If you publish your freewill offerings, it is
excellent; but if you conceal them, and give them
to the poor, that is better for you, and will
acquit you of your evil deeds; God is aware of
the things you do.

Thou art not responsible for guiding them;
but God guides whomsoever He will.

And whatever good you expend is for yourselves,
for then you are expending, being desirous
only of God's Face; and whatever good
you expend shall be repaid to you

in full, and you will not be wronged,
it being for the poor who are restrained
in the way of God, and are unable
to journey in the land; the ignorant man
supposes them rich because of their abstinence,
but thou shalt know them by their mark—
they do not beg of men importunately.
And whatever good you expend, surely God has
knowledge of it.
Those expend their wealth night and day, secretly   275
and in public, their wage awaits them with their Lord,
and no fear shall be on them, neither shall they sorrow.

Those who devour usury shall not rise again
except as he rises, whom Satan of the touch
prostrates; that is because they say,
'Trafficking is like usury.' God has
permitted trafficking, and forbidden usury.
Whosoever receives an admonition
from his Lord and gives over, he shall have
his past gains, and his affair is
committed to God; but whosoever reverts—
those are the inhabitants of the Fire,
therein dwelling forever.
God blots out usury, but freewill offerings
He augments with interest. God loves not
any guilty ingrate.

Those who believe and do deeds of righteousness,
and perform the prayer, and pay the alms—
their wage awaits them with their Lord,
and no fear shall be on them, neither shall they sorrow.

O believers, fear you God; and
give up the usury that is outstanding, if
you are believers.
But if you do not, then take notice that
God shall war with you, and His Messenger; yet
if you repent, you shall have your principal,
unwronging and unwronged.
And if any man should be in difficulties,   280
let him have respite till things are easier; but
that you should give freewill offerings is better for you,
did you but know.
And fear a day wherein you shall be
returned to God, and every soul shall be

paid in full what it has earned; and they
shall not be wronged.

O believers, when you contract a debt
one upon another for a stated term,
write it down, and let a writer
write it down between you justly,
and let not any writer refuse
to write it down, as God has taught him;
so let him write, and let the debtor
dictate, and let him fear God his Lord
and not diminish aught of it. And if
the debtor be a fool, or weak, or unable
to dictate himself, then let his guardian
dictate justly. And call in to witness
two witnesses, men; or if the two
 be not men, then one man and two women,
such witnesses as you approve of,
that if one of the two women errs
the other will remind her; and let the witnesses
not refuse, whenever they are summoned.
And be not loath to write it down,
whether it be small or great, with its term;
that is more equitable in God's sight,
more upright for testimony, and likelier
that you will not be in doubt. Unless it be
merchandise present that you give and take
between you; then it shall be no fault in you
if you do not write it down. And take witnesses
when you are trafficking one with another.
And let not either writer or witness be
pressed; or if you do, that is ungodliness in you.
And fear God; God teaches you, and God has
knowledge of everything.
And if you are upon a journey, and
you do not find a writer, then a pledge
in hand. but If one of you trusts another,
let him who is trusted deliver his trust,
and let him fear God his Lord. And do not
conceal the testimony; whoso conceals it,
his heart is sinful; and God has knowledge of
the things you do.
To God belongs all that is in the heavens and
earth. Whether you publish what is in your hearts
or hide it, God shall make reckoning with you
for it. He will forgive whom He will,

and chastise whom He will; God is powerful
over everything.

The Messenger believes in what was sent down to   285
him from his Lord,
and the believers; each one believes in God
and His angels,
and in His Books and His Messengers; we
make no division
between any one of His Messengers. They say,
'We hear, and obey.
Our Lord, grant us Thy forgiveness; unto Thee
is the homecoming.'

God charges no soul save to its capacity;
standing to its account is what it has earned,
and against its account what it has merited.

Our Lord,
take us not to task
if we forget, or make mistake.
Our Lord,
charge us not with a load such
as Thou didst lay upon those before us.
Our Lord,
do Thou not burden us
beyond what we have the strength to bear.
And pardon us,
and forgive us,
and have mercy on us;
Thou art our Protector.
And help us against the people
of the unbelievers.

Saint Benedict of Nursia

THE BENEDICTINE RULE

The monastic way of life soon spread from Egypt to Palestine and Syria and eventually throughout the Christian Roman Empire. In Italy, Benedict of Nursia (c. 480–547), scion of a wealthy Roman family, founded twelve monasteries, the best known being at Monte Cassino in the mountains of southern Italy. Benedict wrote a set of rules for the governance of his monks; the Benedictine Rule became the model for many monasteries throughout Latin Christendom. In the following extract, Benedict summarizes the purpose and principles of monastic life.

. . . Therefore we are constrained to found a school for the service of the Lord. In its organization we hope we shall ordain nothing severe, nothing burdensome; but if there should result anything a little irksome by the demands of justice for the correction of vices and the persevering of charity, do not therefore, through fear, avoid the way of salvation, which cannot be entered upon save through a narrow entrance, but in which, as life progresses and the heart becomes filled with faith, one walks in the unspeakable sweetness of love; but never departing from His control, and persevering in His doctrine in the monastery until death, let us with patience share in the sufferings of Christ, that we may be worthy to be partakers in His kingdom. . . .

What the Abbot Should Be Like

The abbot who is worthy to rule a monastery ought to remember by what name they are called, and to justify by their deeds the name of a superior. For he is believed to take the place of Christ in the monastery, since he is called by his name, as the apostle says: "Ye have received the spirit of adoption of sons, whereby we call, Abba, Father."

And so the abbot ought not (God forbid) to teach or decree or order anything apart from the precept of the Lord; but his rules and his teaching ought always to be leavened with the leaven of divine justice in the minds of his disciples; and let the abbot be always mindful that in the great judgment of God, both his teaching and the obedience of his disciples will be weighed in the balance. And let the abbot know that whatever the master finds lacking in the sheep will be

Perry, Peden, Von Laue, eds., *Sources of the Western Tradition,* Volume 1, Houghton Mifflin, (ISBN: 0–395–89201–5), original pp. 181–4, (Benedictine Rule).

charged to the fault of the shepherd. Only in case the pastor has shown the greatest diligence in his management of an unruly and disobedient flock, and has given his whole care to the correction of their evil doings, will that pastor be cleared at the judgment of God and be able to say with the prophet, "I have not hid thy righteousness within my heart, I have declared thy faithfulness and thy salvation, but they despising have scorned me"; then let the punishment of eternal death itself fall upon the disobedient sheep of his care.

Therefore when anyone takes on himself the name of abbot, he should govern his disciples by a twofold teaching, that is, let him show forth all the good and holy things by his deeds rather than by his words; to ready disciples he ought to set forth the commands of God in words, but to the hard of heart, and to the simple-minded he ought to illustrate the divine precepts in his deeds. And all things which he has taught his disciples to be wrong, let him demonstrate in his action that they should not be done, lest sometime God should say to him, a sinner: "Why dost thou declare my statutes or take my testimony in thy mouth? Thou hast hated instruction and cast My word behind thee"; and again: "Thou who hast seen the mote in thy brother's eyes, hast not seen the beam in thine own eye."

Let him not be a respecter of persons in the monastery. Let not one be loved more than another, unless he shall have found someone to be better than another in good deeds and in obedience; let not a freeman be preferred to one coming from servitude, unless there be some good and reasonable cause; but if according to the dictates of justice it shall have seemed best to the abbot, let him do this with anyone of any rank whatsoever; otherwise let each keep his own place, since, whether bond or free, we are all one in Christ, and under one God we bear the same burden of service, for there is no respect of persons with God; only in this regard are we distinguished with him if we are found better and more humble than others in our good deeds. Therefore let his love for all be the same, and let one discipline be put upon all according to merit. . . .

About Calling the Brothers to Council

Whenever anything especial is to be done in the monastery, the abbot shall convoke the whole body and himself set forth the matter at issue. And after listening to the advice of the brothers, he shall consider it by himself, and shall do what he shall have judged most useful. Now we say all should be called to the council, because the Lord often reveals to the younger brother what is best to be done.

But let the brothers give advice with all subjection of humility and not presume to defend boldly what seemed good to them, but rather rely on the judgment of the abbot, and all obey him in what he has judged to be for their welfare. But just as it is fitting that the disciples obey the master, so is it incumbent on him to dispose everything wisely and justly.

Therefore, let all follow the rule of the master in all things, and let no one depart from it rashly; let no one in the monastery follow the desire of his own heart. And let no one strive with his abbot shamelessly either within or without the monastery; and if he shall have presumed to do so, let him be subjected to the regular discipline. And let the abbot himself do all things in the fear of God and in the observance of the rule, knowing that he must without doubt render account unto God, the most just judge, for all his judgments.

If there are any matters of minor importance to be done for the welfare of the monastery, let the abbot take the advice only of the elders, as it is written: "Do all things with counsel, and after it is done thou wilt not repent."

Concerning Those Who, Being Often Rebuked, Do Not Amend

If any brother, having frequently been rebuked for any fault, do not amend even after he has been excommunicated, a more severe rebuke shall fall upon him;—that is, the punishment of the lash shall be inflicted upon him. But if he do not even then amend; or, if perchance—which God forbid,—swelled with pride he try even to defend his works: then the abbot shall act as a wise physician. If he have applied . . . the ointments of exhortation, the medicaments [medicines] of the Divine Scriptures; if he have proceeded to the last blasting of excommunication, or to blows with rods, and if he sees that his efforts avail nothing: let him also—what is greater—call in the prayer of himself and all the brothers for him: that God who can do all things may work a cure upon an infirm brother. But if he be not healed even in this way, then at last the abbot may use the pruning knife, as the apostle says: "Remove evil from you," etc.: lest one diseased sheep contaminate the whole flock.

Whether Brothers Who Leave the Monastery Ought Again To Be Received

A brother who goes out, or is cast out, of the monastery for his own fault, if he wish to return, shall first promise every amends for the fault on account of which he departed; and thus he shall be received into the lowest degree—so that thereby his humility may be proved. But if he again depart, up to the third time he shall be received. Knowing that after this every opportunity of return is denied to him.

Concerning Boys Under Age, How They Shall Be Corrected

Every age or intelligence ought to have its proper bounds. Therefore as often as boys or youths, or those who are less able to understand how great is the punishment of excommunication: as often as such persons offend, they shall either be afflicted with excessive fasts, or coerced with severe blows, that they may be healed.

Concerning the Reception of Guests

All guests who come shall be received as though they were Christ; for He Himself said: "I was a stranger and ye took Me in." And to all, fitting honour shall be shown; but, most of all, to servants of the faith and to pilgrims. When, therefore, a guest is announced, the prior or the brothers shall run to meet him, with every office of love. And first they shall pray together; and thus they shall be joined together in peace. Which kiss of peace shall not first be offered, unless a prayer have preceded; on account of the wiles of the devil. In the salutation itself, moreover, all humility shall be exhibited. In the case of all guests arriving or departing: with inclined head, or with prostrating of the whole body upon the ground, Christ, who is also received in them, shall be adored.

> The monks gathered together for prayer seven times in the course of the day. Prayers were chanted from set texts.

Concerning the Art of Singing

Whereas we believe that there is a divine presence, and that the eyes of the Lord look down everywhere upon the good and the evil: chiefly then, without any doubt, we may believe that this is the case when we are assisting at divine service. Therefore let us always be mindful of what the prophets say: "Serve the Lord in all fear"; and before the face of the Divinity and His angels; and let us so stand and again, "Sing wisely"; and "in the sight of the angels I will sing unto thee." Therefore let us consider how we ought to conduct ourselves and sing that our voice may accord with our intention.

Concerning Reverence for Prayer

If when to powerful men we wish to suggest anything, we do not presume to do it unless with reverence and humility: how much more should we supplicate with all humility, and devotion of purity, God who is the Lord of all. And let us know that we are heard, not for much speaking, but for purity of heart and compunction of tears. And, therefore, prayer ought to be brief and pure; unless perchance it be prolonged by the influence of the inspiration of the divine grace. When assembled together, then, let the prayer be altogether brief; and, the sign being given by the prior, let us rise together.

Concerning the Daily Manual Labor

Idleness is the enemy of the soul. And therefore, at fixed times, the brothers ought to be occupied in manual labour; and again, at fixed times, in sacred reading.

Concerning Humility

. . . If we wish to attain to the height of the greatest humility, and to that divine exaltation which is attained by the humility of this present life, we must mount by our own acts that ladder which appeared in a dream to Jacob,[1] upon which angels appeared unto him ascending and descend-

---

[1] Jacob, a patriarch of ancient Israel, had a dream about angels ascending and descending a ladder between heaven and earth; the dream is recounted in the Old Testament.

ing. For that ascent and descent can only be understood by us to be this: to ascend by humility, to descend through pride. . . .

Now the first grade of humility is this: keeping the fear of God before his eyes, let him avoid forgetfulness and ever remember all the precepts of the Lord; and continually consider in his heart that eternal life which is prepared for those who fear God, just as the mockers of God fall into hell. . . .

The fifth grade of humility is this, if one reveals to the abbot in humble confession all the vain imaginings that come into his heart, and all the evil he has done in secret. . . .

This is the eighth grade of humility; if a monk do nothing except what the common rule of the monastery or the examples of his superior urges him to do.

The ninth grade of humility is this: if a monk keep his tongue from speaking and keeping silence speaks only in answer to questions, since the Scripture says that "sin is not escaped by much speaking," and "a talkative man is not established in the earth."

The tenth grade of humility is this, that he be not easily moved nor prompt to laughter, since it is written: "The fool raiseth his voice in laughter."

The eleventh grade of humility is this: if, when the monk speaks, he says few words and those to the point, slowly and without laughter, humbly and gravely; and be not loud of voice, as it is written: "A wise man is known by his few words."

The twelfth grade of humility is this: that a monk conduct himself with humility not only in his heart but also in his bearing, in the sight of all; that is, in the service of God, in the oratory [chapel], in the monastery, in the garden, on the road, in the field; and everywhere, sitting or walking or standing, let him always have his head bowed, and his eyes fixed on the ground. Always mindful of his sins, let him think of himself as being already tried in the great judgment, saying in his heart what that publican, spoken of in the gospel, said with his eyes fixed on the earth: "Lord, I a sinner am not worthy to lift mine eyes to the heavens;" and again with the prophet: "I am bowed down and humbled wheresoever I go." . . .

Saint Thomas Aquinas

SUMMA THEOLOGICA
AND SUMMA CONTRA GENTILES

For most of the middle ages, religious thought was dominated by the influence of Saint Augustine (d. 430), the greatest of the Latin church fathers (see page 185). Augustine placed little value on the study of nature; for him, the City of Man (the world) was a sinful place from which people tried to escape in order to enter the City of God (heaven). Regarding God as the source of knowing, he held that reason by itself was an inadequate guide to knowledge: without faith in revealed truth, there could be no understanding. An alternative approach to that of Augustine was provided by Thomas Aquinas (1225–1274), a friar of the Order of Preachers (Dominicans), who taught theology at Paris and later in Italy. Both Augustine and Aquinas believed that God was the source of all truth, that human nature was corrupted by the imprint of the original sin of Adam and Eve, and that God revealed himself through the Bible and in the person of Jesus Christ. But, in contrast to Augustine, Aquinas expressed great confidence in the power of reason and favored applying it to investigate the natural world.

Aquinas held that as both faith and reason came from God, they were not in opposition to each other; properly understood, they supported each other. Because reason was no enemy of faith, it should not be feared. In addition to showing renewed respect for reason, Aquinas—influenced by Aristotelian empiricism (the acquisition of knowledge of nature through experience)—valued knowledge of the natural world. He saw the natural and supernatural worlds not as irreconcilable and hostile to each other, but as a continuous ascending hierarchy of divinely created orders of being moving progressively toward the Supreme Being. In constructing a synthesis of Christianity and Aristotelianism, Aquinas gave renewed importance to the natural world, human reason, and the creative human spirit. Nevertheless, by holding that reason was subordinate to faith, he remained a typically medieval thinker.

In the opening reading from his most ambitious work, the *Summa Theologica,* Thomas Aquinas asserts that reason by itself is insufficient to lead human beings to salvation. Also included in this grouping is a selection from another work, *Summa Contra Gentiles,* a theological defense of Christian doctrines that relies extensively on natural reason.

Summa Theologica

handwritten notes:
1 Motion
2 Ulvaint cause
3 necessary being
4 perfection in world
5 existance of God as a cause of order

Whether, Besides the Philosophical Sciences, Any Further Doctrine Is Required?

It was necessary for man's salvation that there should be a knowledge revealed by God, besides the philosophical sciences investigated by human reason. First, because man is directed to God as to an end that surpasses the grasp of his reason. . . . But the end must first be known by men who are to direct their thoughts and actions to the end. Hence it was necessary for the salvation of man that certain truths which exceed human reason should be made known to him by divine revelation. Even as regards those truths about God which human reason can investigate, it was necessary that man be taught by a divine revelation. For the truth about God, such as reason can know it, would only be known by a few, and that after a long time, and with the admixture of many errors: whereas man's whole salvation, which is in God, depends upon the knowledge of this truth. Therefore, in order that the salvation of men might be brought about more fitly and more surely, it was necessary that they be taught divine truths by divine revelation. It was therefore necessary that, besides the philosophical sciences investigated by reason, there should be a sacred science by way of revelation.

> In the next selection, Aquinas uses the categories of Aristotelian philosophy to demonstrate through natural reason God's existence.

Whether God Exists?

The existence of God can be proved in five ways.

The first and more manifest way is the argument from motion. It is certain, and evident to our senses, that in the world some things are in motion. Now whatever is moved is moved by another, for nothing can be moved except it is in potentiality to that towards which it is moved; whereas a thing moves inasmuch as it is in act. For motion is nothing else than the reduction of something from potentiality to actuality. But nothing can be reduced from potentiality to actuality, except by something in a state of actuality. Thus that which is actually hot, as fire, makes wood, which is potentially hot, to be actually hot, and thereby moves and changes it. Now it is not possible that the same thing should be at once in actuality and potentiality in the same respect, but only in different respects. For what is actually hot cannot simultaneously be potentially hot; but it is simultaneously potentially cold. It is therefore impossible that in the same

Perry, Peden, Von Laue, eds., *Sources of the Western Tradition*, Volume 1, Houghton Mifflin, (ISBN 0-395-89201-5), original pp. 236–240 (selections from Thomas Aquinas).

respect and in the same way a thing should be both mover and moved, *i.e.,* that it should move itself. Therefore, whatever is moved must be moved by another. If that by which it is moved be itself moved, then this also must needs be moved by another, and that by another again. But this cannot go on to infinity, because then there would be no first mover, and, consequently, no other mover, seeing that subsequent movers move only inasmuch as they are moved by the first mover; as the staff moves only because it is moved by the hand. Therefore it is necessary to arrive at a first mover, moved by no other; and this everyone understands to be God.

The second way if from the nature of efficient cause. In the world of sensible things we find there is an order of efficient causes. There is no case known (neither is it, indeed, possible) in which a thing is found to be the efficient cause of itself; for so it would be prior to itself, which is impossible. Now in efficient causes it is not possible to go on to infinity, because in all efficient causes following in order, the first is the cause of the intermediate cause, and the intermediate is the cause of the ultimate cause, whether the intermediate cause be several, or one only. Now to take away the cause is to take away the effect. Therefore, if there be no first cause among efficient causes, there will be no ultimate, nor any intermediate, cause. But if in efficient causes it is possible to go on to infinity, there will be no first efficient cause, neither will there be an ultimate effect, nor any intermediate efficient causes; all of which is plainly false. Therefore, it is necessary to admit a first efficient cause, to which everyone gives the name of God.

The third way is taken from possibility and necessity, and runs thus. We find in nature things that are possible to be and not to be, since they are found to be generated, and to be corrupted, and consequently, it is possible for them to be and not to be. But it is impossible for these always to exist, for that which can not-be at some time is not. Therefore, if everything can not-be, then at one time there was nothing in existence. Now if this were true, even now there would be nothing in existence, because that which does not exist begins to exist only through something already existing. Therefore, if at one time nothing was in existence, it would have been impossible for anything to have begun to exist; and thus even now nothing would be in existence—which is absurd. Therefore, not all beings are merely possible, but there must exist something the existence of which is necessary. But every necessary thing either has its necessity caused by another, nor not. Now it is impossible to go on to infinity in necessary things which have their necessity caused by another, as has been already proved in regard to efficient causes. Therefore we cannot but admit the existence of some being having of itself its own necessity, and not receiving it from another, but rather causing in others their necessity. This all men speak of as God.

The fourth way is taken from the graduation to be found in things. Among beings there are some more and some less good, true, noble, and the like. But *more* and *less* are predicated of different things according as they resemble in their different ways something which is the maximum, as a thing is said to be hottest according as it more nearly resembles that which is hottest; so that there is something which is truest, something best, something noblest, and, consequently, something which is most being, for those things that are greatest in truth are greatest in being. . . . Now the maximum in any genus is the cause of all in that genus, as fire, which is the maximum of heat, is the cause of all hot things. . . . Therefore there must also be something which is to all beings the cause of their being, goodness, and every other perfection; and this we call God.

The fifth way is taken from the governance of the world. We see that things which lack knowledge, such as natural bodies, act for an end, and this is evident from their acting always, or nearly always, in the same way, so as to obtain the best result. Hence it is plain that they achieve their end, not fortuitously, but designedly. Now whatever lacks knowledge cannot move towards an end, unless it be directed by some being endowed with knowledge and intelligence; as the arrow is directed by the archer. Therefore some intelligent being exists by whom all natural things are directed to their end; and this being we call God.

> The next reading shows Aquinas' great respect for reason. He defines a human being by the capacity to regulate actions through reason and will.

Does Man Choose with Necessity or Freely?

Man does not choose of necessity. . . . For man can will and not will, act and not act . . . can will this or that, and do this or that. The reason for this is to be found in the very power of the reason. For the will can tend to whatever the reason can apprehend as good. Now the reason can apprehend as good not only this, viz., *to will* or *to act,* but also this, viz., *not to will* and *not to act.* Again, in all particular goods, the reason can consider the nature of some good, and the lack of some good, which has the nature of an evil; and in this way, it can apprehend any single one of such goods as to be chosen or to be avoided. . . . Therefore, man chooses, not of necessity, but freely.

> In the following selection Aquinas stresses the necessity of assenting to the truths of faith even if they are beyond the grasp of reason.

Summa Contra Gentiles

Another benefit that comes from the revelation to men of truths that exceed the reason is the curbing of presumption, which is the mother of error. For there are some who have such a presumptuous opinion of their own ability that they deem themselves able to measure the nature of everything: I mean to say that, in their estimation, everything is true that seems to them so, and everything is false that does not. So that the human mind, therefore, might be freed from this presumption and come to a humble inquiry after truth, it was necessary that some things should be proposed to man by God that would completely surpass his intellect.

A still further benefit may also be seen in what Aristotle says in the *Ethics.* There was a certain Simonides who exhorted people to put aside the knowledge of divine things and to apply their talents to human occupations. He said that "he who is a man should know human things, and he who is mortal, things that are mortal." Against Simonides Aristotle says that "man should draw himself towards what is immortal and divine as much as he can." And so he says in the *De animalibus* that, although what we know of the higher substances is very little, yet that little is loved and desired more than all the knowledge that we have about less noble substances. He also says in the *De caelo et mundo* that when questions about the heavenly bodies can be given a modest and merely plausible solution, he who hears this experiences intense joy. From all these considerations it is clear that even the most imperfect knowledge about the most noble realities brings the greatest perfection to the soul. Therefore, although the human reason cannot grasp fully the truths that are above it, yet, if it somehow holds these truths at least by faith, it acquires great perfection for itself.

Therefore it is written: "For many things are shown to thee above the understanding of men" (Ecclus. 3:25). . . .

Those who place their faith in this truth, however, "for which the human reason offers no experimental evidence," do not believe foolishly, as though "following artificial fables" (II Peter 1:16). For these "secrets of divine Wisdom" (Job 11:6) the divine Wisdom itself, which knows all things to the full, has deigned to reveal to men. It reveals its own presence, as well as the truth of its teaching and inspiration, by fitting arguments; and in order to confirm those truths that exceed natural knowledge, it gives visible manifestation to works that surpass the ability of all nature. Thus, there are the wonderful cures of illnesses, there is the raising of the dead. . . . [A]nd what is more wonderful, there is the inspiration given to human minds, so that simple and untutored persons, filled with the gift of the Holy Spirit, come to possess instantaneously the highest wisdom and the readiest eloquence. When these arguments were examined [in Roman times], . . . in the midst of the tyranny of the persecutors, an innumerable throng of people, both simple and most learned, flocked to the Christian faith. In this faith there are truths preached that surpass every human intellect, the pleasures of the flesh are curbed; it is taught that the things of the world should be spurned. Now, for the minds of mortal men to assent to these things is the greatest of miracles, just as it is a manifest work of divine inspiration that, spurning visible things, men should seek only what is invisible. Now, that this has happened . . . as a result of the disposition of God, is clear from the fact that through many pronouncements of the ancient prophets God had foretold that He would do this. The books of these prophets are held in veneration among us Christians, since they give witness to our faith.

Guillaume d' Orange

THE CONQUEST OF ORANGE

Introduction by Constance Bouchard

During the twelfth century "vernacular" literature emerged for the first time, that is, literature written not in the Latin of the church or the schoolroom, but in the everyday spoken
language (early forms of French, German, Italian, and so on). Some of the most popular stories
were those now called epics, tales of adventure, war, conquest, and often death. Most of these
epics had as their heroes semi-legendary, semi-historical figures, usually noble lords and often
kings. By creating these larger-than-life characters and placing them in an imaginary past, the
authors were able to make comments on their own society.

These marvelous, vaguely-historical figures included King Arthur, Charlemagne, and
William of Orange, the hero of the following selection. William was based ultimately on a real
person, a great lord who had served Charlemagne for many years and finally retired to a
monastery, some three centuries before epics were created about him. There were more than
half a dozen different William of Orange epics written in the twelfth century, roughly linked
into a "cycle" of stories. This selection tells how William captured the castle of Orange, a real
city in southern France, located on the Rhone river, which, according to legend, became his
capital.

This particular story is set in the context of conflict between Christians and Muslims. The
southern part of France had been dominated by Muslims during the time of the real William, in
the eighth and ninth centuries, and in the twelfth century the French knights and nobles who
would have enjoyed this story most were also very interested in the conflict between those who
followed the two different religions. The twelfth century was the period of the Crusades, when
many French knights went to the Holy Land to try to conquer the Muslims who controlled the
region, and when many more French knights fought against Muslims in Spain. The person who
wrote this story had no trouble making the Muslims into the villains; clearly he saw little use for
religious tolerance.

As well as highlighting the differences between Christians and Muslims, as perceived by
Christians who actually knew very little about Islam, this story's plot turns on the power of love.
Romantic love, in which people alter their whole life-span after falling for someone, act more
nobly and more bravely because of the beloved's inspiration, and get happily married at the end,
may seem normal in America in the twenty-first century, but it was a real novelty in the twelfth
century. At the time the William of Orange stories were being written, the knights and nobles
who made up their audience mostly took spouses in marriages arranged for them by their

relatives. The presence and power of love in these stories, with its ability to bring together even a Christian and a Muslim, and to inspire both male and female into fearless action, thus had a distinctly subversive quality.

Although most of the stories in the William of Orange cycle were very serious, this one was intended to be funny. Certainly it has moments of tension and danger, but the basic plot of William creeping into a castle in disguise, and his nephew repeatedly blaming him for being about to get them all killed, would certainly have been humorous to those who read this tale or heard it being read. Its humor would not have undercut, and indeed would have strengthened, the author's ideas about courage, religion, and the roles and relations of men and women.

The Conquest of Orange

TRANSLATED BY JOAN M. FERRANTE

i

Listen my lords, and may God give you grace,
the glorious son of Holy Mary,
to a good song that I would offer you.
It is not a tale of pride or folly,
or deception plotted and carried out
but of brave men who conquered in Spain.
They know it well, who have been to St. Gilles,
who have seen the relics kept at Brioude,
the shield of William and the white buckler,
and Bertrand's too, his noble nephew.   10
I think that no clerk will belie me,
nor any writing that's found in a book.
They have all sung of the city of Nîmes,
which William holds among his possessions,
the great high walls and the rooms built of stone,
and the palace and the many castles
and by God, he had not yet won Orange!
There are few men who have told it truly,
but I shall tell what I learned long ago,
how Orange was destroyed and undone.   20
This William did, of the bold countenance.
He expelled the pagans from Almeria,
and the Saracens of Eusce and Pincernie,
those of Baudas and of Tabarie.
He took as his wife Orable the queen—
she had been born of a pagan race—
the wife of Tiebaut, king of Africa.

Guillaume d'Orange: *Four Twelfth-Century Epics* (Joan Ferrante, trans.), Columbia UP, 1991 (ISBN 0231-09634-8),
original pp. 141–195 ("Conquest of Orange" epic).

Then she turned to God, blessed Mary's son,
and founded churches and monasteries.
There are not many who could tell you of them.   30

ii

Hear me, my lords, noble knights and worthy,
if it please you to hear a good deed sung,
how Count William took and destroyed Orange
and took to wife the wise Lady Orable,
who had been Tiebaut of Persia's queen.
Before he was able to win her love,
he had, in truth, to suffer great pains,
many days he fasted, and waked many nights.

iii

It was in May, in the early summer,
the woods blossoming, and the meadows green,   40
the sweet waters withdrawing into streams
and the birds singing sweetly and soft.
One morning Count William arises,
and goes to the church to hear the service.
He comes out when the service is over
and mounts the palace of the heathen Otran,
whom he had conquered by his fierce courage.
He goes to look from the great windows
and gazes far out across the kingdom.
He sees the fresh grass and the rose gardens,   50
he hears the song-thrush and the blackbird sing,
then he remembers the joy and pleasure
that he used to feel when he was in France.
He calls Bertrand: "Sir nephew, come here.
We came out of France in great poverty,
we brought with us no harpers or minstrels,
or young ladies to delight our bodies.
We have our share of fine well-groomed horses,
and strong chain-mail and gilded helmets,
sharp, cutting swords and fine buckled shields,   60
and splendid spears fashioned of heavy iron,
and bread and wine and salted meat and grain;
but God confound the Saracens and Slavs
who leave us to sleep and rest here so long
for they have not yet crossed the sea in force,
to give us the chance to prove ourselves.
It tires me to stay so quiet here,
shut up so tight inside these walls,
as if we were all held as prisoners."
His mind is led astray in this folly,   70

but before the sun is hid or vespers sung,
he will be brought news of such a nature
that he'll be filled with anger and fury.

iv

William stands at the windows in the wind,
sixty of his Franks in attendance,
not one of them without new white ermine,
stockings of silk and cordovan sandals.
Most of them loose their falcons in the wind.
Count William, feeling great joy in his heart,
looks into the valley through the steep mountains;   80
he sees the green grass, the roses in bloom,
and the oriole and the blackbird in song.
He calls Guielin and Bertrand to his side,
his two nephews, whom he loves so well:
"Listen to me, worthy and valiant knights,
we came from France not very long ago;
if only we now had a thousand girls,
maidens from France, with graceful charming forms,
so that our barons might be entertained,
and I too might delight in making love;   90
that would be greatly to my liking.
We have enough fine chargers, swift and strong,
sturdy chain-mail and good shining helmets,
sharp, cutting spears and splendid heavy shields,
good swords whose hilts are fashioned of silver,
and bread and wine, cheeses and salted meat.
God confound the Saracens and Persians
who do not cross the sea to do battle.
Our stay inside here starts to weary me,
for I have no chance to test my courage."   100
He wanders distracted in his folly,
but the sun won't set nor will evening come,
before he is brought such a piece of news,
that it will make him both angry and sad.

v

William is at the windows on the wall,
with him there are a hundred Franks and more;
there is not one who is not clothed in ermine.
He looks below where the Rhone river roars
and to the East, where the roadway runs;
he sees some wretch emerge from the water;   110
it is Gilbert, from the city, Lenu.
He was captured on a bridge of the Rhone,
the Turks, shouting, brought him back to Orange.

Three years they held him in prison there,
until one morning as the day appeared,
when it was God's will that he should escape,
a Saracen untied him by the gate
and then began to beat and insult him.
When the knight had as much as he could bear,
he seized him by the hair and pulled him down;   120
with his huge fist, he struck him such a blow,
that it shattered both his chest and his spine.
Dead at his feet, he has thrown down his foe.
Down from the window, now, he throws himself,
he can no longer be restrained or held.
From there to Nîmes he comes without a stop,
he will report such tidings here today
to our barons, who talk now of trifles,
that will relieve William of his boredom
and bring delight with ladies in the nude.   130

vi
William the noble is at the window.
The fleeing captive has crossed the Rhone,
climbed the hills and gone down the valleys,
from there to Nîmes, he has not made a stop.
He enters the gates of the good city
and finds William beneath the full pine,
and, in his train, many excellent knights.
Beneath the pine, a minstrel is singing
an ancient song, of venerable age.
It is quite good and it pleases the count.   140
And now Gilbert begins to climb the steps;
William sees him and looks at him closely,
he is black and dirty and yet he's pale,
sickly and pallid, tired and thin.
He thinks he must be Saracen or Slav
who has been sent from across the sea
to bring him a message and take one back.
But then the poor wretch begins to greet him:
"May the Lord God who made both wine and grain,
and gives us light and brightness from heaven,   150
who made man and woman to walk and speak,
preserve William, the marquis of the short nose,
the flower of France and his noble knights,
the fighters whom I see assembled here!"
"My good friend and brother, may God bless you!
But tell us now, do not keep it hidden,
who taught you to call this William by name?"
"Sire," he answers, "you will hear the truth now;

inside Orange I have been a long time,
and could not find any way to escape,   160
until one morning as day was breaking,
it was Jesus' will that I be set free."
And William says: "God be praised for that!
But tell me now, do not hide it from me,
what is your name, in what land were you born?"
"Sire," he says, "you will soon hear the truth,
but I have suffered so much torment and pain,
I have waked through the nights and fasted all day,
it is four days since I have eaten at all."
And William says: "You will have all you wish."   170
The count then summons his chamberlains:
"Bring this man plenty of food to eat,
with bread and wine, mixed with spices and honey,
cranes and geese, and peacocks with pepper."
And this was done, as he had commanded.
When he has been richly entertained,
he sits willingly at the feet of the count
and begins to relate the news he brought.

vii

Count William has seen the strange messenger,
he summons him and then asks this question: 180
"Where were you born, friend, and in what country?
What is your name, where in France have you been?"
Gilbert replies, a most valiant knight:
"I am Guion's son, the Duke of Ardennes,
and of Vermendois, which he also holds.
Through Burgundy I came from Alemaigne,
I set sail on the waters of Lausanne,
but a wind caught me and a great tempest
and carried me to the port of Geneva.
Pagans captured me at Lyons on the Rhone   190
and led me off to the port at Orange.
There's no fortress like it from here to the Jordan;
the walls are high, the tower large and wide,
the courtyards, too, and the whole enclosure.
Twenty thousand pagans armed with lances,
seven score Turks, bearing standards—
the city of Orange is guarded well,
for they're afraid that Louis will take it,
and you, sweet lord, and the barons of France.
There's Aragon, a rich Saracen king,   200
the son of Tiebaut, of the land of Spain,
and lady Orable, a noble queen;
there is none so lovely from here to the East,

a beautiful body, slender and fine;
her skin is white, like a flower on the stem.
God, what good is her body or her youth,
she doesn't know God, our father almighty!"
"It's true," says William, "their power is great,
but by Him, in whom I have placed my faith,
I shall not bear shield or lance any more   210
if I do not manage to meet them soon."

viii

Count William has listened to the baron
who is sitting beside him on the step;
he addresses him and speaks with affection:
"Fair brother, friend, you have told quite a tale.
Did the Saracens keep you long in prison?"
"Yes, they did, sire, three years and fifteen days,
and there was no way for me to escape
until one morning when God gave us day,
a Saracen, evil and arrogant,   220
wanted to beat me, as he had each day.
I seized him by the hair on his forehead,
struck him so hard on the neck with my fist,
that I shattered all the bones of his throat.
Then I escaped through the window, alone,
so that not one of the enemy saw.
To Beaucaire, the port at Oriflor, came
Turks and Persians, the king of Aragon,
the elder son of King Tiebaut the Slav;
he is large and heavy and strong and tall,   230
his head is broad and his brow bound with iron,
his nails are long and pointed and sharp,
there is no tyrant like him under the world's cloak.
He murders our Christians and destroys them.
Whoever could win that city and tower
and put to death the treacherous villain,
he would have spent his labor very well."

ix

"Good brother, friend," says Count William the brave,
"Is Orange really as you have described?"
Gilbert answers: "It is even better.   240
If you could see the principal palace,
how high it is and enclosed all around,
as you look at it from any view;
if you were there the first day of summer,
you would hear the birds as they sing there then,

the falcons' cry and the moulting goshawks,
the horses' whinny and the braying mules
that entertain and delight the Saracens.
The sweet herbs smell most fragrant there,
spices and cinammon which he had planted.   250
There you might see the fair Lady Orable
who is the wife of Sir Tiebaut the Slav;
there is no one so fair in all Christendom,
nor in pagan lands wherever you seek.
Her body is lovely, slender and soft,
and her eyes change color like a moulting falcon,
but of what use is all her beauty
when she does not know God and his goodness?
A noble man could be well pleased with her,
she could be saved if she wished to believe."   260
Then William says: "By the faith of St. Omer,
good brother, friend, you sing her praises well.
But by Him who has all mankind to save,
I will not carry lance or shield again
if I don't win the lady and the city."

x

"Good brother, friend, is Orange then so rich?"
The fugitive answers: "God help me, my lord,
if you could see the palace of the city
with its many vaults and its palisades,
as it was built by Grifon of Almeria,   270
a Saracen of most marvelous vice.
No flower grows from here to Pavia
that is not painted there in gold artfully.
Within is Lady Orable, the queen,
the wife of King Tiebaut of Africa.
There is none so lovely in all pagandom,
her body is beautiful, slender and fine,
her skin is as white as the flower of the thorn,
her eyes bright and hazel and always laughing;
But what good is her gay spirit to her   280
when she doesn't know God, blessed Mary's son."
"You have set," William says, "great worth on her,
and by the faith that I owe to my love,
I shall eat no more bread made from flour,
no salted meat, I shall drink no more wine,
until I have seen how Orange is set.
And I must see that tower of marble,
and Lady Orable, the gracious queen.
Love of her has me so in its power,

that I could not describe or conceive it.   290
If I can't have her soon, I shall lose my life."
The fugitive says: "This idea is insane,
if you were now inside that palace
and could see the vast Saracen array,
God confound me, if I thought I should live
long enough to see such a thing achieved.
Best let it be, the whole idea is mad."

xi

Count William listens to the troubled words
that the fugitive has spoken to him.
He summons the people of his country: 300
"Give me advice, noble men of honor.
This poor wretch has praised a city to me,
I was never there, I don't know the land.
But the Rhone runs here, a swift, moving stream,
except for it I should have gone by now."
The fugitive says: "This whole plan is mad.
If you had a hundred thousand with swords,
with beautiful weapons and golden shields,
and you wished to engage the enemy,
if there'd been no water or obstacle   310
before you could even enter the gates,
a thousand blows of the sword would be struck
and belts would be torn and many shields pierced
and many fine men struck down in the streets.
Let it all be, it is madness to try."

xii

"Look here," William says, "You have disturbed me,
you have just told me about this city
that no count or king possesses its like
and you would prevent me from going there.
By St. Maurice, who is sought at Amiens,   320
I tell you, you shall accompany me,
and we shall not take horses or palfreys
or white chain-mail or helmets from Amiens,
no shield or lance or Poitevin spears—
but javelins, like greedy fugitives.
You have spoken enough Turkish in that land
and African, Basque and Bedouin tongues."
The wretch hears him, imagine how he feels—
he wishes he were at Chartres or Blois
or at Paris in the land of the king,   330
for he does not know how to get out of this.

xiii

Now William is angry and filled with wrath,
his nephew Bertrand undertakes to speak:
"Uncle," he says, "give up this madness,
if you were now in that city's palace
and you could look at those Saracen hordes,
you would be known by your bump and your laugh,
they would quickly suspect that you were a spy.
Then, I'm afraid, you'd be brought to Persia,
they would not feed you on bread or flour,   340
nor would they wait long before they killed you;
they would throw you into a stone prison,
and you wouldn't come out again in your lives
until King Tiebaut of Africa came
and Desramé and Golias of Bile,
they would sentence you however they wished.
If, because of love, you come to judgment,
the people of your kingdom will say
that you were cursed for the sight of Orable the queen."
"Look," says William, "I have no fear of that   350
for, by the apostle sought in Galicia,
I would far rather die and lose my life
than go on eating bread made from flour
or salted flesh and fermented wine.
Instead I shall see how Orange is set
and Gloriete with its marble tower
and lady Orable, the gracious queen.
The love of her torments and governs me—
a man in love is reckless and a fool."

xiv
                                                                              360
Now William is troubled about Orange,
his nephew Bertrand begins to chide him:
"Uncle," he says, "you'll bring shame on yourself
and dishonor, and have your limbs torn off."
"Look," says the count, "that is not what I fear,
a man who's in love is completely mad.
I would not give up, though I lose my limbs,
not for any man who might beg me to,
going to see how Orange is set,
and Lady Orable, so worthy of praise.
Love for her has so taken hold of me   370
I can't sleep in the night or take any rest,
I am unable to drink or to eat
or carry arms or to mount on my horse
or go to mass, or to enter a church."

He orders ink ground up in a mortar
and other herbs that the baron knew of;
he and Gilbert, who does not dare leave him,
paint their bodies in front and behind,
their faces and their chests, even their feet,
so they resemble devils and demons.   380
Guielin says: "By St. Riquier's body,
you have both been transformed by a miracle,
now you could wander throughout the world,
you wouldn't be recognized anywhere.
But, by the apostle who's sought in Rome,
I would not give up, though I lose my limbs,
going with you to see how it will be."
With the ointment he too is painted and swabbed;
there are the three all prepared to set forth,
they take their leave and depart the city.   390
"God," says Bertrand, "good and righteous father,
how we have been deceived and betrayed!
In what madness was this affair begun
which will bring us all dishonor and shame,
if God does not help, who must judge us all."

xv

William goes forth, the marquis of the fierce look,
with brave Gilbert and the proud Guielin.
Count Bertrand has already turned back
but these go on without further delay.
Below Beaucaire they have found the Rhone   400
and at Dourance they've crossed over it.
Thereabouts they begin to swim quietly,
they cross the Sorgues without barge or ship.
By Aragon, they have gotten across;
straight towards the walls and moats of Orange
the high halls and the fortified palace
adorned with golden pommels and eagles.
Inside they can hear the little birds sing,
the falcons cry and the moulting goshawks,
the horses whinny and the braying mules,   410
and the Saracens entertained in the tower,
the soft fragrance of spices and cinammon,
all the sweet herbs they have in plenty.
"God," says William, "who gave me life and breath,
what wealth there is in this wondrous city!"
How rich he must be who possesses it."
They do not stop until they reach the gate
and then Gilbert addresses the porter

in his own tongue, he speaks courteously:
"Open these gates, porter, let us come in,   420
we are interpreters from Africa
and men of King Tiebaut the Slav."
The porter says: "I have not heard of you.
What people are you who call me out there?
King Aragon is not yet awake,
and I do not dare to open the gate,
so much do we fear William of the short nose,
who captured Nîmes with such violent force.
You remain here, I shall go to the king;
if he commands, then I'll let you enter."   430
"Go right away," says the baron William,
"quickly so that we lose no more time."
The porter leaves without any delay,
he climbs the marble steps of the palace.
He finds Aragon seated by a pillar,
surrounded by his Saracens and Slavs.
Courteously he begins to address him:
"Sire," he says, "listen to this report:
at the gate there are three honorable Turks
who claim to be from Africa beyond the seas."   440
"Then go, good brother, and let them come in;
there are many things I should like to ask
about my lord who has waited so long."
And so he runs back to open the gate.
Now William has gotten inside Orange,
with him Gilbert and the worthy Guielin.
They will not get out once the gates are shut
before they have suffered distress and pain.

xvi

Now William has gotten inside Orange
with Guielin and the noble Gilbert.   450
They are disguised by alum and black dye,
so that they look like Saracen tyrants.
In the palace they find two Saracens,
they call to them and speak their idiom,
one tells the other: "They're from Africa,
today we shall hear some good news from there."
But Count William keeps walking straight ahead,
towards the palace of the Persian Tiebaut.
The columns and the walls are built of marble
and the windows sculpted of fine silver;   460
a gold eagle sparkles and shines.
The sun doesn't enter, nor a breath of wind.

"God," says William, "redeemer and father—
who ever saw such a splendid palace!
How rich he must be, the lord of this hall,
would it were God's will, who formed all mankind,
that I had with me my palatine Bertrand,
and all the ten thousand Frank warriors!
We would bury the unlucky Saracens.
I would kill a good hundred before noon." 470
He finds Aragon beside a column
and around him fifteen thousand Persians.
William is dead, if he can't deceive them.
Now you shall hear how he speaks to them:
"Emir and lord, noble and valiant knight,
Mohammed greets you and the God Tervagant."
Says the emir: "Baron, you may approach.
Where are you from?" "The African kingdom
of your father, the mighty king Tiebaut.
Yesterday morning as nones was sounded, 480
we got to Nîmes, the strong and rich city,
where we expected to find King Otran
and Sinagon and the tyrant Harpin.
But William had killed him, with his Frank troops;
our men were murdered, bleeding and torn.
He put the three of us in his prison, too,
but he is so rich in family and friends
that somehow we were allowed to escape.
We don't know how—may the devil take him!"
Aragon says: "How sad this makes me. 490
By Mohammed, in whom I believe,
if I had William in my power now,
he would be dead and suffering torment,
his bones and ashes scattered to the winds."
William hears him and he lowers his head.
He wishes that he were at Paris or Sens;
he calls on God, his merciful father:
"Glorious sire, who has formed all mankind,
who was born of the Virgin in Bethlehem,
if the three kings came in search of you 500
and if you were hung on the cross by tyrants,
and by the lance, you were pierced in the side—
Longinus did it, who could not see—
and blood and water ran down from the point;
he rubbed his eyes and the light was restored.
If this is true, just as I have told it,
guard our bodies against death and torment.
Don't let Saracens or Persians kill us!"

xvii

William is in the palace at the tower.
He calls his other companions to him   510
quietly, so the pagans cannot hear:
"My lords," he says, "we shall be in prison
if God does not help by His most holy name."
"Uncle William," Guielin answers him,
"Noble lord, sire, you came here seeking love,
you see Gloriete, the palace and tower,
why don't you ask where the ladies are kept.
You might well find a way to deceive them."
And the count says: "You are right, my young squire."
Now King Aragon begins to question him: 520
"Baron, when were you in Africa?"
"My dear lord, no more than two months ago."
"Did you see King Tiebaut of Aragon?"
"Yes, my good lord, when he was at Vaudon.
He embraced us and sent you this message,
that you maintain his honor and city.
Where is his wife? Will you show her to us?"
"Of course, my lords," says the king Aragon.
"There is none lovelier up to the clouds.
But barons," he adds, "I have need of my father;   530
the Franks are taking our castles and towers.
William is the one, with his two nephews.
But, by Mohammed's and Tervagant's faith,
if I now held William in my prison,
he would soon be burned in fire and coals,
his bones and ashes scattered through the air."
William hears him, he holds his head down
and wishes he could be at Reims or Laon.
He calls on God and His glorious name:
"Glorious father, who made Lazarus,   540
and became incarnate in the Virgin,
preserve my body from death and prison.
Don't let these evil Saracens kill us!"

xviii

Now William is in the noble palace;
pagans and Saracens call for water,
the tables are placed, they sit down to eat.
William sits too and his nephew Guielin;
they speak softly and hold their heads down,
they're in great fear that they will be captured.
King Aragon has them served splendidly.   550
They have plenty of bread and wine at the meal,

cranes and geese and well-roasted peacocks,
and other foods I cannot describe.
There is as much as anyone could wish.
When they have eaten and drunk to their pleasure,
the cup-bearers come to take up the cloths.
Pagan and Saracens start to play chess.
William hears all the palace resound,
which is sculpted of green marble and dark,
he sees the birds and lions depicted: 560
"God," says the count, "who was hung on the cross,
who ever saw so splendid a palace!
If it pleased God, who never deceives us,
that we had the palatine Bertrand here,
and the twenty thousand Franks with their arms,
the pagans would meet a bad end today.
By my head, I would kill eighty myself."

xix
King Aragon has summoned Count William
to sit beside him beneath a pillar
and in his ear he questions him softly: 570
"Noble Turk," he asks, "now tell me the truth,
what sort of man is William of the short nose,
who captured Nîmes with his powerful force
and murdered King Harpin and his brother?
He had you thrown into his prison, too."
And William answers: "You will hear the truth now.
He is so rich, in pride of possessions,
that he has no care for gold or silver;
instead he let us escape for nothing
except that he made us swear by our laws.   580
He sent you a message we cannot hide,
that you flee over seas to Africa,
you will not see the month of May go by
before he attacks with twenty thousand men;
your towers and columns will not save you,
your magnificent halls, nor your deep moats.
With iron clubs they will all be destroyed.
If he captures you, you will suffer torture.
You will hang from the gallows in the wind."
Aragon says: "What madness is this—   590
I shall send overseas to Africa,
my father will come with his mighty nobles,
with Golias and the king Desramé,
Corsolt of Mables, his brother Aceré,
and Clariau and the king Atriblez
and Quinzepaumes and the king Sorgalez,

the king of Egypt and King Codroez,
and King Moranz and the king Anublez,
and the prince of Sorgremont on the sea,
my uncle Borreaus and all his sons,   600
and the thirty kings who were born in Spain.
Each one will bring twenty thousand armed men
and we will fight at the walls and the moats;
William will be dead and go to his end
and his nephews will be hung from the gallows."
William hears him and almost loses his mind;
between his teeth, he answers him softly:
"By God," he says, "you pig, you are lying,
instead three thousand Turks will be killed,
before you conquer or hold Nîmes in fief."   610
If he had arms to equip himself now,
he would hold all the palace in terror
for he can no longer control his rage.

xx

Now William is in the great stone hall:
"King Aragon," he begins his address,
"Sire," he says, "will you show me the queen
whom Africa's emperor seems to love so?"
Aragon says: "It is madness in him,
for he is old and his beard is snow-white,
and she is a young and beautiful girl,   620
there is none so fair in all pagandom.
In Gloriete he enjoys his loves—
better if he loved Soribant of Venice,
a young bachelor who still has his first beard,
who knows how to live with arms and pleasure
better than Tiebaut of Slavonia.
An old man is mad to love a young girl,
he is soon cuckolded and driven mad."
When William hears him he begins to laugh.
"Tell me," asks William, "you don't love her at all?"   630
"Not I, certainly, God curse the woman!
I only wish she were in Africa
or at Baudas, in Almeria."

xxi

In the palace is William the noble,
and Gilbert too and the mighty Guielin;
they go out through the center of the hall,
led by an unsuspecting pagan,
to the queen who is so loved by the king.
Better for them if they would return

beyond the Rhone and go back to Nîmes; 640
before evening comes or the sun can set,
unless God acts with his noble power,
they will suffer what will cause them sorrow.
At Gloriete, they have now arrived,
of marble are its pillars and walls,
and the windows sculpted in fine silver,
the golden eagle, resplendent and bright,
the sun cannot enter, nor does the wind blow;
it is beautifully done, pleasant and charming.
In one part of the chamber, inside, 650
there is a pine grown in such a way,
as you shall hear, if that is your wish:
the branches are long and the leaves are large,
the flower it bears wond'rously fair;
it is white and blue, and even red.
There's an abundance of carob-trees there,
spices, cinnamon, galingale, and incense,
sweet fragrances, of hyssop and allspice.
There sits Orable, the African lady,
dressed in a gown of marvelous stuff, 660
tightly laced on her noble body,
and sewn along the sides with rich silks,
and Rosiane, the niece of Rubiant,
makes a gentle breeze with a silver fan.
She is more white than snow in the sunlight,
she is more red than the most fragrant rose.
William sees her and his blood turns cold,
he greets her nobly and courteously.
"May that God save you, in whom we believe!"
The queen answers: "Baron, please approach me. 670
Mohammed save you, on whom the world depends."
Beside her, she has them sit on a bench,
that is sculpted in silver and gold.
Now they can speak somewhat of their wishes.
"God," says William, "this is paradise here!"
Says Guielin: "I've seen nothing finer,
I would like to spend all my life here.
There would never be a reason to leave."

xxii

Now William is seated in Gloriete,
and Gilbert and the worthy Guielin, 680
near the ladies in the shade of the pine.
There sits Orable, of the bright face,
wearing a piece of ermine fur
and underneath a samite tunic,

tightened with laces on her lovely body.
William sees her, all his body trembles.
"God," says William, "it is Paradise here!"
"If God would help me," Guielin responds,
"I would remain here most willingly.
I would not seek either food or sleep."   690
Then the noble lady begins to ask:
"Where are you from, noble and gentle knight?"
"Lady we are from the Persian kingdom,
from the land of your husband, Tiebaut.
Yesterday morning, when day was breaking,
we were at Nîmes, that marvelous city,
we expected to find people of our race,
King Sinagon and Otran and Harpin,
but Fierebrace had killed all three of them.
The Franks captured us at the gates of the city   700
and led us before the palatine,
but he is so rich and supported by friends
that he does not care for silver or gold.
Instead he let us escape in this way:
first we had to swear an oath by our laws
and carry This message which I bring to you,
that you must flee to the Persian kingdom,
for you will not see the month of April pass
before he comes with twenty thousand men.
The palace and the walls will not save you,   710
nor the broad halls, not the strong palisades,
with iron clubs they will all be destroyed.
If he captures Aragon the Arab,
your stepson, the prince that you love so much,
he will make him die an unpleasant death,
by hanging or burning in fire and flame."
The lady hears him and sighs tenderly.

xxiii

The lady listens to the strange message,
then she asks them, she is anxious to know:
"My lord barons, I am versed in your tongue.   720
What sort of a man is William Fierebrace,
who captured Nîmes, the palace and the halls
and killed my men, and is still threatening me?"
"Indeed," says the count, "he has a fierce heart,
his fists are huge and his arm is mighty.
There is no man from here to Arabia
who, if William strikes him with his sharp sword,
would not be hacked apart, body and arms,
straight to the ground drives that sword as it cuts."

"Indeed," says the lady, "this is distressing.   730
By Mohammed, he will hold great domains.
Happy the lady who possesses his heart."
Then the villainous pagans come in a crowd;
today William will find more trouble
than he has encountered in all his life.
May God protect him against loss and harm!

xxiv
Now William has climbed inside the tower,
and Gilbert and the worthy Guielin;
beside the ladies under the pine,
he sits chatting softly with the queen.   740
The treacherous pagans are massed outside
to watch the barons and look at them.
Unless God helps, who was hung on the cross,
today William will be badly abused,
for there is a pagan, Salatré—
may He confound him who must save us all—
one whom the count had captured at Nîmes,
but one evening the scoundrel had escaped
and had fled through the moats and found his way,
so that he could not be recaptured or found.   750
He causes terrible trouble for William,
as you are about to hear recounted.
To Aragon, the scoundrel now comes,
into his ear he pours out a whole tale:
"By Mohammed, sire, arouse your barons.
We can avenge now the fierce cruelty
that would have struck me at the city of Nîmes.
You see that strong figure in the tower?
That is William, the marquis of the short nose,
and his nephew is the other young knight,   760
the third one, who carries the heavy club,
is the marquis who escaped from here.
To deceive you, they have donned this disguise,
for they hope to capture this good city."
Aragon asks: "Do you tell me the truth?"
"Sire," he answers, "you'll be sorry if you doubt me.
That is William who had me imprisoned,
he would have had me hanging in the wind
if Mohammed had not protected me.
This is the day that he'll be rewarded."   770
Now hear me tell, noble barons and good,
for the love of God who hung on the cross,
of that villain, what evil he worked.
He takes a tunic, made of pure gold,

and hurls it straight into William's face,
it strikes William just above the nose,
he is discovered, his color comes off;
his skin is white like a summer flower.
When William sees this, he almost goes mad,
throughout his body the blood runs cold. 780
He calls on God, the king in majesty:
"Glorious father, who must save us all,
who deigned to become flesh in the Virgin,
all for the people whom You wished to save,
You gave up Your body to pain and torment,
to be wounded and injured upon the cross,
as this is all true, lord, in Your goodness,
guard my body from death and destruction.
Don't let the Slavs and Saracens kill us!"

xxv

When Aragon hears what the Slav tells him, 790
that he recognizes the three companions,
he rises to his feet and begins to speak:
"Sir William, your name is well known here,
you'll be sorry you crossed the Rhone, by Mohammed!
You will all be put to dreadful death,
your bones and ashes scattered in the wind.
I would not, for a dungeon filled with gold,
rescue you from death and burning to coals."
William hears him, his color like ashes;
he wishes he were at Reims or Laon; 800
Guielin sees that they can't hide any longer,
he wrings his hands and tears at his hair.
"God," says William, "by Your most holy name,
glorious Father who made Lazarus
and in the Virgin took on human form,
who saved Jonah in the belly of the whale
and Daniel the prophet in the lion's den,
who granted pardon to Mary Magdalene,
brought the body of St. Peter to Rome,
and converted his companion, St. Paul, 810
who was, at that time, a very cruel man,
but then became one of the believers,
together with them he walked in processions,
as this is true, sire, and we believe it,
protect us against death and foul prison.
Don't let treacherous Saracens kill us!"
He has a stick, large and sturdy and long;
with his two hands, he raises it high
and brings it down on the false Salatré,

who had denounced him to King Aragon.   820
Right through his head comes the blow of the club,
so that his brains pour out on the ground.
"Montjoy!" he cries, "strike ahead, barons!"

xxvi
William has all the palace in terror.
Before the king he has killed a pagan.
Count William has found himself a club
that had been brought there to make a fire.
He runs over to it, swiftly and sweating,
grabs it in his fists and lifts it high.
He strikes Baitaime, the reckless pagan,   830
a vigorous blow of the club on his skull,
which causes his brains to fly from his head.
Before the king he has struck him dead.
And Gilbert, too, goes to strike Quarré,
he shoves his club into his stomach
and forces a good part of it out the side.
He throws him down before the pillar, dead.
"Montjoy!" he cries, "barons, come, strike ahead!
Since we are certainly destined to die,
let's sell ourselves high as long as we last!"   840
Aragon hears; he thinks he will go mad.
Aloud he cries: "Barons, capture these men!
By Mohammed, they will be killed straightway
and tossed and thrown into the Rhone,
or burned in fire and scattered to the wind."
Guielin shouts at them "Barons stand aside,
for by the apostle we seek at Rome,
you won't take me without paying for it."
In fierce anger, he brandishes his stick.
Count William begins to strike with his club   850
and Gilbert with his iron-bound cudgel,
mighty blows the noble barons strike;
fourteen Turks they have thrown to their deaths
and so terrified all the others
that, striking, they chase them out through the gates.
Then the towers are bolted and shut,
and by the great chains, the bridge is hauled up.
May God now help, who was hung on the cross!
For William is in a dangerous spot,
and Gilbert and the worthy Guielin,   860
In Gloriete where they have been trapped,
and the Saracens, the raging cowards,
attack them from outside with no respite.

xxvii

The Saracens are fierce and arrogant,
they attack them by hundreds and thousands,
throwing their lances and piercing steel darts.
The Franks defend themselves like noble knights,
casting those pigs into moats and channels,
more than fourteen have already fallen.
The most fortunate has his neck splintered.   870
Aragon sees it and begins to rage,
from sorrow and anger he is nearly mad.
With a loud, clear voice, he begins to shout:
"Are you up there, William of the fierce look?"
The count answers: "Certainly I am here.
By my prowess I have found good lodging,
may God help me, who was raised on the cross!"

xxviii

Now William has entered Gloriete
and begun to speak to the Saracens:
"Damned be he who thinks he can hide!   880
I entered this city in order to spy
and I have deceived and tricked you so well
that I have chased you out of Gloriete.
Henceforth you will be guardians of this tower,
protect it well, your reward will be high!"
Aragon hears him and begins to rage.
He summons the Saracens and pagans:
"Quickly to arms, now, my noble knights.
The assault must now be begun in force.
Whoever captures this William for me   890
will bear the standard for all my kingdom;
all my treasures will be open to him."
When his men hear this they are pleased and encouraged,
the craven flatterers run for their arms
and attack William in front and behind.
The count sees them and nearly goes mad.
He invokes God, the true and righteous judge.

xxix

Now William is angered and sorrowful,
and brave Guielin and the noble Gilbert.
At Gloriete, where they are trapped inside,   900
they are sought by all of that pagan race,
they throw their lances and piercing steel darts.
William sees them and nearly loses his mind.
"Nephew Guielin, what is holding us back?

Never can we hope to return to France,
if God does not help us, with his power,
we shall not see cousins or family."
But Guielin of the graceful body:
"Uncle William, you're speaking to no end.
Because of your love you made your way here;   910
there is Orable, the African lady,
and none so fair alive in this world.
Go now and sit beside her on the bench,
put both your arms around her lovely form
and don't be slow to embrace and kiss her,
for by the apostle penitents seek,
we shall not have the value of that kiss
unless it costs twenty thousand silver marks
and great suffering to all our people."
"God," says William, "your words so incite me   920
that I can barely keep my reason."

xxx

Count William is now angry and enraged,
and Gilbert and the worthy Guielin;
inside Gloriete where they have been trapped
with the Saracen pagans pressing hard;
they defend themselves like skillful knights,
throwing down clubs and huge heavy cudgels.
Now the queen begins to counsel them:
"Barons," she says, "Franks, give yourselves up.
The villainous pagans hate you fiercely,   930
you will soon see them climbing the steps,
you'll all be dead, murdered, and dismembered."
William hears her, his mind is distraught.
He runs to the chamber beneath the pine
and wildly begins to beg the queen:
"My lady," he says, "please give me armor,
for the love of God who was hung on the cross!
For, by St. Peter, if I live through this,
you will be richly rewarded for it."
The lady hears him and weeps with pity.   940
She runs to the chamber without delay,
to a coffer, which she quickly opens.
She takes from it a good golden shirt of mail
and a bright golden helmet, set with jewels;
William runs to take the things from her,
and to receive what he has so desired.
He dons the hauberk and laces the helm,
and Lady Orable girds on the sword
which belonged to her lord, Tiebaut the Slav.

She had not wished any man to have it, 950
not even Aragon, who wanted it so,
and was the son of her wedded husband.
At his neck she hangs a strong polished shield,
on it a lion wearing a gold crown.
In his fist he holds a good, heavy lance,
its standard held by five golden nails.
"God," says William, "how well armed I am now.
For God, I beg you to think of the others!"

xxxi

When Guielin sees that his uncle is armed,
he too runs into the lady's chamber 960
and calls to her, sweetly begging her aid:
"Lady," he asks, "by St. Peter of Rome,
please give me arms, we have such great need."
"My child," she says, "you are so very young,
if you live long you will be a brave man.
But the Vavars and Hongars hate you to death."
In her chamber she takes out a mail-shirt
which Isaac of Barcelone had forged—
there was no sword that could pierce that mail.
He puts it on and his uncle is glad; 970
he laces the Alfar of Babylon's helm,
the first king who had held that city.
There is no sword that can destroy it
or knock off a stone or ruby flower.
She girds the sword of Tornemont of Valsone
which was stolen from him by thieves at Valdonne,
and then sold to Tiebaut at Voirconbe;
he gave a thousand besants for it
for he hoped to pass it on to his son.
She girds it at his side, the straps are long, 980
at his neck she hangs a large, round shield,
and hands him a lance, my lady of Valronne,
the handle is large and the blade is long.
He is well armed and Gilbert as well.
Today Gloriete will be contested.

xxxii

William and his nephew are now well armed,
and Gilbert, too, and they all rejoice.
On his back a strong, double shirt of mail,
on his head they lace a green barred helmet,
then they gird a sword of steel at his side, 990
and they hang a quartered shield from his neck.
But before he takes the good sharp spear,

the evil pagans have advanced so far
that they are beginning to mount the steps.
Count William goes to strike down Haucebier
and Gilbert, the gate-keeper, Maretant,
and Guielin goes to attack Turfier.
These three pagans do not escape death;
they smash the tips of the pointed spears
so that the splinters shoot up toward the sky.   1000
They are now forced to rely on their swords
which they are anxious to try out and prove.
Count William has drawn his sword of steel,
he strikes a pagan across the back
and cuts him down like an olive branch.
Down into the palace the two halves fall.
And Gilbert goes to strike Gaifier
and sends his head flying into the palace.
Guielin too is not at all frightened.
He holds his sword and grasps his good shield;   1010
whoever he meets is destined to die.
Pagans see him and begin to retreat,
the craven flatterers take to flight.
The Franks chase them, the noble warriors,
more than fourteen they've already destroyed,
and terrified all the others so
that they drive them back out through the gates.
The Franks run to shut them and bolt them;
by the great chains they have pulled up the bridge
and attached it fast against the tower.   1020
Now let God think of them who judges all!
Aragon sees it and his mind rages.

xxxiii

Now William is sorrowful and angry
and Gilbert and the worthy Guielin;
they are pressed hard by the pagan masses
who throw their lances and well-turned darts
and beat down the walls with clubs of iron.
William sees it, he is consumed by rage.
"Nephew Guielin," he asks "what shall we do?
Never, it seems, will we return to France.   1030
Nor will we kiss nephews and relatives again."
"Uncle William, this is useless talk,
for by the apostle who's sought at Rome,
I'll sell myself high before we give up."
They climb down the steps of the tower
and strike the pagans on their rounded helmets;
they cut straight through their chests and their chins

until seventeen lie dead in the sand.
The most fortunate has his lungs cut out.
When the pagans see this, their hearts tremble,   1040
they cry aloud to mighty Aragon:
"Make a truce with them, we'll never get in."
Aragon hears them, nearly dissolved in rage,
he swears by Mohammed he will make them pay.

xxxiv

Aragon sees the pagans hesitate,
he calls them graciously and then he says:
"Sons of bitches, pigs, you'll be sorry you came.
You'll never hold fiefs or marches from me,
you can look for them in fiercer fighting."
And so they do, the miscreant swine,   1050
they throw their darts and miserable lances,
with iron clubs they beat down the walls.
William sees it, nearly mad with fury:
"Nephew Guielin, now what can we do?
We are all dead, and doomed to destruction."
"Uncle William, you're talking like a fool,
for by the apostle we seek in the ark,
I'll make them pay before pagans get me."
The points of their spears have all been shattered,
but each of the three picks up an axe   1060
which the noble Lady Orable gave them.
They go out again, bearing new weapons
and strike the pagans on their red targes,
cutting straight through to their faces and chests.
More than fourteen now lie on the marble,
some of them dead, the others unconscious.
Never did three men do so much damage.
Aragon sees it and nearly goes mad.

xxxv

When Aragon sees his people so pressed,
then he grieves and almost bursts with anger.   1070
In a clear voice, he cries out to the Franks:
"Are you up there, William of the fine body,
the son of Aimeri of Narbonne the great?
Do something for me that I greatly desire,
leave Gloriete, the palace, right now
and go away healthy, safe and alive,
before you lose all your limbs and your blood.
If you refuse, you will suffer for it.
By Mohammed, in whom I believe,
here in this place, a great pyre will be built,   1080

you will all be burned and roasted in there."
William answers: "Your talk is for nothing.
We have plenty of bread and wine and cheese
and salted meat and wines, honeyed and spiced,
and white hauberks and green shining helmets,
excellent swords with hilts of silver,
sharp piercing spears and good heavy shields
and lovely ladies to entertain us.
I shall not leave while I am yet alive,
and soon the noble king Louis will know,   1090
my brother Bernard, who is hoary and white,
and the warrior, Garin of Anseune,
and the mighty duke Bueves of Commarch,
my nephew Bertrand, who is brave and valiant,
whom we just left behind us at Nîmes.
Each one of them, whenever he wishes,
can well send twenty thousand warriors.
When they find out what is happening here,
how we are established here within,
they will come to our aid most graciously   1100
with as many men as they can gather.
I tell you, these walls will be no defense,
nor this palace, where gold shines in splendor;
you will see it shattered in a thousand parts.
If they capture you, it will not go easy,
you will be hooked and hung in the wind."
Aragon says: "We shall grieve all the more."
Pharaon speaks, the king of Bonivent,
"Emir, sire, you are not worth a glove.
By Mohammed, you have very little sense.   1110
Your father was worthy and valiant,
and he left this city to you to defend,
and the palace, Gloriete, as well.
These three scoundrels who are challenging you
have been killing your men and your people;
by Mohammed, you are not worth much
if you can't burn them in stinking Greek fire."

xxxvi

"Pharaon, sir," says the king Aragon,
give me better counsel, for Mohammed's sake,
you see Gloriete, the palace and tower,   1120
whose foundation is set so deep and strong.
All the people from here to Moncontor
could not make any opening in it.
Where the devil would we get the coals?

We have no wooden branches or sticks.
Those three pigs got in there by their arrogance,
but they won't get out in seven years."

xxxvii

"Pharaon, sir," says the king Aragon,
"for Mohammed, whose laws we uphold,
you must advise me immediately.   1130
Behold Gloriete, the splendid palace
the foundation is laid in solid rock.
All the men from here to the port of Vauquois
could not make a hole in its walls in a month.
From what devils could we get the coals
when we haven't a twig of wood or laurel?
In their arrogance those three got inside,
but in seven years, they will not get out."
Now a pagan, Orquenois steps forward,
his beard is black, but his hair white with age,   1140
his eyebrows white, if I judge them rightly.
In a loud voice, he cries out three times:
"Emir, sire, will you listen to me,
and tell me if it would be worth my while
to deliver William the Frank to you
so that you might hold him in your prison?"
Aragon answers: "Yes, by my faith.
Ten mules laden with the best Spanish gold
I would give to one who could tell me that."
Orquenois says: "Then listen to me.   1150
If you will give me your promise straightway,
I shall do it, whatever may happen."
Aragon says: "I swear this to you,
and I pledge faithfully here and now
that when you wish you shall have those riches."
The pagan replies: "I give you my word."

xxxviii

Orquenois says: "By Mohammed, sweet lord,
I shall tell you how to take him with guile:
there is Gloriete, the marble tower,
it foundation set well in the stone.   1160
It was built by Grifaigne of Almeria,
a Saracen of great cleverness.
You never knew what tricks they had designed:
Beneath the earth, a solitary vault,
a portcullis into your palace.
Take a thousand Turks and go there yourself

to lay a siege at the front of the tower
and attack at the same time from behind.
William will soon be dead and in torment."
Aragon says: "By Mohammed, that's true.   1170
You'll be rich for this, by my lord Apollo!"

xxxix
When Aragon has learned of this secret,
that there is a cave in the earth beneath him,
his joy is such that it makes his heart leap.
He takes a thousand Turks, their helmets laced,
and another thousand he leaves in front
to keep up the siege of Guielin and William;
the others turn round and go quickly
not stopping until they reach the entrance,
carrying candles and lanterns along.   1180
They enter the cave, that foul hostile race.
The honorable knights know nothing of them
until they're already inside the palace.
William is the first to find out they are there.
"God," says the count, "glorious in heaven,
we are all dead and delivered to pain."
Guielin says: "By St. Hilaire's body,
as God helps me, Orable has betrayed us.
May God confound the whole Saracen race!"

xl
Count William sees the palace being filled   1190
with Saracens who come there in anger;
he sees the hauberks and the helmets shine.
"God," says the count, "who never deceives us,
we are all dead and doomed to destruction."
"In faith, my good lord," answers Guielin,
"we were betrayed by Orable the fair.
May God confound pagans and Saracens!
This is the day that we must meet our end.
Let us help ourselves, as long as we can,
for we have no friends or relatives here."   1200
Count William brandishes the sword of steel,
in fury he moves to strike a pagan
back-handed and cuts him straight through the middle.
The pagans are terrified by this blow.
They rush at him enraged and distressed.
They defend themselves like emboldened knights;
he strikes great blows, the count palatine.
The assault is fierce and the slaughter great,
but it won't end until they're defeated.

No battle was ever fought so well.   1210
In their defense they have killed thirty Turks.
Who cares, if they can never finish them!
The pagans and Saracens lay hold of him,
Turks and Persians and the Almoravi,
Acoperts, Esclamors and Bedouins;
by Mohammed they swear vengeance will be had.
They will avenge the death of their friends.

xli

William is captured by deadly treason
and with him Gilbert and the brave Guielin.
The Saracen villains have them in their hands   1220
and swear by Mohammed to take revenge.
They send twenty boys into the city
to dig a ditch that will be wide and deep,
and to fill it with kindling wood and twigs
for they intend to grill our barons.
Orable comes, she is fair of visage,
and addresses her stepson Aragon:
"My friend," she says, "give these prisoners to me,
I shall place them in my deepest dungeon,
where toads and adders will feed on them   1230
and small serpents will devour them."
"My lady, queen," says the king Aragon,
"you were the cause of this trouble
when you armed these treacherous swine up there.
Damned be the man who would give them to you!"
The lady hears him and trembles with rage.
"You'll be sorry for that, you bastard pig!
By Mohammed, whom I praise and adore,
if it were not for these other barons,
I would strike you on the nose with my fist.   1240
Get yourself out of my tower quickly,
if you stay longer you will regret it."
She addresses the treacherous villains:
"Vile thieves," she says, "put them in your prison
until Tiebaut returns from Valdon,
and Desramé and Golias the blond.
They will take the vengeance they desire."
"I swear it, lady," says King Aragon,
William is cast into the deep dungeon,
and Guielin and the valiant Gilbert.   1250
For a while we must let our barons be;
when it is time we will come back to them.
Now we must sing of the pagan people.

xlii

King Aragon does not rest with his deed,
he sends his messengers over the seas
and they depart, without pause or halt,
from here to the Rhone they don't rest or stop,
and there they embark on a galley,
on the ship of Maudoine of Nubie.
It is artfully covered with silk,   1260
and does not fear a storm or temptest.
They lift their anchor and hoist their sails,
they take to sea, leave the city behind,
they glide and skim and they steer and they sail,
they have a good wind to carry them straight.
When they reach the port beneath Almeria,
they drop anchor and lower their sails.
Mounting their horses, they still do not stop.
They do not pause or rest from their ride
until they reach the African city.   1270
They dismount in the shade of an olive
and begin to climb to the great stone hall.
They find Tiebaut and his pagan nation
and greet him as Saracen custom bids:
"That Mohammed, who holds all in his power,
preserve King Tiebaut of Esclavonie!
Your son, of the bold look, sends you this plea,
that you come to his aid with all your knights.
He has captured William, I'll hide nothing,
the son of Aimeri, from Narbonne the rich,   1280
inside Orange, the well-protected city;
in disguise he had entered the town,
intending to take it as he had Nîmes
and make love to Lady Orable.
But their devilish scheme did not succeed.
They gave us a hard time from Gloriete
which he managed to hold for seven days;
if it hadn't been for the underground cave
whose stones are set beneath the palace,
you would no longer possess Orable,   1290
your wife, who is such a noble lady.
But Mohammed sent you aid in your need,
we have him now in a lonely prison
from which he will never escape alive.
Vengeance will be taken as you will it."
When Tiebaut hears this he begins to laugh,
he summons the people of his empire.
"Now quickly to arms, noble knights and free!"
and they obey without any delay,

mounting horses from Russia and Puglia.   1300
When Tiebaut leaves the African city,
he takes with him pagans of Almeria
and others from Suite and Esclavonie.
At the head, before him, are sixty thousand.
They don't pause or rest till they reach the sea.
In little time the ships are prepared
with wine and meat and biscuits and grain.
They embark quickly, that Saracen race,
raise their anchors and hoist their sails.
The wind blows hard and drives them straight on,   1310
they reach the sea; they are on their way.
Then might you hear such horns and trumpets,
horses neighing and greyhounds barking,
braying of mules and whinnying chargers,
sparrow-hawks crying out on their perches.
You might hear those sounds from a great distance.
Eight days they sail, on the ninth they arrive,
but before they reach Orange the rich,
Tiebaut will know such sorrow and anger,
as he has not felt in his life before.   1320
For he will lose his fortified city
and his wife, the elegant Orable.

xliii

William is deep inside the prison,
Gilbert too and the noble Guielin.
"God," says the count, "Father and redeemer,
we are dead and abandoned to torment!
God, if only King Louis knew of it,
and my brother Bernard, hoary and white,
and Garin the mighty, of Anseune,
and Bueves the great warrior of Commarch,   1330
and my nephew, Bertrand, valiant and brave,
whom we left behind at the city of Nîmes,
and all twenty thousand fighting Franks.
We could derive great comfort from their aid."
Guielin says, the knight of gracious bearing:
"Uncle William, there's no point to such words.
Send for Orable, the African's lady,
to help, for the love she bears her lover!"
"God," says William "you have taunted me so,
it will not take much for my heart to burst."   1340

xliv

Now William is angry and depressed
and Gilbert too, and the worthy Guielin,

inside the prison where they await death.
But while they are lamenting their lot,
Orable suddenly appears at their cell.
When she sees the counts, she begins to speak:
"Listen to me, noble, valiant knights,
pagans and Saracens hate you unto death.
They intend to hang you tonight or tomorrow."
"We can do nothing, lady," says Guielin,   1350
"but consider, noble, gentle lady,
if we could be let out of this dungeon,
I would become your man by oath and vow
and happily I would render service
whenever you, noble lady, might wish."
"But," says William, "it is she who betrayed us,
because of her we are in this dungeon."
The lady hears him and breathes a sigh.

xlv

"My lord baron," says the gracious Orable,
"by Mohammed, you accuse me wrongly.   1360
It was I who armed you in that tower;
if you could keep fighting in the palace
until word reaches Louis, the son of King Charles,
and Sir Bernard of Brabant and the others,
and Aimeri and all your magnificent line,
the treacherous swine would not know of it
until they had reached the marvelous tower,
and then they'd be able to free this land,
its narrow passes, its fords and gorges."
Guielin replies: "Lady, you've spoken well.   1370
If we were now let out of this prison,
I should be your man the rest of my life."
"By my faith," Orable the queen answers,
"if I thought that my pains would thus be repaid,
if William Fierebrace promised to take me,
I would set all three of you free
and would swiftly become a Christian."
William hears her, his spirit's restored.
"Lady," he says, "I shall give you my gage,
I swear this to you by God and St. James,   1380
and by the apostle we seek in the ark."
"Then," says the lady, "I require no more."
She unlocks all the doors of the prison
and they leave it, valiant men;
each of them rejoices in his heart.

xlvi

Now the lady has received the counts' oaths,
and set them free from their prison;
she leads and guides them into Gloriete.
Up in the palace, they sit down to dine.
When they have all been richly feasted, 1390
the noble lady addresses them thus:
"My lords, barons, listen to me now.
I have taken you out of your prison,
I have led you into my palace,
but I do not know how you will escape.
What I have in mind, I had best tell you:
beneath us here, there is a secret cave
which no man yet born of woman knows,
except my ancestor who had it dug;
from here to the Rhone a tunnel was carved. 1400
If you manage to send a messenger
to Count Bertrand and the other barons,
they might come to speak to you underground,
and the infidel pagans would not know
until they had entered the tiled palace
and begun to strike with their broad swords.
In this way they could set the city free
and all its passes, its gorges and moats."
And William says: "My lady, that is so.
But where can we find a messenger." 1410

xlvii

"Nephew Guielin," Count William then says,
from here to Nîmes do not stop or pause,
you must tell your brother Bertrand of us
and bring him to our aid with all his men."
"Uncle William," says Guielin, "what the devil—
may God help me, this must be a joke.
For by the faith I owe to St. Stephen,
I would rather die in this lovely tower
than in sweet France or at Aix-la-chapelle."

xlviii

"Nephew Guielin," says the noble William, 1420
"you must find your way through the cave below,
not stop for a moment from here to Nîmes,
and tell the palatine Bertrand for me
to bring me help immediately."
"Uncle William, there is no point to all this;
I would not desert you, to save my limbs.
I would rather die inside this tower

than in sweet France among my relatives.
Send Gilbert of Flanders instead."
"Will you go, brother?" asks the good William.   1430
And the baron replies: "I shall go, indeed,
and carry your message faithfully."
"Go, then, good brother, I commend you to Jesus,
and tell the palatine Bertrand for me,
that he must help without any delay.
If he does not, by God the redeemer,
he will never see his uncle again."

xlix

When the messenger hears that he must go,
then he begins to rage and wonder
how he can ever escape from there.   1440
"I've never been there, I don't know where to go."
But the lady says: "I shall guide you there.
You need not fear any man born of woman,
except Jesus Christ, the almighty lord."
Next to a pillar she has a stone moved,
which measures a fathom in length and width.
"My brother," she says, "you can enter here.
At its head, you will find three pillars,
formed and designed with vaulted archways."
He leaves them and begins to wander,   1450
not knowing where, underneath the city.
Count William accompanies him quite far
with lady Orable and baron Guielin.
They do not stop until the three pillars;
through their midst, he reaches the outside
and comes to the Rhone where he finds a boat;
then he moves softly across the water.
Count William has already turned back
with Guielin and Orable of the bright face;
All three of them have entered Gloriete.   1460
It would have been better if they had gone on
and descended to the dungeon below,
for not a thing have they done and plotted
that was not overheard by a pagan
who goes to tell it to King Aragon.

l

This Saracen is evil and deceitful,
he goes to denounce them to King Aragon;
as soon as he sees him, he starts to speak:
"Emir and lord, grant me peace and listen
to what your stepmother has been plotting   1470

with the captives whom you held in your prison.
She has taken them all out of the dungeon
and conducted them up to the palace;
in Gloriete they sat down to a meal."
Aragon asks: "Is this true, messenger?"
"Sire," he answers, "I am not a liar,
I have seen them taking secret counsel
and kissing and embracing one another.
She loves them more, and William in bed,
than your father or the king Haucebier."   1480
Aragon hears and almost loses his mind;
he summons his Saracens and Slavs.
"Barons," he says, "give me counsel on this,
tell me in what way I ought to proceed
against my stepmother who has shamed me,
disgraced me and dishonored my father."

li

Aragon says: "Good and powerful knights,
by Mohammed, gather up all your arms.
Whoever now takes armor and weapons
will pay for it before we capture them."   1490
His men answer: "Just as you command."
Fifteen thousand men rush to arm.
God, what trouble when William finds out,
and Lady Orable and brave Guielin.
In Gloriete where they are hidden,
they play at chess, in all confidence;
they suspect nothing, the noble counts,
when the Slavs and Saracens fall on them.

lii

Aragon finds William beneath the pine,
and Lady Orable and bold Guielin;   1500
the palatine counts know nothing of it
until they are taken by Saracens,
Turks and Persians and evil Bedouins.
By Mohammed they swear they'll have revenge;
Pharaon says, he lays claim to finesse,
"Emir and lord, listen to what I say.
Tiebaut your father is brave and noble,
who left this city to you to protect,
and Gloriete the royal palace.
These swine have dared to challenge you for it,   1510
they have murdered your men, hacked and killed them.
By Mohammed, I am not worth a cent,
if I do not have all their limbs torn off;

and your stepmother, who has shamed you so,
I shall see burn and roast in a fire."
But Escanors, who is white-haired and old:
"King Pharaon, you have not spoken well."

liii

Says Escanors, who is hoary and old:
"King Pharaon, you have not judged this well.
You ought never engage in such folly.   1520
If it once starts, you cannot control it.
Emir, my lord, grant me peace and hear me:
Tiebaut your father is a noble man,
he left this city to you to protect,
and Gloriete, the palace and the fief.
If you were really to burn his lady,
he would only be furious with you.
But have these counts thrown back into prison
and put lady Orable in with them.
Then send a messenger over the seas;   1530
your father will come, with King Haucebier,
and let them decide how they'll be avenged."
Aragon says: "You have spoken well.
You'll be rewarded, you will lack nothing.
But I have already sent a messenger
to my father, the king who rules Africa.
Within eight days he should have returned."
They throw William into prison again
with Guielin, who is bold and skillful.
and Lady Orable is cast in with them.   1540
God save them now, who is judge of us all!

liv

Now William has been cast into prison
with Guielin and the gracious Orable;
the unhappy lady cries in despair.
"God," she says, "our good, heavenly father,
this poor creature has not been baptized yet.
I hoped to become one of God's faithful.
Sir William, your valor has brought me harm,
your noble body and knightly honor,
for you I've been thrown into this dungeon,   1550
in anguish as if I had been a whore."
Guielin says: "What nonsense is this,
you and my uncle are not badly off;
through your great love, you should bear this trouble."
William hears him and rages with anger,
in his fury, he swears by St. James:

"If it were not to my shame and disgrace,
I would give you a good blow on the neck."
Guielin says: "That would only be madness.
From now on I shall say, no matter who hears,   1560
you used to be called William the strong-armed,
but now you will be William the lover.
It was for love that you entered this town."
The count hears him, he looks down at the ground.

lv
Now William is furious and distressed,
and lady Orable and Guielin his nephew,
inside the dungeon where they have been thrown.
"God," says the count, "glorious king of heaven.
We are all dead, betrayed and deceived!"
"What folly it was to start this affair,   1570
by which we are all dishonored and shamed,
unless He, who judges all, rescues us.
Alas, if King Louis the fierce only knew,
my brother Bernard, the white-haired and old,
and valiant Sir Garin of Anseune,
and within Nîmes, the powerful Bertrand.
We certainly have great need of their aid."
"Uncle William," says the fierce Guielin,
"let that be, we have no need of them here.
Here is Orable, the gracious lady,   1580
for you to kiss and embrace as you wish,
I can think of no lovelier lady."
"God," says the count, "now I shall go mad."
The pagans hear them quarrel in the prison,
more than forty, they rush in and seize them
and throw the two men out of their dungeon.
They leave Orable, the gracious lady,
but lead uncle and nephew to the palace.
Pharaon speaks, who is fiercest of all:
"Emir, sire, grant me peace and hear me.   1590
Your father, Tiebaut, must be respected.
He left this city to you to protect
and Gloriete, the palace and the fief.
You see this pig, this young bachelor,
nothing you say does he hold worth a cent.
By Mohammed, you're no more than a clown
if you do not have him torn limb from limb,
him and his uncle, William, the warrior."
Guielin hears him, his sense begins to stray,
he grinds his teeth, his eyes roll in his head;   1600
he steps forward, he has pulled his sleeves back;

with his left fist, he grabs him by the hair,
raises the right and plants it on his neck.
The bone in his throat is almost shattered.
He lets the pagan fall, dead, at his feet.
William watches and rejoices in it.
"God," says the count, "who are judge of us all,
now we are dead and abandoned in pain!"

lvi

William sees Pharaon who has fallen:
"God," says the count, "good king of paradise,   1610
now we are dead, and given up to pain."
"Do not despair, uncle," says Guielin,
"in this palace you are not without friends."
"Indeed," says William, "there are few of those."
Then the young Guielin looks around.
He notices a huge axe near a pillar,
moves forward and seizes it with both hands,
and goes to strike a barbarous pagan.
He cuts through him all the way to the chest.
Aragon looks, almost loses his mind,   1620
he cries aloud: "Seize him, Saracens!
By Mohammed, they shall be abused,
they will be swung and dropped into the Rhone."
Guielin says: "You swine, get away from here.
You have had us led out of your prison
and conducted up here to the palace,
but by the apostle who is blessed at Rome,
you have thus acquired such companions,
they'll make you angry and very sad."
At these words two Saracens appear,   1630
bearing in their hands a serving of wine,
which they intend to serve in the palace,
but when they see such mighty blows struck,
they run away and let everything fall.
Count William runs to seize the huge tray.
Swiftly, he takes it in both his hands
and strikes great blows at pagan Saracens.
Anyone he reaches does not rejoice.

lvii

Now William is inside the tiled palace,
and Guielin his renowned nephew.   1640
One has an axe, the other the tray;
the noble vassals strike great blows with them.
Fourteen Turks have already been killed,
and the others are so terrified,

that they chase them out through the doors,
which they run to bolt and lock after them.
By its great chains, they have pulled up the bridge.
Aragon sees it and his mind rages.
He calls on all his Saracens and Slavs:
"Give me counsel, by Mohammed, my God.   1650
This William has badly abused me,
he has seized my principal palace,
I don't see how we can enter again."
Let us leave the Saracens here for a while,
for we must sing once more of Gilbert,
the messenger who has crossed the Rhone.
He mounts the peaks and descends the valleys,
from here to Nîmes, he has never paused.
It is morning, Count Bertrand has arisen,
he climbs the palace of the heathen Otran   1660
whom he had conquered by his fierce courage.
The count stands at the great windows
and looks down across the kingdom.
He sees the green grass and the rose gardens
and hears the oriole and blackbird sing.
He remembers William of the short nose
and his brother, the highly praised Guielin,
and tenderly then he begins to weep,
grieving for them as you will now hear:
"Uncle William, what madness it was   1670
to go to Orange just to look at it,
disguised in rags like some poor beggar.
Brother Guielin, how worthy you were!
Now you've been killed by Saracens and Slavs,
and I am left all alone in this land.
I see no man here of all my great race
to whom I can go for good counsel.
The Slavs will soon return to this place,
Golias and the king Desramé,
Clareaus and his brother Aceré,   1680
Aguisant and the king Giboé,
and the royal prince of Reaumont by the sea,
the kings Eubron, Borreaus and Lorré,
and Quinzepaumes and his brother Gondrez,
the thirty kings who were born here in Spain.
Each one will have thirty thousand armed men
and they will attack the city of Nîmes;
they will capture me by powerful force,
I shall be dead, murdered or killed.
But there is one thing I have determined: 1690
I would not fail, for the gold of ten cities,

to return to the land where I was born,
and bring back with me all my barons,
whom William of the short nose once led here.
And when I come to the city, Paris,
I will descend on the enameled stones;
sergeants and squires will come to greet me
and they will certainly ask for William,
and for Guielin my worthy brother.
Alas, I will not know what to tell them,   1700
except that the pagans killed them at Orange!"
Twice he falls in a faint on the marble step,
and his barons run to lift him up.

lviii

Count Bertrand is saddened and desolate,
for Guielin and the noble William.
He grieves with fine and courteous words:
"Uncle William, how madly you acted
when you decided to go to Orange
as a poor beggar, disguised in rags.
Brother Guielin, what a good man you were!   1710
Now Persians have killed you and Saracens
and I am alone in this pagan land,
I have no cousin or brother with me.
Now King Tiebaut will return from Africa
and Desramé and the huge Golias,
the thirty kings with their vast forces,
and they will lay siege to me here at Nîmes.
I shall be dead and doomed to torments,
but by the apostle penitents seek,
I shall not, even if I lose my limbs,   1720
give up until I reach Orange the great
to avenge the sorrow and the torment
that Saracens made our people suffer.
Alas, poor wretch, why do I hesitate
to go and present myself before them!"

lix

Count Bertrand is sad and filled with anger,
but just when he is weeping and sighing,
Gilbert arrives and enters the city.
He climbs the steps of the great stone chamber.
Bertrand sees him and he begins to laugh,   1730
in a loud, clear voice he cries out to him:
"You are most welcome, here, good, noble knight!
Where is my uncle of the bold countenance,
and Guielin? Don't hide it from me!"

And Gilbert answers as a noble knight:
"Within Orange, the fortified city,
in Gloriete, the tower of marble;
evil pagans hold them in their power.
It won't be long before they are both killed.
William sent me, I hide nothing from you,   1740
to ask you to help with all of your knights,
immediately, without any delay."
Bertrand hears him, then he begins to laugh.
He calls on everyone who can hear him:
"To arms, now, quickly, my good, noble knights!"
And they obey, without any delay,
mounting their Spanish and Sulian horses.
When Bertrand leaves the city of Nîmes,
he brings every man in his command,
at the head are more than fifteen thousand.   1750
From here to the Rhone they don't pause or stop,
they all embark on ships and galleys.
The Franks put to sea, they sail and steer.
Beneath Orange, there is the vast plains,
the proud companies disembark,
they pitch their tents and raise their pavilions.
Count Bertrand has allowed no delay,
he looks at the messenger and says:
"Now, Sir Gilbert, do not lie to me.
Should we attack this city of Orange,   1760
can we break down the walls and the stone halls?"
Gilbert answers: "Your idea is mad.
She does not fear the whole kingdom of France—
you couldn't take her any day of your life."
Bertrand hears him and nearly goes mad.

lx

"Gilbert, brother," Count Bertrand demands,
"shall we attack the mighty Orange,
could we break down these walls, these high buildings?"
Gilbert answers: "There is no sense in this.
You could not take her in all your lifetime."   1770
Bertrand is enraged by that answer
and the messenger tries to comfort him:
"Sire," he says, "listen to my plan:
I shall get you into the city
without the Persians or Saracens' knowledge."
"Go ahead, good brother, with Jesus' aid!"
He goes, because he knows what is needed,
with thirteen thousand Frankish fighting men,
leaving the others behind at the tents.

They do not stop before they reach the cave,   1780
through the pillars they make their way in—
they are without candles or burning lights—
one after the other in deep darkness.
Bertrand begins to lose heart at this,
he calls the messenger and asks aloud:
"Gilbert, my brother, don't conceal the truth,
my uncle is dead, I'm beginning to see,
and you've sold us to the infidel race."
Gilbert answers: "You're talking nonsense—
I could not do that to save my own limbs.   1790
You will arrive soon inside Gloriete,
by God, I beg you, do it quietly."
"Go on, good brother, with God's protection."
And as they move along, speaking thus,
they suddenly find themselves in Gloriete.
Count William has seen them as they arrive:
"God," says the count, "good father, redeemer,
now I see what I have needed so long."
The valiant fighters unlace their helmets,
they embrace and kiss, weeping in their joy.   1800
Count Bertrand is the first to address him:
"How are you, uncle? Hide nothing from me."
"I'm fine, good nephew, by the grace of God,
though I have suffered great pain and distress.
I didn't expect to see you while I lived,
for the torments of Saracens and Persians."
"Uncle William, you will soon be avenged."
Up in the palace an olifant sounds,
outside in tents and pavilions, men arm.
Count William is bold and valiant.   1810
They approach the gates of the fine city,
the bridge is lowered, they quickly descend
to open the gates as fast as they can,
and the men outside begin to pour in,
shouting "Montjoy!" in the front and the rear.
At their joy, the pagans are terrified,
they run to arm, the treacherous cowards;
from their lodgings they begin to come forth,
running to equip themselves for defense.
But all their armor is not worth a glove,   1820
for there are too many Franks by then;
Bertrand has taken over the city.
To win that strong and valiant fortress,
you might have seen such a furious combat,
so many lances broken and shields crashing,
so many hauberks of Moorish chain pierced,

so many Saracens bleeding and dead.
When Aragon sees his people killed,
his grief is such, he almost goes mad.
He leaps in the saddle of a spirited horse,
grabbing a shield he had taken from a Frank,
he looks on the ground and sees a sharp spear,
he leans down to take it with both his hands
and urges the horse with his sharpened spurs.
He thrusts himself in the thick of the fight.
First he kills our Folquer of Meliant
and then another and a third after him.
Bertrand sees him and almost goes mad,
he draws his sword, whose blade cuts so well,
and strikes Aragon, he does not spare him.
The blow he strikes with such vicious intent,
he cuts through him all the way to his chest.
He knocks him dead from his spirited horse.
Pagans begin to lose force and courage.
But why should I extend this tale further?
Cursed be he who would have escaped it!
Over the earth flows a river of blood.
Count William does not wait any longer,
he runs immediately to the dungeon
and frees Orable of the graceful form.
He calls Bertrand and says this before all:
"Good nephew," he says, "hear what I intend:
this lady of the noble, charming form,
who rescued me, certainly, from death,
I made her a most faithful promise
that I would indeed take her as my wife."
And Bertrand says: "Then why do you delay?
Keep the covenant you have made with her,
and marry her in happiness and joy."
"Nephew," says William, "just as you command."

lxi

Count William is most noble and worthy.
When he has conquered the city by force,
he has a great vessel prepared
and clear water is poured into it.
Then comes the bishop of the city, Nîmes;
they have Orable take off her robes,
and baptize her to the honor of God,
divesting her of her pagan name.
The barons, Bertrand and Guielin, sponsor her
and Gilbert, the worthy and wise.
By Christian law, they call her Guiborc.

1830

1840

1850

1860

1870

To a church consecrated by them,
where Mohammed had once been invoked,
Count William goes to make her his wife.
The mass is sung by the bishop Guimer.
After the mass they return from the church
and the lady is led into Gloriete,
in the paved halls the wedding is splendid.
Count Bertrand serves them as is fitting,
and Gilbert and the worthy Guielin.   1880
Eight days they feast in joy together;
there are harpers and minstrels in plenty,
and robes of silk and delicate ermine,
and mules of Spain and well-groomed horses.

lxii

Count William has married his lady;
now he remains thirty years in Orange,
and no day goes by without a challenge.

Dante

THE DIVINE COMEDY

Introduction by Constance Bouchard

Dante Alighieri (1265–1321), usually known by his first name, is generally considered the greatest vernacular writer of the late Middle Ages. He was from the city of Florence, and his influence was such that the Florentine version of Italian in which he wrote became, and still is, the standard for written Italian. He was born into a noble family of Florence and became involved in the politics and internal quarrels of his hometown. The two major political parties there were the Guelfs and the Ghibellines, the former party further divided among subgroups that called themselves the White and the Black Guelfs. Dante was a prominent figure in the former, and when the Black Guelfs came to power in 1302, he was exiled from his beloved city.

It was during his exile from Florence that he began writing his masterpiece, the *Divine Comedy*. It is not a comedy in the sense of something knee-slappingly hilarious, but rather in the sense of a story in which good triumphs in the end. It was written as a very long poem, divided into short sections of a few pages each, called Cantos. Each Canto in turn is a series of three-line verses, which rhymed in the original Italian, although modern English translators prefer to avoid forcing the lines to rhyme, which can be much more awkward in English than in Italian. The "Comedy" overall is the story of a Pilgrim on a long journey which leads him, over the course of three books, first through Hell, then through Purgatory, and finally to Paradise. The following selection is from the beginning of the first volume, the "Inferno."

The *Divine Comedy* is much more than the story of the human journey toward salvation. Rather, Dante used it as a vehicle to discuss philosophy, theology, politics—especially the relative authority of pope and emperor within the Holy Roman Empire—and history. Most of the people the narrator meets on the course of the journey are historical figures, who would have been well-known to the educated Italian audience for whom Dante was writing. Some were figures out of classical mythology, such as Odysseus (Ulysses). Others were people that Dante had known personally. Virtually all of them are given the opportunity in the poem to speak with the Pilgrim and explain how they ended up in their present position in the afterlife. Dante wrote in a very long tradition of visions of heaven and hell, even though his Divine Comedy is far longer and more complex than any of the earlier accounts of a visit to the afterlife.

A motif that he developed from these previous accounts was that the Pilgrim would need a guide to help direct him and explain what he was seeing. In the "Inferno," the guide is Virgil, the classical Roman poet. Virgil, according to the poem, was chosen to be the Pilgrim's guide by Beatrice, a long-dead lady whom Dante had admired from afar in his youth, and who herself became the Pilgrim's guide when he reached Heaven in the third book (the name means "she who blesses"). Although Virgil, not having been a Christian, would have to remain in Hell according to Christian doctrine (or at least in Limbo, its outermost circle), Dante clearly admired him. It was also appropriate that as Dante set out to write his monumental poem he should have chosen for his first guide Virgil, best known for the *Aeneid,* a monumental poem on the founders of Rome.

The Hell that the Pilgrim and Virgil explore is divided into circles, where people are placed depending on the severity of their sin. The following selection involves only the outer circles, but as they descend into the center of hell, they see Lucifer, frozen on his throne, chewing on the three worst sinners of all, those who had betrayed those who trusted them most: Judas, who betrayed Christ, and Brutus and Cassius, who betrayed Caesar. The inclusion of Caesar's betrayers both indicates the continued relevance of Roman history in Dante's time and, especially, reflects his belief that Roman emperors, of which Caesar was regarded as the first, should have a crucial role in the governance of human society. Among the other people found in Hell were well-known sinners from throughout literature and history, as well as several of Dante's own enemies, and even some popes. Although the *Divine Comedy* is thus a deeply religious work, it thus did not hesitate to criticize where Dante felt criticism was needed, including the organized church.

The Divine Comedy

CANTO I

Halfway through his life, Dante the Pilgrim wakes to find himself lost in a dark wood. Terrified at being alone in so dismal a valley, he wanders until he comes to a hill bathed in sunlight, and his fear begins to leave him. But when he starts to climb the hill his path is blocked by three fierce beasts: first a Leopard, then a Lion, and finally a She-Wolf. They fill him with fear and drive him back down to the sunless wood. At that moment the figure of a man appears before him; it is the shade of Virgil, and the Pilgrim begs for help. Virgil tells him that he cannot overcome the beasts which obstruct his path; they must remain until a "Greyhound" comes who will drive them back to Hell. Rather by another path will the Pilgrim reach the sunlight, and Virgil promises to guide him on the path through Hell and Purgatory, after which another spirit, more fit than Virgil, will lead him to Paradise. The Pilgrim begs Virgil to lead on, and the Guide starts ahead. The Pilgrim follows.

Midway along the journey of our life
    I woke to find myself in a dark wood,
    for I had wandered off from the straight path.   3

How hard it is to tell what it was like,
    this wood of wilderness, savage and stubborn
    (the thought of it brings back all my old fears),   6

a bitter place! Death could scarce be bitterer.
    But if I would show the good that came of it
    I must talk about things other than the good.   9

---

1. The imaginary date of the poem's beginning is the night before Good Friday in 1300, the year of the papal jubilee proclaimed by Boniface VIII. Born in 1265, Dante would be thirty-five years old, which is half the seventy years allotted to man in the Bible.

The Portable Dante (ed. Mark Musa), Viking/Penguin, 1995 (ISBN 0253209307), original pp. 1–31 (first six cantos of Divine Comedy).

How I entered there I cannot truly say,
    I had become so sleepy at the moment
    when I first strayed, leaving the path of truth;   12

but when I found myself at the foot of a hill,
    at the edge of the wood's beginning, down in the valley,
    where I first felt my heart plunged deep in fear,   15

I raised my head and saw the hilltop shawled
    in morning rays of light sent from the planet
    that leads men straight ahead on every road.   18

And then only did terror start subsiding
    in my heart's lake, which rose to heights of fear
    that night I spent in deepest desperation.   21

Just as a swimmer, still with panting breath,
    now safe upon the shore, out of the deep,
    might turn for one last look at the dangerous waters,   24

so I, although my mind was turned to flee,
    turned round to gaze once more upon the pass
    that never let a living soul escape.   27

I rested my tired body there awhile
    and then began to climb the barren slope
    (I dragged my stronger foot and limped along).   30

Beyond the point the slope begins to rise
    sprang up a leopard, trim and very swift!
    It was covered by a pelt of many spots.   33

And, everywhere I looked, the beast was there
    blocking my way, so time and time again
    I was about to turn and go back down.   36

The hour was early in the morning then,
    the sun was climbing up with those same stars
    that had accompanied it on the world's first day,   39

31–51. The three beasts that block the Pilgrim's path could symbolize the three major divisions of Hell. The spotted Leopard (32) represents Fraud (cf. Canto XVI, 106–108) and reigns over the Eighth and Ninth Circles where the Fraudulent are punished (Cantos XVIII-XXXIV). The Lion (45) symbolizes all forms of Violence that are punished in the Seventh Circle (XII-XVII). The She-Wolf (49) represents the different types of Concupisence or Incontinence that are punished in Circles Two to Five (V–VIII).

the day Divine Love set their beauty turning;
    so the hour and sweet season of creation
    encouraged me to think I could get past   42

that gaudy beast, wild in its spotted pelt,
    but then good hope gave way and fear returned
    when the figure of a lion loomed up before me,   45

and he was coming straight toward me, it seemed,
    with head raised high, and furious with hunger—
    the air around him seemed to fear his presence.   48

And now a she-wolf came, that in her leanness
    seemed racked with every kind of greediness
    (how many people she has brought to grief!).   51

This last beast brought my spirit down so low
    with fear that seized me at the sight of her,
    I lost all hope of going up the hill.   54

As a man who, rejoicing in his gains,
    suddenly seeing his gain turn into loss,
    will grieve as he compares his then and now,   57

so she made me do, that relentless beast;
    coming toward me, slowly, step by step,
    she forced me back to where the sun is mute.   60

While I was rushing down to that low place,
    my eyes made out a figure coming toward me
    of one grown faint, perhaps from too much silence.   63

And when I saw him standing in this wasteland,
    "Have pity on my soul," I cried to him,
    "whichever you are, shade or living man!"   66

"No longer living man, though once I was,"
    he said, "and my parents were from Lombardy,
    both of them were Mantuans by birth.   69

---

62. The approaching figure represents (though not exclusively, for he has other meanings) Reason or Natural Philosophy. The Pilgrim cannot proceed to the light of Divine Love (the mountaintop) until he has overcome the three beasts of his sin; and because it is impossible for man to cope with the beasts unaided, Virgil has been summoned to guide the Pilgrim.
63. The voice of Reason has been silent in the Pilgrim's ear for a long time.

I was born, though somewhat late, *sub Julio,*
    and lived in Rome when good Augustus reigned,
    when still the false and lying gods were worshipped.   72

I was a poet and sang of that just man,
    son of Anchises, who sailed off from Troy
    after the burning of proud Ilium.   75

But why retreat to so much misery?
    Why not climb up this blissful mountain here,
    the beginning and the source of all man's joy?"   78

"Are you then Virgil, are you then that fount
    from which pours forth so rich a stream of words?"
    I said to him, bowing my head modestly.   81

"O light and honor of the other poets,
    may my long years of study, and that deep love
    that made me search your verses, help me now!   84

You are my teacher, the first of all my authors,
    and you alone the one from whom I took
    the noble style that was to bring me honor.   87

You see the beast that forced me to retreat;
    save me from her, I beg you, famous sage,
    she makes me tremble, the blood throbs in my veins."   90

"But you must journey down another road,"
    he answered, when he saw me lost in tears,
    "if ever you hope to leave this wilderness;   93

this beast, the one you cry about in fear,
    allows no soul to succeed along her path,
    she blocks his way and puts an end to him.   96

She is by nature so perverse and vicious,
    her craving belly is never satisfied,
    still hungering for food the more she eats.   99

She mates with many creatures, and will go on
    mating with more until the greyhound comes
    and tracks her down to make her die in anguish.   102

---

91. Dante must choose another road because, in order to arrive at the Divine Light, it is necessary first to recognize the true nature of sin, renounce it, and pay penance for it.

He will not feed on either land or money:
> his wisdom, love, and virtue shall sustain him;
> he will be born between Feltro and Feltro.   105

He comes to save that fallen Italy
> for which the maid Camilla gave her life
> and Turnus, Nisus, Euryalus died of wounds.   108

And he will hunt for her through every city
> until he drives her back to Hell once more,
> whence Envy first unleashed her on mankind.   111

And so, I think it best you follow me
> for your own good, and I shall be your guide
> and lead you out through an eternal place   114

where you will hear desperate cries, and see
> tormented shades, some old as Hell itself,
> and know what second death is, from their screams.   117

And later you will see those who rejoice
> while they are burning, for they have hope of coming,
> whenever it may be, to join the blessèd—   120

to whom, if you too wish to make the climb,
> a spirit, worthier than I, must take you;
> I shall go back, leaving you in her care,   123

because that Emperor dwelling on high
> will not let me lead any to His city,
> since I in life rebelled against His law.   126

101–111. The Greyhound has been identified with Henry VII, Charles Martel, and even Dante himself. It seems more plausible that the Greyhound represents Can Grande della Scala, the ruler of Verona from 1308 to 1329, whose "wisdom, love, and virtue" (104) were certainly well-known to Dante. Whoever the Greyhound may be, the prophecy would seem to indicate in a larger sense the establishment of a spiritual kingdom on earth in which "wisdom, love, and virtue" will replace the bestial sins of the world. Perhaps Dante had no specific person in mind.

107. Camilla was the valiant daughter of King Metabus, who was slain while fighting against the Trojans (*Aeneid* XI).

108. Turnus was the king of the Rutulians. Nisus and Euryalus were young Trojan warriors slain during a nocturnal raid on the camp of the Rutulians.

117. The "second" death is that of the soul, which occurs when the soul is damned.

122. Just as Virgil, the pagan Roman poet, cannot enter the Christian Paradise because he lived before the birth of Christ and lacks knowledge of Christian salvation, so Reason can only guide the Pilgrim to a certain point: In order to enter Paradise, the Pilgrim's guide must be Christian Grace or Revelation (Theology) in the figure of Beatrice.

124. Note the pagan terminology of Virgil's reference to God: It expresses, as best it can, his unenlightened conception of the Supreme Authority.

Everywhere He reigns, and there He rules;
    there is His city, there is His high throne.
    Oh, happy the one He makes His citizen!"   129

And I to him: "Poet, I beg of you,
    in the name of God, that God you never knew,
    save me from this evil place and worse,   132

lead me there to the place you spoke about
    that I may see the gate Saint Peter guards
    and those whose anguish you have told me of."   135

Then he moved on, and I moved close behind him.

CANTO II

But the Pilgrim begins to waver; he expresses to Virgil his misgivings about his ability to under-take the journey proposed by Virgil. His predecessors have been Aeneas and Saint Paul, and he feels unworthy to take his place in their company. But Virgil rebukes his cowardice, and relates the chain of events that led him to come to Dante. The Virgin Mary took pity on the Pilgrim in his despair and instructed Saint Lucia to aid him. The Saint turned to Beatrice because of Dante's great love for her, and Beatrice in turn went down to Hell, into Limbo, and asked Virgil to guide her friend until that time when she herself would become his guide. The Pilgrim takes heart at Virgil's explanation and agrees to follow him.

The day was fading and the darkening air
    was releasing all the creatures on our earth
    from their daily tasks, and I, one man alone,   3

was making ready to endure the battle
    of the journey, and of the pity it involved,
    which my memory, unerring, shall now retrace.   6

O Muses! O high genius! Help me now!
    O memory that wrote down what I saw,
    here your true excellence shall be revealed!   9

Then I began: "O poet come to guide me,
    tell me if you think my worth sufficient
    before you trust me to this arduous road.   12

You wrote about young Sylvius's father,
    who went beyond, with flesh corruptible,
    with all his senses, to the immortal realm;   15

but if the Adversary of all evil
    was kind to him, considering who he was,
    and the consequence that was to come from him,   18

this cannot seem, to thoughtful men, unfitting,
    for in the highest heaven he was chosen
    father of glorious Rome and of her empire,   21

and both the city and her lands, in truth,
    were established as the place of holiness
    where the successors of great Peter sit.   24

And from this journey you celebrate in verse,
    Aeneas learned those things that were to bring
    victory for him, and for Rome, the Papal seat;   27

then later the Chosen Vessel, Paul, ascended
    to ring back confirmation of that faith
    which is the first step on salvation's road.   30

But why am I to go? Who allows me to?
    I am not Aeneas, I am not Paul,
    neither I nor any man would think me worthy;   33

and so, if I should undertake the journey,
    I fear it might turn out an act of folly—
    you are wise, you see more than my words express."   36

As one who unwills what he willed, will change
    his purpose with some new second thought,
    completely quitting what he first had started,   39

so I did, standing there on that dark slope,
    thinking, ending the beginning of that venture
    I was so quick to take up at the start.   42

"If I have truly understood your words,"
    that shade of magnanimity replied,
    "your soul is burdened with that cowardice   45

which often weighs so heavily on man,
    it turns him from a noble enterprise
    like a frightened beast that shies at its own shadow.   48

28–30. In his Second Epistle to the Corinthians (12:2–4), the apostle Paul alludes to his mystical elevation to the third heaven and to the arcane messages pronounced there.

To free you from this fear, let me explain
　　the reason I came here, the words I heard
　　that first time I felt pity for your soul: 51

I was among those dead who are suspended,
　　when a lady summoned me. She was so blessed
　　and beautiful, I implored her to command me.   54

With eyes of light more bright than any star,
　　in low, soft tones she started to address me
　　in her own language, with an angel's voice: 57

'O noble soul, courteous Mantuan,
　　whose fame the world continues to preserve
　　and will preserve as long as world there is,   60

my friend, who is no friend of Fortune's, strays
　　on a desert slope; so many obstacles
　　have crossed his path, his fright has turned him back   63

I fear he may have gone so far astray,
　　from what report has come to me in Heaven,
　　that I may have started to his aid too late.   66

Now go, and with your elegance of speech,
　　with whatever may be needed for his freedom,
　　give him your help, and thereby bring me solace.   69

I am Beatrice, who urges you to go;
　　I come from the place I am longing to return to;
　　love moved me, as it moves me now to speak.   72

When I return to stand before my Lord,
　　often I shall sing your praises to Him.'
　　And then she spoke no more. And I began,   75

'O Lady of Grace, through whom alone mankind
　　may go beyond all worldly things contained
　　within the sphere that makes the smallest round,   78

your plea fills me with happy eagerness—
　　to have obeyed already would still seem late!
　　You needed only to express your wish.   81

But tell me how you dared to make this journey
　　all the way down to this point of spacelessness,
　　away from your spacious home that calls you back.'   84

'Because your question searches for deep meaning,
   I shall explain in simple words,' she said,
   'just why I have no fear of coming here.   87

A man must stand in fear of just those things
   that truly have the power to do us harm,
   of nothing else, for nothing else is fearsome.   90

God gave me such a nature through His Grace,
   the torments you must bear cannot affect me,
   nor are the fires of Hell a threat to me.   93

A gracious lady sits in Heaven grieving
   for what happened to the one I send you to,
   and her compassion breaks Heaven's stern decree.   96

She called Lucia and making her request,
   she said, "Your faithful one is now in need
   of you, and to you I now commend his soul."   99

Lucia, the enemy of cruelty,
   hastened to make her way to where I was,
   sitting by the side of ancient Rachel,   102

and said to me: "Beatrice, God's true praise,
   will you not help the one whose love was such
   it made him leave the vulgar crowd for you?   105

Do you not hear the pity of his weeping,
   do you not see what death it is that threatens him
   along that river the sea shall never conquer?"   108

There never was a wordly person living
   more anxious to promote his selfish gains
   than I was at the sound of words like these—   111

to leave my holy seat and come down here
   and place my trust in you, in your noble speech
   that honors you and all those who have heard it!' 114

When she had finished reasoning, she turned
   her shining eyes away, and there were tears.
   How eager then I was to come to you!   117

---

94. The lady is the Virgin Mary.
102. In the Dantean Paradise Rachel is seated by Beatrice.

And I have come to you just as she wished,
    and I have freed you from the beast that stood
    blocking the quick way up the mount of bliss.   120

So what is wrong? Why, why do you delay?
    Why are you such a coward in your heart,
    why aren't you bold and free of all your fear,   123

when three such gracious ladies, who are blessed,
    watch out for you up there in Heaven's court,
    and my words, too, bring promise of such good?"   126

As little flowers from the frosty night
    are closed and limp, and when the sun shines down
    on them, they rise to open on their stem,   129

my wilted strength began to bloom within me,
    and such warm courage flowed into my heart
    that I spoke like a man set free of fear.   132

"O she, compassionate, who moved to help me!
    And you, all kindness, in obeying quick
    those words of truth she brought with her for you—   135

you and the words you spoke have moved my heart
    with such desire to continue onward
    that now I have returned to my first purpose.   138

Let us start, for both our wills, joined now, are one.
    You are my guide, you are my lord and teacher."
    These were my words to him and, when he moved,   141

I entered on that deep and rugged road.

CANTO III

As the two poets enter the vestibule that leads to Hell itself, Dante sees the inscription above the gate, and he hears the screams of anguish from the damned souls. Rejected by God and not accepted by the powers of Hell, the first group of souls are "nowhere," because of their cowardly refusal to make a choice in life. Their punishment is to follow a banner at a furious pace forever, and to be tormented by flies and hornets. The Pilgrim recognizes several of these shades but mentions none by name. Next they come to the River Acheron, where they are greeted by the infernal boatman, Charon. Among those doomed souls who are to be ferried across the river, Charon sees the living man and challenges him, but Virgil lets it be known that his companion must pass. Then across the landscape rushes a howling wind, which blasts the Pilgrim out of his senses, and he falls to the ground.

I AM THE WAY INTO THE DOLEFUL CITY,
   I AM THE WAY INTO ETERNAL GRIEF,
   I AM THE WAY TO A FORSAKEN RACE.   3

JUSTICE IT WAS THAT MOVED MY GREAT CREATOR;
   DIVINE OMNIPOTENCE CREATED ME,
   AND HIGHEST WISDOM JOINED WITH PRIMAL LOVE.   6

BEFORE ME NOTHING BUT ETERNAL THINGS
   WERE MADE, AND I SHALL LAST ETERNALLY.
   ABANDON EVERY HOPE, ALL YOU WHO ENTER.   9

I saw these words spelled out in somber colors
   inscribed along the ledge above a gate;
   "Master," I said, "these words I see are cruel."   12

He answered me, speaking with experience:
   "Now here you must leave all distrust behind;
   let all your cowardice die on this spot.   15

We are at the place where earlier I said
   you could expect to see the suffering race
   of souls who lost the good of intellect."   18

Placing his hand on mine, smiling at me
   in such a way that I was reassured,
   he led me in, into those mysteries.   21

Here sighs and cries and shrieks of lamentation
   echoed throughout the starless air of Hell;
   at first these sounds resounding made me weep: 24

tongues confused, a language strained in anguish
   with cadences of anger, shrill outcries
   and raucous groans that joined with sounds of hands,   27

raising a whirling storm that turns itself
   forever through that air of endless black,
   like grains of sand swirling when a whirlwind blows.   30

And I, in the midst of all this circling horror,
   began, "Teacher, what are these sounds I hear?
   What souls are these so overwhelmed by grief?"   33

5–6. Divine Omnipotence, Highest Wisdom, and Primal Love are, respectively, the Father, the Son, and the Holy Ghost. Thus, the gate of Hell was created by the Trinity moved by Justice.
18. Souls who have lost sight of God.

And he to me: "This wretched state of being
    is the fate of those sad souls who lived a life
    but lived it with no blame and with no praise.   36

They are mixed with that repulsive choir of angels
    neither faithful nor unfaithful to their God,
    who undecided stood but for themselves.   39

Heaven, to keep its beauty, cast them out,
    but even Hell itself would not receive them,
    for fear the damned might glory over them."   42

And I. "Master, what torments do they suffer
    that force them to lament so bitterly?"
    He answered: "I will tell you in few words: 45

these wretches have no hope of truly dying,
    and this blind life they lead is so abject
    it makes them envy every other fate.   48

The world will not record their having been there;
    Heaven's mercy and its justice turn from them.
    Let's not discuss them; look and pass them by."   51

And so I looked and saw a kind of banner
    rushing ahead, whirling with aimless speed
    as though it would not ever take a stand;   54

behind it an interminable train
    of souls pressed on, so many that I wondered
    how death could have undone so great a number.   57

When I had recognized a few of them,
    I saw the shade of the one who must have been
    the coward who had made the great refusal.   60

At once I understood, and I was sure
    this was the sect of evil souls who were
    hateful to God and His enemies.   63

52–69. In the *Inferno* divine retribution assumes the form of the *contrapasso,* i.e., the just punishment of sin, effected by a process either resembling or contrasting to the sin itself. In this canto the *contrapasso* opposes the sin of neutrality, or inactivity: The souls who in their early lives had no banner, no leader to follow, now run forever after one.
60. The coward could be Pontius Pilate, who refused to pass sentence on Christ.

These wretches, who had never truly lived,
    went naked, and were stung and stung again
    by the hornets and the wasps that circled them   66

and made their faces run with blood in streaks;
    their blood, mixed with their tears, dripped to their feet,
    and disgusting maggots collected in the pus.   69

And when I looked beyond this crowd I saw
    a throng upon the shore of a wide river,
    which made me ask, "Master, I would like to know: 72

who are these people, and what law is this
    that makes those souls so eager for the crossing—
    as I can see, even in this dim light?"   75

And he: "All this will be made plain to you
    as soon as we shall come to stop awhile
    upon the sorrowful shore of Acheron."   78

And I, with eyes cast down in shame, for fear
    that I perhaps had spoken out of turn,
    said nothing more until we reached the river.   81

And suddenly, coming toward us in a boat,
    a man of years whose ancient hair was white
    shouted at us, "Woe to you, perverted souls!   84

Give up all hope of ever seeing Heaven:
    I come to lead you to the other shore,
    into eternal darkness, ice, and fire.   87

And you, the living soul, you over there,
    get away from all these people who are dead."
    But when he saw I did not move aside,   90

he said, "Another way, by other ports,
    not here, shall you pass to reach the other shore;
    a lighter skiff than this must carry you."   93

And my guide, "Charon, this is no time for anger!
    It is so willed, there where the power is
    for what is willed; that's all you need to know."   96

These words brought silence to the woolly cheeks
    of the ancient steersman of the livid marsh,
    whose eyes were set in glowing wheels of fire.   99

But all those souls there, naked, in despair,
    changed color and their teeth began to chatter
    at the sound of his announcement of their doom.   102

They were cursing God, cursing their own parents,
    the human race, the time, the place, the seed
    of their beginning, and their day of birth.   105

Then all together, weeping bitterly,
    they packed themselves along the wicked shore
    that waits for every man who fears not God.   108

The devil, Charon, with eyes of glowing coals,
    summons them all together with a signal,
    and with an oar he strikes the laggard sinner.   111

As in autumn when the leaves begin to fall,
    one after the other (until the branch
    is witness to the spoils spread on the ground),   114

so did the evil seed of Adam's Fall
    drop from that shore to the boat, one at a time,
    at the signal, like the falcon to its lure.   117

Away they go across the darkened waters,
    and before they reach the other side to land,
    a new throng starts collecting on this side.   120

"My son," the gentle master said to me,
    "all those who perish in the wrath of God
    assemble here from all parts of the earth;   123

they want to cross the river, they are eager;
    it is Divine Justice that spurs them on,
    turning the fear they have into desire.   126

A good soul never comes to make this crossing,
    so, if Charon grumbles at the sight of you,
    you see now what his words are really saying."   129

He finished speaking, and the grim terrain
    shook violently; and the fright it gave me
    even now in recollection makes me sweat.   132

124–126. It is perhaps a part of the punishment that the souls of all the damned are eager for their punishment to begin; those who were so willing to sin on earth, are in hell damned with a willingness to receive their just retribution.

Out of the tear-drench land a wind arose
   which blasted forth into a reddish light,
   knocking my senses out of me completely,

                              135

and I fell as one falls tired into sleep.

CANTO IV

Waking from his swoon, the Pilgrim is led by Virgil to the First Circle of Hell, known as Limbo, where the sad shades of the virtuous non-Christians dwell. The souls here, including Virgil, suffer no physical torment, but they must live, in desire, without hope of seeing God. Virgil tells about Christ's descent into Hell and His salvation of several Old Testament figures. The poets see a light glowing in the darkness, and as they proceed toward it, they are met by the four greatest (other than Virgil) pagan poets: Homer, Horace, Ovid, and Lucan, who take the Pilgrim into their group. As they come closer to the light, the Pilgrim perceives a splendid castle, where the greatest non-Christian thinkers dwell together with other famous historical figures. Once within the castle, the Pilgrim sees, among others, Electra, Aeneas, Caesar, Saladin, Aristotle, Plato, Orpheus, Cicero, Avicenna, and Averroës. But soon they must leave; and the poets move from the radiance of the castle toward the fearful encompassing darkness.

A heavy clap of thunder! I awoke
   from the deep sleep that drugged my mind—startled,
   the way one is when shaken out of sleep.

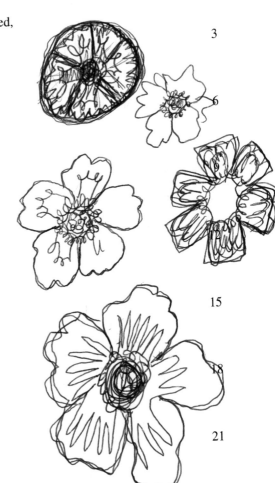

                              3

I turned my rested eyes from side to side,
   already on my feet and, staring hard,
   I tried my best to find out where I was,

                              6

and this is what I saw: I found myself
   upon the brink of grief's abysmal valley
   that collects the thunderings of endless cries.

So dark and deep and nebulous it was,
   try as I might to force my sight below,
   I could not see the shape of anything.

"Let us descend into the sightless world,"
   began the poet (his face was deathly pale):
   "I will go first, and you will follow me."

                              15

And I, aware of his changed color, said:
   "But how can I go on if you are frightened?
   You are my constant strength when I lose heart."

                              18

And he to me: "The anguish of the souls
   that are down here paints my face with pity—
   which you have wrongly taken to be fear.

                              21

Let us go, the long road urges us."
    He entered then, leading the way for me
    down to the first circle of the abyss.   24

Down there, to judge only by what I heard,
    there were no wails but just the sounds of sighs
    rising and trembling through the timeless air,   27

the sounds of sighs of untormented grief
    burdening these groups, diverse and teeming,
    made up of men and women and of infants.   30

Then the good master said, "You do not ask
    what sort of souls are these you see around you.
    Now you should know before we go on farther,   33

they have not sinned. But their great worth alone
    was not enough, for they did not know Baptism,
    which is the gateway to the faith you follow,   36

and if they came before the birth of Christ,
    they did not worship God the way one should;
    I myself am a member of this group.   39

For this defect, and for no other guilt,
    we here are lost. In this alone we suffer:
    cut off from hope, we live on in desire."   42

The words I heard weighed heavy on my heart;
    to think that souls as virtuous as these
    were suspended in that limbo, and forever!   45

"Tell me, my teacher, tell me, O my master,"
    I began (wishing to have confirmed by him
    the teachings of unerring Christian doctrine),   48

"did any leave here, through his merit
    or with another's help, and go to bliss?"
    And he, who understood my hidden question,   51

answered: "I was a novice in this place
    when I saw a mighty lord descend to us
    who wore the sign of victory as his crown.   54

He took from us the shade of our first parent,
    of Abel, his good son, of Noah, too,
    and of obedient Moses, who made the laws;   57

Abram, the Patriarch, David the King,
 Israel with his father and his children,
 with Rachel, whom he worked so hard to win;   60

and many more he chose for blessedness;
 and you should know, before these souls were taken,
 no human soul had ever reached salvation."   63

We did not stop our journey while he spoke,
 but continued on our way along the woods—
 I say the woods, for souls were thick as trees.   66

We had not gone too far from where I woke
 when I made out a fire up ahead,
 a hemisphere of light that lit the dark.   69

We were still at some distance from that place,
 but close enough for me vaguely to see
 that honorable souls possessed that spot.   72

"O glory of the sciences and arts,
 who are these souls enjoying special honor,
 dwelling apart from all the others here?"   75

And he to me: "The honored name they bear
 that still resounds above in your own world
 wins Heaven's favor for them in this place."   78

And as he spoke I heard a voice announce:
 "Now let us honor our illustrious poet,
 his shade that left is now returned to us."   81

And when the voice was silent and all was quiet
 I saw four mighty shades approaching us,
 their faces showing neither joy or sorrow.   84

Then my good master started to explain:
 "Observe the one who comes with sword in hand,
 leading the three as if he were their master.   87

It is the shade of Homer, sovereign poet,
 and coming second, Horace, the satirist;
 Ovid is the third, and last comes Lucan.   90

---

69. The "hemisphere of light" emanates from a "splendid castle" (106), the dwelling place of the virtuous men of wisdom in Limbo. The light is the illumination of human intellect, which those who dwell in the castle had in such high measure on earth.

86–88. Because his name was inseparably linked with the Trojan War, Homer is portrayed by Dante as a sword-bearing poet, one who sang of arms and martial heroes.

Since they all share one name with me, the name
    you heard resounding in that single voice,
    they honor me and do well doing so."   93

So I saw gathered there the noble school
    of the master singer of sublimest verse,
    who soars above all others like the eagle.   96

And after they had talked awhile together,
    they turned and with a gesture welcomed me,
    and at that sign I saw my master smile.   99

Greater honor still they deigned to grant me:
    they welcomed me as one of their own group,
    so that I numbered sixth among such minds.   102

We walked together toward the shining light,
    discussing things that here are best kept silent,
    as there they were most fitting for discussion.   105

We reached the boundaries of a splendid castle
    that seven times was circled by high walls
    defended by a sweetly flowing stream.   108

We walked right over it as on hard ground;
    through seven gates I passed with those wise spirits,
    and then we reached a meadow fresh in bloom.   111

There people were whose eyes were calm and grave,
    whose bearing told of great authority;
    seldom they spoke and always quietly.   114

Then moving to one side we reached a place
    spread out and luminous, higher than before,
    allowing us to view all who were there.   117

106–111. The allegorical construction of the castle is open to question. It may represent natural philosophy unilluminated by divine wisdom, in which case the seven walls serving to protect the castle would be the seven moral and speculative virtues (prudence, justice, fortitude, temperance, intellect, science, and knowledge); and the seven gates that provide access to the castle would be the seven liberal arts that formed the medieval school curriculum (music, arithmetic, geometry, astronomy—the *quadrivium;* and grammar, logic, and rhetoric—the *trivium*). The symbolic value of the stream also remains uncertain; it could signify eloquence, a "stream" that the eloquent Virgil and Dante should have no trouble crossing—and indeed, they "walked right over it as on hard ground" (109).
112–144. The inhabitants of the great castle are important pagan philosophers and poets as well as famous writers. Three of the shades named (Saladin, Avicenna, Averroës) lived only one hundred or two hundred years before Dante. Modern readers might wonder at the inclusion of medieval non-Christians among the virtuous pagans of antiquity, but the three just mentioned were among the non-Christians respected, particularly during the Middle Ages.

And right before us on the lustrous green
  the mighty shades were pointed out to me
  (my heart felt glory when I looked at them).   120

There was Electra standing with a group,
  among whom I saw Hector and Aeneas,
  and Caesar, falcon-eyed and fully armed.   123

I saw Camilla and Penthesilea;
  across the way I saw the Latian King,
  with Lavinia, his daughter, by his side.   126

I saw the Brutus who drove out the Tarquin;
  Lucretia, Julia, Marcia, and Cornelia;
  off, by himself, I noticed Saladin,   129

and when I raised my eyes a little higher
  I saw the master sage of those who know,
  sitting with his philosophic family.   132

All gaze at him, all pay their homage to him;
  and there I saw both Socrates and Plato,
  each closer to his side than any other;   135

Democritus, who said the world was chance,
  Diogenes, Thales, Anaxagoras,
  Empedocles, Zeno, and Heraclitus;   138

---

121. Electra was the daughter of Atlas, the mother of Dardanus, and the founder of Troy; thus, her followers include all members of the Trojan race. She should not be confused with Electra, daughter of Agamemnon, the character in plays by Aeschylus, Sophocles, and Euripides.
122. Among Electra's descendants are Hector, the eldest son of Priam, king of Troy, and Aeneas (cf. Canto I, 73–75; and Canto II, 13–24).
123. Julius Caesar proclaimed himself the first emperor of Rome after defeating numerous opponents in civil conflicts.
124–126. For Camilla see Canto I, note on line 107. Penthesilea was the glamorous queen of the Amazons who aided the Trojans against the Greeks and was slain by Achilles during the conflict. King Latinus commanded the central region of the Italian peninsula, the site where Aeneas founded Rome. He gave Lavinia to the Trojan conqueror in marriage.
127–129. Outraged by the murder of his brother and the rape (and subsequent suicide) of his sister (Lucretia), Lucius Brutus incited the Roman populace to expel the Tarquins, the perpetrators of the offenses. This accomplished, he was elected first consul and consequently became the founder of the Roman Republic. The four women were famous Roman wives and mothers. Lucretia was the wife of Collatinus; Julia the daughter of Julius Caesar and wife of Pompey; Marcia the second wife of Cato of Utica (in the *Convivio* Dante makes her the symbol of the noble soul); and Cornelia the daughter of Scipio Africanus Major and mother of the Gracchi, the tribunes Tiberius and Caius. A distinguished soldier, Saladin became sultan of Egypt in 1174. Medieval opinion of Saladin was favorable; he was lauded for his generosity and his magnanimity.
131. To Dante, Aristotle represented the summit of human reason, that point which man could reach on his own without the benefit of Christian revelation.

I saw the one who classified our herbs:
    Dioscorides I mean. And I saw Orpheus,
    Tully, Linus, Seneca the moralist,

141

Euclid the geometer, and Ptolemy,
    Hippocrates, Galen, Avicenna,
    and Averroës, who made the Commentary.

144

I cannot tell about them all in full;
    my theme is long and urges me ahead,
    often I must omit things I have seen.

147

The company of six becomes just two;
    my wise guide leads me by another way
    out of the quiet into tempestuous air.

150

I come into a place where no light is.

CANTO V

From Limbo Virgil leads his ward down to the threshold of the Second Circle of Hell, where for the first time he will see the damned in Hell being punished for their sins. There, barring their way, is the hideous figure of Minòs, the bestial judge of Dante's underworld; but after strong words from Virgil, the poets are allowed to pass into the dark space of this circle, where can be heard the wailing voices of the Lustful, whose punishment consists in being forever whirled

---

137. Diogenes was the Cynic philosopher who believed that the only good lies in virtue secured through self-control and abstinence. Anaxagoras was a Greek philosopher of the Ionian school (500–428 B.C.). Among his famous students were Pericles and Euripides. Thales (ca. 635–ca. 545 B.C.), an early Greek philosopher born at Miletus, founded the Ionian school of philosophy and in his main doctrine maintained that water is the elemental principle of all things.

140. Dioscorides was a Greek natural scientist and physician of the first century A.D. Orpheus was a mythical Greek poet and musician whose lyrical talent was such that it moved rocks and trees and tamed wild beasts.

141. Tully was Marcus Tullius Cicero, celebrated Roman orator, writer, and philosopher (106–43 B.C.). Linus was a mythical Greek poet and musician who is credited with inventing the dirge. Lucius Annaeus Seneca (4 B.C.–A.D. 65) followed the philosophy of the Stoics in his oral treatises. Dante calls him "the moralist" to distinguish him from Seneca the tragedian, who was thought (erroneously) during the Middle Ages to be another person.

142. Euclid was a Greek mathematician (ca. 300 B.C.) who wrote a treatise on geometry that was the first codification and exposition of mathematical principles. Ptolemy was a Greek mathematician, astronomer, and geographer. The universe, according to the Ptolemaic system (which was accepted by the Middle Ages), so named although he did not invent it, had the earth as its fixed center encircled by nine spheres.

143. Hippocrates was a Greek physician (ca. 460–377 B.C.) who founded the medical profession and introduced the scientific art of healing. Galen was a celebrated physician (ca. A.D. 130–ca. 200) who practiced his art in Greece, Egypt, and Rome. Avicenna (or Ibn-Sina) was an Arabian philosopher and physician (A.D. 980–1037) who was a prolific writer.

144. Ibn-Rushd, called Averroës (ca. A.D. 1126–ca. 1198), was a celebrated Arabian scholar born in Spain. He was widely known in the Middle Ages for his commentary on Aristotle, which served as the basis for the work of St. Thomas Aquinas.

about in a dark, stormy wind. After seeing a thousand or more famous lovers—including Semi-
ramis, Dido, Helen, Achilles, and Paris—the Pilgrim asks to speak to two figures he sees
together. They are Francesca da Rimini and her lover, Paolo, and the scene in which they
appear is probably the most famous episode of the Inferno. *At the end of the scene, the Pilgrim,*
who has been overcome by pity for the lovers, faints to the ground.

This way I went, descending from the first
   into the second round, that holds less space
   but much more pain—stinging the soul to wailing.   3

There stands Minòs grotesquely, and he snarls,
   examining the guilty at the entrance;
   he judges and dispatches, tail in coils.   6

By this I mean that when the evil soul
   appears before him, it confesses all,
   and he, who is the expert judge of sins,   9

knows to what place in Hell the soul belongs;
   the times he wraps his tail around himself
   tell just how far the sinner must go down.   12

The damned keep crowding up in front of him:
   they pass along to judgment one by one;
   they speak, they hear, and then are hurled below.   15

"O you who come to the place where pain is host,"
   Minòs spoke out when he caught sight of me,
   putting aside the duties of his office,   18

"be careful how you enter and whom you trust
   it's easy to get in, but don't be fooled!"
   And my guide said to him: "Why keep on shouting?   21

Do not attempt to stop his fated journey;
   it is so willed there where the power is
   for what is willed; that's all you need to know."   24

And now the notes of anguish start to play
   upon my ears; and now I find myself
   where sounds on sounds of weeping pound at me.   27

[handwritten: allegory story within a story]

---

4. Minòs was the son of Zeus and Europa. As king of Crete he was revered for his wisdom and judicial gifts. For these qualities he became chief magistrate of the underworld in classical literature. (See Virgil, *Aeneid* VI, 432–433.) Although Dante did not alter Minòs' official function, he transformed him into a demonic figure, both in his physical characteristics and in his bestial activity.

I came to a place where no light shone at all,
  bellowing like the sea racked by a tempest,
  when warring winds attack it from both sides.   30

The infernal storm, eternal in its rage,
  sweeps and drives the spirits with its blast:
  it whirls them, lashing them with punishment.   33

When they are swept back past their place of judgment,
  then come the shrieks, laments, and anguished cries;
  there they blaspheme God's almighty power.   36

I learned that to this place of punishment
  all those who sin in lust have been condemned,
  those who make reason slave to appetite;   39

and as the wings of starlings in the winter
  bear them along in wide-spread, crowded flocks,
  so does that wind propel the evil spirits: 42

now here, then there, and up and down, it drives them
  with never any hope to comfort them—
  hope not of rest but even of suffering less.   45

And just like cranes in flight, chanting their lays,
  stretching an endless line in their formation,
  I saw approaching, crying their laments,   48

spirits carried along by the battling winds.
  And so I asked, "Teacher, tell me, what souls
  are these punished in the sweep of the black wind?"   51

"The first of those whose story you should know,"
  my master wasted no time answering,
  "was empress over lands of many tongues;   54

her vicious tastes had so corrupted her
  she licensed every form of lust with laws
  to cleanse the stain of scandal she had spread;   57

she is Semiramis, who, legend says,
  was Ninus' wife as well as his successor;
  she governed all the land the Sultan rules.   60

31–32. The *contrapasso* or punishment suggests that lust (the "infernal storm") is pursued without the light of reason (in the darkness).

The next is she who killed herself for love
    and broke faith with the ashes of Sichaeus;
    and there is Cleopatra, who loved men's lusting.   63

See Helen there, the root of evil woe
    lasting long years, and see the great Achilles,
    who lost his life to love, in final combat;   66

see Paris, Tristan"—then, more than a thousand
    he pointed out to me, and named them all,
    those shades whom love cut off from life on earth.   69

After I heard my teacher call the names
    of all these knights and ladies of ancient times,
    pity confused my senses, and I was dazed.   72

I began: "Poet, I would like, with all my heart,
    to speak to those two there who move together
    and seem to be so light upon the winds."   75

And he: "You'll see when they are closer to us;
    if you entreat them by that love of theirs
    that carries them along, they'll come to you."   78

When the winds bent their course in our direction
    I raised my voice to them, "O wearied souls,
    come speak with us if it be not forbidden."   81

As doves, called by desire to return
    to their sweet nest, with wings raised high and poised,
    float downward through the air, guided by will,   84

---

64. Helen of Troy.

65–66. Enticed by the beauty of Polyxena, a daughter of the Trojan king, Achilles desired her to be his wife, but Hecuba, Polyxena's mother, arranged a counterplot with Paris so that when Achilles entered the temple for his presumed marriage, he was treacherously slain by Paris.

67. Paris was the son of Priam, king of Troy, whose abduction of Helen ignited the Trojan War. Tristan was the central figure of numerous medieval French, German, and Italian romances. Sent as a messenger by his uncle, King Mark of Cornwall, to obtain Isolt for him in marriage, Tristan became enamored of her, and she of him. After Isolt's marriage to Mark, the lovers continued their love affair, and in order to maintain its secrecy they necessarily employed many deceits and ruses. According to one version, Mark, increasingly suspicious of their attachment, finally discovered them together and ended the incestuous relationship by mortally wounding Tristan with a lance.

74. The two are Francesca, daughter of Guido Vecchio da Polenta, lord of Ravenna; and Paolo Malatesta, third son of Malatesta da Verrucchio, lord of Rimini. Around 1275 the aristocratic Francesca was married for political reasons to Gianciotto, the physically deformed second son of Malatesta da Verrucchio. In time a love affair developed between Francesca and Gianciotto's youngest brother, Paolo. One day the betrayed husband discovered them in an amorous embrace and slew them both.

so these two left the flock where Dido is
  and came toward us through the malignant air,
  such was the tender power of my call.   87

"O living creature, gracious and so kind,
  who makes your way here through this dingy air
  to visit us who stained the world with blood,   90

if we could claim as friend the King of Kings,
  we would beseech him that he grant you peace,
  you who show pity for our atrocious plight.   93

Whatever pleases you to hear or speak
  we will hear and we will speak about with you
  as long as the wind, here where we are, is silent.   96

The place where I was born lies on the shore
  where the river Po with its attendant streams
  descends to seek its final resting place.   99

Love, quick to kindle in the gentle heart,
  seized this one for the beauty of my body,
  torn from me. (How it happened still offends me!)   102

Love, that excuses no one loved from loving,
  seized me so strongly with delight in him
  that, as you see, he never leaves my side.   105

Love led us straight to sudden death together.
  Caïna awaits the one who quenched our lives."
  These were the words that came from them to us.   108

When those offended souls had told their story,
  I bowed my head and kept it bowed until
  the poet said, "What are you thinking of?"   111

When finally I spoke, I sighed, "Alas,
  all those sweet thoughts, and oh, how much desiring
  brought these two down into this agony."   114

And then I turned to them and tried to speak;
  I said, "Francesca, the torment that you suffer
  brings painful tears of pity to my eyes.   117

---

107. Caïna was one of the four divisions of Cocytus, the lower part of Hell, wherein those souls who treacherously betrayed their kin are tormented.

But tell me, in that time of your sweet sighing
   how, and by what signs, did love allow you
   to recognize your dubious desires?"   120

And she to me: "There is no greater pain
   than to remember, in our present grief,
   past happiness (as well your teacher knows)!   123

But if your great desire is to learn
   the very root of such a love as ours,
   I shall tell you, but in words of flowing tears.   126

One day we read, to pass the time away,
   of Lancelot, of how he fell in love;
   we were alone, innocent of suspicion.   129

Time and again our eyes were brought together
   by the book we read; our faces flushed and paled.
   To the moment of one line alone we yielded: 132

it was when we read about those longed-for lips
   now being kissed by such a famous lover,
   that this one (who shall never leave my side)   135

then kissed my mouth, and trembled as he did.
   Our Galehot was that book and he who wrote it.
   That day we read no further." And all the while   138

the one of the two spirits spoke these words,
   the other wept, in such a way that pity
   blurred my senses; I swooned as though to die,   141

and fell to Hell's floor as a body, dead, falls.

Petrarch

LETTER TO POSTERITY

Introduction by Michael Levin

Francesco Petrarch (1304–74) is often referred to as "the father of the Italian Renaissance." Born into an exiled Florentine family, Petrarch spent most of his life wandering about Italy, much like Dante. As a young man he attended law school, but he hated it. At one point he took holy orders, but that did not take either—much to his own disgust, Petrarch could never completely renounce the pleasures of the world. His only true loves were classical literature and a woman named Laura, and both would contribute to his profound effect on the Italian Renaissance.

Petrarch felt much more at ease with the history and literature of classical Rome than with the events and people of his own time. He often bemoaned the ignorance and vulgarity of his contemporaries, and longed for a return to the spirit of the classical age. This desire to revive classical ideas and ideals is of course at the heart of the Renaissance (which means "rebirth"), and Petrarch was the first of the Renaissance humanists who sought to rejuvenate their society. It was Petrarch who first coined the term "Dark Ages," referring to the centuries separating classical Rome from himself, and we still owe the idea of the "Middle Ages" to Petrarch and the Renaissance writers who followed his example. In order to return to the virtues of classical Rome, Petrarch advocated the use of the Latin language as the Romans knew it, particularly the great orator and writer Cicero. Petrarch spent his whole life trying to perfect a "Ciceronian" Latin prose style, which subsequently became the model of eloquence for generations of scholars.

But Petrarch isn't important only for his Latin works; his poetry in vernacular Italian was equally influential. Like Dante, Petrarch wrote a great deal of love poetry dedicated to a perfect, unattainable woman. Petrarch's love object was a blonde beauty named Laura, who may or may not have been aware of Petrarch's existence. He wrote a collection of 366 poems about Laura, called the *Canzoniere* ("Songbook"). These poems served as models for love poetry for at least three centuries—Shakespeare's sonnets often echo Petrarch. To the end of his life Petrarch wrestled with his conflicted emotions about earthly love. On the other hand, Laura served as Petrarch's muse, inspiring him to write great poetry. On the other hand Petrarch genuinely yearned to live a pure Christian life, and reject the ephemeral glories of this world. Petrarch expressed this conflict in a work called *Secretum,* in which he imagined a dialogue between himself and St. Augustine, one of the biggest influences on Petrarch's intellectual life. The character of St. Augustine berates Petrarch for caring too much about earthly love and fame, but Petrarch never really changes his mind.

For Petrarch did care about being famous. He promoted the idea of reviving the ancient Roman tradition of granting the title of poet laureate, so that he could win it. And he also wrote the letter we present here, the "Letter to Posterity." Petrarch wrote many letters, to contemporaries and to his long-dead heroes like Cicero. But this letter is written to us, his future readers. Petrarch is often called a "modern" author because of his self-awareness, his individualism, and his desire for immortality through his art. All of these things are evident in this letter. Read this letter and you will hear the voice of a man who has been dead for over six centuries. Petrarch would no doubt be pleased to know his work does indeed live on.

Letter to Posterity

It is possible that some word of me may have come to you, though even this is doubtful, since an insignificant and obscure name will scarcely penetrate far in either time or space. If, however, you should have heard of me, you may desire to know what manner of man I was, or what was the outcome of my labors, especially those of which some description or, at any rate, the bare titles may have reached you.

To begin with myself, then, the utterances of men concerning me will differ widely, since in passing judgment almost every one is influenced not so much by truth as by preference, and good and evil report alike know no bounds. I was, in truth, a poor mortal like yourself, neither very exalted in my origin, nor, on the other hand, of the most humble birth, but belonging, as Augustus Caesar says of himself, to an ancient family. As to my disposition, I was not naturally perverse or wanting in modesty, however the contagion of evil associations may have corrupted me. My youth was gone before I realized it; I was carried away by the strength of manhood; but a riper age brought me to my senses and taught me by experience the truth I had long before read in books, that youth and pleasure are vanity—nay, that the Author of all ages and times permits us miserable mortals, puffed up with emptiness, thus to wander about, until finally, coming to a tardy consciousness of our sins, we shall learn to know ourselves. In my prime I was blessed with a quick and active body, although not exceptionally strong; and while I do not lay claim to remarkable personal beauty, I was comely enough in my best days. I was possessed of a clear complexion, between light and dark, lively eyes, and for long years a keen vision, which however deserted me, contrary to my hopes, after I reached my sixtieth birthday, and forced me, to my great annoyance, to resort to glasses. Although I had previously enjoyed perfect health, old age brought with it the usual array of discomforts.

I have always possessed an extreme contempt for wealth; not that riches are not desirable in themselves, but because I hate the anxiety and care which are invariably associated with them. I certainly do not long to be able to give gorgeous banquets. I have, on the contrary, led a happier existence with plain living and ordinary fare than all the followers of Apicius,[1] with their elaborate dainties. So-called *convivia,* which are but vulgar bouts, sinning against sobriety and good manners, have always been repugnant to me. I have ever felt that it was irksome and profitless to invite others to such affairs, and not less so to be bidden to them myself. On the other hand, the pleasure of dining with one's friends is so great that nothing has ever given me more delight

Kenneth R. Bartlett, ed., *The Civilization of the Italian Renaissance*, Heath, 1992 (ISBN 0669-20900-7), original pp. 17–25 (Petrarch, "Letter to Posterity").

than their unexpected arrival, nor have I ever willingly sat down to table without a companion. Nothing displeases me more than display, for not only is it bad in itself, and opposed to humility, but it is troublesome and distracting.

I struggled in my younger days with a keen but constant and pure attachment, and would have struggled with it longer had not the sinking flame been extinguished by death—premature and bitter, but salutary.[2] I should be glad to be able to say that I had always been entirely free from irregular desires, but I should lie if I did so. I can, however, conscientiously claim that, although I may have been carried away by the fire of youth or by my ardent temperament, I have always abhorred such sins from the depths of my soul. As I approached the age of forty, while my powers were unimpaired and my passions were still strong, I not only abruptly threw off my bad habits, but even the very recollection of them, as if I had never looked upon a woman. This I mention as among the greatest of my blessings, and I render thanks to God, who freed me, while still sound and vigorous, from a disgusting slavery which had always been hateful to me.[3] But let us turn to other matters.

I have perceived pride in others, never in myself, and however insignificant I may have been, I have always been still less important in my own judgment. My anger has very often injured myself, but never others. I make this boast without fear, since I am confident that I speak truly: While I am very prone to take offense, I am equally quick to forget injuries, and have a memory tenacious of benefits. I have always been most desirous of honorable friendships, and have faithfully cherished them. But it is the cruel fate of those who are growing old that they can commonly only weep for friends who have passed away. In my familiar associations with kings and princes, and in my friendship with noble personages, my good fortune has been such as to excite envy. I fled, however, from many of those to whom I was greatly attached; and such was my innate longing for liberty, that I studiously avoided those whose very name seemed incompatible with the freedom that I loved. The greatest kings of this age have loved and courted me. They may know why; I certainly do not. With some of them I was on such terms that they seemed in a certain sense my guests rather than I theirs; their lofty position in no way embarrassing me, but, on the contrary, bringing with it many advantages.

I possessed a well-balanced rather than a keen intellect, one prone to all kinds of good and wholesome study, but especially inclined to moral philosophy and the art of poetry. The latter, indeed, I neglected as time went on, and took delight in sacred literature. Finding in that a hidden sweetness which I had once esteemed but lightly, I came to regard the works of the poets as only amenities. Among the many subjects which interested me, I dwelt especially upon antiquity, for our own age has always repelled me, so that, had it not been for the love of those dear to me, I should have preferred to have been born in any other period than our own. In order to forget my own time, I have constantly striven to place myself in spirit in other ages, and consequently I delighted in history; not that the conflicting statements did not offend me, but when in doubt I accepted what appeared to me most probable, or yielded to the authority of the writer.

My style, as many claimed, was clear and forcible; but to me it seemed weak and obscure. In ordinary conversation with friends, or with those about me, I never gave thought to my language, and I have always wondered that Augustus Caesar should have taken such pains in this respect.[4] When, however, the subject itself, or the place or listener, seemed to demand it, I gave some attention to style, with what success I cannot pretend to say; let them judge in whose presence I spoke. If only I have lived well, it matters little to me how I talked. Mere elegance of language can produce at best but an empty renown.

My parents were honorable folk, Florentine in their origin, of medium fortune, or, I may as well admit it, in a condition verging on poverty. They had been expelled from their native city,[5] and consequently I was born in exile, at Arezzo, in the year 1304 of this latter age which begins with Christ's birth, July the twentieth, on a Monday, at dawn. My life up to the present has, either through fate or my own choice, fallen into the following divisions. A part only of my first year was spent at Arezzo, where I first saw the light. The six following years were, owing to the recall of my mother from exile, spent upon my father's estate at Incisa, about fourteen miles above Florence. I passed my eighth year at Pisa, the ninth and following years in Farther Gaul, at Avignon, on the left bank of the Rhone, where the Roman Pontiff holds and has long held the Church of Christ in shameful exile.[6] It seemed a few years ago as if Urban V was on the point of restoring the Church to its ancient seat, but it is clear that nothing is coming of this effort, and, what is to me the worst of all, the Pope seems to have repented him of his good work, for failure came while he was still living.[7] Had he lived but a little longer, he would certainly have learned how I regarded his retreat. My pen was in my hand when he abruptly surrendered at once his exalted office and his life. Unhappy man, who might have died before the altar of Saint Peter and in his own habitation! Had his successors remained in their capital he would have been looked upon as the cause of this benign change, while, had they left Rome, his virtue would have been all the more conspicuous in contrast with their fault.[8]

But such laments are somewhat remote from my subject. On the windy banks of the river Rhone I spent my boyhood, guided by my parents, and then, guided by my own fancies, the whole of my youth. Yet there were long intervals spent elsewhere, for I first passed four years at the little town of Carpentras, somewhat to the east of Avignon: in these two places I learned as much of grammar, logic, and rhetoric as my age permitted, or rather, as much as it is customary to teach in school: you know how little that is, dear reader. I then set out for Montpellier to study law, and spent four years there, then three at Bologna. I heard the whole body of the civil law, and would, as many thought, have distinguished myself later, had I but continued my studies. I gave up the subject altogether, however, so soon as it was no longer necessary to consult the wishes of my parents.[9] My reason was that, although the dignity of the law, which is doubtless very great, and especially the numerous references it contains to Roman antiquity, did not fail to delight me, I felt it to be habitually degraded by those who practice it. It went against me painfully to acquire an art which I would not practice dishonestly, and could hardly hope to exercise otherwise. Had I made the latter attempt, my scrupulousness would doubtless have been ascribed to simplicity.

So at the age of two and twenty I returned home. I call my place of exile home, Avignon, where I had been since childhood; for habit has almost the potency of nature itself. I had already begun to be known there, and my friendship was sought by prominent men; wherefore I cannot say. I confess this is now a source of surprise to me, although it seemed natural enough at an age when we are used to regard ourselves as worthy of the highest respect. I was courted first and foremost by that very distinguished and noble family, the Colonnesi, who, at that period, adorned the Roman Curia with their presence. However it might be now, I was at that time certainly quite unworthy of the esteem in which I was held by them. I was especially honored by the incomparable Giacomo Colonna, then Bishop of Lombez,[10] whose peer I know not whether I have ever seen or ever shall see, and was taken by him to Gascony; there I spent such a divine summer among the foot-hills of the Pyrenees, in happy intercourse with my master and the members of our company, that I can never recall the experience without a sigh of regret.[11]

Returning thence, I passed many years in the house of Giacomo's brother, Cardinal Giovanni Colonna, not as if he were my lord and master, but rather my father, or better, a most affectionate brother—nay, it was as if I were in my own home.[12] About this time, a youthful desire impelled me to visit France and Germany. While I invented certain reasons to satisfy my elders of the propriety of the journey, the real explanation was a great inclination and longing to see new sights. I first visited Paris, as I was anxious to discover what was true and what fabulous in the accounts I had heard of that city. On my return from this journey I went to Rome, which I had since my infancy ardently desired to visit. There I soon came to venerate Stephano, the noble head of the family of the Colonnesi, like some ancient hero, and was in turn treated by him in every respect like a son. The love and good-will of this excellent man toward me remained constant to the end of his life, and lives in me still, nor will it cease until I myself pass away.

On my return, since I experienced a deep-seated and innate repugnance to town life, especially in that disgusting city of Avignon, which I heartily abhorred, I sought some means of escape. I fortunately discovered, about fifteen miles from Avignon, a delightful valley, narrow and secluded, called Vaucluse, where the Sorgue, the prince of streams, takes its rise. Captivated by the charms of the place, I transferred thither myself and my books. Were I to describe what I did there during many years, it would prove a long story. Indeed, almost every bit of writing which I have put forth was either accomplished or begun, or at least conceived, there, and my undertakings have been so numerous that they still continue to vex and weary me. My mind, like my body, is characterized by a certain versatility and readiness, rather than by strength, so that many tasks that were easy of conception have been given up by reason of the difficulty of their execution. The character of my surroundings suggested the composition of a sylvan or bucolic song.[13] I also dedicated a work in two books upon *The Life of Solitude,* to Philip, now exalted to the Cardinal-bishopric of Sabina. Although always a great man, he was, at the time of which I speak, only the humble Bishop of Cavaillon.[14] He is the only one of my old friends who is still left to me, and he has always loved and treated me not as a bishop (as Ambrose did Augustine), but as a brother.

While I was wandering in those mountains upon Friday in Holy Week, the strong desire seized me to write an epic in an heroic strain, taking as my theme Scipio Africanus the Great, who had, strange to say, been dear to me from my childhood. But although I began the execution of this project with enthusiasm, I straightway abandoned it, owing to a variety of distractions. The poem was, however, christened *Africa,* from the name of its hero, and, whether from his fortunes or mine, it did not fail to arouse the interest of many before they had seen it.[15]

While leading a leisurely existence in this region, I received, remarkable as it may seem, upon one and the same day,[16] letters both from the Senate at Rome and the Chancellor of the University of Paris, pressing me to appear in Rome and Paris, respectively, to receive the poet's crown of laurel.[17] In my youthful elation I convinced myself that I was quite worthy of this honor; the recognition came from eminent judges, and I accepted their verdict rather than that of my own better judgment. I hesitated for a time which I should give ear to, and sent a letter to Cardinal Giovanni Colonna, of whom I have already spoken, asking his opinion. He was so near that, although I wrote late in the day, I received his reply before the third hour on the morrow. I followed his advice, and recognized the claims of Rome as superior to all others. My acceptance of his counsel is shown by my twofold letter to him on that occasion, which I still keep. I set off accordingly; but although, after the fashion of youth, I was a most indulgent judge of my own work, I still blushed to accept in my own case the verdict even of such men as those who summoned me, despite the fact that they would certainly not have honored me in this way, had they not believed me worthy.

Notes

1. Proverbial gourmet from the age of Tiberius.
   SOURCE: Excerpts from D. Thompson (ed. and trans.), *Petrarch: A Humanist Among Princes.* (New York: Harper and Row, 1971), pp. 1–13. Reprinted by permission of HarperCollins Publishers.
2. While it is tempting to see here a reference to Laura, there are chronological difficulties. The period of life described *(adolescentia)* extended from age 15 to 28, but Petrarch's attachment to Laura lasted until her death many years later. Perhaps we must simply accept this as one of those not infrequent instances where Petrarch has altered the account of his life.
3. Though a cleric, Petrarch was the father of two illegitimate children: Giovanni, born in 1337; and Francesca, born six years later.
4. Suetonius, *Life of Augustus,* p. 87.
5. Petrarch's father, a "White" Guelph, was banished by the victorious "Black" Guelphs on October 20, 1302 (nine months after the expulsion of Dante, whom he had known).
6. The French pope, Clement V (1305–14), had moved the papal court to Avignon in 1309.
7. Urban V (1362–70) left Avignon in April, 1367; returned there from Rome in September, 1370; and died on December 19 of the same year.
8. Petrarch had sent metrical epistles to Urban's predecessors, Benedict XII (1334–42) and Clement VI (1342–52), urging them to restore the papacy to Rome.
9. Petrarch left Bologna in April 1326, probably on receiving news of his father's death. His mother had died some years earlier.
10. Some thirty miles southwest of Toulouse. Giacomo had been elected bishop in 1328. He died in 1341.
11. It was during this summer of 1330 that Petrarch formed his lifelong friendship with "Socrates" (the Flemish Ludwig van Kempen, chanter in the chapel of Cardinal Giovanni Colonna), who resided at Avignon; and with "Laelius" (a Roman, Lello di Pietro Stefano dei Tosetti), who also resided at Avignon until the cardinal's death in 1348. Many of Petrarch's letters are addressed to these two friends.
12. As a household chaplain Petrarch was an active member of the cardinal's staff from 1330 to 1337, and an occasionally active member for another ten years. This was his first ecclesiastical appointment. On his ecclesiastical career, see E. H. Wilkins, *Studies in the Life and Works of Petrarch* (Cambridge, Mass., 1955), pp. 3–32.
13. Petrarch conflates his first stay in Vaucluse (1337–41) with his third (1345–47); for the *Bucolicum Carman* and the *De Vita Solitaria* were both begun during the latter period. Petrarch began one or more major works during each of his four periods of residence at Vaucluse.
14. Philippe de Cabassoles, whose diocese included Vaucluse, was about Petrarch's age, and they shared similar tastes for books and country life. Philippe became cardinal in 1368, cardinal-bishop in 1370, and died in 1372.
15. Begun in 1338 or 1339, the *Africa* was never finished; and aside from a fragment that circulated during Petrarch's lifetime, it was not published until after his death. It proved something of a disappointment to Coluccio Salutati and others after they had seen it.
16. September 1, 1340.
17. Albertino Mussato had been crowned with laurel in Padua in 1315; and Dante had been offered a crown by Bologna but had declined (see *Paradiso* XXV, 1–9 on his desire to receive the crown in Florence). For the whole complicated question see E. H. Wilkins, "The Coronation of Petrarch" (*The Making of the "Cansoniere" and Other Petrarchan Studies* [Rome, 1951], pp. 9–69), who concludes: "the sum of the matter would seem to be that Petrarch succeeded, after persistent and varied efforts, in getting two invitations to receive the laurel crown; that the specific basis for the invitations was a rather limited amount of published Latin verse, together with the knowledge that he was engaged in the writing of a grandiose epic; that he had convinced the Colonna family and Roberto de' Bardi [Chancellor at the University of Paris, and a Florentine] that he was in truth a great poet; that their sense of his poetic worth was presumably enhanced by their knowledge that he was engaged in the writing of historical works and by the obvious range of his classical scholarship; and—just possibly—that the beauty of some of his belittled Italian lyrics was in their minds" (p. 35).

Pico della Mirandola

ORATION ON THE DIGNITY OF MAN

In the opening section of the *Oration,* Pico declares that unlike other creatures, human beings have not been assigned a fixed place in the universe. Our destiny is not determined by anything outside us. Rather, God has bestowed upon us a unique distinction: the liberty to determine the form and value our lives shall acquire. The notion that people have the power to shape their own lives is a key element in the emergence of the modern outlook.

I have read in the records of the Arabians, reverend Fathers, that Abdala the Saracen,[1] when questioned as to what on this stage of the world, as it were, could be seen most worthy of wonder, replied: "There is nothing to be seen more wonderful than man." In agreement with this opinion is the saying of Hermes Trismegistus: "A great miracle, Asclepius, is man."[2] But when I weighed the reason for these maxims, the many grounds for the excellence of human nature reported by many men failed to satisfy me—that man is the intermediary between creatures, the intimate of the gods, the kings of the lower beings, by the acuteness of his senses, by the discernment of his reason, and by the light of his intelligence the interpreter of nature, the interval between fixed eternity and fleeting time, and (as the Persians say) the bond, nay, rather, the marriage song of the world, on David's [biblical king] testimony but little lower than the angels. Admittedly great though these reasons be, they are not the principal grounds, that is, those which may rightfully claim for themselves the privilege of the highest admiration. For why should we not admire more the angels themselves and the blessed choirs of heaven? At last it seems to me I have come to understand why man is the most fortunate of creatures and consequently worthy of all admiration and what precisely is that rank which is his lot in the universal chain of Being—a rank to be envied not only by brutes but even by the stars and by minds beyond this world. It is a matter past faith and a wondrous one. Why should it not be? For it is on this very account that man is rightly called and judged a great miracle and a wonderful creature indeed. . . .

. . . God the Father, the supreme Architect, had already built this cosmic home we behold, the most sacred temple of His godhead, by the laws of His mysterious wisdom. The region above the heavens He had adorned with Intelligences, the heavenly spheres He had quickened with eternal souls, and the excrementary and filthy parts of the lower world He had filled with a multitude of animals of every kind. But, when the work was finished, the Craftsman kept wishing

Perry, Peden, Von Laue, eds., *Sources of the Western Tradition,* Volume 1, Houghton Mifflin (ISBN: 0-395-89201-5), original pp. 286–7 (Pico della Mirandola, "Oration on the Dignity of Man").

that there was someone to ponder the plan of so great a work, to love its beauty, and to wonder at its vastness. Therefore, when everything was done (as Moses and Timaeus[3] bear witness), He finally took thought concerning the creation of man. But there was not among His archetypes that from which He could fashion a new offspring, nor was there in His treasurehouses anything which He might bestow on His new son as an inheritance, nor was there in the seats of all the world a place where the latter might sit to contemplate the universe. All was now complete; all things had been assigned to the highest, the middle, and the lowest orders. But in its final creation it was not the part of the Father's power to fail as though exhausted. It was not the part of His wisdom to waver in a needful matter through poverty of counsel. It was not the part of His kindly love that he who was to praise God's divine generosity in regard to others should be compelled to condemn it in regard to himself.

At last the best of artisans [God] ordained that that creature to whom He had been able to give nothing proper to himself should have joint possession of whatever had been peculiar to each of the different kinds of being. He therefore took man as a creature of indeterminate nature and, assigning him a place in the middle of the world, addressed him thus: "Neither a fixed abode nor a form that is thine alone nor any function peculiar to thyself have we given thee, Adam, to the end that according to thy longing and according to thy judgment thou mayest have and possess what abode, what form, and what functions thou thyself shalt desire. The nature of all other beings is limited and constrained within the bounds of laws prescribed by Us. Thou, constrained by no limits, in accordance with thine own free will, in whose hand We have placed thee, shalt ordain for thyself the limits of thy nature. We have set thee at the world's center that thou mayest from thence more easily observe whatever is in the world. We have made thee neither of heaven nor of earth, neither mortal nor immortal, so that with freedom of choice and with honor, as though the maker and molder of thyself, thou mayest fashion thyself in whatever shape thou shalt prefer. Thou shalt have the power to degenerate into the lower forms of life, which are brutish. Thou shalt have the power, out of thy soul's judgment, to be reborn into the higher forms, which are divine."

O supreme generosity of God the Father, O highest and most marvelous felicity of man! To him it is granted to have whatever he chooses, to be whatever he wills. Beasts as soon as they are born (so says Lucilius)[4] bring with them from their mother's womb all they will ever possess. Spiritual beings [angels], either from the beginning or soon thereafter, become what they are to be for ever and ever. On man when he came into life the Father conferred the seeds of all kinds and the germs of every way of life. Whatever seeds each man cultivates will grow to maturity and bear in him their own fruit. If they be vegetative, he will be like a plant. If sensitive, he will become brutish. If rational, he will grow into a heavenly being. If intellectual, he will be an angel and the son of God. And if, happy in the lot of no created thing, he withdraws into the center of his own unity, his spirit, made one with God, in the solitary darkness of God, who is set above all things, shall surpass them all.

Notes

1. Abdala the Saracen possibly refers to the eighth-century A.D. writer Abd-Allah Ibn al-Muqaffa.
2. Ancient writings dealing with magic, alchemy, astrology, and occult philosophy were erroneously attributed to an assumed Egyptian priest, Hermes Trismegistus. Asclepius was a Greek god of healing.
3. Timaeus, a Greek Pythagorean philosopher, was a central character in Plato's famous dialogue *Timaeus*.
4. Lucilius, a first-century A.D. Roman poet and Stoic philosopher, was a close friend of Seneca, the philosopher-dramatist.

CHAPTER ONE

THE NEED FOR WATER

IN ANCIENT SOCIETIES

The title of the course for which you are using this book is probably a variant of "Western Civilization." Why do we use the term "civilization"? What distinguishes human cultures that are labeled civilizations from those that are not? Though great differences separate them, all civilizations share some basic characteristics. The most important of these similarities is the presence of cities; indeed, the word "civilization" comes from the Latin word *civilis* (meaning "civic"), which is also the root of "citizen" and "civil." Historians and archaeologists generally define a city as a place inhabited by more than 5,000 people, and they have discovered the remains of the earliest communities of this size in ancient Mesopotamia, which is present-day Iraq.

Why should the presence of cities be the distinguishing mark of cultural development? It is not the cities themselves but what they imply about a culture that makes them so important. Any society in which thousands of people live in close proximity to one another must have some sort of laws or rules governing human behavior. These may be either part of an oral tradition or, as in ancient Mesopotamia, written down. A city must provide its residents with a constant supply of food, which means developing ways to transport food into the city from the surrounding farmland, to store food throughout the year, and to save it for years marked by poor harvests. Not only does the presence of cities indicate that people could transport and store food effectively, but it also reveals that they were producing enough surplus food to allow for specialization of labor. If all work time had been devoted to farming, it would not have been possible to build roads, produce storage bins, or enforce laws on which the city depended. This specialization of labor, then, gave some members of society the opportunity and time to create and produce goods and artifacts that were not directly essential to daily survival. Urban residents in Mesopotamia began to construct large buildings and decorate them with sculptures, paintings, and mosaics; to write poetry and history; and to develop religious and philosophical ideas, all of which are pursuits we consider essential to a civilization. As the cities themselves grew, they required greater and greater amounts of food to feed their inhabitants, which led to further technological development.

Mesopotamia was in many ways an odd location for the beginning of a civilization. True, the soil is so rich that the region is called the Fertile Crescent, but it does not receive enough natural rainfall to grow crops steadily year after year. In fact, this region is not where agriculture began in the West; that happened closer to the Mediterranean, where the rainfall was more regular. Apparently, as techniques of planting and harvesting crops spread into Mesopotamia, the inhabitants realized that they would be able to use these techniques effectively only through irrigation. They needed to tap the waters flowing in the Tigris and Euphrates Rivers, a project requiring the cooperation of a great many people. Thus, rather than proving a block to further development, the need for irrigation in ancient Mesopotamia may have been one of the reasons that cities first arose there. We may never be able to know this with certainty, because irrigation systems were already in place when written records began and because cities and irrigation expanded at the same time. We do know, however, that in Mesopotamia, neither

could have existed without the other; cities could survive only where irrigation had created a food surplus, and irrigation could survive only where enough people were available to create and maintain ditches and other parts of the system.

Building irrigation systems presented both technical and organizational problems. The Tigris and Euphrates were fast-flowing rivers that carried soil as well as water down from the highlands. This rich soil created new farmland where the rivers emptied into the Persian Gulf. (The ancient Persian Gulf ended more than 100 miles north of its present boundary; all that land was created as the rivers filled in the delta.) The soil also rapidly clogged up the irrigation ditches, which consequently required constant cleaning. Every year these deposits were excavated and piled on the banks until the sides of the ditches grew so tall that cleaning could no longer be easily accomplished. At this point the old ditch was abandoned and a new ditch was cut, tasks that required a great deal of work and the cooperation of everyone whose land was watered by that ditch.

Mesopotamian farmers used several types of irrigation. One technique, known as *basin irrigation*, was to level large plots of land fronting the rivers and main canals and build up dikes around them. In the spring and other times during the year when the water was high, farmers knocked holes in the dikes to admit water and fresh soil. Once the sediment had settled, they let the water flow back into the channel. They also built small waterways between their fields to provide water throughout the year, thereby developing a system of *perennial irrigation*. In the hillier country of northern Mesopotamia, farmers built terraces with water channels running alongside them. The hillside terraces provided narrow strips of flat land to farm, and the waterways were dug to connect with brooks and streams.

Farmers could depend on gravity to bring water to their fields during spring and flood seasons, but at other times they needed water-raising machines. They devised numerous types of machines, some of which are still in use today in many parts of the world. These solved some problems but created others, as farmers with machines could drain an irrigation ditch during times of low water, leaving their neighbors with nothing. How were rights to water to be decided? Solving this problem was crucial to human social organization, and the first recorded laws regarding property rights in fact concern not rights to land but rights to water. In Mesopotamia, land was useless unless it was irrigated.

Many of the irrigation techniques developed in Mesopotamia either spread to Egypt or were developed independently there. Because it received even less rainfall than Mesopotamia, Egypt was totally dependent on the Nile for watering crops. Fortunately, the Nile was a much better source of water than the Tigris and Euphrates because it flooded regularly, allowing easy basin irrigation. The rise and fall of the Nile was so regular, in fact, that the Egyptians based their 365-day calendar on its annual flooding. The Egyptians also constructed waterways and

water-lifting machines to allow for perennial irrigation. As in Mesopotamia, irrigation in Egypt both caused and resulted from the growth of cities. It contributed as well to the power of the kings, whom the Egyptian people regarded as responsible for the flood of the Nile.

Irrigation was more difficult in places that did not have flood-prone rivers, including many parts of North Africa and the Near East. Here people adapted techniques to conserve water from sporadic heavy rainfalls. They dammed the temporary lakes (termed *wadis*) created by these rainfalls and built ditches to convey the water to fields, rather than allowing it simply to flow off onto the desert. Sometimes this wadi irrigation involved a whole series of small dams down the course of rivers that ran only after storms. Besides providing water, wadi irrigation also built up terraces because the rivers carried soil with them.

The earliest water systems were for crop irrigation, but people also began to demand good drinking water. In many parts of the ancient world, the demand for drinking water led to the establishment of a second system because river water that is suitable for irrigation may be brackish, unpleasant, or even unhealthful to drink. In southern Europe, where lakes were often not far from growing cities, people solved the problem by building channels made of timber, stone, or clay earthenware to carry water from the lakes to the city. These channels might be open or closed, depending on the terrain and the level of technical development of the culture that built them. Generally they relied on gravity flow and fed into underground tanks or reservoirs in the city; the oldest known water channels are in Jerusalem and date from about 1000 B.C. The construction of such systems, which demanded even more technical expertise than the building of irrigation ditches, provoked additional legal problems about ownership of the right to this clean, cool water.

When lakes were not located close enough to make aboveground channels feasible, people had to rely on water from *aquifers,* underground water-bearing layers of gravel or porous rock. The water could be obtained from wells drilled in the ground, but wells could supply only a small amount of water at a time. Once an aquifer had been discovered, however, a horizontal channel could be dug to lead the water to an outside channel or reservoir. A horizontal channel worked only in hilly areas where the aquifer stood higher than a nearby valley, but such channels, called *qanats,* have been found in Iran, Syria, Egypt, and Turkey that are over 2,000 years old. If the amount of water it yielded was large enough, the qanat could be used for irrigation as well as drinking water.

When the Romans conquered the Middle East and North Africa in the second century B.C., they inherited irrigation systems that in some cases had already been in existence for more than 2,000 years. The Romans carried many ideas to other parts of their empire and made innovations as the terrain or distance required. Most of the European territory in the Roman Empire received adequate

rainfall for farming without irrigation, but many Roman cities, especially Rome itself, experienced a chronic shortage of drinking water. The Romans solved this problem by building *aqueducts,* covered or uncovered channels that brought water into the cities from lakes and springs. The first of these in Rome was built in 312 B.C., and the system expanded continuously up to about A.D. 150. Over 300 miles of aqueducts served the city of Rome alone, with extensive systems in the outlying provinces as well. Although Roman engineers went to great lengths to avoid valleys, they were occasionally forced to construct enormous bridges to carry the aqueducts over valleys. Some of these bridges were over 150 feet high, and a few, such as the bridge-aqueduct in Segovia, Spain, still bring water to city residents. The Romans' sophisticated architectural and construction techniques—the arch and water-resistant cement, for example— enabled them to build water systems undreamed of in Mesopotamia and Egypt. Legal problems were not as easily solved, however, and disputes about water rights recur frequently throughout the long history of Rome.

Supplying cities with water was not simply a technological problem; it had economic, legal, and political implications. Through their solutions to these complex problems, ancient societies created what we call civilization. Your task in this chapter will be to use both visual and written evidence of ancient water systems to answer the question, How did the need for a steady supply of water shape civilization?

SOURCES AND METHOD

Historians use a wide variety of sources when examining ancient irrigation and water supply systems. Since many of these systems were created before the development of writing, archaeological evidence is extremely important, especially in examining technological development. This evidence may be the actual remains of ancient ditches, machines, or aqueducts, but in many areas these have completely disappeared. This does not mean that they have left no trace, however, for the ancient uses of modern landscapes are often revealed through patterns of depressions and discoloration.

The best way to see these patterns is through aerial photography. Analyzing aerial photographs can be a difficult task, and learning how to read ancient land-use patterns through the overlay of modern development takes a great deal of training. Occasionally the older patterns can be quite clear, however, and only a small amount of additional information is necessary for you to begin to decode them. The first piece of evidence, Source 1, is an aerial photograph of the site of a pre-Roman city in Italy. Examine the picture carefully. Can you see the old grid pattern of irrigation ditches, which shows up as light and dark marsh grass? The dark lines are the outlines of ancient irrigation ditches, the lighter squares are ancient fields, and the white parallel lines superimposed on the top are part of a modern drainage system. To examine the ancient system, you will need to strip away the modern system mentally. What do you think the broader black strip at the top left is? Does this system look like basin or perennial irrigation? Look at the flatness of the landscape. Would silting be a problem?

A more sophisticated type of aerial photography involves the use of satellites rather than airplanes. Satellites can take extremely detailed pictures of the earth's surface that reveal natural and artificially constructed features, both ancient and contemporary. The sharpest images are produced by high-resolution military satellites whose pictures are not available to the public. Low-power images produced by LANDSAT, the only U.S. commercial imaging satellite system, are adequate for most archaeological and historical purposes, however. Source 2 is a map of the major ancient irrigation ditches between the Tigris and Euphrates Rivers that were identifiable in a recent LANDSAT image. What does the size of the system reveal about Mesopotamian technology? What does it imply about the political systems in this area—would you expect, for example, the cities in Mesopotamia to be hostile to one another? New technologies such as LANDSAT imagery not only provide answers to questions, but also guide future research. How could you use this map to plan further investigations of irrigation systems?

Aerial photography provides visual evidence of entire irrigation systems but not of the specific tools and machines used to lift water to the fields. For these we must look to the remains of the tools themselves or to depictions of them in tomb paintings, mosaics, and pottery. Source 3 is the earliest depiction of irrigation ditches that has survived from ancient Egypt, carved on the head of a ceremonial mace dating from around 3100 B.C. The large figure in the middle is one of the early kings of Egypt, who is holding a hoe and who is flanked by two palm-fan bearers and a man holding a basket for the dirt dug up by the hoe. At the bottom are two other workmen, also with hoes, excavating or deepening the ditches. Based on what you already know about Eygptian society, would you expect the king himself to be digging ditches? Why might this mace, which signified royal authority, show the king involved in building irrigation ditches?

Some of the machines depicted in ancient paintings are still in use today, showing that many techniques for lifting water have not changed at all for thousands of years. Sources 4 through 7 show four different machines for raising water that we know were in use in ancient times and are still in use in many parts of the world today: the shaduf, saqiya, Archimedes' screw,[1] and noria. To assess their role and importance, you must consider a number of different factors while carefully examining the four diagrams. Some of these factors are technical: How complicated is the machine to build? Does it have many moving parts that must all be in good repair? How much water can it lift?

How high can it lift the water? Can it work with both flowing and stationary water? Some factors are economic: Does the machine require a person to operate it, thus taking that person away from other types of labor? Does it require a strong adult, or can it be operated by a child? Does it require an animal, which must be fed and cared for? Some factors are both economic and political: Does the machine require a variety of raw materials to build, more than one family might possess? Does it require any raw materials, like metal, that would have to be imported? (Such questions are political because someone has to decide which families get the raw materials necessary for their fields.) Some factors are legal: Does the machine raise so much water that laws about distribution would become necessary? At this point, you may want to make a chart summarizing your assessment of the advantages and disadvantages of each machine, which will help you in making your final conclusions.

We will now turn from visual to written sources. Because water is such a vital commodity, mention of water systems appears very early in recorded human history. The next five sources are written accounts of the construction or operation of water systems. Source 8 contains sections from the Code of Hammurabi, a Babylonian legal code dating from 1750 B.C., that refer to irrigation. Source 9 is a description of the Roman aqueduct system written by Vitruvius during the first century B.C., and Source 10 is a description of the water-system projects undertaken by

1. Archimedes (287–212 B.C.) was a Greek mathematician and inventor who is credited with inventing this machine.

Emperor Claudius during his reign (A.D. 41–54), written by the Roman historian Suetonius. The next selection is a discussion of some of the problems associated with Rome's water system written about A.D. 100 by Frontinus, who was commissioner of the water supply. The last is a proclamation issued by Emperor Theodosius in 438 as part of his code of laws, an edict that had probably been in effect for many earlier decades as well.

As you read these sources, notice first of all the technical issues that the authors are addressing. What problems in tapping, transportation, and storage of water do they discuss? What solutions do they suggest? Then look at legal problems, which you can find most clearly stated in the selection by Frontinus and the law codes of Hammurabi and Theodosius. Keep in mind when you are reading the law codes that laws are generally written to address those problems that already exist, not those

the lawmakers are simply anticipating. The presence of a law, especially one that is frequently repeated, is often a good indication that the prohibited activity was probably happening, and happening often. How did people misuse or harm the water systems? What penalties were provided for those who did? Who controlled the legal use of water, and who decided how water was to be distributed?

The written sources also include information about political and economic factors in ancient water supply systems that is nearly impossible to gain from archaeological evidence. Careful reading can reveal who paid for the construction of such systems and who stood to gain financially from them once they were built. What reasons, other than the simple need for water, might rulers have had for building water systems? What political and economic factors entered into decisions about the ways in which water was to be distributed?

THE EVIDENCE

Source 1 from Leo Deuel, Flights into Yesterday: The Story of Aerial Archeology *(New York: St. Martin's Press, 1969), p. 236. Photo by Fotoaerea Valvassori, Ravenna.*

1. Aerial Photograph of Pre-Roman City in Italy

Source 2 from Robert MaC. Adams, Heartland of Cities: Surveys of Ancient Settlements and Land Use on the Central Floodplains of the Euphrates *(Chicago: University of Chicago Press, 1981), p. 34.*

2. Major Ancient Levees Identifiable in LANDSAT Imagery

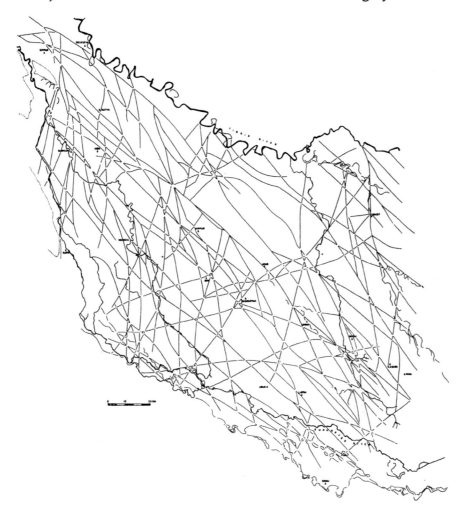

Source 3 from Walter B. Emery, Archaic Egypt *(Baltimore: Penguin, 1961), p. 43.*

3. Early Egyptian King Cutting an Irrigation Ditch, Drawn from Mace-head Carving, 3100 B.C.

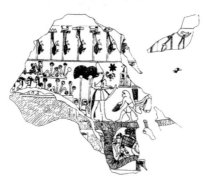

Sources 4 through 7 adapted from sketches by Merry E. Wiesner.

4. Shaduf

5. Saqiya

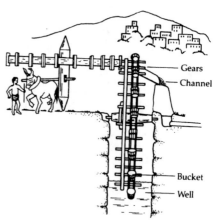

6. Archimedes' Screw

7. Noria

Source 8 from Robert F. Harper, The Code of Hammurabi *(Chicago: University of Chicago Press, 1904).*

8. Sections from the Code of Hammurabi Referring to Irrigation, 1750 B.C.

53. If a man neglects to maintain his dike and does not strengthen it, and a break is made in his dike and the water carries away the farmland, the man in whose dike the break has been made shall replace the grain which has been damaged.

54. If he is not able to replace the grain, they shall sell him and his goods and the farmers whose grain the water has carried away shall divide [the results of the sale].

55. If a man opens his canal for irrigation and neglects it and the water carries away an adjacent field, he shall pay out grain on the basis of the adjacent field.

56. If a man opens up the water and the water carries away the improvements of an adjacent field, he shall pay out ten gur of grain per bur [of damaged land]. . . .

66. If a man has stolen a watering-machine from the meadow, he shall pay five shekels of silver to the owner of the watering-machine.

Sources 9 and 10 from Naphtali Lewis and Meyer Reinhold, editors and translators, Roman Civilization *(New York: Columbia University Press, 1955), pp. 304–306; pp. 151–152. Reprinted with permission of Columbia University Press, 562 W. 113th St., New York, NY 10025, via Copyright Clearance Center, Inc.*

9. Vitruvius's Description of the Roman Aqueduct System, first century B.C.

The supply of water is made by three methods: by channels through walled conduits, or by lead pipes, or by earthenware pipes. And they are arranged as follows. In the case of conduits, the structure must be very solid; the bed of the channel must be leveled with a fall of not less than half a foot in 100 feet. The walled conduits are to be arched over so that the minimum amount of sun may strike the water. When it comes to the city walls, a reservoir is to be made. To this reservoir a triple distribution tank is to be joined to receive the water; and three pipes of equal size are to be placed in the reservoir, leading to the adjoining tanks, so that when there is an overflow from the two outer tanks, it may deliver into the middle tank. From the middle tank pipes will be laid to all basins and fountains; from the second tank to the baths, in order to furnish an annual revenue to the treasury; to avoid a deficiency in the public supply, private houses are to be supplied from the third, for private persons will not be able to divert the water, since they have their own limited supply from the distribution sources. Another reason why I have made these divisions is that those who take private supplies into their houses may by their taxes paid through tax farmers contribute to the maintenance of the water supply.

If, however, there are hills between the city and the source, we must proceed as follows: underground channels are to be dug and leveled to the fall mentioned above. If the bed is of tufa or stone, the channel may be cut in it; but if it is of soil or sand, the bed of the channel and the walls with the vaulting must be constructed, and the water should be thus conducted. Air shafts are to be so constructed that they are 120 feet apart. . . .

Water supply by earthenware pipes has these advantages. First, in the construction: if a break occurs, anybody can repair it. Again, water is much more wholesome from earthenware pipes than from lead pipes. For it seems to be made injurious by lead, because white lead is produced by it; and this is said to be harmful to the human body. So if what is produced by anything is injurious, there is no doubt that the thing itself is not wholesome. We can take an example from the workers in lead who have complexions affected by pallor. For when lead is smelted in casting, the fumes from it settle on the members of the body and, burning them, rob the limbs of the virtues of the blood. Therefore it seems that water should by no means be brought in lead pipes if we desire to have it wholesome. Everyday life can be used to show that the flavor from earthenware pipes is better, because everybody (even those who load their table with silver vessels) uses earthenware to preserve the purity of water.

But if we are to create springs from which the water supplies come, we must dig wells.

But if the soil is hard, or if the veins of water lie too deep, then supplies of water are to be collected from the roofs or higher ground in concrete cisterns. . . . If the cisterns are made double or triple, so that they can be changed by percolation, they will make the supply of water much more wholesome. For when the sediment has a place to settle in, the water will be more limpid and will keep its taste without any smell. If not, salt must be added to purify it.

10. Suetonius's Description of the Water Projects Undertaken by Emperor Claudius (r. A.D. 41–54)

The public works which Claudius completed were great and essential rather than numerous; they were in particular the following: an aqueduct begun by Caligula; also the drainage channel of Lake Fucine and the harbor at Ostia, although in the case of the last two he knew that Augustus had refused the former to the Marsians in spite of their frequent requests, and that the latter had often been considered by the deified Julius but given up because of its difficulty. He brought to the city on stone arches the cool and abundant springs of the Claudian aqueduct . . . and at the same time the channel of the New Anio, distributing them into many beautifully ornamented fountains. He made the attempt on the Fucine Lake as much in the hope of gain as of glory, inasmuch as there were some who offered to drain it at their own cost provided the land that was drained be given them. He finished the drainage canal, which was three miles in length, partly by leveling and partly by tunneling a mountain, a work of great difficulty requiring eleven years, although he had 30,000 men at work all the time without interruption.

Source 11 from B. K. Workman, editor and translator, They Saw It Happen in Classical Times *(New York: Barnes & Noble, 1964), pp. 179–181. Reprinted by permission of Littlefield, Adams & Company and Basil Blackwell Publishers.*

11. Frontinus's Discussion of Rome's Water System, ca A.D. 100

The New Anio[2] is drawn from the river in the district of Sinbrinum, at about the forty-second milestone along the Via Sublacensis. On either side of the

2. An aqueduct completed under the emperor Claudius in A.D. 52.

river at this point are fields of rich soil which make the banks less firm, so that the water in the aqueduct is discoloured and muddy even without the damage done by storms. So a little way along from the inlet a cleansing basin was built where the water could settle and be purified between the river and the conduit. Even so, in the event of rain, the water reaches the city in a muddy state. The length of the New Anio is about 47 miles, of which over 39 are underground and more than 7 carried on structures above the ground. In the upper reaches a distance of about two miles in various sections is carried on low structures or arches. Nearer the city, from the seventh Roman milestone, is half a mile on substructures and five miles on arches. These arches are very high, rising in certain places to a height of 109 feet.

. . . All the aqueducts reach the city at different levels. So some serve the higher districts and some cannot reach loftier ground. For the hills of Rome have gradually increased in height because of the rubble from frequent fires. There are five aqueducts high enough at entrance to reach all the city, but they supply water at different pressures. . . .

Anyone who wants to tap water for private consumption must send in an application and take it, duly signed by the Emperor, to the Commissioner. The latter must take immediate action on Caesar's grant, and enroll one of the Imperial freedmen to help him in the business. . . . The right to water once granted cannot be inherited or bought, and does not go with the property, though long ago a privilege was extended to the public baths that their right should last in perpetuity. . . .

Now that I have explained the situation with regard to private supply, it will be pertinent to give some examples of the ways in which men have broken these very sound arrangements and have been caught red-handed. In some reservoirs I have found larger valves in position than had been granted, and some have not even had the official stamp on them. . . .

Another of the watermen's intolerable practices is to make a new outlet from the cistern when a water-grant is transferred to a new owner, leaving the old one for themselves. I would say that it was one of the Commissioner's chief duties to put a stop to this. For it affects not only the proper protection of the supply, but also the upkeep of the reservoir which would be ruined if needlessly filled with outlets.

Another financial scheme of the watermen, which they call "puncturing," must also be abolished. There are long separate stretches all over the city through which the pipes pass hidden under the pavement. I found out that these pipes were being tapped everywhere by the "puncturers," from which water was supplied by private pipe to all the business premises in the area, with the result that only a meagre amount reached the public utilities. I can estimate the volume of water stolen in this way from the amount of lead piping which was removed when these branch pipes were dug up.

Source 12 from Naphtali Lewis and Meyer Reinhold, editors and translators, Roman Civilization (New York: Columbia University Press, 1955), pp. 479–480. Reprinted with permission of Columbia University Press, 562 W. 113th St., New York, NY 10025, via Copyright Clearance Center, Inc.

12. Proclamation of Emperor Theodosius, A.D. 438

It is our will that the landholders over whose lands the courses of aqueducts pass shall be exempt from extraordinary burdens, so that by their work the aqueducts may be cleansed when they are choked with dirt. The said landholders shall not be subject to any other burden of a superindiction,[3] lest they be occupied in other matters and not be present to clean the aqueducts. If they neglect this duty, they shall be punished by the forfeiture of their landholdings; for the fisc[4] will take possession of the landed estate of any man whose negligence contributes to the damage of the aqueducts. Furthermore, persons through whose landed estates the aqueducts pass should know that they may have trees to the right and left at a distance of fifteen feet from the aqueducts, and your[5] office shall see to it that these trees are cut out if they grow too luxuriantly at any time, so that their roots may not injure the structure of the aqueduct.

QUESTIONS TO CONSIDER

Now that you have looked at both visual and written evidence, you will need to put together the information you have gathered from each type of source to achieve a more complete picture. Because sources for the earliest period of human development are so scanty, we need to use every shred of information available and use it somewhat creatively, making speculations where no specific evidence exists.

Take all the evidence about technical problems first. Keeping in mind that the ancient world had no power equipment and no tools more elaborate than axes, hammers, saws, and drills (the Romans also had planes and chisels), what would you judge to be the most difficult purely technical problem involved in constructing water systems? In keeping them operating? The four diagrams of the water-raising machines are arranged in chronological order of their development: The shaduf may be as old as 2500 B.C., and the other three did not appear until 1,000 years later. Looking at your chart on the advantages and disadvantages of each machine,

3. That is, any special taxes.

4. **fisc**: the imperial treasury.

5. This proclamation was addressed to the administrator of the water supply, the same office that Frontinus held earlier.

in what ways did the later machines improve on the shaduf? What additional problems might these improvements have produced? What types of technological experimentation did the need for water encourage?

Technological advance is not always an unmitigated blessing. For example, water standing in irrigation ditches can become brackish, providing a good breeding ground for mosquitoes and other carriers of disease. Cities that depend on irrigation suffer food shortages and famine when ditches cannot be kept clear or when river levels are low. The diversion of large quantities of water for irrigation makes rivers much smaller when they finally reach their deltas, which means that the deltas become increasingly salty from seawater and unable to support the types of plant and animal life they originally fostered. Judging by the aerial photograph and the LANDSAT map, would you expect any of these problems in ancient Italy or Mesopotamia? Do you find evidence in the written sources for problems in the later Roman water systems that were caused by technical advances? Do the written sources offer suggestions for solving these problems?

Now consider what you have learned about the economic issues associated with water systems. You have doubtless noticed that tremendous numbers of people were needed to construct irrigation ditches and aqueducts. Some of the written sources, such as the extract from Suetonius, provide exact figures. The size and complexity of the systems in the other sources also imply a substantial

work force, given the lack of elaborate equipment. The rulers of Egypt, Mesopotamia, and Rome saw the need for a large labor force as no problem; it was, rather, a solution to the greater problem of unemployment. According to a story told about the Roman emperor Vespasian, when he was offered a labor-saving machine, he refused to allow its use because that would put people out of work and lead to social problems in Rome. We might regard this concern for full employment as a positive social attitude, but it should also tell you something about the value of labor in ancient societies. What would you expect wages to be for construction workers? What class of people would you expect to find working on these water systems?

Large numbers of workers were needed not only to build but also to maintain irrigation systems and to operate water-lifting machines. What does this fact tell you about the value of labor? What would happen with a sudden drop in the population, such as that caused by a famine or epidemic? How would a loss of workers affect the available food supply?

The sources also reveal information about political factors associated with water systems. What does the construction of these systems indicate about the power of rulers to coerce or hire labor? How do rulers control the building and maintenance of machines and ditches? How might their control affect the power and independence of local communities or of individual families? What does this tell you about the role of water in expanding centralized political power?

Finally, the sources provide evidence of alterations in the law made necessary by the search for water. Previously unrestricted and unregulated actions now came under the control of public authorities, which meant that the number of enforcement agents and courts had to increase. What would this do to taxation levels? In what ways would political concerns shape the regulations?

Political issues affect not only the types of laws to be passed, but also the stringency or selectivity with which those laws are enforced. We have very little information about how rigidly law codes were implemented in ancient societies, for few legal documents have survived; law codes were frequently recopied and reissued, but the outcome of individual cases was not.

It is therefore dangerous to assume that the prescribed penalties were actually levied or that the law was regularly obeyed. (Think for a minute the mistake a person 2,000 years from now would make in describing traffic patterns in twentieth-century America if he or she assumed that the posted speed limit described the actual speed at which traffic moved!) Looking again at the law codes of Hammurabi and Theodosius, would you expect the penalties to be carried out, or do they appear to serve more as a strong warning? How would the penalties differ in their effects on poor and rich people?

You are now ready to answer the question posed at the beginning of the chapter. How did the need for a steady supply of water affect the development of civilization in the West?

EPILOGUE

The irrigation and water supply systems of the ancient world not only required huge amounts of labor, but also made necessary a strong central authority to coerce or hire that labor and to enforce laws to keep the channels flowing. At first, each Mesopotamian city managed its own irrigation system, but the wealthy and advanced cities were attractive targets for foreign conquerors. The political history of ancient Mesopotamia was one of wave after wave of conquerors coming down from the north—the Akkadians, Babylonians, Assyrians, Persians, Greeks, and finally the Romans. Most of these conquerors realized the importance of irrigation and ordered the conquered residents to maintain or expand their systems. When the Muslims invaded the region in the seventh century, they also learned Mesopotamian techniques and spread these westward into North Africa and Spain, where Roman irrigation systems had in many places fallen apart.

Irrigation could also be overdone, however, and during periods of political centralization many areas were overirrigated, which led to salinization, making the land useless for farming. This, combined with the rivers of Mesopotamia changing their courses, meant that many cities could not survive. Centuries of irrigation combined with too little fertilization made even land that was not salinized less and less productive.

The benefits and problems produced by irrigation are not limited to the ancient world, however; they can be seen in many modern societies. One of the best modern examples comes from the same part of the world we have been studying in this chapter. Throughout the twentieth century, Egypt expanded its irrigation system watered by the Nile with a series of dams, culminating in the Aswan High Dam; this dam, begun in 1960, was designed to provide hydroelectric power and limit the free flow of water at the height of the flood season. The enormous reservoir formed by the dam can also be tapped at low-water times to allow for perennial irrigation. The Aswan Dam serves all its intended purposes very well, but it has also created some unexpected problems. The river's regular flooding had brought new fertile soil to the Nile Valley and carried away the salts that resulted from evaporation. Once the dam stopped the flooding, Egyptian fields needed artificial fertilizer to remain productive, a commodity many farmers could not afford. The soil of the Nile Valley has a high clay content, rendering drainage difficult, and a steady supply of water makes many fields waterlogged and unusable. The large reservoir created by the dam sits in the middle of the Sahara, allowing a tremendous amount of evaporation and significantly decreasing the total flow of water in the Nile; it has also put many acres of farmland under water and forced the relocation of tens of thousands of people. Ending the flooding allowed snails carrying bilharzia or schistosomiasis—an intestinal parasite that makes people very weak—to proliferate in the fields and irrigation ditches. The high water table resulting from the dam is destroying many ancient monuments, such as the temples of Luxor and Karnak, that have survived for millennia. Thus, like the lead pipes that brought water to the Romans, the Aswan High Dam has proved a mixed blessing in modern Egypt.

As you reflect on what you have discovered in this chapter, you may want to think about problems associated with the distribution of water in your own region. How does the need for water affect the political and economic structures of your city or state? What technological solutions has your region devised, and how have these worked? Thinking more globally, why might analysts be predicting that by the end of the twenty-first century the distribution of water will be a far greater political and economic issue than the distribution of oil?

CHAPTER TWO

THE IDEAL AND THE REALITY

OF CLASSICAL ATHENS

THE PROBLEM

Athens during the fifth century B.C. is often identified as one of the main sources of Western values and standards. Later Europeans and Americans regarded the Athenians as the originators of democracy, drama, representational or realistic art, history, philosophy, and science. At different times over the past 2,500 years they have attempted to imitate this "Golden Age" of classical Athens in everything from buildings to literature. Many U.S. state capitols and government buildings are modeled on the Parthenon or other temples, complete with statuary of former governers in the manner of Greek gods. We still divide drama into tragedies and comedies in the same way the Athenians did, though now we sometimes use a prerecorded laugh track instead of grinning masks to indicate that a given work is a comedy. During some historical periods, such as the Renaissance, thinkers and writers made conscious attempts to return to classical ideals in all areas of life, combing the works of Athenian authors for previously overlooked material in their quest to draw guidance and learn everything possible from this unique flowering of culture.

Even more than as a model for literature and art, classical Athens has continued to serve as a relevant source for answers to basic questions about human existence. Though all cultures have sought to identify the ultimate aim and meaning of human life, the ancient Greeks, especially the Athenians, were the first in the West to provide answers that were not expressed in religious or mythological terms. Their thoughts on these matters grew out of speculations on the nature of the universe made by earlier Greeks, particularly Thales and his followers Anaximander and Heraclitus. These thinkers, living in the seventh and sixth centuries B.C., theorized about how the universe had been formed and what it was made of by means of rational explanations drawn from observation rather than from myth or religious tradition. Because they believed the natural universe could be explained in other than supernatural

monolotry:

terms, they are often termed the first true scientists or first philosophers.

During the fifth century B.C., several Athenian thinkers turned their attention from the world around them to the human beings living in that world. They used this new method of philosophical inquiry to question the workings of the human mind and the societies humans create. They asked such questions as, How do we learn things? What should we try to learn? How do we know what is right or wrong, good or bad? If we can know what is good, how can we create things that are good? What kind of government is best? This type of questioning is perhaps most often associated with Socrates (469–399 B.C.) and his pupil Plato (427?–347 B.C.), who are generally called the founders of Western philosophy. Thales and his followers are thus known as the pre-Socratics; and a twentieth-century philosopher, Alfred North Whitehead, noted—only half jokingly—that "the European philosophical tradition . . . consists of a series of footnotes to Plato."

Both Socrates and Plato believed that goodness is related to knowledge and that excellence could be learned. For Plato especially, true knowledge was gained not by observation of the world but by contemplation of what an ideal world would be like. In their view, to understand goodness, justice, or beauty, it is necessary to think about what pure and ultimate goodness, justice, or beauty means. Plato thus introduced into Western thought a strong strain of idealism and was the first to write works on what an ideal society or set of laws would look like. He also

described the education required to train citizens for governing this ideal state and the social and economic structure necessary to keep them at their posts. Though he probably recognized that these standards could never be achieved, he believed that the creation of ideals was an important component of the discipline of philosophy, a sentiment shared by many Western thinkers after him.

Plato's most brilliant pupil, Aristotle (384–322 B.C.), originally agreed with his teacher but then began to depart somewhat from idealism. Like the pre-Socratics, Aristotle was fascinated by the world around him, and many of his writings on scientific subjects reveal keen powers of observation. Even his treatises on standards of human behavior, such as those concerning ethics and politics, are based on close observation of Athenian society and not simply on speculation. Aristotle further intended that these works should not only describe ideal human behavior or political systems, but also provide suggestions about how to alter current practice to conform more closely to the ideal. Thus, although Aristotle was still to some degree an idealist, both the source and the recipient of his ideals was the real world.

In classical Athens, human nature was a subject contemplated not only by scientists and philosophers, but also by historians, such as Herodotus and Thucydides. They, too, searched for explanations about the natural order that did not involve the gods. For Herodotus and Thucydides, the Persian and Peloponnesian wars were caused by human failings, not by actions of vengeful gods such as those that Homer, following tradition, depicted in the *Iliad* as causing the Trojan War. Like Aristotle, they were interested in describing real events and finding explanations for them; like Plato, they were also interested in the possible as well as the actual. History, in their opinion, was the best arena for observing the true worth of various ideals to human society.

To the Athenians, war was the ultimate test of human ideals, morals, and values, but these could also be tested and observed on a much smaller scale in the way people conducted their everyday lives. Although for Plato the basis of an ideal government was the perfectly trained ruler or group of rulers, for Aristotle and other writers it was the perfectly managed household, which they regarded as a microcosm of society. Observing that the household was the smallest economic and political unit in Athenian society, Aristotle

began his consideration of the ideal governmental system with thoughts on how households should be run. Other writers on politics and economics followed suit, giving advice after observing households they regarded as particularly well managed.

Whereas Plato clearly indicated that he was describing an ideal, in the case of Aristotle and other Athenians, it is sometimes difficult to determine whether they were attempting to describe reality, what they wished reality was, or a pure ideal. Your task in this chapter will be to examine the relationship between idealism and reality in the writings of several Athenian philosophers, historians, and commentators and in an architectural diagram of an Athenian house. What ideals do the writers set forth for the individual, the household, and the government? How are these ideals reflected in more realistic descriptions of life in Athens and in the way Athenians built their houses?

SOURCES AND METHOD

All the written sources we will use come from Athenians who lived during the classical period and are thus what we term original or primary sources. They differ greatly from modern primary sources, however, in that their textual accuracy cannot be checked. Before the development of the printing press, the only way to obtain a copy of a work was to write it out by hand yourself or hire someone to do so. Therefore, each manuscript copy might be slightly different. Because the

originals of the works of Aristotle or Thucydides have long since disappeared, what we have to work with are translations of composites based on as many of the oldest copies still in existence after 2,500 years that the translators could find.

The problem of accuracy is further complicated with some of the authors we will read because they did not actually write the works attributed to them. Many of Aristotle's works, for instance, are probably copies of his students' notes combined with (perhaps) some of his own. If you think of the way in which you record your own instructors' remarks, you can see why we must be cautious about assuming that these secondhand works contain everything Aristotle taught exactly as he intended it. Socrates, in fact, wrote nothing at all; all his ideas and words come to us through his pupil Plato. Scholars have long debated how much of the written record represents Socrates and how much represents Plato, especially when we consider that Socrates generally spoke at social gatherings or informally while walking around Athens, when Plato was not taking notes. These problems do not mean that we should discount these sources; they simply mean that these sources differ from the printed documents and tape-recorded speeches of later eras.

We will begin our investigation with what is probably the most famous description of classical Athens: a funeral speech delivered by Pericles. Pericles, one of the leaders of Athens when the Peloponnesian War opened, gave this speech in 430 B.C. in honor of those who had died during the first year of the war. It was recorded by Thucydides and, though there is some disagreement over who actually wrote it, reflects Pericles' opinions. Read the speech carefully. Is Pericles describing an ideal he hopes Athens will achieve or reality as he sees it? How does he depict Athenian democracy and the Athenian attitude toward wealth? How does he compare Athens with Sparta? How does Athens treat its neighbors? What role does Pericles see for Athenian women? Before going on to the next readings, jot down some words that you feel best describe Athens and the Athenians.

Would you want to live in the Athens Pericles describes?

Source 2 comes from a later section of Thucydides' *Peloponnesian War*, and it describes Athenian actions in the sixteenth year of the war. As you read it, think about the virtues that Pericles ascribed to the Athenians. Are these virtues reflected in the debate with the Melians or in the actions against them? How do the Athenians justify their actions? After reading this selection, jot down a few more words that you think describe the Athenians. Would you now erase some entries from your first list?

Source 3 is taken from the first book of Aristotle's *The Politics*. In this selection, he describes the proper functioning of a household and the role of each person in it. As you read it, you will notice that Aristotle is concerned equally with the economic role of household members and their moral status. What qualities does he see as important in the ideal head of household? The ideal wife or child? The ideal slave? How does he justify the differences between household members? How do these qualities compare with those described by Pericles or exhibited by the Athenians in their contact with the Melians? Add a few more words to your list describing the Athenians.

The fourth selection, by an unknown author, presents another view of Athenian democracy and the Athenian empire. This passage was written about five years after the speech made by Pericles and about ten years before the Melian debate. How does this author view democracy and Athens's relations with its neighbors?

What words might he add to your list to describe his fellow Athenians? How do you think he would have responded had he been in the audience listening to Pericles' funeral speech?

The fifth selection is a discussion of household management cast in the form of a dialogue, from a treatise by Xenophon called *The Economist*. What does the main speaker, whose name is Ischomachus, see as the main roles of husband and wife? Would he have agreed with Aristotle's conclusions about the qualities necessary in an ideal husband and wife? What suggestions does he make for encouraging ideal behavior in wives and slaves? Does he appear to be describing an actual or an ideal marital relationship? What words would you now add to or subtract from your list?

The sixth selection is a very small part of *The Republic*, in which Plato sets out his views on the ideal government. Plato did not favor democracy; he advocated training a group of leaders, whom he called *guardians*, to work for the best interests of all. What qualities does Plato feel are most important in the guardians?

What economic and family structures does he feel will help them maintain these qualities? How does his description of the ideal female guardian compare with Pericles' and Xenophon's descriptions of the ideal Athenian wife? Do the qualities he finds important in guardians match up with any of those on your list?

Once you have read all the selections carefully, go back to Pericles' speech and read it again. Do you still have the same opinion about whether he is describing the ideal or reality? Which of the words describing Athens that were on your original list are left?

Now look at Source 7, the floor plan of a house from fifth-century B.C. Olynthus. Since it is based on archaeological discoveries, it is a clear representation of physical reality in classical Greece, but it tells us something about ideals as well, for people construct the space they live in according to their ideas about how society should operate. Does the actual house correspond to the one described by Xenophon? How does the layout of the house reinforce the roles prescribed for the ideal husband and wife?

THE EVIDENCE

Sources 1 and 2 from Thucydides, History of the Peloponnesian War, *translated by Richard Crawley (New York: Modern Library, 1951), pp. 103–106; p. 109.*

1. Pericles' Funeral Speech, 430 B.C.

That part of our history which tells of the military achievements which gave us our several possessions, or of the ready valour with which either we or our fathers stemmed the tide of Hellenic or foreign aggression, is a theme too familiar to my hearers for me to dilate on, and I shall therefore pass it by. But what was the road by which we reached our position, what the form of government under which our greatness grew, what the national habits out of which it sprang; these are questions which I may try to solve before I proceed to my panegyric upon these men: since I think this to be a subject upon which on the present occasion a speaker may properly dwell, and to which the whole assemblage, whether citizens or foreigners, may listen with advantage.

Our constitution does not copy the laws of neighbouring states; we are rather a pattern to others than imitators ourselves. Its administration favours the many instead of the few; this is why it is called a democracy. If we look to the laws, they afford equal justice to all in their private differences; if to social standing, advancement in public life falls to reputation for capacity, class considerations not being allowed to interfere with merit; nor again does poverty bar the way, if a man is able to serve the state, he is not hindered by the obscurity of his condition. The freedom which we enjoy in our government extends also to our ordinary life. There, far from exercising a jealous surveillance over each other, we do not feel called upon to be angry with our neighbour for doing what he likes, or even to indulge in those injurious looks which cannot fail to be offensive, although they inflict no positive penalty. But all this ease in our private relations does not make us lawless as citizens. Against this fear is our chief safeguard, teaching us to obey the magistrates and the laws, particularly such as regard the protection of the injured, whether they are actually on the statute book, or belong to that code which, although unwritten, yet cannot be broken without acknowledged disgrace.

Further, we provide plenty of means for the mind to refresh itself from business. We celebrate games and sacrifices all the year round, and the elegance of our private establishments forms a daily source of pleasure and helps to banish the spleen; while the magnitude of our city draws the produce of the world into our harbour, so that to the Athenian the fruits of other countries are as familiar a luxury as those of his own.

If we turn to our military policy, there also we differ from our antagonists. We throw open our city to the world, and never by alien acts exclude foreigners from any opportunity of learning or observing, although the eyes of an enemy may occasionally profit by our liberality; trusting less in system and policy than to the native spirit of our citizens; while in education, where our rivals from their very cradles by a painful discipline seek after manliness, at Athens we live exactly as we please, and yet are just as ready to encounter every legitimate danger. In proof of this it may be noticed that the Lacedæmonians[1] do not invade our country alone, but bring with them all their confederates; while we Athenians advance unsupported into the territory of a neighbour, and fighting upon a foreign soil usually vanquish with ease men

---

1. **Lacedæmonians:** Spartans.

who are defending their homes. Our united force was never yet encountered by any enemy, because we have at once to attend to our marine and to despatch our citizens by land upon a hundred different services; so that, wherever they engage with some such fraction of our strength, a success against a detachment is magnified into a victory over the nation, and a defeat into a reverse suffered at the hands of our entire people. And yet if with habits not of labour but of ease, and courage not of art but of nature, we are still willing to encounter danger, we have the double advantage of escaping the experience of hardships in anticipation and of facing them in the hour of need as fearlessly as those who are never free from them.

Nor are these the only points in which our city is worthy of admiration. We cultivate refinement without extravagance and knowledge without effeminacy; wealth we employ more for use than for show, and place the real disgrace of poverty not in owning to the fact but in declining the struggle against it. Our public men have, besides politics, their private affairs to attend to, and our ordinary citizens, though occupied with the pursuits of industry, are still fair judges of public matters; for, unlike any other nation, regarding him who takes no part in these duties not as unambitious but as useless, we Athenians are able to judge at all events if we cannot originate, and instead of looking on discussion as a stumbling-block in the way of action, we think it an indispensable preliminary to any wise action at all. Again, in our enterprises we present the singular spectacle of daring and deliberation, each carried to its highest point, and both united in the same persons; although usually decision is the fruit of ignorance, hesitation of reflexion. But the palm of courage will surely be adjudged most justly to those, who best know the difference between hardship and pleasure and yet are never tempted to shrink from danger. In generosity we are equally singular, acquiring our friends by conferring not by receiving favours. Yet, of course, the doer of the favour is the firmer friend of the two, in order by continued kindness to keep the recipient in his debt; while the debtor feels less keenly from the very consciousness that the return he makes will be a payment, not a free gift. And it is only the Athenians who, fearless of consequences, confer their benefits not from calculations of expediency, but in the confidence of liberality.

In short, I say that as a city we are the school of Hellas; while I doubt if the world can produce a man, who where he has only himself to depend upon, is equal to so many emergencies, and graced by so happy a versatility as the Athenian. And that this is no mere boast thrown out for the occasion, but plain matter of fact, the power of the state acquired by these habits proves. For Athens alone of her contemporaries is found when tested to be greater than her reputation, and alone gives no occasion to her assailants to blush at the antagonist by whom they have been worsted, or to her subjects to question her title by merit to rule. Rather, the admiration of the present and succeeding ages will be ours, since we have not left our power without witness, but have shown it by mighty proofs; and far from needing a Homer for our panegyrist, or other of his craft whose verses might charm for the moment only for the impression which they gave to melt at the touch of fact, we have forced every sea and land to be the highway of our daring, and everywhere, whether for evil or for good, have left imperishable monuments behind us. Such is the Athens for which these men, in the assertion of their resolve not to lose her, nobly fought and died; and well may every one of their survivors be ready to suffer in her cause. . . .

[I]f I must say anything on the subject of female excellence to those of you who will now be in widowhood, it will be all comprised in this brief exhortation. Great will be your glory in not falling short of your natural character; and greatest will be hers who is least talked of among the men whether for good or for bad.

My task is now finished. I have performed it to the best of my ability, and in words, at least, the requirements of the law are now satisfied. If deeds be in question, those who are here interred have received part of their honours already, and for the rest, their children will be brought up till manhood at the public expense: the state thus offers a valuable prize, as the garland of victory in this race of valour, for the reward both of those who have fallen and their survivors. And where the rewards for merit are greatest, there are found the best citizens.

And now that you have brought to a close your lamentations for your relatives, you may depart.

2. The Melian Debate, 415 B.C.

The Athenians also made an expedition against the isle of Melos with thirty ships of their own, six Chian, and two Lesbian vessels, sixteen hundred heavy infantry, three hundred archers, and twenty mounted archers from Athens, and about fifteen hundred heavy infantry from the allies and the islanders. The Melians are a colony of Lacedæmon[2] that would not submit to the Athenians like the other islanders, and at first remained neutral and took no part in the struggle, but afterwards upon the Athenians using violence and plundering their territory, assumed an attitude of open hostility. Cleomedes, son of Lycomedes, and Tisias, son of Tisimachus, the generals, encamping in their territory with the above armament, before doing any harm to their land, sent envoys to negotiate. These the Melians did not bring before the people, but bade them state the object of their mission to the magistrates and the few; upon which the Athenian envoys spoke as follows: . . .

ATHENIANS: We will now proceed to show you that we are come here in the interest of our empire, and that we shall say what we are now going to say, for

2. **Lacedæmon:** Sparta.

the preservation of your country; as we would fain exercise that empire over you without trouble, and see you preserved for the good of us both.

MELIANS: And how, pray, could it turn out as good for us to serve as for you to rule?

ATHENIANS: Because you would have the advantage of submitting before suffering the worst, and we should gain by not destroying you.

MELIANS: So that you would not consent to our being neutral, friends instead of enemies, but allies of neither side.

ATHENIANS: No; for your hostility cannot so much hurt us as your friendship will be an argument to our subjects of our weakness, and your enmity of our power.

MELIANS: Is that your subjects' idea of equity, to put those who have nothing to do with you in the same category with peoples that are most of them your own colonists, and some conquered rebels?

ATHENIANS: As far as right goes they think one has as much of it as the other, and if any maintain their independence it is because they are strong, and that if we do not molest them it is because we are afraid; so that besides extending our empire we should gain in security by your subjection; the fact that you are islanders and weaker than others rendering it all the more important that you should not succeed in baffling the masters of the sea.

MELIANS: But do you consider that there is no security in the policy which we indicate? For here again if you debar us from talking about justice and invite us to obey your interest, we also must explain ours, and try to persuade you, if the two happen to coincide. How can you avoid making enemies of all existing neutrals who shall look at our case and conclude from it that one day or another you will attack them? And what is this but to make greater the enemies that you have already, and to force others to become so who would otherwise have never thought of it?

ATHENIANS: Why, the fact is that continentals generally give us but little alarm; the liberty which they enjoy will long prevent their taking precautions against us; it is rather islanders like yourselves, outside our empire, and subjects smarting under the yoke, who would be the most likely to take a rash step and lead themselves and us into obvious danger.

MELIANS: Well then, if you risk so much to retain your empire, and your subjects to get rid of it, it were surely great baseness and cowardice in us who are still free not to try everything that can be tried, before submitting to your yoke.

ATHENIANS: Not if you are well advised, the contest not being an equal one, with honour as the prize and shame as the penalty, but a question of self-preservation and of not resisting those who are far stronger than you are. . . .

Of the gods we believe, and of men we know, that by a necessary law of their nature they rule wherever they can. And it is not as if we were the first to make this law, or to act upon it when made: we found it existing before us, and shall leave it to exist for ever after us; all we do is to make use of it, knowing that you and everybody else, having the same power as we have, would do the same as we do. . . . You will surely not be caught by that idea of disgrace, which in dangers that are disgraceful, and at the same time too plain to be mistaken, proves so fatal to mankind; since in too many cases the very men that have their eyes perfectly open to what they are rushing into, let the thing called disgrace, by the mere influence of a seductive name, lead them on to a point at which they become so enslaved by the phrase as in fact to fall wilfully into hopeless disaster, and incur disgrace more disgraceful as the companion of error, than when it comes as the result of misfortune. This, if you are well advised, you will guard against; and you will not think it dishonourable to submit to the greatest city in Hellas, when it makes you the moderate offer of becoming its tributary ally, without ceasing to enjoy the country that belongs to you; nor when you have the choice given you between war and security, will you be so blinded as to choose the worse. And it is certain that those who do not yield to their equals, who keep terms with their superiors, and are moderate towards their inferiors, on the whole succeed best. Think over the matter, therefore, after our withdrawal, and reflect once and again that it is for your country that you are consulting, that you have not more than one, and that upon this one deliberation depends its prosperity or ruin.

The Athenians now withdrew from the conference; and the Melians, left to themselves, came to a decision corresponding with what they had maintained in the discussion, and answered, 'Our resolution, Athenians, is the same as it was at first. We will not in a moment deprive of freedom a city that has been inhabited these seven hundred years; but we put our trust in the fortune by which the gods have preserved it until now, and in the help of men, that is, of the Lacedæmonians; and so we will try and save ourselves. Meanwhile we invite you to allow us to be friends to you and foes to neither party, and to retire from our country after making such a treaty as shall seem fit to us both. . . .'

The Athenian envoys now returned to the army; and the Melians showing no signs of yielding, the generals at once betook themselves to hostilities, and drew a line of circumvallation[3] round the Melians, dividing the work among the different states. Subsequently the Athenians returned with most of their army, leaving behind them a certain number of their own citizens and of the allies to keep guard by land and sea. The force thus left stayed on and besieged the place. . . .

Meanwhile the Melians attacked by night and took the part of the Athenian lines over against the market, and killed some of the men, and brought

---

3. **circumvallation:** ramparts and walls.

in corn and all else that they could find useful to them, and so returned and kept quiet, while the Athenians took measures to keep better guard in future.

Summer was now over. The next winter . . . the Melians again took another part of the Athenian lines which were but feebly garrisoned. Reinforcements afterwards arriving from Athens in consequence, under the command of Philocrates, son of Demeas, the siege was now pressed vigorously; and some treachery taking place inside, the Melians surrendered at discretion to the Athenians, who put to death all the grown men whom they took, and sold the women and children for slaves, and subsequently sent out five hundred colonists and inhabited the place themselves.

Source 3 from Aristotle, The Politics, *translated by T. A. Sinclair and revised by Trevor J. Saunders (Baltimore: Penguin, 1962, 1981), pp. 26–27, 31, 34, 50–53. Copyright © the estate of T. A. Sinclair, 1962; revised material copyright © Trevor J. Saunders, 1981. Reprinted with permission.*

3. From Aristotle, *The Politics*

We shall, I think, in this as in other subjects, get the best view of the matter if we look at the natural growth of things from the beginning. . . .

It was out of the association formed by men with these two, women and slaves, that the first household was formed; and the poet Hesiod was right when he wrote, "Get first a house and a wife and an ox to draw the plough." (The ox is the poor man's slave.) This association of persons, established according to the law of nature and continuing day after day, is the household. . . .

Now property is part of a household and the acquisition of property part of the economics of a household; for neither life itself nor the good life is possible without a certain minimum standard of wealth. Again, for any given craft the existence of the proper tools will be essential for the performance of its task. Tools may be animate as well as inanimate; a ship's captain uses a lifeless rudder, but a living man for watch; for the worker in a craft is, from the point of view of the craft, one of its tools. So any piece of property can be regarded as a tool enabling a man to live; and his property is an assemblage of such tools, including his slaves; and a slave, being a living creature like any other servant, is a tool worth many tools. . . .

The "slave by nature" then is he that can and therefore does belong to another, and he that participates in the reasoning faculty so far as to understand but not so as to possess it. For the other animals serve their owner not by exercise of reason but passively. The use, too, of slaves hardly differs at all from that of domestic animals; from both we derive that which is essential for our bodily needs. . . . It is clear then that in household management the people are of greater importance than the material property, and their quality of more account than that of the goods that make up their wealth, and also that free men are of more account than slaves. About slaves the first question to be asked is whether in addition to their value as tools and servants there is some other quality or virtue, superior to these, that belongs to slaves. Can they possess self-respect, courage, justice, and virtues of that kind, or have they in fact nothing but the serviceable quality of their persons?

The question may be answered in either of two ways, but both present a difficulty. If we say that slaves have these virtues, how then will they differ from free men? If we say that they have not, the position is anomalous, since they are human beings and capable of reason. Roughly the same question can be put in relation to wife and child: Have not these also virtues? Ought not a woman to be self-respecting, brave, and just? Is not a child sometimes naughty, sometimes good? . . .

This mention of virtue leads us straightaway to a consideration of the soul; for it is here that the natural ruler and the natural subject, whose virtue we regard as different, are to be found. In the soul the difference between ruler and ruled is that between the rational and the nonrational. It is therefore clear that in other connexions also there will be natural differences. And so generally in cases of ruler and ruled; the differences will be natural but they need not be the same. For rule of free over slave, male over female, man over boy, are all natural, but they are also different, because, while parts of the soul are present in each case, the distribution is different. Thus the deliberative faculty in the soul is not present at all in a slave; in a female it is inoperative, in a child undeveloped. We must therefore take it that the same conditions prevail also in regard to the ethical virtues, namely that all must participate in them but not all to the same extent, but only as may be required by each for his proper function. The ruler then must have ethical virtue in its entirety; for his task is simply that of chief maker and reason is chief maker. And the other members must have what amount is appropriate to each. So it is evident that each of the classes spoken of must have ethical virtue. It is also clear that there is some variation in the ethical virtues; self-respect is not the same in a man as in a woman, nor justice, nor courage either, as Socrates thought; the one is courage of a ruler, the other courage of a servant, and likewise with the other virtues.

If we look at the matter in greater detail it will become clearer. For those who talk in generalities and say that virtue is "a good condition of the soul," or that it is "right conduct" or the like, delude themselves. Better than those who look for general definitions are those who, like Gorgias, enumerate the different virtues. So the poet Sophocles singles out "silence" as "bringing credit to a woman," but that is not so for a man. This method of assessing virtue according to function is one that we should always follow. Take the child: he is not yet fully developed and his function is to grow up, so we cannot speak of his virtue as belonging absolutely to him, but only in relation to the progress of his development and to whoever is in charge of him. So too with slave and master; we laid it down that a slave's function is to perform menial tasks; so the amount of virtue required will not be very great, only enough to ensure that he does not neglect his work through loose living or mere fecklessness.

Source 4 from B. K. Workman, editor and translator, They Saw It Happen in Classical Times *(New York: Barnes & Noble, 1964), pp. 32–34. Reprinted by permission of Littlefield, Adams & Company and Basil Blackwell, Publishers.*

4. An Unknown Author's View of Athenian Democracy

Insolent conduct of slaves and resident aliens is everywhere rife in Athens. You cannot strike a slave there, and he will not get out of your way in the street. There is good reason for this being the local custom. If the law allowed a free-born citizen to strike a slave, an alien, or a freedman, then you would often strike an Athenian citizen in the mistaken impression that he was a slave. For the common people dress as poorly as slaves or aliens and their general appearance is no better. . . .

The common people take no supervisory interest in athletic or aesthetic shows, feeling that it is not right for them, since they know that they have not the ability to become expert at them. When it is necessary to provide men to put on stageshows or games or to finance and build triremes,[4] they know that impresarios come from the rich, the actors and chorus from the people. In the same way, organizers and ship-masters are the rich, while the common people take a subordinate part in the games and act as oarsmen for the triremes. But they do at least think it right to receive pay for singing or running or dancing or rowing in the fleet, to level up the incomes of rich and poor. The same holds good for the law courts as well; they are more interested in what profit they can make than in the true ends of justice. . . .

Of the mainland cities in the Athenian Empire, the large ones are governed by fear, the small ones by want. For all states must import and export, and this they cannot do unless they remain subject to the mistress of the seas.

---

4. **trireme:** standard Greek warship, about 120 feet long and rowed by 150 to 175 men; a ram on the bow was the trireme's main weapon.

5. From Xenophon,
The Economist

"Here's another thing I'd like to ask you," said I. "Did you train your wife yourself or did she already know how to run a house when you got her from her father and mother?"

"What could she have known, Socrates," said he, "when I took her from her family? She wasn't yet fifteen. Until then she had been under careful supervision and meant to see, hear, and ask as little as possible. Don't you think it was already a lot that she should have known how to make a cloak of the wool she was given and how to dole out spinning to the servants? She had been taught to moderate her appetites, which, to my mind, is basic for both men's and women's education."

"So, apart from that," I asked, "it was you, Ischomachus, who had to train and teach her her household duties?"

"Yes," said Ischomachus, "but not before sacrificing to the gods. . . . And she solemnly swore before heaven that she would behave as I wanted, and it was clear that she would neglect none of my lessons."

"Tell me what you taught her first. . . ."

"Well, Socrates, as soon as I had tamed her and she was relaxed enough to talk, I asked her the following question: 'Tell me, my dear,' said I, 'do you understand why I married you and why your parents gave you to me? You know as well as I do that neither of us would have had trouble finding someone else to share our beds. But, after thinking about it carefully, it was you I chose and me your parents chose as the best partners we could find for our home and our children. Now, if God sends us children, we shall think about how best to raise them, for we share an interest in securing the best allies and support for our old age. For the moment we only share our home. . . .'"

"My wife answered, 'But how can I help? What am I capable of doing? It is on you that everything depends. My duty, my mother said, is to be well behaved.'"

" 'Oh, by Zeus,' said I, 'my father said the same to me. But the best behavior in a man and woman is that which will keep up their property and increase it as far as may be done by honest and legal means.'"

" 'And do you see some way,' asked my wife, 'in which I can help in this?'"

" '. . . It seems to me that God adapted women's nature to indoor and man's to outdoor work. . . . As Nature has entrusted woman with guarding the household supplies, and a timid nature is no disadvantage in such a job, it has endowed woman with more fear than man. . . . It is more proper for a woman to stay in the house than out of doors and less so for a man to be indoors instead of out. If anyone goes against the nature given him by God and leaves his appointed post . . . he will be punished. . . . You must stay indoors and send out the servants whose work is outside and supervise those who work indoors, receive what is brought in, give out what is to be spent, plan ahead what should be stored and ensure that provisions for a year are not used up in a month. When the wool is brought in, you must see to it that clothes are made from it for whoever needs them and see to it that the corn is still edible. . . . Many of your duties will give you pleasure: for instance, if you teach spinning and weaving to a slave who did not know how to do this when you got her, you double her usefulness to yourself, or if you make a good housekeeper of one who didn't know how to do anything. . . .' Then I took her around the family living rooms, which are pleasantly decorated, cool in summer and warm in winter. I pointed out how the whole house faces south so as to enjoy the winter sun. . . . I showed her the women's quarters which are separated from the men's by a bolted door to prevent anything being improperly removed and also to ensure that the slaves should not have children without our permission. For good slaves are usually even more devoted once they have a family; but good-for-nothings, once they begin to cohabit, have extra chances to get up to mischief."

Source 6 from B. Jowett, translator, The Dialogues of Plato, *revised edition, vol. 3 (Oxford: Oxford University Press, 1895, revised 1924), pp. 58, 100–101, 103, 106, 140–142, 147–148, 151, 159.*

6. From Plato, *The Republic*

Is not the love of learning the love of wisdom, which is philosophy?

They are the same, he replied.

And may we not say confidently of man also, that he who is likely to be gentle to his friends and acquaintances, must by nature be a lover of wisdom and knowledge?

That we may safely affirm.

Then he who is to be a really good and noble guardian of the State will require to unite in himself philosophy and spirit and swiftness and strength?

Undoubtedly.

Then we have found the desired natures; and now that we have found them, how are they to be reared and educated? Is not this an enquiry which may be expected to throw light on the greater enquiry which is our final end—How do justice and injustice grow up in States?

Adeimantus thought that the enquiry would be of great service to us. . . .

Come then, and let us pass a leisure hour in storytelling, and our story shall be the education of our heroes.

By all means.

And what shall be their education? Can we find a better than the traditional sort?—and this has two divisions, gymnastic for the body, and music[5] for the soul.

True. . . .

Very good, I said; then what is the next question? Must we not ask who are to be rulers and who subjects?

Certainly.

There can be no doubt that the elder must rule the younger.

Clearly.

And that the best of these must rule.

That is also clear.

Now, are not the best husbandmen those who are most devoted to husbandry?

Yes.

And as we are to have the best of guardians for our city, must they not be those who have most the character of guardians?

Yes. . . .

Then there must be a selection. Let us note among the guardians those who in their whole life show the greatest eagerness to do what is for the good of their country, and the greatest repugnance to do what is against her interests.

Those are the right men.

And they will have to be watched at every age, in order that we may see whether they preserve their resolution, and never, under the influence either of force or enchantment, forget or cast off their sense of duty to the State. . . . And he who at every age, as boy and youth and in mature life, has come out of the trial victorious and pure, shall be appointed a ruler and guardian of the State; he shall be honoured in life and death, and shall receive sepulture[6] and other memorials of honour, the greatest that we have to give. But him who fails, we must reject. I am inclined to think that this is the sort of way in which our rulers and guardians should be chosen and appointed. I speak generally, and not with any pretension to exactness.

And, speaking generally, I agree with you, he said. . . .

Then let us consider what will be their way of life, if they are to realize our idea of them. In the first place, none of them should have any property of his own beyond what is absolutely necessary; neither should they have a private house or store closed against any one who has a mind to enter; their provisions should be only such as are required by trained warriors, who are men of temperance and courage; they should agree to receive from the citizens a fixed rate of pay, enough to meet the expenses of the year and no more; and they will go to mess and live together like soldiers in a camp. Gold and silver

5. By "music," the Athenians meant all that was sacred to the **muses**, the patron goddesses of the arts and sciences.

6. **sepulture:** a special burial ceremony.

we will tell them that they have from God; the diviner metal is within them, and they have therefore no need of the dross which is current among men, and ought not to pollute the divine by any such earthly admixture; for that commoner metal has been the source of many unholy deeds, but their own is undefiled. And they alone of all the citizens may not touch or handle silver or gold, or be under the same roof with them, or wear them, or drink from them. And this will be their salvation, and they will be the saviours of the State. But should they ever acquire homes or lands or moneys of their own, they will become housekeepers and husbandmen instead of guardians, enemies and tyrants instead of allies of the other citizens; hating and being hated, plotting and being plotted against, they will pass their whole life in much greater terror of internal than of external enemies, and the hour of ruin, both to themselves and to the rest of the State, will be at hand. For all which reasons may we not say that thus shall our State be ordered, and that these shall be the regulations appointed by us for our guardians concerning their houses and all other matters?

Yes, said Glaucon. . . .

The part of the men has been played out, and now properly enough comes the turn of the women. Of them I will proceed to speak, and the more readily since I am invited by you.

For men born and educated like our citizens, the only way, in my opinion, of arriving at a right conclusion about the possession and use of women and children is to follow the path on which we originally started, when we said that the men were to be the guardians and watchdogs of the herd.

True.

Let us further suppose the birth and education of our women to be subject to similar or nearly similar regulations; then we shall see whether the result accords with our design.

What do you mean?

What I mean may be put into the form of a question. I said: Are dogs divided into hes and shes, or do they both share equally in hunting and in keeping watch and in the other duties of dogs? or do we entrust to the males the entire and exclusive care of the flocks, while we leave the females at home, under the idea that the bearing and suckling of their puppies is labour enough for them?

No, he said, they share alike; the only difference between them is that the males are stronger and the females weaker.

But can you use different animals for the same purpose, unless they are bred and fed in the same way?

You cannot.

Then, if women are to have the same duties as men, they must have the same nurture and education?

Yes. . . .

My friend, I said, there is no special faculty of administration in a state which a woman has because she is a woman, or which a man has by virtue of his sex, but the gifts of nature are alike diffused in both; all the pursuits of men are the pursuits of women also, but in all of them a woman is inferior to a man.

Very true.

Then are we to impose all our enactments on men and none of them on women?

That will never do.

One woman has a gift of healing, another not; one is a musician, and another has no music in her nature?

Very true.

And one woman has a turn for gymnastic and military exercises, and another is unwarlike and hates gymnastics?

Certainly.

And one woman is a philosopher, and another is an enemy of philosophy; one has spirit, and another is without spirit?

That is also true.

Then one woman will have the temper of a guardian, and another not. Was not the selection of the male guardians determined by differences of this sort?

Yes.

Men and women alike possess the qualities which make a guardian; they differ only in their comparative strength or weakness.

Obviously.

And those women who have such qualities are to be selected as the companions and colleagues of men who have similar qualities and whom they resemble in capacity and in character?

Very true. . . .

The law, I said, which is the sequel of this and of all that has preceded, is to the following effect—"that the wives of our guardians are to be common, and their children are to be common, and no parent is to know his own child, nor any child his parent."

Yes, he said, that is a much greater wave [i.e. obstacle to be overcome] than the other; and the possibility as well as the utility of such a law are far more questionable. . . .

Both the community of property and the community of families, as I am saying, tend to make them more truly guardians; they will not tear the city in pieces by differing about "mine" and "not mine"; each man dragging any acquisition which he has made into a separate house of his own, where he has a separate wife and children and private pleasures and pains; but all will be affected as far as may be by the same pleasures and pains because they are all of one opinion about what is near and dear to them, and therefore they all tend towards a common end.

Certainly, he replied.

Source 7 adapted from Orestis B. Doumanis and Paul Oliver, editors, Shelter in Greece (Athens: Architecture in Greece Press, 1974), p. 25.

7. Floor Plan of a House from Olynthus, Fifth century B.C.

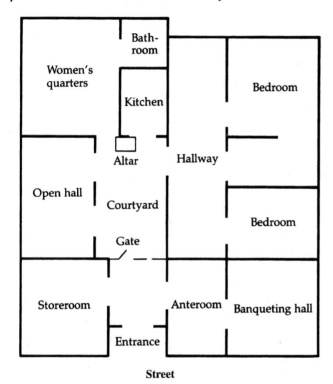

Street

QUESTIONS TO CONSIDER

Before you start to think about the questions in this section, you may want to turn to your text to read (or reread) the section on Athens during the classical period. This can give you more background on the authors and on the political events that might have affected what they wrote.

Though some of the written selections in this chapter clearly describe ideals and others reality, still others blend realism and idealism, creating an idealized view of actual persons or situations. Which selections would you put in this last category? Why would these authors describe reality in an idealized manner? (To answer this question, you need to think about both the purpose of each selection and whether the author truly thought that what he was describing actually existed—in other words, whether this was a conscious or unconscious alteration of reality.)

Once you have labeled the written sources as ideals, reality, and idealizations of reality, go back to your list of the personal qualities of Athenians. Which qualities would you put in each of these three categories? Now that you know you are describing only an ideal or real characteristic, would you add any further qualities? The next step is to divide your list into categories of persons, for it is clear that most of the authors make great distinctions between male and female, adult and child, slave and free. Do all the authors agree on the qualities important in an ideal man, woman, or slave? Which authors have opposing ideas? Why might this be so? Sometimes distinctions between categories are not clearly set out by the author; when Pericles, for instance, uses the words "person" and "people" in his funeral oration, one might think he was talking about all Athenians. Looking at your list divided into categories, of whom is Pericles speaking when he says "person" and "people"? Do any of the authors make distinctions between individuals of the same category based on such factors as wealth or education; for example, do they describe wealthy men differently than poor men, or set out different ideals for women who are interested in learning than for those who are not?

Turning from the individual to social units, what qualities should the ideal Athenian household possess? How might real households work to emulate these ideals? Judging from information in the selections and in your text about Athenian marriage patterns, family life, and social life in general, did real Athenian households approach the ideal at all? How did their beliefs about the way households should be run affect the way Athenians designed their houses? How did the layout of a house work to make reality correspond with those ideals?

The qualities of governments as presented in the selections may also be classified as real, ideal, or idealized. Were any of the words you used to describe the Athenian government after first reading Pericles included in your final list? Does his idealized view of Athens come closer to the realistic view provided in the Melian debate or to the purely ideal view of Plato? After reading all the selections, would you put the quality "democracy" into the real or the ideal column for Athens? How would Athenians define democracy? Do all the authors agree that democracy is a desirable form of government? Judging from information in your text about politics in Athens in the fifth century, why would authors disagree on this matter? If you put democracy in the ideal column, what changes in existing conditions would have been necessary for it to become a reality?

The selections you have read offer varying opinions on a great many subjects, including the benefits of wealth and private property, the relationship between dominant and dependent states and between dominant and dependent individuals, the reasons for the differences between men and women, the role of naval power in foreign policy, and the causes of imperialism. All these issues have both ideal and real components, and you may want to think about them before you draw your final conclusions about classical Athens. How well did Athens live up to the ideals it set for itself? How did the different ideals held up for different categories of persons affect their participation in Athenian life?

EPILOGUE

We can find the ideals of the Athenians expressed not only in their philosophy, history, and architecture, as you have discovered here, but also in their drama, poetry, and sculpture. Indeed, most of the original sources we have from Athens are not realistic descriptions but either thoughts about ideals or idealizations of actual persons and episodes. That they are idealizations may be very clear to us as modern skeptical readers, but for a long time the statements in these sources were taken as literal truth. To give you an example, here is a quotation from Edith Hamilton, one of the foremost historians of Greece, published in 1930:

> For a hundred years Athens was a city where the great spiritual forces that war in men's minds flowed together along in peace; law and freedom, truth and religion, beauty and goodness, the objective and the subjective—there was a truce to their eternal warfare, and the result was the balance and clarity, the harmony and completeness, that the word Greek has come to stand for.[7]

Given what you have just read, would you agree with her? Do you think everyone living in classical Athens would have agreed with her?

No matter how you have judged the relationship between ideal and reality in classical Athens, the ideals for the individual and state created there have significantly shaped the development of Western philosophy and social institutions. Roman philosophers closely studied Plato's *Republic,* and medieval philosophers were strongly influenced by Aristotle's *Politics.* Writers from the Renaissance to the present have invented ideal societies, "utopias" guided by wise leaders like Plato's guardians. Occasionally small groups of people have actually tried to set up working replicas of these ideal societies, frequently forbidding private property and the nuclear family as Plato did. Educational theorists have devised "perfect" school systems that, if not entirely successful when put into practice, have had their effect on real-life pedagogy. The Athenian ideal of government by the people is reflected in the constitutions of modern democratic states, with the category "people" now including groups unthinkable to Pericles.

In terms of Athenian history, democracy was an extremely short-lived phenomenon. Widespread revolt broke out in the Athenian empire, and Sparta ultimately defeated Athens, bringing the Peloponnesian War to a close after twenty-seven years. This did not end

7. Edith Hamilton, *The Greek Way* (New York: Norton, 1930), p. 206.

warfare in Greece, however, as the city-states continued to battle among themselves. Finally, in 338 B.C., Greece was conquered by Philip of Macedon, and Athens became simply one small part of a much larger empire. From that point on, Athenian ideals of individual behavior would be emulated in Western culture, but democratic government would not again be attempted as an experiment in the real world for another 2,000 years.

CHAPTER THREE

THE ACHIEVEMENTS

OF AUGUSTUS

For many centuries, the seat of power in Rome was the senate, a body of men drawn from the most powerful and prominent Roman families that made all major political and military decisions. Under the leadership of the senate, Rome had gradually taken control of the entire Italian peninsula. It then conquered southern France and much of Spain, and, after defeating Carthage in the Punic Wars, occupied northern Africa. These territorial conquests altered the nature of power in Rome, however, because the armies that conquered and held the new territories pledged loyalty to their military leaders and not to the senate. During the first century before Christ, several of these semi-independent armies challenged the senate's power, and civil war erupted in many parts of the Roman territory. The city itself was plundered several times by rival legions, and trade and communications were frequently disrupted. In 60 B.C., three army generals—Pompey, Crassus, and Julius Caesar—decided to form a political alliance, the triumvirate, leaving the senate intact but without much actual power.

All three of these generals were ambitious men who were unwilling to share power with anyone for very long. The senate was especially worried about Julius Caesar, who was gathering an increasingly larger army in Gaul (present-day France), and decided to put its trust in Pompey, whose base of power lay in Greece. (Crassus had meanwhile died in battle.) It ordered Caesar to disband his army and not to return to Rome, setting the Rubicon River near Ravenna in northern Italy as the line he must not cross. In 49 B.C., Caesar crossed the Rubicon (an expression we still use for an irrevocable decision), directly challenging the power of the senate and of Pompey. His armies quickly defeated those of the senate in Italy, and within a few months he held the entire Italian peninsula. From there Caesar turned his attention to Pompey's army, which his forces also defeated in 48 B.C., leaving him in control of all the Roman territory. Though he did not disband the senate, he did begin to shape the government to his liking, appointing officials and army officers and directly overseeing the administration of the provinces. He increased the size of the senate from 600 to 900 members by padding it with his followers, many of whom came from the provinces.

Caesar's meteoric and extralegal rise to power created great resentment among many Roman senators. Intensely proud of Roman traditions and of their own families' long-standing political power, they felt that Caesar was degrading the senate by adding unsophisticated rural representatives. A group of senators, led by Brutus and Cassius, decided to assassinate Caesar, which they did on the steps of the Roman senate on March 15, 44 B.C. The conspirators had not thought much beyond this act, however, and Caesar's death led not to peace but to a renewal of civil war. Some of the army was loyal to the assassins; some to Mark Antony, an associate of Caesar; and some to Caesar's nephew and adopted son, Octavian. At first Mark Antony and Octavian cooperated to defeat the assassins, but then they turned against each other. The war dragged on for over a decade, with Octavian's forces gradually gaining more territory. Octavian won the support of many Romans by convincing them that Antony was plotting with Cleopatra, queen of Egypt, and in 31 B.C. his forces decisively defeated

those of Antony at the naval battle of Actium. Antony and his ally Cleopatra committed suicide, leaving Octavian sole ruler of the Mediterranean world.

The problem now facing Octavian was the same one Julius Caesar had confronted twelve years earlier: how to transform a state won by military force into a stable political system. Caesar's answer—personal, autocratic rule—had led to his assassination at the hands of disgruntled senators. This lesson was not lost on Octavian, who realized that directly opposing the strong republican tradition in Rome could be very dangerous.

This tradition had arisen from both political reality—the senate had held actual power for many generations—and Roman political theory. The Romans held that their form of government had been given to them by the gods, who had conferred authority on Romulus, the mythical founder of Rome. That authority was later passed on to the senate, whose original function was to consult the gods about actions Rome should take. The senate in turn passed on authority to the rest of the government bureaucracy and to male heads of household, for in Rome households were considered, as in Athens, the smallest unit of government. Only male heads of household could sit in the senate, for only such individuals were regarded as worthy enough to consult the gods on matters of great importance to the state. This meant that Roman society was extremely patriarchal, with fathers having (at least in theory) absolute control over their wives, children, and servants.

This divinely ordained authority could always be distributed downward as the political bureaucracy grew, but to do away with existing institutions was extremely dangerous. Any radical transformation of the structure of government, especially any change in the authority of the senate, would have been regarded as impious.

Octavian had himself grown up in this tradition and at least to some degree shared these ideas about authority and the divine roots of the Roman political system. He realized that he could be more effective—and probably would live longer—if he worked through, rather than against, existing political institutions. Moreover, serious problems existed that had to be faced immediately, and after years of civil war, the government bureaucracy

was no longer firmly in place to deal with them. Octavian needed to appoint officials and governors and reestablish law and order throughout Roman territory without offending the senate by acting like an autocrat or dictator.

In the eyes of many of his contemporaries, Octavian accomplished this admittedly difficult task very well. The senate conferred on him the name he is usually known by, Augustus, meaning "blessed" or "magnificent." Later historians regarded Augustus, rather than Julius Caesar, as the creator of the Roman Empire. Your task in this chapter will be to evaluate these judgments. How did Augustus transform the Roman republic into an empire? Why was he successful where Julius Caesar had not been?

SOURCES AND METHOD

As you think about these questions, you can see that they involve two somewhat different components: the process by which Augustus made changes and the results of these changes, or what we might term the "means" and the "ends." Both are important to consider in assessing the achievements of any political leader, and both have been used by the contemporaries of Augustus, later Roman writers, and modern historians in evaluating the first Roman emperor's reign.

One of the best sources for observing the process of political change is laws, especially basic laws such as constitutions that set out governmental

structure. Rome was a society in which law was extremely important and was explicitly written down, unlike many early societies, in which laws were handed down orally from generation to generation. As the Romans conquered Europe and the Mediterranean, they brought their legal system with them; consequently, Roman law forms the basis of most modern Western legal systems, with England and thus the United States the most notable exceptions.

We encounter some serious difficulties in using laws as our source material for the reign of Augustus, however. Given Roman ideas about authority and the strength of Roman tradition, would you expect him to have made major legal changes? Augustus, after all, described his aims and his actions as restoring republican government; if we use only the constitution of Rome as a source, we might be tempted to believe him. No new office was created for the emperor. Instead, he carefully preserved all traditional offices while gradually taking over many of them himself. Augustus was both a consul and a tribune, although the former office was usually reserved for a patrician and the latter for a plebeian. Later the senate appointed him *imperator,* or commander-in-chief of the army, and gave him direct control of many of the outlying provinces. These provinces furnished grain supplies essential to the people of Rome as well as soldiers loyal to Augustus rather than to the senate. The senate also gave him the honorary title of *princeps* (or "first citizen"), the title he preferred, which gradually lost its republican origins and gained the overtones of "monarch" evident in its modern English derivative, "prince." Augustus recognized the importance of religion to most Romans, and in 12 B.C. he had himself named *pontifex maximus,* or "supreme priest." He encouraged the building of temples dedicated to "Rome and Augustus," laying the foundations for the growth of a ruler cult closely linked with patriotic loyalty to Rome.

None of these innovations required any alteration in the basic constitution of Rome. What did change, however, was the tone of many laws, particularly those from the outlying provinces, where Augustus could be more open about the transformation he was working without bringing on the wrath of the senate. Our first two

selections, then, are decrees and laws from Roman territories, where we can perhaps see some hint of the gradual development of the republic into an empire.

Source 1 is a decree by Augustus himself, an inscription dated 4 B.C. from the Greek city of Cyrene. Like all laws, it was passed in response to a perceived problem. What problem does the decree confront? What procedure does it provide to solve this problem? What complications does it anticipate, and how does it try to solve them? You will notice that the decree itself is set within a long framework giving the reasons it was issued. This is true for many laws, including the American Constitution, which begins, "We the people of the United States, in order to form a more perfect union, establish justice, insure domestic tranquillity." Why does Augustus say he is passing this law? This framework can also give you clues to the relationship between Augustus and the senate. How is this relationship described, and what does Augustus's attitude appear to be?

The second law is an inscription dated A.D. 11 from an altar in the city of Narbonne in southern France. This law was passed by the local government, not the central Roman authorities. What does it order the population to do? Although the law itself does not state why it was passed, what might some reasons have been? What does the law indicate about attitudes toward Augustus and toward Roman authorities?

Another valuable source for examining the achievements of Augustus consists of the comments of his contemporaries and later Roman historians. Because Romans had such a strong sense of their own traditions, they were fascinated by history and were ever eager to point out how the hand of the gods operated in a way that allowed Rome to conquer most of the Western world. In the century before Augustus took over, it looked to many Romans as if the gods had forgotten Rome, leaving its citizens to kill each other in revolutions and civil wars. Augustus's military successes and political acumen seemed to show that he had the gods on his side, so writers delighted in extolling his accomplishments. Augustus's astuteness also extended to the world of literature and the arts, and he hired writers, sculptors, architects, and painters to glorify Rome, causing his own reputation no harm in the process. Many of the poems and histories are blatant hero worship, others communicate a more balanced view, and, because Augustus was not totally successful at winning everyone over to his side, some authors are openly critical.

Sources 3 through 6 are assessments by various Romans of Augustus's rule. As you read them, first try to gauge each author's basic attitude toward Augustus. What does he find to praise or blame? Does his judgment appear overly positive or negative? Does he sound objective? In answering these questions, you will need to pay attention not only to the content of the selection but also to the specific words each author chooses. What kinds of adjectives does he use to describe Augustus's person and political actions? Once you have

assessed the basic attitude of each author, identify what he regards as important in Augustus's reign. To what factors does he attribute Augustus's success? How does he describe the process by which the Roman republic was turned into an empire? What reasons does he give for Augustus's success and Julius Caesar's failure?

A bit of background on each of these selections will help you put them in better perspective. Source 3 was written by Horace, a poet living at the court of Augustus. This is an excerpt from his *Odes*, a literary rather than a primarily historical work. Source 4, an excerpt from Suetonius's biography of Augustus, was composed during the first half of the second century. Suetonius, private secretary to the emperor Hadrian, was keenly interested in the private as well as the public lives of the Roman emperors. Source 5 is taken from the long history of Rome by the politician and historian Dio Cassius (ca 150–235). Source 6 is drawn from the *Annals* of Tacitus, an orator and historian from a well-to-do Roman family. Sources 4 through 6 were written between one and two centuries after the events they present and are thus "history" as we know it, describing events after they happened.

Source 7 is a third type of evidence, namely, Augustus's own description of his rule. Usually called the *Res Gestae Divi Augusti*, it is an inscription he composed shortly before the end of his life. In this piece, following a long Roman tradition of inscriptions commemorating distinguished citizens, he describes the honors conferred on him as well as his accomplishments. Like all autobiographical statements, it is intended not simply as an objective description of a ruler's deeds but specifically as a vehicle for all that Augustus most wanted people to remember about this reign. Even though it is subjective, the *Res Gestae* is unique and invaluable as a primary source because it gives us Augustus's own version of the transformations he wrought in Roman society. As you read it, compare Augustus's descriptions of his deeds with those of the historians you have just read. What does Augustus regard as his most important accomplishments?

Many of the best sources for Augustus, of course, as for all of ancient history, are not written but archaeological. In fact, two of the sources we have looked at so far, the decree issued by Augustus and the inscription from Narbonne (Sources 1 and 2), are actually archaeological as well as written sources because they are inscriptions carved in stone. Thus, unlike other texts from the ancient world, including such basic ones as Plato's *Republic*, we have the original text and not a later copy.

Inscriptions are just one of many types of archaeological evidence. As the Romans conquered land after land, they introduced not only their legal code but their monetary system as well. Roman coins have been found throughout all of Europe and the Near East, far beyond the borders of the Roman Empire. *Numismatics*, the study of coins, can thus provide us with clues available from no other source, for coins have the great advantage of being both durable and valuable. Though their value sometimes

works to render them less durable—people melt them down to make other coins or to use the metal in other ways—it also makes them one of the few material goods that people hide in great quantities. Their owners intend to dig them up later, of course, but die or forget where they have buried them, leaving great caches of coins for later archaeologists and historians.

Roman coins differ markedly from modern coins in some respects. Though the primary function of both is to serve as a means of exchange, Roman coins were also transmitters of political propaganda. One side usually displayed a portrait of the emperor, chosen very carefully by the emperor himself to emphasize certain qualities. The reverse side often depicted a recent victory, anniversary, or other important event, or the personification of an abstract quality of virtue such as health or liberty. Modern coins also feature portraits, pictures, and slogans, but they tend to stay the same for decades, and so we pay very little attention to what is on them. Roman emperors, on the other hand, issued new coins frequently, expecting people to look at them. Most of the people who lived in the Roman Empire were illiterate, with no chance to read about the illustrious deeds of the emperor, but they did come into contact with coins nearly every day. From these coins they learned what the emperor looked like, what he had recently done, or what qualities to associate with him, for even illiterate people could identify the symbols for such abstract virtues as liberty or victory. Over one hundred different portraits of Augustus have been found on coins, providing us with additional clues about the achievements he most wanted to emphasize.

Once you have read the written documents, look at the two illustrations of coins, Sources 8 and 9. On the first, issued in 2 B.C., the lettering reads CAESAR AUGUSTUS DIVI F PATER PATRIAE, or "Augustus Caesar, son of a God, Father of the Fatherland." (Julius Caesar had been deified by the senate after his assassination, which is why Augustus called himself "son of a God.") Augustus is crowned with what appears to be a wreath of wheat stalks; this crown was the exclusive right of the priests of one of Rome's oldest religious groups that honored agricultural gods. The second coin, issued between 20 and 16 B.C., shows Augustus alongside the winged figure of the goddess Victory in a chariot atop a triumphal arch that stands on top of a viaduct; the inscription reads QUOD VIAE MUN SUNT, "because the roads have been reinforced." Think about the message Augustus was trying to convey with each of these coins. Even if you could not read the words, what impression of the emperor would you have from coins like these?

Issuing coins was one way for an emperor to celebrate and communicate his achievements; building was another. As you will read in Augustus's autobiography, he had many structures—stadiums, marketplaces, and temples—built for various purposes. He, and later Roman emperors, also built structures that were purely symbolic, the most impressive of which were celebratory arches,

built to commemorate an achievement or a military victory. The second coin shows Augustus standing on top of such an arch; Source 10 is a photograph of the arch of Augustus that still stands at Rimini. This arch was built at one end of the Flaminian Way, which Augustus reconstructed, as you will read in his autobiography; a similar arch was built at the other end in Rome. As you did when looking at the coins, think about the message such an arch conveys. It was put up with the agreement of the senate; does it give you a sense of republicanism or empire?

Roads are another prime archaeological source, closely related to the aqueducts we examined in Chapter 1. The Romans initially built roads to help their army move more quickly; once built, however, the road system facilitated trade and commerce as well. Roads are thus symbols of power as well as a means to maintain and extend it. Archaeologists have long studied the expansion of the Roman road system, and their findings can most easily be seen diagrammed on maps. Though maps do not have the immediacy of actual archaeological remains, they are based on such remains and enable us to detect patterns and make comparisons over time.

Selections 11 and 12 are maps of the major Roman roads existing before the reign of Augustus, those built or reconstructed during his reign, and the Roman road system at its farthest extent. Compare the first map with the information you have obtained from Augustus himself about his expansion of the frontiers of

Rome (Source 7, paragraph 26). Notice that he mentions only the western part of the Roman Empire; do the roads built during his reign reflect this western orientation? What do the later road-building patterns shown in Source 12 tell us about the goals and successes of later Roman emperors?

THE EVIDENCE

Sources 1 through 3 from Naphtali Lewis and Meyer Reinhold, editors and translators, Roman Civilization, *vol. 2,* The Empire *(New York: Columbia University Press, 1955), pp. 39–42; p. 62; p. 20. Reprinted with permission of Columbia University Press, 562 W. 113th St., New York, NY 10025, via Copyright Clearance Center, Inc.*

1. Decree Issued by Emperor Augustus, 4 B.C.

The Emperor Caesar Augustus, *pontifex maximus,* holding the tribunician power for the nineteenth year, declares:

A decree of the senate was passed in the consulship of Gaius Calvisius and Lucius Passienus, with me as one of those present at the writing. Since it affects the welfare of the allies of the Roman people, I have decided to send it into the provinces, appended to this my prefatory edict, so that it may be known to all who are under our care. From this it will be evident to all the inhabitants of the provinces how much both I and the senate are concerned that none of our subjects should suffer any improper treatment or any extortion.

DECREE OF THE SENATE

Whereas the consuls Gaius Calvisius Sabinus and Lucius Passienus Rufus spoke "Concerning matters affecting the security of the allies of the Roman people which the Emperor Caesar Augustus, our *princeps,* following the recommendation of the council which he had drawn by lot from among the senate, desired to be brought before the senate by us," the senate passed the following decree:

Whereas our ancestors established legal process for extortion so that the allies might more easily be able to take action for any wrongs done them and recover moneys extorted from them, and whereas this type of process is sometimes very expensive and troublesome for those in whose interest the law was enacted, because poor people or persons weak with illness or age are dragged from far-distant provinces as witnesses, the senate decrees as follows:

If after the passage of this decree of the senate any of the allies, desiring to recover extorted moneys, public or private, appear and so depose before one of the magistrates who is authorized to convene the senate, the magistrate—except where the extorter faces a capital charge—shall bring them before the senate as soon as possible and shall assign them any advocate they themselves request to speak in their behalf before the senate; but no one who has in accordance with the laws been excused from this duty shall be required to serve as advocate against his will. . . .

The judges chosen shall hear and inquire into only those cases in which a man is accused of having appropriated money from a community or from private parties; and, rendering their decision within thirty days, they shall order him to restore such sum of money, public or private, as the accusers prove was taken from them. Those whose duty it is to inquire into and pronounce judgment in these cases shall, until they complete the inquiry and pronounce their judgment, be exempted from all public duties except public worship. . . .

The senate likewise decrees that the judges who are selected in accordance with this decree of the senate shall pronounce in open court each his several findings, and what the majority pronounces shall be the verdict.

2. Inscription from the City of Narbonne, A.D. 11

In the consulship of Titus Statilius Taurus and Lucius Cassius Longinus, September 22. Vow taken to the divine spirit of Augustus by the populace of the Narbonensians in perpetuity: "May it be good, favorable, and auspicious to the Emperor Caesar Augustus, son of a god, father of his country, *pontifex maximus*, holding the tribunician power for the thirty-fourth year; to his wife, children, and house; to the Roman senate and people; and to the colonists[1] and residents of the Colonia Julia Paterna of Narbo Martius,[2] who have bound themselves to worship his divine spirit in perpetuity!"

The populace of the Narbonensians has erected in the forum at Narbo an altar at which every year on September 23—the day on which the good fortune of the age bore him to be ruler of the world—three Roman *equites*[3] from the populace and three freedmen shall sacrifice one animal each and shall at their own expense on that day provide the colonists and residents with incense and wine for supplication to his divine spirit. And on September 24 they shall likewise provide incense and wine for the colonists and residents. Also on January 1 they shall provide incense and wine for the colonists and residents. Also on January 7, the day on which he first entered upon the command of the world, they shall make supplication with incense and wine, and

---

1. The word "colonist" has a very specific meaning in Roman history. **Colonists** were Romans, often retired soldiers, who were granted land in the outlying provinces in order to build up Roman strength there. They were legally somewhat distinct from native residents, which is why this law uses the phrase "colonists and residents" to make it clear that both groups were required to follow its provisions.

2. The long phrase "Colonia Julia Pasterna of Narbo Martius" is the official and complete Roman name for the town of Narbo, which we now call Narbonne.

3. **equites:** cavalry of the Roman army.

shall sacrifice one animal each, and shall provide incense and wine for the colonists and residents on that day. And on May 31, because on that day in the consulship of Titus Statilius Taurus and Manius Aemilius Lepidus he reconciled the populace to the decurions,[4] they shall sacrifice one animal each and shall provide the colonists and residents with incense and wine for supplication to his divine spirit. And of these three Roman *equites* and three freedmen one . . . [The rest of this inscription is lost.]

3. From Horace, *Odes*

Thine age, O Caesar, has brought back fertile crops to the fields and has restored to our own Jupiter the military standards stripped from the proud columns of the Parthians;[5] has closed Janus' temple[6] freed of wars; has put reins on license overstepping righteous bounds; has wiped away our sins and revived the ancient virtues through which the Latin name and the might of Italy waxed great, and the fame and majesty of our empire were spread from the sun's bed in the west to the east. As long as Caesar is the guardian of the state, neither civil dissension nor violence shall banish peace, nor wrath that forges swords and brings discord and misery to cities. Not those who drink the deep Danube shall violate the orders of Caesar, nor the Getae, nor the Seres,[7] nor the perfidious Parthians, nor those born by the Don River. And we, both on profane and sacred days, amidst the gifts of merry Bacchus, together with our wives and children, will first duly pray to the gods; then, after the tradition of our ancestors, in songs to the accompaniment of Lydian flutes we will hymn leaders whose duty is done.

Source 4 from Suetonius, The Lives of the Twelve Caesars, *edited and translated by Joseph Gavorse (New York: Modern Library, 1931), p. 89.*

4. From Suetonius, *Life of Augustus*

The whole body of citizens with a sudden unanimous impulse proffered him the title of "father of his country"—first the plebs, by a deputation sent to

4. **decurion:** member of a town council.

5. The Parthians were an empire located in the region occupied by present-day Iraq. They had defeated Roman armies led by Mark Antony and had taken the Roman military standards, that is, the flags and banners of the army they defeated. Augustus recovered these standards, an important symbolic act, even though he did not conquer the Parthians.

6. This was a small temple in Rome that was ordered closed whenever peace reigned throughout the whole Roman Empire. During the reign of Augustus it was closed three times.

7. The Getae and the Seres were people who lived in the regions occupied by present-day Romania and Ukraine.

Antium, and then, because he declined it, again at Rome as he entered the theater, which they attended in throngs, all wearing laurel wreaths; the senate afterwards in the senate house, not by a decree or by acclamation, but through Valerius Messala. He, speaking for the whole body, said: "Good fortune and divine favor attend thee and thy house, Caesar Augustus; for thus we feel that we are praying for lasting prosperity for our country and happiness for our city. The senate in accord with the Roman people hails thee 'Father of thy Country.'" Then Augustus with tears in his eyes replied as follows (and I have given his exact words, as I did those of Messala): "Having attained my highest hopes, members of the senate, what more have I to ask of the immortal gods than that I may retain this same unanimous approval of yours to the very end of my life?"

Sources 5 through 7 from Naphtali Lewis and Meyer Reinhold, editors and translators, Roman Civilization, vol. 2, The Empire (New York: Columbia University Press, 1955), pp. 4–8; p. 4; pp. 9–10, 12, 14–16, 17, 19. Reprinted with permission of Columbia University Press, 562 W. 113th St., New York, NY 10025, via Copyright Clearance Center, Inc.

5. From Dio Cassius, *Roman History*

In this way the power of both people and senate passed entirely into the hands of Augustus, and from this time there was, strictly speaking, a monarchy; for monarchy would be the truest name for it, even if two or three men later held the power jointly. Now, the Romans so detested the title "monarch" that they called their emperors neither dictators nor kings nor anything of this sort. Yet, since the final authority for the government devolves upon them, they needs must be kings. The offices established by the laws, it is true, are maintained even now, except that of censor; but the entire direction and administration is absolutely in accordance with the wishes of the one in power at the time. And yet, in order to preserve the appearance of having this authority not through their power but by virtue of the laws, the emperors have taken to themselves all the offices (including the titles) which under the Republic possessed great power with the consent of the people—with the exception of the dictatorship. Thus, they very often become consuls, and they are always styled proconsuls whenever they are outside the *pomerium*.[8] The title *imperator* is held by them for life, not only by those who have won victories in battle but also by all the rest, to indicate their absolute power, instead of the title "king" or "dictator." These latter titles they have never assumed since they fell out of use in the constitution, but the actuality of those offices is secured to them by the appellation *imperator*. By virtue of the titles named, they secure the right to make levies, collect funds, declare war, make peace,

8. **pomerium:** the city limits of Rome.

and rule foreigners and citizens alike everywhere and always—even to the extent of being able to put to death both *equites* and senators inside the *pomerium*—and all the other powers once granted to the consuls and other officials possessing independent authority; and by virtue of holding the censorship they investigate our lives and morals as well as take the census, enrolling some in the equestrian and senatorial orders and removing others from these orders according to their will. By virtue of being consecrated in all the priesthoods and, in addition, from their right to bestow most of them upon others, as well as from the fact that, even if two or three persons rule jointly, one of them is *pontifex maximus,* they hold in their own hands supreme authority over all matters both profane and sacred. The tribunician power, as it is called, which once the most influential men used to hold, gives them the right to nullify the effects of the measures taken by any other official, in case they do not approve, and makes their persons inviolable; and if they appear to be wronged in even the slightest degree, not merely by deed but even by word, they may destroy the guilty party as one accursed, without a trial.

Thus by virtue of these Republican titles they have clothed themselves with all the powers of the government, so that they actually possess all the prerogatives of kings without the usual title. For the appellation "Caesar" or "Augustus" confers upon them no actual power but merely shows in the one case that they are the successors of their family line, and in the other the splendor of their rank. The name "Father" perhaps gives them a certain authority over us all—the authority which fathers once had over their children; yet it did not signify this at first, but betokened honor and served as an admonition both to them to love their subjects as they would their children; and to their subjects to revere them as they would their fathers. . . .

The senate as a body, it is true, continued to sit in judgment as before, and in certain cases transacted business with embassies and envoys from both peoples and kings; and the people and the plebs, moreover, continued to come together for the elections; but nothing was actually done that did not please Caesar. At any rate, in the case of those who were to hold office, he himself selected and nominated some; and though he left the election of others in the hands of the people and the plebs, in accordance with the ancient practice, yet he took care that no persons should hold office who were unfit or elected as the result of factious combinations or bribery.

Such were the arrangements made, generally speaking, at that time; for in reality Caesar himself was destined to have absolute power in all matters for life, because he was not only in control of money matters (nominally, to be sure, he had separated the public funds from his own, but as a matter of fact he spent the former also as he saw fit) but also in control of the army. At all events, when his ten-year period came to an end, there was voted him another five years, then five more, after that ten, and again another ten, and then ten for the fifth time, so that by the succession of ten-year periods he continued to be sole ruler for life. And it is for this reason that the subsequent monarchs, though no longer appointed for a specified period but for their whole life once for all, nevertheless always held a celebration every ten years, as if then renewing their sovereignty once more; and this is done even at the present day.

Now, Caesar had received many privileges previously, when the question of declining the sovereignty and that of apportioning the provinces were under discussion. For the right to fasten laurels to the front of the imperial residence and to hang the civic crown above the doors was then voted him to symbolize the fact that he was always victorious over enemies and savior of the citizens. The imperial palace is called Palatium, not because it was ever decreed that this should be its name but because Caesar dwelt on the Palatine and had his military headquarters there. . . . Hence, even if the emperor resides somewhere else, his dwelling retains the name of Palatium.

And when he had actually completed the reorganization, the name Augustus was at length bestowed upon him by the senate and by the people. . . . He took the title of Augustus, signifying that he was more than human; for all most precious and sacred objects are termed *augusta*. For which reason they called him also in Greek *sebastos* . . . meaning an august person.

6. From Tacitus, *Annals*

After the death of Brutus and Cassius, there was no longer any army loyal to the Republic. . . . Then, laying aside the title of triumvir and parading as a consul, and professing himself satisfied with the tribunician power for the protection of the plebs, Augustus enticed the soldiers with gifts, the people with grain, and all men with the allurement of peace, and gradually grew in power, concentrating in his own hands the functions of the senate, the magistrates, and the laws. No one opposed him, for the most courageous had fallen in battle or in the proscription. As for the remaining nobles, the readier they were for slavery, the higher were they raised in wealth and offices, so that, aggrandized by the revolution, they preferred the safety of the present to the perils of the past. Nor did the provinces view with disfavor this state of affairs, for they distrusted the government of the senate and the people on account of the struggles of the powerful and the rapacity of the officials, while the protection afforded them by the laws was inoperative, as the provinces were repeatedly thrown into confusion by violence, intrigue, and finally bribery. . . .

At home all was peaceful; the officials bore the same titles as before. The younger generation was born after the victory of Actium, and even many of the older generation had been born during the civil wars. How few were left who had seen the Republic!

Thus the constitution had been transformed, and there was nothing at all left of the good old way of life. Stripped of equality, all looked to the directives of a *princeps* with no apprehension for the present, while Augustus in the vigorous years of his life maintained his power, that of his family, and peace.

7. From Augustus, *Res Gestae Divi Augusti*

1. At the age of nineteen, on my own initiative and at my own expense, I raised an army by means of which I liberated the Republic, which was oppressed by the tyranny of a faction. For which reason the senate, with honorific decrees, made me a member of its order in the consulship of Gaius Pansa and Aulus Hirtius, giving me at the same time consular rank in voting, and granted me the *imperium*. It ordered me as propraetor, together with the consuls, to see to it that the state suffered no harm. Moreover, in the same year, when both consuls had fallen in the war, the people elected me consul and a triumvir for the settlement of the commonwealth.

2. Those who assassinated my father I drove into exile, avenging their crime by due process of law; and afterwards when they waged war against the state, I conquered them twice on the battlefield.

3. I waged many wars throughout the whole world by land and by sea, both civil and foreign, and when victorious I spared all citizens who sought pardon. Foreign peoples who could safely be pardoned I preferred to spare rather than to extirpate. . . . Though the Roman senate and people unitedly agreed that I should be elected soul guardian of the laws and morals with supreme authority, I refused to accept any office offered me which was contrary to the traditions of our ancestors. . . .

9. The senate decreed that vows for my health should be offered up every fifth year by the consuls and priests. In fulfillment of those vows, games were often celebrated during my lifetime, sometimes by the four most distinguished colleges of priests, sometimes by the consuls. Moreover, the whole citizen body, with one accord, both individually and as members of municipalities, prayed continuously for my health at all the shrines.

10. My name was inserted, by decree of the senate, in the hymn of the Salian priests. And it was enacted by law that I should be sacrosanct in perpetuity and that I should possess the tribunician power as long as I live. I declined to become *pontifex maximus* in place of a colleague while he was still alive, when the people offered me that priesthood, which my father had held. A few years later, in the consulship of Publius Sulpicius and Gaius Valgius, I accepted this priesthood, when death removed the man who had taken possession of it at a time of civil disturbance; and from all Italy a multitude flocked to my election such as had never previously been recorded at Rome. . . .

17. Four times I came to the assistance of the treasury with my own money, transferring to those in charge of the treasury 150,000,000 sesterces. And in the consulship of Marcus Lepidus and Lucius Arruntius I transferred out of my own patrimony 170,000,000 sesterces to the soldiers' bonus fund, which was

established on my advice for the purpose of providing bonuses for soldiers who had completed twenty or more years of service.

18. From the year in which Gnaeus Lentulus and Publius Lentulus were consuls, whenever the provincial taxes fell short, in the case sometimes of 100,000 persons and sometimes of many more, I made up their tribute in grain and in money from my own grain stores and my own patrimony. . . .

20. I repaired the Capitol and the theater of Pompey with enormous expenditures on both works, without having my name inscribed on them. I repaired the conduits of the aqueducts which were falling into ruin in many places because of age, and I doubled the capacity of the aqueduct called Marcia by admitting a new spring into its conduit. I completed the Julian Forum and the basilica which was between the temple of Castor and the temple of Saturn, works begun and far advanced by my father, and when the same basilica was destroyed by fire, I enlarged its site and began rebuilding the structure, which is to be inscribed with the names of my sons; and in case it should not be completed while I am still alive, I left instructions that the work be completed by my heirs. In my sixth consulship I repaired eighty-two temples of the gods in the city, in accordance with a resolution of the senate, neglecting none which at that time required repair. In my seventh consulship I reconstructed the Flaminian Way from the city as far as Ariminum,[9] and also all the bridges except the Mulvian and the Minucian. . . .

22. I gave a gladiatorial show three times in my own name, and five times in the names of my sons or grandsons; at these shows about 10,000 fought. Twice I presented to the people in my own name an exhibition of athletes invited from all parts of the world, and a third time in the name of my grandson. I presented games in my own name four times, and in addition twenty-three times in the place of other magistrates. On behalf of the college of fifteen, as master of that college, with Marcus Agrippa as my colleague, I celebrated the Secular Games[10] in the consulship of Gaius Furnius and Gaius Silanus. In my thirteenth consulship I was the first to celebrate the Games of Mars, which subsequently the consuls, in accordance with a decree of the senate and a law, have regularly celebrated in the succeeding years. Twenty-six times I provided for the people, in my own name or in the names of my sons or grandsons, hunting spectacles of African wild beasts in the circus or in the Forum or in the amphitheaters; in these exhibitions about 3,500 animals were killed.

---

9. Present-day Rimini, Italy.

10. The Secular Games were an enormous series of athletic games, festivals, and banquets that Augustus ordered held in 17 B.C. Though called "secular," they were held in honor of the gods and were directed by the College of Fifteen, a board that oversaw sacrifices to the gods. All adult Roman citizens were expected to view the games out of religious duty.

23. I presented to the people an exhibition of a naval battle across the Tiber where the grove of the Caesars now is, having had the site excavated 1,800 feet in length and 1,200 feet in width. In this exhibition thirty beaked ships, triremes or biremes, and in addition a great number of smaller vessels engaged in combat. On board these fleets, exclusive of rowers, there were about 3,000 combatants. . . .

26. I extended the frontiers of all the provinces of the Roman people on whose boundaries were peoples subject to our empire. I restored peace to the Gallic and Spanish provinces and likewise to Germany, that is, to the entire region bounded by the Ocean from Gades to the mouth of the Elbe River. I caused peace to be restored in the Alps, from the region nearest to the Adriatic Sea as far as the Tuscan Sea, without undeservedly making war against any people. My fleet sailed the Ocean from the mouth of the Rhine eastward as far as the territory of the Cimbrians,[11] to which no Roman previously had penetrated either by land or by sea. . . .

34. In my sixth and seventh consulships, after I had put an end to the civil wars, having attained supreme power by universal consent, I transferred the state from my own power to the control of the Roman senate and people. For this service of mine I received the title of Augustus by decree of the senate, and the doorposts of my house were publicly decked with laurels, the civic crown was affixed over my doorway, and a golden shield was set up in the Julian senate house, which, as the inscription on this shield testifies, the Roman senate and people gave me in recognition of my valor, clemency, justice, and devotion. After that time I excelled all in authority, but I possessed no more power than the others who were my colleagues in each magistracy.

35. When I held my thirteenth consulship, the senate, the equestrian order, and the entire Roman people gave me the title of "father of the country" and decreed that this title should be inscribed in the vestibule of my house, in the Julian senate house, and in the Augustan Forum on the pedestal of the chariot which was set up in my honor by decree of the senate. At the time I wrote this document I was in my seventy-sixth year.

---

11. Near present-day Hamburg, Germany.

Sources 8 and 9 from the American Numismatic Society, New York.

8. Roman Coin Issued 2 B.C.

9. Roman Coin Issued 20–16 B.C.

Source 10 from Alinari/Art Resource. Photo by Stab D. Anderson, 1931.

10. Arch of Augustus at Rimini

Source 11 adapted from sketches by Merry E. Wiesner.

11. Main Roman Roads, 31 B.C.–A.D. 14

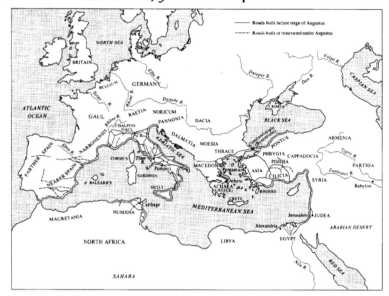

Source 12 from Victor W. Von Hagen, The Roads That Led to Rome *(Cleveland and New York: World Publishing Co., © 1967 by George Weidenfeld and Nicolson, London), pp. 18–19.*

12. Main Roman Roads at Their Greatest Extent, A.D. 180

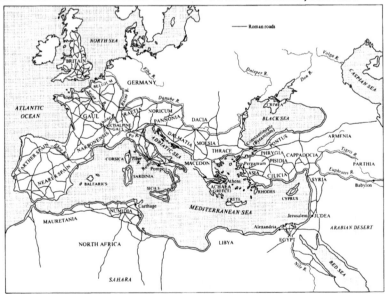

QUESTIONS TO CONSIDER

Now that you have examined various pieces of evidence, you need to put them together to arrive at a conclusion that you can support. Do not worry about not having all the evidence you need; no historian can ever discover "all" the facts about an event or person. He or she makes conclusions on the basis of the evidence available, alters those conclusions when new material is discovered, and uses those conclusions as a framework for further research. In this respect, historians operate just like physicists learning how the universe works. Do not worry if some of your sources disagree; ten people who witness an auto accident often come up with ten quite contradictory accounts of the event. Why might accounts of Augustus's rule be even more contradictory?

The sources have made you aware of the operation of Roman government on two levels: that of the formal constitution, which remained a republic, and that of the actual locus of power, which was increasingly the emperor. The changes that Augustus instituted thus took place at the second level, and in many areas we can ignore the formal constitution of Rome in describing the process of change. Comparing all the sources, how would you describe the means by which Augustus transformed the republic into a different type of government? Which steps were most important? Which observers seemed to have the clearer view of this process, Augustus himself and those living during his lifetime, or later historians?

In considering this last question, you need to think about the advantages and disadvantages of eyewitness reports versus later, secondary accounts.

The second question concerns results, not process: Why was Augustus successful? To answer this, we must consider not only the changes themselves, but people's perceptions of them. A ruler's place in history depends not only on real accomplishments but also on how these accomplishments are perceived and judged by later generations. Rulers perceived as good or successful are often given credit for everything good that happened during their reigns, even if they had nothing to do with it. Conversely, rulers regarded as unsuccessful, weak, or bad get blamed for many things that were not their fault. A reputation is generally based on actual achievements, but occasionally it is also determined by a ruler's successful manipulation of public opinion, and sometimes by that manipulation alone.

Augustus clearly recognized the importance of public opinion, which in Rome was tied to upholding tradition. How does he make use of Roman traditions in the laws and coins he issues? How do other observers judge his connection with tradition? Many of Rome's traditions were incorporated into public rituals and ceremonies. What sorts of ceremonies did Romans participate in or view? How did Augustus use these ceremonies to demonstrate his power or his personal connections with Roman tradition? Along with rituals, titles are also important demonstrations of power.

What does Augustus call himself and what do others call him, both in the written documents and on the coins? Why is there so much discussion of his accepting or not accepting various titles?

Now that you have considered the opinions of a range of commentators, assessed some actual legal changes and road-building patterns, examined some coins, and heard from Augustus himself, you are ready to answer the questions: How did Augustus transform the Roman republic into an empire? Why was he successful? Once you have made your assessment, think about how you would use it to structure future research. What other evidence would be useful in supporting your conclusions? Where might you go to find that evidence?

EPILOGUE

Though Augustus said that his aim was a restoration of the republic, in reality he transformed Roman government into an empire ruled by one individual. His reign is generally termed the *Principate,* a word taken from Augustus's favorite title *princeps,* but the rulers of Rome after him did not hesitate to use the title *emperor.* Like him, they also retained the titles *pontifex maximus,* supreme priest, and *imperator,* commander-in-chief. It is interesting to see how many of our words denoting aspects of royal rule come from Augustus: not only "prince," "emperor," and "czar" (the Russian variant of "Caesar") but also "palace," from Palatine, the hill where Augustus had his house.

The emperors who came after Augustus built on his achievements, both literally and figuratively. They extended the borders of the Roman Empire even farther, so that at its largest it would stretch from Scotland to the Sudan and from Spain to Syria. The Roman road system was expanded to over 50,000 miles, longer than the current interstate highway system in the United States; some of those roads are still usable today. Roman coins continued to be stamped with the emperor's picture and have been found as far away as southern India. Later emperors continued Augustus's building projects in Rome and throughout the empire. Vespasian built the Colosseum, which could seat 50,000 people; Trajan, the Forum with a number of different buildings and an enormous 125-foot column with his statue on top; Hadrian, the Pantheon and a wall dividing England and Scotland. The emperor Nero may have even ordered part of Rome burned to make room for his urban renewal projects.

Augustus's successors also continued his centralization of power. His stepson Tiberius stripped the assemblies of their right to elect magistrates, and later emperors took this power away from the senate as well. Bureaucrats appointed by the emperor oversaw the grain trade, the army, and the collection of taxes, with the senate gradually dwindling into a rubber stamp for the emperor's decisions. New territories were ruled directly by the emperor through governors and generals; in these jurisdictions, the senate did not have even the pretense of power.

The cult of ruler worship initiated somewhat tentatively in the provinces under Augustus grew enormously after his death, when, like Julius Caesar, he was declared a god. Though Romans officially deified only the *memory* of deceased emperors, some emperors were not willing to wait that long. Caligula declared himself a god at the age of twenty-five, spent much of his time in the temple of Castor and Pollux, and talked to the statue of Jupiter as an equal. Though Caligula was probably insane and later was stabbed to death, ruler worship in general was serious business for most Romans, closely linked as it was to tradition and patriotism. Groups like the Christians who did not offer sacrifices to the emperor or at least to the emperor's "genius" were felt to be unpatriotic, disloyal, and probably traitorous.

Thus in many ways Augustus laid the foundation for the success and durability of his empire. Historians have always been fascinated with the demise of the Roman Empire, but considering the fact that it lasted more than 400 years after Augustus in western Europe—and, in a significantly altered form, almost 1,500 years in eastern Europe—a more appropriate question might be why it lasted so long. Though the weaknesses that led to the empire's eventual collapse were also outgrowths of the reign of Augustus, the latter still represents a remarkable success story.

We must be careful of attributing too much to one man, however. As we have seen, Augustus had an extremely effective network of supporters and advisers, including Rome's most important men of letters. Their rendering of the glories of Roman civilization and the brilliance of Augustus has shaped much of what has been written about Rome since; you may only need to check the adjectives used in your text to describe Augustus to confirm this. Myths or exaggerations told about a ruler die hard, especially those that have been repeated for nearly 2,000 years.

CHAPTER FOUR

PHILOSOPHY AND FAITH:

THE PROBLEM OF ANCIENT SUICIDE

Life itself is our most precious possession, and every civilization has viewed suicide, representing as it does the rejection of all human society, as an act of supreme importance, charged with religious, philosophical, and even legal significance. Indeed, the French philosopher Albert Camus (1913–1960) wrote, "There is only one truly philosophical problem, and that is suicide. Judging whether life is or is not worth living amounts to answering the fundamental question of philosophy."[1] Camus was only one of the most recent in a long line of thinkers, extending back at least to the civilization of ancient Egypt, who have written on the fundamental issues raised by the act of self-destruction. This extensive discourse on suicide can afford us a revealing glimpse of the intellectual life of past civilizations by allowing us to compare the evolution of their thinkers' ideas on this important act.

In the twentieth century, for example, most of us understand suicide in terms defined by the modern social, psychological, and medical sciences. Emile Durkheim (1858–1917), the pioneering French sociologist, identified several kinds of suicide, but concentrated particularly on the role of modern society in eroding the integrative and regulative aspects of traditional society, resulting, he claimed, in an increase in suicide. We now know that Durkheim's statistical evidence for the increase in suicide in modern times was defective, but his conclusion that suicide is a particular side effect of modern society has endured, even though deprived of its statistical support. Sigmund Freud (1856–1940), the father of modern psychoanalysis, and others of his discipline focused modern attention on the psychological problems that often produce suicide. And since the work of the German physician Emil Kraepelin (1865–1926), medical professionals have sought to treat the organic

1. Albert Camus, *The Myth of Sisyphus and Other Essays*, translated by Justin O'Brien (New York: Vintage Books, 1991), p. 3.

causes of depressive disorders that can end in self-destruction.

The earliest Western societies, on the other hand, lacking our modern scientific knowledge, viewed the act of self-destruction in very different, often spiritual terms. Such societies certainly condemned suicide because it robbed their ranks of productive members. But primitive peoples also believed that the spirits of those who took their own lives would not rest in the world of the dead, but would return to haunt the realm of the living.

In the present chapter we will examine the thought of the ancient world on suicide. The practice was common for much of the period, and ancients seem to have taken their lives for a number of reasons. One had to do with personal honor. Examples abound of ancients extolled in the literature of their time for their nobility in ending their lives to preserve their honor. Perhaps the most famous of these suicides was that of Cato the Younger (95–46 B.C.), a leader of the senatorial opposition to Julius Caesar's attempt to control Rome. With his forces defeated in the field, and facing Caesar's imminent attack on Utica, the stronghold under his command, Cato assured the escape of his followers and took his own life rather than surrender to the man he regarded as a tyrant. Other ancients took their own lives to avoid the pains of old age, perhaps because they saw mental and physical decline as diminishing their honor. Thus, the Greek philosopher Zeno (ca 334–ca 262) took his own life at the age of seventy-two when breaking a bone in a minor accident seemed to convince

him of impending physical decline. Love for a dead spouse also led to suicide. Portia, the daughter of Cato and the wife of Caesar's assassin, Brutus, took her own life after her husband's suicide upon his defeat by Caesar's heir, Octavian, in 42 B.C. Ancients also took their lives in the belief that their deaths could advance a cause, and we will look at such an act in the death of Samson. Indeed, we will examine ancient thought on such acts of self-destruction among the Greeks, the Romans, the Hebrews of the Old Testament, and early Christians.

Historians date Hellenic, or classical Greek, civilization from about 800 B.C., when growing commercial wealth and the development of an efficient writing system promoted the economic and intellectual flowering of Greek city-states on the Greek mainland, the islands of the Aegean, Asia Minor (modern Turkey), and the shores of the Black Sea. The epics of Homer helped to shape early Hellenic culture, with the heroes providing role models for young Greeks and the tales of the gods forming the basis for early belief in a cluster of deities, presided over by Zeus, inhabiting the heights of Mount Olympus. These religious beliefs of the Greeks had little of the creedal structure of modern religion, but emphasized instead the duty of citizens of an independent city-state (as most Greeks were) to live in accord with the community. For the early Greeks, as for most Mediterranean peoples of that period, death simply represented the spirit's journey to a shadowy realm of the dead.

The greatest accomplishment of Hellenic intellectuals was to begin to transcend this traditional Greek religion—which explained events in this life in terms of divine action—and to apply reason to their understanding of natural phenomena and human events. As they replaced myth with reason, the Greeks first attempted to explain the physical world around them. The Cosmologists, thinkers concerned with the origins, structure, and operation of the universe, including Thales (ca 624–548 B.C.), Anaximander (ca 611–547 B.C.), and Pythagoras (ca 580–507 B.C.), sought natural explanations for the origins of the universe and advanced the concept that the physical world operates according to mathematical, scientific laws. Greek philosophers also evaluated human society, examining political and ethical problems through the use of reason. Socrates (ca 469–399 B.C.) and Plato (ca 429–347 B.C.), philosophers we will study in this chapter, in particular led the Greek inquiry into ethical problems.

A political event fundamentally transformed the Hellenic age, however. In 338 B.C. King Philip of Macedon (382–336 B.C.), a primitive state in northern Greece, conquered the city-states of Greece and ended their independence by subjecting them to the rule of his growing empire. Philip planned further military campaigns; these were carried out after his death by his son, Alexander the Great (356–323 B.C.). Alexander conquered Greece's historic enemy, the Persian Empire, and created an empire that stretched to the borders of India.

Although Alexander's empire dissolved into several smaller monarchies after his death, his conquests began a new Hellenistic age. Greek became the language of administration and intellectual life in the eastern Mediterranean world, and contact with eastern ideas reshaped Hellenic thought. Hellenistic philosophy reflected a search for intellectual peace for the individual in a world far less democratic and secure than that of the independent city-states of the Hellenic age.

Epicurus (342–270 B.C.) began to teach philosophy in Athens in the late fourth century, creating Epicureanism, one of the great schools of Hellenistic philosophy. Seeking intellectual tranquillity in a much less secure age, Epicurus urged his followers to withdraw from public affairs and civic responsibilities, which had been central to the earlier period of city-states. He also taught his students to abandon pursuit of worldly success. The wise person, Epicurus taught, would seek spiritual tranquillity instead, and he taught his students not to fear even divine interruptions of that peace. He affirmed the gods' existence, but held that they played no role in human affairs. Adopting the thought of the Cosmologist Democritus (ca 460–370 B.C.), Epicurus taught that the physical world consisted of matter made up of atoms governed by mechanical principles and unaffected by divine action. Death released the atoms making up the human form to constitute new matter, and so the peace Epicurus sought to instill in his followers was very much one of this world.

Zeno, who, as we have seen, committed suicide, founded a second school of Hellenistic philosophy. He taught on the *stoa poecile* (the "painted porch") near the agora, or marketplace, of Athens. As a consequence, his ideas came to be called Stoicism. Stoics accepted the new realities of the Greek and, later, Roman worlds by emphasizing the universality of human society. As expressed by Zeno, "All men should regard themselves as members of one city and people, having one life and order as a herd feeding together on a common pasture."[2] Stoics believed that the universe inhabited by such a society received order from divine reason, or Logos. Animals followed this divine order by instinct, and inanimate objects necessarily adhered to the physical laws of the universe— for example, those governing the regular movements of the heavenly bodies. Humans, however, had free will and could choose to reject the divine plan. But Stoics taught that the virtuous person could achieve happiness only by living in harmony with the Logos, subjecting personal emotions to reason, and accepting life's trials as part of the overall plan of the universe.

While Epicureans withdrew from the world and Stoics sought to live in accord with the Logos, the Cynics, a third group of Hellenistic philosophers led by Diogenes of Sinope (ca 412–323 B.C.), rejected social conventions. They urged their followers to give up material possessions and the complexities of human society and live lives of self-sufficiency and high personal ethics. Because material matters meant little to Cynics, they were prepared to commit suicide if anything blocked their quest for the virtuous life. Indeed, Diogenes reportedly said that the conduct of life required either reason or the noose.

Imperial expansion fundamentally shaped Roman civilization. Thus, in the fourth century B.C., the Romans came into contact with the Greek settlements in the south of their native Italy, and Roman equivalents of the Greek deities soon replaced traditional Roman religion, which was centered on the gods of home and family. In philosophy, the Romans similarly embraced Hellenistic Epicureanism and Stoicism. But, ultimately, the fundamental force reshaping Roman thought as the empire conquered the Mediterranean world was religious. Rome's world empire only increased the sense of alienation and personal insecurity that we identified in the Hellenistic age, and while educated Romans adopted Stoicism and other rational solutions to these problems, others often sought religious answers. Popular among such people were the mystery religions, so called because they involved secret rituals known only to initiates. These religions, whose attraction only grew as the Roman Empire weakened, offered their adherents spiritual immortality in · an afterlife. But the greatest religious force transforming Rome was Christianity, whose roots we must seek in the Jewish experience beginning in

2. Quoted in D. Brendan Nagle, *The Ancient World: A Social and Cultural History* (Englewood Cliffs, N.J.: Prentice-Hall, 1979), p. 206.

the Middle East in the late second millennium B.C.

The founders of this religious tradition, the Hebrews, originated a faith that was unique in the ancient Middle East. By the late second millennium B.C., their Judaism was a monotheistic religion centered on the deity Yahweh, who demanded ethical behavior of his followers. In this ethical monotheism of the early Hebrews, Yahweh enforced his laws by divine intervention in this life. There was no belief in a last judgment, and afterlife beliefs were quite similar to those of the Greeks; the Jews' Sheol was a dark underworld of the dead.

By the first century B.C., new ideas were taking root among the Jews of Palestine, dividing them into four main sects. The Sadducees, often drawn from the elite of Jewish society, maintained traditional beliefs and ceremonies and the letter of ancient religious law dating back to the days of the lawgiver Moses. The Pharisees, quite possibly representing the majority of Jews in Palestine, challenged the Sadducees by their willingness to admit the law to interpretation and by their acceptance of the eastern idea of a life after death, with the possibility of spiritual salvation through resurrection. The Essenes, the third group within first-century Judaism, also accepted the idea of resurrection, but formed a monastic-style community near the Dead Sea where they awaited the imminent establishment of the Kingdom of God on earth. The fourth sect, the Zealots, refused to accept Roman conquest of their homeland and engaged in violent resistance, culminating in a Jewish revolt in Palestine in A.D. 66.

A widely held belief among first-century Jews in Palestine was that they would be delivered from foreign domination by a Messiah. Many Jews conceived of the Messiah as a military leader, but when a peaceful figure, Jesus of Nazareth (ca 4 B.C.–ca A.D. 29), declared that he was the Messiah, many Jews saw him as fulfilling their expectation, and Jesus soon had a growing following. Grounded in Jewish monotheism, Jesus' teachings called on his followers to repent their sins in order to enter the Kingdom of God and thus achieve spiritual salvation in a life after death. But to conservative Jews like the Sadducees, Jesus was defying traditional religious law, and they turned him over to Roman authorities. In a difficult province of their empire, these officials certainly saw Jesus as an unsettling presence who counted Zealots among his closest followers, and they ordered his execution.

Jesus' followers proclaimed his resurrection three days after his death as fulfillment of his teachings, and the nature of his following shortly began to change. More and more Gentiles, or non-Jews, joined Jesus' original Jewish followers, as Saint Paul (ca 5–ca A.D. 67) emphasized that adherence to traditional Jewish law, including dietary rules and circumcision, was not required for membership in the Christian community. In the Hellenized culture of the Middle East, Jesus increasingly was referred to as "Christ," from the Greek *Christos*, or "the Anointed," a translation of the

Hebrew word *Messiah*. Thus, a new faith, Christianity, quite distinct from Judaism, emerged and grew steadily because of its promise of other-worldly rewards in a society already seeking such spiritual comfort in the mystery religions. Soon the Christian community grew large enough to attract the attention of Roman authorities to a faith that seemed subversive in its nonviolence and refusal even superficially to conform to the Roman civic practice of venerating the emperor. Imperial authorities responded with sporadic, often brutal, persecutions of Christians, beginning in A.D. 64. But the continued growth of the new faith led first to its legalization under Emperor Constantine in A.D. 313 and finally to its elevation to the status of Rome's official religion by Emperor Theodosius I in A.D. 392.

As it achieved legitimacy, Christianity also defined its belief system in an atmosphere of theological controversy. Many theologians whose ideas came to be viewed by the Church as false doctrines, or heresies, sought to promote their ideas in the Christian community. Thus, the followers of Arius (A.D. 250–326), a Greek priest of Alexandria, denied the absolute divinity of Christ, who had declared that he was the son of God. Arians, who taught that Christ was certainly no mere mortal but that neither was he God's equal, received the Church's condemnation at the Council of Nicaea in A.D. 325. Another heretical group was the Donatists, who rejected the idea, held by the majority of Christians, that the Church should be a universal, or catholic, church embracing all, sinners as well as those meriting salvation. Donatists believed that the Church should include only the elect. Other heresies also spread, but the work of a group of theologians remembered as Church Fathers eventually imposed doctrinal uniformity on the early Church.

Your goal in this chapter is to analyze the thought of these ancient peoples on three levels defined by the central questions of this chapter. The first is very specific to the issue of suicide: What does the author of each selection say about suicide? The second asks you to place these ideas in their intellectual context: How do each author's ideas on self-destruction represent his own thought system and the intellectual outlook of the society in which he lived? The third requires that you perform one of the essential tasks of the historian and examine change over an extended period of time: What change in attitudes toward self-destruction do you see over the extended time period covered by these selections?

SOURCES AND METHOD

This chapter, like Chapter 2, offers us ancient primary sources that present certain analytical challenges. Again, we must recognize that the absolute accuracy of these texts cannot be verified the way records of modern scholars' writings can be checked in their printed works or in recordings or transcripts of their lectures.

Products of a pre-print age, the handwritten originals of most of these sources have long ago disappeared, and students must rely on texts based on ancient scribes' transcriptions of the originals, which may not always be entirely faithful to the authors' precise words. Furthermore, because much ancient writing has failed to survive, it is often difficult to determine whether a given work represents all that its author had to say on a subject.

We also will encounter again sources that are not actually the work of those to whom they are attributed. As we saw in Chapter 2, we can know the thought of Socrates, who wrote nothing, only through the work of his student Plato, and scholars still disagree as to which ideas in the latter's writings are his own and which are those of his teacher. Such considerations require some analysis for all our sources in this chapter.

Source 1 is the work of Plato, an Athenian philosopher who, in the course of his long career, wrote on just about all the philosophical problems that have occupied Western thinkers since his death. His surviving works include letters and a number of dialogues. The dialogues replicate in written form the teaching method of Socrates. Socrates particularly concerned himself with the search for the values by which he and his fellow Athenians might live lives of moral excellence. Socrates believed that these values were not imparted to humanity by a deity, but rather that the individual could discover them through rational inquiry, and

he devised a mode of inquiry, dialectics, to facilitate that search. As practiced by Socrates and his followers, dialectics represented a logical discussion, propelled by the teacher's questions to the student, that forced the student to clarify and justify his thought. Thus, in Source 1, from Plato's dialogue *The Phaedo*, questions are posed by Socrates.

Many scholars divide Plato's dialogues into two chief categories, according to the order in which they probably were written. They call the earlier dialogues, including *The Apology*, *The Meno*, and *The Gorgias*, "Socratic" because they seem to express chiefly the ideas of Socrates. The later dialogues, including *The Phaedo*, seem more nearly to express the ideas of Plato himself.

Plato divided knowledge into two realms. One of these was knowledge of the material world, which can be gathered through sensory perceptions. The other, higher realm of knowledge was that of absolute reality and perfect virtues, the realm of forms or ideas for Plato, which could be achieved only intellectually.

In Source 1, one of the most dramatic episodes of ancient literature, Plato describes the execution of Socrates. Plato's teacher had employed his dialectic method not only with his students, but with his fellow citizens as well, in the hope of leading them to more ethical lives. Indeed, he became the Athenians' "gadfly," and he made more than a few enemies. When Athens lost the Peloponnesian War with Sparta, many of those enemies led Athenians who were seeking an explanation for their defeat to charge Socrates with having had a role in the military disaster. Indeed, several of Socrates' former students had betrayed their city in the war, and his enemies charged him with having led the youth of Athens away from the traditional gods and thereby contributed to the Spartan victory.

As was customary in Athens, the trial of Socrates took place before a jury with wide-ranging powers; the jury not only judged guilt or innocence but also determined the sentence. Plato's accounts of the procedure in The Apology make it clear that Socrates could have escaped serious penalty by going into voluntary exile before trial or, perhaps after conviction, by admitting error and promising to stop teaching. But when the jury found him guilty and asked him to suggest a punishment, Socrates almost mockingly proposed what amounted to civic honors. Even though he subsequently suggested a fine, the jury clearly took offense at his remarks; more jurors voted for the penalty of death by taking poison (hemlock) than had voted for the verdict of guilty.

Socrates' behavior at his trial and his subsequent refusal to approve the efforts of his friends Simmias and Cebes, who arrived with money to finance an escape from confinement, suggest to many scholars a sort of death wish. These scholars propose that the philosopher's end represented not so much an execution as a suicide. Indeed, self-destruction figures prominently in The Phaedo,

which opens on Socrates' execution day (which had been delayed by Athenian religious observances). Socrates spent that day surrounded by friends, and one of these, Cebes, asked Socrates, on behalf of the poet Evenus, why he had lately taken to writing poetry. Socrates replied that he had no wish to rival Evenus, but simply wrote in response to a dream demanding that he "make music"; he wrote only so as to leave no duty undone as he met his end. Our selection from The Phaedo opens in the midst of the discussion of poetry. In that selection, why does Socrates think that philosophers in particular should welcome death? How should death open to philosophers the realm of ideas or forms? Does Socrates suggest any divine limitation on an individual's right to self-destruction? What suggests to you that Socrates believed that a divine necessity now permitted his death and that he welcomed his end as a remedy for the problems of this life? What in the thought of Socrates strikes you as characteristic of a philosopher who was a free citizen of a democratic city-state? What about Plato's thought might suggest to you that he was less optimistic than his teacher about finding perfection in this life?

While important portions of Plato's work have survived for modern study, the work of some other ancient philosophers comes to us less directly. This is the case with both Epicurus (ca 341–270 B.C.), of whose vast writings only fragments have survived, and Epictetus (ca 50–ca A.D.

138), whose thought survives only in writings of a disciple, Arrian, based on notes of Epictetus' words.

Much of what we know of the life and thought of Epicurus comes from *Lives of Eminent Philosophers* by Diogenes Laertius, an author about whom scholars know very little. He wrote this history of ancient philosophers in Greek, and the contents of the book suggest that he composed it early in the third century after the birth of Christ. *Lives of Eminent Philosophers* is a remarkable source for ancient history because Diogenes Laertius included many writings that subsequently were lost and, therefore, are available nowhere else. The author illustrated his accounts of philosophers' lives with quotations from their philosophical writings as well as from decrees, letters, wills, and epitaphs. Indeed, Source 2 opens with a letter from Epicurus and concludes with a brief portion of the maxims that he expected his students to memorize, all drawn from *Lives of Eminent Philosophers*.

In the excerpts from the works of Epicurus in Source 2, what aim in life does he urge on his followers? How are they to attain that goal? Why will death be "nothing" to Epicureans? How did his thought relate to self-destruction? Why did the Roman thinker Cicero (106–43 B.C.) write the following passage?

For my part I think that in life we should observe the rule which is followed at Greek banquets:—"Let him either drink," it runs, "or go!" And rightly; for either he should enjoy the pleasure of tippling along with the others or get away early, that a sober man may not be a victim to the violence of those who are heated with wine. Thus by running away one can escape the assaults of fortune which one cannot face. This is the same advice as Epicurus gives.[3]

How does this quotation embody developments we have examined in the Hellenistic and Roman worlds?

Source 3 presents a selection from the *Discourses* of Epictetus recorded by Arrian (ca A.D. 95–175), who was a cosmopolitan figure indeed. A Greek born in Asia Minor, he entered Roman service and combined success as a governor and general with scholarship. Writing in Greek, he was the author of several histories, including one of Alexander the Great, and as a student of philosophy, Arrian wrote the only record of the thought of his teacher, Epictetus.

Like Arrian a Greek born in Asia Minor, Epictetus was the son of a slave woman and was a slave himself for many years. Taken to Rome as a youth, he studied philosophy there; once freed, perhaps at his master's death, he taught first in the imperial capital and then at Nicopolis in Greece. The teaching of Epictetus reflected this former slave's love of freedom and placed him in the ranks of the foremost Stoics.

Stoicism proved particularly attractive to the Romans, many of whom believed that their empire represented the Stoic ideal of a universal

3. Cicero, *Tusculan Disputations*, translated by J. E. King (Cambridge, Mass.: Harvard University Press, 1960), pp. 543–545.

human community. For Roman audiences, Epictetus called Logos "God" in Source 3. What evidence do you find of the philosopher's love of freedom? What is the concern of "the good and excellent man" in life? When may such a person terminate his life? What similarity do you find between these circumstances and those in which Plato found suicide justifiable? How does the thought of Epictetus perhaps reflect problems of the Roman world?

With Sources 4 through 9, we move from the classical tradition of Greece and Rome to the roots of the Judeo-Christian heritage in Palestine. Sources 4 through 8 are from the thirty-nine books of the Hebrew scriptures that Jews refer to as *Tanak* and that Christians call the Old Testament of the Bible. Written between the thirteenth and second centuries B.C., the Hebrew scriptures provide a remarkable record of the experience of the Jewish people before the birth of Christ, and we must examine their utility as a work of history.

The compilers of the Old Testament were not historians but religious thinkers concerned with Jewish faith, law, and literature, as well as history. The Old Testament thus is the foundation of the modern Jewish and Christian faiths. Students of history find the Old Testament an invaluable source, but they also find that this work of religious inspiration sometimes contains historical contradictions and occasional factual errors, and so scholars must verify biblical accounts of events against records in other sources. Nevertheless, the Old Testament, a collection of works by many authors, contains a consistent expression of values and belief and is our best source for understanding the religion of the Hebrews, and it is from that perspective that we will consider Sources 4 through 8.

We draw Sources 4 through 8 from the Hebrew scriptures' books of Judges, 1 and 2 Samuel, and 1 Kings, books that recount the teachings and careers of the great Hebrew prophets and leaders. These books contain all the acts of self-destruction that are found in the Hebrew scriptures. Sources 4 and 5 come from the Book of Judges, which describes the period in Hebrew history between the deaths of Moses and Joshua—who had led their people out of captivity in Egypt and into the promised land of Canaan—and the advent of kings as rulers among the Hebrews. Source 4 is from the Book of Judges' account of political instability among the Hebrews as they evolved from nomadic tribesmen into a more settled people who needed nontribal, permanent institutions of government. In search of that government, they offered the crown to the prophet Gideon, who rejected the overture, proclaiming that God alone should rule. After Gideon's death, his son Abimelech slew all but one of his brothers and seized the crown his father had rejected. Established as king, Abimelech brutally put down rebellions against his authority and, as told in Source 4, engaged in an attack on the rebellious city of Thebez. How did Abimelech meet his end? Why may we consider this suicide? Beyond the statement that Abimelech's death represented divine retribution, do you find any textual condemnation of the death of Abimelech?

Source 5 also comes from the Book of Judges; it is part of the account of the mighty Samson, a judge, or leader, of the Hebrews. According to this account, Samson possessed extraordinary strength, which he used against the pagan Philistines, who were enemies of the Hebrews. Samson's long hair represented his vows of devotion to God, and when the woman Delilah learned of this, she cut his hair, depriving Samson of his strength. The Philistines then captured Samson, blinded him, and enslaved him. But his hair grew back, and with it his strength, a fact unnoticed by the Philistines when they put him on display in a temple to their god, Dagon. What does Source 5 show Samson doing in the temple? While this is an act of martyrdom, why must it also be considered a suicide? Understanding that among many ancient peoples, burial in the family tomb was an honor, what can you conclude about the Hebrews' perception of Samson's death?

In Source 6 we have an account of the first anointed king of the Hebrews, Saul. Selected as king by the great judge Samuel, Saul disobeyed God's commands, and Samuel designated David as the new and rightful king. Nevertheless, Saul retained the crown, fighting David in a civil war, while continuing to battle the historic enemies of the Hebrews, the Philistines. What action did Saul, facing defeat by the Philistines atop Mount Gilboa, take in Source 6? Why must you conclude that Saul's death was a suicide? What is the reaction of

the Hebrews to Saul's death? How does the following response of David to the death of Saul and his son Jonathan reinforce your conclusion about the Hebrews' reaction to Saul's self-destruction?

Thy glory, O Israel, is slain upon
    thy high places!
How are the mighty fallen!
    . . . . .
Saul and Jonathan, beloved and
    lovely!
In life and death they were not
    divided;
They were swifter than eagles,
    they were stronger than lions.[4]

Saul's death allowed David to gain the crown, but David's rule did not go unchallenged. He faced a rebellion by his son Absalom and his former counselor, Ahithophel. The advice of Ahithophel was highly esteemed, for "in those days the counsel which Ahithophel gave was as if one consulted the oracle of God."[5] Nevertheless, Absalom rejected the strategy proposed by Ahithophel, "For the Lord had ordained to defeat the good counsel of Ahithophel, so that the Lord might bring evil on Absalom."[6] What does Source 7 indicate was Ahithophel's response to Absalom's humiliating him by ignoring his advice? What happened to Ahithophel's remains? What response does this in-

4. 2 Samuel 1:19, 23, in *The Oxford Annotated Bible with the Apocrypha* (New York: Oxford University Press, 1965), p. 375.

5. 2 Samuel 16:23, in *The Oxford Annotated Bible*, p. 397.

6. 2 Samuel 17:14, in *The Oxford Annotated Bible*, p. 398.

dicate that Ahithophel's contemporaries had to his death?

After the death of King David's son and heir, Solomon, the Hebrew kingdom divided into Israel and Judah, and Source 8 recounts an event in Israel. Zimri, a powerful military leader, killed King Elah and seized the throne. Zimri's coup did not go unopposed, however, and the forces of the army commander, Omri, besieged the usurper in the city of Tirzah. What end overtook Zimri, according to Source 8? While the text certainly suggests that God's punishment was a factor in Zimri's death, did the author in any way condemn the act of suicide?

Source 9 also is a biblical selection, but it comes from the writings commonly known among Christians as the New Testament. These Christian scriptures consist of the twenty-seven books that recount the life of Jesus Christ and record his teachings and those of his followers. They are central to the belief of all Christians. Source 9 describes the death of one of the twelve apostles of Jesus, Judas Iscariot. For thirty silver coins, Judas had betrayed Jesus' location to priests of the Temple in Jerusalem who opposed his teachings. Christ was arrested and executed by crucifixion, a mode of punishment commonly employed by the Roman authorities. Source 9 describes the suicide of Judas. Why, according to this account, did Judas take his own life? Is there any textual condemnation of this act of self-destruction? What response to suicide seems common to both Hebrew and Christian texts?

Source 10 is the work of Josephus, one of the greatest ancient historians. Josephus (37–ca A.D. 100) was a complex individual, and we require an understanding of his background in order to interpret his writings. A Jew born in Jerusalem, his early studies led Josephus to join the Pharisees. When Palestine erupted in a Jewish rebellion against Roman rule in A.D. 66, the scholarly Josephus took an active role, commanding rebel forces in Galilee. Roman legions eventually crushed the rebellion, and Josephus won the favor of their commander, Titus Flavius Vespasian; he even added "Flavius" to his own name. Vespasian went on to become emperor of Rome, and Josephus Flavius enjoyed imperial patronage in the capital. There he wrote in Greek several important histories, including *Jewish Antiquities,* a history of the Jews from Adam and Eve to the first century A.D., and *The Jewish War,* a history of the Jewish rebellion against Roman rule in Palestine.

Scholars detect many influences on Josephus that we must identify before reading his work. Certainly he was a devout Jewish Pharisee whose work represented an apology of sorts for his people's rebellion. At the same time, Josephus was a Roman citizen who had been thoroughly imbued with the Greco-Roman culture of the first century A.D. And we must not forget that Josephus enjoyed an imperial pension, which might have affected his portrayal of events in his histories.

Source 10 presents perhaps the most famous event in the Jewish rebellion, the last stand of the Zealots at the mountain fortress of Masada in 73 A.D. Faced with inevitable defeat, what step did the Zealots' leader, Eleazar, urge upon them? How did the garrison respond? How many persons perished, according to Josephus? How does he portray this mass suicide? How does this portrayal replicate reactions to suicide in other ancient sources?

Our final source, Source 11, is the work of Saint Augustine (A.D. 354–430), one of the greatest early Church Fathers. Saint Augustine lived in turbulent times, when the Roman Empire in the West was in marked decline and heretical ideas challenged Christian doctrine. Raised as a Christian in his native North Africa, Augustine abandoned that faith during a rather dissolute period as a young man and adopted the Manichaean heresy, an eastern belief system founded upon the idea that the world was a battleground between the forces of good and evil deities. Eventually, in Milan, Italy, Augustine encountered the eloquent preaching of another Church Father, Saint Ambrose, bishop of Milan, which helped to win him back to Christianity.

Augustine returned to North Africa, became bishop of Hippo, and produced a large body of writings that helped to define Christian doctrine and to defend it against the numerous heresies of the day. *The City of God Against the Pagans*, excerpted in Source 11, is the most important of these. Saint Augustine wrote it in response to the sack of Rome by the Visigoths in 410. Non-Christians blamed this disaster on the Christianity that had won over much of the

empire in the fourth century A.D. They saw the event as the revenge of the old gods that had been abandoned by many Romans and as the result of Christians' refusal to perform military service. Saint Augustine denied such charges and reasoned that, while imperial Rome was the greatest city that humanity could realize, the true object of the Christian life should be attainment to the heavenly City of God. In short, the rise and fall of empires was unimportant compared to the individual's spiritual journey to heavenly salvation.

Saint Augustine also used *The City of God* to further his mission of defending Christian doctrine. An issue that particularly concerned him was how his contemporaries, Christians and heretics alike, fulfilled Christ's injunction in Mark 8:34–35: "If any man would come after me, let him deny himself and take up his cross and follow me. For whoever would save his life will lose it; and whoever loses his life for my sake and the gospel's will save it."[7] Early Christians sometimes actually sought martyrdom at the hands of Roman officers assigned to enforce the superficial rites of official veneration of the emperor. Such suicidal self-sacrifice especially occurred among Donatists.

This enthusiastic martyrdom caused several early Christian thinkers to distinguish between true martyrdom and suicide. Saint Augustine takes up this theme in Source 11 as part of his discussion of the plunder of Rome in 410, when a number of women committed suicide rather than suffer sex-

---

7. *The Oxford Annotated Bible,* p. 1225.

ual assault by the Visigothic attackers. How does Saint Augustine view suicide? How does Saint Augustine's interpretation of the deaths of Samson and Judas differ from the accounts in Sources 5 and 9? In what circumstances would Saint Augustine permit suicide? What religious change did these conditions reflect? What new approach to suicide did Saint Augustine introduce?

Using this background on ancient philosophy and theology, now examine the evidence. As you read each source, you should seek answers for the central questions of this chapter. What does the author of each selection say about suicide? How do each author's ideas on self-destruction represent his own thought system and the intellectual outlook of the society in which he lived? What change in attitude toward self-destruction do you observe over the extended time period covered by these selections?

Source 1 from Plato with English Translation, *vol. 1*, Euthyphro, Apology, Crito, Phaedo, Phaedrus, *translated by Harold North Fowler (Cambridge, Mass.: Harvard University Press, 1953), pp. 213–233, 399–403. Reprinted with permission of the publishers and the Loeb Classical Library.*

1. Plato, *The Phaedo*

"So tell Evenus that, Cebes, and bid him farewell, and tell him, if he is wise, to come after me as quickly as he can. I, it seems, am going to-day; for that is the order of the Athenians."

And Simmias said, "What a message that is, Socrates, for Evenus! I have met him often, and from what I have seen of him, I should say that he will not take your advice in the least if he can help it."

"Why so?" said he. "Is not Evenus a philosopher?"

"I think so," said Simmias.

"Then Evenus will take my advice, and so will every man who has any worthy interest in philosophy. Perhaps, however, he will not take his own life, for they[8] say that is not permitted." And as he spoke he put his feet down on the ground and remained sitting in this way through the rest of the conversation.

Then Cebes asked him: "What do you mean by this, Socrates, that it is not permitted to take one's life, but that the philosopher would desire to follow after the dying?" . . .

---

8. **they:** Socrates refers here to the Pythagorean philosophers, including Philolaus, who opposed suicide. Pythagoreans believed that the soul was imprisoned in the body as punishment for sins in an earlier life. Thus, self-destruction was akin to a prison escape and was unacceptable to them.

"Why in the world do they say that it is not permitted to kill oneself, Socrates? I heard Philolaus, when he was living in our city, say the same thing you just said, and I have heard it from others, too, that one must not do this; but I never heard anyone say anything definite about it."

"You must have courage," said he, "and perhaps you might hear something. But perhaps it will seem strange to you that this alone of all laws is without exception, and it never happens to mankind, as in other matters, that only at some times and for some persons it is better to die than to live; and it will perhaps seem strange to you that these human beings for whom it is better to die cannot without impiety do good to themselves, but must wait for some other benefactor."

And Cebes, smiling gently, said, "Gawd knows it doos," speaking in his own dialect.

"It would seem unreasonable, if put in this way," said Socrates, "but perhaps there is some reason in it. Now the doctrine that is taught in secret about this matter, that we men are in a kind of prison and must not set ourselves free or run away, seems to me to be weighty and not easy to understand. But this at least, Cebes, I do believe is sound, that the gods are our guardians and that we men are one of the chattels of the gods. Do you not believe this?"

"Yes," said Cebes, "I do."

"Well, then," said he, "if one of your chattels should kill itself when you had not indicated that you wished it to die, would you be angry with it and punish it if you could?"

"Certainly," he replied.

"Then perhaps from this point of view it is not unreasonable to say that a man must not kill himself until god sends some necessity upon him, such as has now come upon me."

"That," said Cebes, "seems sensible. But what you said just now, Socrates, that philosophers ought to be ready and willing to die, that seems strange if we were right just now in saying that god is our guardian and we are his possessions. For it is not reasonable that the wisest men should not be troubled when they leave that service in which the gods, who are the best overseers in the world, are watching over them. A wise man certainly does not think that when he is free he can take better care of himself than they do. A foolish man might perhaps think so, that he ought to run away from his master, and he would not consider that he must not run away from a good master, but ought to stay with him as long as possible; and so he might thoughtlessly run away; but a man of sense would wish to be always with one who is better than himself. And yet, Socrates, if we look at it in this way, the contrary of what we just said seems natural; for the wise ought to be troubled at dying and the foolish to rejoice." . . .

. . . "I wish now to explain to you, my judges, the reason why I think a man who has really spent his life in philosophy is naturally of good courage when he is to die, and has strong hopes that when he is dead he will attain the greatest blessings in that other land. So I will try to tell you, Simmias, and Cebes, how this would be.

"Other people are likely not to be aware that those who pursue philosophy aright study nothing but dying and being dead. Now if this is true, it would be absurd to be eager for nothing but this all their lives, and then to be troubled when that came for which they had all along been eagerly practising."

And Simmias laughed and said, "By Zeus, Socrates, I don't feel much like laughing just now, but you made me laugh. For I think the multitude, if they heard what you just said about the philosophers, would say you were quite right, and our people at home would agree entirely with you that philosophers desire death, and they would add that they know very well that the philosophers deserve it."

"And they would be speaking the truth, Simmias, except in the matter of knowing very well. For they do not know in what way the real philosophers desire death, nor in what way they deserve death, nor what kind of a death it is. Let us then," said he, "speak with one another, paying no further attention to them. Do we think there is such a thing as death?"

"Certainly," replied Simmias.

"We believe, do we not, that death is the separation of the soul from the body, and that the state of being dead is the state in which the body is separated from the soul and exists alone by itself and the soul is separated from the body and exists alone by itself? Is death anything other than this?" "No, it is this," said he.

"Now, my friend, see if you agree with me; for, if you do, I think we shall get more light on our subject. Do you think a philosopher would be likely to care much about the so-called pleasures, such as eating and drinking?"

"By no means, Socrates," said Simmias.

"How about the pleasures of love?"

"Certainly not."

"Well, do you think such a man would think much of the other cares of the body—I mean such as the possession of fine clothes and shoes and the other personal adornments? Do you think he would care about them or despise them, except so far as it is necessary to have them?"

"I think the true philosopher would despise them," he replied.

"Altogether, then, you think that such a man would not devote himself to the body, but would, so far as he was able, turn away from the body and concern himself with the soul?"

"Yes."

"To begin with, then, it is clear that in such matters the philosopher, more than other men, separates the soul from communion with the body?"

"It is." . . .

"Now, how about the acquirement of pure knowledge? Is the body a hindrance or not, if it is made to share in the search for wisdom? What I mean is this: Have the sight and hearing of men any truth in them, or is it true, as the poets are always telling us, that we neither hear nor see anything accurately? And yet if these two physical senses are not accurate or exact, the rest are not likely to be, for they are inferior to these. Do you not think so?"

"Certainly I do," he replied.

"Then," said he, "when does the soul attain to truth? For when it tries to consider anything in company with the body, it is evidently deceived by it."

"True."

"In thought, then, if at all, something of the realities becomes clear to it?"

"Yes."

"But it thinks best when none of these things troubles it, neither hearing nor sight, nor pain nor any pleasure, but it is, so far as possible, alone by itself, and takes leave of the body, and avoiding, so far as it can, all association or contact with the body, reaches out toward the reality."

"That is true."

"In this matter also, then, the soul of the philosopher greatly despises the body and avoids it and strives to be alone by itself?"

"Evidently."

"Now how about such things as this, Simmias? Do we think there is such a thing as absolute justice or not?"

"We certainly think there is."

"And absolute beauty and goodness."

"Of course."

"Well, did you ever see anything of that kind with your eyes?"

"Certainly not," said he.

"Or did you ever reach them with any of the bodily senses? I am speaking of all such things, as size, health, strength, and in short the essence or underlying quality of everything. Is their true nature contemplated by means of the body? Is it not rather the case that he who prepares himself most carefully to understand the true essence of each thing that he examines would come nearest to the knowledge of it?"

"Certainly."

"Would not that man do this most perfectly who approaches each thing, so far as possible, with the reason alone, not introducing sight into his reasoning nor dragging in any of the other senses along with his thinking, but who employs pure, absolute reason in his attempt to search out the pure, absolute essence of things, and who removes himself, so far as possible, from eyes and ears, and, in a word, from his whole body, because he feels that its companionship disturbs the soul and hinders it from attaining truth and wisdom? Is not this the man, Simmias, if anyone, to attain to the knowledge of reality?"

"That is true as true can be, Socrates," said Simmias.

"Then," said he, "all this must cause good lovers of wisdom to think and say one to the other something like this: 'There seems to be a short cut which leads us and our argument to the conclusion in our search that so long as we have the body, and the soul is contaminated by such an evil, we shall never attain completely what we desire, that is, the truth. . . .

. . . "For, if pure knowledge is impossible while the body is with us, one of two thing[s] must follow, either it cannot be acquired at all or only when we are dead; for then the soul will be by itself apart from the body, but not before. And while we live, we shall, I think, be nearest to knowledge when we avoid, so far as possible, intercourse and communion with the body, except what is absolutely necessary, and are not filled with its nature, but keep ourselves pure from it until God himself sets us free. And in this way, freeing ourselves from the foolishness of the body and being pure, we shall, I think, be with the pure and shall know of ourselves all that is pure—and that is, perhaps, the truth. For it cannot be that the impure attain the pure.' Such words as these, I think, Simmias, all who are rightly lovers of knowledge must say to each other and such must be their thoughts. Do you not agree?"

"Most assuredly, Socrates."

"Then," said Socrates, "if this is true, my friend, I have great hopes that when I reach the place to which I am going, I shall there, if anywhere, attain fully to that which has been my chief object in my past life, so that the journey which is now imposed upon me is begun with good hope; and the like hope exists for every man who thinks that his mind has been purified and made ready." . . .

Thereupon Crito nodded to the boy who was standing near. The boy went out and stayed a long time, then came back with the man who was to administer the poison, which he brought with him in a cup ready for use. And when Socrates saw him, he said: "Well, my good man, you know about these things; what must I do?" "Nothing," he replied, "except drink the poison and walk about till your legs feel heavy; then lie down, and the poison will take effect of itself."

At the same time he held out the cup to Socrates. He took it, and very gently, Echecrates, without trembling or changing colour or expression, but looking up at the man with wide open eyes, as was his custom, said: "What do you say about pouring a libation[9] to some deity from this cup? May I, or not?" "Socrates," said he, "we prepare only as much as we think is enough." "I understand," said Socrates; "but I may and must pray to the gods that my departure hence be a fortunate one; so I offer this prayer, and may it be granted." With these words he raised the cup to his lips and very cheerfully and quietly drained it. Up to that time most of us had been able to restrain our tears fairly well, but when we watched him drinking and saw that he had drunk the poison, we could do so no longer. . . . He walked about and, when he said his legs were heavy, lay down on his back, for such was the advice of the attendant. The man who had administered the poison laid his hands on him and after a while examined his feet and legs, then pinched his foot hard and asked if he

---

9. **libation:** the ritual pouring out of wine or holy oil as an offering to a deity.

felt it. He said "No"; then after that, his thighs; and passing upwards in this way he showed us that he was growing cold and rigid. And again he touched him and said that when it reached his heart, he would be gone. The chill had now reached the region about the groin, and uncovering his face, which had been covered, he said—and these were his last words—"Crito, we owe a cock to Aesculapius.[10] Pay it and do not neglect it." "That," said Crito, "shall be done; but see if you have anything else to say." To this question he made no reply, but after a little while he moved; the attendant uncovered him; his eyes were fixed. And Crito when he saw it, closed his mouth and eyes.

Such was the end, Echecrates, of our friend, who was, as we may say, of all those of his time whom we have known, the best and wisest and most righteous man.

Source 2 from Diogenes Laertius, Lives of Eminent Philosophers, *vol. 2, translated by Robert Drew Hicks (New York: G. P. Putnam's Sons, 1925), pp. 651–653, 657, 665.*

2. Epicurus on the Meaning of Death

[From a letter]

"Accustom thyself to believe that death is nothing to us, for good and evil imply sentience,[11] and death is the privation of all sentience; therefore a right understanding that death is nothing to us makes the mortality of life enjoyable, not by adding to life an illimitable time, but by taking away the yearning after immortality. For life has no terrors for him who has thoroughly apprehended that there are no terrors for him in ceasing to live. Foolish, therefore, is the man who says that he fears death, not because it will pain when it comes, but because it pains in the prospect. Whatsoever causes no annoyance when it is present, causes only a groundless pain in the expectation. Death, therefore, the most awful of evils, is nothing to us, seeing that, when we are, death is not come, and, when death is come, we are not. It is nothing, then, either to the living or to the dead, for with the living it is not and the dead exist no longer. But in the world, at one time men shun death as the greatest of all evils, and at another time choose it as a respite from the evils in life. The wise man does not deprecate life nor does he fear the cessation of life. The thought of life is no offence to him, nor is the cessation of life regarded as an evil. And even as men choose of food not merely and simply the larger portion, but the more pleas-

10. **Aesculapius:** sometimes also rendered "Asclepius," this was the chief god of healing. It was common in the ancient world to offer animal sacrifices to deities as part of prayerful entreaties or as offerings of thanks.

11. **sentience:** the capacity for feeling or sensation.

ant, so the wise seek to enjoy the time which is most pleasant and not merely that which is longest. . . .

"When we say, then, that pleasure is the end and aim, we do not mean the pleasures of the prodigal or the pleasures of sensuality, as we are understood to do by some through ignorance, prejudice, or wilful misrepresentation. By pleasure we mean the absence of pain in the body and of trouble in the soul. It is not an unbroken succession of drinking-bouts and of revelry, not sexual love, not the enjoyment of the fish and other delicacies of a luxurious table, which produce a pleasant life; it is sober reasoning, searching out the grounds of every choice and avoidance, and banishing those beliefs through which the greatest tumults take possession of the soul. Of all this the beginning and the greatest good is prudence. Wherefore prudence is a more precious thing even than philosophy; from it spring all the other virtues, for it teaches that we cannot lead a life of pleasure which is not also a life of prudence, honour, and justice; nor lead a life of prudence, honour, and justice, which is not also a life of pleasure. For the virtues have grown into one with a pleasant life, and a pleasant life is inseparable from them. . . .

> *[From the maxims]*

Death is nothing to us; for the body, when it has been resolved into its elements, has no feeling, and that which has no feeling is nothing to us.

Source 3 from Epictetus, The Discourses as Reported by Arrian, the Manual, and Fragments, *vol. 2, translated by W(illiam) A(bbott) Oldfather (New York: G. P. Putnam's Sons, 1926), pp. 215–217.*

3. Epictetus on Ending Life

For this reason the good and excellent man, bearing in mind who he is, and whence he has come, and by whom he was created, centres his attention on this and this only, how he may fill his place in an orderly fashion, and with due obedience to God. "Is it Thy will that I should still remain? I will remain as a free man, as a noble man, as Thou didst wish it; for Thou hast made me free from hindrance in what was mine own. And now hast Thou no further need of me? Be it well with Thee. I have been waiting here until now because of Thee and of none other, and now I obey Thee and depart." "How do you depart?" "Again, as Thou didst wish it, as a free man, as Thy servant, as one who has perceived Thy commands and Thy prohibitions. But so long as I continue to live in Thy service, what manner of man wouldst Thou have me be? An official or a private citizen, a senator or one of the common people, a soldier or a general, a teacher or the head of a household? Whatsoever station and post Thou assign me, I will die ten thousand times, as Socrates says, or ever I abandon it.[12] And where wouldst Thou have me be? In Rome, or in Athens, or in Thebes, or in Gyara? Only remember me there. If Thou sendest me to a place where men have no means of living in accordance with nature, I shall depart this life, not in disobedience to Thee, but as though Thou wert sounding for me the recall. I do not abandon Thee—far be that from me! but I perceive that Thou hast no need of me. Yet if there be vouchsafed a means of living in accordance with nature, I will seek no other place than that in which I am, or other men than those who are now my associates."

Sources 4 through 9 from the Revised Standard Version of the Bible, pp. 307–308; p. 316; p. 373; p. 399; p. 441; p. 1209. Copyright 1946, 1952, 1971 by the Division of Christian Education of the National Council of the Churches of Christ in the U.S.A. Used by permission.

4. The Death of Abimelech
(Judges 9:50–56)

Then Abim'elech went to Thebez, and encamped against Thebez, and took it. But there was a strong tower within the city, and all the people of the city fled to it, all the men and women, and shut themselves in; and they went to the roof of the tower. And Abim'elech came to the tower, and fought against it, and drew near to the door of the tower to burn it with fire. And a certain woman threw an upper millstone upon Abim'elech's head, and crushed his skull. Then he called hastily to the young man his armor-bearer, and said to him, "Draw your sword and kill me, lest men say of me, 'A woman killed him.' " And his young man thrust him through, and he died. And when the men of Israel saw that Abim'elech was dead, they departed every man to his home. Thus God requited the crime of Abim'elech, which he committed against his father in killing his seventy brothers.

5. The Death of Samson
(Judges 16:23–31)

Now the lords of the Philistines gathered to offer a great sacrifice to Dagon their god, and to rejoice; for they said, "Our god has given Samson our enemy into our hand." And when the people saw him, they praised their god; for they said, "Our god has given our enemy into our hand, the ravager of our country, who has slain many of us." And when their hearts were merry, they said, "Call Samson, that he may make sport for us." So they called Samson out of the prison, and he made sport before them. They made him stand between the pillars; and Samson said to the lad who held him by the hand, "Let me feel

12. This is a paraphrase of the words of Socrates in Plato's dialogue *The Apology,* which recounts the philosopher's defense at his trial.

the pillars on which the house rests, that I may lean against them." Now the house was full of men and women; all the lords of the Philistines were there, and on the roof there were about three thousand men and women, who looked on while Samson made sport.

Then Samson called to the LORD and said, "O Lord GOD, remember me, I pray thee, and strengthen me, I pray thee, only this once, O God, that I may be avenged upon the Philistines for one of my two eyes." And Samson grasped the two middle pillars upon which the house rested, and he leaned his weight upon them, his right hand on the one and his left hand on the other. And Samson said, "Let me die with the Philistines." Then he bowed with all his might; and the house fell upon the lords and upon all the people that were in it. So the dead whom he slew at his death were more than those whom he had slain during his life. Then his brothers and all his family came down and took him and brought him up and buried him between Zorah and Esh'ta-ol in the tomb of Mano'ah his father. He had judged Israel twenty years.

6. The Deaths of Saul and His Armor-Bearer (1 Samuel 31:1–13)

Now the Philistines fought against Israel; and the men of Israel fled before the Philistines, and fell slain on Mount Gilbo'a. And the Philistines overtook Saul and his sons; and the Philistines slew Jonathan and Abin'adab and Mal'chishu'a, the sons of Saul. The battle pressed hard upon Saul, and the archers found him; and he was badly wounded by the archers. Then Saul said to his armor-bearer, "Draw your sword, and thrust me through with it, lest these uncircumcised come and thrust me through, and make sport of me." But his armor-bearer would not; for he feared greatly. Therefore Saul took his own sword, and fell upon it. And when his armor-bearer saw that Saul was dead, he also fell upon his sword, and died with him. Thus Saul died, and his three sons, and his armor-bearer, and all his men, on the same day together. And when the men of Israel who were on the other side of the valley and those beyond the Jordan saw that the men of Israel had fled and that Saul and his sons were dead, they forsook their cities and fled; and the Philistines came and dwelt in them.

On the morrow, when the Philistines came to strip the slain, they found Saul and his three sons fallen on Mount Gilbo'a. And they cut off his head, and stripped off his armor, and sent messengers throughout the land of the Philistines, to carry the good news to their idols and to the people. They put his armor in the temple of Ash'taroth; and they fastened his body to the wall of Beth-shan. But when the inhabitants of Ja'besh-gil'ead heard what the Philistines had done to Saul, all the valiant men arose, and went all night, and took the body of Saul and the bodies of his sons from the wall of

Beth-shan; and they came to Jabesh and burnt them there. And they took their bones and buried them under the tamarisk tree in Jabesh, and fasted seven days.

7. The Death of Ahithophel
(2 Samuel 17:23)

When Ahith'ophel saw that his counsel was not followed, he saddled his ass, and went off home to his own city. And he set his house in order, and hanged himself; and he died, and was buried in the tomb of his father.

8. The Death of Zimri
(1 Kings 16:18–19)

And when Zimri saw that the city was taken, he went into the citadel of the king's house, and burned the king's house over him with fire, and died, because of his sins which he committed, doing evil in the sight of the Lord, walking in the way of Jerobo'am,[13] and for his sin which he committed, making Israel to sin.

9. The Death of Judas
(Matthew 27:1–8)

When morning came, all the chief priests and the elders of the people took counsel against Jesus to put him to death; and they bound him and led him away and delivered him to Pilate the governor.

When Judas, his betrayer, saw that he was condemned, he repented and brought back the thirty pieces of silver to the chief priests and the elders, saying, "I have sinned in betraying innocent blood." They said, "What is that to us? See to it yourself." And throwing down the pieces of silver in the temple, he departed; and he went and hanged himself. But the chief priests, taking the pieces of silver, said, "It is not lawful to put them into the treasury, since they are blood money." So they took counsel, and bought with them the potter's field, to bury strangers in. Therefore that field has been called the Field of Blood to this day.

---

13. **Jeroboam:** a traitor and idolater in the Old Testament who led an unsuccessful revolt of the north of the Hebrew state against King David's son, Solomon. He later led a successful rebellion against Solomon's son, King Rehoboam, and established an independent state in which he encouraged the worship of idols, not Yahweh.

Source 10 from Josephus with English Translation, vol. 3, The Jewish War, Books IV–VII, *translated by Henry St. John Thackeray (New York: G. P. Putnam's Sons, 1928), pp. 595–603, 613–619.*

10. Josephus on Mass Suicide at Masada, 73 A.D.

However, neither did Eleazar himself contemplate flight, nor did he intend to permit any other to do so. Seeing the wall consuming in the flames, unable to devise any further means of deliverance or gallant endeavour, and setting before his eyes what the Romans, if victorious, would inflict on them, their children and their wives, he deliberated on the death of all. And, judging, as matters stood, this course the best, he assembled the most doughty of his comrades and incited them to the deed by such words as these:

"Long since, my brave men, we determined neither to serve the Romans nor any other save God, for He alone is man's true and righteous Lord; and now the time is come which bids us verify that resolution by our actions. At this crisis let us not disgrace ourselves; we who in the past refused to submit even to a slavery involving no peril, let us not now, along with slavery, deliberately accept the irreparable penalties awaiting us if we are to fall alive into Roman hands. For as we were the first of all to revolt, so are we the last in arms against them. Moreover, I believe that it is God who has granted us this favour, that we have it in our power to die nobly and in freedom—a privilege denied to others who have met with unexpected defeat. Our fate at break of day is certain capture, but there is still the free choice of a noble death with those we hold most dear. For our enemies, fervently though they pray to take us alive, we can no more prevent this than we can now hope to defeat them in battle. . . .

. . . Let our wives thus die undishonoured, our children unacquainted with slavery; and, when they are gone, let us render a generous service to each other, preserving our liberty as a noble winding-sheet. But first let us destroy our chattels and the fortress by fire; for the Romans, well I know, will be grieved to lose at once our persons and the lucre. Our provisions only let us spare; for they will testify, when we are dead, that it was not want which subdued us, but that, in keeping with our initial resolve, we preferred death to slavery."

Thus spoke Eleazar; but his words did not touch the hearts of all hearers alike. Some, indeed, were eager to respond and all but filled with delight at the thought of a death so noble,[14] but others, softer-hearted, were moved with

14. Scholars disagree about the precise translation of the original Greek text at this point. Some render "filled with delight at the thought of a death so noble" as "filled with pleasure supposing such a death to be noble." The latter translation significantly modifies the meaning of Josephus.

compassion for their wives and families, and doubtless also by the vivid prospect of their own end, and their tears as they looked upon one another revealed their unwillingness of heart. Eleazar, seeing them flinching and their courage breaking down in face of so vast a scheme, feared that their whimpers and tears might unman even those who had listened to his speech with fortitude. Far, therefore, from slackening in his exhortation, he roused himself and, fired with mighty fervour, essayed a higher flight of oratory on the immortality of the soul. Indignantly protesting and with eyes intently fixed on those in tears, he exclaimed:

"Deeply, indeed, was I deceived in thinking that I should have brave men as associates in our struggles for freedom—men determined to live with honour or to die. But you, it seems, were no better than the common herd in valour or in courage, you who are afraid even of that death that will deliver you from the direst ills, when in such a cause you ought neither to hesitate an instant nor wait for a counsellor. For from of old, since the first dawn of intelligence, we have been continually taught by those precepts, ancestral and divine—confirmed by the deeds and noble spirit of our forefathers—that life, not death, is man's misfortune. For it is death which gives liberty to the soul and permits it to depart to its own pure abode, there to be free from all calamity; but so long as it is imprisoned in a mortal body and tainted with all its miseries, it is, in sober truth, dead, for association with what is mortal ill befits that which is divine. . . .

. . . Unenslaved by the foe let us die, as free men with our children and wives let us quit this life together! This our laws enjoin, this our wives and children implore of us. The need for this is of God's sending, the reverse of this is the Romans' desire, and their fear is lest a single one of us should die before capture. Haste we then to leave them, instead of their hoped-for enjoyment at securing us, amazement at our death and admiration of our fortitude."

He would have pursued his exhortation but was cut short by his hearers, who, overpowered by some uncontrollable impulse, were all in haste to do the deed. Like men possessed they went their way, each eager to outstrip his neighbour and deeming it a signal proof of courage and sound judgement not to be seen among the last: so ardent the passion that had seized them to slaughter their wives, their little ones and themselves. . . . They had died in the belief that they had left not a soul of them alive to fall into Roman hands; but an old woman and another, a relative of Eleazar, superior in sagacity and training to most of her sex, with five children, escaped by concealing themselves in the subterranean aqueducts, while the rest were absorbed in the slaughter. The victims numbered nine hundred and sixty, including women and children; and the tragedy occurred on the fifteenth of the month Xanthicus.[15]

15. May 2, A.D. 73.

The Romans, expecting further opposition, were by daybreak under arms and, having with gangways formed bridges of approach from the earthworks, advanced to the assault. Seeing none of the enemy but on all sides an awful solitude, and flames within and silence, they were at a loss to conjecture what had happened. At length, as if for a signal to shoot, they shouted, to call forth haply any of those within. The shout was heard by the women-folk, who, emerging from the caverns, informed the Romans how matters stood, one of the two lucidly reporting both the speech and how the deed was done. But it was with difficulty that they listened to her, incredulous of such amazing fortitude; meanwhile they endeavoured to extinguish the flames and soon cutting a passage through them entered the palace. Here encountering the mass of slain, instead of exulting as over enemies, they admired the nobility of their resolve and the contempt of death displayed by so many in carrying it, unwavering, into execution.

Source 11 *from Saint Augustine,* The City of God Against the Pagans, *translated by George E. McCracken (Cambridge, Mass.: Harvard University Press, 1957), pp. 77–79, 91–101, 109–113. Reprinted by permission of the publishers and the Loeb Classical Library.*

11. Saint Augustine, *The City of God*, Book I

XVII

ON SUICIDE CAUSED BY FEAR OF PUNISHMENT OR DISGRACE.

For if it is not right on individual authority to slay even a guilty man for whose killing no law has granted permission, certainly a suicide is also a homicide, and he is guilty, when he kills himself, in proportion to his innocence of the deed for which he thought he ought to die. If we rightly execrate Judas' deed, and truth pronounces that when he hanged himself, he increased rather than expiated the crime of that accursed betrayal, since by despairing of God's mercy, though he was at death repentant, he left himself no place for a saving repentance, how much more should the man who has no guilt in him to be punished by such means refrain from killing himself!

When Judas killed himself, he killed an accursed man, and he ended his life guilty not only of Christ's death but also of his own, because, though he was killed to atone for his crime, the killing itself was another crime of his. Why, then, should a man who has done no evil do evil to himself, and in doing away with himself do away with an innocent man so as not to suffer from the crime of another, and perpetrate upon himself a sin of his own, so that another's may not be perpetrated on him?

XX
THAT THERE IS NO AUTHORITY THAT ALLOWS CHRISTIANS IN ANY CASE THE RIGHT TO DIE OF THEIR OWN WILL.

Not for nothing is it that in the holy canonical books no divinely inspired order or permission can be found authorizing us to inflict death upon ourselves, neither in order to acquire immortality nor in order to avert or divert some evil. For we must certainly understand the commandment as forbidding this when it says: "Thou shalt not kill,"[16] particularly since it does not add "thy neighbour," as it does when it forbids false witnessing. . . .

On this basis some try to extend this commandment even to wild and domestic animals and maintain that it is wrong to kill any of them. Why not then extend it also to plants and to anything fixed and fed by roots in the earth? For things of this kind, though they have no feeling, are said to live, and therefore can also die, and hence, when violence is exercised, be slain. Thus the Apostle, when he speaks of seeds of this sort, says: "That which thou sowest is not quickened except it die,"[17] and we find in a psalm, "He killed their vines with hail."[18] Do we from this conclude, when we hear "Thou shalt not kill," that it is wrong to pull up a shrub? Are we so completely deranged that we assent to the Manichaean error?

Hence, putting aside these ravings, if when we read, "Thou shalt not kill," we do not understand this phrase to apply to bushes, because they have no sensation, nor to the unreasoning animals that fly, swim, walk or crawl, because they are not partners with us in the faculty of reason, the privilege not being given them to share it in common with us—and therefore by the altogether righteous ordinance of the Creator both their life and death are a matter subordinate to our needs—the remaining possibility is to understand this commandment, "Thou shalt not kill," as meaning man alone, that is, "neither another nor thyself," for in fact he who kills himself kills what is no other than a man.

XXI
WHAT CASES OF HOMICIDE ARE EXCEPTED FROM THE CHARGE OF MURDER?

This very same divine law, to be sure, made certain exceptions to the rule that it is not lawful to kill a human being. The exceptions include only such persons as God commands to be put to death, either by an enacted law or by special decree applicable to a single person at the given time—but note that the man who is bound to this service under orders, as a sword is bound to be the tool of him who employs it, is not himself the slayer, and consequently there is no breach of this commandment, which says, "Thou shalt not kill," in the case of those who by God's authorization have waged wars, or, who, repre-

16. Exodus 20:16. Saint Augustine makes frequent biblical references in his text.
17. 1 Corinthians 15:36.
18. Psalms 78:46.

senting in their person the power of the state, have put criminals to death in accordance with God's law, being vested, that is, with the imperial prerogative of altogether righteous reason. Abraham too not only was not blamed for cruelty, but was even praised for piety, because he resolved to slay his son, not with criminal motives but in obedience to God. And it is properly a question whether we should regard it as equivalent to a command of God when Jephthah slew his daughter who ran to meet him after he had vowed to sacrifice to God the first victim that met him as he returned victorious from battle.[19] Nor is Samson acquitted of guilt on any other plea, inasmuch as he crushed himself by the collapse of the house along with his enemies, than the plea that the Spirit who through him had been working miracles,[20] had secretly ordered this. With these exceptions then, those slain either by application of a just law or by command of God, the very fount of justice, whoever kills a human being, either himself or no matter who, falls within the meshes of the charge of murder.

XXII

WHETHER SUICIDE IS EVER A SIGN OF GREATNESS OF MIND.

Those who have laid violent hands upon themselves are perhaps to be admired for the greatness of their souls, but not to be praised for the soundness of their wisdom. If, however, you take reason more carefully into account, you will not really call it greatness of soul which brings anyone to suicide because he or she lacks strength to bear whatever hardships or sins of others may occur. For the mind is rather detected in weakness, if it cannot bear whether it be the harsh enslavement of its own body, or the stupid opinion of the mob; and a mind might better be called greater that can endure instead of fleeing from a distressful life, and that can in the light of pure conscience despise the judgement of men, especially that of the mob, which as a rule is wrapped in a fog of error.

Therefore, if suicide can be thought to be a great-souled act, this quality of greatness of soul was possessed by that Theombrotus[21] of whom they say that, when he had read Plato's book containing a discussion of the immortality of the soul,[22] he hurled himself headlong from a wall and so departed from this life to that which he thought a better. He was not urged to this act by any calamity of fortune or accusation, false or true, that he had not strength to bear and so made away with himself. Nay, his sole motive for seeking death and breaking the sweet bonds of this life was his greatness of soul. Nevertheless, this Plato himself whom he had read could have borne witness that he

19. Judges 11:29–40.
20. Judges 16:28–30.
21. **Theombrotus:** a philospher of Ambracia, Greece.
22. Plato's dialogue *The Phaedo*.

acted greatly rather than well, for assuredly Plato would have made this act the first step and the most important step he took himself, and might well have pronounced in favour of it too, had he not, with that intellect by which he saw the soul's immortality, reached the conclusion that suicide should not be committed, nay more, should be forbidden.

Yet in fact many have killed themselves to prevent falling into the hands of the enemy. We are not now asking whether this was done but whether it should have been done. Sound reasoning, naturally, is to be preferred even to precedents, but there are precedents for that matter not discordant with reason—such, be it noted, as are precedents the more worthy of imitation as they are more outstanding in piety. No case of suicide occurred among patriarchs, among prophets, among apostles, seeing that the Lord Christ himself, when he advised them, if they suffered persecution, to flee from city to city,[23] might then have advised them to lay hands upon themselves to avoid falling into the hands of their persecutors. Furthermore, granted that he gave no command or advice to His disciples to employ this means of departing from life, though he promised that he would prepare everlasting mansions for them when they departed, then, no matter what precedents are brought forward by heathen that know not God, it is obvious that suicide is unlawful for those who worship the one true God.

XXVI

WHAT EXPLANATION WE SHOULD ADOPT TO ACCOUNT FOR
THE SAINTS' DOING CERTAIN THINGS THAT THEY ARE KNOWN
TO HAVE DONE WHICH IT IS NOT LAWFUL TO DO.

But, they say, in time of persecution certain saintly women, to avoid the pursuers of their chastity, cast themselves into a river that would ravish and drown them, and in that way they died and their memorial shrines are frequented by great numbers who venerate them as martyrs in the Catholic Church.

With regard to these women I dare not give any rash judgement. I do not know whether the divine authority has counselled the church by some trustworthy testimonies to honour their memory in this, and it may be so. For what if the women acted as they did, not by human misconception, but by divine command, and they did not go astray in their act, but were obedient? Compare the case of Samson, where it would be sin to hold any other view. When God, moreover, gives a command and makes it clear without ambiguity that he gives it, who can summon obedience to judgement? Who can draw up a brief against religious deference to God? . . .

. . . Let anyone, therefore, who is told that he has no right to kill himself, do the deed if he is so ordered by him whose orders must not be slighted. There is just one proviso: he must be sure that his divine command is not made pre-

---

23. Matthew 10:5–15.

carious by any doubt. It is through the ear that we take note of men's thoughts; we do not arrogate to ourselves any right to judge such as are kept secret. No one "knows what goes on in a man except the spirit of the man that is in him."[24]

This we say, this we declare, this we by all means endorse: that no man ought to inflict on himself a voluntary death, thinking to escape temporary ills, lest he find himself among ills that are unending; that no one ought to do so because of another's sins, lest by the very act he bring into being a sin that is his own, when he would not have been polluted by another's; that on one ought to do so on account of any past sins, inasmuch as he needs this life the more to make possible their healing by repentance; that no one ought to do so thinking to satisfy his hunger for the better life for which we hope after death, inasmuch as the better life after death does not accept those who are guilty of their own death.

24. 1 Corinthians 2:11.

QUESTIONS TO CONSIDER

The evidence in this chapter all deals with the central issue of suicide, but it comes from sources originating over an extraordinarily long period, about a millennium and one-half of the ancient period. Our objective in spanning such a period is to examine the continuities and changes in ancient thought on the subject of self-destruction by asking you to address three progressively more probing central questions based on the sources.

The first question asks that you consider each of the selections individually by identifying every author's thought on the suicide that was common in much of the ancient world. How do all of the authors, except Saint Augustine, implicitly or more directly accept suicide as justifiable? What sort of ethical considera-tions does the act raise for each author? What limitations, if any, does each place on self-destruction?

The second question requires that you place each of the sources in the intellectual context within which its author wrote. You must consider the religious beliefs and philosophical outlook of each period represented in the sources: the Hellenic and Hellenistic ages, the Roman Empire, Old and New Testament Palestine, and the early Christian era. How did the ideas of the various thinkers reflect the religious and philosophical orientations of their respective ages?

The third question asks that you examine the evolution of ancient ideas on suicide over an extended period of time. What basic continuities on this subject do you note in ancient thought? At what point did ancient thought on suicide change? What aspects of Christian doctrine and the controversies surrounding this faith in the third and fourth centuries A.D. promoted the viewpoint advanced by Saint Augustine? On what basis did he deny that the acts of self-destruction in the Bible were true suicides? Why might you assume that Saint Augustine's theology heavily influenced Western attitudes toward suicide in the Christian era that emerged from the decline and fall of the Roman Empire?

As you consider your answers to these questions, you should better comprehend the ancients' views on suicide, but even more importantly, you should understand the philosophical and theological foundations for those ideas.

EPILOGUE

Very few ancient thinkers unconditionally condemned the act of self-destruction, although as we have seen, Socrates noted one such group, the Pythagoreans. [We must add that Neoplatonists like Plotinus (205–270) also condemned suicide. They held that since one's standing in the afterlife rested on the state of one's soul at death, suicide was inadmissible because the possibility of moral improvement existed as long as life endured.] Thus, Saint Augustine's general condemnation of suicide reflected a distinct break with the past. Indeed, his dictum that suicide was murder, reaffirmed by later theologians, including Saint Thomas Aquinas (1225–1274), shaped the religious and legal response of the Christian West to the act of self-destruction into the twentieth century.[25]

Religiously, Saint Augustine's condemnation of all forms of suicide, perhaps reinforced by primitive suicide taboos among the Germanic tribes overwhelming late ancient Rome, became part of canon law. That law always relieved persons of diminished psychological capacity from the spiritual consequence of suicide. But for suicides of apparently sound mind, the act of self-destruction incurred severe spiritual penalties. Theologians believed suicides by such individuals represented despair and thus rejection of the Christian message, perhaps reflecting Satanic possession. Thus at the Council of Braga in 563, the Roman Catholic Church denied religious burial to these persons, a practice many Protestant groups perpetuated after the Reformation of the sixteenth century.

25. Indeed, the very word *suicide* did not exist in Western languages prior to the early seventeenth century, and some variation of the phrase "murder of oneself" described the act of self-destruction in most European tongues. The word *suicide* seems first to have appeared in a work of the Englishman Sir Thomas Browne, *Religio medici*, published in 1642. The use of the term slowly gained ground in English usage, and in the eighteenth century it found its way into French, Italian, Portuguese, and Spanish lexicons. Literally translated from its Latin roots as "to strike oneself mortally," the word itself is highly significant because it eschews the more condemnatory term *murder*.

Legally, most medieval and early modern Western states reflected canon law by adopting statutes recognizing suicide as a form of murder. Thus, persons taking their own lives might incur worldly as well as spiritual penalties if a postmortem judicial proceeding determined that they had, indeed, ended their own lives while in a sound mental state. Worldly penalties typically included two elements. The first was financial in nature. Under laws dating from at least as early as the thirteenth century in England and France, the state confiscated the property of the successful suicide. In the second form of punishment, the authorities desecrated the corpse of the suicide in ceremonies that included the spiritual penalty of denied burial. Thus, in Catholic France prior to the Revolution, judicial authorities dragged suicides' corpses through the streets, frequently displayed the remains to the public, and disposed of the bodies without burial rites, often as refuse. In England, after the Reformation, the authorities buried suicides' remains without religious sacraments at crossroads. Because of popular fears that the spirits of suicides might return to the world of the living, the authorities often drove stakes through the bodies and into the ground to prevent the return of the deceased from their graves. Other Western countries engaged in similar practices that long endured, and attempted suicide was a capital offense in many legal codes for centuries.

Only in the late seventeenth and eighteenth centuries, in a process that historians have called a "secularization of suicide,"[26] did many Western thinkers begin to view the act of self-destruction as a social, psychological, or medical problem rather than the moral and theological issue defined by Saint Augustine. Nevertheless, the law long reflected this earlier attitude, and the act of suicide persistently excited basic religious and philosophical controversies. Suicide remained a crime in France until 1791, and the last English crossroads burial occurred in 1823. Attempted suicide continued to be a crime in England until 1961, and until that same year, those of sound mind who took their own lives might be denied burial rites by the Church of England. Attempted suicide remains a criminal offense in a small number of American states today.

26. This terminology was introduced by the work of Michael MacDonald and Terence Murphy, *Sleepless Souls: Suicide in Early Modern England* (Oxford: Oxford University Press, 1990).

CHAPTER FIVE

THE DEVELOPMENT

OF ORTHODOXY

IN EARLY CHRISTIANITY

THE PROBLEM

The world in which Christianity began was one in which people practiced many different religions. The Romans generally tolerated the religions of the people they conquered as long as they did not appear to be politically or socially revolutionary, and as long as the people would also participate in ceremonies that honored and appeased the Roman gods. Like most of the peoples of the ancient world, the Romans were *polytheists* who honored many gods and easily added new gods or goddesses to their belief systems. In fact, Romans often adopted the gods of conquered peoples, believing that additional gods would simply make the Roman state stronger. In their religious life, most people who lived in the Roman Empire were *syncretistic*, that is, they not only easily added new deities, but also combined parts of various religious and philosophical systems together in an individualized way.

One group living within the Roman Empire had very different religious ideas, however. These were the Jews, who were strictly *monotheistic*, believing that they were to worship only one single god, whom they termed *Yahweh*. They would thus not participate in events that honored other gods or those in which living or deceased Roman emperors were described as divine. Though one would think this would have led to trouble with Roman authorities, usually it did not, for the Romans recognized that Jewish monotheism had a long tradition behind it. The Romans' respect for their own traditions led them to make an exception in the case of the Jews; the Jews were also not actively seeking converts, so the Romans did not have to worry that Judaism would spread.

Though all Jews were monotheistic, during the lifetime of Jesus of Nazareth (ca 5 B.C.–A.D. 29), on whose ideas Christianity was based, there were a number of groups within Judaism that stressed different parts of the Jewish tradition or had slightly different ideas. Thus when Jesus' early followers—all of them Jews—began to talk about his ideas, they appeared to Roman authorities as simply another Jewish sect. In fact, many of Jesus' early followers, who regarded him as the Messiah (the one foretold in Jewish prophecy who would bring about a period of happiness for Jews), thought of their movement as one primarily to reform Judaism.

By the last half of the first century, this way of thinking began to change, as those who followed Jesus' ideas began to set themselves apart from other Jews by participating in a special commemorative meal and by aggressively preaching. Many of them began to preach to non-Jews (termed *Gentiles*), leading to disagreements about whether those who accepted Jesus' ideas first had to become Jews to become full members of the movement. This issue was resolved at a meeting in Jerusalem in favor of the more universalist position, for it was decided that Gentile followers should have equal status without having to be circumcised or follow Jewish laws and customs. This decision enabled the movement to spread much more widely, with men and women traveling as missionaries throughout the Roman Empire. Instead of being a group within Judaism, Jesus' followers were now a distinct religion, taking the name that the Romans had first given them, *Christians*, a word derived from Christ, a Greek translation of the Hebrew word *Messiah* and a title given to Jesus by his followers.

Though Christians separated themselves from Jews, they took many of their religious ideas from Judaism, most importantly its monotheism, moral standards, and refusal to honor other gods. Christians also refused to participate in public religious ceremonies or honor the emperor as divine, but because their ideas were new and not part of a long-standing tradition, Romans did not feel that they warranted the same respect that Jews did. Beginning with the reign of the emperor Nero (54–68), Roman authorities began to persecute Christians, decreeing the death penalty for any who would not recant. These persecutions were stepped up during periods of unrest in the Empire, when Christians were blamed for provoking the displeasure of the traditional gods by refusing to honor them, so that the gods allowed turmoil and crisis. Many Christian beliefs and practices also appeared to be suspect or dangerous to Roman eyes: They talked about their king, who sounded like a rival to the emperor, and held ceremonies in which they claimed to eat the body and blood of this king, which to Romans appeared to be cannibalism; husbands and wives called each other brother and sister, suggesting incest; Christians spoke of an imminent end of the world, which would of course mean the end of the Roman Empire, and so appeared to be preaching political revolution. Christians' refusal to participate in the state cult implied disloyalty to Rome. They held secret meetings, which only the initiates could attend; this suggested they had something to hide and contrasted sharply with the public religious ceremonies common in Roman polytheism.

Despite Roman suspicion, however, the campaigns against Christians were never very thorough. Most of the emperors and the governors of Roman provinces followed the advice of the emperor Trajan (98–117) that Christians were not to be sought out, but only arrested if a responsible citizen accused them, and only executed if they did not recant. He recommended that authorities avoid general investigations or listening to rumors, and called for the arrest of anyone who accused someone of being a Christian without clear proof. Trajan and many of the emperors who followed him thus did not take Christianity very seriously, and let local governors decide how to handle Christians in their territories. The persecutions that did take place often led to dramatic public martyrdoms, giving Christianity great publicity and convincing many people throughout the Roman Empire that this new religion offered something distinctive.

The heroism of the early martyrs combined with the sporadic nature of the persecutions gave Christianity breathing space to expand. The number of Christians, particularly in urban areas, grew slowly but steadily, and began to include highly educated people who were familiar with a wide variety of religious and philosophical ideas. This was a time in the Roman Empire when many people appear to have been dissatisfied with traditional religion, and a number of groups that offered salvation to converts gained in popularity. Because it combined a promise of life after death with a spirit of community and gave believers a sense of purpose in life, Christianity grew faster than most other religions. This growth created problems for Christianity, however, for there was great diversity among early Christian communities, with each interpreting the accounts of Jesus' life related to them by missionaries and the main points of his message slightly differently. Because they had been brought up in a tradition of religious syncretism, many people adopted only some of the ideas of Christianity or combined Christian ideas with those from other sources. The sayings of Jesus and the accounts of his preaching were often enigmatic, so that people were able to use them in support of widely differing ideas.

This diversity was troubling to many of the leaders of early Christianity, who thought it extremely important that there be unity among all those who called themselves Christians. They thus began to declare certain ideas as *orthodox*, that is, acceptable or correct, and others as *heretical*, that is, unacceptable or incorrect, breaking with the Greco-Roman tradition of religious syncretism and toleration. They realized this could not be done simply on their own authority, but that some type of standards needed to be devised by which to judge ideas and practices. The establishment of orthodox ideas and authoritative standards did not happen in a vacuum, however, but was shaped by the preconceptions of early Church leaders and the social and political situation of the Roman Empire in which they lived. Your task in this chapter will be to use the writings of both those authors judged orthodox and those judged heretical to assess the way in which early Christianity developed. How was the initial diversity of Christianity transformed into a split between orthodoxy and heresy? What ideas and institutions came to be the most important determinants of orthodoxy?

SOURCES AND METHOD

Studying the history of any religious movement poses special problems for historians, for sources are very rarely objective. Even in the tolerant Roman Empire, some religious ideas were judged dangerous or deviant, so the writings of these groups were destroyed or not preserved, and the only record we have of them is from hostile observers. This is even more the case with Christianity, for most of our records come from those whose ideas were later judged orthodox. It is thus important for us to remember when using such sources that orthodoxy and heresy are relative terms. Only those who don't accept a belief label it as a heresy; those who accept it regard it as correct, of course, so that in their minds the others are the heretics. What we now call heresies within Christianity are beliefs that were rejected as orthodoxy was established.

Along with problems created by subjective sources, we may also have more difficulties in achieving unbiased assessments of the history of religion than other historical topics because we have an intellectual, spiritual, or emotional commitment to certain religious ideas. This does not mean, however, that we should avoid religious topics, particularly when studying Western history in which Judaism, Christianity, and Islam have been key factors, but that we should be cognizant of our own prejudices. Our job as historians is to understand people's religious ideas within their historical context and to see how religious faith manifested itself in historically observable phenomena; it is not to judge whether certain religious ideas are right or wrong. The people we are studying (and perhaps we ourselves) may believe certain developments to be the result of divine will or action, but as historians, we must use the same standards about how or why something happened that we would use in evaluating any event in the past and concentrate on the human actors. Perhaps the most important part of our methodology in exploring religious topics is thus to approach them with both objectivity and respect.

Not only are many of our sources subjective, but very few of them were written simply to describe things that have happened. Rather, they were written to bolster the faith of other followers, to correct perceived errors, or to win converts. You can see this clearly in studying the earliest decades of Christianity. The only contemporary written sources that describe the events in the life of Jesus and in the lives of his first followers were recorded by those who regarded themselves as Christians.

These writings were later termed gospels (*evangelium* in Latin), a word that means "good news," and were written primarily to spread the "good news" of Jesus' message and not simply to record the biographical details of his life. We can extract historical information from them and compare them with one another, but we have no way of checking them against non-Christian sources except for their references to political events such as the reigns of emperors.

Because gospels are some of the earliest Christian writings that have survived, they are a good place to start our exploration of the development of orthodoxy. During the early centuries of Christianity, many different gospels circulated, but gradually four—those of Matthew, Mark, Luke, and John—came to be considered orthodox and the rest heretical, or at least not as central as Matthew, Mark, Luke, and John. By comparing these orthodox Gospels with those which were excluded, we can see some of the ideas that became central to orthodoxy very early.

The first two sources are from the Gospels of Luke and Matthew, and form the basis for the orthodox interpretation of the resurrection of Jesus and his handing on of authority. In Source 1, who first discovers the empty tomb? What are they told has happened to the body of Jesus? What was the reaction of Jesus' other followers to their report? What point is Jesus trying to make about his own resurrection in verses 36–43? According to Luke, is the resurrection physical or spiritual? Source 2 is the very end of the Gospel of Matthew, and

describes Jesus' final words to his followers. According to this account, to whom does Jesus give authority? What is the source and extent of the authority he is delegating? To whom does Jesus say his message should be communicated?

Sources 3 and 4 offer quite a different view of Jesus' resurrection and handing on of authority, though these were also written by people calling themselves Christians in the first two centuries after the death of Jesus. They come from a movement termed *gnosticism*, with which you may be less familiar than with Christian orthodoxy. Gnosticism was not an organized group, but a diffuse body of beliefs drawn from Greek philosophy, Judaism, Persian religions, and then Christianity. While gnostics disagreed with each other about many things and their beliefs are often very complex, they generally agreed that they had special knowledge, revealed to them by a messenger sent from the creative power or supreme being of the universe; the term *gnostic*, in fact, comes from the Greek word *gnosis*, which means "to know." This special knowledge would enable them to understand the world, and particularly the presence of evil in it, and teach them how to act in order to gain deliverance from the world and achieve salvation. Gnostics believed that the supreme being was totally spiritual and that the material world was either accidentally created or was evil; they were thus uninterested in the things of this world such as politics or human society and were very pessimistic about them. They did feel that a small group of humans would be able to return to the purely spiritual world on death—those who had been given the secret knowledge, which would enable the "pure" spirit to escape the "impure" body.

People who were interested in these ideas found much in Christian teachings that appealed to them, and many gnostics became Christian. They created their own body of literature slightly later than the gospels you have read so far, the bulk of which was lost or destroyed. Until quite recently scholars had only fragments of certain gnostic texts and discussions of gnostic ideas in the writings of orthodox thinkers, so that it was difficult to get an unbiased picture. This changed when in 1945 near the town of Nag Hammadi, an Egyptian peasant accidentally found a jar filled with gnostic books, copies made probably in 350–400 of texts first written down as much as three centuries earlier. These were gradually transcribed and translated, and turned out to be fifty-two texts, some of them also labeled "gospels." Sources 3 and 4 are from two of these Nag Hammadi texts, 3 from the gospel of Mary Magdalene and 4 from a text titled "The Wisdom of Jesus Christ."

Source 3 begins with the same event described in the Gospel of Matthew, but then goes on to relate a series of events not included in the orthodox Gospels. How do the instructions Jesus gives his followers differ from those included in Matthew? Who emerges as the strongest of Jesus' followers? What gives her special authority? What is the reaction of Jesus' other followers to this? Source 4 describes an appearance of Jesus to his followers after his crucifixion. How does its description of his appearance differ from that in the Gospel of Luke? How does the group to whom Jesus appears differ from that described in Matthew? Whom does Jesus say will receive true knowledge? How does this group differ from those whom Matthew describes as the audience of his message?

As you can see from your readings so far, there was great diversity among early Christians in regard to such basic things as the nature of Jesus' Resurrection, the intended audience for his message, and the nature of the group responsible for spreading this message. During the second century, however, many Church leaders felt that this diversity was dangerous, and began to declare certain ideas and interpretations orthodox. The remaining sources in this chapter all stem from second-century orthodox writers, and will help you discover both what ideas were rejected as heresy and the standards devised by Church leaders to make. this rejection. We will focus on gnostic ideas, as these were regarded as the most divergent from what became orthodoxy, though the gnostics were not the only heretics in early Christianity. Indeed, many church leaders, including some bishops and the philosopher Origen (185?–254?) held ideas that were, either during their lifetimes or after they died, judged to be heretical. Because of the Nag Hammadi find, however, we have more direct access to gnostic ideas than those of most other heretical thinkers.

Source 5 comes from a work generally known as *Against Heresies,* written in the late second century by Irenaeus of Lyons (ca 130–ca 202), a Greek theologian who became bishop of Lyons in France and who was one of the first to systematize Christian doctrine. In *Against Heresies,* Irenaeus seeks to refute gnostic ideas. In this extract, he describes three different types of gnosticism, each of which had different ideas about who Jesus was and the relation between Jesus and the creator of the universe. As you read these three descriptions, it might be useful to write down the variant gnostic answers to the following questions: What was the nature of Jesus—spirit? Human? What actually happened at the crucifixion? What was Jesus' chief purpose while on earth? What is the nature of human salvation—spiritual? Bodily? Because of this, what is the proper attitude of humans toward their bodies—indifference? Rejection?

Though they spent much of their time describing and refuting gnostic ideas, Irenaeus and other leaders recognized that it was also important to devise a positive formulation of the ideas that would be considered orthodox. They took this from the words that many Christian groups were already using when they baptized new initiates, and put together what was termed the "symbol of the faith," or what we would call a creed. This second-century creed became the basis for what later came to be called the Apostles' Creed, first given

that name in a letter of St. Ambrose, the bishop of Milan, in about 390, and assuming its present form in about 650 (Source 6). As you read this source, note which clauses directly refute the various gnostic answers to the questions posed above. What is becoming the orthodox answer to these questions?

The sources thus far have mainly touched on the substance of orthodoxy—the second of the central questions for this chapter—but those remaining will address the first question, regarding the process of the establishment of orthodoxy, more directly. We have already seen, perhaps without noticing, one step in this process—the devising of a uniform statement of belief, with clauses that are unacceptable to most gnostics. Sources 7 and 8 describe another element of this process. Source 7 is another section of Irenaeus's *Against Heresies,* in which he describes the ideas of Marcion, a second-century religious leader influenced by the gnostics. What ideas does Marcion hold that disagree with the statement of faith in the Apostles' Creed? How does Marcion alter the works of other authors so that they support him? Marcion's alteration of Luke and Paul's works led other Church leaders to the realization that some decision needed to be made about which writings from the earliest followers of Jesus were to be accepted as authoritative, and what standards were to be used to make this decision. Source 8 is a fragment from a Greek text probably dating from the late second century, in which the unknown author sets out what he feels are the books and letters (termed *epistles*) that should have special status. This is the earliest known *canon,* or list of the books that later came to be included in the Christian New Testament, and is called the *Muratorian Canon* after the Italian historian who discovered the text. As you read this, note the reasons the author gives for including certain books and excluding others, or for why the authors of these books wrote what they did. How is Luke's authority to write a gospel established, considering that he was not one of the original disciples? What inspires John to write a gospel? In writing Acts, why does Luke exclude certain events? Why does the author feel that the personal letters he regards as written by Paul (to Philemon, Titus, and Timothy) should be included?

As you have probably discovered, the way in which this author judged which books should be included was the same way that orthodox leaders gave authority to their statement of faith—by linking it with the apostles, that is, with Jesus' early followers. As you remember from the first four readings, however, there were wide variations as to whom should be regarded as Jesus' closest followers; Mark speaks of eleven men, "The Wisdom of Jesus Christ" of twelve men and seven women. Mark represents what came to be the orthodox interpretation, which included as true apostles eleven of Jesus' original disciples plus a few other men—most notably Paul, as Source 7 makes clear. By this standard, the works of the gnostics were judged not to be orthodox not only because of their content, but also because they were generally not as old as the books included in the Christian New Testament. In addition, they did not always make a claim of connection with one of the apostles. The problem for orthodox leaders was now to affirm their own connection with this original group of men. Sources 9 through 11 give you the writings of three early orthodox leaders on this issue. Source 9 is from a letter of Clement of Rome, the bishop of Rome who was martyred about 97 A.D., to Christians at Corinth in Greece, written at the end of the first century. Source 10 is another section from Irenaeus of Lyons's *Against Heresies,* and Source 11 is a section from *Prescription Against the Heretics,* written by Tertullian (ca 160–ca 230), a theologian from North Africa. As you read these, note the ways in which the idea of apostolic succession, like the creed and canon, was also shaped by gnosticism. How would you compare Clement's discussion of the initial mood of the apostles with that described in the *Gospel of Mary*? How does the way in which Clement alters the Old Testament text of Isaiah help support his argument? How does Irenaeus use apostolic succession to refute the gnostic idea that there was a secret tradition revealed only to a few? Do the authors give evidence of events that contradict their notion of a unity among "true" churches? Whom exactly do they regard as the contemporary holders of apostolic authority?

Before you answer the central questions for this chapter, you may wish to reread all the sources to assess the ways in which the two questions are interrelated. How might the process by which orthodoxy was established have affected the content of orthodox ideas? And, conversely, how might the content of those ideas have shaped the institutions that established orthodoxy?

THE EVIDENCE

Sources 1 and 2 from New Oxford Annotated Bible *(Revised Standard Version) (New York: Oxford University Press, 1971), p. 1283; p. 1284.*

1. The Gospel of Luke, Chapter 24

But on the first day of the week, at early dawn, they went to the tomb, taking the spices which they had prepared. 2And they found the stone rolled away from the tomb, 3but when they went in they did not find the body. 4While they were perplexed about this, behold, two men stood by them in dazzling apparel; 5and as they were frightened and bowed their faces to the ground, the men said to them, "Why do you seek the living among the dead? 6Remember how he told you, while he was still in Galilee, 7that the Son of man must be delivered into the hands of sinful men, and be crucified, and on the third day rise." 8And they remembered his words, 9and returning from the tomb they told all this to the eleven and to all the rest. 10Now it was Mary Mag'-dalene and Jo-an-'na and Mary the mother of James and the other women with them who told this to the apostles; 11but these words seemed to them an idle tale and they did not believe them. . . .

> [*Jesus then appeared to two men in a village near Jerusalem, who returned to Jerusalem to tell the disciples what they had seen.*]

36As they were saying this, Jesus himself stood among them. 37But they were startled and frightened, and supposed that they saw a spirit. 38And he said to them, "Why are you troubled, and why do questionings rise in your hearts? 39See my hands and my feet, that it is I myself; handle me, and see; for a spirit has not flesh and bones as you see that I have."[1] 41And while they still disbelieved for joy, and wondered, he said to them, "Have you any-

---

1. Other ancient authorities add verse 40, *And when he had said this, he showed them his hands and feet.*

thing here to eat?" [42]They gave him a piece of broiled fish, [43]and he took it and ate before them.

2. The Gospel of Matthew, Chapter 28

[16]Now the eleven disciples went to Galilee, to the mountain to which Jesus had directed them. [17]And when they saw him they worshiped him; but some doubted. [18]And Jesus came and said to them, "All authority in heaven and on earth has been given to me. [19]Go therefore and make disciples of all nations, baptizing them in the name of the Father and of the Son and of the Holy Spirit, [20]teaching them to observe all that I have commanded you; and lo, I am with you always, to the close of the age."

Sources 3 and 4 from James M. Robinson, editor, The Nag Hammadi Library in English, *3d edition (San Francisco: Harper and Row, 1988), pp. 525–527; pp. 222–224.*

3. The Gospel of Mary Magdalene

When the blessed one[2] had said this, he greeted them all, saying, "Peace be with you. Receive my peace to yourselves. Beware that no one lead you astray, saying, 'Lo here!' or 'Lo there!' For the Son of Man is within you. Follow after him! Those who seek him will find him. Go then and preach the gospel of the kingdom. Do not lay down any rules beyond what I appointed for you, and do not give a law like the lawgiver lest you be constrained by it." When he had said this, he departed.

But they were grieved. They wept greatly, saying, "How shall we go to the gentiles and preach the gospel of the kingdom of the Son of Man? If they did not spare him, how will they spare us?" Then Mary stood up, greeted them all, and said to her brethren, "Do not weep and do not grieve nor be irresolute, for his grace will be entirely with you and will protect you. But rather let us praise his greatness, for he has prepared us and made us into men." When Mary said this, she turned their hearts to the Good, and they began to discuss the words of the [Savior].

Peter said to Mary, "Sister, we know that the Savior loved you more than the rest of women. Tell us the words of the Savior which you remember— which you know (but) we do not, nor have we heard them." Mary answered and said, "What is hidden from you I will proclaim to you." And she began to speak to them these words: "I," she said, "I saw the Lord in a vision and I said

2. **the blessed one:** Jesus.

to him, 'Lord, I saw you today in a vision.' He answered and said to me, 'Blessed are you, that you did not waver at the sight of me. For where the mind is, there is the treasure.' I said to him, 'Lord, now does he who sees the vision see it ⟨through⟩ the soul ⟨or⟩ through the spirit?' The Savior answered and said, 'He does not see through the soul nor through the spirit, but the mind which [is] between the two—that is [what] sees the vision and it is [. . .].'

> [*The next several pages are lost, and then
> Mary goes on to describe the ascent of
> the soul.*]

"[. . .] it. And desire that, 'I did not see you descending, but now I see you ascending. Why do you lie, since you belong to me?' The soul answered and said, 'I saw you. You did not see me nor recognize me. I served you as a garment, and you did not know me.' When it had said this, it went away rejoicing greatly.

"Again it came to the third power, which is called ignorance. [It (the power)] questioned the soul saying, 'Where are you going? In wickedness are you bound. But you are bound; do not judge!' And the soul said, 'why do you judge me although I have not judged? I was bound though I have not bound. I was not recognized. But I have recognized that the All is being dissolved, both the earthly (things) and the heavenly.'

When the soul had overcome the third power, it went upwards and saw the fourth power, (which) took seven forms. The first form is darkness, the second desire, the third ignorance, the fourth is the excitement of death, the fifth is the kingdom of the flesh, the sixth is the foolish wisdom of flesh, the seventh is the wrathful wisdom. These are the seven [powers] of wrath. They ask the soul, 'Whence do you come, slayer of men, or where are you going, conqueror of space?' The soul answered and said, 'What binds me has been slain, and what surrounds me has been overcome, and my desire has been ended, and ignorance has died. In a [world] I was released from a world, [and] in a type from a heavenly type, and (from) the fetter of oblivion which is transient. From this time on will I attain to the rest of the time, of the season, of the aeon, in silence.' "

When Mary had said this, she fell silent, since it was to this point that the Savior had spoken with her. But Andrew answered and said to the brethren, "Say what you (wish to) say about what she has said. I at least do not believe that the Savior said this. For certainly these teachings are strange ideas." Peter answered and spoke concerning these same things. He questioned them about the Savior: "Did he really speak with a woman without our knowledge (and) not openly? Are we to turn about and all listen to her? Did he prefer her to us?"

Then Mary wept and said to Peter, "My brother Peter, what do you think? Do you think that I thought this up myself in my heart, or that I am lying about the Savior?" Levi answered and said to Peter, "Peter, you have always been hot-tempered. Now I see you contending against the woman like the adversaries. But if the Savior made her worthy, who are you indeed to reject her? Surely the Savior knows her very well. That is why he loved her more than us. Rather let us be ashamed and put on the perfect man and acquire him for ourselves as he commanded us, and preach the gospel, not laying down any other rule or other law beyond what the Savior said." When [. . .] and they began to go forth [to] proclaim and to preach.

4. "The Wisdom of Jesus Christ"

The Sophia[3] of Jesus Christ.

After he rose from the dead, his twelve disciples and seven women continued to be his followers and went to Galilee onto the mountain called "Divination and Joy." When they gathered together and were perplexed about the underlying reality of the universe and the plan and the holy providence and the power of the authorities and about everything that the Savior is doing with them in the secret of the holy plan, the Savior appeared, not in his previous form, but in the invisible spirit. And his likeness resembles a great angel of light. But his resemblance I must not describe. No mortal flesh could endure it, but only pure (and) perfect flesh, like that which he taught us about on the mountain called "Of Olives" in Galilee. And he said: "Peace be to you! My peace I give to you!" And they all marveled and were afraid.

The Savior laughed and said to them: "What are you thinking about? (Why) are you perplexed? What are you searching for?" Philip said: "For the underlying reality of the universe and the plan."

The Savior said to them: "I want you to know that all men born on earth from the foundation of the world until now, being dust, while they have inquired about God, who he is and what he is like, have not found him. Now the wisest among them have speculated from the ordering of the world and (its) movement. But their speculation has not reached the truth. For it is said that the ordering is directed in three ways by all the philosophers, (and) hence they do not agree. For some of them say about the world that it is directed by itself. Others, that it is providence (that directs it). Others, that it is fate. But it is none of these. Again, of the three voices I have just mentioned, none is close to the truth, and (they are) from man. But I, who came from Infinite Light, I am here—for I know him (Light)—that I might speak to you about the precise nature of the truth. For whatever is from itself is a polluted life; it is self-made. Providence has no wisdom in it. And fate does not discern.

But to you it is given to know; and whoever is worthy of knowledge will receive (it), whoever has not been begotten by the sowing of unclean rubbing but by First Who Was Sent, for he is an immortal in the midst of mortal men."

---

3. **Sophia:** Greek word for "wisdom."

Source 5 from Henry Bettenson, editor and translator, Documents of the Christian Church, 2d edition (London: Oxford University Press, 1963), pp. 35–37.

5. Descriptions of the Ideas of Several Gnostic Thinkers, from Irenaeus of Lyons's *Against Heresies*

Saturninus[4] was of Antioch.[5] . . . Like Menander,[4] he taught that there is one Father, utterly unknown, who made Angels, Archangels, Virtues, Powers; and that the world, and all things therein, was made by certain angels, seven in number. . . .

The Saviour he declared to be unborn, incorporeal and without form, asserting that he was seen as a man in appearance only. The God of the Jews, he affirms, was one of the Angels; and because all the Princes wished to destroy his Father, Christ came to destroy the God of the Jews, and to save them that believed on him, and these are they who have a spark of his life. He was the first to say that two kinds of men were fashioned by the Angels, one bad, the other good. And because the demons aid the worst, The Saviour came to destroy the bad men and the Demons and to save the good. But to marry and procreate they say is of Satan. . . .

Basilides,[4] that he may seem to have found out something higher and more plausible, vastly extends the range of his teaching, declaring that Mind was first born of the Unborn Father, then Reason from Mind, from Reason, Prudence, from Prudence, Wisdom and Power, and from Wisdom and Power the Virtues, Princes and Angels, whom he also calls "the First." By them the First Heaven was made; afterwards others were made, derived from these, and they made another Heaven like to the former, and in like manner others . . . [in all, 365 Heavens].

4. Those Angels who hold sway over the later Heaven, which is seen by us, ordered all things that are in the world, and divided among them the earth and the nations upon the earth. And their chief is he who is held to be the God of the Jews. He wished to subdue the other nations beneath his own people, the Jews, and therefore all the other Princes resisted him and took measures against him. . . . Then the Unborn and Unnamed Father . . . sent his First-begotten Mind (and there is he they call Christ), for the freeing of them that believe in him from those who made the world. And he appeared to the nations of them as a man on the earth, and performed deeds of virtue. Wherefore he suffered not, but a certain Simon, a Cyrenian, was impressed to bear his cross for him; and Simon was crucified in ignorance and error, having been transfigured by him, that men should suppose him to be Jesus, while Jesus himself

4. **Saturninus, Menander, Basilides,** and **Cerinthus:** gnostic thinkers.
5. **Antioch:** a city in Syria.

took on the appearance of Simon and stood by and mocked them. . . . If any therefore acknowledge the crucified, he is still a slave and subject to the power of them that made our bodies; but he that denies him is freed from them, and recognises the ordering of the Unborn Father.

A certain Cerinthus[4] also in Asia taught that the world was not made by the first God, but by a certain Virtue far separated and removed from the Principality which is above all things, a Virtue which knows not the God over all. He added that Jesus was not born of a virgin but was the son of Joseph and Mary, like other men, but superior to all others in justice, prudence and wisdom. And that after his baptism Christ descended upon him in the form of a dove, from that Principality which is above all things; and that then he revealed the Unknown Father and performed deeds of virtue, but that in the end Christ flew back, leaving Jesus, and Jesus suffered and rose again, but Christ remained impassible, being by nature spiritual.

6. The Apostles' Creed: Adapted from a Letter of St. Ambrose of Milan, 390

I believe in God, the Father Almighty, maker of heaven and earth, and in Jesus Christ his only Son our Lord, conceived by the Holy Spirit and born of the Virgin Mary. He suffered under Pontius Pilate, was crucified, died and was buried. He descended into hell. On the third day he rose again from the dead. He ascended into heaven and sits at the right hand of God the Father Almighty. From whence he shall come again to judge the quick and the dead. I believe in the Holy Spirit, the Holy catholic[6] church, the communion of saints, the forgiveness of sins, the resurrection of the body, and the life everlasting.

Sources 7 through 11 from Henry Bettenson, editor and translator, Documents of the Christian Church, *2d edition (London: Oxford University Press 1963), p. 37; pp. 28–29; p. 63; pp. 68–70; p. 71.*

7. Description of the Ideas of Marcion, from Irenaeus of Lyons's *Against Heresies*

Marcion of Pontus took his [Cerdon's[7]] place and amplified his teaching, impudently blaspheming him who is declared to be God by the Law and the Prophets; calling him a worker of evils, delighting in wars, inconstant in

6. "Catholic" in this instance means worldwide.
7. **Cerdon:** a gnostic thinker.

judgement and self-contradictory. While he alleges that Jesus came from the Father who is above the God that made the world; that he came to Judaea in the time of Pontius Pilate the governor, who was the procurator of Tiberius Caesar, and was manifest in the form of a man to all that were in Judaea, destroying the prophets and the Law and all the works of that God who made the world, whom he calls also the Ruler of the Universe. Moreover he mutilated the Gospel according to Luke, removing all the narratives of the Lord's birth, and also removing much of the teaching of the discourses of the Lord wherein he is most manifestly described as acknowledging the maker of this universe to be his father. Thus he persuaded his disciples that he himself was more trustworthy than the apostles, who handed down the Gospel; though he gave to them not a Gospel but a fragment of a Gospel. He mutilated the Epistles of the Apostle Paul in the same manner, removing whatever is manifestly spoken by the Apostle concerning the God who made the world, where he says that he is the father of our Lord Jesus Christ, and setting aside all the Apostle's teaching drawn from the Prophetic writings which predict the advent of the Lord.

2. And then he says that salvation will be of our souls only, of those souls which have learned his teaching; the body, because forsooth it is taken from the earth, cannot partake in salvation.

8. The Muratorian Canon

... The third book of the Gospel is that according to Luke. Luke, the physician, when, after the Ascension of Christ, Paul had taken him to himself as one studious of right [or, probably, as travelling companion] wrote in his own name what he had been told [or in order], although he had not himself seen the Lord in the flesh. He set down the events as far as he could ascertain them, and began his story with the birth of John.

The fourth gospel is that of John, one of the disciples. ... When his fellow-disciples and bishops exhorted him he said, 'Fast with me for three days from to-day, and then let us relate to each other whatever may be revealed to each of us.' On the same night it was revealed to Andrew, one of the Apostles, that John should narrate all things in his own name as they remembered them. ...

Moreover the Acts of all the Apostles are included in one book. Luke addressed them to the most excellent Theophilus, because the several events took place when he was present; and he makes this plain by the omission of the passion of Peter and of the journey of Paul when he left Rome for Spain.

For the Epistles of Paul ... he wrote to not more than seven churches, in this order: the first to the Corinthians, the second to the Ephesians, the third to the Philippians, the fourth to the Colossians, the fifth to the Galatians, the sixth to the Thessalonians, the seventh to the Romans. ... He wrote besides these one to Philemon, one to Titus, and two to Timothy. These were written in personal affection; but they have been hallowed by being held in honour by the Catholic Church for the regulation of church discipline. There are extant also a letter to the Laodiceans and another to the Alexandrians, forged under Paul's name to further the heresy of Marcion. And there are many others which cannot be received into the Catholic Church. For it is not fitting for gall to be mixed with honey.

The Epistle of Jude indeed, and two bearing the name of John, are accepted in the Catholic Church; also Wisdom, written by the friends of Solomon in his honour. We receive also the Apocalypse of John and that of Peter, which some of us refuse to have read in the Church. But the *Shepherd* was written very recently in our time by Hermas, in the city of Rome, when his brother, Bishop Pius, was sitting in the Chair of the Church of Rome. Therefore it ought also to be read; but it cannot be publicly read in the Church to the people, either among the Prophets, since their number is complete [?], or among the Apostles, to the end of time. . . .

9. Clement of Rome, Letter to the Christians at Corinth

. . . The Apostles for our sakes received the gospel from the Lord Jesus Christ; Jesus Christ was sent from God. Christ then is from God, and the Apostles from Christ. Both therefore came in due order from the will of God. Having therefore received his instructions and being fully assured through the Resurrection of our Lord Jesus Christ, they went forth with confidence in the word of God and with full assurance of the Holy Spirit, preaching the gospel that the Kingdom of God was about to come. And so, as they preached in the country and in the towns, they appointed their firstfruits (having proved them by the Spirit) to be bishops and deacons [overseers and ministers] of them that should believe. And this was no novelty, for of old it had been written concerning bishops and deacons; for the Scripture says in one place, 'I will set up their bishops in righteousness, and their deacons in faith' (Is. lx. 17).[8]

Our Apostles knew also, through our Lord Jesus Christ, that there would be strife over the dignity of the bishop's office. For this reason therefore, having received complete foreknowledge, they appointed the aforesaid, and after a time made provision that on their death other approved men should succeed to their ministry. . . .

8. Clement is here changing the original wording of Isaiah 60: 17, which reads *overseers* and *taskmasters* instead of *bishops* and *deacons*.

10. Discussion of Succession from Irenaeus's *Against Heresies*

... Those that wish to discern the truth may observe the apostolic tradition made manifest in every church throughout the world. We can enumerate those who were appointed bishops in the churches by the Apostles, and their successors [or successions] down to our own day, who never taught, and never knew, absurdities such as these men produce. For if the Apostles had known hidden mysteries which they taught the perfect in private and in secret, they would rather have committed them to those to whom they entrusted the churches. For they wished those men to be perfect and unblameable whom they left as their successors and to whom they handed over their own office of authority. But as it would be very tedious, in a book of this sort, to enumerate the successions in all the churches, we confound all those who in any way, whether for self-pleasing, or vainglory, or blindness, or evilmindedness, hold unauthorized meetings. This we do by pointing to the apostolic tradition and the faith that is preached to men, which has come down to us through the successions of bishops; the tradition and creed of the greatest, the most ancient church, the church known to all men, which was founded and set up at Rome by the two most glorious Apostles, Peter and Paul. For with this church, because of its position of leadership and authority, must needs agree every church, that is, the faithful everywhere; for in her the apostolic tradition has always been preserved by the faithful from all parts.

2. The blessed Apostles, after founding and building up the church, handed over to Linus the office of bishop. Paul mentions this Linus in his epistles to Timothy (2 Tim. iv. 21). He was succeeded by Anacletus, after whom, in the third place after the Apostles, Clement was appointed to the bishopric. He not only saw the blessed Apostles but also conferred with them, and had their preaching ringing in his ears and their tradition before his eyes. In this he was not alone; for many still survived who had been taught by the Apostles. Now while Clement was bishop there arose no small dissension among the brethren in Corinth, and the church in Rome sent a most weighty letter to the Corinthians urging them to reconciliation, renewing their faith and telling them again of the tradition which he had lately received from the Apostles. ...

3. Euarestus succeeded this Clement, Alexander followed Euarestus; then Sixtus was appointed, the sixth after the Apostles. After him came Telesphorus, who had a glorious martyrdom. Then Hyginus, Pius, Anicetus and Soter; and now, in the twelfth place from the Apostles, Eleutherus occupies the see. In the same order and succession the apostolic tradition in the Church and the preaching of the truth has come down to our time. ...

4. And then Polycarp, besides being instructed by the Apostles and acquainted with many who had seen the Lord, was also appointed by the Apos-

tles from Asia as bishop of the church in Smyrna.[9] Even I saw him in my early youth; for he remained with us a long time, and at a great age suffered a martyrdom full of glory and renown and departed this life, having taught always the things which he had learnt from the Apostles, which the Church hands down, which alone are true. There testify to these things all the churches throughout Asia, and the successors of Polycarp down to this day, testimonies to the truth far more trustworthy and reliable than Valentinus[10] and Marcion and the other misguided persons.

Polycarp, when staying in Rome in the time of Anicetus, converted many of the before-mentioned heretics to the Church of God, declaring that he had received this one and only truth from the Apostles, the truth which has been handed down by the Church. There are also some who heard him relate that John, the disciple of the Lord, went to the baths at Ephesus; and seeing Cerinthus[10] inside he rushed out without taking a bath, saying, 'Let us flee, before the baths fall in, for Cerinthus the enemy of the truth is inside.' . . .

iv. 1. Since therefore there are so many proofs, there is now no need to seek among others the truth which we can easily obtain from the Church. For the Apostles have lodged all that there is of the truth with her, as with a rich bank, holding back nothing. And so anyone that wishes can draw from her the draught of life. This is the gateway of life; all the rest are thieves and robbers. . . .

Therefore we ought to obey only those presbyters who are in the Church, who have their succession from the Apostles, as we have shown; who with their succcession in the episcopate have received the sure gift of the truth according to the pleasure of the Father. The rest, who stand aloof from the primitive succession, and assemble in any place whatever, we must regard with suspicion, either as heretics and evil-minded; or as schismatics, puffed up and complacent; or again as hypocrites, acting thus for the sake of gain and vainglory. All these have fallen from the truth.

11. Discussion of Succession from Tertullian, *Prescription Against the Heretics*

But if any of these [heresies] are bold enough to insert themselves into the Apostolic age, in order to seem to have been handed down from the Apostles because they existed under the Apostles, we can say: Let them then produce the origins of their churches; let them unroll the list of their bishops, an unbroken succession from the beginning so that that first bishop had as his precursor and the source of his authority one of the Apostles or one of the apostolic men who, though not an Apostle, continued with the Apostles. This is how

9. **Smyrna:** a city in Asia Minor (present-day Turkey).
10. **Valentinus and Cerinthus:** gnostic thinkers.

the apostolic churches report their origins; thus the church of the Smyrnaeans relates that Polycarp was appointed by John, the church of Rome that Clement was ordained by Peter. . . .

QUESTIONS TO CONSIDER

As scholars have discovered more about the diversity of early Christian beliefs and practices, they have been increasingly interested in explaining not only *how*, but also *why* certain ideas became identified as orthodox and others were rejected, and why orthodoxy ultimately triumphed. Answers to these questions take us far beyond the sources included here, but you can use the sources, combined with information from your textbook about Roman society in the first centuries after Jesus, to begin to address them. Considering these questions will also allow you to deepen your understanding of the process of this change as you answer the questions for this chapter.

Thinking about gnostic ideas in general, why might the gnostic view that Jesus' true mission was to an elite group able to understand secret knowledge have reduced its popularity among early converts to Christianity? How did the gnostic notion that the inner experience or vision of Christ was what mattered, an experience that anyone could have, challenge Roman ideas of proper structures of authority? How did the gnostic idea that the true message of Jesus had primarily been communicated orally both allow for and limit the spread of gnostic ideas?

Taking some of the actions in the establishment of orthodoxy, why might orthodox views of the crucifixion, which emphasized its bodily nature, be especially appealing at a time when Christians were persecuted by Roman authorities? How did orthodoxy's setting up of objective criteria for membership (that is, taking in anyone who would accept orthodox doctrines and agree to be governed by bishops) increase its appeal as compared to gnosticism's demand for special spiritual insight? Once bishops were established as figures of authority, why would it be increasingly difficult to promote gnostic ideas? How did setting up the criterion of "apostolic" as the central determinant of orthodoxy limit the importance of visions such as that described by Mary Magdalene in Source 3? How would the idea of apostolic authority have worked against groups such as the gnostics who did not think it important to link themselves with the apostles?

Once you begin to understand what ideas became central to orthodox Christianity, you can see that certain events surrounding the life of Jesus were somewhat problematic because they seemed to point to an alternative interpretation. One of these events is that related in Source 1, the fact that the empty tomb was discovered by women, not by the disciples, and that women first heard the message that Jesus had risen. How did this conflict with notions of authority being developed in orthodoxy? One solution for problems such as this was to alter the account somewhat, and, in fact, some ancient texts of Luke add an additional verse after verse 11 in Source 1, which reads: "But Peter rose and ran to the tomb; stooping and looking in, he saw the linen cloths by themselves; and he went home wondering at what had happened." How might this addition change one's interpretation of the event?

As we search for human reasons for the developments traced in this chapter, it is important not to forget that the people we are studying regarded these events as signs of divine providence, of God working in history. Early Christians and many non-Christian Romans expected God (or the gods) to act through human agents and so did not regard human explanations as disproof of the divine or miraculous. If the question of how and why orthodoxy triumphed had been put to someone like Irenaeus, how might he have answered? Comparing his hypothetical answer to yours, how have ideas of causation in history changed since ancient times?

EPILOGUE

The transformation of Christianity from its original diversity to a religion with clear lines between heresy and orthodoxy was not something that was accomplished by A.D. 200, but has continued to the present day. The original pattern set by the confrontation with gnosticism has been largely followed, however. Christianity generally defined what would be considered orthodoxy only when confronted by a group taking a firm alternative position; the development of Christian theology has thus been reactive rather than spontaneous, and Christianity has tolerated *heterodoxy*, or a range of opinions, on many issues for a long time.

Because of its many denominations, modern Christianity appears at first glance to be a return to diversity and heterodoxy, yet the ideas and institutions you have traced in this chapter are still present in many Christian denominations. Contemporary theological disputes, particularly within Roman Catholicism but also within Eastern Orthodoxy and many Protestant denominations, are still being decided upon by reference to apostolic authority and the texts of the New Testament. Bishops in many Christian denominations still have a great amount of power, and people still recite the Apostles' Creed. Though it would be hard to find an idea that all Christian denominations today regard as heresy, those of the gnostics would probably come the closest.

The ideas and interpretations put forth by gnostics did not completely die out in the second century, however. Not only did gnostic Christianity survive for several more centuries, but gnostic ideas reemerged in the Middle Ages and in many

Christian thinkers down to the present day. The gnostic texts rediscovered at Nag Hammadi have also become increasingly popular with people searching for spiritual answers today. Both those who wish to remain within a Christian tradition but are uncomfortable with the institutionalization and stress on authority that came to mark orthodoxy, and those who are again developing syncretistic personal religions from a variety of traditions have turned to gnosticism for inspiration.

CHAPTER SIX

SLAVE LAW IN ROMAN AND

GERMANIC SOCIETY

In all the cultures of the ancient Mediterranean, some people were slaves, owned as property by other people. In Mesopotamia and Egypt, people became slaves in a variety of ways, and the earliest law codes, such as that of Hammurabi (ca 1780 B.C.), include provisions regarding slavery. Many slaves were war captives, brought into the area from outside along with other types of booty. Some were criminals, for whom slavery was the punishment for a crime. Some had been sold into slavery by their parents or had sold themselves into slavery in times of economic hardship. Others became slaves to repay debts, a condition that was often temporary. In these cultures, slaves performed a variety of tasks, from farming to highly skilled professional and administrative work, but the proportion of slaves in the population was not very great and most work was carried out by free persons. Thus, historians describe Mesopotamia and Egypt as slave-using but not slave societies.

By contrast, republican Rome was truly a slave society, in which a significant proportion of the population were slaves—perhaps one-quarter or one-third by the second century B.C.—and in which slaves did much of the productive labor. The military conquests of Rome during the second and first centuries B.C. provided many new war captives and also increased the wealth of Rome's elite, who invested in huge agricultural estates (termed *latifundia*). These estates were too large to be worked by single peasant families—who were often migrating to the cities in any case—and so an increasing share of agricultural production was carried on by large labor gangs of slaves under the supervision of overseers, who might themselves be slaves. The owners of both the land and the slaves were often absentee, living in Rome or another urban center rather than out on the latifundia themselves. This system of agricultural slavery continued into the Roman Empire, although the influx of new slaves lessened somewhat as military expansion slowed and laws were passed prohibiting the enslavement of subjects of the Empire. In addition, urban slaves who worked as household servants, artisans, teachers, gladiators, or shopkeepers continued to be very common.

The Germanic tribes that gradually migrated into the Roman Empire beginning in the second century were also slave-owning cultures, although the relative number of slaves among them was probably less than that in Rome. When they conquered Roman lands, they generally took a proportion of the slaves and the land for themselves, leaving the rest to the existing Roman proprietors. However, the breakdown in communication and political control that accompanied the disintegration of the Roman Empire in the West made it increasingly difficult for absentee owners to control their estates and to ship their products safely to distant markets. Thus, like many other aspects of life during this period, slavery became increasingly localized and less economically significant than it had been earlier in these areas, although it did not disappear.

Slavery in both Roman and Germanic societies was based not on racial distinctions but on notions of personal freedom that could be very complex. At the heart of this complexity was the issue that a slave was both a person, able to engage in relationships with other persons and to act on his or her own, and a thing, owned by another person. Law codes developed by both Romans and Germans had to balance these two aspects of being a slave, as well as regulate other matters concerning slaves and slavery. They had to establish and protect the boundaries between slave and free, but also establish ways in which those boundaries could be crossed, as slavery was not necessarily a permanent status. Your task in this chapter will be to investigate Roman and Germanic laws regarding slavery during the period 400 to 1000, in order to answer the following questions: How were legal distinctions between slave and free established, structured, and maintained, and how could they be overcome? What similarities and differences are there in Roman and Germanic laws regarding slavery?

SOURCES AND METHOD

When historians investigate legal developments, they often use law codes in conjunction with court records and other documents to examine the actual workings of the law, or to contrast legal theory with reality. For the period we are investigating in this chapter, sources describing actual legal practice in central and western Europe are virtually nonexistent, and so our focus will be strictly on the law codes. (Other sources regarding slavery in the Roman Empire do exist, such as economic treatises, histories of slave revolts, and philosophical discussions of slavery, but there are no parallel sources for early Germanic societies.) We must thus keep in mind that everything we read is essentially legal theory, describing what is supposed to happen rather than what actually does happen. Law codes are not written in a vacuum, however. They reflect not only the ideals of the legal and political authorities who were their authors, but also these authorities' assumptions about what people—in this case slaves, their owners, and people who came into contact with slaves and their owners—might actually do. In some cases laws also explicitly describe actual conduct, generally as a preamble to a prohibition of this conduct, or a succession of laws implies actual conduct, as prohibitions are made more specific or penalties are made more stringent.

It is important in this chapter, then, to keep in mind the limitations of using law codes as a source, and it is also important to recognize that the law codes we will be using come from two cultures that had very different notions concerning the origin, function, and purpose of law. Roman law began during the republican period as a set of rules governing the private lives of citizens, and was later expanded to include the handling of disputes between Romans and non-Romans and between foreigners under Roman jurisdiction. The first written codification, the Twelve Tables, was made in the middle of the fifth century B.C. and posted publicly, giving at least those Romans who could read direct access to it. Legal interpreters called *praetors* and judges

called *judices* made decisions based on explicit statutes and also on their own notions of what would be fair and equitable, which gave them a great deal of flexibility. Praetors generally followed the laws set by their predecessors, announcing publicly at the beginning of their terms of office that they would do this, but they also added to the body of law as new issues arose. Thus Roman law was adaptable to new conditions, with jurists in the Empire regarding their work as building on that of earlier centuries rather than negating it. Ultimately all those living within the boundaries of the Roman Empire were regarded as subject to the same law, the *ius gentium*, or "law of peoples."

Roman law regarding slavery—like all Roman law—for most of the republican and imperial periods was a mixture of senatorial statutes, edicts of elected officials, opinions of learned jurists, imperial decrees, and rulings by lesser officials. Under Emperor Theodosius II (r. 408–450), an attempt was made to compile some of the actual imperial decrees, and the resultant Theodosian Code promulgated in 435–438 contained all of the imperial laws issued since the time of the emperor Constantine (r. 311–337) that were still in effect, including those on slavery. Theodosius ruled the eastern half of the Roman Empire (which later came to be called the Byzantine Empire), but his laws were promulgated for both the eastern and western halves. The Theodosian Code was expanded under the direction of the Byzantine Emperor Justinian (r. 527–565), with older and newer laws and the opinions of jurists added. Justinian's Code, promulgated in 529–533 and officially termed the *Corpus Juris Civilis*, became the basis of Byzantine legal procedure for nearly a millennium.

In contrast to Roman written statutory law, Germanic law remained a body of traditions handed down orally for almost a thousand years after the first codification of Roman law. Like all systems of customary law around the world, it was regarded as binding because it represented the immemorial customs of a specific tribe. The ultimate authority in this legal system was not an abstract body of laws or a group of legal interpreters, but the king, whose chief legal function was to "speak the law"—that is, to decide cases based on existing oral tradition; neither the king nor anyone else could (at least in theory) make new laws. This body of custom was regarded as the inalienable possession of all members of a tribe, no matter where they happened to be, and was thus attached to persons rather than to geographic areas the way Roman (and today's) statutory law codes were.

At roughly the same time that codifications of Roman law were promulgated by the emperors Theodosius and Justinian, Germanic kings in western Europe supported the initial written codifications of what had been oral customary law. These codes usually bore the name of the tribe, such as the Lombard Law, the Burgundian Law, or the Salic Law (the law of the Salian Franks). On the continent of Europe, such law codes were written down in Latin, often by Roman jurists employed by Germanic kings, so that they sometimes included Roman legal tradition as well as Germanic customs, particularly in southern Europe, where Roman culture was strongest. In northern Europe and in England—where the laws were initially written in the West Saxon dialect that became Old English—Roman influences were weaker, making the codes of these areas, such as those of the Frisians and the Anglo-Saxons, more purely customary in origin.

When the Germanic tribes came into the Empire, these two notions of the law—statutory and geographic versus customary and personal—came into direct conflict. The problem was solved initially by letting Romans be judged according to written Roman law while non-Romans were judged by their own oral customs. As the Germanic kingdoms became more firmly established, their rulers saw the merits of a written code, but two legal systems—one for Romans and one for Germanic people—often existed side by side for centuries in these areas. Only in cases that involved a conflict between a Roman and a German was the former expected to follow the new Germanic code. As noted above, however, Roman principles did shape these Germanic codes to some degree. Though the initial codifications claimed to be simply the recording of long-standing customs, in reality the laws often modified customs that no longer fit the needs of the Germanic peoples as they became more settled and adopted some aspects of the more sophisticated Roman culture. Later kings were also not hesitant to make new laws when situations demanded it and to state explicitly that this is what they were doing. Thus Germanic codes gradually evolved from records of tribal customs based on moral sanctions and notions of a common tradition into collections of royal statutes based on the political authority of kings. They remained more closely linked to the ruler than Roman law and never included the opinions of legal commentators the way Justinian's Code did, but, like Roman law, they were eventually tied to a geographic area rather than to a group of people.

There were thus significant differences between Roman and Germanic societies in the function and complexity of law, but the legal codes of all these societies included provisions regarding slavery. The sources for this chapter come from seven different law codes, two from Roman tradition—the Theodosian Code and Justinian's Code—and five from Germanic tradition—Burgundian, Salic, Lombard, Alemannic, and Anglo-Saxon. Many of these law codes exist in multiple manuscript versions, with the earliest extant version often dating from centuries after the code was first compiled. This provides much fuel for scholarly disagreement about exactly when they were drawn up, exactly which sections date from the initial codification and which from later revisions, and exactly how certain sections are supposed to read. (Scholars can often trace the path manuscripts followed by noting which errors were recopied by subse-

quent scribes; often this does not help in determining which versions are more "authentic," however.) For this chapter, we have used the version of these codes most widely accepted by recent scholarship, but you should be aware that any edition or translation of texts like these from manuscript cultures involves a decision on the part of the editor as to which version to use.

To explore the legal definitions of and boundaries between slavery and freedom, we will be examining four basic issues in this chapter: (A) How could a person become a slave, or a slave become free? (B) How were slaves valued, in comparison to other things a person might own, and what limits were placed on the treatment of slaves by their owners? (C) How were personal relationships between slave and free regulated? (D) How were slaves differentiated from free persons in terms of criminal actions committed by them or against them? To assist you in working through the issues in this chapter, provisions in the laws have been grouped according to these four topics rather than being presented in the order in which they appear in the codes. (In many of these codes, particularly the Germanic ones, laws are arranged completely haphazardly in any case, so that the order makes no difference.) Thus, as you are taking notes on the sources, it would be a good idea to draw up a chart for each issue. Other than this, your basic method in this chapter is careful reading.

Source 1 includes selections from the Theodosian Code. According to the selections in Source 1A, what are some of the ways in which one could become a slave in the late Roman Empire? What are some ways in which slaves could become free? According to 1B, what would happen to a master who beat his slaves? According to 1C, what would happen to a woman who had sexual relations with or married one of her slaves? To a man who had sexual relations with one of his slaves? To a decurion (a man who was a member of a local municipal council) who did so? According to 1D, what would happen to rebellious slaves?

Source 2 contains selections from Justinian's Code, which was itself divided into three parts: the *Codex,* actual imperial legislation, including much that was contained in the Theodosian Code; the *Digest,* the opinions of various jurists from throughout the history of Rome; and the *Institutes,* an officially prescribed course for first-year law students, in which some of the opinions found in the *Digest* are repeated. The legal opinions included in the *Digest* sometimes refer to specific imperial statutes, and sometimes simply describe what the commentator saw as Roman tradition in regard to legal categories or procedures. Like legal opinions today, however, the judgments of these jurists shaped the handling of cases, for later judges and lawyers looked to earlier precedents and opinions when making their decisions. They are thus much more important than the opinion of a private person on an issue would be, and all the selections included here come from the *Digest.* According to Source 2A, what were some of the ways in which one could

become a slave or become free? Would becoming free remove all obligations a slave had toward his master? According to 2C, did slaves have family relationships? According to 2D, what would happen to someone who killed a slave? To slaves whose master was killed while they were within earshot? To runaway slaves and those who protected them?

Putting the information from Sources 1 and 2 together, you can begin to develop an idea about the legal status of slaves in the later Roman Empire. What are some of the ways one could cross from slave to free? From free to slave? Is this a hard boundary, as the writers of the *Digest* imply in 2A, or are there intermediate steps? How do restrictions on slave/free sexual relationships help to maintain the boundaries? Why do you think there are gender differences in such restrictions? In what ways do the laws in 1D and 2D regard the slave as a thing? In what ways as a person?

Sources 3 through 7 are selections from Germanic law codes, which were often written down under the reign of one king and then expanded under his successors. Compared with Roman law, Germanic codes were extremely short and consist solely of statements of law, with no juristic opinions such as those contained in the *Digest.* They thus offer a less full picture of slave life than does Roman law, but slaves are mentioned in many of their clauses. In Germanic society, murder, injuries, or insults to honor had resulted in feuds between individuals and families, but by the time the law codes were written down, a system of monetary compensatory payments—called *wergeld* in the case of murder or *composition* in the case of lesser injuries—was being devised as a substitute. These compensatory payments were set according to the severity of the loss or injury, and also according to the social status of the perpetrator and the victim.

Source 3 comes from one of the earliest Germanic law codes, the Law of Gundobad, drawn up for his Burgundian subjects by King Gundobad (r. 474–516), who ruled the Burgundian kingdom in what is now southeastern France. (Following the principle that customary law applied to persons and not territories, Gundobad also drew up a separate code for his Roman subjects, the *Lex Romana Burgundionem*, at about the same time.) According to the laws in Source 3A, what were some of the ways in which one could become a slave or be freed if one were a slave? According to 3C, what were the penalties for rape of freewomen and slaves? For women who willingly had sexual relations with slaves? According to 3D, what was the relative value of slaves as compared to that of free persons and freedmen (former slaves), at least in regard to their teeth and female honor?

Source 4 comes from the Germanic tribe known as the Franks, who conquered the Burgundian kingdom in 534. The original Frankish code, the *Pactus Legis Salicae*, was issued by King Clovis in about 510 and was amended and revised by many of his successors. (Like all Germanic codes,

it did not apply to everyone living under Frankish overlordship; Burgundians living within the Frankish kingdom continued to be judged by Burgundian law for centuries after the conquest.) It includes no laws on how one becomes a slave or is released from slavery, but it does include sections on sexual relations with slaves, and on slaves who steal or run away. According to the laws in Source 4C, in the first group, what would happen to a freeman or freewoman who marries or has sexual intercourse with a slave? To a slave who marries or has sexual intercourse with a free person or another slave? According to 4D, how were the slave's owners' rights balanced against those of the person from whom the slave stole? How were those who encouraged slaves to run away to be punished? How does this punishment compare with that set for slaves who steal?

Source 5 contains selections from the Lombard Laws, written down between 643 and 755 under the direction of various Lombard kings, including King Rothair (issued in 643), King Luitprand (issued 713–735), and King Aistulf (issued 750–755). The Lombards invaded Italy in 568, after the Franks, Burgundians, and other tribes had already established successor kingdoms in parts of the old Roman Empire, and established a kingdom in central and northern Italy that lasted until 774, when it was conquered by the Frankish ruler Charlemagne. Like Burgundian law, Lombard law remained in force for Lombards within Frankish territory for centuries—in fact, until the city-states of Italy began to adopt Roman legal principles and the *Corpus Juris Civilis* in the twelfth century. Lombard law was more comprehensive than the Burgundian and Frankish codes, and included provisions regarding all of the issues we are investigating in this chapter. According to the laws in Source 5A, what were some of the ways in which a person could become a slave in Lombard society? How could a slave be freed? According to 5B, what was the relative value of slaves as compared to horses? According to 5C, how were marriages between slaves, freed persons, and free people to be handled? According to 5D, how were fugitive slaves and slaves who revolted to be handled?

Source 6 comes from the Germanic tribe known as the Alamans, who settled in what is now southern Germany and Switzerland in the third century A.D. and wrote their law codes between 613 and 713. Like other Germanic codes, Alamannic law set compensatory payments for various injuries and actions, and also used slavery as a punishment for certain crimes. According to Source 6A, what was one of the ways in which people could become slaves? According to 6B, were there limits on a master's treatment of slaves? According to 6C, what would happen to a freewoman who married a slave? According to 6D, what were the relative values placed on men and women from the three basic social groups, free persons, freedpersons, and slaves? How was the rape of slaves to be compensated?

Source 7, the final source for this chapter, contains provisions from Anglo-Saxon law codes from the various kingdoms of England, dating from the sixth through the tenth centuries. These codes were written in Old English, not in Latin, and show no signs of Roman influence, although many of their provisions are similar to those we have seen in other Germanic codes. According to Source 7A, laws issued by Edward the Elder (dated between 901 and 925), what was one way in which a person could become a slave? According to 7B, from the laws of Ine (688–695), what were some of the limitations on a master's treatment of his slaves? According to 7D, laws of Aethelbert of Kent (565–604) and Alfred (890–899), what was the punishment for rape of a slave? How did this differ depending on the status of the slave and the perpetrator?

You now need to put together the Germanic material in the same way that you did the Roman. How could people in Germanic society move from free to slave? From slave to free? Are there intermediate steps between these two, and how do the rights of these people differ from those of free people and slaves? What are the consequences of various types of slave/free sexual relationships? Are there hierarchies of status and value among slaves? On what are these based? Do the laws regarding crimes against slaves and crimes committed by slaves tend to view slaves as things or as persons?

Source 1 from Clyde Pharr, editor, The Theodosian Code *(Princeton, N.J.: Princeton University Press, 1952), Sections 3.3.1; 4.6.7; 5.6.3; 5.9.1; 7.13.16; 7.18.4; 9.12.1–2; 9.9.1–3, 6; 10.10.33; 14.18.1. Copyright © 1952 by Clyde Pharr, Princeton University Press. Renewed 1980 by Roy Pharr. Reprinted by permission of Princeton University Press.*

1. Theodosian Code

A. Slave to Free/Free to Slave

[3.3.1] All those persons whom the piteous fortune of their parents has consigned to slavery while their parents thereby were seeking sustenance shall be restored to their original status of free birth. Certainly no person shall demand repayment of the purchase price, if he has been compensated by the slavery of a freeborn person for a space of time that is not too short.

INTERPRETATION: If a father, forced by need, should sell any freeborn child whatsoever, the child cannot remain in perpetual slavery, but if he has made compensation by his slavery, he shall be restored to his freeborn status without even the repayment of the purchase price.

[4.6.7] We sanction that the name of natural children shall be placed upon those who have been begotten and brought into this world as the result of a lawful union without an honorable performance of the marriage ceremony. But it is established that children born from the womb of a slave woman are slaves, according to the law . . . [I]f natural children have been born from a slave woman and have not been manumitted by their master, they are reckoned among the slaves belonging to his inheritance.

[5.6.3] We have subjected the Scyrae, a barbarian nation, to Our power after We had routed a very great force of Chuni, with whom they had allied themselves. Therefore We grant to all persons the opportunity to supply their own fields with men of the aforesaid race.

[5.9.1] If any person should take up a boy or a girl child that has been cast out of its home with the knowledge and consent of its father or owner, and if he should rear this child to strength with his own sustenance, he shall have the right to keep the said child under the same status as he wished it to have when he took charge of it, that is, as his child or as a slave, whichever he should prefer.

[14.18.1] If there should be any persons who adopt the profession of mendicancy[1] and who are induced to seek their livelihood at public expense, each of

---

1. **mendicancy:** begging.

them shall be examined. The soundness of body and the vigor of years of each one of them shall be investigated. In the case of those who are able, the necessity shall be placed upon them that the zealous and diligent informer shall obtain the ownership of those beggars who are held bound by their servile status, and such informer shall be supported by the right to the perpetual colonate² of those beggars who are attended by only the liberty of their birth rights, provided that the informer should betray and prove such sloth.

[7.13.16] In the matter of defense against hostile attacks,³ We order that consideration be given not only to the legal status of soldiers, but also to their physical strength. Although We believe that freeborn persons are aroused by love of country, We exhort slaves⁴ also, by the authority of this edict, that as soon as possible they shall offer themselves for the labors of war, and if they receive their arms as men fit for military service, they shall obtain the reward of freedom, and they shall also receive two solidi each for travel money. Especially, of course, do We urge this service upon the slaves of those persons who are retained in the armed imperial service, and likewise upon the slaves of federated allies and of conquered peoples, since it is evident that they are making war also along with their masters.

[7.18.4] [In the case of deserters,] if a slave should surrender such deserter, he shall be given freedom. If a freeborn person of moderate status should surrender such deserter, he shall gain immunity.⁵

B. Value and Treatment of Slaves

[9.12.1–2] If a master should beat a slave with light rods or lashes or if he should cast him into chains for the purpose of custody, he shall not endure any fear of criminal charges if the slave should die, for We abolish all consideration of time limitations and legal interpretation.⁶ The master shall not, indeed, use his own right immoderately, but he shall be guilty of homicide if he should kill the slave voluntarily by a blow of a club or of a stone, at any rate if he should use a weapon and inflict a lethal wound or should order the slave to be hanged by a noose, or if he should command by a shameful order that he be thrown from a high place or should administer the virus of a poison or should lacerate his body by public punishments,⁷ that is, by cutting through

---

2. **colonate:** forced labor on farms.

3. At this time the Roman Empire was gradually crumbling from the attacks of the barbarians.

4. In violation of long-established Roman custom.

5. From compulsory public services, including taxes.

6. The references seem to be to preceding laws, which specified distinctions depending on whether a slave died immediately or after a period of time, and which contained various technicalities.

7. Types of punishment that were inflicted for certain public crimes.

his sides with the claws of wild beasts[8] or by applying fire and burning his body, or if with the savagery of monstrous barbarians he should force bodies and limbs weakening and flowing with dark blood, mingled with gore, to surrender their life almost in the midst of tortures.

Whenever such chance attends the beating of slaves by their masters that the slaves die, the masters shall be free from blame if by the correction of very evil deeds they wished to obtain better conduct on the part of their household slaves. . . .

INTERPRETATION: If a slave should die while his master is punishing a fault, the master shall not be held on the charge of homicide, because he is guilty of homicide only if he is convicted of having intended to kill the slave. For disciplinary correction is not reckoned as a crime.

C. Slave/Free Relations

[9.9.1–6] If any woman is discovered to have a clandestine love affair with her slave, she shall be subject to the capital sentence, and the rascally slave shall be delivered to the flames. All persons shall have the right to bring an accusation of this public crime; office staffs shall have the right to report it; even a slave shall have permission to lodge information, and freedom shall be granted to him if the crime is proved, although punishment threatens him if he makes a false accusation. 1. If a woman has been so married[9] before the issuance of this law, she shall be separated from such an association, shall be deprived not only of her home but also of participation in the life of the province, and shall mourn the absence of her exiled lover. 2. The children also whom she bears from this union shall be stripped of all the insignia of rank. They shall remain in bare freedom, and neither through themselves nor through the interposition of another person shall they receive anything under any title of a will from the property of the woman. 3. Moreover, the inheritance of the woman, in case of intestacy, shall be granted either to her children, if she has legitimate ones, or to the nearest kinsmen and cognates, or to the person whom the rule of law admits, so that whatever of their own property her former lover and the children conceived from him appear by any chance to have had shall be joined to the property of the woman and may be vindicated by the aforesaid successors. . . .

6. For after the issuance of this law We punish by death those persons who commit this crime. But those who have been separated in accordance with this

---

8. Implements of torture, actually made of metal.

9. A loose use of the word *marriage*, as slaves could not enter legally recognized marriages (*conubia*) because those were contracts available only to free persons. Instead they were joined in less formal unions termed *contubernia*.

law and secretly come together again and renew the forbidden union and who are convicted by the evidence of slaves or that of the office of the special investigator or also by the information of nearest kinsmen shall sustain a similar penalty.

INTERPRETATION: If any freeborn woman should join herself secretly to her own slave, she shall suffer capital punishment. A slave also who should be convicted of adultery with his mistress shall be burned by fire. Whoever wishes shall have it in his power to bring accusation of a crime of this kind. Even slaves or maidservants, if they should bring an accusation of this crime, shall be heard, on this condition, however, that they shall obtain their freedom if they prove their accusation; that if they falsify, they shall be punished. The inheritance of a woman who defiles herself with such a crime shall be granted either to her children, if they were conceived from her husband, or to those near kinsmen who succeed according to law.

[12.1.6] Although it appears unworthy for men, even though not endowed with any high rank, to descend to sordid marriages with slave women, nevertheless this practice is not prohibited by law; but a legal marriage cannot exist with servile persons, and from a slave union of this kind, slaves are born. We command, therefore, that decurions shall not be led by their lust to take refuge in the bosom of the most powerful houses. For if a decurion should be secretly united with any slave woman belonging to another man and if the overseers and procurators should not be aware of this, We order that the woman shall be cast into the mines through sentence of the judge, and the decurion himself shall be deported to an island; his movable property and his urban slaves shall be confiscated; his landed estates and rustic slaves shall be delivered to the municipality of which he had been a decurion, if he had been freed from paternal power and has no children or parents, or even close kinsmen, who may be called to his inheritance, according to the order of the law. But if the overseers or procurators of the place in which the disgraceful act was committed were aware of it and were unwilling to divulge this crime of which they were aware, they shall be cast into the mines. But if the master permitted such offense to be committed of afterwards learned of the deed and concealed it, and if indeed, it was perpetrated on his farm, the farm with the slaves and flocks and all other things which are used in rural cultivation shall be [confiscated].

D. Criminal Actions
by/toward Slaves

[10.10.33] The lawful distinction between slavery and freedom shall stand firm. We sanction the rights of masters by the restitution of their slaves, who shall not rebel with impunity.

Source 2 from S. P. Scott, translator, Corpus Juris Civilis: The Civil Law (Cincinnati, Ohio: The Central Trust, 1932), Sections 1.5.4–5; 9.2.2; 11.4.1; 29.5.1; 37.14.1, 19; 38.10.10; 40.1.5.

2. Selections from the *Digest* of Justinian's Code

A. *Slave to Free/Free to Slave*

[1.5.4] Liberty is the natural power of doing whatever anyone wishes to do unless he is prevented in some way, by force or by law.

(1) Slavery is an institution of the Law of Nations by means of which anyone may subject one man to the control of another, contrary to nature.

(2) Slaves are so called for the reason that military commanders were accustomed to sell their captives, and in this manner to preserve them, instead of putting them to death.

(3) They are styled *mancipia*, because they are taken by the hands [*manus*] of their enemies.

[1.5.5] One condition is common to all slaves; but of persons who are free some are born such, and others are manumitted.

(1) Slaves are brought under our ownership either by the Civil Law or by that of Nations. This is done by the Civil Law where anyone who is over twenty years of age permits himself to be sold for the sake of sharing in his own price. Slaves become our property by the Law of Nations when they are either taken from the enemy, or are born of our female slaves.

(2) Persons are born free who are born from a free mother, and it is sufficient for her to have been free at the time when her child was born, even though she may have been a slave when she conceived; and, on the other hand, if she was free when she conceived, and was a slave when she brought forth, it has been established that her child is born free, nor does it make any difference whether she conceived in a lawful marriage or through promiscuous intercourse; because the misfortune of the mother should not be a source of injury to her unborn child.

(3) Hence the following question arose, where a female slave who was pregnant, has been manumitted, and is afterwards again made a slave, or, after having been expelled from the city, should bring forth a child, whether that child should be free or a slave? It was very properly established that it was born free; and that it is sufficient for a child who is unborn that its mother should have been free during the intermediate time.

[40.1.5] If a slave should allege that he was purchased with his own money, he can appear in court against his master, whose good faith he impugns, and complain that he has not been manumitted by him; but he must do this at Rome, before the Urban Prefect, or in the provinces before the Governor, in accordance with the Sacred Constitutions of the Divine Brothers; under the penalty, however, of being condemned to the mines, if he should attempt this and not prove his case; unless his master prefers that he be restored to him, and then it should be decided that he will not be liable to a more severe penalty.

(1) Where, however, a slave is ordered to be free after having rendered his accounts, an arbiter between the slave and his master, that is to say, the heir, shall be appointed for the purpose of having the accounts rendered in his presence.

[37.14.1] Governors should hear the complaints of patrons against their freedmen, and their cases should be tried without delay; for if a freedman is ungrateful, he should not go unpunished. Where, however, the freedman fails in the duty which he owes to his patron, his patroness, or their children, he should only be punished lightly, with a warning that a more severe penalty will be imposed if he again gives cause for complaint, and then be dismissed. But if he is guilty of insult or abuse of his patrons, he should be sent into temporary exile. If he offers them personal violence, he must be sentenced to the mines.

[37.14.19] A freedman is ungrateful when he does not show proper respect for his patron, or refuses to manage his property, or undertake the guardianship of his children.

C. Slave/Free Relations

[38.10.10] We make use of this term, that is to say, cognates, even with reference to slaves. Therefore, we speak of the parents, the children, and the brothers of slaves; but cognation is not recognized by servile laws.

D. Criminal Actions
by/toward Slaves

[11.4.1] He who conceals a fugitive slave is a thief.

(1) The Senate decreed that fugitive slaves shall not be admitted on land or be protected by the superintendents or agents of the possessors of the same, and prescribed a fine. But, if anyone should, within twenty days, restore fugitive slaves to their owners, or bring them before magistrates, what they had previously done will be pardoned; but it was afterwards stated in the same Decree of the Senate that immunity is granted to anyone who restores fugitive slaves to their masters, or produces them before a magistrate within the prescribed time, when they are found on his premises. . . .

(4) And the magistrates are very properly notified to detain them carefully in custody to prevent their escape. . . .

(7) Careful custody permits the use of irons.

[9.2.2] It is provided by the first section of the *Lex Aquilia* that, "Where anyone unlawfully kills a male or female slave belonging to another, or a quadruped included in the class of cattle, let him be required to pay a sum equal to the greatest value that the same was worth during the past year."

[29.5.1] As no household can be safe unless slaves are compelled, under peril of their lives, to protect their masters, not only from persons belonging to his family, but also from strangers, certain decrees of the Senate were enacted with reference to putting to public torture all the slaves belonging to a household in case of the violent death of their master . . . , for the reason that slaves are punished whenever they do not assist their master against anyone who is guilty of violence towards him, when they are able to do so. . . . Whenever slaves can afford assistance to their master, they should not prefer their own safety to his. Moreover, a female slave who is in the same room with her mistress can give her assistance, if not with her body, certainly by crying out, so that those who are in the house or the neighbors can hear her; and this is evident even if she should allege that the murderer threatened her with death if she cried out. She ought, therefore, to undergo capital punishment, to prevent other slaves from thinking that they should consult their own safety when their master is in danger.

Source 3 from Katherine Fischer Drew, translator, The Burgundian Code *(Philadelphia: University of Pennsylvania Press, 1972), Sections 26, 30, 33, 35, 88, Constitutiones Extravagantes 21.9. Copyright © University of Pennsylvania Press. Reprinted by permission of the publisher.*

3. Selections from
The Burgundian Code

A. Slave to Free/Free to Slave

[Constitutiones Extravagantes, 21.9] If anyone shall buy another's slave from the Franks, let him prove with suitable witnesses how much and what sort of price he paid and when witnesses have been sworn in, they shall make oath in the following manner: "We saw him pay the price in our presence, and he who purchased the slave did not do so through any fraud or connivance with the enemy." And if suitable witnesses shall give oaths in this manner, let him receive back only the price which he paid; and let him not seek back the cost of support and let him return the slave without delay to his former owner.

[88] Since the title of emancipation takes precedence over the law of possession, great care must be exercised in such matters. And therefore it should be observed, that if anyone wishes to manumit a slave, he may do so by giving him his liberty through a legally competent document; or if anyone wishes to give freedom to a bondservant without a written document, let the manumis-

sion thus conferred by confirmed with the witness of not less than five or seven native freemen, because it is not fitting to present a smaller number of witnesses than is required when the manumission is in written form.

C. Slave/Free Relations

[30] OF WOMEN VIOLATED.

1. Whatever native freeman does violence to a maidservant, and force can be proved, let him pay twelve solidi to him to whom the maidservant belongs.
2. If a slave does this, let him receive a hundred fifty blows.

[35] OF THE PUNISHMENT OF SLAVES WHO COMMIT A CRIMINAL ASSAULT ON FREEBORN WOMEN.

1. If any slave does violence to a native freewoman, and if she complains and is clearly able to prove this, let the slave be killed for the crime committed.
2. If indeed a native free girl unites voluntarily with a slave, we order both to be killed.
3. But if the relatives of the girl do not wish to punish their own relative, let the girl be deprived of her free status and delivered into servitude to the king.

D. Criminal Actions by/toward Slaves

[26] OF KNOCKING OUT TEETH.

1. If anyone by chance strikes out the teeth of a Burgundian of the highest class, or of a Roman noble, let him be compelled to pay fifteen solidi.
2. For middle-class freeborn people, either Burgundian or Roman, if a tooth is knocked out, let composition be made in the sum of ten solidi.
3. For persons of the lowest class, five solidi.
4. If a slave voluntarily strikes out the tooth of a native freeman, let him be condemned to have a hand cut off; if the loss which has been set forth above has been committed by accident, let him pay the price for the tooth according to the status of the person.
5. If any native freeman strikes out the tooth of a freedman, let him pay him three solidi. If he strikes out the tooth of another's slave, let him pay two solidi to him to whom the slave belongs.

[33] OF INJURIES WHICH ARE SUFFERED BY WOMEN.

1. If any native freewoman has her hair cut off and is humiliated without cause (when innocent) by any native freeman in her home or on the road, and

this can be proved with witnesses, let the doer of the deed pay her twelve solidi, and let the amount of the fine be twelve solidi.

2. If this was done to a freedwoman, let him pay her six solidi.

3. If this was done to a maidservant, let him pay her three solidi, and let the amount of the fine be three solidi.

4. If this injury (shame, disgrace) is inflicted by a slave on a native freewoman, let him receive two hundred blows; if a freedwoman, let him receive a hundred blows; if a maidservant, let him receive seventy-five blows.

5. If indeed the woman whose injury we have ordered to be punished in this manner commits fornication voluntarily (i.e., if she yields), let nothing be sought for the injury suffered.

Source 4 from Katherine Fischer Drew, translator, The Laws of the Salian Franks *(Philadelphia: University of Pennsylvania Press, 1991), Sections 25, 39, 40, 98. Copyright © 1991 University of Pennsylvania Press. Reprinted by permission of the publisher.*

4. Selections from Salic Law

C. Slave/Free Relations

[25] ON HAVING INTERCOURSE WITH SLAVE GIRLS OR BOYS

1. The freeman who has intercourse with someone else's slave girl, and it is proved against him . . . , shall be liable to pay six hundred denarii (i.e., fifteen solid[i]) to the slave girl's lord.

2. The man who has intercourse with a slave girl belonging to the king and it is proved against him . . . , shall be liable to pay twelve hundred denarii (i.e., thirty solidi).

3. The freeman who publicly joins himself with (i.e., marries) another man's slave girl, shall remain with her in servitude.

4. And likewise the free woman who takes someone else's slave in marriage shall remain in servitude.

5. If a slave has intercourse with the slave girl of another lord and the girl dies as a result of this crime, the slave himself shall pay two hundred forty denarii (i.e., six solidi) to the girl's lord or he shall be castrated; the slave's lord shall pay the value of the girl to her lord.

6. If the slave girl has not died . . . , the slave shall receive three hundred lashes or, to spare his back, he shall pay one hundred twenty denarii (i.e., three solidi) to the girl's lord.

7. If a slave joins another man's slave girl to himself in marriage without the consent of her lord . . . , he shall be lashed or clear himself by paying one hundred twenty denarii (i.e., three solidi) to the girl's lord.

[98] CONCERNING THE WOMAN WHO JOINS HERSELF TO HER SLAVE

1. If a woman joins herself in marriage with her own slave, the fisc[10] shall acquire all her possessions and she herself will be outlawed.

2. If one of her relatives kills her, nothing may be required from that relative or the fisc for her death. The slave shall be placed in the most severe torture, that is, he shall be placed on the wheel. And if one of the relatives of the woman gives her either food or shelter, he shall be liable to pay fifteen solidi.

D. Criminal Actions
by/toward Slaves

[40] CONCERNING THE SLAVE ACCUSED OF THEFT

1. In the case where a slave is accused of theft, if [it is a case where] a freeman would pay six hundred denarii (i.e., fifteen solidi) in composition, the slave stretched on a rack shall receive one hundred twenty blows of the lash.

2. If he [the slave] confesses before torture and it is agreeable to the slave's lord, he may pay one hundred twenty denarii (i.e., three solidi) for his back [i.e., to avoid the lashes]; and the slave's lord shall return the value of the property stolen to its owner. . . .

4. . . . If indeed he [the slave] confessed in the earlier torture, i.e., before the one hundred twenty lashes were completed, let him [the slave] be castrated or pay two hundred forty denarii (i.e., six solidi); the lord should restore the value of the property stolen to its owner.

5. If he [the slave] is guilty of a crime for which a freeman or a Frank would be liable to pay eight thousand denarii (i.e., two hundred solidi), let the slave compound fifteen solidi (i.e., six hundred denarii). If indeed the slave is guilty of a more serious offense—one for which a freeman would be liable to pay eighteen hundred denarii (i.e., forty-five solidi)—and the slave confessed during torture, he shall be subjected to capital punishment. . . .

11. If indeed it is a female slave accused of an offense for which a male slave would be castrated, then she should be liable to pay two hundred forty denarii (i.e., six solidi)—if it is agreeable for her lord to pay this—or she should be subjected to two hundred forty lashes.

[39] ON THOSE WHO INSTIGATE SLAVES TO RUN AWAY

1. If a man entices away the bondsmen of another man and this is proved against him . . . , he shall be liable to pay six hundred denarii (i.e., fifteen solidi) [in addition to return of the bondsmen plus a payment for the time their labor was lost] .

---

10. **fisc:** king's treasury.

Source 5 from Katherine Fischer Drew, translator, The Lombard Laws *(Philadelphia: University of Pennsylvania Press, 1973), Sections Rothair 156, 217, 221, 222, 267, 280, 333, 334; Luitprand 55, 63, 80, 140, 152. Copyright © 1973 University of Pennsylvania Press. Reprinted with permission of the publisher.*

5. Selections from
Lombard Laws

A. Slave to Free/Free to Slave

[Rothair 156] In the case of a natural son who is born to another man's woman slave, if the father purchases him and gives him his freedom by the formal procedure . . . , he shall remain free. But if the father does not free him, the natural son shall be a slave to him to whom the mother slave belongs.

[Luitprand 63] He who renders false testimony against anyone else, or sets his hand knowingly to a false charter, and this fraud becomes evident, shall pay his wergeld as composition,[11] half to the king and half to him whose case it is. If the guilty party does not have enough to pay the composition, a public official ought to hand him over as a slave to him who was injured, and he [the offender] shall serve him as a slave.

[Luitprand 80] In connection with thieves, each judge shall make a prison underground in his district. When a thief has been found, he shall pay composition for his theft, and then the judge shall seize him and put him in prison for two or three years, and afterwards shall set him free.

If the thief is such a person that he does not have enough to pay the composition for theft, the judge ought to hand him over to the man who suffered the theft, and that one may do with him as he pleases.

If afterwards the thief is taken again in theft, he [the judge] shall shave . . . and beat him for punishment as befits a thief, and shall put a brand on his forehead and face. If the thief does not correct himself and if after such punishment he has again been taken in theft, then the judge shall sell him outside the province, and the judge shall have his sale price provided, nevertheless, that it be a proved case for the judge ought not to sell the man without certain proof.

[Luitprand 152] If the man who is prodigal or ruined, or who has sold or dissipated his substance, or for other reasons does not have that with which to pay composition, commits theft or adultery or a breach of the peace . . . or injures another man and the composition for this is twenty solidi or more, then a public representative ought to hand him over as a slave to the man who suffered such illegal acts.

11. **composition:** restitution.

[Luitprand 55] If anyone makes his slave folkfree and legally independent . . . or sets him free from himself in any manner by giving him into the hand of the king or by leading him before the altar of a church, and if afterwards that freedman [continues] to serve at the will of his patron, the freedman ought at frequent intervals to make clear his liberty to the judge and to his neighbors and [remind them] of the manner in which he was freed.

Afterward the patron or his heirs may at no time bring complaints against him who was freed by saying that because [he continues to serve] he ought still to obey, for it was only on account of the goodness of his lord that the former slave continued to serve his commands of his own free will. He shall remain permanently free.

[Luitprand 140] If a freeman has a man and woman slave, or aldius and aldia,[12] who are married, and, inspired by hatred of the human race, he has intercourse with that woman whose husband is the slave or with the aldia whose husband is the aldius, he has committed adultery and we decree that he shall lose that slave or aldius with whose wife he committed adultery and the woman as well. They shall go free where they wish and shall be as much folkfree . . . as if they had been released by the formal procedure for alienation . . .—for it is not pleasing to God that any man should have intercourse with the wife of another.

B. Value and Treatment of Slaves

[Rothair 333] On mares in foal. He who strikes a mare in foal and causes a miscarriage shall pay one solidus as composition. If the mare dies, he shall pay as above for it and its young.

[Rothair 334] On pregnant woman slaves. He who strikes a woman slave large with child and causes a miscarriage shall pay three solidi as composition. If, moreover, she dies from the blow, he shall pay composition for her and likewise for the child who died in her womb.

C. Slave/Free Relations

[Rothair 217] On the aldia who marries a slave. The aldia or freedwoman who enters another man's house to a husband and marries a slave shall lose her liberty. But if the husband's lord neglects to reduce her to servitude, then when her husband dies she may go forth together with her children and all the property which she brought with her when she came to her husband. But

12. **aldius** and **aldia:** freedman and freedwoman.

she shall have no more than this as an indication of her mistake in marrying a slave.

[Rothair 221] The slave who dares to marry a free woman or girl shall lose his life. With regard to the woman who consented to a slave, her relatives have the right to kill her or to sell her outside the country and to do what they wish with her property. And if her relatives delay in doing this, then the king's gastald or schultheis[13] shall lead her to the king's court and place her there in the women's apartments among the female slaves.

[Rothair 222] On marrying one's own woman slave. If any man wishes to marry his own woman slave, he may do so. Nevertheless he ought to free her, that is, make her worthy born . . . , and he ought to do it legally by the proper formal procedure. . . . She shall then be known as a free and legal wife and her children may become the legal heirs of their father.

D. Criminal Actions
by/toward Slaves

[Rothair 267] The boatman who knowingly transports fugitive bondsmen, and it is proved, shall search for them and return them together with any properties taken with them to their proper owner. If the fugitives have gone elsewhere and cannot be found, then the value of those bondsmen together with the sworn value of the property which they carried with them shall be paid by that ferryman who knowingly transported the fugitives. In addition, the ferryman shall pay twenty solidi as composition to the king's fisc.

[Rothair 280] On seditious acts committed by field slaves. If, for any reason, rustics[14] . . . associate together for plotting or committing seditious acts such as, when a lord is trying to take a bondsman or animal from his slave's house, blocking the way or taking the bondsman or animal, then he who was at the head of these rustics shall either be killed or redeem his life by the payment of a composition equal to that amount at which he is valued. And each of those who participated in this evil sedition shall pay twelve solidi as composition, half to the king and half to him who bore the injury or before whom he presumed to place himself. And if that one who was trying to take his property endures blows or suffers violence from these rustics, composition for such blows or violence shall be paid to him just as is stated above, and the rustics shall suffer such punishment as is noted above for this presumption. If one of the rustics is killed no payment shall be required because he who killed him did it while defending himself and in protecting his own property.

13. **gastald** and **schultheis:** royal officials.
14. **rustics:** field slaves.

Source 6 from Theodore John Rivers, translator, Laws of the Alamans and Bavarians *(Philadelphia: University of Pennsylvania Press, 1977), Alamannic Law, Sections 17, 18, 37, 39, 75. Copyright © 1977 University of Pennsylvania Press. Reprinted by permission of the publisher.*

6. Laws of the Alamans

A. *Slave to Free/Free to Slave*

[39] We prohibit incestuous marriages. Accordingly, it is not permitted to have as wife a mother-in-law, daughter-in-law, step-daughter, step-mother, brother's daughter, sister's daughter, brother's wife, or wife's sister. Brother's children and sister's children are under no pretext to be joined together. If anyone acts against this, let them [the married pair] be separated by the judges in that place, and let them lose all their property, which the public treasury shall acquire. If there are lesser persons who pollute themselves through an illicit union, let them lose their freedom; let them be added to the public slaves.

B. *Value and Treatment of Slaves*

[37] 1. Let no one sell slaves . . . outside the province, whether among pagans or Christians, unless it is done by the order of the duke.

C. *Slave/Free Relations*

[17] 1. Concerning maidservants.[15] If a freewoman was manumitted by a charter or in a church, and after this she married a slave, let her remain permanently a maidservant of the church.

2. If, however, a free Alamannic woman marries a church slave and refuses the servile work of a maidservant, let her depart. If, however, she gives birth to sons or daughters there, let them remain slaves and maidservants permanently, and let them not have the right of departure.

D. *Criminal Actions by/toward Slaves*

[18] 1. Concerning waylayers . . . , [if a man blocks the way of a freeman] , let him pay six solidi.

2. If it is a freedman [who is blocked] , let the perpetrator pay four solidi.

3. If it is a slave, three solidi.

4. If he does this to a free Alamannic woman, let him compensate with twelve solidi.

15. **maidservants:** here, female slaves.

5. If it is a freedwoman, let him compensate with eight solidi.

6. If it is a maidservant, let him pay four solidi.

7. If a man seizes her hair, [let him compensate similarly].

[75] 1. If anyone lies with another's chambermaid against her will, let him compensate with six solidi.

2. And if anyone lies with the first maid of the textile workshop against her will, let him compensate with six solidi.

3. If anyone lies with other maids of the textile workshop against their will, let him compensate with three solidi.

Source 7 from F. L. Attenborough, editor, Laws of the Earliest English Kings, *Laws of Edward the Elder, Section 6; Laws of Ine, Section 3. Laws of Aethelbert, Sections 10, 11, 16; Laws of Alfred, Section 25.*

7. Laws of Anglo-Saxon Kings

A. Slave to Free/Free to Slave

[Edward the Elder 6] If any man, through [being found guilty of] an accusation of stealing, forfeits his freedom and gives up his person to his lord, and his kinsmen forsake him, and he knows no one who will make legal amends for him, he shall do such servile labour as may be required, and his kinsmen shall have no right to his wergeld [if he is slain].

B. Value and Treatment of Slaves

[Ine 3] If a slave works on Sunday by his lord's command, he shall become free, and the lord shall pay a fine of 30 shillings.

§1. If, however, the slave works without the cognisance of his master, he shall undergo the lash or pay the fine in lieu thereof.

§2. If, however, a freeman works on that day, except by his lord's command, he shall be reduced to slavery, or [pay a fine of] 60 shillings. A priest shall pay a double fine.

D. Criminal Actions
by/toward Slaves

[Aethelbert 10] If a man lies with a maiden belonging to the king, he shall pay 50 shillings compensation.

[Aethelbert 11] If she is a grinding slave, he shall pay 25 shillings compensation. [If she is of the] third [class], [he shall pay] 12 shillings compensation.

[Aethelbert 16] If a man lies with a commoner's serving maid, he shall pay 6 shillings compensation; [if he lies] with a slave of the second class, [he shall pay] 50 sceattas[16] [compensation] ; if with one of the third class, 30 sceattas.

[Alfred 25] If anyone rapes the slave of a commoner, he shall pay 5 shillings to the commoner, and a fine of 60 shillings.[17]
   §1. If a slave rapes a slave, castration shall be required as compensation.

16. 20 sceattas = one shilling.
17. The 60 shillings went to the king's treasury.

QUESTIONS TO CONSIDER

The central questions for this chapter ask you to do two things: investigate the boundaries between slave and free in various law codes, and then compare these issues in Roman and Germanic cultures. Your answers to the second question are based, of course, on your answers to the first, and the Sources and Method section suggests some of the questions you might ask yourself about slave law in each of these two cultures.

In addition to these, in the Roman codes, what role does military conquest play in the determination of slave and free? Does conquest simply provide slaves, or does it also offer them opportunities? What limitations were placed on a male owner's treatment of his slaves? On a female owner's treatment of her slaves? What obligations does—or could—the status of freedman or freedwoman entail? Do these obligations make this status appear closer to that of a slave or that of a free person? How are family relationships among slaves regarded legally? The provi-sion in Justinian's Code (Source 2D) that slaves who did not prevent a master's being killed were to be killed themselves may seem very harsh. Why do you think this was part of Roman slave law? What other provisions strike you as especially harsh, and why might these have been enacted? Given the role of slavery in the Roman economy, why were there such strong provisions about runaway slaves? Other than the restrictions on those who aided runaways, what laws discuss actions by those who were neither owners nor slaves? How might these have shaped general attitudes toward slavery and slaves?

Turning now to the Germanic codes, what are the hierarchies you find among slaves based on? Given the nature of Germanic society, in which tribes often moved around a great deal, why do you think there was so much concern about not taking slaves away to other areas, even if it was their owners who were taking them? Historians often point out the importance of personal honor in Germanic societies. Do you find evidence of this? Do slaves have honor?

Do any of their actions affect the honor of others in ways that the actions of free people do not? A close examination of the laws indicates that the only nonpunishable sexual relation between slave and free was a man marrying his own slave among the Lombards, mentioned in Source 5C. Why do you think this was allowed? What must a man do before he does this, and why do you think this was important?

You are now ready to investigate some comparative questions: In what ways do the different notions of the law in Roman and Germanic cultures—territorial versus personal, statutory versus traditional—emerge in laws regarding slavery? When comparing Germanic culture to Roman, historians often point to the relative propensity to interpersonal violence and the importance of the family among the Germans. Do the laws regarding slavery from these two cultures provide evidence of these factors? What evidence do you see of the different economic structures in the two cultures, i.e., of the greater complexity of the Roman economic system?

Comparing two cultures involves exploring continuities along with contrasts. One of the issues in slave systems was how to punish slaves without harming their owners. How do the laws handle this? Do you see much difference between Roman and Germanic cultures in this? How do the laws handle the issue that slaves do not own property? How are the actions and obligations of freed slaves toward their former masters handled in both cultures? Why do you think it was important in both cultures to have an intermediate status between slave and free? Do you see much difference with regard to laws concerning sexual relations between slaves and free in the two cultures? Why might there have been continuity in this?

After putting all of this material together, you are now ready to answer the central questions for this chapter: How were legal distinctions between slave and free established, structured, and maintained, and how could they be overcome? What similarities and differences are there in Roman and Germanic law regarding slavery?

EPILOGUE

During the Renaissance, scholars and thinkers began to divide the history of Europe into three stages, ancient, medieval, and modern, a division that has persisted until today. They viewed the end of the Roman Empire as a dramatic break in history, and

saw the Germanic successor states as sharply different from Rome. This view is increasingly being modified today as historians point to a number of continuities between late ancient and early medieval society.

As you have discovered in this chapter, the slave system was one of those continuities, for slavery did not disappear from the European scene with the fall of Rome, nor did the spread of Christianity lead to an end of slavery. (Christianity did not oppose slavery on moral grounds, although it did praise those who chose to free their slaves and pushed for slaves being allowed to marry in legally binding ceremonies.) Gradually, however, more people came to occupy the intermediate stage between slave and free that you have seen in these laws, which became known as serfdom. Serfdom was a legal condition in which people were personally free—not owned by another individual as slaves were—but were bound to the land, unable to move and owing labor obligations to their lord. For former slaves, serfdom was a step up; for others, however, it was a step down, for the bulk of the serfs in Europe probably came from families that had originally been free peasants, but had traded their labor and freedom to move in return for protection. In any case, serfdom did not immediately replace slavery; both continued side by side for centuries, and the laws you have seen here regarding slaves often shaped later laws regarding serfs. Law codes alone, of course, cannot tell us about relative numbers of slaves or serfs, and they sometimes hide major changes. The transformation of slave to serf was so gradual that it occasioned little comment in the codes, which had, as we have seen, long included discussion of intermediate stages between slave and free and of hierarchies among slaves.

The laws you have seen here also had great influence beyond Europe.

As you have discovered, Germanic law did not break sharply with Roman on many issues regarding slavery, indicating that Justinian's Code probably influenced some early medieval Germanic codes. Justinian's Code was also rediscovered in western Europe in the eleventh century, and became the basis of legal education at the law schools that were established in southern Europe in the twelfth century. It influenced national and local codes in this era of expanding states and growing cities, and ultimately all of the legal systems of western Europe except for that of England became based on Roman law. When Portugal and Spain set up slave systems extending into the New World, Roman law was the basis of many provisions regarding slavery. Thus, two of the New World's most heavily slave societies—the French Caribbean and Brazil—based their systems on Roman law.

The other slave societies in the New World—the British Caribbean and the southern United States before the Civil War—did not base their laws as directly on those of Rome, but their laws did grow out of Germanic codes such as those you have seen here. Though these systems were different from the Roman and Germanic systems in that slavery came to be based on race, many of the laws—those concerning owners' freedom to treat slaves as they wished, sexual relations between slave and free, punishment of those who aided runaway slaves—were remarkably similar. Once slavery came to be racially based, however, the permeable boundary between slave and free that you have traced in this chapter, with slavery not necessarily being a permanent status, became much harder to cross. Poverty, begging, theft, debt, capture in war, false testimony, or incest did not make a white person a slave, nor did turning in deserters, marriage to an owner, or—except in rare instances—military service make a black person free.

CHAPTER SEVEN

THE DEVELOPMENT OF

THE MEDIEVAL STATE

THE PROBLEM

The governments of medieval Europe are generally described as "feudal," a word that perhaps confuses more than it clarifies. The term "feudalism" was unknown in the Middle Ages; it was invented only later to describe the medieval system of landholding and government. Used correctly, *feudalism* denotes a system of reciprocal rights and obligations, in which individuals who fought (knights) promised their loyalty, aid, and assistance to a king or other powerful noble, becoming what were termed *vassals* of that lord. The lord in turn promised his vassals protection and material support, which in the Early Middle Ages was often board and room in the lord's own household. As their vassals became more numerous or lived farther away, lords increasingly gave them grants of land as recompense for their allegiance. This piece of land, termed a *fief* (*feudum* in Latin), theoretically still belonged to the lord, with the vassal obtaining only the use of it. Thus feudalism involved a mixture of personal and property ties. Unlike the systems of property ownership in the Roman Empire or most modern governments, it did not involve any ties to an abstract state or governmental system, but was simply a personal agreement between individuals.

Because this promise of allegiance and support could be made only by free individuals, the serfs who were tied to the land were not actually part of the feudal system. In the economic structure of medieval Europe, estates or *manors* of various sizes were worked by slaves, serfs, and free peasants. The whole economic system is termed *manorialism.* Fiefs were generally made up of manors and included the peasants who lived on them, but *manorialism* and *feudalism* are not synonymous.

Though serfs were not included in the feudal system, church officials were. Rulers rewarded church officials with fiefs for their spiritual services or promises of allegiance. In addition, the Church held pieces of land on its own, and granted fiefs in return for promises of assistance from knightly vassals. Abbots and abbesses of monasteries, bishops, and archbishops were either lords[1] or vassals in many feudal arrangements. In addition, both secular and clerical vassals further subdivided their fiefs, granting land to people who became their vassals, a process known as *subinfeudation*. Thus the same person could be a lord in one relationship and a vassal in another.

This system could easily become chaotic, particularly as it was easy to forget, once a family had held a piece of land for several generations, that the land actually belonged to the lord. This is more or less what happened from 700 until 1050, with political power becoming completely decentralized and vassals ruling their fiefs quite independently. About 1050 this began to change, however, and rulers started to manipulate feudal institutions to build up rather than diminish their power.

The rulers of England after the Norman Conquest in 1066 were particularly successful at manipulating feudal institutions to build up their own power. William the Conqueror (1066–1087) and Henry II (1154–1189) dramatically increased royal authority, as did later rulers of France, especially Philip II Augustus (1180–1223), and of Germany, especially

Frederick Barbarossa (1152–1190). Gradually the feudal system was transformed into one that is sometimes termed *feudal monarchy*. Because monarchs in the High Middle Ages had so much more power than they had had in the Early Middle Ages, however, some historians no longer term such governments feudal at all, but simply monarchies, and see in them the origins of the modern state.

In asserting their power, the rulers of western Europe had to suppress or limit the independent powers of two groups in medieval society—their noble vassals and church officials. The challenge provided by each group was somewhat different. Noble vassals often had their own armies, and the people living on their fiefs were generally more loyal to them than to any faraway ruler. During the period before the mid-eleventh century, vassals often supervised courts, which heard cases and punished crimes, and regarded themselves as the supreme legal authority in their fief. Though they were vassals of the ruler, church officials also owed allegiance to an independent, international power—the papacy in Rome. Throughout the Middle Ages, the pope and higher church officials claimed that all church personnel, down to village priests and monks, were not subject to any secular legal jurisdiction, including that of a ruler. They also argued that the spiritual hierarchy of Western Christianity, headed by the pope, was elevated by God over all secular hierarchies, so that every ruler was subject to papal authority.

1. Because abbesses and, in some parts of Europe, noblewomen who inherited land could grant fiefs and have vassals, the word "lord" in the context of feudalism did not always mean a man. It simply means "the person who holds the rights of lordship."

In this chapter we will be exploring the ways in which medieval monarchs asserted their authority over their vassals and the Church. We will use both visual and written evidence in answering the question, How did the rulers of the High Middle Ages overcome challenges to their power and begin the process of recentralization of power?

SOURCES AND METHOD

Traditionally, political history has been seen as the history of politics, and has used as its sources laws, decrees, parliamentary debates, and other written documents that give information about political changes. These are still important, but recently political history has been seen more broadly as the history not only of politics but of all relations involving power, and a wider range of sources is now used to understand the power relationships in past societies. Picking up techniques from anthropologists, political historians now use objects as well as written documents to explore the ways in which power is externally expressed and symbolized as well as the ways in which it is manipulated in relationships. The rulers of medieval western Europe were aware of the power of symbols, and along with actual military and legal moves to increase their authority, they also demonstrated that authority symbolically.

A symbol is basically something that stands for something else, that has a meaning beyond the actual object or words. Symbols can be used consciously or unconsciously, and can be interpreted differently by different observers or readers. Anthropologists have pointed out that symbols can often be read at many different levels, so understanding them in all their meanings can be very complicated. The symbols we will be looking at here are less complicated than many, however, because they were consciously employed by rulers and officials who wanted to be very sure that their correct meaning was understood. Since many of the observers were not highly educated or even literate, rulers chose simple symbols and repeated them so that their meaning would certainly be grasped. Because many of these symbols have much the same meaning to us today, you will find them easier to analyze than the symbols from unfamiliar cultures that are often the focus of anthropologists' studies. As we explore the ways in which rulers asserted their authority, then, we must keep in mind both the tactical and the symbolic impact of their actions.

The first four sources all provide evidence of one of the ways in which William the Conqueror and his successors gained power over the English nobility. Source 1 is from a history of England written in the early twelfth century by Ordericus Vitalis, a monk who was half Anglo-Saxon and half Norman. The author provides a relatively objective account of William's reign, and here describes how William subdued one of the many rebellions against him. Read the selection carefully. Rather than simply sending out armies, what does William do to establish royal power? Why does Ordericus feel this was effective in ending the rebellion?

Visual depictions of Norman castles may help you judge whether Ordericus's opinion about their importance was valid, so turn to the next three sources. Sources 2 and 3 are photographs of castles built by English kings. The first was begun at Richmond in 1089, and the second was built at Harlech between 1283 and 1290. Source 4 is a map of all the castles built in England by William the Conqueror during his reign, from 1066 to 1087. Many of these were wooden fortifications rather than the enormous stone castles shown in Sources 2 and 3, but William's successors expanded these simpler castles into larger stone ones as quickly as time and resources permitted. As you look at these, try to imagine yourself as a vassal or subject confronted by castles that looked like these in all the places you see on the map. What message would you get about the power of the king? What strategic value is gained by placing a castle on a hill? How would this also increase the castle's symbolic value? What other features of the castles depicted increase either their strategic value as fortresses or their symbolic value? The map indicates that the castles built by William were not evenly distributed. Given what your text tells you about the Norman Conquest and the problems that William faced, why

might he have built his castles where he did? Does this pattern of castle building surprise you? (A clue here is to keep in mind that castles are both symbols of power and a means to enforce that power, and that these castles may not all have been built for the same reason.)

Source 5 provides evidence of another way in which William and his successors both gained and demonstrated authority over their vassals. It is an excerpt from *The Anglo-Saxon Chronicle* describing William's requirement in 1086 that all vassals swear loyalty to him in what became known as the Salisbury Oath. Rulers such as William recognized that people regarded oaths as very serious expressions of their duties as Christians, and so they required their vassals to swear allegiance regularly in person in ceremonies of *homage* (allegiance) and *fealty* (loyalty). They expanded the ceremonies of knighthood, impressing on young knights their duties of obedience and loyalty. After you read this short selection, think about how the fact that the vassals had to leave their fiefs to swear the Oath might have also helped increase royal power.

After William, Henry II was the most innovative fashioner of royal power in medieval England. In 1166, he issued the Assize[2] of Clarendon (the location of the king's hunting lodge), which set up inquest juries to report to the king's sheriff or traveling judges the name of anyone suspected of having committed a major crime. Source 6 gives you some of the

2. **assize:** a decree made by an assembly.

clauses from the Assize of Clarendon. As you read it, note the ways in which the independent powers of the vassals in their territories are restricted. Who does it state is the ultimate legal authority? Who gains financially from these provisions?

Henry II directly limited not only the legal power of his vassals, but also that of the Church in England. Two years before the Assize of Clarendon, he issued the Constitutions of Clarendon, which purported to be a codification of existing practices governing relations between the Church and the state. Source 7 is an extract from this document. Read it carefully, noting first under whose authority Henry issues it. Who does he say has agreed to its provisions? How do these provisions limit the legal power of the Church over its own clergy? Over laypeople? What role is the king to play in the naming of church officials? In hearing cases involving clergy? How are church officials to be reminded of their duties as the king's vassals?

The Constitutions of Clarendon are perhaps the strongest statement of the power of a secular ruler over the Church to emerge from the Middle Ages, and, as we will see in the epilogue to this chapter, they were quickly opposed by the Church. This was not the only time a ruler asserted his power over the Church, however, for on the Continent German kings and emperors also claimed extensive powers over all aspects of church life up to and including the papacy. Source 8 gives an example of this assertion of power. It is a selection from the biography of the German emperor

Frederick Barbarossa (1152–1190), begun by Bishop Otto of Freising. Otto was Frederick's uncle, so although he was a bishop of the Church, he was quite favorably inclined toward the emperor. In this selection, Otto describes Frederick's coronation and some later responses by the emperor to papal ambassadors. What roles do church officials play in Frederick's coronation? What does Otto view as a further symbol of Frederick's right to rule? What role does Otto report that the pope claimed to have played in granting Frederick power? What, in contrast to this, does Frederick view as the source of his authority? What does he see to be his religious duties as emperor?

Along with actions such as constructing castles or requiring oaths of loyalty, both of which combined tactical with symbolic assertions of power, medieval rulers also demonstrated their power over vassals and the Church in purely symbolic ways. The final sources in this chapter provide examples of some of these. Source 9 is a description of the coronation ceremony of Richard the Lionhearted, Henry II's son, in 1189. More than the much shorter description of Frederick Barbarossa's coronation, which you have already read, it gives evidence of the way in which kings and other territorial rulers expanded their coronation ceremonies, turning them into long, spectacular celebrations of royal wealth and power. As you read it, look first for things that symbolize power relationships. What titles are used to describe the participants? What objects are used in the ceremonies?

Who is in attendance, and what roles do they play? What actions are required of the various participants, either during the ceremony or as part of their later duties?

Living in the media age as we do, we are certainly used to the manipulation of symbols to promote loyalty and allegiance. We may even be a bit jaded by flag-waving and military bands. Medieval people did not live in a world as full of visual stimulation, so the ceremonies surrounding a monarch were truly extraordinary.

Coronation ceremonies were rare events, and rulers also used symbols in more permanent visual demonstrations of their power, such as paintings and statuary, which they commissioned or which were designed in a way to gain their approval. The next three sources all depict rulers. Source 10 is a manuscript-illumination portrait of the German emperor Otto III (983–1002) seated on his throne. Source 11 is a section of the Bayeux tapestry showing on the left King Harold of England (1053–1066) seated on the throne. In the center, Englishmen acclaim him as king and point up to Halley's Comet (identified in the tapestry as a star). Because we no longer live in a world of royal authority, you may need some assistance in interpreting the meaning of the objects shown with the rulers, although medieval people would have understood them immediately. Many of these objects had both a secular and a religious meaning: the crown represented royal authority (the points symbolized the rays of the sun) and the crown of thorns worn by Jesus before the Crucifixion; the orb (the ball

surmounted by a cross) represented the ruler's domination of the land and protection of the Church; the scepter also represented Church and state power by being ornamented with both religious and secular designs. Seeing a monarch in full regalia or a portrait of a monarch would impress on anyone that this was not just the greatest of the nobles, but also someone considered sacred, whose authority was supported by Scripture. Monarchs also demonstrated the sacred aspects of their rule with purely religious symbols, such as crosses and chalices.

Now look carefully at the pictures. What symbols are used to depict the sources of royal authority? How do these communicate the ruler's secular and religious authority? What types of individuals are shown with the ruler? What does this indicate about the relationship between lord and vassal, and between Church and state? Why might the appearance of the heavenly body that came to be known as Halley's Comet have been viewed as an appropriate symbol of monarchy?

You have now examined evidence of a number of ways in which rulers increased their own authority, decreased that of their noble vassals and church officials, and expressed their greater power symbolically. As you assess how all of these helped rulers overcome challenges to their authority, it will be useful to recognize that symbols are not just passive reflections of existing power relationships, but are actively manipulated to build up or decrease power. Therefore it is often difficult to separate what we might term the real or tactical effect of an action or legal change from the symbolic. As you answer the central question in this chapter, then, think about the ways in which symbols and real change are interwoven.

Source 1 from Ordericus Vitalis, The Ecclesiastical History of England and Normandy, *trans. Thomas Forester (London: Henry G. Bohn, 1854). This source taken from a reprint of this edition (New York: AMS Press, 1968), vol. 2, pp. 17–20.*

1. From Ordericus Vitalis's *The Ecclesiastical History of England and Normandy*

The same year [1068], Edwin and Morcar, sons of Earl Algar, and young men of great promise, broke into open rebellion, and induced many others to fly to arms, which violently disturbed the realm of Albion.[3] King William, however, came to terms with Edwin, who assured him of the submission of his brother and of nearly a third of the kingdom, upon which the king promised to give him his daughter in marriage. Afterwards, however, by a fraudulent decision of the Normans, and through their envy and covetousness, the king refused to give him the princess who was the object of his desire, and for whom he had long waited. Being, therefore, much incensed, he and his brother again broke into rebellion, and the greatest part of the English and Welsh followed their standard. The two brothers were zealous in the worship of God, and respected good men. They were remarkably handsome, their relations were of high birth and very numerous, their estates were vast and gave them immense power, and their popularity great. The clergy and monks offered continual prayers on their behalf, and crowds of poor daily supplications. . . .

At the time when the Normans had crushed the English, and were overwhelming them with intolerable oppressions Blethyn, king of Wales, came to the aid of his uncles, at the head of a large body of Britons. A general assembly was now held of the chief men of the English and Welsh, at which universal complaints were made of the outrages and tyranny to which the English were subjected by the Normans and their adherents, and messengers

---

3. **Albion:** England.

were dispatched into all parts of Albion to rouse the natives against their enemies, either secretly or openly. All joined in a determined league and bold conspiracy against the Normans for the recovery of their ancient liberties. The rebellion broke out with great violence in the provinces beyond the Humber. The insurgents fortified themselves in the woods and marshes, on the estuaries, and in some cities. York was in a state of the highest excitement, which the holiness of its bishop was unable to calm. Numbers lived in tents, disdaining to dwell in houses lest they should become enervated; from which some of them were called savages by the Normans.

In consequence of these commotions, the king carefully surveyed the most inaccessible points in the country, and, selecting suitable spots, fortified them against the enemy's excursions. In the English districts there were very few fortresses, which the Normans call castles; so that, though the English were warlike and brave, they were little able to make a determined resistance. One castle the king built at Warwick, and gave it into the custody of Henry, son of Roger de Beaumont.[4] Edwin and Morcar, now considering the doubtful issue of the contest, and not unwisely preferring peace to war, sought the king's favour, which they obtained, at least, in appearance. The king then built a castle at Nottingham, which he committed to the custody of William Peverell.

When the inhabitants of York heard the state of affairs, they became so alarmed that they made hasty submission, in order to avoid being compelled by force; delivering the keys of the city to the king, and offering him hostages. But, suspecting their faith, he strengthened the fortress within the city walls, and placed in it a garrison of picked men. At this time, Archill, the most powerful chief of the Northumbrians, made a treaty of peace with the king, and gave him his son as a hostage. The bishop of Durham, also being reconciled to King William, became the mediator for peace with the king of the Scots, and was the bearer into Scotland of the terms offered by William. Though the aid of Malcolm had been solicited by the English, and he had prepared to come to their succour with a strong force, yet when he heard what the envoy had to propose with respect to a peace, he remained quiet, and joyfully sent back ambassadors in company with the bishop of Durham, who in his name swore fealty to King William. In thus preferring peace to war, he best consulted his own welfare, and the inclinations of his subjects; for the people of Scotland, though fierce in war, love ease and quiet, and are not disposed to disturb themselves about their neighbours' affairs, loving rather religious exercises than those of arms. On his return from this expedition, the king erected castles at Lincoln, Huntingdon, and Cambridge, placing in each of them garrisons composed of his bravest soldiers.

4. **Roger de Beaumont:** a Norman noble.

Source 2 from the British Tourist Authority.

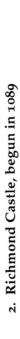

2. **Richmond Castle, begun in 1089**

Source 3: *Photograph courtesy of the British Tourist Authority. Ground plan courtesy of the Ministry of Public Building and Works.*

3. View and Ground Plan of Harlech Castle, Built by Edward I Between 1283 and 1290

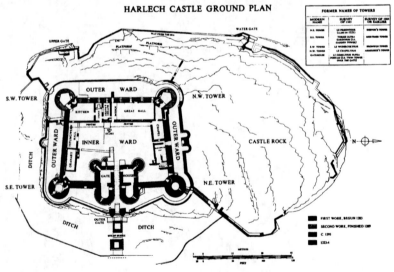

HARLECH CASTLE GROUND PLAN

Source 4 adapted from map in H. C. Darby, Domesday England *(Cambridge: Cambridge University Press, 1977), p. 316.*

4. Major Royal Castles Built During the Reign of William the Conqueror, 1066–1087

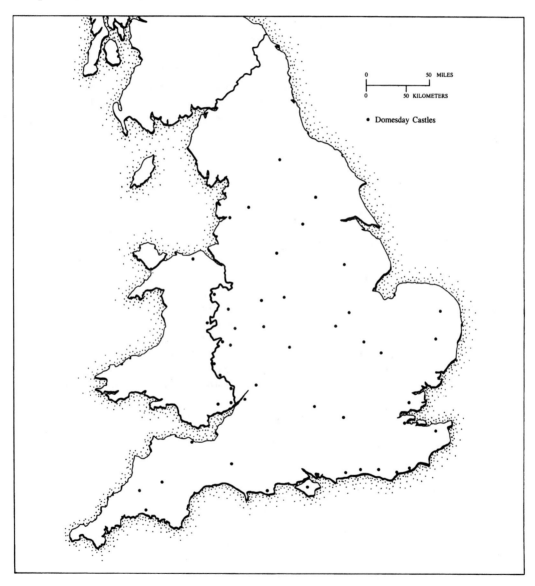

0 ___ 50 MILES
0 ___ 50 KILOMETERS

• Domesday Castles

Source 5 from The Anglo-Saxon Chronicle *(London: Eyre and Spottiswoode, 1961, and New Brunswick, N.J.: Rutgers University Press), p. 162.*

5. From *The Anglo-Saxon Chronicle*

1086—In this year the king wore his crown and held his court at Winchester for Easter, and travelled so as to be at Westminster for Whitsuntide, and there dubbed his son, Henry, a knight. Then he travelled about so as to come to Salisbury at Lammas,[5] and there his councillors came to him, and all the people occupying land who were of any account all over England, no matter whose vassals they might be; and they all submitted to him and became his vassals, and swore oaths of allegiance to him, that they would be loyal to him against all other men. . . .

Sources 6 and 7 from Edward P. Cheyney, editor, "English Constitutional Documents," Translations and Reprints from the Original Sources of European History *(Philadelphia: University of Pennsylvania, 1900), vol. 1, no. 6, pp. 22–25; pp. 26–30.*

6. Assize of Clarendon

Here begins the Assize of Clarendon, made by King Henry II, with the assent of the archbishops, bishops, abbots, earls and barons of all England.

1. In the first place, the aforesaid King Henry, with the consent of all his barons, for the preservation of the peace and the keeping of justice, has enacted that inquiry should be made through the several counties and through the several hundreds,[6] by twelve of the most legal men of the hundred and by four of the most legal men of each manor, upon their oath that they will tell the truth, whether there is in their hundred or in their manor, any man who has been accused or publicly suspected of himself being a robber, or murderer, or thief, or of being a receiver of robbers, or murderers, or thieves, since the lord king has been king. And let the justices make this inquiry before themselves, and the sheriffs before themselves.

2. And let any one who has been found by the oath of the aforesaid to have been accused or publicly suspected of having been a robber, or murderer, or thief, or a receiver of them, since the lord king has been king, be arrested and go to the ordeal of water and let him swear that he has not been a robber, or murderer, or thief, or receiver of them since the lord king has been king, to the value of five shillings, so far as he knows. . . .

5. **Lammas:** the wheat-harvest festival, August 1.

6. **hundred:** a division of a county.

4. And when a robber, or murderer, or thief, or receiver of them shall have been seized through the above-mentioned oath, if the justices are not to come very soon into that country where they have been arrested, let the sheriffs send word to the nearest justice by some intelligent man that they have arrested such men, and the justices will send back word to the sheriffs where they wish that these should be brought before them; and the sheriffs shall bring them before the justices; and along with these they shall bring from the hundred and the manor where they have been arrested, two legal men to carry the record of the county and of the hundred as to why they were seized, and there before the justice let them make their law.

5. And in the case of those who have been arrested through the aforesaid oath of this assize, no one shall have court, or judgment, or chattels,[7] except the lord king in his court before his justices, and the lord king shall have all their chattels. In the case of those, however, who have been arrested, otherwise than through this oath, let it be as it has been accustomed and ought to be. . . .

17. And if any sheriff shall have sent word to any other sheriff that men have fled from his county into another county, on account of robbery or murder or theft, or the reception of them, or for outlawry or for a charge concerning the forest of the king, let him arrest them. And even if he knows of himself or through others that such men have fled into his county, let him arrest them and hold them until he shall have secured pledges from them.

18. And let all sheriffs cause a list to be made of all fugitives who had fled from their counties; and let them do this in the presence of their county courts, and they will carry the written names of these before the justices when they come first before these, so that they may be sought through all England, and their chattels may be seized for the use of the king. . . .

7. Constitutions of Clarendon

In the year of the incarnation of the Lord, 1164, of the papacy of Alexander, the fourth year, of the most illustrious king of the English, Henry II, the tenth year, in the presence of the same king, has been made this memorial or acknowledgment of a certain part of the customs and franchises and dignities of his predecessors, that is to say of King Henry, his grandfather, and of other kings, which ought to be observed and held in the kingdom. And on account of the discussions and disputes which have arisen between the clergy and the justices of our lord and king and the barons of the kingdom concerning the customs and dignities, this acknowledgment is made in the presence of the archbishops and bishops and clergy and earls and barons and principal men of the kingdom. And these customs, acknowledged by

---

7. **chattels:** all items of property and goods except land.

the archbishops and bishops and earls and barons, and by the most noble and ancient of the kingdom, Thomas, archbishop of Canterbury, and Roger, archbishop of York, . . . [plus 12 bishops and 38 named barons] and many others of the principal men and nobles of the kingdom, as well clergy as laity.

Of these acknowledged customs and dignities of the realm, a certain part is contained in the present writing. Of this part the heads are as follows:

1. If any controversy has arisen concerning the advowson[8] and presentation of churches between laymen and ecclesiastics, or between ecclesiastics, it is to be considered or settled in the courts of the lord king.

2. Churches of the fee of the lord king cannot be given perpetually without his assent and grant.

3. Clergymen charged and accused of anything, when they have been summoned by a justice of the king shall come into his court, to respond there to that which it shall seem good to the court of the king for them to respond to, and in the ecclesiastical court to what it shall seem good should be responded to there; so that the justice of the king shall send into the court of holy church to see how the matter shall be treated there. And if a clergyman shall have been convicted or has confessed, the church ought not to protect him otherwise.

4. It is not lawful for archbishops, bishops, and persons of the realm to go out of the realm without the permission of the lord king. And if they go out, if it please the lord king, they shall give security that neither in going nor in making a stay nor in returning will they seek evil or loss to the king or the kingdom. . . .

7. No one who holds from the king in chief, nor any one of the officers of his demesnes shall be excommunicated, nor the lands of any one of them placed under an interdict, unless the lord king, if he is in the land, first agrees, or his justice, if he is out of the realm, in order that he may do right concerning him. . . .

8. Concerning appeals, if they should occur, they ought to proceed from the archdeacon to the bishop, from the bishop to the archbishop. And if the archbishop should fail to show justice, it must come to the lord king last, in order that by his command the controversy should be finally terminated in the court of the archbishop, so that it ought not to proceed further without the assent of the lord king. . . .

10. If any one who is of a city or a castle or a borough or a demesne manor of the lord king has been summoned by the archdeacon or the bishop for any offence for which he ought to respond to them, and is unwilling to make answer to their summons, it is fully lawful to place him under an interdict, but he ought not to be excommunicated before the principal officer of the lord

8. **advowson:** the right to recommend candidates for vacant church positions that carried with them capital assets.

king for that place agrees, in order that he may adjudge him to come to the answer. And if the officer of the king is negligent in this, he himself will be at the mercy of the lord king, and afterward the bishop shall be able to coerce the accused man by ecclesiastical justice.

11. Archbishops, bishops, and all persons of the realm, who hold from the king in chief, have their possessions from the lord king as a barony, and are responsible for them to the justices and officers of the king, and follow and perform all royal rules and customs; and just as the rest of the barons ought to be present at the judgment of the court of the lord king along with the barons, at least till the judgment reaches to loss of limbs or to death.

12. When an archbishopric or bishopric or abbacy or priorate of the demesne of the king has become vacant, it ought to be in his hands, and he shall take thence all its rights and products just as demesnes. And when it has come to providing for the church, the lord king ought to summon the more powerful persons of the church, and the election ought to be made in the chapel of the lord king himself, with the assent of the lord king and with the agreement of the persons of the realm whom he has called to do this. And there the person elected shall do homage and fealty to the lord king as to his liege lord, concerning his life and his limbs and his earthly honor, saving his order, before he shall be consecrated. . . .

This acknowledgment of the aforesaid royal customs and dignities has been made by the aforesaid archbishops, and bishops, and earls, and barons, and the more noble and ancient of the realm, at Clarendon, on the fourth day before the Purification of the Blessed Mary, perpetual Virgin, Lord Henry being there present with his father, the lord king. There are, however, many other and great customs and dignities of holy mother church and of the lord king, and of the barons of the realm, which are not contained in this writing. These are preserved to holy church and to the lord king and to his heirs and to the barons of the realm, and shall be observed inviolably forever.

8. Coronation of Emperor Frederick Barbarossa, 1152

[*From* Gesta Friderici]

In the year . . . 1152, after the most pious King Conrad had died in the spring . . . in the city of Bamberg . . . there assembled in the city of Frankfort from the vast expanse of the transalpine kingdom [Germany], marvellous to tell, the whole strength of the princes, not without certain of the barons from Italy, in one body, so to speak. Here, when the primates were taking counsel about the prince to be elected—for the highest honour of the Roman Empire claims this point of law for itself, as if by special prerogative, namely, that the kings do not succeed by heredity but are created by the election of the princes—finally Frederick, duke of Swabia, son of Duke Frederick, was desired by all, and with the approval of all, was raised up as king. . . .

When the king had bound all the princes who had assembled there in fealty and homage, he, together with a few whom he had chosen as suitable, having dismissed the others in peace, took ship with great joy on the fifth day and, going by the Main and Rhine, he landed at the royal palace of Sinzig. There, taking horse, he came to Aachen on the next Saturday; on the following day, Sunday [March 9th] . . . led by the bishops from the palace to the church of the blessed Virgin Mary, and with the applause of all present, crowned by Arnold, archbishop of Cologne, assisted by the other bishops, he was set on the throne of the Franks, which was placed in the same church by Charles the Great. Many were amazed that in such a short space of time not only so many of the princes and nobles of the kingdom had assembled but also that not a few had come even from western Gaul, where, it was thought, the rumour of this event could not yet have penetrated. . . .

Nor should I pass over in silence that on the same day in the same church the bishop-elect of Münster, also called Frederick, was consecrated as bishop by the same bishops who had consecrated the king; so that in truth the highest king and the priest believed this to be a sort of prognostication[9] in the present joyfulness that, in one church, one day saw the unction[10] of two persons, who

9. **prognostication:** prophecy.
10. **unction:** anointing.

alone are anointed sacramentally with the institution of the old and new dispensations and are rightly called the anointed of Christ. . . .

[*From "The Deeds of Frederick
Barbarossa"*]

In the middle of the month of October (1157) the emperor set out for Burgundy to hold a diet at Besançon. . . . We must speak of the ambassadors of the Roman pontiff, Hadrian. . . . The personnel of the embassy consisted of Roland, cardinal priest of the title of St. Mark and chancellor of the Holy Roman Church, and Bernard, cardinal priest of the title of St. Clement, both distinguished for their wealth, their maturity of view, and their influence, and surpassing in prestige almost all others in the Roman Church. . . . When this letter had been read and carefully set forth by Chancellor Rainald in a faithful interpretation, the princes who were present were moved to great indignation, because the entire content of the letter appeared to have no little sharpness and to offer even at the very outset an occasion for future trouble. But what had particularly aroused them all was the fact that in the aforesaid letter it had been stated, among other things, that the fullness of dignity and honor had been bestowed upon the emperor by the Roman pontiff, that the emperor had received from his hand the imperial crown, and that he would not have regretted conferring even greater benefits (*beneficia*) upon him. . . . And the hearers were led to accept the literal meaning of these words and to put credence in the aforesaid explanation because they knew that the assertion was rashly made by some Romans that hitherto our kings had possessed the imperial power over the City, and the kingdom of Italy, by gift of the popes, and that they made such representations and handed them down to posterity not only orally but also in writing and in pictures. . . .

They returned without having accomplished their purpose, and what had been done by the emperor was published throughout the realm in the following letter (October, 1157):

"Whereas the Divine Sovereignty, from which is derived all power in heaven and on earth, has entrusted unto us, His anointed, the kingdom and the empire to rule over, and has ordained that the peace of the churches is to be maintained by the imperial arms, not without the greatest distress of heart are we compelled to complain to Your Benevolence that from the head of the Holy Church, on which Christ has set the imprint of his peace and love, there seem to be emanating causes of dissentions and evils, like a poison, by which, unless God avert it, we fear the body of the Church will be stained, its unity shattered, and a schism created between the temporal and spiritual realms. . . . And since, through election by the princes, the kingdom and the empire are ours from God alone, Who at the time of the passion of His Son Christ subjected the world to dominion by the two swords, and since the apostle Peter taught the world this doctrine: 'Fear God, honor the king,' whosoever says that we received the imperial crown as a benefice (*pro beneficio*) from the lord pope contradicts the divine ordinance and the doctrine of Peter and is guilty of a lie. . . ."

Source 9 from J. A. Giles, translator and editor, Roger of Wendover's Flowers of History *(London: H. G. Bohn, 1849), vol. 2, pp. 79–81.*

9. Coronation of Richard the Lionhearted, 1189

Duke Richard, when all the preparations for his coronation were complete, came to London, where were assembled the archbishops of Canterbury, Rouen, and Treves, by whom he had been absolved for having carried arms against his father after he had taken the cross. The archbishop of Dublin was also there, with all the bishops, earls, barons, and nobles of the kingdom. When all were assembled, he received the crown of the kingdom in the order following: First came the archbishops, bishops, abbots, and clerks, wearing their caps, preceded by the cross, the holy water, and the censers, as far as the door of the inner chamber, where they received the duke, and conducted him to the church of Westminster, as far as the high altar, in a solemn procession. In the midst of the bishops and clerks went four barons carrying candlesticks with wax candles, after whom came two earls, the first of whom carried the royal sceptre, having on its top a golden cross; the other carried the royal sceptre, having a dove on its top. Next to these came two earls with a third between them, carrying three swords with golden sheaths, taken out of the king's treasury. Behind these came six earls and barons carrying a chequer,[11] over which were placed the royal arms and robes, whilst another earl followed them carrying aloft a golden crown. Last of all came Duke Richard, having a bishop on the right hand, and a bishop on the left, and over them was held a silk awning. Proceeding to the altar, as we have said, the holy Gospels were placed before him together with the relics of some of the saints, and he swore, in presence of the clergy and people, that he would observe peace, honour, and reverence, all his life, towards God, the holy Church and its ordinances: he swore also that he would exercise true justice towards the people committed to his charge, and abrogating all bad laws and unjust customs, if any such might be found in his dominions, would steadily observe those which were good. After this they stripped him of all his clothes except his breeches and shirt, which had been ripped apart over his shoulders to receive the unction. He was then shod with sandals interwoven with gold thread, and Baldwin archbishop of Canterbury anointed him king in three places, namely, on his head, his shoulders, and his right arm, using prayers

11. **chequer:** a small table.

composed for the occasion: then a consecrated linen cloth was placed on his head, over which was put a hat, and when they had again clothed him in his royal robes with the tunic and gown, the archbishop gave into his hand a sword wherewith to crush all the enemies of the Church; this done, two earls placed his shoes upon his feet, and when he had received the mantle, he was adjured by the archbishop, in the name of God, not to presume to accept these honours unless his mind was steadily purposed to observe the oaths which he had made: and he answered that, with God's assistance, he would faithfully observe everything which he had promised. Then the king taking the crown from the altar gave it to the archbishop, who placed it upon the king's head, with the sceptre in his right hand and the royal wand in his left; and so, with his crown on, he was led away by the bishops and barons, preceded by the candles, the cross and the three swords aforesaid. When they came to the offertory of the mass, the two bishops aforesaid led him forwards and again led him back. At length, when the mass was chanted, and everything finished in the proper manner, the two bishops aforesaid led him away with his crown on, and bearing in his right hand the sceptre, in his left the royal wand, and so they returned in procession into the choir, where the king put off his royal robes, and taking others of less weight, and a lighter crown also, he proceeded to the dinner-table, at which the archbishops, bishops, earls, and barons, with the clergy and people, were placed, each according to his rank and dignity, and feasted splendidly, so that the wine flowed along the pavement and walls of the palace.

Source 10 © Bettman/CORBIS.

10. Portrait of Emperor Otto III

Source 11 from Giraudon/Art Resource, New York.

11. Portion of the Bayeux Tapestry Showing King Harold Seated on the Throne of England, with Halley's Comet Above

QUESTIONS TO CONSIDER

The power relationships we have been investigating involve three main groups in medieval society: the nobles, the Church, and the rulers. To understand changes in the balance of power among them, you will need to extract information from each of the sources about them, and then compare your findings.

Take the nobles first. How would you compare the role of the nobles in the ceremonies of homage such as the Salisbury Oath with their role in the coronation ceremonies? How is their relationship to the ruler expressed in the pictures of Otto III and Harold? How does this compare with the way this relationship is expressed in the Assize of Clarendon? What differences do you see in the role of the nobles in Germany and those in England, as expressed in the coronation accounts?

Turning to the Church, what types of religious objects appear in the ceremonies and depictions of rulers? Do they serve to express the power of the Church as an institution or of someone else? What do they reveal to you about medieval religious beliefs and practices? What do the pictures of Otto III and Harold indicate about the relationship between the ruler and church officials? How does this compare with the expression of this relationship in the Constitutions of Clarendon?

The claim of rulers such as Henry II and Frederick Barbarossa to religious authority was accompanied in the High Middle Ages by changes in the theory underlying kingship. In the Early Middle Ages, the king was viewed as simply the greatest of the nobles, whose power derived from the agreements he had made with his vassals. This idea continued into the High Middle Ages, but alongside it developed the idea that the king got his power from God as well. Rulers were increasingly viewed not only as the apex of a pyramid of vassals, but also as the representative to God for their entire kingdom. They were not regarded as divine in the way that ancient rulers such as the Egyptian pharaohs and Roman emperors had been, for Christianity would not allow this, but they were considered sacred in some ways. What evidence of this new idea of kingship can you find in either the Constitutions of Clarendon or the statements of Frederick Barbarossa? The two coronation ceremonies, Sources 8 and 9, are from the period of the building up of the monarchy. What evidence do you see in them of both the older idea of the king as the greatest of the nobles, and the newer idea of the king as ordained by God?

Remember that most literate people in the Middle Ages were clerics, so that all of the documents included here were probably written by priests or monks. How might this have affected their account of the events? Given what you have read and looked at here, what actions would you now regard as most significant in the creation of the medieval state?

EPILOGUE

The moves undertaken by rulers to increase their power during the High Middle Ages did not go unchallenged. The Constitutions of Clarendon were immediately opposed by church officials, including Henry II's friend Thomas Becket, whom Henry had made the Archbishop of Canterbury. The controversy between them grew very bitter, and ended with Becket's murder by several of Henry's nobles. After this the Constitutions were officially withdrawn, but Henry continued to enforce many of their provisions anyway.

In the area ruled by the German emperors, the Church was better able to assert its independent power; in fact, constant disputes with the pope were one of the reasons that the German emperors were not successful at establishing a unified country. Church officials patterned themselves after secular rulers and began in the twelfth century to demand regular oaths of homage and loyalty. They made sure that church power was clearly symbolized in any royal ceremony and in all ceremonies of knighthood. As rulers built castles, they built cathedrals, permanent monuments in stone to both the glory of God and the authority of the Church. The consecrations of churches and cathedrals rivaled the coronations of monarchs in splendor and pomp. The Church was fortunate in this regard, for opportunities for special ceremonies and celebrations were much more frequent than they were for secular rulers. Even the regular mass could be used to convey the Church's might to all who observed it. The king may have had sacred authority, but church officials wanted to make sure that everyone knew that they did as well.

Nobles in England also opposed the growth of royal power, and were more effective than the Church in enforcing limits to royal authority. The most famous of these was the Magna Carta in 1215, which King John was forced to sign at a meeting in Runnymede, giving the higher nobles of England the right to participate in government. This document said nothing about the rights of the vast majority of English people, but it is still unusual in its limitation of the power of the king, though John immediately refuted it once he left Runnymede.

Despite opposition, however, the expansion of royal power at the expense of the nobles and Church continued, for this expansion had only begun during the High Middle Ages. Monarchs in the later Middle Ages, the Renaissance, and the early modern period continued to build up their power, devising new methods of taxation to raise revenue, creating a centralized legal system under firm royal control, reducing the role of or doing away with feudal assemblies of nobles, hiring middle-class lawyers and bureaucrats as their advisers and officials, and forbidding the nobles to maintain their own armies while building up royal armies led by generals whom they chose for loyalty.

This expansion of royal power was made easier in many countries in the sixteenth century because of the Protestant Reformation. Many rulers, such as Henry VIII of England, resented any independent power of the Church; they thus found Protestant theology, which declared the papacy to be evil and the ruler the proper source of all religious authority, very attractive. Some rulers became Protestant out of sincere religious conviction, but for others the chance to take over church property and appoint church officials was the strongest motivation.

The growth of actual royal power was accompanied, as you would expect after working through this chapter, by changes in the theory underlying kingship and in the symbols used to portray the king. Political theorists developed the idea of the divine right of kings, whereby kings got their power directly and pretty much only from God, and so were not answerable to their subjects for their behavior. You can see this idea beginning in the documents you have just read, and it would be developed to its furthest extent in seventeenth-century absolutism.

Centralized monarchy did not develop in all parts of Europe, however. Germany and Italy remained divided, and in fact did not become unified nations until the late nineteenth century, just a little over a hundred years ago. From the description of Frederick Barbarossa's coronation, you can see one reason for this, the fact that the emperorship was elected rather than hereditary. The lack of strong central governments in Germany and Italy was one reason for their decreasing political importance in the early modern period. The rulers of western Europe had much greater financial resources, and so could field larger armies and encourage economic development. After the voyages of the Portuguese and Spanish revealed new lands and new ways to the East, these rulers also supported exploration and colonization, which further increased royal and national power. Some type of feudal structure existed in most parts of western Europe in the High Middle Ages, but it was the rulers of France, England, and Spain who were most successful at manipulating both actual power and the symbols of that power to build up their own authority and end the feudal system.

CHAPTER EIGHT

LIFE AT A

MEDIEVAL UNIVERSITY

In Europe during the classical period, education was handled by private tutors and small schools, and during the Early Middle Ages most education was carried out by monasteries and convents, which gave children basic training in Latin. Some monasteries provided more advanced education for the few individuals who would become leaders in the Church or administrators for secular rulers. Beginning in the eleventh century, schools attached to cathedrals in some cities also began offering more advanced subjects and developed a curriculum based on the works of Christian and classical authors. These cathedral schools took in boys and young men who had learned their Latin in monasteries or through tutors. One of the earliest cathedral schools was that in Paris, where students were drawn by excellent teachers such as Peter Abelard. Because only an official of the bishop, called the *scholasticus* or chancellor, had the authority to issue licenses to teach, students and teachers clustered around the cathedral of Notre Dame, located on an island in the Seine. This educational community soon grew so large that it required additional housing on the left bank of the river, which came to be known as the "Latin Quarter" after the official academic language. Special residence halls for students, called *colleges*, were opened, though the teachers themselves had no classrooms and simply rented rooms on their own for lecturing.

As the number of students in Paris increased, the teachers joined together into a "universal society of teachers," or *university* for short. Believing that the chancellor often either granted the right to teach to unqualified parties or simply sold licenses outright, they began to require that prospective teachers pass an examination set by the university besides getting the chancellor's approval. This certificate to teach was the earliest form of academic degree, granting the holder one of the titles, *master* or *doctor,* that we still use today. (Bachelor's degrees were to come later.) Most of the students studied theology, and Paris became the model for later universities such as Oxford and Cambridge in England and Heidelberg in Germany.

Colleges at many universities changed their character over the centuries. Originally no more than residence halls, the colleges gradually began to sponsor lectures and arrange for courses, and the university became simply the institution that granted degrees. This process was especially noticeable at the English universities of Oxford and Cambridge. When colleges were first established in the United States, they generally modeled themselves on the colleges of Oxford and Cambridge; because they were not part of larger universities, the colleges also granted degrees themselves. Thus modern U.S. colleges may be either completely independent institutions or part of a university, such as the College of Engineering or the College of Letters and Science found at many universities. In most cases, colleges that are part of modern universities have completely lost their original function as residences.

The University of Bologna had somewhat different roots and a different emphasis. Bologna was located at the crossing of the main trade routes in northern Italy, and so was a center of commerce and trade. In the late eleventh century, a manuscript of the Roman emperor Justinian's law code was discovered in the area. Scholars studying the text realized that Roman law provided better ways of handling complex business transactions than did existing customary law, and they began teaching Roman law at professional schools for lawyers, notaries, and merchants in Bologna. The university developed from these professional schools, and consequently the students were older and more sophisticated than those at Paris. Here, the students themselves banded into a university; they determined the fees teachers would be paid, the hours of classes, and the content of lectures. The most important course of study at Bologna was law, though other subjects were added later. Bologna became the model for European universities such as Orleans or Padua, where students have retained their traditional power through modern times.

Because all those associated with the universities were literate, a great many records survive detailing every aspect of university life, both inside and outside the classroom. We can observe the process by which universities were established, read the rules students were required to live by, and learn what they were supposed to be studying (as well as what they actually spent time doing!). Much of medieval university life will seem familiar to us, for modern colleges and universities have inherited a great deal from their medieval predecessors. Indeed, most of the universities that had their beginning in the Middle Ages are still thriving today, making universities one of the few medieval institutions we can evaluate to some extent as insiders, rather than the outsiders we are when we look at such vanished social forms as serfdom or feudalism.

Because of the many parallels between medieval and modern universities, your task in this chapter will be twofold. First, you will be asked to use a variety of records to answer this question: What was life like for students at a medieval university? You can then use this description and your own experiences as a student to answer the second question: How would you compare medieval with modern student life, and what factors might account for the differences?

SOURCES AND METHOD

You will be using four types of sources in this chapter. The first type (Sources 1 through 4) consists of rules for university or college life issued by the founders. These are prescriptive documents, setting forth standards of functioning and behavior. The second type (Sources 5 through 8), written by teachers at medieval universities, describes their methods of teaching or presents the area on which they concentrated. The third type (Source 9) is a critique of university teaching by an individual outside the university structure. These sources provide us with information about how and what students studied or were supposed to study and so have both prescriptive and descriptive qualities. Selections of the fourth type (Sources 10 through 13) describe actual student life or were written by students themselves. These sources are thus fully descriptive, recounting real events or the problems and desires of real students.

As you read each selection, keep in mind the identity of its author and his position in the university. (No women were allowed to attend medieval universities in any capacity, so we can be sure that all authors, even anonymous students, were male.) Then as now, the perspective of administrators, those who established and ran the universities, was very different from that of students and faculty. It is also important to identify the source as prescriptive or descriptive. Prescriptive rules were often written in response to real problems, but the standards they laid down should never be mistaken for reality.

Begin your analysis of medieval university life with a careful reading of Sources 1 through 4. Source 1 describes privileges granted to the students at the University of Paris by the king of France in 1200. Though the University of Paris was originally started by the teachers themselves, the king took the scholars under his special protection and guaranteed them certain extraordinary rights. What privileges are they granted in this document?

Source 2 consists of the statutes issued for the University of Paris by Cardinal Robert Courçon in 1215. Courçon, a representative of Pope Innocent III, took a special interest in the university and approved rules governing academic life. Innocent had been a student at Paris himself and wanted to ensure the university's tradition of theological orthodoxy and high levels of scholarship and behavior. As you read the selection, note the restrictions placed on those allowed to teach the arts. What restrictions are placed on teachers of

560

theology? Why would Innocent be stricter about theology? What other areas did he believe important to regulate? What matters were the masters and students allowed to decide for themselves?

Source 3 contains further statutes issued for the University of Paris by Pope Gregory XI in 1231. What rules did he set for the chancellor's granting of teaching licenses? What issues was the university permitted to decide for itself? What special legal protections did students and teachers have? As pope, Gregory was particularly concerned with the manner in which theology was taught. What special restrictions did he lay down for students and teachers of theology? How would you compare these rules with the earlier ones established by Innocent III?

Source 4 is a series of rules governing life in one of the residential colleges, not the university as a whole. They were issued by Robert de Sorbon, the chaplain of King Louis IX, who established the college in the thirteenth century. This college was originally a residence hall for students of theology. By the sixteenth century, however, the word *Sorbonne* was used to describe the faculty of theology; since the nineteenth century the entire University of Paris has been called the Sorbonne.

As you can see from Source 4, Sorbon's establishment was simply a residence hall, with none of the broader functions that colleges later assumed. What aspects of student life did he regulate? What qualities did he attempt to encourage in the students living at his college?

By reading these four prescriptive sources, you have gained some information about the structure of one university (Paris), the hierarchy of authority, special student privileges, daily life in a residential college, and the handling of rule infractions. You have also learned something about the ideals held by authorities and patrons, for the popes and Sorbon established these rules because they held certain beliefs about how students should behave. What qualities would their ideal student exhibit? What did they see as the ultimate aim of the university? You can also use these sources to assess how church and secular leaders reacted to scholars, students, and the university in general. How would you describe their attitude—patronizing, respectful, hostile? How might their opinions about members of the university community have influenced other citizens of these university towns?

Besides informing us of standards, rules can also expose real-life problems because those who set the regulations were often responding to events in their environment. Which rules were specifically aimed at halting acts that were already taking place? Which rules seem most likely to have been a response to actual behavior? What kinds of acts did the authorities appear most upset about? Why do you think they believed these acts were important? Judging by the information in these sources, how would you describe relations between university students and the other residents of Paris? Before you go on to the next selections, write a brief description of medieval university life as you now see it. What types of sources would help you test whether your assumptions at this point are correct?

You have probably realized that so far you do not know very much about what or how students actually studied, other than those writings the popes recommended or forbade. The next four selections provide specific academic information. Sources 5 and 6 were written by teachers of theology and philosophy at Paris; Sources 7 and 8, by teachers of law at Bologna. Source 5 is the introduction to Peter Abelard's *Sic et Non*, a philosophical treatise introducing students and other readers to the *scholastic method* of inquiry, which applied logic to Christian theology. Source 6 is a demonstration of the scholastic method by one philosopher, Anselm of Canterbury, to prove the existence of God. If you are not familiar with philosophical works, you will need to read these excerpts very carefully, with special attention to the author's main points and the way in which logic is used to advance arguments. Because scholastic philosophers regarded logic as the most important aid to human understanding, it is fair for you to be critical if you see any flaws in their own logic. In making this analysis, you will be engaging in an activity that students in medieval universities both did themselves and were encouraged to do.

Begin with Abelard's introduction. How did he suggest to students that they read the works of the church fathers? How were they to handle seeming contradictions? Was all literature to be treated in this way? What, for Abelard, was the most important quality a student could possess? How was education supposed to strengthen this quality? Proceed to Anselm's proof, which you may need to read a number of times. Do you see any flaws in the logic? If you were a student disputing his proof, where would you begin?

Source 7 is an announcement of lectures in law by Odofredus, a teacher at the University of Bologna, written about 1255. Although later in the thirteenth century the city of Bologna began to pay teachers in order to control the university faculty more closely, at this point teachers were still paid directly by their students, and so Odofredus did not simply announce his course, he advertised it in a way that would make it attractive. What did he see as the positive qualities of his teaching method? How did he propose to handle a text? What specific skills was he trying to teach his students?

Source 8 is the introduction to the *Digest*, the main part of the collection of laws and commentaries made by the Emperor Justinian in the sixth century and one of the basic legal texts taught by Odofredus and his colleagues at Bologna. Like many textbooks, it opens with definitions of what would be taught. What distinctions among types of law does it present? What is the ultimate aim of legal education to be? Return to the description of university life you wrote after reading the first group of sources. What can you now add about the way teachers approached their subjects or the way in which material was taught? What do you now know about the content of courses in medieval universities?

Though teachers of theology and law used both logic and reason as means of analysis, there were some thinkers in the Middle Ages who questioned their value, particularly in matters of theology. Source 9 is an excerpt from two letters of St. Bernard of Clairvaux (1090–1153), a very influential French abbot, mystic, and adviser to the papacy. What does Bernard object to in Abelard's teaching? Why does he view Abelard's ideas as dangerous? What is his opinion of the scholastic method being developed at that time in the universities?

Students did not spend all their time studying, nor did they always behave in the ways popes or patrons hoped they would. The final group of sources come from students themselves or describe what might be termed their extracurricular activities. Source 10 is an anonymous account of a riot in Oxford in 1298, and Source 11 is a description of student life at Paris written by Jacques de Vitry, a high-minded scholar and historian who had studied at Paris himself. Source 12 consists of two letters, one from a student at Oxford to his father and another from a father to his son, a student at Orleans; Source 13 contains three anonymous short poems written originally in Latin by twelfth-century students.

The account of the riot is relatively straightforward and objective, like a story you might read in a newspaper today. What does this incident indicate about the relations between university scholars and townspeople? Whom did the two

sets of disputants ask to decide the matter?

The other selections are more subjective than this account, so you must keep the point of view and the intent of the authors in mind as you read them. What kind of language does Vitry use to describe students? With what authority did he criticize their actions? How would you describe his general opinion of university life? How would you compare his critique of logic and the philosophers who used it with Bernard's? What tactics did the student use to convince his father to send money? How would you compare the father's attitude with Vitry's?

Most medieval student poetry was written by young scholars who wandered from university to university and took much longer at their studies than normal, if they ever finished at all. It is important when reading from this genre to remember that the authors were not describing the daily grind but celebrating their wild escapades, in the same way you might talk about an academic year in terms of homecoming parties, weekend bashes, and early morning cramming for exams. This does not mean that we should reject their poetry as a valid historical source; rather, we must simply be aware of its intent and limitations. Keeping this in mind, how do the poets describe themselves and their problems? How does this description of student life reinforce or change what you have learned so far?

Return to your original description of university life. What would you add now?

THE EVIDENCE

Sources 1 through 3 from Dana Carleton Munro, editor and translator, Translations and Reprints from the Original Sources of European History, *vol. 2, no. 3 (Philadelphia: University of Pennsylvania Press, no date), pp. 4–5; pp. 12–15; pp. 7–11.*

1. Royal Privileges Granted to the University of Paris by the King of France, 1200

In the Name of the sacred and indivisible Trinity, amen. Philip, by the grace of God, King of the French. . . .

Concerning the safety of the students at Paris in the future, by the advice of our subjects we have ordained as follows: we will cause all the citizens of Paris to swear that if any one sees an injury done to any student by any layman, he will testify truthfully to this, nor will any one withdraw in order not to see [the act]. And if it shall happen that any one strikes a student, except in self-defense, especially if he strikes the student with a weapon, a club or a stone, all laymen who see [the act] shall in good faith seize the malefactor or malefactors and deliver them to our judge; nor shall they withdraw in order not to see the act, or seize the malefactor, or testify to the truth. Also, whether the malefactor is seized in open crime or not, we will make a legal and full examination through clerks or laymen or certain lawful persons; and our count and our judges shall do the same. And if by a full examination we or our judges are able to learn that he who is accused, is guilty of the crime, then we or our judges shall immediately inflict a penalty, according to the quality and nature of the crime; notwithstanding the fact that the criminal may deny the deed and say that he is ready to defend himself in single combat, or to purge himself by the ordeal by water.

Also, neither our provost nor our judges shall lay hands on a student for any offence whatever; nor shall they place him in our prison, unless such a crime has been committed by the student, that he ought to be arrested. And in that case, our judge shall arrest him on the spot, without striking him at all, unless he resists, and shall hand him over to the ecclesiastical judge, who ought to guard him in order to satisfy us and the one suffering the injury. And if a serious crime has been committed, our judge shall go or shall send to see what is done with the student.

2. Statutes for the University
of Paris Issued by Robert
Courçon, 1215

R., servant of the cross of Christ, by the divine mercy cardinal priest of the title of St. Stephen in Monte Celio and legate of the apostolic seat, to all the masters and scholars at Paris—eternal safety in the Lord.

Let all know, that having been especially commanded by the lord pope to devote our energy effectively to the betterment of the condition of the students at Paris, and wishing by the advice of good men to provide for the tranquillity of the students in the future, we have ordered and prescribed the following rules:

No one is to lecture at Paris in arts before he is twenty-one years old. He is to listen in arts at least six years, before he begins to lecture. He is to promise that he will lecture for at least two years, unless he is prevented by some good reason, which he ought to prove either in public or before the examiners. He must not be smirched by any infamy. When he is ready to lecture, each one is to be examined according to the form contained in the letter of lord P. bishop of Paris (in which is contained the peace established between the chancellor and the students by the judges appointed by the lord pope, approved and confirmed namely by the bishop and deacon of Troyes and by P., the bishop, and J., the chancellor of Paris).

The treatises of Aristotle on logic, both the old and the new, are to be read in the schools in the regular and not in the extraordinary courses. The two Priscians,[1] or at least the second, are also to be read in the schools in the regular courses. On the feast-days nothing is to be read except philosophy, rhetoric, *quadrivialia*,[2] the Barbarism, the Ethics, if they like, and the fourth book of the Topics. The books of Aristotle on Metaphysics or Natural Philosophy, or the abridgements of these works, are not to be read, nor the writings of Master David of Dinant, the heretic Amauri, or the Spaniard Mauricius.[3]

In the promotions and meetings of the masters and in the confutations or arguments of the boys or youths there are to be no festivities. But they may call in some friends or associates, but only a few. We also advise that donations of garments and other things be made, as is customary or even to a greater extent, and especially to the poor. No master lecturing in arts is to

1. **Priscian:** a Roman grammarian whose two works presented models of correct letters and legal documents.

2. *quadrivialia:* the four more advanced fields of study within the seven liberal arts: arithmetic, geometry, astronomy, and music.

3. Aristotle's treatises on metaphysics and natural philosophy were forbidden by the pope because they stated that the world was eternal (rather than created by God) and that the human soul was not immortal. The last three authors the Church regarded as heretics.

wear anything except a cope,[4] round and black and reaching to the heels—at least, when it is new. But he may well wear a pallium.[5] He is not to wear under the round cope embroidered shoes and never any with long bands.

If anyone of the students in arts or theology dies, half of the masters of arts are to go to the funeral one time, and the other half to the next funeral. They are not to withdraw until the burial is completed, unless they have some good reason. If any master of arts or theology dies, all the masters are to be present at the vigils, each one is to read the psalter or have it read. Each one is to remain in the church, where the vigils are celebrated, until midnight or later, unless prevented by some good reason. On the day when the master is buried, no one is to lecture or dispute.

We fully confirm to them the meadow of St. Germain in the condition in which it was adjudged to them.

Each master is to have jurisdiction over his scholars. No one is to receive either schools or a house without the consent of the occupant, if he is able to obtain it. No one is to receive a license from the chancellor or any one else through a gift of money, or furnishing a pledge or making an agreement. Also, the masters and students can make among themselves or with others agreements and regulations, confirmed by a pledge, penalty or oath, about the following matters: namely, if a student is killed, mutilated or receives some outrageous injury—if justice is not done; for fixing the prices of lodgings; concerning the dress, burial, lectures and disputations; in such a manner, however, that the university is not scattered or destroyed on this account.

We decide concerning the theologians, that no one shall lecture at Paris before he is thirty-five years old, and not unless he has studied at least eight years, and has heard the books faithfully and in the schools. He is to listen in theology for five years, before he reads his own lectures in public. No one of them is to lecture before the third hour on the days when the masters lecture. No one is to be received at Paris for the important lectures or sermons unless he is of approved character and learning. There is to be no student at Paris who does not have a regular master.

3. Statutes for the University of Paris Issued by Pope Gregory XI, 1231

Gregory, the bishop, servant of the servants of God, to his beloved sons, all the masters and students of Paris—greeting and apostolic benediction. . . .

4. **cope:** a long cloak or cape.

5. **pallium:** a white stole usually worn by popes and archbishops as a symbol of their authority. In this case, a master teacher was allowed to wear one as an indication of his level of academic achievement and its corresponding institutional authority; the pallium thus served a function similar to the master's or doctoral hood.

Concerning the condition of the students and schools, we have decided that the following should be observed: each chancellor, appointed hereafter at Paris, at the time of his installation, in the presence of the bishop, or at the command of the latter in the chapter at Paris—two masters of the students having been summoned for this purpose and present in behalf of the university—shall swear that, in good faith, according to his conscience, he will not receive as professors of theology and canon law any but suitable men, at a suitable place and time, according to the condition of the city and the honor and glory of those branches of learning; and he will reject all who are unworthy without respect to persons or nations. Before licensing anyone, during three months, dating from the time when the license is requested, the chancellor shall make diligent inquiries of all the masters of theology present in the city, and of all other honest and learned men through whom the truth can be ascertained, concerning the life, knowledge, capacity, purpose, prospects and other qualities needful in such persons; and after the inquiries, in good faith and according to his conscience, he shall grant or deny the license to the candidate, as shall seem fitting and expedient. The masters of theology and canon law, when they begin to lecture, shall take a public oath that they will give true testimony on the above points. The chancellor shall also swear, that he will in no way reveal the advice of the masters, to their injury; the liberty and privileges being maintained in their full vigor for the canons at Paris, as they were in the beginning. Moreover, the chancellor shall promise to examine in good faith the masters in medicine and arts and in the other branches, to admit only the worthy and to reject the unworthy.

In other matters, because confusion easily creeps in where there is no order, we grant to you the right of making constitutions and ordinances regulating the manner and time of lectures and disputations, the costume to be worn, the burial of the dead; and also concerning the bachelors,[6] who are to lecture and at what hours, and on what they are to lecture; and concerning the prices of the lodgings or the interdiction of the same; and concerning a fit punishment for those who violate your constitutions or ordinances, by exclusion from your society. And if, perchance, the assessment of the lodgings is taken from you, or anything else is lacking, or an injury or outrageous damage, such as death or the mutilation of a limb, is inflicted on one of you; unless through a suitable admonition satisfaction is rendered within fifteen days, you may suspend your lectures until you have received full satisfaction. And if it happens that any one of you is unlawfully imprisoned, unless the injury ceases on a remonstrance from you, you may, if you judge it expedient, suspend your lectures immediately.

We command, moreover, that the bishop of Paris shall so chastise the excesses of the guilty, that the honor of the students shall be preserved and evil

6. **bachelor:** a student who had his first degree and could teach beginning-level subjects.

deeds shall not remain unpunished. But in no way shall the innocent be seized on account of the guilty; nay rather, if a probable suspicion arises against anyone, he shall be detained honorably and on giving suitable bail he shall be freed, without any exactions from the jailors. But if, perchance, such a crime has been committed that imprisonment is necessary, the bishop shall detain the criminal in his prison. The chancellor is forbidden to keep him in his prison. We also forbid holding a student for a debt contracted by another, since this is interdicted by canonical and legitimate sanctions. Neither the bishop, nor his official, nor the chancellor shall exact a pecuniary penalty for removing an excommunication or any other censure of any kind. Nor shall the chancellor demand from the masters who are licensed an oath, or obedience, or any pledge; nor shall he receive any emolument[7] or promise for granting a license, but be content with the above-mentioned oath.

Also, the vacation in summer is not to exceed one month, and the bachelors, if they wish, can continue their lectures in vacation time. Moreover, we prohibit more expressly the students from carrying weapons in the city, and the university from protecting those who disturb the peace and study. And those who call themselves students but do not frequent the schools, or acknowledge any master, are in no way to enjoy the liberties of the students.

Moreover, we order that the masters in arts shall always read one lecture on Priscian, and one book after the other in the regular courses. Those books on natural philosophy which for a certain reason were prohibited in a provincial council, are not to be used at Paris until they have been examined and purged of all suspicion of error. The masters and students in theology shall strive to exercise themselves laudably in the branch which they profess; they shall not show themselves philosophers, but they shall strive to become God's learned. And they shall not speak in the language of the people, confounding the sacred language with the profane. In the schools they shall dispute only on such questions as can be determined by theological books and the writings of the holy fathers.

It is not lawful for any man whatever to infringe this deed of our provision, constitution, concession, prohibition and inhibition or to act contrary to it, from rash presumption. If anyone, however, should dare to attempt this, let him know that he incurs the wrath of almighty God and of the blessed Peter and Paul, his apostles.

Given at the Lateran, on the Ides of April [April 13], in the fifth year of our pontificate.

---

7. **emolument:** fee.

Source 4 from University Records and Life in the Middle Ages *by Lynn Thorndike, ed. Copyright © 1944 Columbia University Press. Reprinted with permission of the publisher.*

4. Robert de Sorbon's
Regulations for His College,
before 1274

I wish that the custom which was instituted from the beginning in this house by the counsel of good men may be kept, and if anyone ever has transgressed it, that henceforth he shall not presume to do so.

No one therefore shall eat meat in the house on Advent, nor on Monday or Tuesday of Lent, nor from Ascension Day to Pentecost.

Also, I will that the community be not charged for meals taken in rooms. If there cannot be equality, it is better that the fellow eating in his room be charged than the entire community.

Also, no one shall eat in his room except for cause. If anyone has a guest, he shall eat in hall. If, moreover, it shall not seem expedient to the fellow to bring that guest to hall, let him eat in his room and he shall have the usual portion for himself, not for the guest. If, moreover, he wants more for himself or his guest, he should pay for it himself. . . .

Also, the fellows should be warned by the bearer of the roll that those eating in private rooms conduct themselves quietly and abstain from too much noise, lest those passing through the court and street be scandalized and lest the fellows in rooms adjoining be hindered in their studies. . . .

Also, the rule does not apply to the sick. If anyone eats in a private room because of sickness, he may have a fellow with him, if he wishes, to entertain and wait on him, who also shall have his due portion. What shall be the portion of a fellow shall be left to the discretion of the dispenser. If a fellow shall come late to lunch, if he comes from classes or a sermon or business of the community, he shall have his full portion, but if from his own affairs, he shall have bread only. . . .

Also, all shall wear closed outer garments, nor shall they have trimmings of vair or grise[8] or of red or green silk on the outer garment or hood.

Also, no one shall have loud shoes or clothing by which scandal might be generated in any way.

Also, no one shall be received in the house unless he shall be willing to leave off such and to observe the aforesaid rules.

Also, no one shall be received in the house unless he pledges faith that, if he happens to receive books from the common store, he will treat them carefully as if his own and on no condition remove or lend them out of the

---

8. **vair:** squirrel fur. **grise:** any type of gray fur.

house, and return them in good condition whenever required or whenever he leaves town.

Also, let every fellow have his own mark on his clothes and one only and different from the others. And let all the marks be written on a schedule and over each mark the name of whose it is. And let that schedule be given to the servant so that he may learn to recognize the mark of each one. And the servant shall not receive clothes from any fellow unless he sees the mark. And then the servant can return his clothes to each fellow. . . .

Also, for peace and utility we propound that no secular person living in town—scribe, corrector, or anyone else—unless for great cause eat, sleep in a room, or remain with the fellows when they eat, or have frequent conversation in the gardens or hall or other parts of the house, lest the secrets of the house and the remarks of the fellows be spread abroad.

Also, no outsider shall come to accountings or the special meetings of the fellows, and he whose guest he is shall see to this.

Also, no fellow shall bring in outsiders frequently to drink at commons, and if he does, he shall pay according to the estimate of the dispenser.

Also, no fellow shall have a key to the kitchen.

Also, no fellow shall presume to sleep outside the house in town, and if he did so for reason, he shall take pains to submit his excuse to the bearer of the roll. . . .

Also, no women of any sort shall eat in the private rooms. If anyone violates this rule, he shall pay the assessed penalty, namely, sixpence.[9] . . .

Also, no one shall form the habit of talking too loudly at table. Whoever after he has been warned about this by the prior shall have offended by speaking too loudly, provided this is established afterwards by testimony of several fellows to the prior, shall be held to the usual house penalty, namely two quarts of wine.

The penalty for transgression of statutes which do not fall under an oath is twopence, if the offenders are not reported by someone, or if they were, the penalty becomes sixpence in the case of fines. I understand "not reported" to mean that, if before the matter has come to the attention of the prior, the offender accuses himself to the prior or has told the clerk to write down twopence against him for such an offence, for it is not enough to say to the fellows, "I accuse myself."

---

9. This was a substantial amount for most students to pay.

Source 5 from James Harvey Robinson, editor and translator, Readings in European History, *vol. 1 (Boston: Ginn, 1904), pp. 450–452.*

5. Introduction to Peter
Abelard's *Sic et Non,* ca 1122

There are many seeming contradictions and even obscurities in the innumerable writings of the church fathers. Our respect for their authority should
not stand in the way of an effort on our part to come at the truth. The
obscurity and contradictions in ancient writings may be explained upon many
grounds, and may be discussed without impugning the good faith and
insight of the fathers. A writer may use different terms to mean the same
thing, in order to avoid a monotonous repetition of the same word. Common,
vague words may be employed in order that the common people may understand; and sometimes a writer sacrifices perfect accuracy in the interest
of a clear general statement. Poetical, figurative language is often obscure
and vague.

Not infrequently apocryphal works are attributed to the saints. Then, even
the best authors often introduce the erroneous views of others and leave the
reader to distinguish between the true and the false. Sometimes, as Augustine
confesses in his own case, the fathers ventured to rely upon the opinions of
others.

Doubtless the fathers might err; even Peter, the prince of the apostles, fell
into error; what wonder that the saints do not always show themselves
inspired? The fathers did not themselves believe that they, or their companions, were always right. Augustine found himself mistaken in some cases
and did not hesitate to retract his errors. He warns his admirers not to look
upon his letters as they would upon the Scriptures, but to accept only those
things which, upon examination, they find to be true.

All writings belonging to this class are to be read with full freedom to
criticise, and with no obligation to accept unquestioningly; otherwise the way
would be blocked to all discussion, and posterity be deprived of the excellent
intellectual exercise of debating difficult questions of language and presentation. But an explicit exception must be made in the case of the Old and
New Testaments. In the Scriptures, when anything strikes us as absurd, we
may not say that the writer erred, but that the scribe made a blunder in
copying the manuscripts, or that there is an error in interpretation, or that
the passage is not understood. The fathers make a very careful distinction
between the Scriptures and later works. They advocate a discriminating, not
to say suspicious, use of the writings of their own contemporaries.

In view of these considerations, I have ventured to bring together various dicta of the holy fathers, as they came to mind, and to formulate certain questions which were suggested by the seeming contradictions in the

statements. These questions ought to serve to excite tender readers to a zealous inquiry into truth and so sharpen their wits. The master key of knowledge is, indeed, a persistent and frequent questioning. Aristotle, the most clear-sighted of all the philosophers, was desirous above all things else to arouse this questioning spirit, for in his *Categories* he exhorts a student as follows: "It may well be difficult to reach a positive conclusion in these matters unless they be frequently discussed. It is by no means fruitless to be doubtful on particular points." By doubting we come to examine, and by examining we reach the truth.

> [*Abelard provides arguments for and*
> *against 158 different philosophical or*
> *theological propositions. The following are*
> *a few of the questions he discusses.*]

Should human faith be based upon reason, or no?
Is God one, or no?
Is God a substance, or no?
Does the first Psalm refer to Christ, or no?
Is sin pleasing to God, or no?
Is God the author of evil, or no?
Is God all-powerful, or no?
Can God be resisted, or no?
Has God free will, or no?
Was the first man persuaded to sin by the devil, or no?
Was Adam saved, or no?
Did all the apostles have wives except John, or no?
Are the flesh and blood of Christ in very truth and essence present in the
    sacrament of the altar, or no?
Do we sometimes sin unwillingly, or no?
Does God punish the same sin both here and in the future, or no?
Is it worse to sin openly than secretly, or no?

Source 6 from Roland H. Bainton, The Medieval Church *(Princeton, N.J.: D. VanNostrand, 1962), pp. 128–129.*

6. St. Anselm's Proof of the Existence of God, from His *Monologium*, ca 1070

I sought if I might find a single argument which would alone suffice to demonstrate that God exists. This I did in the spirit of faith seeking understanding. . . . Come now, O Lord my God, teach my heart where and how it may seek Thee. O Lord, if Thou art not here where shall I seek Thee absent, and if Thou art everywhere why do I not see Thee present? Surely Thou dwellest in light inaccessible. When wilt Thou enlighten our eyes? I do not presume to penetrate Thy profundity but only in some measure to understand Thy truth, which my heart believes and loves, for I seek not to understand that I may believe, but I believe in order that I may understand.

Now the fool will admit that there can be in the mind something than which nothing greater can be conceived. This, being understood, is in the mind, but it cannot be only in the mind, because it is possible to think of something which exists also in reality and that would be greater. If, therefore, that than which nothing greater can be conceived is only in the mind, that than which a greater cannot be conceived is that than which a greater can be conceived and this certainly cannot be. Consequently, without doubt, that than which nothing greater can be conceived exists both in the mind and in reality. This, then, is so sure that one cannot think of its not being so. For it is possible to think of something which one cannot conceive not to exist which is greater than that which cannot be conceived can be thought not to exist, it is not that a greater than which cannot be conceived. But this does not make sense. Therefore, it is true that something than which a greater cannot be conceived is not able to be conceived as not existing. This art Thou, O Lord, my God.

Source 7 from Lynn Thorndike, editor and translator, University Records and Life in the Middle Ages *(New York: Columbia University Press, 1944), pp. 66–67. Reprinted with permission of Columbia University Press, 562 W. 113th St., New York, NY 10025, via Copyright Clearance Center, Inc.*

7. Odofredus Announces His Law Lectures at Bologna, ca 1255

If you please, I will begin the *Old Digest*[10] on the eighth day or thereabouts after the feast of St. Michael[11] and I will finish it entire with all ordinary and extraordinary, Providence permitting, in the middle of August or thereabouts. The *Code*[12] I will always begin within about a fortnight of the feast of St. Michael and I will finish it with all ordinary and extraordinary, Providence permitting, on the first of August or thereabouts. The extraordinary lectures used not to be given by the doctors. And so all scholars including the

10. **Old Digest:** the first part of the *Digest,* the emperor Justinian's collation of laws, commentaries, and interpretations of laws by Roman jurists.
11. **feast of St. Michael:** September 29.
12. *Code:* another part of Justinian's collation of laws reflecting the additions to Roman law that came about after Christianity became the official religion of the empire.

unskilled and novices will be able to make good progress with me, for they will hear their text as a whole, nor will anything be left out, as was once done in this region, indeed was the usual practice. For I shall teach the unskilled and novices but also the advanced students. For the unskilled will be able to make satisfactory progress in the position of the case and exposition of the letter; the advanced students can become more erudite in the subtleties of questions and contrarieties. I shall also read all the glosses, which was not done before my time. . . .

For it is my purpose to teach you faithfully and in a kindly manner, in which instruction the following order has customarily been observed by the ancient and modern doctors and particularly by my master, which method I shall retain. First, I shall give you the summaries of each title before I come to the text. Second, I shall put forth well and distinctly and in the best terms I can the purport of each law. Third, I shall read the text in order to correct it. Fourth, I shall briefly restate the meaning. Fifth, I shall solve conflicts, adding general matters (which are commonly called *brocardica*) and subtle and useful distinctions and questions with the solutions, so far as divine Providence shall assist me. And if any law is deserving of a review by reason of its fame or difficulty, I shall reserve it for an afternoon review.

Source 8 from Anders Piltz, The World of Medieval Learning, *translated by David Jones (Totowa, N.J.: Barnes & Noble, 1981), p. 97.*

8. Introduction to *Digest* of Emperor Justinian, sixth century

Public law is the legislation which refers to the Roman state, *private law* on the other hand is of value to the individual. Common law contains statutes about sacrifices, the priesthood and civil servants. Private law can be divided into three parts: it comprises regulations based on natural law and regulations governing the intercourse of nations and of individuals. *Natural law* is what is taught to all living creatures by nature itself, laws which apply not only to mankind but to every living creature on the earth, in the heavens or in the seas. It is this that sanctions the union of man and woman, which is called marriage, and likewise the bearing and upbringing of children: we can see that other living creatures also possess understanding of this law. *International law* is the [commonly recognized set of] laws applied by every nation of the world. As can be seen it differs from natural law in that the latter is the same for all living creatures whereas the former only concerns human intercourse. . . . *Civil law* does not deviate completely from natural law but neither is it subordinate to it . . . . It is either written or unwritten . . . . Its sources are laws, popular decisions, decisions of the senate, the decrees of princes and the opinions of jurists.... *Justice* is the earnest and steadfast desire to give every man the rights he is entitled to. The injunctions of the law are these: live honestly, do no man injury, give to every man what he is entitled to.

Jurisprudence is knowledge of divine and human things, the study of right and wrong.

Source 9 from The Letters of St. Bernard of Clairvaux, *translated by Bruno Scott James (Chicago: Henry Regnery Co. 1953), pp. 321, 328.*

9. Extracts from *The Letters of St. Bernard of Clairvaux*, 1140

Master Peter Abelard is a monk without a rule, a prelate without responsibility.... He speaks iniquity openly. He corrupts the integrity of the faith and the chastity of the Church. He oversteps the landmarks placed by our Fathers in discussing and writing about faith, the sacraments, and the Holy Trinity; he changes each thing according to his pleasure, adding to it or taking from it. In his books and in his works he shows himself to be a fabricator of falsehood, a coiner of perverse dogmas, proving himself a heretic not so much by his error as by his obstinate defence of error. He is a man who does not know his limitations, making void the virtue of the cross by the cleverness of his words. Nothing in heaven or on earth is hidden from him, except himself.... He has defiled the Church; he has infected with his own blight the minds of simple people. He tries to explore with his reason what the devout mind grasps at once with a vigorous faith. Faith believes, it does not dispute. But this man, apparently holding God suspect, will not believe anything until he has first examined it with his reason. When the Prophet says, "Unless you believe, you shall not understand," this man decries willing faith as levity, misusing that testimony of Solomon: "He that is hasty to believe is light of head." Let him therefore blame the Blessed Virgin Mary for quickly believing the angel when he announced to her that she should conceive and bring forth a son. Let him also blame him who, while on the verge of death, believed those words of One who was also dying: "This day thou shalt be with me in Paradise."

Source 10 from Cecil Headlam, The Story of Oxford *(London: Dent, 1907), pp. 234–235.*

10. Anonymous Account of a Student Riot at Oxford, 13th century

They [the townsmen] seized and imprisoned all scholars on whom they could lay hands, invaded their inns, made havoc of their goods and trampled their books under foot. In the face of such provocation the Proctors[13] sent their bedels[14] about the town, forbidding the students to leave their inns. But all commands and exhortations were in vain. By nine o'clock next morning, bands of scholars were parading the streets in martial array. If the Proctors failed to restrain them, the mayor was equally powerless to restrain his townsmen. The great bell of S. Martin's rang out an alarm; oxhorns were sounded in the streets; messengers were sent into the country to collect rustic allies. The clerks,[15] who numbered three thousand in all, began their attack simultaneously in various quarters. They broke open warehouses in the Spicery, the Cutlery and elsewhere. Armed with bows and arrows, swords and bucklers, slings and stones, they fell upon their opponents. Three they slew, and wounded fifty or more. One band, led by Fulk de Neyrmit, Rector of Piglesthorne, and his brother, took up a position in High Street between the Churches of S. Mary and All Saints', and attacked the house of a certain Edward Hales. This Hales was a longstanding enemy of the clerks. There were no half measures with him. He seized his crossbow, and from an upper chamber sent an unerring shaft into the eye of the pugnacious rector. The death of their valiant leader caused the clerks to lose heart. They fled, closely pursued by the townsmen and country-folk. Some were struck down in the streets, and others who had taken refuge in the churches were dragged out and driven mercilessly to prison, lashed with thongs and goaded with iron spikes.

Complaints of murder, violence and robbery were lodged straight-way with the King by both parties. The townsmen claimed three thousand pounds' damage. The commissioners, however, appointed to decide the matter, condemned them to pay two hundred marks, removed the bailiffs, and banished twelve of the most turbulent citizens from Oxford. Then the terms of peace were formally ratified.

13. **proctor:** university official who maintained order and supervised examinations.
14. **bedel:** assistant to the proctor.
15. **clerks:** here, students and teachers.

Source 11 from Dana Carleton Munro, editor and translator, Translations and Reprints from the Original Sources of European History, *vol. 2, no. 3 (Philadelphia: University of Pennsylvania Press, no date), pp. 19–21.*

11. Jacques de Vitry's Description of Student Life at Paris, ca 1225

Almost all the students at Paris, foreigners and natives, did absolutely nothing except learn or hear something new. Some studied merely to acquire knowledge, which is curiosity; others to acquire fame, which is vanity; others still for the sake of gain, which is cupidity and the vice of simony. Very few studied for their own edification, or that of others. They wrangled and disputed not merely about the various sects or about some discussions; but the differences between the countries also caused dissensions, hatreds and virulent animosities among them, and they impudently uttered all kinds of affronts and insults against one another.

They affirmed that the English were drunkards and had tails; the sons of France proud, effeminate and carefully adorned like women. They said that the Germans were furious and obscene at their feasts; the Normans, vain and boastful; the Poitevins, traitors and always adventurers. The Burgundians they considered vulgar and stupid. The Bretons were reputed to be fickle and changeable and were often reproached for the death of Arthur. The Lombards were called avaricious, vicious and cowardly; the Romans, seditious, turbulent and slanderous; the Sicilians, tyrannical and cruel; the inhabitants of Brabant, men of blood, incendiaries, brigands and ravishers; those of Flanders, fickle, prodigal, gluttonous, yielding as butter, and slothful. After such insults, from words they often came to blows.

I will not speak of those logicians, before whose eyes flitted constantly "the lice of Egypt," that is to say, all the sophistical subtleties, so that no one could comprehend their eloquent discourses in which, as says Isaiah, "there is no wisdom." As to the doctors of theology, "seated in Moses' seat," they were swollen with learning, but their charity was not edifying. Teaching and not practicing, they have "become as sounding brass or a tinkling cymbal," or like a canal of stone, always dry, which ought to carry water to "the bed of spices." They not only hated one another, but by their flatteries they enticed away the students of others; each one seeking his own glory, but caring not a whit about the welfare of souls.

Having listened intently to these words of the Apostle, "If a man desire the office of a bishop, he desireth a good work," they kept multiplying the prebends,[16] and seeking after the offices; and yet they sought the work

---

16. **prebends:** that part of church revenues paid as a clergyman's salary.

decidedly less than the preëminence, and they desired above all to have "the uppermost rooms at feasts and the chief seats in the synagogue, and greetings in the market." Although the Apostle James said, "My brethren, be not many masters," they on the contrary were in such haste to become masters, that most of them were not able to have any students, except by entreaties and payments. Now it is safer to listen than to teach, and a humble listener is better than an ignorant and presumptuous doctor. In short, the Lord had reserved for Himself among them all, only a few honorable and timorous men, who had not stood "in the way of sinners," nor sat down with the others in the envenomed seat.

Sources 12 and 13 from Charles Homer Haskins, The Rise of Universities *(Ithaca, N.Y.: Cornell University Press, 1957), pp. 77–80; pp. 85–87.*

12. Two Letters, thirteenth century

B. to his venerable master A., greeting. This is to inform you that I am studying at Oxford with the greatest diligence, but the matter of money stands greatly in the way of my promotion,[17] as it is now two months since I spent the last of what you sent me. The city is expensive and makes many demands; I have to rent lodgings, buy necessaries, and provide for many other things which I cannot now specify. Wherefore I respectfully beg your paternity that by the promptings of divine pity you may assist me, so that I may be able to complete what I have well begun. For you must know that without Ceres and Bacchus Apollo[18] grows cold.

To his son G. residing at Orleans P. of Besançon sends greetings with paternal zeal. It is written, "He also that is slothful in his work is brother to him that is a great waster." I have recently discovered that you live dissolutely and slothfully, preferring license to restraint and play to work and strumming a guitar while the others are at their studies, whence it happens that you have read but one volume of law while your more industrious companions have read several. Wherefore I have decided to exhort you herewith to repent utterly of your dissolute and careless ways, that you may no longer be called a waster and your shame may be turned to good repute.

17. **promotion:** that is, attaining his degree.
18. **Ceres:** Roman god of grain. **Bacchus:** god of wine. **Apollo:** god of wisdom.

13. Three Anonymous Student Poems, twelfth century

I, a wandering scholar lad,
  Born for toil and sadness,
Oftentimes am driven by
  Poverty to madness.

Literature and knowledge I
  Fain would still be earning,
Were it not that want of pelf[19]
  Makes me cease from learning.

These torn clothes that cover me
  Are too thin and rotten;
Oft I have to suffer cold,
  By the warmth forgotten.

Scarce I can attend at church,
  Sing God's praises duly;
Mass and vespers both I miss,
  Though I love them truly.

Oh, thou pride of N——,
  By thy worth I pray thee
Give the suppliant help in need,
  Heaven will sure repay thee.

Take a mind unto thee now
  Like unto St. Martin;
Clothe the pilgrim's nakedness,
  Wish him well at parting.

So may God translate your soul
  Into peace eternal,
And the bliss of saints be yours
  In His realm supernal.

We in our wandering,
Blithesome and squandering,
  Tara, tantara, teino!

Eat to satiety,
Drink with propriety;
  Tara, tantara, teino!

Laugh till our sides we split,
Rags on our hides we fit;
  Tara, tantara, teino!

Jesting eternally,
Quaffing infernally:
  Tara, tantara, teino!
            etc.

Some are gaming, some are drinking,
Some are living without thinking;
And of those who make the racket,
Some are stripped of coat and jacket;
Some get clothes of finer feather,
Some are cleaned out altogether;
No one there dreads death's invasion,
But all drink in emulation.

19. **pelf:** a contemptuous term for money.

QUESTIONS TO CONSIDER

You have now examined medieval universities and colleges from four points of view—those of the authorities who established them, the teachers who taught in them, the church officials who criticized them, and the students who attended them. In refining your description of university life, think first about points on which a number of sources agree. What role did religious and secular authorities play in the universities, both in their founding and in day-to-day operations? What privileges were extended to teachers and students, and how did these benefits affect their relationship with townspeople? Given these privileges along with student attitudes and actions, what opinion would you expect townspeople to have of students? Which of Sorbon's rules would you expect to have been frequently broken? What qualities did authorities and teachers alike see as vital to effective teaching? What qualities did both try to encourage in students? Would students have agreed about any of these? What problems did the authorities, teachers, and students all agree were most pressing for students?

Now turn to points on which you have contradictory information. How would you compare Abelard's beliefs about the role of logic in education with those of Bernard and de Vitry? How might Bernard and de Vitry have viewed Anselm's attempt to prove the existence of God through reason? Would Abelard have believed that the rules for students set out in Sources 1 through 4 helped or hindered the learning process? What suggestions for educational improvements might a philosopher like Abelard have made? A churchman like Bernard? Would Anselm and Odofredus have agreed about the proper methods and aims of education?

De Vitry's critique and the student poetry have pointed out that the rules for student life set out in Sources 1 through 4 were not always followed. The consequences of St. Bernard's criticism similarly demonstrate that Abelard's assertion of the need for free discussion of all topics was an ideal and not always the reality in medieval universities. In 1140, St. Bernard convinced the church leadership at the Council of Sens to condemn Abelard's teachings. Abelard appealed to the pope, who upheld the council's decision, and Abelard retired to a monastery, never to teach again. What does this incident indicate about where the ultimate authority in the university lay? Does this assertion of papal authority contradict any of the ideas expressed in other sources for this chapter besides Abelard's writings?

Some of the contradictions you have discovered are inherent in the highly different points of view of the four groups and are irreconcilable. You must, however, make some effort to resolve those contradictions that involve conflicting points of *fact* rather than simply conflicting *opinions*. Historians resolve contradictions in their sources by a variety of methods: by assessing the authors' intent and possible biases, giving weight to evidence that is likely to be most objective; by judging each source as partially valid, speculating on how each author's point of view might have affected his or her description; by trying to find additional information confirming one side or the other. At this point you can use the first two methods in your own thinking: Which observers do you judge to be most objective? Why did the students, teachers, and officials have different viewpoints in the first place? (You can also think about the third method historians use to resolve contradictions in their evidence: What other types of sources would you examine to confirm what you have discovered here?) Once you have made these judgments, you can complete your description of medieval university life.

Now move on to the second part of your task in this chapter, which is to compare medieval and modern university life. Some of the more striking contrasts have probably already occurred to you, but the best way to proceed is to think first about your evidence. What types of sources would give you the information for modern universities that you have unearthed for medieval ones? What are the modern equivalents of the medieval rules and ordinances? Of descriptions of student actions? Of student poetry? Of course announcements? Of philosophical treatises? Besides such parallel sources, where else can you find information about modern universities? What types of sources generated from modern universities,

or from their students and teachers, have no medieval equivalent?

After considering these points of similarity and difference in sources, we are ready to make a specific comparison of university life in medieval and modern times. Because higher education in the United States is so diverse—some colleges and universities are public and some private, some religious and some nonsectarian, some residential and some commuter—it would be best if you compared your own institution with the more generalized description of medieval universities that you have developed. Do you see any modern equivalents to the privileges granted students by popes and kings? To the frequent clashes between universities and their surrounding communities? To the pope's restriction of "academic freedom" in the case of Abelard? How would you compare the relationship between religious and political authorities in medieval universities and in your own institution? The concern of authorities for the methods and content of higher education? How would you compare student residential life? Student problems? The students themselves? Relations between students and their parents? How would you compare the subjects taught? The method of teaching? The status of the faculty? Relations between students and teachers? Teachers' and students' views of the ultimate aims of education?

Once you have drawn up your comparison, you will need to perform what is often the most difficult task of any historical inquiry, which is to suggest reasons for what you have discovered. In doing this, you need to speculate not only about why some things have changed, but also about why others have remained the same. In your view, what is the most important difference between medieval and modern universities, and why?

The pattern set by Paris and Bologna was a popular one; by 1500, more than eighty universities were in existence throughout Europe. Students often traveled from university to university in search of the best teachers or most amenable surroundings; because there were no admission forms or credits required for graduation, transferring from school to school was much easier in the Middle Ages than it is today.

As you have deduced from the sources, medieval students and teachers were criticized for all the seven deadly sins: greed, sloth, pride, lust, gluttony, envy, and anger. Toward the end of the Middle Ages, the university system itself came under increasing attack for being too remote from worldly concerns, providing students only with useless philosophical information that would never help them in the real world of politics and business. Especially in Italy, independent teachers of speech and writing began to offer young men who wanted an education an alternative to universities, setting up academies to teach practical rhetorical and literary skills for those who planned to engage in commerce, banking, or politics. This new program of study, called *humanism,* emphasized language and literature rather than theology and philosophy.

Though the universities initially opposed the humanist curriculum, by the sixteenth century a considerable number, especially the newer ones, began to change their offerings. They established endowed chairs for teachers of Latin, Greek, and Hebrew, particularly because students who had trained at humanist secondary schools demanded further language training.

The gradual introduction of humanism set a pattern that universities were to follow when any new body of knowledge or subject matter emerged. Innovative subjects and courses were at first generally taught outside the universities in separate academies or institutes, then slowly integrated into the university curriculum. In the seventeenth and eighteenth centuries, natural science was added in this way; in the nineteenth century, the social sciences and modern languages; and in the twentieth, a whole range of subjects, such as agriculture, engineering, and the fine arts. Thus, even though the university has survived since the Middle Ages, Peter Abelard or Robert de Sorbon might have difficulty recognizing the institution in its present-day form.

CHAPTER NINE

CAPITALISM AND CONFLICT

IN THE MEDIEVAL CLOTH TRADE

During the Early Middle Ages, western Europe was largely a rural society. Most of the cities of the Roman Empire had shrunk to villages, and the roads the Romans had built were allowed to fall into disrepair. Manors and villages were relatively self-sufficient in basic commodities such as grain and cloth, and even in times of famine they could not import the food they needed because the cost of transportation was too high. Much local trade was carried out by barter, and any long-distance trade that existed was handled by Jews, Greeks, and Syrians, who imported luxury goods like spices, silks, and perfumes from the Near East. These extremely expensive commodities were purchased only by nobles and high-ranking churchmen. The lack of much regional trade is reflected in the almost complete absence of sources about trade before the tenth century. Commercial documents are extremely rare, and both public and private records testify to the agrarian nature of early medieval society.

This situation began to change in the tenth century, when Vikings in the north and Italians in the south revived long-distance European commerce. The Vikings initially raided and plundered along the coasts of northern Europe, but they soon turned to trading with the very people whose lands they had threatened. At the same time, merchants from the cities of Genoa, Pisa, and Florence were taking over former Muslim trade routes in the western Mediterranean. These Italian merchants began to keep increasingly elaborate records of their transactions and devised new methods of bookkeeping to keep track of their ventures. They developed new types of partnerships to share the risks and found ways to get around the medieval Christian church's prohibition of the lending of money at interest (termed *usury*). These changes, combined with the growth in trade, led to a transformation of the European economy often called the *Commercial Revolution*.

Once western European merchants began to trade more extensively with the East, particularly after the Crusades in the twelfth century, it became clear that the balance of trade favored the East; Eastern luxuries such as spices and silks were paid for primarily in gold. Gradually, however, western European merchants began to add high- and medium-quality woolen cloth, with Italian merchants trading cloth made in Flanders (modern-day Belgium and northeast France) to Asia and Africa, carrying it all the way to the court of Genghis Khan. They also shipped increasing quantities of cloth to other locations in Europe, eventually importing raw wool from England to supply the Flemish cloth-makers and handling both long-distance and regional trade.

The reinvigoration of trade in the Commercial Revolution came with, and was one of the causes of, a rebirth of town life. Especially in Italy and the Low Countries, but in many other parts of Europe as well, towns began to spring up around cathedrals, monasteries, and castles or at locations favorable for trade, such as ports or major crossroads. Many of these became cloth-producing centers, as weavers and other artisans involved in the many stages of cloth production gathered together to manufacture goods for regional and long-distance traders. Cloth merchants in these towns—sometimes in combination with the merchants of other types of products—joined together to form a merchants' guild that prohibited nonmembers from trading in the town. These same merchants often made up

the earliest town government, serving as mayors and members of the city council, so that a town's economic policies were determined by its merchants' self-interest. Acting through the city council, the merchants' guilds determined the hours that markets would be open, decided which coins would be accepted as currency, and set prices on imported and local goods. Foreign affairs were also guided by the merchants, and cities formed alliances, termed *hanses,* with other cities to gain trading benefits.

From its beginnings, the trade in fine cloth was organized as a capitalist enterprise. Cloth merchants, called *drapers,* purchased raw materials, hired workers for all stages of production, and then sold the finished cloth; they rarely did any production themselves, and in some parts of Europe they were actually forbidden to do so. Some stages of production might be carried out in drapers' homes or in buildings that they owned, but more often production was carried out in the houses of those that they hired, who were paid by the piece rather than by the hour or day; these workers, especially those who wove cloth, might in turn hire several people to weave alongside them.

Cloth went through many stages from sheep to finished cloth. Once the sheep were sheared, the wool was sorted, beaten, and washed; it was then carded and spun by women using either hand spindles or, after the thirteenth century, spinning wheels. Next, the thread was prepared for weaving by *warpers,* who wound the long threads for the warp (warp threads are those that run lengthwise on a piece of cloth), and by *spoolers*, who wound woof threads (woof threads are those that run crosswise). The prepared thread went to the weavers, who used horizontal treadle looms. After the cloth was woven, it went to *fullers*, who stamped the cloth with their feet in troughs full of water, alkaline earth, and urine to soften it and fill in the spaces between the threads. (In the thirteenth century in some parts of Europe, fulling began to take place in water-powered fulling mills.) The cloth was then cleaned, hung to dry on wooden frames called *tenters*, and stretched to the correct width. The cloth was finished by repeatedly brushing it with thistle-like plants called *teasles* set in rows on a frame and then shearing the resulting fuzz off with large shears. It could be dyed at any stage in this process, as wool, thread, or whole cloth.

Some of these processes, such as dyeing, weaving, and shearing, required great skill and were usually reserved for men; others, such as spinning, sorting, and stretching on the tenter, called for less skill and were often carried out by women or young people. Once the cloth had been sheared for the final time, it went to the drapers, who monopolized all cutting of bolts of cloth and, thus, all retail sales. In areas where merchants organized production on a huge scale, such as Florence, there was a distinction between merchants and drapers, with the major merchants doing no actual cloth cutting themselves but simply hiring drapers; in most parts of Europe, however, merchants cut as well as sold, and were often called merchant-drapers.

Especially in Flanders and Florence, the merchants who controlled the cloth trade attempted to regulate everything down to the smallest detail. They set up precise standards of quality with severe penalties for those who did not meet them, regulated the length of the workday and the wages of all workers, and sent out inspectors regularly to enforce the ordinances and handle disputes. At first there was little opposition, but, beginning in the twelfth and thirteenth centuries in many areas, cloth workers challenged the merchants' control through strikes and revolts, and attempted to form their own organizations, called *craft guilds*. (At the same time, those who produced or handled many other sorts of products, such as shoemakers, butchers, and blacksmiths, were also forming separate craft guilds.) In some areas, such as Florence, the cloth merchants were successful at stopping all organizing and suppressing all rebellions, but in others, such as many cities in Flanders, the merchants lost, and the wool workers were able to form their own guilds and even become part of the city government for at least a short period of time. In some places, those artisans who were highly skilled and who owned some of their own equipment, such as weavers, fullers, dyers, and shearers, were able to form guilds, whereas the less-skilled spinners and sorters were not.

In periods during which they were able to form independently, the craft guilds took over the regulation of production from the merchant guilds. They set quality standards for their particular product and regulated the size of workshops, the training period, and the conduct of members. In most cities, individual guilds, such as those of weavers or dyers, achieved a monopoly in the production of one particular product, forbidding non-members to work. The craft guild then chose some of its members to act as inspectors and set up a court to hear disputes between members, although the city court remained the final arbiter, particularly in cases involving conflict between merchants and artisans or between members of craft guilds and those who were not members.

Each guild set the pattern by which members were trained. If one wanted to become a dyer, for instance, one spent four to seven years as an apprentice and then at least that long as a journeyman, working in the shop of a master dyer, after which one could theoretically make one's masterpiece. If the masterpiece was approved by the other master dyers and if they thought the market in their town was large enough to allow for another dyer, one could then become a master and start a shop. Though the amount of time a candidate had to spend as an apprentice and a journeyman varied slightly from guild to guild, all guilds—both those in the cloth industry and those in other sorts of production—followed this same three-stage process. The apprentices and journeymen generally lived with the master and his family, and were often forbidden to marry. Conversely, many guilds required that masters be

married, as they believed a wife was absolutely essential to the running of the shop and the household, and also felt that married men were likely to be more stable and dependable.

The master's wife assisted in running the shop, often selling the goods her husband had produced. Their children, both male and female, also worked alongside the apprentices and journeymen; the sons were sometimes formally apprenticed, but the daughters generally were not, since many guilds limited formal membership to males. Most guilds did allow a master's widow to continue operating a shop for a set period of time after her husband's death, for they recognized that she had the necessary skills and experience. Such widows paid all guild dues but did not vote or hold office in the guilds because they were not considered full members. The fact that women were not formally guild members did not mean that they did not work in guild shops, however, for alongside the master's wife and daughters, female domestic servants often performed the less-skilled tasks. In addition, there were a few all-female guilds in several European cities, particularly Cologne and Paris, in which girls were formally apprenticed in the same way boys were in regular craft guilds.

Both craft and merchants' guilds were not only economic organizations but also systems of social support. Though they were harsh against outsiders, they were protective and supportive of their members. They took care of elderly masters who could no longer work, and often supported masters' widows and orphans. They maintained an altar at a city church, and provided for the funerals of members and baptisms of their children. Guild members marched together in city parades, and reinforced their feelings of solidarity with one another by special ceremonies and distinctive dress.

Whether workers were able to form separate craft guilds or not, conflicts between merchants and workers over the cloth trade were a common feature of medieval town life in the major centers of cloth production. These conflicts often disrupted cloth production from a certain area, allowing other areas to expand their trade. In the late fourteenth century, for example, mass rebellions in Florence and Flanders benefited English weavers, who began to turn a greater percentage of English wool into cloth rather than exporting it as raw wool to the Continent. Government policy in England also helped the English weavers, as the crown in 1347 imposed a 33 percent tariff on the export of raw wool, while setting only a 2 percent tariff on the export of finished cloth. The crown also ordered people to wear English cloth (a provision that was very difficult to enforce) and encouraged Flemish cloth-makers

displaced by unrest in their own towns to settle in England. Flemish cloth-makers also migrated to many towns in Germany, and by the sixteenth century the production of wool cloth was more dispersed throughout Europe than it had been several centuries earlier.

Often the change from the medieval to the modern economy is described as "the rise of capitalism," a change accompanied by "the rise of the middle class." Though specialists in the period disagree about many aspects of the development of capitalism, they agree that cloth production and trade was the earliest and most important capitalist enterprise in medieval Europe. Thus we can see in the cloth trade many of the issues that would emerge later in other parts of the economy, and that are still issues facing business and governments today. Your task in this chapter will be to use a variety of sources regarding cloth production from several parts of Europe to answer these questions: What were the key economic and social goals of governments, merchant-capitalists, and artisans regarding the cloth trade, and how did they seek to achieve these aims? What economic and social conflicts emerged as the cloth trade grew and changed?

SOURCES AND METHOD

In analyzing the development of the cloth trade, historians have a wide variety of documents at their disposal. Because cloth was regarded by city

and national governments as so important, their records include many laws that refer to the cloth trade, and often describe royal or municipal actions that encouraged cloth production. Some of the earliest attempts by governments to gather statistical information also refer to wool and cloth. The merchants' and later craft guilds themselves kept records—both regulations and ordinances, and records of judgments against those who broke these ordinances. Private business documents and personal documents such as contracts also often refer to aspects of the cloth trade.

In general, these sources can be divided into two basic types, a division that holds equally for sources from many other historical periods. The first type is *prescriptive*—laws, regulations, and ordinances that describe how the cloth trade was supposed to operate and how the guild or government officials who wrote the ordinances hoped things would be. These documents do not simply describe an ideal, however; they were generally written in response to events already taking place, so they can tell us about real problems and the attitudes of guilds and officials toward these problems. It is sources such as these that will allow us to answer the first of our questions, for they tell us specifically about goals and efforts to achieve them. What they cannot tell us is if any of these efforts worked, or what problems these efforts might have caused. For this we need to turn to a second type of primary evidence, *descriptive* documents such as court records and statistical information. Through these records we can observe how regulations were actually enforced, and assess—to a limited degree, because medieval statistics must always be used very carefully—the results of government and guild efforts to build up the cloth trade. As you are reading the sources, then, the

first question you have to ask yourself is whether the record is prescriptive or descriptive, for confusing the two can give a very skewed view of medieval economic and social issues. (This kind of discrimination must be applied to any historical source, of course, and is not always an easy task. Sometimes even prominent historians have built a whole pyramid of erroneous theories about the past by assuming that prescriptive sources accurately described reality.)

The first three selections are all laws regarding the wool trade issued by territorial rulers. Source 1 comes from what are termed the laws of King Edward the Confessor of England (though they were written after his reign, sometime after 1115), setting out what were termed the "Liberties of London," or what we would term the rights accorded the citizens of London by the king. Source 2 is a similar law of the count of Holland regarding the city of Dortrecht. Read each of these carefully. What special privileges were granted to the citizens of these towns by their rulers? Source 3 is a proclamation of the countess of Flanders in 1224. What extra inducement did she offer to encourage wool production in the town of Courtrai? At this point you may want to begin a three-column list or chart, one column for the goals stated either explicitly or implicitly in the sources, a second for the actions taken to achieve those goals, and a third for the conflicts alluded to or discussed.

The next three sources are regulations regarding those who worked in cloth production issued by merchants' guilds or by the city councils, which were usually dominated by the merchants. Source 4 is from the English town of Winchester, Source 5 from the German town of Stendal, and Source 6 from the Flemish town of Arras. Read each of these sources carefully and add the information there to your three-column list. What were the most important aims of the merchants? What punishments did they set for those who broke the regulations, and how did they otherwise enforce their rules? Do the kinds of distinctions they make between groups—citizens and foreigners; those who make cloth and those who cut and sell it; members of artisans' families and nonmembers; masters, journeymen, and apprentices in a shop—suggest or perhaps contribute to social conflicts? What other types of conflicts are mentioned explicitly? (In all of these sources, the word "guest" or "foreigner" is used for someone who comes from a different town or village, and not necessarily from a different country.)

Though in many cities we do not have complete records of how well the provisions set forth in the ordinances were actually carried out, we can get glimpses from court records and similar sources from some cities. Through these we can see some instances of the enforcement of regulations and of the conflicts that this could cause. Sources 7 through 10 are examples of actual cases involving disputes in the cloth trade; Sources 7 and 8 are from fourteenth-century Flanders, and Sources 9 and 10 from sixteenth-century Germany. In Source 7, what is Jacquemars des Mares's aim? That of the cloth inspectors and the city

council? How well do the actions of the city councils in Sources 7, 8, and 9 reinforce the aims of the merchants as set out in Sources 4, 5, and 6? Though the ultimate decisions of the city council in Source 10 are not known, from the supplication itself we can get a good idea of actions taken by members of the weavers' guild. Do these fit with the aims of the merchants, or are the aims of these artisans somewhat different? Why might women have appealed to the city council, made up largely of merchants, to rectify actions taken against them by artisans?

Along with government records, private records can give us additional information about the cloth trade. Most private business documents are primarily descriptive in nature, although they can also contain information about the aims of those who drew them up. Source 11 contains two apprenticeship contracts from the thirteenth century. What were the aims of the parents involved and of the master weavers? Can we get any hints of potential conflicts that arose in apprenticeships? Source 12 contains several insurance contracts for wool and cloth shipments from a fourteenth-century Italian merchant. Why would wool traders have wanted to enlist his services? How does their using an insurer fit with their other actions?

The final sources for this chapter are statistical and rely on both official and private records. Source 13 consists of two charts of the total number of cloths produced in Florence and Ypres in Flanders, based on guild records. Source 14 consists of two charts of the export of raw wool and wool cloth from England, based on customs records that began after customs duties were imposed in 1347. These records do not include cloth made for use in England and report *only* exports that went through the customs office (there was a great deal of smuggling, so they may significantly underreport the total amounts exported), but we can use them in conjunction with the charts of Source 13 to ascertain general trends. How would you compare the trends in cloth production for the three areas? How would you assess the success of English government policies that encouraged weaving? How might the decline in the amount of raw wool exported from England have affected weaving in Florence, Ypres, and other areas, despite the efforts there of governments or merchants?

THE EVIDENCE

Source 1 from Benjamin Thorpe, Ancient Laws and Institutes of England *(London: Eyre and Spottiswoode, 1840), p. 462.*

1. Laws Regarding Foreign Merchants Under King Edward the Confessor of England, after 1115

And after he has entered the city, let a foreign merchant be lodged wherever it please him. But if he bring dyed cloth, let him see to it that he does not sell his merchandise at retail, but that he sell not less than a dozen pieces at a time. And if he bring pepper, or cumin, or ginger, or alum, or brasil wood, or resin, or incense, let him sell not less than fifteen pounds at a time. But if he bring belts, let him sell not less than a thousand at a time. And if he bring cloths of silk, or wool or linen, let him see that he cut them not, but sell them whole.

Also a foreign merchant may not buy dyed cloth, nor make the dye in the city, nor do any work which belongs by right to the citizens.

Source 2 from C. Gross, The Gild Merchant *(Oxford: Clarendon, 1890), vol. 1, p. 293.*

2. Law Regarding Cloth Cutting Under the Count of Holland, 1200

I, Theodore, by the grace of God, Count of Holland, and Adelaide, Countess of Holland, my wife, wish it to be known to all, both present and future, that we decree that our townsmen of Dortrecht may enjoy in their own right the following freedom in the said town, namely, that it is permitted to no one in Dortrecht to cut cloth for retail sale except to those who are designated by this trade, being called cutters of cloth, and except they be in the hanse[1] and fraternity of the townsmen belonging to Dortrecht. And that this charter, instituted by us, may forever be secure and intact, we corroborate it by affixing our seals thereto, and the signatures of witnesses.

These are the witnesses. . . .

Source 3 from Roy C. Cave and Herbert H. Coulson, A Source Book for Medieval Economic History *(New York: Biblo and Tannen, 1965), p. 374.*

3. Proclamation Regarding Taxes by the Countess of Flanders, 1224

I, Joan, Countess of Flanders and Hainault, wish it to be known to all both now and in the future, that I and my successors cannot and ought not to take any tax or payment from the fifty men who shall come to live at Courtrai, for as long as they remain here, to work in the woolen industry from this day on. But their heirs, after the decease of their parents, shall serve me just as my other burgesses do. Given at Courtrai, in the year of the Lord 1224, on the feast of St. Cecilia.

1. **hanse:** in this instance, the merchants' guild.

Source 4 from Beverley Town Documents, *edited by A. F. Leach, Publications of the Selden Society, vol. 14 (London: Selden Society, 1900), appendix II, pp. 134–135.*

4. City Ordinances Regarding Weavers in Winchester, England, ca 1209

This is the law of the Fullers and Weavers of Winchester: Be it known that no weaver or fuller may dry or dye cloth nor go outside the city to sell it. They may sell their cloth to no foreigner, but only to merchants of the city. And if it happens that, in order to enrich himself, one of the weavers or fullers wishes to go outside the city to sell his merchandise, he may be very sure that the honest men of the city will take all his cloth and bring it back to the city, and that he will forfeit it in the presence of the aldermen and honest men of the city. And if any weaver or fuller sell his cloth to a foreigner, the foreigner shall lose his cloth, and the other shall remain at the mercy of the city for as much as he has. Neither the weaver nor the fuller may buy anything except for his trade but by making an agreement with the mayor. No free man[2] can be accused by a weaver or a fuller, nor can a weaver or a fuller bear testimony against a free man. If any of them become rich, and wish to give up his trade, he may forswear it and turn his tools out of the house, and then do as much for the city as he is able in his freedom.

Sources 5 and 6 from Roy C. Cave and Herbert H. Coulson, A Source Book for Medieval Economic History *(New York: Biblo and Tannen, 1965), pp. 246–248; pp. 250–252.*

5. City Ordinances Regarding Guilds in Stendal, Germany, 1231 and 1233

We make known . . . that we, . . . desiring to provide properly for our city of Stendal, have changed, and do change, for the better, the laws of the gild [*sic*] brethren, and of those who are called cloth-cutters, so that they might have the same laws in this craft as their gild brethren the garment-cutters in Magdeburg have been accustomed to observe in the past.

These are the laws:

1. No one shall presume to cut cloth, except he be of our craft; those who break this rule will amend to the gild with three talents.[3]

2. **free man:** a citizen of Winchester. The weavers and fullers were not fully citizens at this point, but probably came from outside Winchester.

3. **talents, denarii, solidi:** different coins in circulation in Stendal. A mark was worth about 160 denarii; a solidus was worth about 25 denarii. The value of a talent varied widely.

2. Thrice a year there ought to be a meeting of the brethren, and whoever does not come to it will amend according to justice.

3. Whoever wishes to enter the fraternity whose father was a brother and cut cloth will come with his friends to the meeting of the brethren, and if he conduct himself honestly, he will be able to join the gild at the first request on payment of five solidi, and he will give six denarii to the master. And if he be dishonest and should not conduct himself well, he should be put off until the second or third meeting. But any of our citizens who wish to enter the gild, if he be an honest man, and worthy, will give a talent to the brethren on entry into the gild, and will present a solidus to the master. But if a guest who is an honest man should decide to join our fraternity, he will give thirty solidi to the gild on his entry, and eighteen denarii to the master. . . . But if any brother should make cloth against the institutions of the brethren, and of their decrees, which he ought on the advice of the consuls to observe, he will present to the consuls by way of emendation one talent for each offense or he will lose his craft for a year.

4. But if any one be caught with false cloth, his cloth will be burned publicly, and verily, the author of the crime will amend according to justice. . . .

9. If any one should marry a widow whose husband was of the craft, he will enter the fraternity with three solidi.

6. Shearers' Charter from Arras, Flanders, 1236

Here is the Shearers' Charter, on which they were first founded.

This is the first ordinance of the shearers, who were founded in the name of the Fraternity of God and St. Julien, with the agreement and consent of those who were at the time mayor and aldermen.

1. Whoever would engage in the trade of a shearer shall be in the Confraternity of St. Julien, and shall pay all the dues, and observe the decrees made by the brethren.

2. That is to say: first, that whoever is a master shearer shall pay 14 solidi to the Fraternity. And there may not be more than one master shearer working in a house. And he shall be a master shearer all the year, and have arms for the need of the town.

3. And a journeyman shall pay 5 solidi to the Fraternity.

4. And whoever wishes to learn the trade shall be the son of a burgess or he shall live in the town for a year and a day; and he shall serve three years to learn this trade.

5. And he shall give to his master 3 *muids*[4] for his bed and board; and he ought to bring the first *muid* to his master at the beginning of his apprenticeship, and another *muid* a year from that day, and a third *muid* at the beginning of the third year.

6. And no one may be a master of this trade of shearer if he has not lived a year and a day in the town, in order that it may be known whether or not he comes from a good place. . . .

9. And whoever does work on Saturday afternoon, or on the Eve of the Feast of Our Lady, or after Vespers on the Eve of the Feast of St. Julien, and completes the day by working, shall pay, if he be a master, 12 denarii, and if he be a journeyman, 6 denarii. And whoever works in the four days of Christmas, or in the eight days of Easter, or in the eight days of Pentecost, owes 5 solidi. . . .

11. And an apprentice owes to the Fraternity for his apprenticeship 5 solidi. . . .

13. And whoever does work in defiance of the mayor and aldermen shall pay 5 solidi. . . .

16. And those who are fed at the expense of the city shall be put to work first. And he who slights them for strangers owes 5 solidi: but if the stranger be put to work he cannot be removed as long as the master wishes to keep him. . . . And when a master does not work hard he pays 5 solidi, and a journeyman 2 solidi. . . .

18. And after the half year the mayor and aldermen shall fix such wages as he ought to have. . . .

20. And whoever maligns the mayor and aldermen, that is while on the business of the Fraternity, shall pay 5 solidi. . . .

23. And if a draper or a merchant has work to do in his house, he may take such workmen as he wishes into his house, so long as the work be done in his house. And he who infringes this shall give 5 solidi to the Fraternity. . . .

25. And each master ought to have his arms when he is summoned. And if he has not he should pay 20 solidi. . . .

32. And if a master does not give a journeyman such wage as is his due, then he shall pay 5 solidi.

33. And he who overlooks the forfeits of this Fraternity, if he does not wish to pay them when the mayor and aldermen summon him either for the army or the district, then he owes 10 solidi, and he shall not work at the trade until he has paid. Every forfeit of 5 solidi, and the fines which the mayor and aldermen command, shall be written down. All the fines of the Fraternity ought to go for the purchase of arms and for the needs of the Fraternity.

4. **muid:** a silver coin in circulation in Arras.

34. And whatever brother of this Fraternity shall betray his confrère for others shall not work at the trade for a year and a day. . . .

36. And should a master of this Fraternity die and leave a male heir he may learn the trade anywhere where there is no apprentice.

37. And no apprentice shall cut to the selvage[5] for half a year, and this is to obtain good work. And no master or journeyman may cut by himself because no one can measure cloth well alone. And whoever infringes this rule shall pay 5 solidi to the Fraternity for each offense.

38. Any brother whatsoever who lays hands on, or does wrong to, the mayor and aldermen of this Fraternity, as long as they work for the city and the Fraternity, shall not work at his trade in the city for a year and a day.

And if he should do so, let him be banished from the town for a year and a day, saving the appeal to Monseigneur the King and his Castellan. . . .

Sources 7 and 8 from Carolly Erickson, The Records of Medieval Europe, *translated by Carolly Erickson (Garden City, N.Y.: Anchor, 1971), p. 238.*

7. Judgment Against a Draper in Flanders, mid-14th century

When Jacquemars des Mares, a draper, brought one of his cloths to the great cloth hall of Arras and sold it, the aforesaid cloth was examined by the *espincheurs*[6] as is customary, and at the time they had it weighed, it was half a pound over the legal weight. Then, because of certain suspicions which arose, they had the cloth dried, and when it was dry, it weighed a half pound less than the legal weight. The *espincheur* brought the misdeed to the attention of the Twenty;[7] Jacquemars was fined 100 shillings.

8. Dispute Between Master Fullers and Their Apprentices in Flanders, 1345

A point of discussion was mooted between the apprentice fullers on the one hand, and the master fullers on the other. The apprentices held that, as they laid out in a letter, no one could have work done in his house without taking apprentices. . . . For they complained of fulling masters who had their children work in their houses, without standing [for jobs] in the public square like the other apprentices, and they begged that their letter be answered. The fulling masters

5. **selvage:** very edge of the cloth.
6. **espincheur:** cloth inspector.
7. **Twenty:** court of twenty men, made up of members of the city council.

stated certain arguments to the contrary. The aldermen sent for both parties and for the Twenty also and asked the masters if indeed they kept their children as apprentices; each master said he did. It was declared by the aldermen that every apprentice must remain in the public square, as reason demanded.

Done in the year of 1344 [1345], in the month of February, and through a full sitting of the aldermen.

Source 9 from Merry E. Wiesner, translator, unpublished decisions in Nuremberg Stadtarchiv, Quellen zur Nürnbergische Geschichte, Rep. F5, no. 68/I, fol. 58 (1577).

9. Decision by the Nuremberg City Council, 1577

The honorable city council has decided to deny the request of Barbara Hansmesser that she be allowed to dye wool because the blanketweavers' guild has so adamantly opposed it. Because her husband is not a citizen, they are both ordered to get out of the city and find work in some other place, with the warning that if they are found in the vicinity of this city, and are doing any work here, work will be taken from them and the yarn cut to pieces. They can count on this.

Source 10 from Merry E. Wiesner, translator, unpublished supplications in Frankfurt Stadtarchiv, Zünfte, Ugb. C-32, R, no. 1.

10. Widow's Supplication to the Frankfurt City Council, late sixteenth century

Most honorable and merciful gentlemen, you certainly know what a heavy and hard cross God has laid on me, and in what a miserable situation I find myself, after the much too early death of my late husband, with my young children, all of them still minors and some still nursing. This unfortunate situation is well known everywhere.

Although in consideration of my misfortune most Christian hearts would have gladly let me continue in my craft and occupation, and allowed me to earn a little piece of bread, instead the overseers of the woolweavers' guild came to me as soon as my husband had died, in my sorrow and even in my own house. Against all Christian charity, they began to order changes in my workshop with very harsh and menacing words. They specifically ordered that my apprentice, whom I had raised and trained at great cost and who had just come to be of use to me in the craft, leave me and go to them, which would be to their great advantage but my greater disadvantage. They ordered this on the pretense that there was no longer a master here so he could not finish his training.

Honorable sirs, I then humbly put myself under the protection of the lord mayors here, and asked that the two journeymen and the apprentice be allowed to continue on in their work as they had before unimpeded until a final judgment was reached in the matter. Despite this, one of the weavers began to shout at my journeymen whenever he saw them, especially if there were other people on the street. In his unhindered and unwarranted boldness, he yelled that my workshop was not honorable, and all journeymen who worked there were thieves and rascals. After doing this for several days, he and several others came into my workshop on a Saturday, and, bitter and jealous, pushed my journeymen out. They began to write to all places where this craft is practiced to tell other masters not to accept anyone who had worked in my workshop.

I now humbly beg you, my honorable and gracious sirs, protect me and my hungry children from such abuse, shame, and insult. Help my journeymen, who were so undeservedly insulted, to regain their honor. I beg you, as the protector of humble widows, to let my apprentice stay with me, as apprentices are allowed to stay in the workshops of widows throughout the entire Holy Roman Empire, as long as there are journeymen, whether or not there is a master present. Protect me from any further insults of the woolweavers' guild, which does nothing to increase the honor of our city, which you, honorable sirs, are charged to uphold. I plead with you to grant me my request, and allow me to continue my workshop.

Source 11 from Roy C. Cave and Herbert H. Coulson, A Source Book for Medieval Economic History *(New York: Biblo and Tannen, 1965), pp. 256–257.*

11. Two Apprenticeship Contracts, thirteenth century

Be it known to present and future aldermen that Ouede Ferconne apprentices Michael, her son, to Matthew Haimart on security of her house, her person, and her chattels,[8] and the share that Michael ought to have in them, so that Matthew Haimart will teach him to weave in four years, and that he (Michael) will have shelter, and learn his trade there without board. And if there should be reason within two years for Michael to default she will return him, and Ouede Ferconne, his mother, guarantees this on the security of her person and goods. And if she should wish to purchase his freedom for the last two years she may do so for thirty-three solidi, and will pledge for that all that has been stated. And if he should not free himself of the last two years let him return, and Ouede Ferconne, his mother, pledges this with her person and her goods. And the said Ouede pledges that if Matthew Haimart suffers either loss or damage through Michael, her son, she will restore the loss and damage on the security of herself and all her goods, should Michael do wrong.

8. **chattels:** personal property.

April the ninth. I, Peter Borre, in good faith and without guile, place with you, Peter Feissac, weaver, my son Stephen, for the purpose of learning the trade or craft of weaving, to live at your house, and to do work for you from the feast of Easter next for four continuous years, promising you by this agreement to take care that my son does the said work, and that he will be faithful and trustworthy in all that he does, and that he will neither steal nor take anything away from you, nor flee nor depart from you for any reason, until he has completed his apprenticeship. And I promise you by this agreement that I will reimburse you for all damages or losses that you incur or sustain on my behalf, pledging all my goods, etc.; renouncing the benefit of all laws, etc. And I, the said Peter Feissac, promise you, Peter Borre, that I will teach your son faithfully and will provide food and clothing for him.

Done at Marseilles, near the tables of the money-changers. Witnesses, etc.

Source 12 from Robert S. Lopez and Irving W. Raymond, editors and translators, Medieval Trade in the Mediterranean World *(New York: Columbia University Press, 1955), pp. 263–265, no. 138.*

12. Insurance Contracts from Pisa, 1384

This is a book of Francesco of Prato and partners, residing in Pisa, and we shall write in it all insurances we shall make in behalf of others. May God grant us profit from these and protect us from dangers.

[*Seal of Francesco son of Marco*]

A memorandum that on September 7, 1384, in behalf of Baldo Ridolfi and partners we insured for 100 gold florins wool in the ship of Guilhem Sale, Catalan, [in transit] from Peñiscola to Porto Pisano. And from the said 100 florins we received 3 gold florins in cash, and we insured against all risks, as is evident by a record by the hand of Gherardo d'Ormanno which is undersigned by our hand.

Said ship arrived safely in Porto Pisano and unloaded on . . . October, 1384, and we are free from the insurance.

A memorandum that on September 10 in behalf of Ambrogio, son of Bino Bini, we insured for 200 gold florins Milanese cloth in the ship of Bartolomeo Vitale, [in transit] from Porto Pisano to Palermo. And from the said 200 florins we received 8 gold florins, charged to the debit account of Ambrogio on *c.* 174, and no other record appears [written] by the hand of any broker.

Arrived in Palermo safely.

First graph in Source 13 from R. S. Lopez, "Hard Times and Investment in Culture," The Renaissance: Medieval or Modern *(Boston: D. C. Heath, 1959); second graph from H. van Werveke, "De omgang van de Ieperse lakenproductie in de veertiende eeuw,"* Medelelingen, K. Vlaamse Acad. voor Wetensch., Letteren en schone Kunsten van Belgie *(1947). Both reprinted in Harry A. Miskimin,* The Economy of Early Renaissance Europe, 1300–1460 *(Englewood Cliffs, N.J.: Prentice Hall, 1969), p. 94.*

13. Trends in the Cloth Trade in Florence and Ypres

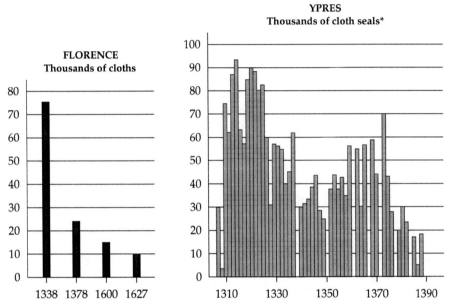

*The drapers' guild attached a seal to each cloth that it handled.

Table in Source 14 from A. R. Bridbury, Economic Growth: England in the Later Middle Ages (London: G. Allen and Unwin, 1962), p. 32. Used by permission of the author; graphs adapted from H. C. Darby, editor, A New Historical Geography of England (Cambridge, England: Cambridge University Press, 1973), p. 219. Reprinted with permission of Cambridge University Press.

14. English Exports of Raw Wool and Cloth, Based on Customs Records, ca 1350–1550

Years	Raw wool (sacks)	Woollen cloths (as equivalent to sacks of raw wool)
1361–70	28,302	3,024
1371–80	23,241	3,432
1381–90	17,988	5,521
1391–1400	17,679	8,967
1401–10	13,922	7,651
1411–20	13,487	6,364
1421–30	13,696	9,309
1431–40	7,377	10,051
1441–50	9,398	11,803
1471–80	9,299	10,125
1481–90	8,858	12,230
1491–1500	8,149	13,891

1   Raw Wool Exports

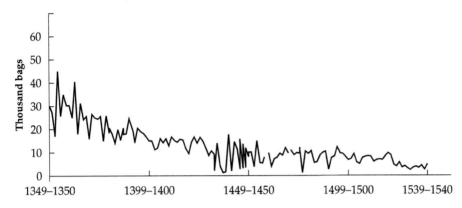

2   Cloth Exports

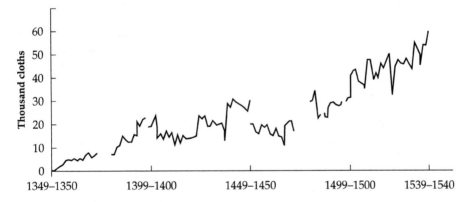

QUESTIONS TO CONSIDER

The records you have read shed some light on a wide variety of issues in the medieval cloth trade, as well as providing information on other social and economic matters. To draw some general conclusions and answer the questions for this chapter, you will need to go back to your list of goals, actions, and conflicts, and put together the information from the various sources. Because our focus here is on cloth production and sales, you will also need to leave aside what you have learned about other issues, though this may be very interesting to you. Investigating social and economic questions often involves not only uncovering sources that deal with your problem directly, but also extracting small bits of information from sources that cover a great many other areas, such as the city council records of Sources 9 and 10. Being a social historian requires that you discipline yourself to stick to the topic; though it may be fascinating to read every entry about every issue, this will not help with the completion of your research project.

Go back, then, to your list: How would you describe the key aims of territorial rulers regarding the cloth trade? Of local ruling bodies such as city councils? Do the sources you have read here lead you to support the thesis that city ordinances generally reflect the aims of cloth merchants? How might the aims of territorial rulers and merchants come into conflict? (For one example, how might cloth merchants or artisans already working in cloth production in Courtrai feel about the tax breaks that the Countess of Flanders gave to immigrants into the city in Source 3? What might cloth merchants do in response to this to maintain their monopoly on the cloth trade? For another, how might merchants in raw wool have regarded the changing nature of English exports as traced in Source 14 and the government tariff policies that were responsible for this?) In addition to shaping government policies, what private actions do you find merchants engaging in to achieve their goals?

Turning to the relationship of the merchants—or the city councils, usually dominated by merchants—to the artisans: What actions by artisans are explicitly prohibited in city ordinances or guild charters? (See Sources 4, 5, and 6.) How do these prohibitions

reflect merchant aims? How would you describe the attitudes of merchants toward artisans—suspicious, friendly, hostile, paternalistic, fraternal? How did groups or individuals use the conflicts between these two to their own advantage? (The best examples here are the supplication quoted in Source 10 and the dispute recorded in Source 8. To whom did the widow and the apprentices turn for help, and about which groups were they complaining? In the widow's supplication, what sort of language does she use to persuade authorities to help her?)

Turning to the workplace itself: How would you characterize the atmosphere in the houses of most woolworkers—collegial and friendly, or divided and somewhat hostile? As you have no doubt noticed, ordinances regulated not simply individual workers, but their families as well. What special privileges were given to members of the master's family? Who objected to these privileges, and why? How did the guilds treat widows of their members? Do you see any discrepancy in the discussion of widows in the ordinances and in the actual treatment of a member's widow in Source 10? How do the guilds react to women working who were not the wives or widows of guild members? Would you regard the guilds as generally helpful to families or helpful to only certain types of families? Along with the privileges accorded to the master's family members, what other sources of dispute between masters and journeymen, and between masters and apprentices, are mentioned in the sources? How might the goals of the craft guild masters and those of the merchants come into conflict in the handling of these disputes?

You are now ready to answer the questions posed by this chapter: What were the key economic and social goals of governments, merchant-capitalists, and artisans regarding the cloth trade, and how did they seek to achieve these aims? What economic and social conflicts emerged as the cloth trade grew and changed?

EPILOGUE

Because of its capitalist organization and complex division of labor, the medieval cloth trade is often seen as a harbinger of modern economic developments. As you have read the sources for this chapter, you have probably discovered other areas in which there are parallels between the medieval cloth trade and the modern economy. Many of the goals of governments, merchants, and artisans that we have seen expressed in the medieval sources are shared by modern governments, corporations, and unions: the expansion of domestic production, the maintenance of order in the workplace, the limitation of risk, the highest level of profit, steady wages and job security, protection from foreign competition, the replacement of exports of raw materials with exports of manufactured products. As they were in the Middle Ages, these goals are often contradictory, if not mutually exclusive.

Many of the actions taken by medieval authorities and individuals continue to appear on the evening news as it reports economic developments: protectionist legislation, tax breaks to promote the development of industry and job creation, preferential treatment for certain groups, the transfer of jobs to places where wages are lower or workers are less likely to strike, immigration policies that promote the immigration of workers with specific skills, fraud and falsification of merchandise in an attempt to increase profits.

Many of the conflicts we have seen here still beset workplaces in the twentieth century: disputes over wage levels and the right to work; disagreements between labor and management over who controls certain aspects of the workplace; conflicts between older and younger workers, now often expressed as issues of seniority; and demands that employers pay more attention to the family responsibilities of their employees and make the workplace more "family friendly." Methods of enforcing aims and resolving conflicts that were tried in the Middle Ages are still often tried today, such as the use of outside authorities or arbitrators, revolts and strikes, and blacklisting and fines.

Though in the contemporary economy production of many types of goods often faces conflicts—automobiles, electronic and computer equipment, and agricultural products usually gain the most headlines—cloth and clothing production is still an important issue for many nations, corporations, and unions. Many of the commercials promoting the retail giant Wal-Mart's policy of buying products made in the United States highlight cloth and clothing manufacturers. The attempts by U.S. immigration authorities to make employers responsible for making sure their foreign-born employees have the necessary work permits have targeted sportswear makers in New York and California who hire undocumented aliens. Lawsuits by U.S. companies charging copyright infringement are often brought against foreign manufacturers of such items as T-shirts and beach towels. Just as cloth production in the Middle Ages was a harbinger of trends and conflicts in the modern economy, cloth production in the early twenty-first century may also be a harbinger of the future. The internationalization of the marketplace and work force that it points to perhaps would not seem so strange to the countess of Flanders or Francesco of Prato, nor would the difficulties that can result from this seem so strange to the woolworkers of Florence or Ypres.

CHAPTER TEN

LAY PIETY AND

HERESY IN

THE LATE MIDDLE AGES

During the late Middle Ages, the Christian church went through a period of turmoil and disunity, with corruption and abuse evident at all levels of its hierarchy. Though the Church was officially an independent institution, many of its officials, such as bishops and archbishops, were actually chosen by secular nobles and rulers, who picked their own relatives or others who would do as they were told. Officials who were elected or appointed from within the Church itself were often selected for their administrative and legal skills, not for their piety, high moral standards, or religious devotion. These problems extended all the way to the papacy, which for much of the fourteenth century was located not in Rome but in Avignon in southern France, where it was dominated by the French monarchy. During this time the papacy lost its stature as an international power and had difficulty raising revenue from many parts of Europe, especially from the English, who rightly suspected that money sent to the pope might end up in the coffers of the French king, with whom they were at war. The Avignon popes had ever-increasing needs for revenue because they had to hire mercenaries to keep the Papal States in Italy under control, build palaces and churches in Avignon that reflected the power and prestige of the papacy, and pay the salaries of a growing corps of lawyers and bureaucrats who administered the papal empire.

The papacy devised a number of ways to meet its increasing need for money. Though the outright selling of Church offices, termed *simony*, was strictly forbidden, the popes required all candidates to pay for the privilege of taking over a vacant office, then hand over a large share of their first year's revenues directly to the papacy. Official prohibitions, such as those against priests having concubines or giving Church land to family members, could be ignored if the cleric paid the pope for a special dispensation. The papacy also collected money directly from laypeople, charging fees for clerical services such as marriage or baptism and for dispensations that legitimized children born out of wedlock.

The most lucrative source of income for the papacy proved to be the granting of *indulgences*. Indulgences were based on three doctrines developed by the medieval Church—the sacrament of penance, the concept of Purgatory, and the Treasury of Merit. To partake of the sacrament of penance, a believer was to confess all sins to a priest and be truly sorry, or contrite, for them, after which the priest absolved the believer, often requiring him or her to carry out certain acts as penance for these sins, such as saying prayers or going on pilgrimages. According to Church doctrine, penance did not end with death but might be extended into Purgatory, where Christians spent time atoning for the sins for which they had not done earthly penance. Only after a set time in Purgatory could most Christians be admitted to heaven. (Those who were going to hell, on the other hand, went directly there.)

Along with the doctrines of penance and Purgatory, the Church also developed the idea of the Treasury of Merit. This treasury was seen as a collection of all the superlative good deeds and meritorious acts that the

apostles, saints, and other good people had done during their lives, which the pope as head of the Church could dispense as he wished through the granting of indulgences. The recipient of an indulgence received a share in the Treasury of Merit that took the place of having to do individual penance. Originally granted to people who performed special services for the Church, such as participating in crusades, indulgences gradually came to be exchanged for cash contributions. Though official theology taught that priestly absolution and true contrition were still necessary, unscrupulous indulgence peddlers often sold indulgences outright as easy substitutes for penance. Indulgences also began to be granted to relieve people of time in Purgatory and even to allow believers to shorten deceased relatives' time in Purgatory. To many people, it seemed that the Church was teaching that one could buy one's way into heaven, though this was not actually so.

Because Church officials at all levels were often chosen for their family connections or their legal and financial skills, they also bent official doctrines and saw their posts primarily in terms of income rather than spiritual duties. Bishops spent much of their time at the papal court trying to win the pope's favor and squeezed all possible revenues out of their dioceses in order to pay for their offices. These absentee officials, who left the affairs of the diocese in the hands of substitutes, often had very little idea about the needs or problems of their territory. Those who were successful in gaining papal backing might be appointed to many different offices simultaneously; they collected the income from all their posts, appointed badly paid proxies to carry out their duties, and might actually never even visit the diocese over which they were bishop.

With so little supervision, parish priests and monks were sometimes lax in their standards of morality and spiritual observance. Frequently parish priests were poor and badly educated, for most of the Church's wealth stayed in the hands of higher officials, who provided no opportunity for priests to gain an education; some priests did not even know Latin, but simply recited the Mass by rote without understanding what they were saying. During the week they farmed just as their parishioners did, for the income from tithes was not sufficient to support them. Some of the monasteries and convents maintained high standards, but others, caught in the squeeze for revenue, admitted any applicant who would pay the entrance fee, without determining if the person was fit for the monastic life.

With the Church embroiled in these problems, we might expect that people would turn away from religion to concentrate on other aspects of life, but this was not the case. Religion continued to dominate the lives of people in the late Middle Ages, which was in fact perhaps the most religious period in all of European history. What did change, however, was how people expressed and experienced their Christian faith. Not surprisingly, they turned away somewhat from the institutional Church and sought more direct paths to God through individual actions.

Much of this lay piety was supported by the Church hierarchy because it did not question basic theological doctrines such as life after death; the importance of the sacraments of baptism, communion, and penance; the honor owed to saints and their relics; and the right of the pope to grant indulgences, collect taxes, and determine correct doctrine. Pious laypeople also made frequent donations, which swelled the Church's revenue. Some individuals and groups went beyond personal piety, however, to question the Church's wealth and many of its central doctrines. The Church declared such people heretics and set up inquisitorial courts to investigate, try, and condemn them.

Your task in this chapter will be to examine late medieval lay piety and religious practices, both those approved by the institutional Church and those condemned as heresy. How did common people in the Middle Ages experience and express their religious faith? How did the Church as an institution respond to laypeople's ideas and actions?

SOURCES AND METHOD

Medieval Christianity, multifaceted in nature, may be explored from a number of angles. Christianity was a faith shared by most people living in Europe, whether they were highly educated or uneducated, wealthy or poor. We can find information about how educated men understood and interpreted Christianity fairly easily by reading theological treatises and official Church decisions, but these may not accurately reflect the religious views of the majority. For this perspective, we must turn to a much smaller group of sources that throw light on the religious beliefs of the common people.

Learning about and reconstructing the ideas of common people in the premodern period is extremely difficult, for such people were by and large illiterate. The surviving written records of their thoughts and actions thus all come through the filter of literate observers, whose perspective and understanding of events might differ radically from the participants'. This is especially a problem when we are examining religious ideas, for most people who could read and write in the Middle Ages were clerics and thus part of the institutional Church. It was often hard for such observers to be objective about criticism directed against the Church, or even to comprehend how uneducated people interpreted and understood theological concepts.

Because of these problems, we must ask several questions before turning to any written source about popular religious belief. Who actually wrote the document? Was the writer recording the words of an illiterate person or simply describing actions he or she had observed? Why was this piece written? If the writer is recording the words of someone else, did he or she clearly understand the language being spoken, or might there be some problems because of dialect? Is the writer translating a vernacular language such as English or French into Latin, and so possibly mistranslating religious ideas? Why were this person's thoughts recorded—did that person wish it or did the authorities, as was the case with trial records?

Artistic evidence might seem more direct, for people who could not read or write sculpted, painted, and made stained-glass windows. They did not always choose their own subject matter or sign their works, however, so medieval art does not directly express the individual personality and concerns of the artist in the way that modern art does. What it does reveal, however, is how common people learned about religion from windows and statues depicting biblical and other Christian scenes. We can also use frequently recurring images as a rough guide to popular religious sentiments, for individuals and groups commissioned art that reflected their own concerns. The dominance of certain images shifted throughout the Middle Ages as people's attitudes toward the Church and the right way to approach God changed.

Using artistic evidence as a source of information about popular belief requires a different set of initial questions from those needed for written evidence. Where and when was the piece probably made? Can we learn anything about the artist or patron, such as his or her identity? Where was the piece originally displayed? Are the materials simple enough that the piece could have been ordered or purchased by someone who was not wealthy? Is the image common or unusual?

Keeping in mind the limitations we have noted, turn now to the written sources. The first two are *sermon stories*, tales of miracles that learned preachers used in their public sermons; later they were collected by many different preachers and used widely in sermons all over Europe. These stories are consequently not written *by* laypeople but *for* them and reflect official Church doctrines. They do not present sophisticated theology, however, but show us how common people learned about Christianity. As you read, note the kinds of people who appear as main characters. Why would preachers use characters like these?

In the first sermon, to whom does the woman turn for assistance? When her prayers are not answered immediately, what does she do? Why would the preacher condone such a dramatic action? (To answer this question, think about the impact this story would have on the female members of the audience; Mary may not have responded instantly to prayer, but, like most mothers, she did so immediately once her child

was taken from her.) What qualities of Mary does this story emphasize?

The second sermon discusses an important element in lay piety, the belief in saints and relics. Does the author support or condemn these beliefs? Is it the relics themselves or faith in them that is important? Why would the author, himself a priest, describe the priest in the story as "wily" and "wicked"? (Again, keep in mind the audience. Given the problems most people recognized in the Church, how would a lay audience respond to a story in which the hero is also a layperson?)

Though most laypeople in the Middle Ages could not read, some of them could, and one of the most popular types of reading material was stories about the lives of saints, termed *hagiography*. Like sermon stories, hagiography often presented quite ordinary people whose lives were touched by God and who could serve as an inspiration. Source 3 comes from the best-known collection of saints' lives, *The Golden Legend*, first composed in the late thirteenth century by an Italian bishop, and then translated and recopied throughout Europe during the late Middle Ages. It describes events from the life of St. Nicholas (the original Santa Claus) and miracles attributed to him after his death, and would have been familiar even to those who could not read because they would have heard this story from those who could. What type of people does Nicholas assist? What sort of problems does he solve for them?

Taking these three sources together, what types of actions do you think preachers and writers of hagiography were trying to encourage in people? What traits of lay piety did they praise?

The remaining written sources directly record the thoughts and actions of laypeople, some of whom the Church supported and some of whom it condemned. None could read or write Latin, and so they qualified as unlearned by medieval standards, though some could read their own vernacular language. Source 4 is taken from the *Revelations* of Bridget of Sweden, a noblewoman who lived from 1303 to 1373. After her husband's death, Bridget traveled to Rome, where she began to see visions and give advice based on these visions to both laypeople and Church officials. Because she could not speak Latin, she wrote or dictated her visions in Swedish; these were later translated by her confessors and eventually were published in Latin. At the end of her life, Bridget made a pilgrimage to Jerusalem, where she had the visions reprinted here. How would you describe these visions? How did the fact that she was a woman shape her religious experience?

Source 5 is drawn from the first autobiography ever written in English, that of Margery Kempe, who was probably born in 1373, the same year Bridget died. Kempe, a middle-class woman from the town of King's Lynn, was illiterate in English as well as Latin. Although she was married and had fourteen children, she began to see visions in which Christ demanded that she set herself apart from most women. At the end of her most unusual life, she dictated her autobiography to several male scribes, who wrote it down in English. As you read, note how Kempe describes her actions and behavior. What made her most open to criticism? How does she defend her actions? She refers to herself, always in the third person, as "this creature." What does this practice indicate about her self-consciousness? Do her actions reflect this self-image? What aspects of Christianity most inspire or disturb her? How was the official reaction to her influenced by the fact that she was a woman?

The last two written sources come from trial records. Source 6 contains six testimonies from the Inquisition carried out between 1318 and 1325 by Jacques Fournier, Bishop of Pamiers in southern France. All six accused were illiterate peasants who spoke Occitan, a regional dialect; their words were translated by scribes into Latin. Fournier launched the Inquisition because he suspected large numbers of people in his district to be *Albigensians* (also called Cathars), followers of a heretical movement that rejected many basic Church doctrines. Albigensians regarded the material world as evil and not made by God and did not believe in the possibility of eternal life. They denied the power of many Church ceremonies and rituals and urged that any Church leader, including the pope, should not be obeyed if he did not live up to rigorous moral standards.

As you read the testimonies, note which specific Christian beliefs were being challenged. Given their statements, would you call the peasants who were being questioned Christians? How might problems of translation have affected the records? How might the fact that this was a trial have affected what the individuals said?

Source 7 comes from a heresy trial of sixty people suspected of Lollard beliefs, conducted in the diocese of Norwich, England, between 1428 and 1431. Lollards followed the ideas of John Wyclif, an English scholar who lived in the fourteenth century; the selection itself presents all of the basic Lollard beliefs. Most of the trial record is in Latin because it was conducted by ecclesiastical authorities and recorded by clerics, but a few of the confessions were written down in English. The selection here is one of those, with the spelling modernized. What does the accused admit to having believed? The list of unacceptable beliefs in many heresy trials reflects not only the ideas of the person confessing but also those the inquisitors thought were especially dangerous and in need of suppression. What did the inquisitors in this case appear particularly concerned about? How would this emphasis have shaped the confession? How was the accused to prove he had given up his heresy? Given his beliefs, would you call the person under questioning a Christian?

Now examine the two visual sources. Both are wooden statues carved in the fourteenth or fifteenth centuries by unknown artists and originally placed in churches in southern Germany. They are examples of the two most common religious images of the late Middle Ages. What aspects of popular belief that you have identified from the written sources do they reflect? Mary is shown wearing a crown and holding an orb, a sphere representing the world that normally was carried by monarchs. What qualities are emphasized through this depiction? Christ is shown in a dramatic pose of suffering. What does this attitude emphasize about his nature? Given what you now know about how common people understood Christianity, why would these two subjects be the most popular? Why do you think there is no depiction of God the Father?

████ THE EVIDENCE ████

Source 1 from C. C. S. Bland, editor and translator, Miracles of the Blessed Virgin Mary *(London: Routledge, 1928), p. 118.*

1. A Sermon Story About the Virgin Mary, 13th century

A certain woman of simple and upright life used to worship the Holy Mary, Mother of God, often strewing flowers and herbs before her image.

Now it chanced that the woman's only son was taken prisoner. And the mother weeping for him would not be comforted, and prayed with all her heart to the Blessed Virgin Mary for her son's deliverance. But seeing it was all in vain, she entered the church and thus addressed the image of the Blessed Virgin, "O Blessed Virgin Mary, often have I asked thee for the deliverance of my son and thou hast not heard me. Therefore, as my son was taken from me, so will I take away thine and will put him in durance as hostage for mine."

And taking the image of the Child from the bosom of Mary, she went home, wrapped him up in a clean cloth, and shut him up carefully in a chest. And, behold, the following night the Blessed Mary appeared to the captive youth bidding him to go forth and said to him: "Tell your mother to give me my Son." And he coming to his mother, described how he had been set free. But she with great rejoicing carried back the image of Jesus to Mary and gave her thanks.

Source 2 from Dana Carleton Munro, editor and translator, Translations and Reprints from the Original Sources of European History, *vol. 2, no. 4 (Philadephia: University of Pennsylvania Press, no date), p. 14.*

2. A Sermon Story About Relics, 13th century

A certain knight loved most ardently the above-mentioned martyr, St. Thomas of Canterbury,[1] and sought everywhere to obtain some relic of him. When a certain wily priest, in whose house he was staying, heard of this he said to him, "I have by me a bridle which St. Thomas used for a long time,

---

1. **Thomas Becket**: the Archbishop of Canterbury who was murdered on the steps of the cathedral on the orders of Henry II for opposing the king's wishes. He was quickly made a saint, and Canterbury became the most popular pilgrimage site in England.

and I have often experienced its virtues." When the knight heard this, and believed it, he joyfully paid the priest the money which the latter demanded and received the bridle with great devotion.

God truly, to whom nothing is impossible, wishing to reward the faith of the knight and for the honor of his martyr, deigned to work many miracles through the same bridle. The knight seeing this founded a church in honor of the martyr and in it he placed as a relic the bridle of that most wicked priest.

Source 3 from Iacobus de Voragine, The Golden Legend, *included in* Lives of the Saints, *translated by William Caxton and selected and edited by George V. O'Neill, S.J. (Cambridge: Cambridge University Press, 1914), pp. 62–71.*

3. Extracts from the Life of St. Nicholas, *The Golden Legend*, ca 1270

Nicholas, citizen of the city of Patras, was born of rich and holy kin, and his father was Epiphanes and his mother Johane. In his young age he eschewed the plays and japes[2] of other young children. He used and haunted gladly holy Church; and all that he might understand of holy Scripture he executed it in deed and work after his power. And when his father and mother were departed out of this life, he began to think how he might distribute his riches, and not to the praising of the world but to the honor and glory of God. And it was so that one, his neighbor, had then three daughters, virgins, and he was a nobleman: but for the poverty of them together, they were constrained and in very purpose to abandon them to sin. And when the holy man Nicholas knew hereof he had great horror of this, and threw by night secretly into the house of the man a mass of gold wrapped in a cloth. And when the man arose in the morning, he found this mass of gold, and rendered to God therefor great thankings, and therewith he married his oldest daughter. And a little while after this holy servant of God threw in another mass of gold; which the man found, and thanked God, and purposed to wake for to know him that so had aided him in his poverty. And after a few days Nicholas doubled the mass of gold, and cast it into the house of this man. He awoke by the sound of the gold, and followed Nicholas, which fled from him, and he said to him: "Sir, flee not away so but that I may see and know thee." Then he ran after him more hastily, and knew that it was Nicholas; and anon he kneeled down, and would have kissed his feet, but the holy man would not, but required him not to tell nor discover this thing as long as he lived.

2. **japes:** toys.

It is read in a chronicle that the blessed Nicholas was at the Council of Nice; and on a day, as a ship with mariners were in perishing on the sea, they prayed and required devoutly Nicholas, servant of God, saying: "If those things that we have heard of thee said to be true, prove them now." And anon a man appeared in his likeness, and said: "Lo! see ye me not? ye called me"; and then he began to help them in their exploit of the sea, and anon the tempest ceased. And when they were come to his church, they knew him without any man to show him to them, and yet they had never seen him. And then they thanked God and him of their deliverance. And he bade them to attribute it to the mercy of God and to their belief, and nothing to his merits.

It was so on a time that all the province of S. Nicholas suffered great famine, in such wise that vitaille[3] failed. And then this holy man heard say that certain ships laden with wheat were arrived in the haven. And anon he went thither and prayed the mariners that they would succor the perished at least with an hundred muyes of wheat of every ship. And they said: "Father, we dare not, for it is meted and measured, and we must give reckoning thereof in the garners[4] of the emperor in Alexandria." And the holy man said to them: "Do this that I have said to you, and I promise, in the truth of God, that it shall not be lessed or minished when ye shall come to the garners." And when they had delivered so much out of every ship, they came into Alexandria and delivered the measure that they had received. And then they recounted the miracle to the ministers of the emperor, and worshipped and praised strongly God and his servant Nicholas. Then this holy man distributed the wheat to every man after that he had need, in such wise that it sufficed for two years, not only for to sell but also to sow. . . .

And when it pleased Our Lord to have him depart out this world, he prayed Our Lord that he would send him his angels; and inclining his head he saw the angels come to him, whereby he knew well that he should depart, and began this holy Psalm: "In te domine speravi," unto "in manus tuas," and so saying: "Lord, into thine hands I commend my spirit," he rendered up his soul and died, the year of Our Lord three hundred and forty-three. . . .

There was a Jew that saw the virtuous miracles of S. Nicholas, and did do make an image of the saint, and set it in his house, and commanded him that he should keep well his house when he went out, and that he should keep well all his goods, saying to him: "Nicholas, lo! here be all my goods, I charge thee to keep them, and if thou keep them not well, I shall avenge me on thee in beating and tormenting thee." And on a time, when the Jew was out, thieves came and robbed all his goods, and left unborne away only the image. And when the Jew came home he found him robbed of all his goods. He areasoned the image, saying these words: "Sir Nicholas, I had set you in my house for to keep my goods from thieves, wherefore have ye not kept them? Ye shall receive sorrow and torments, and shall have pain for the thieves. I shall

3. **vitaille:** food.
4. **garners:** storehouses for grain.

avenge my loss and refrain my woodness in beating thee." And then took the Jew the image, and beat it, and tormented it cruelly. Then happed a great marvel, for when the thieves departed the goods, the holy saint, like as he had been in his array, appeared to the thieves, and said to them: "Wherefore have I been beaten so cruelly for you and have so many torments? See how my body is hewed and broken; see how that the red blood runneth down by my body; go ye fast and restore it again, or else the ire of God Almighty shall make you as to be one out of his wit, and that all men shall know your felony, and that each of you shall be hanged." And they said: "Who art thou that sayest to us such things?" And he said to them: "I am Nicholas the servant of Jesu Christ, whom the Jew hath so cruelly beaten for his goods that ye bare away." Then they were afeared, and came to the Jew, and heard what he had done to the image, and they told him the miracle, and delivered to him again all his goods. And thus came the thieves to the way of truth, and the Jew to the way of Jesu Christ.

A man, for the love of his son, that went to school for to learn, hallowed,[5] every year, the feast of S. Nicholas much solemnly. On a time it happed that the father had to make ready the dinner, and called many clerks to this dinner. And the devil came to the gate in the habit of a pilgrim for to demand alms; and the father anon commanded his son that he should give alms to the pilgrim. He followed him as he went for to give to him alms, and when he came to the quarfox[6] the devil caught the child and strangled him. And when the father heard this he sorrowed much strongly and wept, and bare the body into his chamber, and began to cry for sorrow, and say: "Bright sweet son, how is it with thee? S. Nicholas, is this the guerdon[7] that ye have done to me because I have so long served you?" And as he said these words, and other semblable,[8] the child opened his eyes, and awoke like as he had been asleep, and arose up tofore all, and was raised from death to life.

Source 4 from Katharina M. Wilson, editor, Medieval Women Writers *(Athens: University of Georgia Press, 1984), p. 245. Selection translated by Barbara Obrist.*

4. Two Visions of Bridget of Sweden, 1370s

After this the Virgin Mary appeared again to me, in the same place, and said: it has been a long time since in Rome I promised you that I would show you here in Bethlehem how my offspring had been born. And although in Naples I showed you something of it, that is to say the way I was standing when I gave

5. **hallowed:** honored.
6. **quarfox:** crossroads.
7. **guerdon:** reward.
8. **semblable:** similar ones.

birth to my son, you still should know for sure that I stood and gave birth such as you have seen it now—my knees were bent and I was alone in the stable, praying; I gave birth to him with such exultation and joy of my soul that I had no difficulties when he got out of my body or any pain. Then I wrapped him in swaddling clothes that I had prepared long ago. When Joseph saw this he was astonished and full of joy and happiness, because I had given birth without any help.

At the same place where the Virgin Mary and Joseph were adoring the boy in the cradle, I also saw the shepherds, who had been watching their flocks, coming so that they could look at the child and adore it. When they saw the child, they first wanted to find out whether it was a male or a female, for angels had announced to them that the savior of the world had been born, and they had not said that it was a savioress. Then the Virgin Mary showed to them the nature and the male sex of the child. At once they adored him with great awe and joy. Afterward they returned, praising and glorifying God for all they had heard and seen.

Source 5 from W. Butler-Bowdon, editor, The Book of Margery Kempe *(London: Oxford University Press, 1936), pp. 41–42, 86–88, 161–165, 167–168. Reprinted by permission of Oxford University Press.*

5. From the Autobiography of Margery Kempe, ca 1430

This creature, when Our Lord had forgiven her her sin, as has been written before, had a desire to see those places where He was born, and where He suffered His Passion,[9] and where He died, with other holy places where He was in His life, and also after His resurrection.

As she was in these desires, Our Lord bade her, in her mind, two years ere she went, that she should go to Rome, to Jerusalem and to Saint James,[10] and she would fain have gone but she had no money.

And then she said to Our Lord:—"Where shall I get money to go with to these Holy Places?"

Our Lord answered to her:—"I shall send thee friends enough in divers countries of England to help thee. And, daughter, I shall go with thee in every country and provide for thee, I shall lead thee thither, and bring thee back again in safety. And no Englishman shall die in the ship that thou art in. I shall

9. **Passion:** the crucifixion.
10. **St. James of Compostella:** a cathedral in northwestern Spain.

keep thee from all wicked men's power. And, daughter, I say to thee that I will that thou wearest clothes of white and no other colour, for thou shalt be arrayed after My will."

"Ah! Dear Lord, if I go arrayed in other manner than other chaste women do, I dread the people will slander me. They will say I am a hypocrite and wonder at me."

"Yea, daughter, the more ridicule that thou hast for My love, the more thou pleasest Me."

Then this creature durst not otherwise do than she was commanded in her soul. . . .

So they went forth into the Holy Land till they could see Jerusalem. And when this creature saw Jerusalem, riding on an ass, she thanked God with all her heart, praying Him for His mercy that, as He had brought her to see His earthly city of Jerusalem, He would grant her grace to see the blissful city of Jerusalem above, the city of Heaven. Our Lord Jesus Christ, answering her thought, granted her to have her desire.

Then for the joy she had, and the sweetness she felt in the dalliance with Our Lord, she was on the point of falling off her ass, for she could not bear the sweetness and grace that God wrought in her soul. Then two pilgrims, Duchemen, went to her, and kept her from falling; one of whom was a priest, and he put spices in her mouth to comfort her, thinking she had been sick. And so they helped her on to Jerusalem, and when she came there, she said:—

"Sirs, I pray you be not displeased though I weep sore in this holy place where Our Lord Jesus Christ was quick and dead."

Then went they to the temple in Jerusalem and they were let in on the same day at evensong time, and abode there till the next day at evensong time. Then the friars lifted up a cross and led the pilgrims about from one place to another where Our Lord suffered His[11]. . . and His Passion, every man and woman bearing a wax candle in one hand. And the friars always, as they went about, told them what Our Lord suffered in every place. The aforesaid creature wept and sobbed as plenteously as though she had seen Our Lord with her bodily eye, suffering His Passion at that time. Before her in her soul she saw Him verily by contemplation, and that caused her to have compassion. And when they came up on to the Mount of Calvary,[12] she fell down because she could not stand or kneel, and rolled and wrested with her body, spreading her arms abroad, and cried with a loud voice as though her heart would have burst asunder; for, in the city of her soul, she saw verily and clearly how Our Lord was crucified. Before her face, she heard and saw, in her ghostly sight, the mourning of Our Lady, of Saint John, and Mary Magdalene and of many others that loved Our Lord.

11. Word missing in manuscript.
12. **Calvary:** where Jesus is believed to have been crucified.

And she had such great compassion and such great pain, at seeing Our Lord's pain that she could not keep herself from crying and roaring though she should have died for it. And this was the first cry[13] that ever she cried in any contemplation. And this manner of crying endured many years after this time, for aught any man might do, and therefore, suffered she much despite and much reproof. The crying was so loud and so wonderful that it made the people astounded unless they had heard it before, or unless they knew the cause of the crying. And she had them so often that they made her right weak in her bodily might, and especially if she heard of Our Lord's Passion. . . .

[*She returned to England, where her crying upset many people and she was called to appear before the Archbishop of York.*]

On the next day she was brought into the Archbishop's Chapel, and there came many of the Archbishop's retinue, despising her, calling her "Lollard" and "heretic" and swearing many a horrible oath that she should be burnt.

And she, through the strength of Jesus, spoke back to them:—

"Sirs, I dread ye shall be burnt in Hell without end, unless ye amend in your swearing of oaths, for ye keep not the Commandments of God. I would not swear as ye do for all the money in this world."

Then they went away, as if they had been shamed. She then, making her prayer in her mind, asked grace so to be demeaned that day as was most pleasure to God, and profit to her own soul, and good example to her fellow Christians.

Our Lord, answering her, said it should be right well. At the last, the said Archbishop came into the chapel with his clerks, and sharply he said to her:—

"Why goest thou in white? Art thou a maiden?"

She kneeling on her knees before him, said:—

"Nay, sir, I am no maiden. I am a wife."

He commanded his retinue to fetch a pair of fetters and said she should be fettered, for she was a false heretic.

Then she said:—"I am no heretic, nor shall ye prove me one."

The Archbishop went away and left her standing alone. Then she made her prayers to Our Lord God Almighty to help her and succour her against all her enemies, ghostly and bodily, a long while, and her flesh trembled and quaked wonderfully, so that she was fain to put her hands under her clothes, so that it should not be espied.

Afterwards the Archbishop came again into the Chapel with many clerks, amongst whom was the same doctor who had examined her before, and the monk that had preached against her a little time before in York. Some of the

---

13. **cry**: outcry, scream.

people asked whether she were a Christian woman or a Jew; some said she was a good woman; some said "Nay."

Then the Archbishop took his seat and his clerks also, each of them in his degree, many people being present.

And during the time while the people were gathering together and the Archbishop taking his seat, the said creature stood all behind, making her prayers for help and succour against her enemies with high devotion, so long that she melted all into tears.

And at the last she cried aloud therewith, so that the Archbishop and his clerks and many people had great wonder of her, for they had not heard such crying before. When her crying was passed, she came before the Archbishop and fell down on her knees, the Archbishop saying full boisterously unto her:—

"Why weepest thou, woman?"

She, answering, said:—"Sir, ye shall wish some day that ye had wept as sore as I."

Then anon, the Archbishop put to her the Articles of our Faith,[14] to which God gave her grace to answer well and truly and readily without any great study, so that he might not blame her. Then he said to the clerks:—

"She knoweth her Faith well enough. What shall I do with her?"

The clerks said:—"We know well that she can say the Articles of Faith, but we will not suffer her to dwell amongst us, for the people hath great faith in her dalliance, and, peradventure, she might pervert some of them.". . .

Then said the Archbishop to her:—"Thou shalt swear that thou wilt neither teach nor challenge the people in my diocese."

"Nay, sir, I shall not swear," she said, "for I shall speak of God, and rebuke those that swear great oaths wheresoever I go, unto the time that the Pope and Holy Church hath ordained that no man shall be so bold as to speak of God, for God Almighty forbiddeth not, sir, that we shall speak of Him. And also the Gospel maketh mention that, when the woman had heard Our Lord preach, she came before Him with a loud voice and said:—'Blessed be the womb that bore Thee, and the teats that gave Thee suck.' Then Our Lord again said to her, 'Forsooth, so are they blessed that hear the word of God and keep it.' And therefore, sir, methinketh that the Gospel giveth me leave to speak of God."

"Ah! Sir," said the clerks, "here wot we well that she hath a devil within her, for she speaketh of the Gospel."

As quickly as possible, a great clerk brought forth a book and laid Saint Paul, for his part, against her, that no woman should preach.[15]

14. **Articles of Faith:** a standard series of questions, in which a person suspected of heresy was asked if he or she believed in the central doctrines of Christianity—the Trinity, the Virgin Birth, the efficacy of the sacraments, heaven and hell, the power of the Pope.

15. The first letter to Timothy in the New Testament, which until recently was believed to have been written by the apostle Paul, orders women to keep silent in church.

She answering thereto said:—"I preach not, sir; I come into no pulpit, I use but communication and good words, and that I will do while I live." . . .

She, kneeling down on her knees, asked his blessing. He, praying her to pray for him, blessed her and let her go.

Then she, going again to York, was received by many people and full worthy clerks, who rejoiced in Our Lord, Who had given her, unlettered, wit and wisdom to answer so many learned men without disgrace or blame, thanks be to God.

Source 6 from Edward Peters, editor, Heresy and Authority in Medieval Europe: Documents in Translation *(Philadelphia: University of Pennsylvania Press, 1980), pp. 259–261. Selection translated by Steven Sargent. Reprinted by permission.*

6. Testimony from the Inquisition Led by Jacques Fournier, Bishop of Pamiers, 1318–1325

Testimony of Arnaud de Savinhan

"He said that as long as he could remember, which might be about thirty years since he was then about forty-five years old, he had believed completely that God had not made the world, namely heaven, earth, and the elements, but that it had always been existing in and of itself, and was not made by God nor by anyone else. Nevertheless he always had believed that Adam was the first man and that God had made him, and thereafter there had been human generation. But before God had made Adam, the world had lasted infinitely into the past; and he [the witness] did not believe that the world had had a beginning.

"He also said that he had believed for all that time up to the beginning of May in the present year that the world had never had a beginning, and thus that it would never end, and that the world would go on in the same way in the future as it did now; and that just as men were generated now and as they had been generated from Adam onward, there would always be in the future the generation of men, and of vines, and of the other plants, and of all animals; nor would that generation ever end. He believed that there was no other world except the present one."

Testimony of Raimond de l'Aire, of Tignac

An older man told him that a mule has a soul as good as a man's "and from this belief he had by himself deduced that his own soul and those of other men are nothing but blood, because when a person's blood is taken away, he dies. He also believed that a dead person's soul and body both die, and that after death nothing human remains, because he didn't see anything leave the mouth of a person when he dies. From this he believed that the human soul after death has neither good nor evil, and that there is no hell or paradise in another world where human souls are rewarded or punished."

Testimony of Guillemette Benet

"Asked if, since she believed that human souls died with the bodies, she also believed that men would be resurrected and would live again after death, she answered that she did not believe that the resurrecting of the human body would happen, since she believed that as the dead body was buried, the soul was buried with the body; and since she saw that the body putrefied, she believed that it would never be resurrected. . . .

"Asked if she believed that the soul of Jesus Christ, who died on the cross, had died with his body, she answered yes, because although God is not able to die, nevertheless Jesus Christ died and therefore, even though she believed that God always existed, nevertheless she did not believe that Christ's soul lived and existed. . . .

"Asked if she believed that Christ was resurrected, she said yes and that God had done this."

Testimony of Arnaud Gelis, of Pamiers

Arnaud's beliefs	Roman Catholic orthodoxy
1. The souls of dead people do not do any other penance except to wander from church to church, some faster, some slower according to their sinfulness.	1. All souls of dead people go to purgatory, where they do the penance they had not completed on earth. And when this is done they go to the heavenly paradise where Christ, Mary, the angels, and the saints reside.
2. After they are finished going around to churches through the streets, the souls go to the place of rest, which is on this earth. They stay there until the judgment day.	2. When their penance is done, the souls of the dead go to the joy of the celestial paradise, which is no place of rest on earth, but rather in heaven.
3. No soul of any man except the most saintly goes directly to heaven or the heavenly kingdom. Souls do this on the day of judgment.	3. All souls of the dead, when their penance is done in purgatory (if they had need of it), enter the heavenly kingdom.

4. Souls of children who died before baptism go to an obscure place until the judgment day. There they feel neither pain nor pleasure. After the judgment day they enter paradise.

4. The souls of unbaptized children will never be saved or enter the kingdom of heaven.

5. No soul of a dead person, no matter how evil, has entered or will enter hell.

5. The souls of all evil persons—i.e., those who perpetrate great crimes that they do not confess or do penance for—go immediately after death to hell, where they stay and are punished for their sins.

6. At the last judgment God will have mercy on all who held the Christian faith and no one will be damned, no matter how evil he was.

6. All souls that held the Christian faith and accepted its sacraments and obeyed its commandments will be saved; but those who, even though holding the faith and accepting the sacraments, did not live according to the commandments will be damned.

7. Christ will have mercy on the souls of all heretics, Jews, and pagans; therefore none of them will be damned.

7. All souls of heretics, pagans, and Jews, who did not want to believe in Christ, will be damned. They will be punished eternally in hell.

8. Human souls, both before the body's death and after, have their own bodily form just like their external body. And the souls have distinct members like hands, eyes, feet, and the rest.

8. Human souls, both while in the body and after its death, because they are spirits, are not corporeal, nor do they have corporeal members, nor do they eat or drink, nor do they suffer such corporeal necessities.

9. Hell is a place only for demons.

9. Hell is a place for demons and for wicked people, where each is punished eternally as he deserves.

Disbelief in Indulgences: Testimony of Guillelme Cornelhano

"He also said that about two years before around the feast of Pentecost . . . a seller of indulgences passed by [him and Guillelma Vilara, wife of Arnald Cuculli] who had with him many indulgences. And after he had left them, Guillelma said, "Do you believe that any man is able to indulge or absolve anyone of his sins? Don't believe it, because no one can absolve anyone except God." And when he himself said that the pope and all priests could absolve man from sins, Guillelma answered that it was not so, only God could [do that]."

Testimony of Peter Sabatier

"When questioned, Peter said and confessed willingly that about three years ago on a certain day in the village of Varillis . . . when he returned from the church [to his house], he said that whatever things the priests and clerics were chanting and singing in the church were lies and tricks; but he never doubted, rather always believed, that the sacraments of the church and its articles of faith were true."

He persisted in this belief "for about a year, and believed out of silliness that priests and clerics, in singing and chanting those things in the church while performing the divine offices, sang and chanted in order to have the contributions, and that there was no good effect wrought by those divine of-fices."

Source 7 from Norman P. Tanner, editor, Heresy Trials in the Diocese of Norwich, 1428–1431, *Camden Fourth Series, vol. 20 (London: Royal Historical Society, 1977), pp. 111–113. Selection translated by Merry E. Wiesner.*

7. A Norwich Heresy Trial, 1428–1431

In the name of God, before you, the worshipful father in Christ, William, by the grace of God bishop of Norwich, I, John Reve, a glover from Beccles in your diocese, your subject, feeling and understanding that I have held, believed, and affirmed errors and heresies which be counted in this confession, that is to say:

That I have held, believed, and affirmed that the sacrament of baptism done in water in the form customary to the church is of no avail and not to be demanded if the father and mother of the child are christened and of Christian beliefs.

Also that the sacrament of confirmation done by a bishop is not profitable or necessary to man's salvation.

Also that confession ought not to be made to any priest, but only to God, for no priest has the power to forgive a man of sin.

Also that I have held, believed and affirmed that no priest has the power to make God's body in the sacrament of the altar, and that after the sacramental words said by a priest at mass nothing remains except a loaf of material bread.

Also that only consent of love in Jesus Christ between a man and woman of Christian beliefs is sufficient for the sacrament of matrimony, without any contract of words or solemnizing in church.

Also that I have held, believed and affirmed that only God has power to make the sacraments, and no other creature.

Also that I have held, believed and affirmed that no creature of Christian belief is required to fast in Lent, on the Umber Days, Fridays, vigils of saints nor any other times which the Church commands should be fasted, but it is lawful for people of Christian beliefs to eat meat at all such times and days. And in affirming this opinion I have eaten meat on Fridays and the other aforementioned days.

Also I have held, believed and affirmed that it is lawful for all Christ's people to do all bodily work on Sundays and all other days which the Church has commanded to be held holy, if people keep themselves from other sins at such days and times.

Also I have held, believed and affirmed that every man may lawfully and without sin withhold and withdraw his tithes and offerings from churches and curates, if it is done prudently.

Also I have held, believed and affirmed that it is lawful for God's people to act contrary to the precepts of the Church.

Also that censures of the Church and sentences of cursing whether from bishops, prelates, or other ordinaries are not to be taken into account or dreaded, for as soon as such bishops or ordinaries curse any man, Christ himself assails him.

Also that I have believed, held, and affirmed that no manner of worship ought to be done to any images of the crucifix, of Our Lady or of any other saints.

Also that no manner of pilgrimages ought to be done to any places of saints, but only to poor people.

Also that I have held and believed that it is not lawful to swear in any case.

Also that I have held, believed, and affirmed that the pope of Rome is the Antichrist and has no power in the Holy Church as St. Peter had unless he follows in the steps of Peter in his manner of living.

Also that all bishops, prelates and priests of the Church are the Antichrist's disciples.

Also that I have held, believed and affirmed that it is as meritorious and as profitable to all Christ's people to be buried in meadows or in wild fields as it is to be buried in churches or churchyards.

Because of which and many other errors and heresies which I have held, believed, and affirmed within your diocese, I am called before you, worshipful father, who has the cure of my soul. And you are fully informed that the said my holding, believing, and affirming are judged errors and heresies and contrary to the Church of Rome, wherefore I willingly follow the doctrine of holy Church and depart from all manner of heresy and error and turn with good heart and will to the unity of the Church. Considering that holy Church will not spare her bosom to him that will return nor God will the death of a sinner but rather that he be returned and live, with a pure heart I confess, detest and despise my said errors and heresies, and the said opinions I confess as heretical and erroneous and repugnant to the faith of the Church at Rome and all universal holy Church. And for as much as I showed myself corrupt and unfaithful through the said things that I so held, believed, and affirmed, from henceforth I will show myself uncorrupt and faithful, and I promise to keep the faith and doctrine of the holy Church truly. And I abjure and forswear all manner of error and heresy, doctrine and opinion against the holy Church and the determination of the Church of Rome—namely the opinions listed before—and swear by these holy gospels which I am bodily touching that from henceforth I shall never hold error nor heresy nor false doctrine against the faith of holy Church and the determination of the Church of Rome. No such things shall I obstinately defend. I shall defend no person holding or teaching such things openly or privately. I shall never after this time be an assistor, counselor, or defender of heretics or of any person suspected of heresy. I shall never ally myself with them. I shall not wittingly show fellowship to them, nor give them counsel, gifts, succor, favor, or comfort. If I know any heretics or any persons suspected of heresy, or people who counsel, assist or defend them, or any persons holding private conventicles or meetings, or holding any singular opinions different from the common doctrine of the Church, I shall let you, worshipful father, or your vicar general in your absence or the diocesans of such persons know soon and immediately. So help me God at holy doom and these holy gospels.

In witness of which things I subscribe here with my own hand a cross—X. And to this part intended to remain in your register I set my sign. And that other part I receive with your seal to keep with me until my life's end. Given at Norwich in the chapel of your palace, xviii day of the month of April in the year of our Lord one thousand four hundred and thirty.

Source 8 from Bavarian National Museum, Munich.

8. Madonna, Germany, ca 1430

Source 9 from Cathedral of St. Vitus, Prague (Foto Marburg/Art Resource, NY).

9. Crucifix, Germany, 14th century

QUESTIONS TO CONSIDER

The written sources and the religious statues have provided you with evidence for the two central questions of this chapter. Looking again at those questions, you can see that the first concerns the religious beliefs and practices of laypeople, and the second the official Church reaction to those beliefs and practices. You now need to sort through the sources to separate the information you have gained about each question.

Look first at lay piety itself. Which Christian beliefs were numbers of people attracted to? Why were these beliefs especially appealing? Why might it have been difficult for most people to respond to more esoteric points of theology such as the Trinity? Many of the sources have described or depicted the extremely important role of the Virgin Mary in lay piety. Why do you think people turned to her, rather than to God the Father, in their prayers and devotions? In official Christian theology, Mary is not a goddess but completely human, and believers were urged to honor but not to worship her. From the sources, do you think most laypeople understood this distinction? Looking at the first sermon story, which relates beliefs and practices approved of by the Church, was this distinction always made clear to laypeople?

You have seen that religion was not simply a matter of belief for most people but also of real-world practices and acts. What practices were most popular? How did people see these as contributing to their spiritual lives? One of the sermon stories, the life of St. Nicholas, and the works of Bridget and Margery Kempe refer matter-of-factly to visions and miracles. What does this imply about the divisions between the natural and supernatural in most people's minds?

The two heresy trials record beliefs that deviated from those officially accepted. Do you find evidence of similar beliefs, though perhaps not carried so far, in any of the other sources? For example, what religious beliefs and practices of Margery Kempe opened her to the accusation of heresy? How would you compare the two heresies from the sources reprinted here? Does either appear to deviate further from official Church teachings than the other? Which teachings do both dispute? Can you make any generalizations about late medieval heresy from these examples, or are the differences between them more striking than the similarities?

Now turn to the second question. Official Church reaction to lay piety was both positive and negative. Positive reactions included attempts by preachers and priests to shape popular belief and to encourage certain actions that they felt strengthened the Church. Judging by the sermon stories and the life of St. Nicholas, what beliefs and practices were preachers and hagiographers trying to encourage? Did the religious statuary encourage similar ideas? How did the archbishop try to influence Margery Kempe? Negative reactions included the Church's attempts to eradicate unacceptable beliefs and behavior, with sanctions ranging from mild scoldings to execution for heresy. Judging from the heresy trials and Margery Kempe's autobiography, what kinds of beliefs were Church officials especially worried about? Did they appear to be more concerned with beliefs or with behavior?

Many of those charged with heresy or with suspect beliefs in the late Middle Ages were women, and the Church hierarchy was of course totally male. Thinking particularly of the experience of Margery Kempe, do you find evidence of gender differences in official attitudes toward lay piety? Even women whose ideas were initially accepted could later be judged heretical. For example, Bridget of Sweden was made a saint less than twenty years after her death, but only forty years later the authenticity of her visions was questioned and she was dismissed by some Church officials as a chatterbox deluded by the devil. Do you find anything in the visions printed here that might have been disturbing to the all-male clerical establishment?

Both lay piety and official reaction to it were shaped by political and economic factors as well as by theology and doctrine. From your sources, which beliefs and practices encouraged or condemned by the Church would have had economic repercussions? Especially in the Norwich heresy trial, which ideas did the Church view as a political threat? Why would the ideas expressed in that trial have been seen as more dangerous than those of Margery Kempe? Reread the discussion in your text of the political and economic changes that late medieval Europe experienced. How was the Church involved in these changes? Do your sources provide evidence for any of the developments described in your text?

You are now ready to answer the two central questions of this chapter: How did common people in the Middle Ages experience and express their religious faith? How did the Church as an institution respond to laypeople's beliefs and practices? Are your answers more complex or less complex than you expected?

EPILOGUE

Most of the strong lay piety in the late Middle Ages remained inside the boundaries judged acceptable by the Church. Groups branded as heretics were usually small, and they were quite successfully wiped out by intensive inquisitions and campaigns of persecution such as those carried out against the Albigensians and Lollards.

Persecution did not put an end to dissatisfaction with the institutional Church, however, nor were preachers and priests ever able to exert total control over the beliefs or activities of common people. Indeed, the more historians study the beliefs of "unlearned" people, the more they discover that people do not passively absorb what they are told but add to it their own ideas. Illiteracy does not preclude imagination or intelligence, and influence between the learned elite and the common people runs in both directions.

Though lay dissatisfaction persisted, it did not cause the institutional Church to change or initiate reforms during the late Middle Ages. In 1377, the papacy returned to Rome, and when the pope died the following year the Roman people forced the college of cardinals, the body of church officials who chose the popes, to elect an Italian pope. This pope, Urban VI, tried to reform some of the Church's problems but did so in such a belligerent way that he set most of the college of cardinals against him. They responded by declaring that the pope's election was invalid because they had been put under duress and, calling for his resignation, elected another pope. Urban did not step down, however, and a forty-year power split began in which two and later three popes simultaneously excommunicated the others, collected taxes, made appointments, and granted indulgences. The Great Schism, as this period is called, was probably the low point in the history of organized Christianity in the West, but the eventual reunification of the Church in 1417 did not resolve all problems. For the next century, the popes con-

centrated their energies on artistic patronage and expansion of their political power in Italy. Despite several major attempts at reform and increasing recognition of internal problems by many Church officials and scholars throughout Europe, low standards of discipline and morality, and high levels of corruption, persisted.

Martin Luther's break with the Catholic church in the early sixteenth century began as yet another attempt at reform but quickly grew into a revolution that split Western Christianity from that time on. The swift and widespread acceptance of Luther's ideas gave vivid testimony to the depth of popular dissatisfaction with the Church. At the very beginning, at least, common people in many parts of Germany saw the Protestant Reformation as the change they had been looking for, a movement that emphasized personal piety and played down the priest's role in the individual's salvation. Supporting Luther initially, they quickly realized that he was not the leader they had hoped for and that he attacked many of the practices, such as pilgrimages or the veneration of Mary, that were dearest to them. Thus the strong lay piety movement of the late Middle Ages is an important factor in understanding not just medieval Christianity in all its complexity but the roots of the Reformation as well.

CHAPTER ELEVEN

THE RENAISSANCE

MAN AND WOMAN

The age we know as the Renaissance had its beginnings in the fourteenth century as a literary movement among educated, mostly upper-class men in northern Italian cities, notably Florence. Such writers as Petrarch attempted to emulate as closely as possible the literary figures of ancient Rome, believing that these men, especially Cicero, had attained a level of style and a command of the Latin language that had never since been duplicated. Petrarch's fascination with antiquity did not stop with language, however, but also included an interest in classical architecture and art; he spent long hours wandering around the large numbers of Roman ruins remaining in Italy. His obsession with the classical past also led him to reject the thousand-year period between his own time and that of Rome, viewing this as a "dark," "gothic," or at best "middle" age—a deep trough between two peaks of civilization.

Though Petrarch himself did not call his own period the *Renaissance*—a word that means "rebirth"—he clearly believed he was witnessing the dawning of a new age.

Writers and artists intending to recapture the glory that was Rome would have to study Roman models, and Petrarch proposed an appropriate course of study or curriculum termed the *studia humanitates*, or simply "liberal studies" or the "liberal arts." Like all curricula, it contained an implicit philosophy, a philosophy that came to be known as *humanism*. Humanism was not a rigorous philosophical system like Aristotelianism, or an all-encompassing belief system like Christianity, but what we might better call an attitude toward learning and toward life.

This new attitude had a slow diffusion out of Italy, with the result that the Renaissance "happened" at very different times in different parts of Europe. Because it was not a single historical event in the same sense as the French Revolution or the

Peloponnesian War, the Renaissance is difficult to date. Roughly, we can say it began in Italy in the fourteenth century; spread to France, Germany, and Spain by the end of the fifteenth century; to England by the early part of the sixteenth century; and not until the seventeenth century to Scandinavia. Thus the Renaissance preceded the Reformation—which *was* an event—in most of Europe, took place at the same time as the Reformation in England, and came after the Reformation in Scandinavia. Shakespeare, for example, is considered a "Renaissance" writer even though he lived 250 years after Petrarch.

Though the chronology may be somewhat confusing, there are certain recurring features of humanism through the centuries. One of these is a veneration of the classical past. Petrarch concentrated primarily on Latin and ancient Rome, but during the mid-fifteenth century humanists also began to emphasize Greek language, art, architecture, philosophy, and literature. Though they disagreed about the relative merits of the classical philosophers and writers, all agreed that classical philosophy and literature were of paramount importance to their own culture.

Another feature of humanism is its emphasis on individualism. Medieval society was corporate—that is, oriented toward, and organized around, people acting in groups. Medieval political philosophy dictated that the smallest component of society was not the individual but the family. An individual ruler stood at the top of medieval society, but this ruler was regarded as tightly bound to the other nobles by feudal alliances and, in some ways, as simply the greatest of the nobles. Workers banded together in guilds; pious people formed religious confraternities; citizens swore an oath of allegiance to their own city. Even art was thought to be a group effort, with the individual artist feeling no more need to sign a work than a baker did to sign each loaf of bread. (We know the names of some medieval artists from sources such as contracts, bills of sale, and financial records, but rarely from the paintings or sculptures themselves.)

Christianity encouraged this sense of community as well. Though Christians were baptized and participated in most other sacraments as individuals, the priest represented the whole community when he alone drank wine at communion, and Christ was believed to have embodied all of Christianity when he died. Christians were encouraged to think of themselves as part of one great "Christendom" and to follow the example of Christ by showing humility and meekness rather than the self-assurance that draws attention to the individual.

These attitudes began to shift during the Renaissance. The family, the guild, and other corporate groups remained important social forces, but some individuals increasingly viewed the group as simply a springboard to far greater individual achievement that could be obtained through talent or hard work. Rather than defining themselves primarily within the context of the group, some prized their own sense of uniqueness and individuality, hiring artists to paint or sculpt their portraits and writers to produce verbal likenesses. Caught up in this new individualism, artists and writers themselves began to paint their own self-portraits and write autobiographies. Visual artists, believing that their skill at painting or sculpture was a result not simply of good training but of individual genius, began to sign their works. Rather than the vices they were to medieval Christians, self-confidence and individualism became virtues for many people. Humanists wrote not only biographies of prominent individuals but also treatises that described the attributes of the ideal person. In their opinion, that person should be well rounded and should also exhibit the quality of *virtù*—a word that does not mean "virtue" but rather the ability to make an impact in one's chosen field of endeavor.

The notion of individualism includes a belief that the people and objects of this world are important, at least important enough to warrant a picture or a verbal description. This belief, usually called *secularism*, is also a part of humanism. "Secularism" is a highly charged word in modern American political jargon— even more so when expanded to "secular humanism"—and may be too strong a term to apply to Renaissance thinkers. No one in the Renaissance denied the existence of God or the central importance of religion in human life. What they did reject was the idea that it was necessary to forsake the material world and retire to a life of contemplation in order to

worship God. God had created this world full of beauty, including the human body, to be appreciated. The talents of each person should be developed to their fullest through education and then displayed to the world because those talents came from God. Studying pre-Christian philosophers such as Plato or Aristotle could enhance an understanding of Christianity because God could certainly have endowed these thinkers with great wisdom even though they were not Christian.

The basis for all these features of humanism—classicism, individualism, secularism—was learning, and humanists all agreed on the importance of education, not just for the individual but also for society as a whole. During the mid-fifteenth century many humanists, such as Leonardo Bruni, began to stress that a proper liberal education was based on training for service to society as well as on classical models. Medieval education had been primarily an organ of the Church, oriented to its needs. Church and cathedral schools trained students to read and write so that they could copy manuscripts, serve as church lawyers, and write correspondence. Monks, priests, and nuns also used their education to honor the glory of God by reciting prayers, studying the Bible and other religious works, composing and singing hymns, or simply speculating on the nature of God. In the Middle Ages the ultimate aim of human life was to *know,* and particularly to know God, so medieval education was often both inwardly directed and otherworldy, helping individuals to come to a better understanding of God. The Renaissance humanists, on the other hand, believed the ultimate aim of human life was to *act*, so humanist education was resoundingly outwardly directed and this-worldly, emphasizing practical skills such as public speaking and writing that would benefit any politician, diplomat, military leader, or businessman. This education was not to be used in a monastery where only God could see it, but in the newly expanding cities and towns of northern Italy, cities that were growing steadily richer thanks to the development of trade we examined in Chapter 9. The primarily classical humanism of the fourteenth century was gradually transformed into civic humanism as humanists took employment as city secretaries and historians and as merchants and bankers sent their sons to humanist schools.

Humanism underwent a further transformation in the sixteenth century, when the governing of the cities of northern Italy was taken over by powerful noblemen. These rulers hired humanists as secretaries, tutors, diplomats, and advisers, and they established humanist academies in their capital cities. Unlike medieval rulers, who saw themselves primarily as military leaders, Renaissance rulers saw themselves as the leaders of all facets of life in their territories. Thus they supported poets and musicians as well as generals, learned several languages, and established their court as the cultural as well as political center of the territory.

Reflecting this new courtly milieu, humanists began to write biographies of rulers and to reflect on the qualities that were important in the ideal ruler and courtier. The trait of *virtù*, so vital in an individual, was even more critical in a ruler. For a ruler, *virtù* meant the ability to shape society as a whole and leave an indelible mark on history. Humanists held up as models worthy of emulation such classical rulers as Alexander the Great and Julius Caesar.

In many ways, then, Renaissance thinkers broke with the immediate medieval past in developing new ideals for human behavior. For one group, however, this break was not so complete. When humanists described the ideal woman, she turned out to be much more like her medieval counterpart than the "Renaissance man" was. The problem of female education was particularly perplexing for humanists. Medieval women, like medieval men, had been educated to serve and know God. Renaissance men were educated to serve the city or the state, which no humanist felt was a proper role for women. If women were not to engage in the type of public activities felt to be the proper arena for displaying talent and education, why should they be educated at all? Should the new virtues of self-confidence and individualism be extended to include women? Or should women be the link with the older Christian virtues of modesty and humility? How could women properly show *virtù*— a word whose roots lie in the word *vir*, which meant "man"—when to do so required public actions? Should women, perhaps, be even more encouraged to remain within the private sphere of home and family, given the opinions of classical philosophers such as Aristotle (which we saw in Chapter 3) about the proper role of women? In their consideration of the proper "Renaissance woman," humanists often exhibited both the tension between, and their attempts to fuse, the pagan classical and medieval Christian traditions.

In this chapter, you will examine the writings of several humanists describing the ideal educational program for boys and girls, the ideal male and female courtier, and the ideal ruler. In addition, you will read one short section from the autobiography of a humanist and another from the biography of a ruler written by a humanist; you will also look at several portraits. How do these authors describe the ideal man, woman, and ruler? How were these ideals expressed in written descriptions and visual portraits of actual Renaissance people?

SOURCES AND METHOD

The written sources in this chapter are primarily prescriptive; in other words, they present ideals that their humanist authors hoped people would emulate. Our questions and methodology are those of intellectual historians, who are interested in the development of ideas as well as in how those ideas relate to other types of changes. Intellectual history is an especially important dimension of the Renaissance, which was primarily an intellectual rather than a political or social movement. The questions you need to keep most in mind, then, relate to the ideas set forth here: What qualities was the ideal man, woman, or ruler supposed to possess? How were these qualities to be inculcated in young people? On the basis of these qualities, what did humanists think was most important in human existence? How did authors and artists portraying real people—in biographies, autobiographies, or portraits—express similar ideas?

Whenever we use prescriptive literature as our historical source, we must first inquire into the author's motives. Why did our Renaissance writers believe that people had to be instructed in matters of behavior? Were they behaving badly, or were they confronting new situations in which they would not know how to act? The intentions of these humanist authors were fairly straightforward because they believed themselves to be living in a new age, a rebirth of classical culture. In their minds, people needed to be informed about the values of this new age and instructed in the means for putting these values into practice. The humanist authors were thus attempting to mold new types of people to fit a new world, not simply correcting attitudes and behavior they felt were wrong or misguided. Consequently, humanist prescriptive literature concentrates on the positive, telling people what to do rather than what not to do (unlike much other prescriptive literature, such as the Ten Commandments).

Before you read the written selections, look at the three portraits. The first is a self-portrait by the German artist Albrecht Dürer; the second a portrait of an Italian woman known simply as Simonetta, by the Italian artist Sandro Botticelli or a member of his workshop; the third a sculpture of the Venetian general Bartolommeo Colleoni by Andrea del Verrocchio. How would you describe the expressions of the subjects in each of these portraits? Do any of them exhibit the qualities prized by the humanists— individualism, *virtù*, self-confidence? What other traits did the artist choose to emphasize? What differences do you see in the portrait of the woman compared with those of the two men? Now proceed to the written evidence.

Sources 4 and 5 are letters from humanists to members of the nobility. The first, discussing the proper education for men, is from Peter Paul Vergerius to Ubertinus, the son of the ruler of Padua, Italy; the second, discussing the proper education for women, is from Leonardo Bruni to Lady Baptista Malatesta, the daughter of the Duke of Urbino. As you read them, note both the similarities and the differences in the two courses of study. What factors might account for this? What is the ultimate purpose of the two educational programs?

Sources 6 and 7 are taken from one of the most popular advice manuals ever written, Baldassare Castiglione's *The Courtier*. Castiglione was himself a courtier in Urbino, Mantua, and Milan, and he wrote this discussion

of the perfect courtier and court lady in the form of a dialogue between noblemen. As you did for Sources 4 and 5, compare the qualities prescribed for men and women, respectively. How do these relate to the educational program discussed in Sources 4 and 5?

Source 8 comes from one of the most widely read pieces of political advice ever written, Machiavelli's *The Prince*. Like Castiglione, Niccolo Machiavelli had served various governments and had watched rulers and states rise and fall in late-fifteenth- and early-sixteenth-century Italy. What does he believe is the most critical factor or factors in the training of a prince? What qualities should a ruler possess to be effective and display *virtù*?

The first five documents are all straightforward prescriptive literature, as the authors' frequent use of such words as "ought" and "should" indicates. This was not the only way humanists communicated their ideals, however; biographies of real people also expressed these ideals. To use biographies as a source of ideas, we must take a slightly more subtle approach, identifying those personal characteristics the author chose to emphasize, those that might have been omitted, and the way in which each biographer manipulated the true personality of his subject to fit the humanist ideal. These are points to consider as you read the next two documents. Source 9 is from the autobiography of Leon Battista Alberti, which you will note is written in the third person. How does Alberti describe himself? How did his life reflect the new humanist ideals? Why might he have chosen to write in the third person instead of saying "I"? Source 10 is Polydore Vergil's description of Henry VII of England, who ruled from 1485 to 1509. What does it tell us about Renaissance monarchs and also about the author?

Once you have read the written selections, return to the portraits. Do you find anything there that you did not see before?

THE EVIDENCE

Source 1 from German Information Center.

1. Albrecht Dürer, *Self-Portrait in a Fur Coat*, 1500

Source 2 from Staatliche Museen zu Berlin—Preussischer Kulturbesitz Gemaldegalerie. Photograph: Jorg P. Anders.

2. Workshop of Botticelli (ca 1444–1510), So-called *Simonetta*

Source 3 from Venice (Alinari/Art Resource, New York).

3. Andrea del Verrocchio (ca 1435–1488), Sculpture of General Bartolommeo Colleoni

Sources 4 and 5 from W. H. Woodward, editor and translator, Vittorino da Feltre and Other Humanist Educators *(London: Cambridge University Press, 1897), pp. 102, 106–107, 109, 110; pp. 126–129, 132, 133.*

4. Peter Paul Vergerius, Letter to Ubertinus of Padua, 1392

3. We call those studies *liberal* which are worthy of a free man; those studies by which we attain and practice virtue and wisdom; that education which calls forth, trains, and develops those highest gifts of body and of mind which ennoble men, and which are rightly judged to rank next in dignity to virtue only. For to a vulgar temper gain and pleasure are the one aim of existence, to a lofty nature, moral worth and fame. It is, then, of the highest importance that even from infancy this aim, this effort, should constantly be kept alive in growing minds. . . .

We come now to the consideration of the various subjects which may rightly be included under the name of "Liberal Studies." Amongst these I accord the first place to History, on grounds both of its attractiveness and of its utility, qualities which appeal equally to the scholar and to the states-man. Next in importance ranks Moral Philosophy, which indeed is, in a pe-culiar sense, a "Liberal Art," in that its purpose is to teach men the secret of true freedom. History, then, gives us the concrete examples of the precepts inculcated by Philosophy. The one shows what men should do, the other what men have said and done in the past, and what practical lessons we may draw therefrom for the present day. I would indicate as the third main branch of study, Eloquence, which indeed holds a place of distinction amongst the refined arts. By philosophy we learn the essential truth of things, which by eloquence we so exhibit in orderly adornment as to bring conviction to differing minds. And history provides the light of experience—a cumulative wisdom fit to supplement the force of reason and the persuasion of eloquence. For we allow that soundness of judgment, wisdom of speech, integrity of conduct are the marks of a truly liberal temper. . . .

4. The principal "Disciplines" have now been reviewed. It must not be supposed that a liberal education requires acquaintance with them all: for a thorough mastery of even one of them might fairly be the achievement of a lifetime. Most of us, too, must learn to be content with modest capacity as with modest fortune. Perhaps we do wisely to pursue that study which we find most suited to our intelligence and our tastes, though it is true that we cannot rightly understand one subject unless we can perceive its relation to the rest. The choice of studies will depend to some extent upon the character of individual minds. . . .

Respecting the general place of liberal studies, we remember that Aristotle would not have them absorb the entire interests of life: for he kept steadily in view the nature of man as a citizen, an active member of the State. For the man who has surrendered himself absolutely to the attractions of Letters or of speculative thought follows, perhaps, a self-regarding end and is useless as a citizen or as prince.

5. Leonardo Bruni, Letter to Lady Baptista Malatesta, ca 1405

There are certain subjects in which, whilst a modest proficiency is on all accounts to be desired, a minute knowledge and excessive devotion seem to be a vain display. For instance, subtleties of Arithmetic and Geometry are not worthy to absorb a cultivated mind, and the same must be said of Astrology. You will be surprised to find me suggesting (though with much more hesitation) that the great and complex art of Rhetoric should be placed in the same category. My chief reason is the obvious one, that I have in view the cultivation most fitting to a woman. To her neither the intricacies of debate nor the oratorical artifices of action and delivery are of the least practical use, if indeed they are not positively unbecoming. Rhetoric in all its forms—public discussion, forensic argument, logical fence, and the like—lies absolutely outside the province of women.

What Disciplines then are properly open to her? In the first place she has before her, as a subject peculiarly her own, the whole field of religion and morals. The literature of the Church will thus claim her earnest study. Such a writer, for instance, as St. Augustine affords her the fullest scope for reverent yet learned inquiry. Her devotional instinct may lead her to value the help and consolation of holy men now living; but in this case let her not for an instant yield to the impulse to look into their writings, which, compared with those of Augustine, are utterly destitute of sound and melodious style, and seem to me to have no attraction whatever.

Moreover, the cultivated Christian lady has no need in the study of this weighty subject to confine herself to ecclesiastical writers. Morals, indeed, have been treated of by the noblest intellects of Greece and Rome. What they have left to us upon Continence, Temperance, Modesty, Justice, Courage, Greatness of Soul, demands your sincere respect. . . .

But we must not forget that true distinction is to be gained by a wide and varied range of such studies as conduce to the profitable enjoyment of life, in which, however, we must observe due proportion in the attention and time we devote to them.

First amongst such studies I place History: a subject which must not on any account be neglected by one who aspires to true cultivation. For it is our duty to understand the origins of our own history and its development; and the achievements of Peoples and of Kings.

For the careful study of the past enlarges our foresight in contemporary affairs and affords to citizens and to monarchs lessons of incitement or warning in the ordering of public policy. From History, also, we draw our store of examples of moral precepts. . . .

The great Orators of antiquity must by all means be included. Nowhere do we find the virtues more warmly extolled, the vices so fiercely decried. From them we may learn, also, how to express consolation, encouragement, dissuasion or advice. . . .

I come now to Poetry and the Poets—a subject with which every educated lady must shew herself thoroughly familiar. For we cannot point to any great mind of the past for whom the Poets had not a powerful attraction. . . . Hence my view that familiarity with the great poets of antiquity is essential to any claim to true education. For in their writings we find deep speculations upon Nature, and upon the Causes and Origins of things, which must carry weight with us both from their antiquity and from their authorship. Besides these, many important truths upon matters of daily life are suggested or illustrated. All this is expressed with such grace and dignity as demands our admiration.

But I am ready to admit that there are two types of poet: the aristocracy, so to call them, of their craft, and the vulgar, and that the latter may be put aside in ordering a woman's reading. A comic dramatist may season his wit too highly: a satirist describe too bluntly the moral corruption which he scourges: let her pass them by. . . .

But my last word must be this. . . . All sources of profitable learning will in due proportion claim your study. None have more urgent claim than the subjects and authors which treat of Religion and of our duties in the world; and it is because they assist and illustrate these supreme studies that I press upon your attention the works of the most approved poets, historians and orators of the past.

Sources 6 and 7 from Baldassare Castiglione, The Book of the Courtier, *trans. Charles S. Singleton, ed. Edgar Mayhew (Garden City, New York: Doubleday, 1959), pp. 32, 34, 70–71; pp. 206–208, 211–212. Copyright © 1959 by Charles S. Singleton and Edgar de N. Mayhew. Used by permission of Doubleday, a division of Random House, Inc.*

6. From Baldassare Castiglione, *The Courtier,* 1508–1516

"I hold that the principal and true profession of the Courtier must be that of arms which I wish him to exercise with vigor; and let him be known among the others as bold, energetic, and faithful to whomever he serves. And the repute of these good qualities will be earned by exercising them in every time and place, inasmuch as one may not ever fail therein without great blame.

And, just as among women the name of purity, once stained, is never restored, so the reputation of a gentleman whose profession is arms, if ever in the least way he sullies himself through cowardice or other disgrace, always remains defiled before the world and covered with ignominy. Therefore, the more our Courtier excels in this art, the more will he merit praise." . . .

Then signor Gasparo replied: "As for me, I have known few men excellent in anything whatsoever who did not praise themselves; and it seems to me that this can well be permitted them, because he who feels himself to be of some worth, and sees that his works are ignored, is indignant that his own worth should lie buried; and he must make it known to someone, in order not to be cheated of the honor that is the true reward of all virtuous toil. Thus, among the ancients, seldom does anyone of any worth refrain from praising himself. To be sure, those persons who are of no merit, and yet praise themselves, are insufferable; but we do not assume that our Courtier will be of that sort."

Then the Count said: "If you took notice, I blamed impudent and indiscriminate praise of one's self: and truly, as you say, one must not conceive a bad opinion of a worthy man who praises himself modestly; nay, one must take that as surer evidence than if it came from another's mouth. I do say that whoever does not fall into error in praising himself and does not cause annoyance or envy in the person who listens to him is indeed a discreet man and, besides the praises he gives himself, deserves praises from others; for that is a very difficult thing." . . .

"I would have him more than passably learned in letters, at least in those studies which we call the humanities. Let him be conversant not only with the Latin language, but with Greek as well, because of the abundance and variety of things that are so divinely written therein. Let him be versed in the poets, as well as in the orators and historians, and let him be practiced also in writing verse and prose, especially in our own vernacular; for, beside the personal satisfaction he will take in this, in this way he will never want for pleasant entertainment with the ladies, who are usually fond of such things. And if, because of other occupations or lack of study, he does not attain to such a perfection that his writings should merit great praise, let him take care to keep them under cover so that others will not laugh at him, and let him show them only to a friend who can be trusted; because at least they will be of profit to him in that, through such exercise, he will be capable of judging the writing of others. For it very rarely happens that a man who is unpracticed in writing, however learned he may be, can ever wholly understand the toils and industry of writers, or taste the sweetness and excellence of styles, and those intrinsic niceties that are often found in the ancients.

"These studies, moreover, will make him fluent, and (as Aristippus said to the tyrant) bold and self-confident in speaking with everyone. However, I would have our Courtier keep one precept firmly in mind, namely, in this as in everything else, to be cautious and reserved rather than forward, and take care not to get the mistaken notion that he knows something he does not know."

7. From Baldassare Castiglione, *The Courtier*, 1508–1516

I think that in her ways, manners, words, gestures, and bearing, a woman ought to be very unlike a man; for just as he must show a certain solid and sturdy manliness, so it is seemly for a woman to have a soft and delicate tenderness, with an air of womanly sweetness in her every movement. . . .

[Again] . . . many virtues of the mind are as necessary to a woman as to a man; also, gentle birth; to avoid affectation, to be naturally graceful in all her actions, to be mannerly, clever, prudent, not arrogant, not envious, not slanderous, not vain, not contentious, not inept, to know how to gain and hold the favor of her mistress [queen or presiding lady at court] and of all others, to perform well and gracefully the exercises that are suitable for women. And I do think that beauty is more necessary to her than to the Courtier, for truly that woman lacks much who lacks beauty. . . . I say that, in my opinion, in a Lady who lives at court a certain pleasing affability is becoming above all else, whereby she will be able to entertain graciously every kind of man with agreeable and comely conversation suited to the time and place and to the station of the person with whom she speaks, joining to serene and modest manners, and to that comeliness that ought to inform all her actions, a quick vivacity of spirit whereby she will show herself a stranger to all boorishness; but with such a kind manner as to cause her to be thought no less chaste, prudent, and gentle than she is agreeable, witty, and discreet: thus, she must observe a certain mean (difficult to achieve and, as it were, composed of contraries) and must strictly observe certain limits and not exceed them.

Now, in her wish to be thought good and pure, this Lady must not be so coy, or appear so to abhor gay company or any talk that is a little loose, as to withdraw as soon as she finds herself involved, for it might easily be thought that she was pretending to be so austere in order to hide something about herself which she feared others might discover; for manners so unbending are always odious. Yet, on the other hand, for the sake of appearing free and amiable she must not utter unseemly words or enter into any immodest and unbridled familiarity or into ways such as might cause others to believe about her what is perhaps not true; but when she finds herself present at such talk, she ought to listen with a light blush of shame. . . .

And to repeat briefly a part of what has already been said. I wish this Lady to have knowledge of letters, of music, of painting, and know how to dance and how to be festive, adding a discreet modesty and the giving of a good impression of herself to those other things that have been required of the

Courtier. And so, in her talk, her laughter, her play, her jesting, in short in everything, she will be most graceful and will converse appropriately with every person in whose company she may happen to be, using witticisms and pleasantries that are becoming to her.

Source 8 from Niccolo Machiavelli, The Prince and the Discourses, *translated by Luigi Ricci, revised by E. R. P. Vincent (New York: Random House, 1950), pp. 4, 53, 55, 56, 61–62. Reprinted by permission of Oxford University Press.*

8. From Niccolo Machiavelli,
The Prince, 1513

I desire no honour for my work but such as the novelty and gravity of its subject may justly deserve. Nor will it, I trust, be deemed presumptuous on the part of a man of humble and obscure condition to attempt to discuss and direct the government of princes; for in the same way that landscape painters station themselves in the valleys in order to draw mountains or high ground, and ascend an eminence in order to get a good view of the plains, so it is necessary to be a prince to know thoroughly the nature of the people, and one of the populace to know the nature of princes. . . .

A prince should therefore have no other aim or thought, nor take up any other thing for his study, but war and its organisation and discipline, for that is the only art that is necessary to one who commands, and it is of such virtue that it not only maintains those who are born princes, but often enables men of private fortune to attain to that rank. And one sees, on the other hand, that when princes think more of luxury than of arms, they lose their state. The chief cause of the loss of states, is the contempt of this art, and the way to acquire them is to be well versed in the same. . . .

But as to exercise for the mind, the prince ought to read history and study the actions of eminent men, see how they acted in warfare, examine the causes of their victories and defeats in order to imitate the former and avoid the latter, and above all, do as some men have done in the past, who have imitated some one, who has been much praised and glorified, and have always kept his deeds and actions before them. . . .

It now remains to be seen what are the methods and rules for a prince as regards his subjects and friends. . . .

From this arises the question whether it is better to be loved more than feared, or feared more than loved. The reply is, that one ought to be both feared and loved, but as it is difficult for the two to go together, it is much safer to be feared than loved, if one of the two has to be wanting. For it may be said of men in general that they are ungrateful, voluble, dissemblers, anxious to avoid danger, and covetous of gain; as long as you benefit them, they are entirely yours; they offer you their blood, their goods, their life, and their children, as I have before said, when the necessity is remote; but when it approaches, they revolt. And the prince who has relied solely on their words, without making other preparations, is ruined; for the friendship which is gained by purchase and not through grandeur and nobility of spirit is bought but not secured, and at a pinch is not to be expended in your service. And men have less scruple in offending one who makes himself loved than one who makes himself feared; for love is held by a chain of obligation which, men being selfish, is broken whenever it serves their purpose; but fear is maintained by a dread of punishment which never fails.

Still, a prince should make himself feared in such a way that if he does not gain love, he at any rate avoids hatred; for fear and the absence of hatred may well go together, and will be always attained by one who abstains from interfering with the property of his citizens and subjects or with their women. And when he is obliged to take the life of any one, let him do so when there is a proper justification and manifest reason for it; but above all he must abstain from taking the property of others, for men forget more easily the death of their father than the loss of their patrimony. Then also pretexts for seizing property are never wanting, and one who begins to live by rapine will always find some reason for taking the goods of others, whereas causes for taking life are rarer and more fleeting.

But when the prince is with his army and has a large number of soldiers under his control, then it is extremely necessary that he should not mind being thought cruel; for without this reputation he could not keep an army united or disposed to any duty.

Source 9 from James Bruce Ross and Mary Martin McLaughlin, editors, The Portable Renaissance Reader *(New York: Viking, 1953), pp. 480–485, 490–492. Selection translated by James Bruce Ross. Copyright 1953, renewed 1981 by Viking Penguin Inc. Used by permission of Viking Penguin, a division of Penguin Putnam, Inc.*

9. From Leon Battista Alberti, *Autobiography*, after 1460(?)

In everything suitable to one born free and educated liberally, he was so trained from boyhood that among the leading young men of his age he was considered by no means the last. For, assiduous in the science and skill of dealing with arms and horses and musical instruments, as well as in the pursuit of letters[1] and the fine arts, he was devoted to the knowledge of the most strange and difficult things. And finally he embraced with zeal and forethought everything which pertained to fame. To omit the rest, he strove so hard to attain a name in modelling and painting that he wished to neglect

1. **letters:** Alberti means the humanist program of study, primarily the study of languages and literature.

nothing by which he might gain the approbation of good men. His genius was so versatile that you might almost judge all the fine arts to be his. Neither ease nor sloth held him back, nor was he ever seized by satiety in carrying out what was to be done.

He often said that not even in letters had he noticed what is called the satiety of all things among mortals; for to him letters, in which he delighted so greatly, seemed sometimes like flowering and richly fragrant buds, so that hunger or sleep could scarcely distract him from his books. At other times, however, those very letters swarmed together like scorpions before his eyes, so that he could see nothing at all but books. Therefore, when letters began to be displeasing to him, he turned to music and painting and exercise.

He played ball, hurled the javelin, ran, leaped, wrestled, and above all delighted in the steep ascent of mountains; he applied himself to all these things for the sake of health rather than sport or pleasure. . . .

At length, on the orders of his doctors, he desisted from those studies which were most fatiguing to the memory, just when they were about to flourish. But in truth, because he could not live without letters, at the age of twenty-four he turned to physics and the mathematical arts. He did not despair of being able to cultivate them sufficiently, because he perceived that in them talent rather than memory must be employed. At this time he wrote for his brother *On the Advantages and Disadvantages of Letters*, in which booklet, taught by experience, he discussed whatever could be thought about letters. And he wrote at this time for the sake of his soul several little works: *Ephebia, On Religion, Deiphira*, and more of this sort in prose; then in verse, *Elegies* and *Eclogues*, and *Discourses*, and works on love of such a kind as to inculcate good habits in those who studied them and to foster the quiet of the soul. . . .

Although he was affable, gentle, and harmful to no one, nevertheless he felt the animosity of many evil men, and hidden enmities, both annoying and very burdensome; in particular the harsh injuries and intolerable insults from his own relatives. He lived among the envious and malevolent with such modesty and equanimity that none of his detractors or rivals, although very hostile towards him, dared to utter a word about him in the presence of good and worthy men unless it was full of praise and admiration. Even by these envious ones he was received with honour face to face. But, in truth, when he was absent, those who had pretended to love him most slandered him with every sort of calumny, wherever the ears of the fickle and their like lay open. For they took it ill to be exceeded in ability and fame by him who, far inferior to them in fortune, had striven with such zeal and industry. There were even some among his kinsmen (not to mention others) who, having experienced his humanity, beneficence, and liberality, conspired against him most ungratefully and cruelly in an evil domestic plot, and those barbarians aroused the boldness of servants to strike him with a knife, blameless as he was.

He bore injuries of this kind from his kinsmen with equanimity, more in silence than by indignantly resorting to vengeance or permitting the shame and ignominy of his relatives to be made public. . . .

He could endure pain and cold and heat. When, not yet fifteen, he received a serious wound in the foot, and the physician, according to his custom and skill, drew together the broken parts of the foot and sewed them through the skin with a needle, he scarcely uttered a sound of pain. With his own hands, though in such great pain, he even aided the ministering doctor and treated his own wound though he was burning with fever. And when on account of a pain in his side he was continually in an icy sweat, he called in musicians, and for about two hours he strove by singing to overcome the force of the malady and the agony of the pain. His head was by nature unable to endure either cold or wind; but by persistence he learned to bear them, gradually getting used to riding bareheaded in summer, then in winter, and even in raging wind. By some defect in his nature he loathed garlic and also honey, and the mere sight of them, if by chance they were offered to him, brought on vomiting. But he conquered himself by force of looking at and handling the disagreeable objects, so that they came to offend him less, thus showing by example that men can do anything with themselves if they will. . . .

When his favourite dog died he wrote a funeral oration for him.

Source 10 from Denys Hay, editor and translator, The Anglia Historia of Polydore Vergil, *AD 1485–1537, book 74 (London: Camden Society, 1950), p. 147.*

10. From Polydore Vergil, *Anglia Historia,* ca 1540

Henry reigned twenty-three years and seven months. He lived for fifty-two years. By his wife Elizabeth he was the father of eight children, four boys and as many girls. He left three surviving children, an only son Henry prince of Wales, and two daughters, Margaret married to James king of Scotland, and Mary betrothed to Charles prince of Castile. His body was slender but well built and strong; his height above the average. His appearance was remarkably attractive and his face was cheerful, especially when speaking; his eyes were small and blue, his teeth few, poor and blackish; his hair was thin and white; his complexion sallow. His spirit was distinguished, wise and prudent; his mind was brave and resolute and never, even at moments of the greatest danger, deserted him. He had a most pertinacious memory. Withal he was not devoid of scholarship. In government he was shrewd and prudent, so that no one dared to get the better of him through deceit or guile. He was gracious and kind and was as attentive to his visitors as he was easy of access. His hospitality was splendidly generous; he was fond of having foreigners at his court and he freely conferred favours on them. But those of his subjects who were indebted to him and who did not pay him due honour or who were generous only with promises, he treated with harsh severity. He well knew how to maintain his royal majesty and all which appertains to kingship at every time and in every place. He was most fortunate in war, although he was constitutionally more inclined to peace than to war. He cherished justice above all things; as a result he vigorously punished violence, manslaughter and every other kind of wickedness whatsoever. Consequently he was greatly regretted[2] on that account by all his subjects, who had been able to conduct their lives peaceably, far removed from the assaults and evil doing of scoundrels. He was the most ardent supporter of our faith, and daily participated with great piety in religious services. To those whom he considered to be worthy priests, he often secretly gave alms so that they should pray for his salvation. He was particularly fond of those Franciscan friars whom they call Observants, for whom he founded many convents, so that with his help their rule should continually flourish in his kingdom. But all these virtues were obscured latterly only by avarice, from which (as we showed above) he suffered. This avarice is surely a bad enough vice in a private individual, whom it forever torments; in a monarch indeed it may be considered the worst vice, since it is harmful to everyone, and distorts those qualities of trustfulness, justice and integrity by which the state must be governed.

2. **regretted:** missed after he died.

QUESTIONS TO CONSIDER

The first step in exploring the history of ideas is to focus on and define the ideas themselves. Once you have done that by reading the selections and thinking about the questions proposed in Sources and Method, you need to take the next step, which is to compare the ideas of various thinkers. In this way you can trace the development of ideas, how they originate and mature and change in the mind of one thinker after another. First, ask specific questions, such as: What would Bruni think of Castiglione's court lady? How would Leon Battista Alberti be judged by Castiglione's standards? Did Polydore Vergil and Machiavelli have the same ideas about the personal qualities of a ruler? Would a man educated according to the ideas of Vergerius have fitted into Castiglione's ideal court? Would a ruler have wanted him? Would Bruni's learned lady have made a good member of Castiglione's court? Would Botticelli's Simonetta? Does Machiavelli's prince display the qualities Vergerius envisioned in a liberally educated man? How do the main qualities of Machiavelli's prince compare with those of Castiglione's courtier? Why might they be quite different? From the portrait, how might Dürer have been judged by each of the writers? Could we think of Verrocchio's sculpture of Colleoni as a portrait of a Machiavellian ruler? How did the artists' ideals for men, women, and rulers differ from the writers'?

Once you have made these specific comparisons, you can move on to broader comparisons of the basic assumptions of the authors and artists: What was the underlying view of human nature for these writers? Was this the same for men and women? You have probably noticed that all the writers and artists presented here are male. Given what you have now learned about ideals for men and women, would you have expected most Renaissance writers to be male?

Many intellectual historians are interested not only in the history of ideas themselves but also in their social and political origins. These historians want to know what people thought and why they thought the way they did. This type of intellectual history is called the *sociology of knowledge* because it explores the societal context of ideas in the same way that sociology examines past and present social groups. The sociology of knowledge is a more speculative field than the history of ideas alone because it attempts to discover the underlying reasons that cause people to develop different ways of thinking in different historical periods—a process that can be quite difficult to discern. Nevertheless, from the information your text provides about the social and political changes occurring during the Renaissance, you can also consider some sociology of knowledge questions: Why did humanism first arise in northern Italy and not elsewhere in Italy? Why was religion regarded as especially important for women? How did Castiglione's career affect his view of politics? How did

Machiavelli's? What transformation of the status of artists during the Renaissance allowed both Alberti and Dürer to depict themselves in the ways they did? Given that the documents range from 1392 to 1540, what political changes might have accounted for the varying ideals proposed for the individual? How did the ideals proposed for rulers reflect the actual growth of centralized political power? How might the growth of that power have shaped the ideals set forth by Machiavelli and Polydore Vergil? Questions such as these take us somewhat beyond the scope of our original enquiry, but they are important to ask in looking at any ideological change, particularly a sensibility as far-reaching as the Renaissance. Humanism did not spring up in a vacuum but at a very specific time and place.

We must also be careful, however, not to overemphasize social and political background in tracing the development of ideas. Intellectual historians prefer to speak of "necessary conditions" or "background factors" rather than "causes." A movement as diffuse and long lasting as humanism necessarily stemmed from a wide variety of factors, so do not feel concerned if you find yourself qualifying your answers to the questions in the last paragraph with such words as "might," "perhaps," and "possibly."

EPILOGUE

Scholars and writers throughout Western history have attempted to revive the classical past, but none of these efforts before or after were to produce the long-lasting effects of the Italian Renaissance. In many ways Petrarch was right: It was the dawn of a new age. As the ideas and ideals of humanism spread, writers all over Europe felt that they had definitely broken with the centuries-long tradition that directly preceded them. It was at this point that historians began the three-part division of Western history that we still use today: antiquity, the Middle Ages or medieval period, and the modern period. (If you pause to reflect on what "middle" implies, you will see that no one living in the tenth century would have described him- or herself as living in the "Middle Ages.")

The effects of the Renaissance were eventually felt far beyond the realms of literature and art. Humanist schools and academies opened throughout Europe, and eventually the older universities changed their curricula to add courses in Latin, Greek, and Hebrew language and literature. In northern Europe, humanists became interested in reforming the Church, bringing it back to the standards of piety and morality they believed had been present in the early Church, in the same way that Petrarch had tried to return the Latin language to its ancient standards. This movement, termed *Christian humanism*, would be one of the background factors behind the Protestant Reformation, as learned people began to realize from their studies that the Church was now far removed from the ideas and standards of the early Christians. The intense Renaissance interest in the physical world, combined with monetary greed and missionary impulses, led to the exploration and eventual colonization of much of the non-European world. This secular spirit was also important in setting the stage for the Scientific Revolution of the seventeenth century.

Humanist ideas about the perfect man, woman, and ruler were originally directed at the upper classes but would eventually find a much larger audience. Castiglione's *The Courtier* was translated into every European language, and the personal characteristics he outlined for the ideal courtier became those expected of the middle-class gentleman. Echoes of the Renaissance ideal for women are still with us; a glance at women's magazines or at contemporary advice manuals for girls will show you that physical beauty, morality, femininity, and religion are often still seen to be the most important personal qualities a woman can possess. Machiavelli's *The Prince* has more dramatic echoes, as many modern dictators clearly would agree that it is more important to be feared than loved.

We should not overemphasize the effects of the intellectual changes of the Renaissance on people living during that period, however. Only a very small share of the population, primarily wealthy, urban, and, as we have seen, male, participated at all in cultural life, whether as consumers or as producers. Most people's lives were shaped much more during this period by economic changes and by religious practices than by the cultural changes we looked at in this chapter. In fact, in their efforts to stress the elitism of Renaissance culture, some historians have questioned whether the term "Renaissance" itself is a valid one, and prefer simply to use the more neutral phrase "late medieval and early modern period."

Even among the elites, many aspects of the Middle Ages continued during the Renaissance. Despite the emergence of individualism, family background remained the most important determinant of a person's social and economic standing. Despite an emphasis on the material, secular world, religion remained central to the lives of the elite as well as the common people. Though some artists were recognized as geniuses, they were still expected to be dependable, tax-paying members of society—that is, members of the community like everybody else. The fact that so many humanists felt it necessary to set standards and describe ideal behavior gives us a clue that not everyone understood or accepted that they were living in a new age: People have no need to be convinced of what they already believe is true.